Learning
Corel® Office
Professional 7

Iris Blanc & Cathy Vento

Acknowledgments

To Our Families
Alan, Pamela and Jaime
Jim, Chris, Dirk, Jimmy, and Anthony

Project Manager
Marni Ayers
New York, NY

English Editors
Rebecca Fiala
Cambridge, MA

Monique Peterson
New York, NY

Technical Editors
Carol Havlicek
Long Beach, NY

Hollywood P Co.
Dover, NJ

Neal Ehrenberg
E. Northport, NY

Aegina Berg
New York, NY

Design and Layout
Shu Y. Chen
New York, NY

Paul Wray
New York, NY

Published by DDC Publishing

First DDC Publishing Inc. Printing

ISBN: 1-56243-334-2
Catalog Number: Z12

10 9 8 7 6 5 4 3 2

Printed in the United States of America.

Contents

ABOUT COREL® OFFICE PROFESSIONAL 7

- Corel® Office Professional 7 version includes Corel WordPerfect® 7, Quattro® Pro 7, Borland® Paradox® 7, Corel Presentations™ 7, Envoy™, Corel InfoCentral and a host of bonus applications such as Corel Draw™ 6, CorelFLOW™3, Sidekick®95, Dashboard® 95 and more. More than 10,000 clip art images and 150 typographical fonts are included as well. Each of the applications and utilities included in the package can be used separately or they can be used together to produce professional looking documents.

    ✓ *If you are using the standard Corel Office 7 suite package, Borland® Paradox® and some bonus applications will not be included. Bonus applications are not covered in this book.*

- The following software applications will be covered in Learning Corel Office Professional 7:

    - **Corel WordPerfect 7**, a word processing program, used for creating and editing documents.

    - **Corel Quattro Pro 7**, a spreadsheet program, used for analyses and graphing of numerical data.

    - **Borland Paradox 7**, a database program, used for organizing and sorting information.

    - **Corel Presentations** 7, a presentation graphics program, used for creating visual presentations.

- The information created in one application can be shared with other applications. For instance, a spreadsheet created in Quattro Pro, or a database created in Paradox, can easily be incorporated into a memo or letter that is created in WordPerfect. Data created in WordPerfect, Quattro Pro or Paradox can be incorporated into Presentations. Such integration is further demonstrated in the Integration section of this text.

ABOUT THIS BOOK

- Learning Corel Office Professional 7 will teach you to use and integrate the four mentioned applications in the Corel Office Professional 7 suite package on an IBM PC or compatible computer.

- Each lesson in this book explains concepts, provides numerous exercises to apply those concepts and illustrates the necessary keystrokes or mouse actions required to complete the exercises. Lesson summary exercises are provided at the end of each lesson to challenge and reinforce the concepts learned.

- After completing the exercises in this book, you will be able to use the basic features of each application in the Corel Office Professional 7 suite with ease.

HOW TO USE THIS BOOK

- Each exercise contains four parts:

    - **NOTES** explain the Corel Office Professional 7 concept and application being introduced.

    - **EXERCISE DIRECTIONS** explain how to complete the exercise.

    - **EXERCISES** allow you to apply the new concept.

    - **KEYSTROKES** outline the keystroke shortcuts and mouse actions required for completing an exercise.

    ✓ *Keystrokes and mouse actions are only provided when a new concept is being introduced. Therefore, if you forget the keystroke or mouse action required to perform a task, you can use the Corel Office Professional 7 Help feature (explained in the Introductory Basics section) or the index of this book to find the procedure.*

- Before you begin working on the exercises in any Corel Office Professional 7 application, you should read the first introductory section entitled Basics. This section will explain the screens, the Help feature, working in Windows, Toolbars, menus, and other necessary preliminary information.

THE DATA AND SOLUTION DISKS

- Data and solutions disks may be purchased separately from DDC Publishing. You may use the data files on the data disk to complete an exercise without typing lengthy text or data. However, exercise directions are provided for both data disk and non-data disk users. Exercise directions will include a keyboard icon 🖮 to direct non data disk users to open documents created in a previous exercise and a diskette icon 💾 to direct data disk users to open the document available on disk. For example, a typical direction might read: Open 🖮TRY or 💾03TRY.

- The data disk contains WordPerfect, Quattro Pro, Paradox and Presentations files. Each filename begins with the corresponding exercise number and contains an extension that correlates with the program in which the file was created. For example, **03TRY.WPD** would indicate a WordPerfect document, whereas **03TRY.WB3** would indicate a Quattro Pro document.

- In order to maintain the integrity of the data disk, be sure to make a back up copy of the disk, open data files as Read Only, and use the Save As method to save each file under a new name (see explanations of Read Only and Save As in the WordPerfect section of this text).

- The Solution disk may be used for you to compare your work with the final version or solution on disk. Each solution filename begins with the letter "S" and is followed by the exercise number and descriptive filename to which it pertains. For example, **S03TRY** would contain the final solution to the exercise directions in exercise three.

- A directory of data disk and solutions disk filenames are provided in the Log of Exercises section of this book.

  ✓ *Saving files to a network will automatically truncate all filenames to a maximum of eight characters. Therefore, though Windows 95 allows for longer filenames, a maximum of eight characters will be used in naming data and solution files.*

THE INSTRUCTOR'S GUIDE

- While this book can be used as a self-paced learning book, a comprehensive Instructor's Guide is also available. The instructor's guide contains the following:

  - Lesson objectives
  - Exercise objectives
  - Related vocabulary
  - Points to emphasize
  - Exercise settings

FEATURES OF THIS TEXT

- Lesson objectives
- Exercise objectives
- Application concepts and vocabulary
- A Log of Exercises, which lists filenames in exercise number order
- A Directory of Documents, which lists filenames alphabetically along with the corresponding exercise numbers.
- Exercises to apply each concept
- End of lesson summary exercises to review and test your knowledge of lesson concepts
- Keystrokes and mouse actions necessary to complete each application

Log of Exercises

Directory of Documents

File Name	Exercises	Page
WordPerfect		
ABC	11	53
AGELESS	40	159
ANNOUNCE	49	212
BRAZIL	34	136
BROWN	28, 47	110, 199
BUYD	44	186
BUYF	44	186
BUYFI	44	186
CAREER	27	108
COLLEGE	34	136
COLORFUL	16	72
CRUISE	41, 42	164, 171
CRUISE	42	171
DUEDAT	43	182
DUEFRM	43	182
FILM	30, 33, 36	119, 131, 143
FISH	17	74
FRANCE	26, 35	106, 143
FRANCE1	36	147
INVDAT	43	182
INVFI	43	182
INVFRM	43	182
JOIN	12	56
JOURNEY	40, 50	159, 215
MARATHON	8, 18, 21, 23	42, 78, 88, 94
MASON	24, 29, 36	97, 115, 143
MENU	14, 15	64, 68
NET	32, 36	128, 143
NEWFILM	47	199
NEWLAND	33	131
NEWLAND1	31	124
NEWLAND2	31	124
RAFFLE	3, 9	27, 45
RELAX	45, 46	190, 194
RELAXING	46	194
RELEASE	36	153
SALARY	41, 42	164, 171
SETTLE	38	153
SURVIVAL	19, 25, 48	82, 103, 205
SURVIVAL2	48	205
THANKYOU	4	30
TIPS	20, 22, 36	85, 91, 143
TIVOLI	12, 13	56, 61, 205

Corel Office Basics

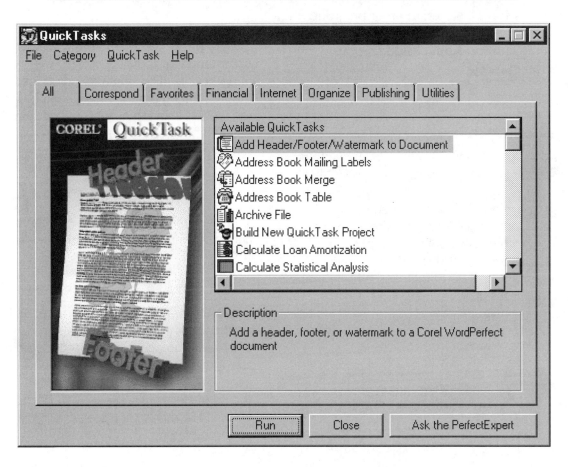

<table>
<tr><td>Exercise
1</td><td>■ **About Corel Office 7** ■ **Desktop Application Director (DAD)**
■ **Mouse and Keyboard** ■ **Start Corel Office 7**
■ **Close an Application Using the Mouse**</td></tr>
</table>

NOTES

About Corel Office 7

■ Corel Office Professional 7® provides a full range of powerful tools that may be used independently or in an integrated fashion to perform various office tasks efficiently. Corel Office 7 includes WordPerfect® (Word processing tool), Quattro Pro® (spreadsheet tool), Presentations® (presentation tool), Paradox® (database tool), Envoy (publishing tool), and InfoCentral 7 (a calendar and information management tool). *Envoy and InfoCentral 7 will not be covered in this book.*

■ After the software is installed, a program group for Corel Office 7 appears on the desktop. In addition, the **Desktop Application Director**, also referred to as **DAD**, appears on the Taskbar.

Desktop Application Director (DAD)

■ The Desktop Application Director (DAD) displays icons (symbols) that represent most Corel Office Professional 7® applications and utilities. DAD is displayed at all times so that you can easily access any Corel Office 7 Application from within windows or easily switch between applications. DAD contains icons for WordPerfect®, Quattro Pro®, Presentations®, Paradox®, and other Corel Office 7® utilities.

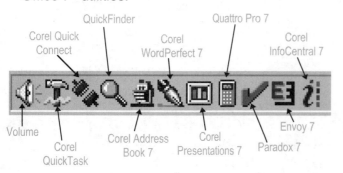

- To identify each DAD icon, place the mouse pointer on the icon. A **QuickTip** will appear with the name or function of the button.

- DAD may be customized to add other applications or utilities you may have installed in your system.

✓ *The volume icon will only appear if a sound card is installed in your system.*

■ All Corel Office Professional 7® applications and utilities have similar Toolbars, menus, commands, and dialog boxes. The skills learned in one application, such as using the Toolbars, menus, dialog boxes, and Online help features (as well as moving around the screen) are used consistently in all Corel Office Professional 7® applications.

Mouse and Keyboard

■ You may use the mouse or the keyboard to choose commands and perform tasks.

Using the Mouse

■ When the mouse is moved on the tabletop, a corresponding movement of the mouse pointer occurs on the screen. The mouse pointer changes shape depending on the tool being used, the object it is pointing to, and the action it will be performing. The mouse pointer will not move if the mouse is lifted up and placed back on the tabletop.

- The mouse terminology and the corresponding actions described below will be used throughout the book:

Point to	Move the mouse (on the tabletop) so the pointer touches a specific item.
Click	Point to item and quickly press and release the left mouse button.
Right-click	Point to item and press and release the right mouse button.
Double-click	Point to item and press the left mouse button twice in rapid succession.
Drag	Point to item and press and hold down the left mouse button while moving the mouse. When the item is in the desired position, release the mouse button to place the item.
Right-Drag	Point to item and press and hold down the right mouse button while moving the mouse. When the item is in the desired position, release the mouse button to place the item.

- All references to the use of mouse buttons in this book refer to the *left* mouse button unless otherwise specified.

Using the Keyboard

- Computers contain specialized keyboard keys:

  - **Function keys** (F1 through F10 or F12) perform special functions and are located across the top of the keyboard.

  - **Modifier keys** (Shift, Alt, Ctrl) are used in conjunction with other keys to select certain commands or perform actions. To use a modifier key with another key, you must hold down the modifier key while tapping the other key.

- **Numeric keys**, found on keyboards with a number pad, allow you to enter numbers quickly. When Num Lock is ON, the number keys on the pad are operational, as is the decimal point. When Num Lock is OFF, the cursor control keys (Home, PgUp, End, PgDn) are active. The numbers on the top row of the keyboard are always active.

- **Escape key** (Esc) is used to cancel some actions, commands, menus, or an entry.

- **Enter keys** (there are two on most keyboards) are used to complete an entry of data in some applications.

- **Directional arrow keys** are used to move the active screen insertion point as determined by the tool being used.

Start Corel Office 7

There are two ways to start a Corel Office Professional 7 application:

- **Using the Windows Taskbar:** The Windows Taskbar appears at the bottom of the screen in all programs running Windows 95. The Taskbar is used to start applications as well as to switch between applications.

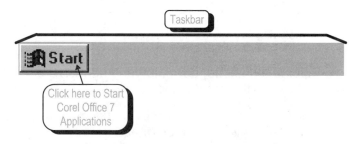

- After you install Corel Office Professional 7 software, a **Corel Office 7** menu item appears when Start is accessed from the Taskbar. Slide the mouse to highlight Corel Office 7, then slide the mouse to highlight the other applications. Click the left mouse to select the application you wish to access.

■ **Using DAD [Desktop Application Director] on the Taskbar:** Click the desired application icon.

- To start a second application, hold down Ctrl and click on a second application icon.

Close an Application Using the Mouse

■ To quickly exit an application using the mouse, click the **Program Close** button ⊠ in the upper right corner of the screen. In the illustration below, you will note two Close buttons. The top Close button closes the program; the bottom Close button closes the document window. Closing a document will be covered in Exercise 2.

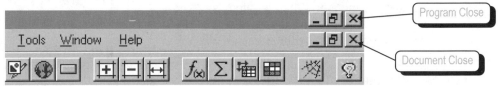

In this exercise, you will use the mouse to start and close Corel Office Professional 7 applications.

EXERCISE DIRECTIONS

1. Roll the mouse up, down, left and right on the tabletop or the mouse pad.

2. Place the mouse pointer over each icon on the Desktop Application Director and note the QuickTip notation for each application.

3. Click the DAD icon for Corel WordPerfect 7.

4. Click on the top Close button to exit the WordPerfect program.

5. Click Start on the Windows 95 Taskbar.

6. Highlight Corel Office 7, then Corel Quattro Pro 7, and then click to select Corel Quattro Pro 7.

7. Click on the top Close button to exit Quattro Pro.

KEYSTROKES

START A COREL OFFICE 7 APPLICATION

1. Click Start on Taskbar .... 🏁Start
2. Highlight Corel Office 7.

3. Highlight application.
4. Press Enter .... Enter
OR
1. Point to application icon on DAD Toolbar.
2. Click to open application.

CLOSE AN APPLICATION

Click Program Close Button ....

<table>
<tr><td>Exercise
2</td><td>■ **Corel Office 7 Windows** ■ **Menus, Toolbars, and Commands**
■ **QuickMenus** ■ **Select Menu Items** ■ **The Dialog Box** ■ **Zoom**</td></tr>
</table>

NOTES

Corel Office 7 Windows

■ When you access each Corel Office 7 application, you will see its opening screen.

■ The common parts of all Corel Office 7 application windows will be discussed using the WordPerfect screen. The specific screen parts for each Corel Office 7 tool will be detailed in the appropriate sections of this book.

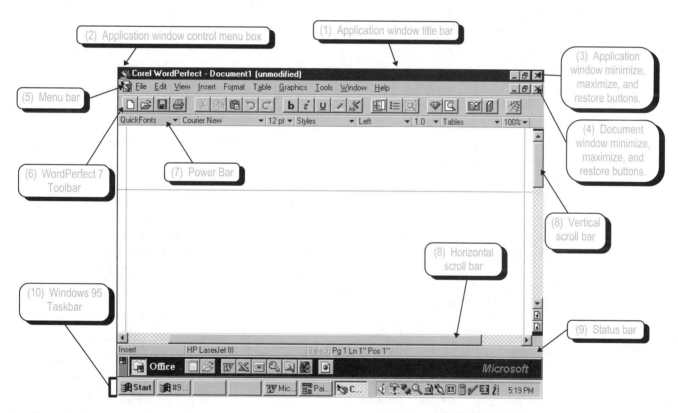

✓ *Note the following universal window parts:*

• There are many different bars available in WordPerfect 7 which display when the screen appears. They are: application window title bar, menu bar, Toolbar, Power Bar, scroll bar(s) and status bar.

• The (1) **application window title bar**, located at the top of the application window, displays

the program name (WordPerfect, Quattro Pro, etc.) and may also display the name of an opened file if the window is maximized.

• The (2) **application window control menu box**, located to the left of the application window title bar, can be clicked to access a drop-down menu from which you can choose commands that control the window.

- The (3) **application window minimize, maximize, and restore buttons** are located on the right side of the application window title bar. Clicking the minimize button shrinks the window to an icon. Clicking the maximize button enlarges the window to a full screen. Once the window has been maximized, the maximize button changes to the restore button. Clicking the restore button restores the window to its previous size.

- The (4) **document window minimize, maximize, and restore buttons** function the same as the application window buttons, but only the current document is affected.

- The (5) **menu bar**, located below the title bar, displays menu names from which drop-down menus may be accessed.

- The (6) **WordPerfect 7 Toolbar**, located below the menu bar, contains buttons that represent some of the most commonly performed WordPerfect tasks. The Toolbar may only be accessed with the mouse.

- The (7) **Power Bar**, located below the Toolbar, contains pull-down lists that represent the most frequently used text editing and text layout features. The Power Bar provides quick access to styles, font faces and sizes, tables and columns. The Power Bar features may be accessed only with the mouse.

- Pointing to and resting the pointer on a Toolbar button or Power Bar drop-down list displays the tool's name and an explanation of its function.

- The (8) **horizontal and vertical scroll bars** are used to move the screen view horizontally or vertically. The scroll box on the vertical scroll bar can be dragged up or down to move more quickly toward the beginning or end of the document.

- The (9) **status bar**, located at the bottom of the window, displays information about the current mode or operation.

- The (10) **Windows 95 Taskbar**, located at the bottom of the screen, displays the start button, all minimized windows, and the Desktop Application Director.

Menus, Toolbars, and Commands

- The menu bar and Toolbars may be used to access commands. Each application contains a menu bar and two Toolbars.

- The main Toolbar, located below the menu bar, contains icons that accomplish many common tasks easily, like saving and printing a file.

- The Power Bar, located below the main Toolbar, contains functions that easily change the appearance of data. While each application contains both bars and many of the same icons, each application contains buttons unique to that tool.

- You may display the Toolbars at the top of your screen, or you may hide one or both of them to make room on your screen for text or data. You may also change to one of the other specialized Toolbars available in each application.

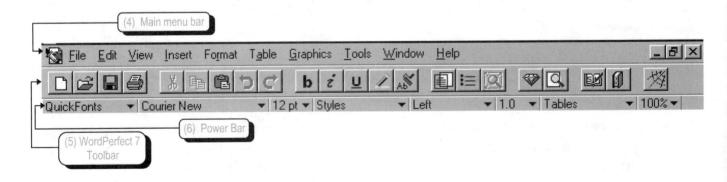

QuickMenus

- Clicking the right mouse button displays a QuickMenu that lists options that may be used to select tasks. The QuickMenus display different options depending on the location of the insertion point when the right mouse button is pressed, as illustrated below.

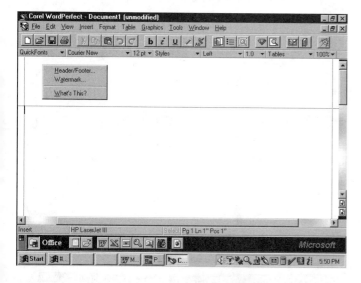

Select Menu Items

- You may use the keyboard, the mouse, or a combination of both to select menu items. Keyboard shortcut keys may also be used to accomplish tasks.

- To access menu bar items:

  - Use the mouse to point to a menu item on the menu bar and click once,

    OR

- Press Alt + underlined letter in the menu name. A drop-down menu will appear.

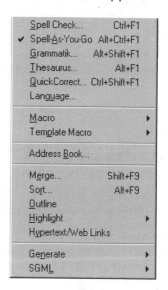

- To select an item from the drop-down menu:

  - Use the mouse to point to the command on the drop-down menu and click once, or
  - Press the underlined letter in the command name, or
  - Use the up or down arrow key to highlight the command, then press Enter.
  - Some menu options are dimmed, while others appear black. Dimmed options are not available for selection at this time, while black options are.
  - A check mark next to a drop-down menu item means the option is currently selected.
  - A menu item followed by an arrow opens a submenu with additional choices.
  - A menu item followed by an ellipsis (...) indicates that a dialog box (which requires you to provide additional information to complete a task) will be forthcoming.

- Procedures for completing a task will be illustrated as follows throughout this book: Mouse actions are illustrated on the left, keystroke procedures are illustrated on the right, and keyboard shortcut keys are illustrated below the heading. Use whichever method you find most convenient.

  For Example:

  SAVE A FILE
  Ctrl + S
  - Click **File**.....Alt + F
  - Click **Save**.........S

The Dialog Box

- A dialog box contains different methods to obtain information in order to complete a task.

  The parts of a dialog box are explained below:

  - The **title bar** identifies the title of the dialog box.

  - The **text box** is a location where you type information.

  - **Command buttons** carry out actions described on the button. When command names have an ellipsis following them, they will access another dialog box.

  - The **drop-down list** is marked with a down arrow. Clicking the drop-down list arrow accesses a short list of options from which a choice should be made.

  - An **increment box** provides a space for typing a value. An up or down arrow (usually to the right of the box) gives you a way to select a value with the mouse.

  - A **named tab** is used to display options related to the tab's name in the same dialog box.

  - **Option buttons** are small circular buttons marking options appearing as a set. You may choose only one option from the set. A selected option button contains a dark circle.

  - A **check box** is a small square box where an option may be selected or deselected. An "X" or "✓" in the box indicates that the option has been selected. If several check boxes are offered, you may select more than one.

  - A **list box** displays a list of items from which selections can be made. A list box may have a scroll bar that can be used to show hidden items in the list.

  - A **scroll bar** is a horizontal or vertical bar providing scroll arrows and a scroll box that can be dragged up or down to move more quickly through the available options.

  - A **preview window** allows you to see the result of your selection.

  - ✓ *Note the labeled parts in the dialog boxes below:*

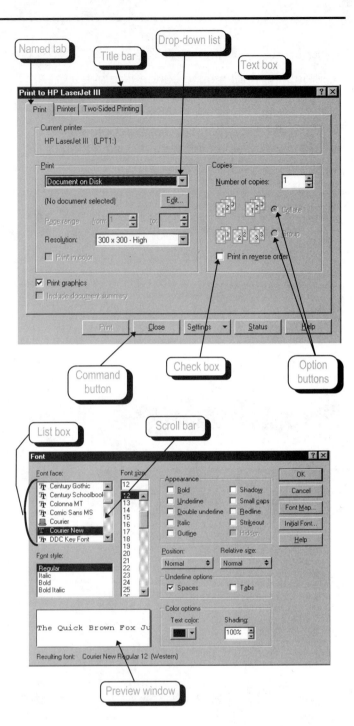

Zoom

- The View menu contains a Zoom option that allows you to set the magnification of the data on the screen. When Zoom is selected, the following dialog box appears:

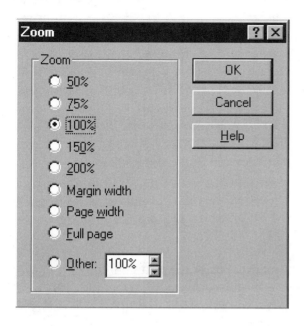

■ Clicking a Zoom option button displays document text at 200%, 100%, 75%, etc. You can also access the Zoom feature by clicking the Zoom button on the Power Bar and selecting a magnification amount. This method does not open a dialog box.

In this exercise, you will practice using Toolbars, Menus, and Commands.

EXERCISE DIRECTIONS

1. Open the WordPerfect application.

2. Select View from the menu bar.

3. Select Toolbars/Ruler.

4. Deselect Power Bar.

5. Deselect WordPerfect 7 Toolbar and click OK.
   ✓ *Note the change in the screen.*

6. Select View Toolbars/Ruler and reselect Power Bar and WordPerfect 7 Toolbar to return them to the screen.

7. Select View; select Two Page.
   ✓ *Note the changes.*

8. Restore the screen to the default view by selecting Page from the View menu.

9. Type your name on the screen.

10. Select 100% from the Power bar.

11. Select the 200% magnification option.
    ✓ *Note the change.*

12. Repeat steps 10-11 using the 75% option.

13. Return to 100% magnification.

14. Right-click at the top of the page and note the QuickMenu. Left-click anywhere on the screen to clear menu.

15. Right-click in the middle of the screen and note QuickMenu. Left-click anywhere on the screen to clear the menu.

16. Exit WordPerfect.

KEYSTROKES

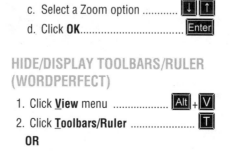

MAGNIFICATON/ZOOM

1. Click 100%
   button on Power Bar .... `100% ▼`

2. Select a zoom option.
   OR
   a. Click **View** .... `Alt`+`V`
   b. Click **Zoom** .... `Z`

   c. Select a Zoom option .... `↓` `↑`
   d. Click **OK** .... `Enter`

HIDE/DISPLAY TOOLBARS/RULER (WORDPERFECT)

1. Click **View** menu .... `Alt`+`V`
2. Click **Toolbars/Ruler** .... `T`
   OR

- Point to the Toolbar.
- Right-click.
- Select desired Toolbar.

Exercise

3

■ **Get Help**

NOTES:

Get Help

■ Help may be accessed by clicking <u>H</u>elp on the menu bar or by pressing F1. Each application's Help menu has some commands in common; in addition, each application has tool-specific help commands.

✓ *If you are in a Help window, F1 will close the window and open the How to Use Help screen.*

✓ *Note the following Help menus from WordPerfect 7 and Paradox 7 and the discussion of the standard commands.*

✓ *You may also get help on a particular screen item by pressing Shift + F1, then pointing to any screen icon or location and clicking the left mouse button. A help screen appears explaining the item in question.*

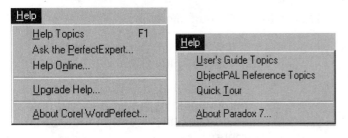

• After you select <u>H</u>elp and then <u>H</u>elp Topics, the Help Topics dialog box displays with various tabs. Ask the PerfectExpert may be accessed by selecting Ask the <u>P</u>erfectExpert from the <u>H</u>elp menu or by clicking on the Ask the PerfectExpert button 💡 on the Toolbar.

• **Ask the PerfectExpert** searches for answers to your question about a particular topic. In the **What do you want to know?** text box, enter your question and click the <u>S</u>earch button. A series of topics in answer to your question displays in the <u>S</u>earch Results list box. Double-click any topic in the list box or select the topic and click <u>D</u>isplay to view the help screen. Note the Ask the PerfectExpert screen below:

✓ *Ask the PerfectExpert is not available in Paradox 7.*

- **Contents** provides the overall contents of the Help system. Double-clicking the book icon to the left of a topic opens a new set of subtopics. Note the WordPerfect Help Contents page:

- **Index** allows you to enter the first few letters of your topic; the index feature brings you to the index entry. Double-click the entry or select the entry and click Display. The help screen related to your topic is then displayed.

- **Find** accesses the Help database feature. It allows you to search the Help database for the occurrence of any word or phrase in the help topic. The Index and Find features are similar; however, Find offers more options to search for a topic.

- **Show Me** allows you to select a topic and have the program play a demo of the topic. The demo steps you through the procedure for completing the task, or actually does the procedure for you (QuickTasks). Show Me is only available in the WordPerfect and Presentations applications.

- **Upgrade Help** provides information to help you easily make the transition from other software packages to Corel Office 7.

- **About Corel WordPerfect.../About Corel Quattro Pro** provides system status information.

To Exit Help:

- Click Cancel or Close **X** or press Escape to exit Help.

In this exercise, you will gain practice using the help menus.

EXERCISE DIRECTIONS:

1. Open the Quattro Pro application.

2. Select Help from the menu bar.

3. Select Help Topics.

4. Select the Contents tab. Do the following:
   - Double-click How Do I.
   - Double-click Learn the Essentials.
   - Double-click Toolbars.
   - Click the Close button.

5. Select Help from the menu bar.

6. Select Help Topics.

7. Select the Index tab. Do the following:
   - Type **menu** in the text box.
   - Select the topic, **menu bar**, in the list.
   - Click the Display button.
     - ✓ *Note search results.*
   - Click Cancel, then click cancel again.

8. Select the Help menu.

9. Select Ask the PerfectExpert.
   - Type, **change column width**.
   - Click Search.
     - ✓ *Note search results.*

10. Click Cancel to exit PerfectExpert.

11. Close Quattro Pro.

KEYSTROKES

GET HELP

F1
1. Click **Help** menu .... Alt + H
2. Select desired option.

Corel WordPerfect 7

Lesson 1: **Create, Save, and Print Documents**

Lesson 2: **Open and Edit Documents; Manage Files**

Lesson 3: **Text Alignment and Enhancements**

Lesson 4: **Format and Edit Documents**

Lesson 5: **Work with Multiple Pages**

Lesson 6: **Work with Multiple Documents; Macros**

Lesson 7: **Columns, Tables, Merge**

Lesson 8: **Create Graphics, Templates, Envelopes, and Labels**

Exercise

1

- Start WordPerfect ■ The WordPerfect Screen
- Document Window Displays
- Close a Document Window/Exit WordPerfect ■ If You Make an Error...
- View Modes ■ Default Settings ■ Create a New Document
- Save a New Document ■ Close a Document

NOTES

Start WordPerfect

- If you worked with WordPerfect 6.1, you will note that the interface, or the look of the window, is somewhat different. The Windows 95 Taskbar appears at the bottom of the screen on all programs running in Windows 95. WordPerfect may be started using one of the following procedures:

- **Using the Start button on the Taskbar:** The Taskbar allows you to start applications and/or switch between them. After installing Corel Office 7, a Corel Office 7 menu item appears when Start is accessed from the Taskbar. Slide the mouse to highlight Corel Office 7, then slide the mouse to highlight Corel WordPerfect 7, and finally click the left mouse button to select the program.

- **Using DAD [Desktop Application Director] on the Taskbar** (If you are using WordPerfect within the Corel Office 7 Suite): Click Corel WordPerfect 7 icon 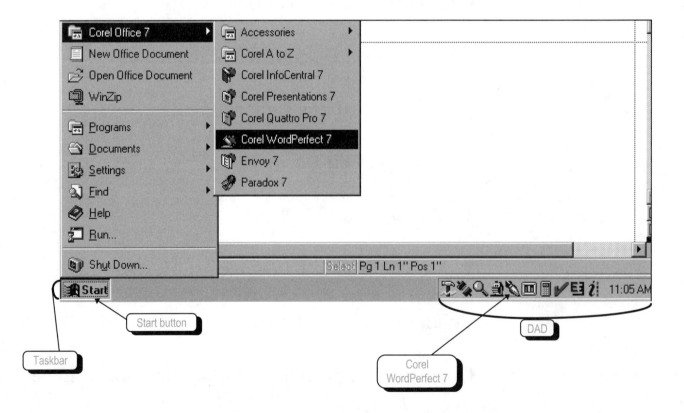.

The WordPerfect Screen

- After you launch the WordPerfect program, the following editing screen appears. Note the names and descriptions of each screen part:

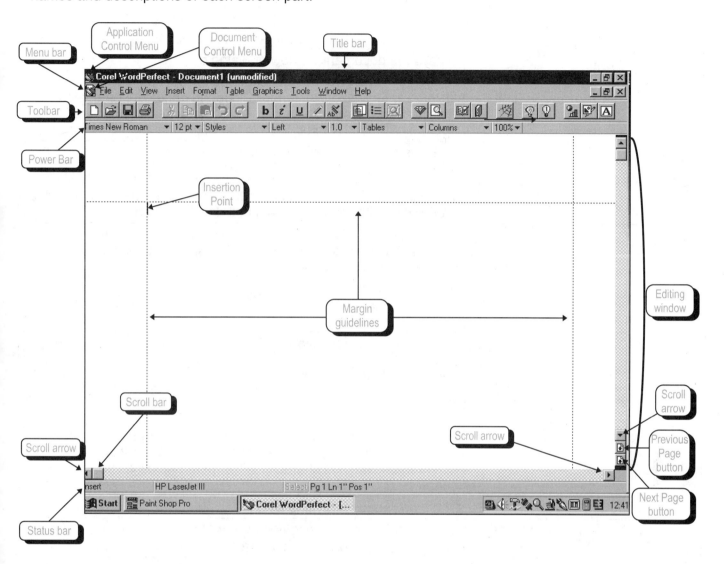

Part	Description
Application Window	The window within which WordPerfect runs.
Application Control Buttons/Menu:	
Minimize button	Shrinks the window to an icon.
Maximize button	Enlarges the window to a full screen.
Restore button	Causes the icon to change to a maximize button.
Close button	Closes the window or dialog box.
Application Control Menu	Clicking the WordPerfect 7 application icon accesses a menu to Maximize, Minimize, Restore, or Close the WordPerfect 7 window. Closing the WordPerfect window will exit WordPerfect.

Part	Description
Document Control Buttons/Menu:	
Minimize button	Shrinks the document window to an icon.
Maximize button	Enlarges the document window to a full screen.
Restore button	Causes the icon to change to a maximize button.
Close button	Closes the document window or dialog box.
Document Control Menu	Clicking the WordPerfect 7 document icon accesses a menu to Maximize, Minimize, Restore or Close the document on screen. Closing the document will exit it. If the document is not saved, the operator will be prompted to save the document before closing.
Title bar	Displays the program and document name.
Menu bar	Displays items that you can select to execute specific commands.
	When an item is selected using either the keyboard or the mouse, a group of sub-items appears in a pull-down submenu.
Toolbar	Displays a collection of icons (pictures) that enables you to accomplish many common word processing tasks easily, such as saving and printing a file.
	When you point to a button on the Toolbar, a QuickTip displays with an explanation of that button's function displayed below the icon. You must use the mouse to access Toolbar buttons.
Power Bar	Displays buttons that allow you to change the appearance of your document easily, such as font size and style options. You must use the mouse to access Power Bar buttons.
Margin guidelines	Blue dashed lines at the top, bottom, left, and right, display the current margins.
Insertion point	The blinking vertical line that appears in the upper left-hand corner when the WordPerfect document window appears. It indicates where the next typed character will appear and blinks between characters.
Editing window	The blank space for typing text.
Previous and Next Page buttons	The top button moves pages backward through a document; the bottom button moves pages forward through a document.
Scroll arrows	Used to move the screen view horizontally or vertically. The scroll box on the vertical scroll bar can be dragged up or down to move the screen view quickly toward the beginning or end of the document. The horizontal scroll box on the horizontal scroll bar can be dragged left or right.
Status bar Items:	Appears at the bottom of the screen and displays:
General Status	Whether Insert or Typeover mode is active. Or provides the status of columns, tables, macros, and merge features.
Printer	Displays the current printer.
Select on/off	Indicates whether text or codes are selected. Double click to switch on or off.
Combined Position	Displays page number, vertical line position of insertion point, (as measured from the top of the page) and horizontal position (as measured from the left edge of the page).

Document Window Displays

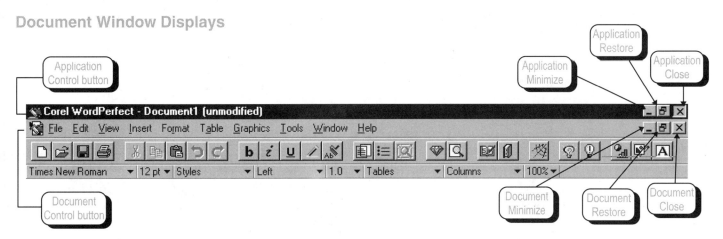

- The Document Control button ![icon], located to the left of the menu bar, can be clicked to access a pull-down menu from which you can choose commands to control the document window.

- The document window minimize, restore and close buttons are located on the right of the menu bar. Clicking the minimize button ![icon] shrinks the window to an icon which displays at the bottom of the screen. Clicking the restore button ![icon] creates a document window (below the Toolbars) including a document title bar.

- The document title bar contains the document control icon and the minimize, restore and close buttons which appear on the menu bar. Clicking the restore button on the document title bar returns the window to the default opening screen. Clicking the Close button closes the document.

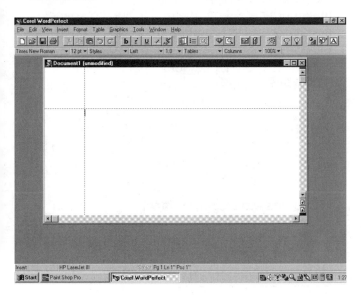

- Document window after clicking restore button (Note: Restore button is now a maximize button).

Close a Document Window/Exit WordPerfect

- To quickly exit an application using the mouse, click the Close button ![X]. In the illustration below, you will note two Close buttons. The top Close button closes the WordPerfect application; the bottom Close button closes the document window.

If You Make an Error...

- The following keys will get you out of trouble:

  - **Backspace** Will erase characters to the immediate left of the insertion point.

  - **Escape** Or clicking a Cancel button, will back you out of most commands without executing them.

  - **F1** Will access the Help Topics dialog box.

View Modes

- WordPerfect provides various ways to view documents on the screen. You may change view modes by selecting a particular view from the **View** menu.

  - **Page mode** is the default. It allows you to view a document just as it will look when printed. This view allows you to see headers and footers, footnotes and endnotes, columns, etc.

- **Draft mode** displays your document without headers, footers, page numbers, or other page formatting features. More of the document can be seen on screen in this mode.

- **Two Page mode** displays two pages side by side.

Default Settings

- Default settings are preset conditions within the program. Settings such as margins, tabs, line spacing, font style, font size, and text alignment are automatically set by the WordPerfect program. These settings may be changed as desired. Changing margins, tabs, etc., will be covered in later exercises.

  - **Margins** are set at 1" on the left, right, top, and bottom. Margins are measured from the edges of the page. WordPerfect assumes you are working on a standard 8.5" x 11" page. The line (Ln) and position (Pos) indicators on the status bar are displayed in inches. When the insertion point is at the left margin, the Pos indicator displays 1", indicating a 1" top margin.

  - **Tab stops** are set every half inch.

- The Power Bar (shown below) displays some default settings. When settings are changed, the new settings will display on the Power Bar.

  - **Font face** (the design of your characters) is set to Times New Roman.

- **Font size** is set to 12 point. (Font size is measured in points.)

- **Text alignment** is set to Left.

- **Line spacing** is set to single (1.0).

Create a New Document

- When you start WordPerfect, a blank screen with guidelines appears, ready for you to begin typing text. WordPerfect assigns "Document1" in the title bar as the document name (until you provide a name).

- The insertion point will be flashing at the beginning of the document. Text appears at this point when you start typing.

- The **Pos** indicator on the status bar shows the insertion point's horizontal position on the page, as measured in inches from the left of the page; the **Ln** indicator shows the insertion point's vertical position, as measured in inches from the top of the page.

- As you type text, the insertion point automatically advances to the next line. This feature is called **word wrap** or **wraparound**. It is only necessary to use the Enter key at the end of a short line or to begin a new paragraph.

Save a New Document

- Documents must be given a name for identification. A filename can contain a maximum of 255 characters, including spaces, and an optional three-character file extension. Filenames and extensions are separated by a period. If you choose not to include a filename extension, WordPerfect automatically assigns the file extension **.wpd**.

- It is recommended that you allow WordPerfect to insert the **.wpd** file extension for you. Doing so will display the document as a WordPerfect 7 file on your computer.

- Filenames are displayed in the letter case in which they are originally typed. For instance, if you type a filename in uppercase, it will appear

Power Bar

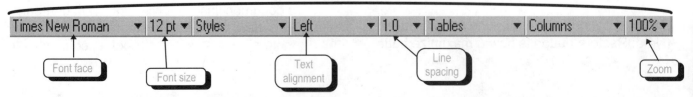

in uppercase. You cannot, however, save one filename in uppercase and save another using the same name in lowercase.

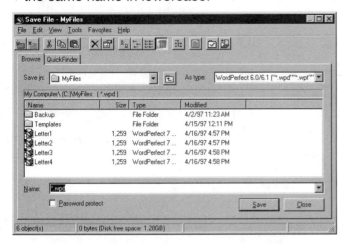

✓ *Note the Save in text box. WordPerfect displays the current location, or folder, where you can save your file. The large area below the Save in text box displays the contents of the current folder.*

■ When saving a file, you must indicate the location where you wish to save it. Documents may be saved on a removable disk or on an internal hard drive. If you save a file to a removable disk, you must indicate that you are saving to the A or B drive. The hard drive is usually designated as the C drive.

■ If you save to the hard drive, WordPerfect provides folders that you may use to save your work. Or, you may create your own folders in which to save your work. You will learn to create folders (or directories) in a later exercise. You should use a floppy disk to save the exercises in this book.

■ When saving a file for the first time, select Save from the File menu or click the Save button 🖫 on the Toolbar. The following Save File dialog box appears:

■ If you wish to save your file to a removable disk, click the list arrow next to the Save in text box and double-click 3½" Floppy (A:).

■ Once this location is specified, the large area below the Save in text box displays the contents of the disk located in the A drive. Enter a desired filename, or use the one that WordPerfect assigns, in the Name text box, and click the Save button to save the document.

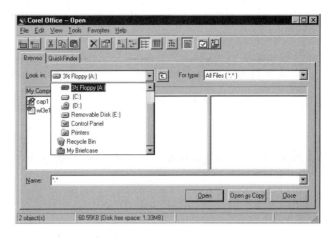

■ You can save your document in a format other than WordPerfect by selecting As type and selecting a desired format from the drop-down list. Use this option if you intend to use your file with another software program.

■ Once your document is named, the filename appears in the Title bar.

■ After saving your document for the first time, you can save the document again and continue working (updating it) by selecting Save from the File main menu or by clicking the Save button 🖫 on the Toolbar. Once the file has been named, the Save File dialog box does not reappear; any changes you have made to your file are simply saved. *Save often to prevent losing data.*

■ Documents may also be saved by selecting Save As from the File main menu. Use this command when you want to save your document under a different filename or in a different drive/directory (folder).

Close a Document

■ When a document has been saved, it remains on your screen. If you wish to clear the screen, you may close the document window by selecting Close from the File menu, or double-clicking the Document Control icon.

■ You automatically get a new blank document after closing another.

■ If you attempt to close a document before saving it, WordPerfect will prompt you to save it before exiting. You may type Y for Yes or N for No.

■ If you make a mistake and would like to begin the document again, close the document window without saving it.

> *In this exercise, you will create a two paragraph document using the word wrap feature and use the backspace key to correct any errors.*

EXERCISE DIRECTIONS

1. Start with a clear screen.

2. Begin the exercise at the top of your screen (Ln 1").

3. Type the first paragraph below, allowing the text to word wrap to the next line.

4. Correct detected errors immediately using the Backspace key.

   ✓   *Ignore red wavy lines below errors that remain at this time.*

5. Close the file without saving it.

6. Begin the exercise again and complete it. Press the Enter key twice before starting the second paragraph.

7. Save the document; name it TRY.

8. Close the document window.

As you type, notice the Pos indicator on your status bar change as the position of your insertion point changes.

The wraparound feature allows the operator to decide on line endings, making the use of the Enter unnecessary except at the end of a paragraph or short line. Each file is saved on a disk or hard drive for recall. Documents must be given a name for identification.

KEYSTROKES

START WORDPERFECT

Using the Taskbar

1. Click **Start** .... Ctrl + Esc
2. Highlight Corel Office 7
3. Select Corel WordPerfect 7

Using the DAD Bar

   Click Corel WordPerfect 7 icon .... 🔧

SAVE A NEW DOCUMENT

Ctrl + S

Click **Save** icon .... 💾
OR
1. Click **File** .... Alt + F
2. Click **Save** .... S
3. Click **Save in** text box .... Alt + I
   to select drive or folder.

4. Select desired .... ↓ , Enter
   drive or folder.
5. To select .... Tab , ↓ , Enter
   subfolder, Double-click folder.
6. Double-click File .... Alt + N
   name text box.
7. Type filename .... *filename*
8. Click **Save** .... Alt + S or Enter

CLOSE A DOCUMENT

1. Double-click **document control** icon.
2. Click **Yes** .... Y
   to save changes.
OR
Click **No** .... N
to abandon changes.
OR
1. Click **File** .... Alt + F
2. Click **Close** C

3. Click **Yes** .... Y
   to save changes.
OR
Click **No** .... N
to abandon changes.

EXIT WORDPERFECT

Alt + F4

1. Click **File** .... Alt + F
2. Click **Exit** X
OR
1. Click WordPerfect Program Control
   Box .... 🔧
2. Click **Close** C
OR
Double-click WordPerfect Program
Control Box .... 🔧

Exercise 2

- **QuickCorrect** ■ **Spell-As-You-Go**
- **Spell Check** ■ **Document (Properties)**

Spell Check

NOTES

QuickCorrect

- The **QuickCorrect** feature automatically replaces common spelling errors and mistyped words with the correct text as soon as you press the spacebar.

- There are numerous words already in the user word list. However, you can enter words that you commonly misspell into the user word list by selecting QuickCorrect from the Tools main menu.

- If you find this feature annoying, you can deselect the Replace words as you type option in the QuickCorrect dialog box.

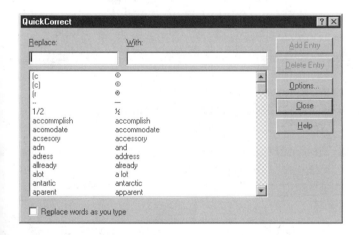

- By clicking the Options button in the QuickCorrect dialog box, you can specify other types of corrections in the QuickCorrect Options dialog box which follows:

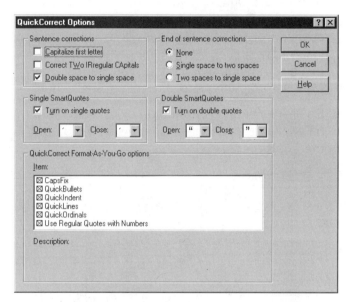

- **Capitalize first letter** automatically capitalizes the first letter of a sentence.

- **Correct TWo IRregular CApitals** automatically converts two initial capital letters of a word to an initial capital letter and a lowercase second letter.

- **Double space to single space** automatically converts a double space between words in a sentence to one space.

- **Single space to two spaces** automatically converts a single space at the end of a sentence to two spaces.

- **Two spaces to single space** automatically converts two spaces at the end of a sentence to a single space.

- **Turn on single quotes/ double quotes** allows you to use quotation characters you select from the drop-down list.

- **QuickCorrect Format-As-You-Go options** allow you to select from additional corrections to be included in QuickCorrect.

Spell-As-You-Go

- The **Spell-As-You-Go** feature underlines spelling errors with red dashes as you type. To correct a misspelled word, point to the underlined error with your mouse and click the *right* mouse button. A QuickMenu displays with suggested corrections. Click the correctly spelled word in the list and it will replace the incorrectly spelled word in the document. You can also add the word to the WordPerfect user word list, skip the word, or begin a Spell Check.

- Spell-As-You-Go is turned on by default. To turn off this feature, deselect Spell-As-You-Go from the Tools menu.

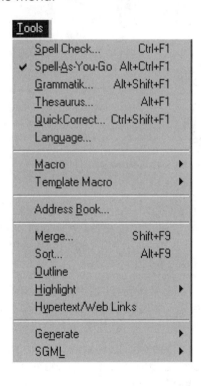

Spell Check

- WordPerfect's **Spell Check** feature checks your document for general spelling errors, double words, words containing numbers, and irregular capitalizaiton.

- A word, a sentence, a section of a page, an entire page, or an entire document may be checked for spelling errors. When a misspelled or unrecognized word is found, Spell Check offers possible alternatives so you can replace the error.

- Spell Check may be accessed by selecting Spell Check from the Tools menu or by clicking the Spell Check button on the Toolbar. You may also click the *right* mouse button in the document window and select Spell Check. The following Writing Tools dialog box will appear:

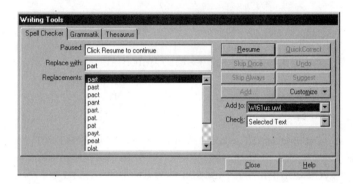

- Words may be added to a **user word list** (.uwl) (the default) or to a document word list.

- A **document word list** is automatically attached to every document. The word list is saved as part of the document and is only used with that document. To add a word to the document word list, click the Add to text box list arrow in the Writing Tools dialog box and select Document Word List.

- Words may be added to the user or document word list before, after, or during the spell check session.

- To avoid having proper names flagged as incorrect spellings during the spell check session, add them to the user or document word list.

- Spell Check does not find errors in word usage (example: using *their* instead of *there*). Finding usage errors will be covered when Grammatik is introduced in Lesson 4.

- You can use QuickCorrect inside Spell Check to add a word and its replacement to the correction list. Any word added to the correction list (through the QuickCorrect option button) will be automatically corrected during the Spell Check session.

Document (Properties)

- The Document Properties feature provides you with a statistical summary of your document. Document Properties may be accessed by selecting Document, then Properties from the File menu.

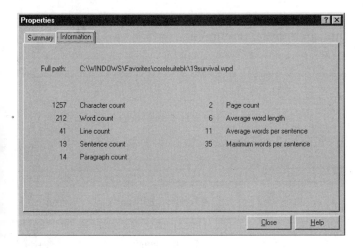

- The Information tab in the Properties dialog box lists the number of characters, words, lines, sentences, paragraphs, and pages in your document. In addition, it indicates the average word length, average words per sentence, and maximum words per sentence. This is a particularly useful feature when you are required to submit a report with a specified word or page count.

- The Summary tab allows you to save summary information with each document, such as a descriptive name and type, creation and revision dates, author and typist name(s), and subject.

In this exercise, you will type two short paragraphs using word wrap and purposely misspell several words. After typing the word incorrectly and pressing the Spacebar, you will note that the correct spelling appears. You will then use either the Spell-As-You-Go feature on the QuickMenu or the Spell Check feature to correct the other misspellings.

EXERCISE DIRECTIONS

1. Start with a clear screen.

2. Begin the exercise at the top of your screen.

3. Access the QuickCorrect feature. Be sure Replace words as you type has been selected.

4. Type the paragraphs on the next page exactly as shown, including the circled, misspelled words. Allow the text to word wrap to the next line.

5. Press the Enter key twice to begin a new paragraph, and press the Tab key once to indent the paragraph.

6. Use the Spell Check or Spell-As-You-Go feature to correct the misspellings in the document.

7. Using the Document Properties feature, fill out the following summary information about your document:

> **Descriptive Name:** .... WordPerfect Information
> **Descriptive Type:** ....Report
> **Author:**...Your name
> **Typist:** ....Your name
> **Subject:**......................Promotion for WordPerfect

8. Save the exercise using the Save button on the Toolbar; name it TRYAGAIN.

9. Close the document window.

Corel WordPerfect is simple to use since you can begin typing as soon as you enter teh program.

THe way text will lay out or "format" on a page is set by the WordPerfect program. For example, margins are set for 1" on the left and 1" on the right; line spaceing is automatic; tabs are set to advance the insersion point 1/2 inch each time the Tab key is pressed. Formats may be changed at any time and as many times as desired throughtout the document.

KEYSTROKES

QUICKCORRECT

Ctrl + Shift + F1

1. Click **Tools** .... Alt + T
2. Click **QuickCorrect** .... Q
3. Select **Replace words as you type**
   option .... Alt + E

   To add words to QuickCorrect dictionary:

   a. Click **Replace** text box .... Alt + R
   b. Type commonly misspelled word to be included.
   c. Click **With** text box .... Alt + W
   d. Type corrected version of word.

   To select QuickCorrect options:

   a. Click **Options** .... Alt + O
   b. Click desired options.
   c. Click **OK** .... Enter
4. Click **Close** .... Alt + C

SPELL CHECK

Ctrl + F1

Click Speller button on Toolbar .... 🔠

OR

1. Position mouse on word with error.
2. Click *right* mouse.
3. Select correct spelling.

OR

4. Click **Spell Check** L
5. Follow Step 3 below.

OR

1. Click **Tools** .... Alt + T
2. Click **Spell Check** .... S
3. Select Spell Checker tab.

   To check anything other than the full document:

   a. Click in **Check** text box ...... Alt + K
   b. Click list arrow and select a Spell Check option:

   - **Document**
   - **Number of Pages**
   - **Page**
   - **Paragraph**
   - **Selected Text**
   - **Sentence**
   - **To End of Document**
   - **Word**
4. Click **Start** .... Alt + S

   If an error is found, click on one or more options:

   - **Replace**. .... Alt + R
     to replace word with correctly spelled word.
   - **Skip Once** .... Alt + O
     to ignore selected word and continue.
   - **Skip Always** .... Alt + A
     to ignore all occurrences of word in document.
   - **QuickCorrect** .... Alt + Q
     to correct a word in the QuickCorrect dictionary.
   - **Add** .... Alt + D
     to add word to WP dictionary.
   - **Suggest** .... Alt + U
     to see offered spelling suggestions.

- **Replace With** .... Alt + W
- Highlight correct spelling from list of **Replacements** .... Alt + P

If correct spelling is not found:

- Enter correct spelling of word in **Replace With** text box .... Alt + W
- Click **Replace** .... Alt + R
5. Click **Close** .... Alt + C

SPELL-AS-YOU-GO

1. Place mouse on red wavy underlined word.
2. Press *right* mouse button.
3. Click correct spelling word.

   OR

- Double-click book icon on status bar.
- Click correct spelling on Shortcut menu.

DOCUMENT PROPERTIES

1. Click **File** .... Alt + F
2. Click **Document** .... D
3. Click **Properties** .... T
4. Click **Summary** or **Information** Tab.
5. Click **OK** or **Close** .... Enter

Exercise 3

■ **Insertion Point Movements** ■ **QuickSpots** ■ **Scroll a Document**
■ **Create a Business Letter** ■ **The Date Feature**

NOTES

Insertion Point Movements

■ As noted earlier, the insertion point is the blinking vertical bar that shows you where the next typed character will appear. The arrow keys on the numeric keypad, or the separate arrow keys located to the left of the keypad, are used to move the insertion point in the direction indicated by the arrow. You may move the insertion point using the keyboard or the mouse:

- **Keyboard:** Press the arrow key in the direction you wish the insertion point to move. You may use the arrow keys located on the numeric keypad or (depending on your keyboard) the separate arrow keys located to the left of the numeric keypad. You can "express" move the insertion point from one point on the document to another using special key combinations (*see keystrokes at the end of this exercise*).

- **Mouse:** Move the mouse pointer to where you want to place the insertion point. You will note that when the mouse pointer is moved, a light vertical line moves with it. This light vertical line is called the **shadow cursor**. It allows you to see where the insertion point will be placed in the document. When the shadow cursor is in the desired position, click the *left* mouse button to place the insertion point.

■ The insertion point will only move through text, spaces, or codes. The insertion point cannot be moved before the beginning or past the end of your document.

QuickSpots

■ As you pass the mouse pointer over paragraphs, tables, or graphics, small boxes display on screen. These are called **QuickSpots**. Clicking a QuickSpot will display a Paragraph dialog box of editing options that relate to the paragraph, table, or graphic. You will learn to use QuickSpots for editing in a later exercise.

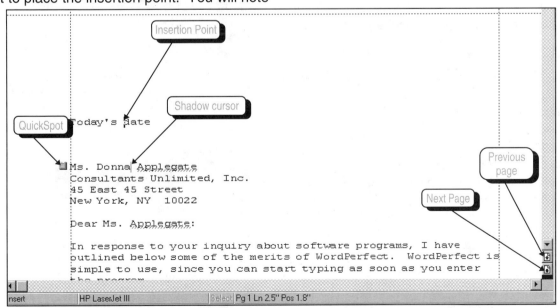

Scroll a Document

■ To move the insertion point to a part of the document that does not appear on screen, you can scroll your document vertically by clicking with your mouse on the scroll arrows (up/down arrows) on the right of your document screen.

■ To quickly scroll through a document, you may click and drag the scroll box (located on the scroll bar) up or down. Dragging the scroll box down or clicking the scroll down arrow moves the page up; dragging the scroll box up or clicking the scroll up arrow moves the page down.

■ You can also click in the gray area between the scroll box and the arrows to move a screen up down, right, or left. When the part of the document you wish to work with is in view, position your mouse pointer within the document and click where you wish to place the insertion point.

■ To scroll one page up or down, you may click on the Previous or Next Page buttons. While the horizontal scroll bars are seldom used, they move (or scroll) a document horizontally. You may choose to hide scroll bars so they do not display on the screen.

Create a Business Letter

■ There are a variety of letter styles for business and personal use. The parts of a business letter and the vertical spacing of letter parts are the same regardless of the style used. A business letter is composed of eight parts:

- date
- inside address (to whom and where the letter is going)
- salutation
- body
- closing
- signature line
- title line
- reference initials (the first set of initials belongs to the person who wrote the letter; the second set belongs to the person who typed the letter).
  - ✓ *Whenever you see* yo *as part of the reference initials in an exercise in this book, substitute* your own *initials.*

■ The letter style illustrated in this exercise is a full-block business letter with the date, closing, signature, and title lines beginning at the left margin.

■ In later exercises, you will learn to use a template to create a business letter and use other letter styles.

■ A letter generally begins 2.5" from the top of a page. If the letter is long, it may begin 2" from the top of the page. If the letter is short, it may begin 3" or more from the top.

■ Margins and the size of the characters may also be adjusted to make a letter more balanced on the page.
  - ✓ *Changing margins and font size will be covered in a later lesson.*

The Date Feature

■ The **Date** feature enables you to insert the current date into your document automatically.

■ To insert the date, select <u>D</u>ate from the <u>I</u>nsert menu. Then, select Date <u>T</u>ext or Date <u>C</u>ode. If you wish to change the date format, select Date <u>F</u>ormat and a dialog box will display listing date format options.

■ The Date feature gives you two options for inserting the date. If you select Date <u>T</u>ext, the current date is inserted into your document. If you select Date <u>C</u>ode, the date will automatically update whenever the document is opened or printed.

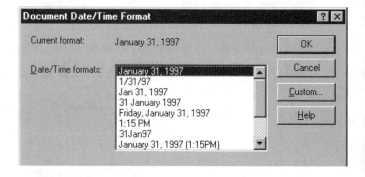

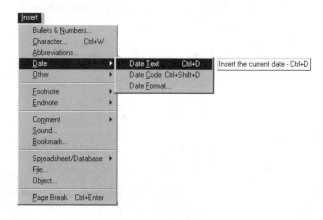

In this exercise, you will create a full-block letter and practice moving the insertion point through the document.

EXERCISE DIRECTIONS

1. Start with a clear screen.

2. Type the letter on the following page exactly as shown. Press the Enter key between parts of the letter as directed in the exercise.

3. Use the default margins and tabs.

4. Begin the date at approximately Ln 2.5". Use the Date Text feature to insert today's date.

5. Access the QuickCorrect feature. Be sure the Replace words as you type option has been selected.

6. Use the Spell Check or Spell-As-You-Go feature to correct the misspellings in the document.

7. Move the mouse pointer over the first paragraph. Note the shadow cursor. Move the insertion point to the top of the screen (Ctrl + Home) and then back to the end of the document (Ctrl + End).

8. Use the scroll box to scroll to the top of the document.

9. Click on a QuickSpot and note the options on the Paragraph dialog box. Click the Close button on the dialog box.

10. Save the document; name it RAFFLE.

11. Close the document window.

KEYSTROKES

INSERT CURRENT DATE

Ctrl + D

1. Click **Insert** .... `Alt`+`I`
2. Click **Date** .... `D`
3. Click **Date Text** .... `T`

INSERT DATE CODE

Ctrl + Shift + D

1. Click **Insert** .... `Alt`+`I`
2. Click **Date** .... `D`
3. Click **Date Code** .... `C`

CHANGE DATE FORMAT

1. Click **Insert** .... `Alt`+`I`
2. Click **Date** .... `D`
3. Click **Date Format** .... `F`
4. Click desired format.
5. Click **OK** .... `Enter`

SCROLL

Click up/down/left/right arrows on scroll bar until desired text is in view, or click and drag the scroll box up/down to express move the window.

EXPRESS INSERTION POINT MOVEMENT KEYSTROKES

TO MOVE:	PRESS:
One character left	`←`
One character right	`→`
One line up	`↑`
One line down	`↓`
Previous word	`Ctrl`+`←`
Next word	`Ctrl`+`→`
Top of screen	`Page Up`
Bottom of screen	`Page Down`
Beginning of document	`Ctrl`+`Home`
End of document	`Ctrl`+`End`
Beginning of line	`Home`
End of line	`End`
First line on previous page	`Alt`+`Page Up`
First line on next page	`Alt`+`Page Down`

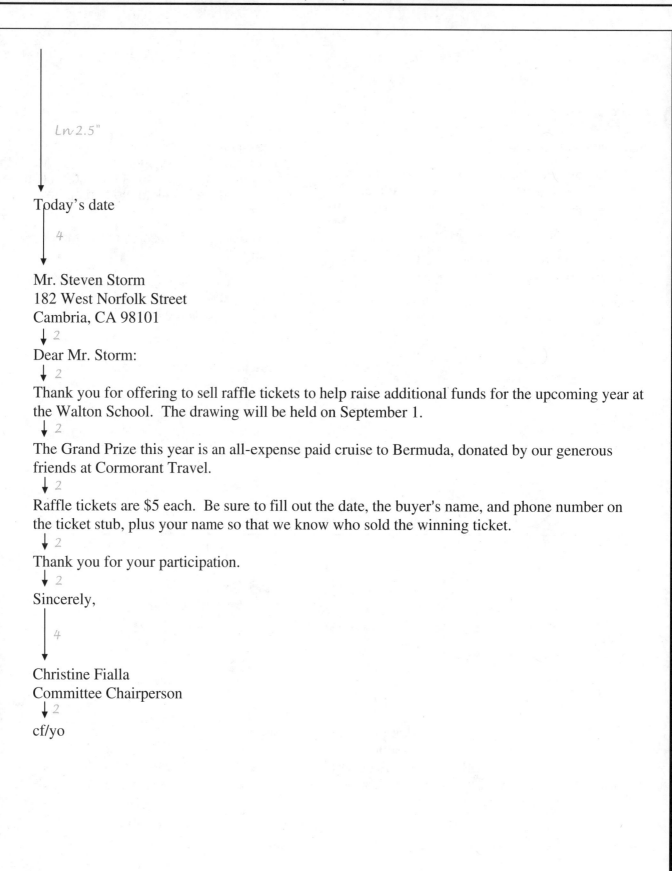

Ln 2.5"

Today's date

4

Mr. Steven Storm
182 West Norfolk Street
Cambria, CA 98101

↓ 2

Dear Mr. Storm:

↓ 2

Thank you for offering to sell raffle tickets to help raise additional funds for the upcoming year at the Walton School. The drawing will be held on September 1.

↓ 2

The Grand Prize this year is an all-expense paid cruise to Bermuda, donated by our generous friends at Cormorant Travel.

↓ 2

Raffle tickets are $5 each. Be sure to fill out the date, the buyer's name, and phone number on the ticket stub, plus your name so that we know who sold the winning ticket.

↓ 2

Thank you for your participation.

↓ 2

Sincerely,

4

Christine Fialla
Committee Chairperson

↓ 2

cf/yo

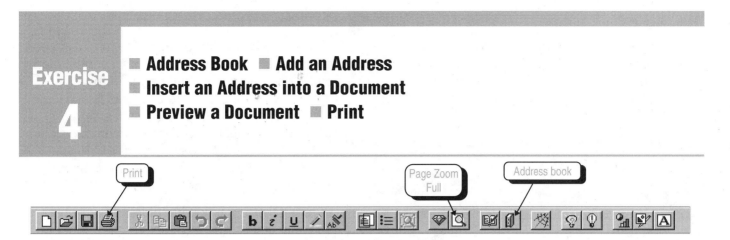

Exercise 4

- **Address Book** ■ **Add an Address**
- **Insert an Address into a Document**
- **Preview a Document** ■ **Print**

Print   Page Zoom Full   Address book

NOTES

Address Book

- The **Address Book** feature allows you to keep the names, addresses, and phone numbers of people to whom you send letters frequently. After entering names and addresses into WordPerfect's address book, you can retrieve them into a document when you desire by clicking the Address Book button on the Toolbar and selecting the name and address you desire.

- To enter a name and address into the address book, click the Address Book button on the Toolbar, or select Address <u>B</u>ook from the <u>T</u>ools menu.

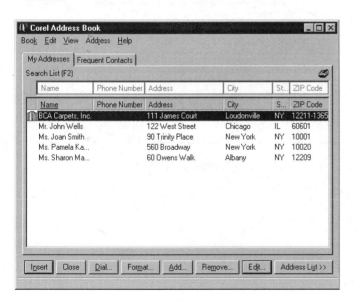

- In the Address Book dialog box, two tabs display: My Addresses and Frequent Contacts. Each tab is considered an individual address book. You can create other address books to allow you to group individuals' phone and address information. For example, you could create an address book (tab) which reads Computer Club. You would then enter the names and addresses of contacts within that organization or club.

Add an Address

- To add an address, click the Tab where you wish to save your information, then click the <u>A</u>dd button. In the New Entry dialog box, you will be asked to indicate whether the entry is a person or an organization. Make the appropriate selection. In the Properties for New Entry dialog box which follows, fill out the entry form as desired.
  - ✓ *Precede each first name entry with a title: Mr., Ms., Dr., etc., so that the title is included when the address is inserted into a document.*

- If you wish to add more than one name at a time, click the Ne<u>w</u> button instead of OK when one name is completed.

- In the address book list, a small building icon displays next to each organization entry to distinguish it from a personal address entry.

Insert an Address into a Document

- To insert a name and address into a document, click the Address Book button on the Toolbar, then double-click the desired address to be inserted, or select the address and click I<u>n</u>sert.

Preview a Document

- To see how your document will format, or appear on a page, you may preview your work by clicking the Page/Zoom Full button on the Toolbar ⬜ or by selecting Zoom, Full Page from the View menu.

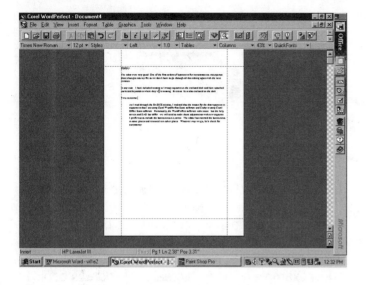

Print

- By default, WordPerfect prints the full, on-screen document. However, you can also print a page of the document, selected pages of the document, or one or more blocks of text within the document. You may also print a single document or multiple documents from a disk without retrieving them to the screen. In this exercise, you will print a full document from a window on your screen.

- Before you send a document to print, always check to see that your printer is turned on and that paper is loaded.

- There are three ways to print an entire document:

  - Click the Print button 🖨 on the Toolbar.

  - Select File, Print from the menu bar. In the Print dialog box which displays, click Print.

  - Press Ctrl + P.

In this exercise, you will enter name and address information using the existing address books that were created by WordPerfect. You will then create a full-block letter using the Date feature and print one copy of the document.

EXERCISE DIRECTIONS

1. Access the Address Book. Enter the following names and addresses of persons within the My Addresses Tab. Change the Format to Name, Title and Company.

   - Mr. John Wells, 122 West Street, Chicago, IL 60601
   - Ms. Sharon Mason, 60 Owens Walk, Albany, NY 12209
   - Ms. Pamela Kavaler, Manager, L. & J. Company, 560 Broadway, New York, NY 10020

2. Use the default margins and tabs.

3. Type the letter on the following page as shown:

   - Use the Date Text feature to insert today's date approximately 2.5" from the top of the page.
   - Press the Enter key between parts of the letter as directed in the exercise.
   - Use the Address Book to insert the inside address.

4. Access the QuickCorrect feature. Be sure the Replace words as you type option has been selected.

5. Spell check.

6. Preview the document.

7. Print one copy using any of the three methods outlined above.

8. Save the document; name it THANKYOU.

9. Close the document window.

Today's date

Ms. Sharon Mason
60 Owens Walk
Albany, NY 12209

Dear Ms. Mason:

Thank you for your generous contribution to our annual Holiday Fund-raising event.

Your generosity and commitment to helping underprivileged children is most appreciated.
The Holiday Banquet will be held on Saturday, December 19. We would be delighted to have
you attend. An invitation will be forthcoming under separate cover.

Once again, thank you for helping a child.

Sincerely,

Wendy Ashton
Events Chairperson

wa/yo

KEYSTROKES

CREATE A NEW ADDRESS BOOK

Click Address Book button on
Toolbar .... 🚪

OR

1. Click **Tools** .... Alt + T
2. Click **Address Book** .... B
3. Click **Book** .... Alt + K
4. Click **New** .... N
5. Type name of your address book (e.g.,
   Friends)
6. Click **OK** .... Enter

ADD NAMES TO ADDRESS BOOK

1. Click Address Book button on
   Toolbar.. 🚪
2. Click **Tools** .... Alt + T
3. Click **Address Book** .... B
4. Click Tab where you want to add
   names and address (e.g. Frequent
   Contacts or Friends).
5. Click **Add** .... Alt + A
6. Choose Person or Organization in
   Select entry type list box.
7. Enter the appropriate information.
8. Click **OK** .... Enter

INSERT ADDRESS INTO A DOCUMENT

1. Position insertion point where address
   is to be inserted.
2. Click Address Book button on
   Toolbar.. 🚪

OR

3. Click **Tools** .... Alt + T
4. Click **Address Book** .... B
5. Click the desired tab.
6. Double click name you wish to insert
   into your document.

OR

7. Click **Insert** .... Alt + N

PREVIEW A DOCUMENT

Click Page/Zoom Full button on
Toolbar... 🔍

OR

1. Click **View** .... Alt + V
2. Click **Zoom** .... Z
3. Click **Full Page** .... F
4. Click **OK**............................... Enter

EXIT PREVIEW

Click Page/Zoom Full button on
Toolbar... 🔍

OR

1. Click **View**............................ Alt + V
2. Click **Zoom** .... Z
3. Click **100%** 1
4. Click **OK** .... Enter

PRINT

F5 or Ctrl + P

1. Click Print button on Toolbar.......... 🖨

   OR

   a. Click **File** .... Alt + F
   b. Click **Print** .... P
2. Click **Print tab**.
3. Click Print list arrow to select a print
   option .... Alt + P , ↓ ↑
4. Click **Print**............................ Enter

CANCEL PRINT JOB

1. Click Print button on Toolbar.......... 🖨

   OR

   a. Click **File** .... Alt + F
   b. Click **Print** .... P
2. Click **Status** .... Alt + S
3. Click document to cancel.
4. Click **Document** .... Alt + D
5. Click **Cancel Printing**.................... C
6. Click **Close** .... Alt + C

Exercise

5

■ **Summary**

In this exercise, you will create a full-block letter using the Date, Address Book, and Spell check features. You will then Preview and print one copy of the completed document.

EXERCISE DIRECTIONS

1. Type the letter below in full-block style.
2. Use the default margins and tabs.
3. Use the Date Text feature to insert today's date.
4. Use the Address Book to insert the inside address.

5. Spell check.
6. Preview the document.
7. Print one copy.
8. Save the document; name it VACANCY.
9. Close the document window.

Today's date Mr. John Wells, 122 West Street, Chicago, IL 60601 Dear Mr. Wells: Thank you for your inquiry regarding employment with our firm.⧾We have reviewed your qualifications with several members of our firm. We regret to report that we do not have an appropriate vacancy at this time.⧾We will retain your resume in our files in the event that an opening occurs in your field.⧾Your interest in our organization is very much appreciated. We hope to be able to offer you a position at another time. Very truly yours, Christine Ford, PERSONNEL MANAGER cf/yo

<table>
<tr><td rowspan="3">Exercise
6</td><td>■ **Open and Revise a Document** ■ **Open a Recently Saved File**</td></tr>
<tr><td>■ **Open a Document not Recently Saved** ■ **Specify a File**</td></tr>
<tr><td>■ **QuickFinder to Find Files** ■ **File Details** ■ **Sort Files**
■ **Insert Text** ■ **Save Changes to a Document**</td></tr>
</table>

NOTES

Open and Revise a Document

■ A document is revised when corrections or adjustments need to be made. **Proofreaders' marks** are symbols on a printed copy of a document that indicate changes to be made. As each proofreaders' mark is introduced in an exercise in this text, it will be explained and illustrated.

■ Before a document can be revised or edited, it must be opened from the disk to the screen.

Open a Recently Saved File

■ WordPerfect lists the nine most recently opened files at the bottom of the File menu. To open a recently opened file, select the desired filename on the list of recently opened files.

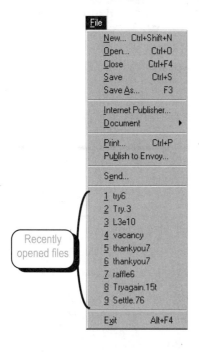

Open a Document Not Recently Saved

■ After you select Open from the File menu or click the Open button 📂 on the Toolbar, the Open dialog box appears, listing all files that have been saved.

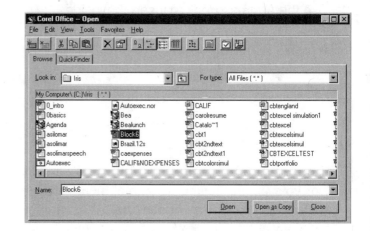

Specify a File

■ To specify a file you want opened, type the filename in the Name text box, or double-click the filename from the list of documents displayed in the window. If the desired file is not listed in the current folder shown in the Look in text box, click the list arrow next to the Look in text box and select a desired drive and/or folder.

■ You may also select a file from the history list. Clicking the list box arrow next to the Name text box displays the last ten recently saved files.

QuickFinder to Find Files

- **QuickFinder** allows you to search for filenames, patterns in words, or items contained in document summaries in the current folder, subfolder, or the entire drive.

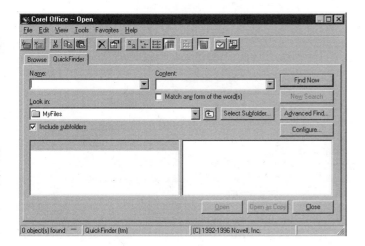

- QuickFinder may be accessed by selecting Open from the File menu and selecting the QuickFinder tab.

- In the dialog box which displays, you may enter the filename you are trying to find in the Name text box. If you are uncertain of the file's name, you can enter a word or phrase from the document in the Content text box. You can search a particular folder by entering the folder name in the Look in text box, or if you are uncertain of the folder which may contain the file, click the list arrow next to the Look in text box and select a drive you wish to search.

File Details

- The Open dialog box may also be used to obtain detailed information about a file or group of files. Selecting a file and clicking the Details button at the top of the dialog box displays the name, size, and type of file as well as the date/time the file was last modified.

Sort Files

- To sort files in ascending order by Name, Size, Type of file, or date/time last modified, click the column header (Name, Size, Type, Modified). To sort files in descending order, click the column header again.

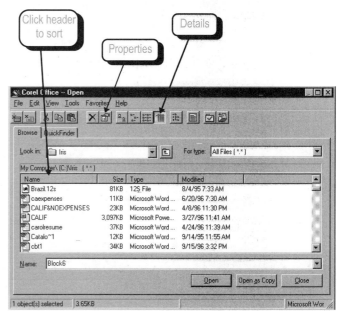

- Selecting a file and clicking the Properties button displays summary information such as title, author, and keywords that the user added when creating the document.

Insert Text

- To make corrections, use the insertion point movement keys to move to the point of correction, or use the mouse to click at the point of correction.

- Text is inserted immediately before the insertion point when Insert mode is on. (Insert is the default keyboarding mode indicated at the bottom left of the Status bar.) When typing inserted text, the existing text moves to the right. When inserting a word, the space following the word must also be inserted.

- To create a new paragraph in existing text, place the insertion point immediately to the left of the first character in the new paragraph and press the Enter key twice.

- Another way to edit text is to type over existing text with new text. To put WordPerfect in Typeover mode, press the Insert (Ins) key once. In this mode, existing text does not move to the right—it is typed over. (After pressing the Insert key, note the bottom left of the status bar— Typeover mode is displayed).

- Press the Insert key again to return to Insert mode.

- When a document is opened and revisions are made, the revised or updated version must be resaved or replaced. When a document is resaved, the old version is replaced with the new version.

Save Changes to a Document

- You may save your changes as you are working or you may save your changes after all corrections have been made. Click the Save button 🖫 on the Toolbar or select <u>S</u>ave from the <u>F</u>ile menu. Your file will be updated, and the document will remain on the screen for you to continue working.

- It is recommended that you save often to prevent loss of data.

- The proofreaders' mark for insertion is: ∧

- The proofreaders' mark for a new paragraph is: ⌗

In this exercise, you will open a previously saved document and insert new text.

EXERCISE DIRECTIONS

1. Open ▱TRY, or open ▱06TRY.

2. Make the insertions indicated below.

3. Use Typeover mode to insert the word "determine" in the second paragraph. Return to Insert mode immediately following this step.

4. Save your work.

5. Spell check.

6. Print one copy.

7. Close the file.

8. Close the document window.

As you type, *you will* notice the Pos indicator on your status bar change as the position of your insertion point changes.

The "wraparound" feature allows the *computer* operator to ~~decide on~~ *determine* line endings, making the use of *the* Enter unnecessary except at the end of a paragraph or short line. ⌗Each file is saved on a *data* disk or hard drive for recall. Documents must be given a name *or number* for identification.

key

KEYSTROKES

OPEN A DOCUMENT

CTRL + O

1. Click Open File button .... 🗁
2. Double-click desired filename.

OR

1. Click <u>F</u>ile .... `Alt` + `F`
2. Click <u>O</u>pen .... `O`
3. Select or type desired filename.
4. Click **OK** .... `Enter`

OR

1. Click <u>F</u>ile .... `Alt` + `F`
2. Select desired filename .... `↓`
   from list of recently opened files.

RESAVE A DOCUMENT

Click **Save** button .... 🖫

OR

1. Click <u>F</u>ile .... `Alt` + `F`
2. Click <u>S</u>ave .... `S`

OR

1. Click <u>F</u>ile .... `Alt` + `F`
2. Click <u>C</u>lose .... `C`
3. Click <u>Y</u>es .... `Y`
   when prompted to save changes.

INSERT TEXT

1. Place insertion point to left of character that will immediately follow inserted text.
2. Type text.

TYPEOVER

1. Place insertion point where text is to be overwritten.
2. Press **Insert** .... `Ins`
3. Type text.
4. Press **Insert** .... `Ins`
   to exit Typeover mode.

Exercise 7

- **Open as Copy (Read-Only Document)** ■ **Save As**
- **Undo** ■ **Redo**

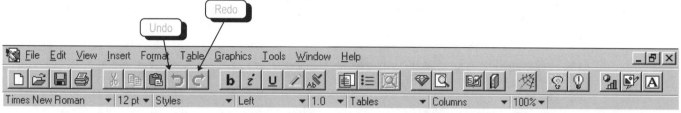

NOTES

Open as Copy (Read-Only Document)

- If you wish to open a document but not make changes to it, you can click the Open as Copy option in the Open File dialog box. This will make the document a read-only copy and will require you to save it with a different file name, preventing you from accidentally affecting the file.

Click to open as a read-only file.

- If you save, close, or exit a document that you opened using the Open as Copy option, WordPerfect automatically displays the Save As dialog box for you to give the file another name, thus leaving the original document intact.

Save As

- If you wish to save any document under a different filename or in a different location, you may select Save As from the File menu. When any document is saved under a new filename, the original document remains intact.

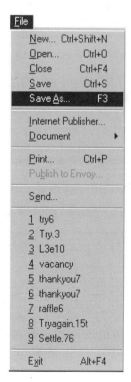

Undo

- The **Undo** feature lets you undo the last change you made to the document.

- WordPerfect remembers up to 300 actions in a document and allows you to undo any or all of them. You can undo all your recent actions by repeatedly clicking the Undo button ⤺ on the Toolbar, or you can undo a selected action by selecting Undo/Redo History from the Edit menu and choosing the action to undo from the list presented.

Redo

- The **Redo** feature allows you to reverse the last undo. Like Undo, Redo allows you to reverse up to 300 actions in a document. You can redo an action by repeatedly clicking the Redo button on the Toolbar ⤻, or you can redo a selected action by selecting Undo/Redo History from the Edit menu and choosing the action to redo.

In this exercise, you will insert text at the top of the page and create a full-block letter. To insert the date, press the Enter key eight times to bring the Ln indicator to 2.57". Remember to use the automatic Date feature. After inserting the date, you will use the address book to insert the inside address. Text will adjust as you continue creating the letter.

EXERCISE DIRECTIONS

1. Open 🖾TRYAGAIN as an Open as Copy file, or open 🖫07TRYAGA from the data disk as an Open as Copy file.

2. Make the indicated insertions. Follow the spacing for a full-block letter illustrated in Exercise 3.

3. Use the Date Text feature to insert today's date.

4. Use Typeover mode to insert the word "start" in the second paragraph; return to Insert mode immediately.

5. After typing the initials (jo/yo) in lowercase, undo the action several times to remove the initials.

6. Retype the initials in uppercase.

7. Preview your work.

8. Modify the document summary information (Properties) as follows:

   Descriptive Name:....... Software Inquiry Response
   Descriptive Type: ....Letter
   Author: .... Your name
   Typist: .... Your name
   Subject:..................................Response to Inquiry

9. Access the Information tab in the Properties dialog box and note the number of words in this document.

10. Print one copy.

11. Use Undo to remove the uppercase initials; retype them in lowercase.

12. Close the file; save as TRYIT.

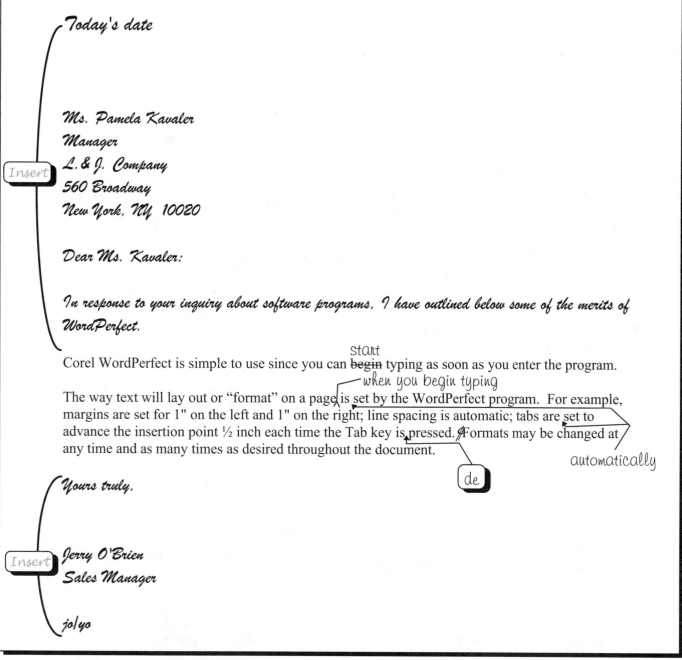

Today's date

Insert

Ms. Pamela Kavaler
Manager
L. & J. Company
560 Broadway
New York, NY 10020

Dear Ms. Kavaler:

In response to your inquiry about software programs, I have outlined below some of the merits of WordPerfect.

Corel WordPerfect is simple to use since you can ~~begin~~ ^{start} typing as soon as you enter the program.

when you begin typing

The way text will lay out or "format" on a page is set by the WordPerfect program. For example, margins are set for 1" on the left and 1" on the right; line spacing is automatic; tabs are set to advance the insertion point ½ inch each time the Tab key is pressed. ¶ Formats may be changed at any time and as many times as desired throughout the document.

automatically

de

Yours truly,

Insert

Jerry O'Brien
Sales Manager

jo/yo

KEYSTROKES

SAVE AS

F3

1. Click **File**.............................. Alt + F
2. Click **Save As** .... A
3. Keyboard new filename.
4. Click **OK** .... Enter

UNDO

Ctrl + Z

This procedure is to be used immediately after executing the command you wish to undo.

- Click **Undo** button .... ↩

OR

1. Click **Edit**............................. Alt + E
2. Click **Undo**................................. U

REDO

This procedure is to be used immediately after undoing a command.

- Click **Redo** button .... ↪

OR

1. Click **Edit** .... Alt + E
2. Click **Redo**.................................. R

<table>
<tr><td>Exercise
8</td><td>■ **Delete Text** ■ **Select Text**
■ **Undelete** ■ **Undelete vs. Undo**</td></tr>
</table>

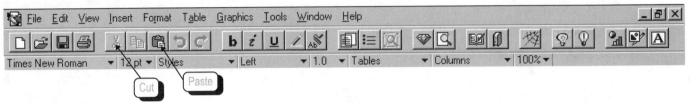

NOTES

Delete Text

■ The **Delete** feature allows you to remove text, graphics, or codes from a document.

■ Procedures for deleting text vary depending upon what is being deleted: a character, previous character, word, line, paragraph, page, remainder of page, or a blank line.

■ The Backspace key may be used to delete characters and close up spaces to the left of the insertion point.

■ To delete a character or a space, place the insertion point immediately to the left of the character or space to delete, then press the Delete (Del) key (located on the right side of your keyboard).

■ A block of text (words, sentences, or paragraphs) may be deleted by selecting (highlighting) the block and either:

• Pressing the Delete key.

• Clicking the Cut button ✂ on the Toolbar.

• Right-clicking the mouse button and selecting Cut.

(See Select Text right.)

■ When text is deleted using the Cut button, it disappears from the screen and is placed on the Clipboard. The Clipboard is a temporary storage area in the computer's memory. The text most recently sent to the Clipboard may be retrieved by clicking the Paste button on the Toolbar 📋.

Select Text

■ Text may be highlighted or selected in several ways:

• **Using the keyboard**, by holding down the Shift key while pressing the insertion point movement keys.

• **Using the keyboard in combination with the mouse**, by clicking where the selection should begin, holding down the Shift key, and clicking where the selection will end.

• **Using the mouse**, by dragging the mouse pointer over desired text.

• **Using the mouse**, by clicking in the left margin opposite the desired sentence.

✓ *When you move the mouse pointer into the left margin, the mouse pointer changes to the shape of an arrow pointing upward toward the top right of the screen.*

✓ *Clicking and holding the left mouse button and dragging the mouse pointer up or down in the margin will allow you to highlight or select as many lines of text as you wish.*

• **Using the F8 key**, which anchors the insertion point and allows you to use the insertion point movement keys to highlight or select text in any direction from the position of the insertion point. You may extend the selection to any character or symbol by pressing that character or symbol on the keyboard. WordPerfect will instantly highlight from the insertion point to the next occurrence of that character or symbol. Press F8 to cancel the selection.

- To abandon any selection process, release the mouse button and click once anywhere on the WordPerfect screen.

Undelete

- Text may be restored after it has been deleted. Your insertion point should be in the location where you wish the text to be restored when accessing this task. WordPerfect remembers your last three deletions and allows you to restore them.

- Undelete may be accessed by selecting Undelete from the Edit menu, or by pressing Ctrl + Shift + Z.

Undelete vs. Undo

- Undelete lets you restore the most recent deletion or up to three previous deletions at the insertion point. Undo lets you restore deleted information in its original location or reverse the last change or action made to the document.

- When using Undo to restore deleted text, you must use the command immediately after the deletion is made.

- Common proofreaders' marks for deleting or moving text are:

  delete: ℓ

  close up space: ⌒

  move text to the left: [or {

KEYSTROKES

SELECT (HIGHLIGHT) BLOCKS OF TEXT

– USING THE KEYBOARD –

Place insertion point where highlight is to begin.

To Highlight:	Press:
One character to the left	Shift + ←
One character to the right	Shift + →
One line up	Shift + ↑
One line down	Shift + ↓
To the end of a line	Shift + End
To the beginning of a line	Shift + Home
To the end of a word	Shift + Ctrl + →
To the beginning of a word	Shift + Ctrl + ←
Top of Page	Shift + Page Up
Bottom of Page	Shift + Page Down
To the end of a paragraph	Shift + Ctrl + ↓
To the beginning of a paragraph	Shift + Ctrl + ↑
To the end of the document	Shift + Ctrl + End
To the beginning of the document	Shift + Ctrl + Home
Entire document	Ctrl + A

– USING F8 –

1. Place insertion point where block highlighting is to begin.
2. Press **F8** F8
3. Press any of the insertion movement keys to extend the highlighting.

   OR

   Press any character, punctuation, or symbol to highlight to the next occurrence of that key.

– USING THE MOUSE –

1. Place insertion point where block highlighting is to begin.
2. Hold down the left mouse button and drag the insertion point to desired location.
3. Release the mouse button.

   OR

1. Place insertion point where block highlighting is to begin.
2. Point to where selection should end.
3. Press **Shift** .... Shift
   and click left mouse button.

MOUSE SELECTION SHORTCUTS

To select a word:

1. Place insertion point anywhere in word.
2. Double-click left mouse button.

To select a sentence:

1. Place insertion point anywhere in sentence.
2. Hold down **Ctrl** .... Ctrl
   and triple click left mouse button.

To select a paragraph:

1. Place insertion point anywhere in paragraph.
2. Quadruple-click left mouse button.

   OR

1. Place mouse pointer in **left margin**, opposite desired paragraph.

   Mouse pointer will point to the right when you're in the left margin area.

2. Click left mouse button once.

To select an entire document:

Ctrl + A

1. Click **E**dit .... Alt + E
2. Click Se**l**ect L
3. Click A**l**l L

To cancel a selection:

Click anywhere outside the selection.

(continued)

DELETE

Character:

1. Place insertion point to the left of character to delete.
2. Press **Delete** .... Del

OR

1. Place insertion point to the right of character to delete.
2. Press **Backspace** .... Backspace

Word:

1. Double-click desired word.
2. Press **Delete** .... Del

OR

1. Place insertion point to the right of word to delete.
2. Press **Ctrl+Backspace** .... Ctrl + Backspace

Block of Text:

1. Select (highlight) block to delete using procedures described above.
2. Click **Cut** icon .... to place text on clipboard.

OR

Press **Delete** .... Del

✓ *The **clipboard** is a temporary storage area in computer memory. The text most recently sent to the clipboard may be retrieved by clicking the **Paste** button on the Toolbar or by pressing **Ctrl + V**.*

REPLACE DELETED TEXT WITH TYPED TEXT

1. Select (highlight) text to replace using procedures described above.
2. Type new text .... *text*

UNDELETE

Ctrl + Shift + Z

1. Click **Edit** .... Alt + E
2. Click **Undelete** .... N
3. Select desired option:
   - **Restore** to restore last deletion .... R
   - **Next** or **Previous** to cycle through last three deletions .... N or P
4. Click **Restore** .... R

In this exercise you will use various deletion methods to edit a document. Use block highlighting procedures to delete sentences, words, or blocks of text.

EXERCISE DIRECTIONS

1. Start with a clear screen.
2. Create the exercise as shown in Part I, or open 08MARATH.
3. Use the default margins.
4. Begin the exercise on Ln 1".
5. Using the selection and deletion procedures indicated in Part II of the exercise, make the revisions.
6. After deleting the last paragraph, undelete it.
7. Using another deletion method, delete the last paragraph again.
8. Spell check.
9. Print one copy.
10. Close the file; save as MARATHON.
11. Close the document window.

RUNNING A MARATHON
SO YOU WANT TO RUN A MARATHON?

TWO MAJOR STEPS TO GO THE LONG DISTANCE

It doesn't take a major miracle to run a marathon. Going the distance can be easy. Depending upon your level of fitness, you can take anywhere from up to three months to a year to properly train for a marathon. Don't be discouraged; you'll build your strength over time and be on your way to crossing the finish line.

Training for Endurance
Endurance training is what is needed to building strength, speed and overall improved performance. The key is to run relaxed and focused. While running, keep your wrists, hands and jaw loose. Keep your feet under your entire body and try to avoid leaning forward.

Training for Strength
Strength training builds incredible power; it allows you to lengthen your stride and get more distance with every step. The best way to build up your strength is by running hills.
During strength training, the key is to focus on form, not speed. Remember to adjust your form according to the grade: shorten your stride, pump your arms, and increase your tempo.

RUNNING A MARATHON   *Triple click, press delete*
SO YOU WANT TO RUN A MARATHON?

TWO MAJOR STEPS TO GO THE LONG DISTANCE   *Double-click Press Del*   *Double-click, Right-click, cut*

It doesn't take a major miracle to run a marathon. Going the distance can be easy. Depending upon your level of fitness, you can take anywhere from up to three months to a year to properly train for a marathon. Don't be discouraged; you'll build your strength over time and be on your way to crossing the finish line   *Triple-Click, Press Del*

Training for Endurance
Endurance training is what is needed to building strength, speed and overall improved performance. The key is to run relaxed and focused. While running, keep your wrists, hands and jaw loose. Keep your feet under your entire body and try to avoid leaning forward.

Select w/mouse, Right-click, cut

Training for Strength
Strength training builds incredible power; it allows you to lengthen your stride and get more distance with every step. The best way to build up your strength is by running hills.
During strength training, the key is to focus on form, not speed. Remember to adjust your form according to the grade: shorten your stride, pump your arms, and increase your tempo.

Move mouse pointer on left margin, Right-click, choose paragraph, Press Del

Exercise 9

■ **Reveal Codes** ■ **Show Symbols** ■ **Delete/Edit**

NOTES

Reveal Codes

■ As a document is created in WordPerfect, codes are inserted that determine the document's appearance. These codes are not displayed on the screen, but can be revealed when necessary either through the **Reveal Codes** or **Show Symbols** features.

■ When the Reveal Codes feature is selected, the document window is divided into two parts. The top part is the normal editing area; the bottom part displays the same text with the codes. The divider line splits the two parts of the window.

■ Reveal Codes may be accessed by pressing Alt + F3, by selecting Reveal Codes from the View menu or by right-clicking the mouse and selecting Reveal Codes.

■ As you point to a code with your mouse, a QuickTip explains the code. An example of this screen and its codes appears below.

■ Reveal Codes may be deselected by pressing Alt + F3 again, or by deselecting the Reveal Codes option under the View menu.

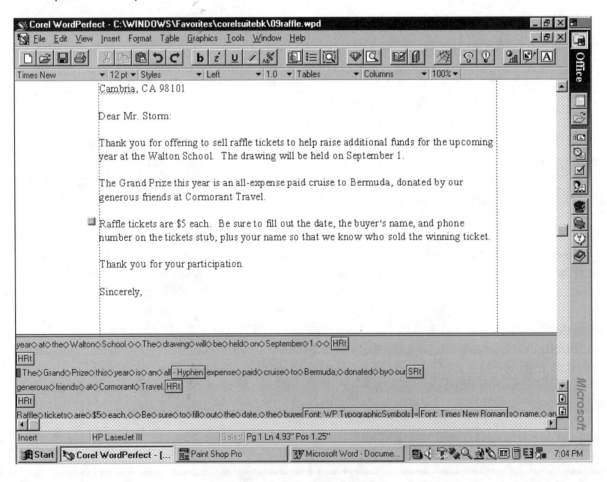

Show Symbols

- When the Show (¶) Symbols feature is selected, all the codes that were inserted when the document was created are displayed on screen as various symbols.

- Show Symbols may be accessed by selecting Show ¶ from the View menu or by pressing Ctrl + Shift +F3.

- A hard return code is represented by a paragraph symbol (¶); a tab code is represented by an arrow (→); a space is represented by a small solid circle (•). An example of a document with symbols displayed is shown below.

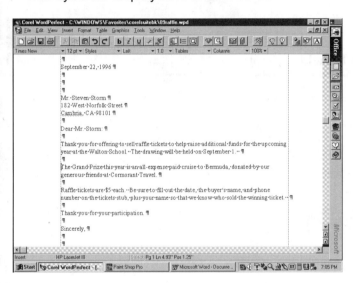

- Show Symbols may be deselected by pressing Ctrl + Shift + F3 or by deselecting the Show ¶ option.

Delete/Edit Codes

- **To delete a code in Reveal Codes mode**, use the mouse pointer to click on the code (the insertion point, represented by a red indicator, appears before the code), and press the Delete key. Or, use the mouse pointer to drag the code out of the Reveal Codes window.

- To edit a code in Reveal Codes mode, double-click the code, and a dialog box relating to the feature displays.

- **To delete a code in Show Symbols mode,** move the insertion point to the left of the code and press the Delete key.

- To combine two paragraphs into one, the hard returns that separate the paragraphs must be deleted. Therefore, deleting the paragraph symbols will delete the code. This may be done in either Reveal Codes or Show Symbols mode.

In this exercise, you will edit an exercise you created earlier.

EXERCISE DIRECTIONS

1. Start with a clear screen.

2. Open ⬚RAFFLE or open ⬚09RAFFLE from the data disk as a read-only file (Open As Copy).

3. Reveal codes. Point to each code and view the QuickTip.

4. To combine the two paragraphs, delete the hard return codes in the Reveal Codes screen.

5. Make the remaining corrections.

6. Preview your work.

7. Print one copy.

8. Close the file; save the changes.

September 22, 199-

Mr. Steven Storm
182 West Norfolk Street
Cambria, CA 98101

Dear Mr. Storm:

Thank you for offering to sell raffle tickets to help raise ~~additional~~ funds for the ~~upcoming year at the~~ Walton School. The drawing will be held on September 1.

The Grand Prize ~~this year~~ is an all-expense paid cruise to Bermuda, donated by our generous friends at Cormorant Travel.

Raffle tickets are $5 each. Be sure to fill out the date, *your name,* the buyer's name, and phone number on the ticket stub, ~~plus your name so that we know who sold the winning ticket~~.

Thank you for your participation *in this fund-raising event*

Sincerely,

Christine Fialla
Committee Chairperson

cf/yo

KEYSTROKES

REVEAL CODES

Alt + F3

1. Click **V**iew .... `Alt`+`V`
2. Click **Reveal Codes** .... `C`

To exit Reveal Codes:

Repeat steps 1 and 2 above.

DELETE CODES

1. Reveal codes.
2. Point to and click on code to be deleted.
3. Press Delete .... `Del`

OR

4. Use the mouse pointer to drag the code out of the Reveal Codes window.

SHOW SYMBOLS

Ctrl + Shift + F3

1. Click **V**iew .... `Alt`+`V`
2. Click **Show** ¶ .... `S`

To exit Show Symbols:

1. Click **V**iew .... `Alt`+`V`
2. Click **Show** .... `S`

Exercise 10

- **Change Toolbars** - **Hard Space** - **Convert Case**
- **Set Margins** - **Set Tabs** - **Relative vs. Absolute Tabs**

NOTES

Change Toolbars

- WordPerfect 7 provides 15 specialized Toolbars to make accessing features easier.

- To change Toolbars, point to the current Toolbar, right-click and select a new Toolbar from the list provided. The WordPerfect 7 Toolbar is the default.

- The selected Toolbar will stay until a new Toolbar is selected, even if a new document is created.

Hard Space

- To prevent two or more words from splitting during word wrap, a **hard space** code can be inserted between words. This feature is particularly useful when keyboarding first and last names, dates, equations, and time.

- The procedure for inserting a hard space is to delete the existing space, and then hold down the Control key as you press the space bar.

Convert Case

- The **Convert Case** feature lets you change an existing block of text to Lowercase, Uppercase or Initial Caps. When you choose Initial Caps, the first word in each sentence remains capitalized. To change case, select Convert Case from the Edit menu and select a convert option.

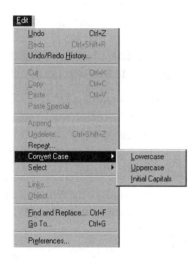

Set Margins

- WordPerfect measures margins in inches. The default margins are 1" on the left and right and 1" on the top and bottom of the page.

- There are three ways to change left and right margins:

  - **Drag margin guidelines.** This method is the most convenient way to adjust margins and see the effect on the document text.

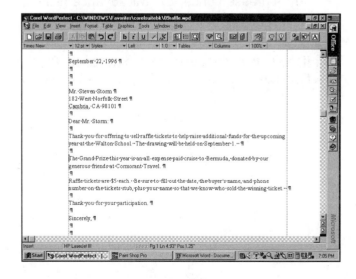

Format Toolbar

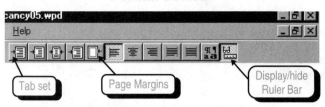

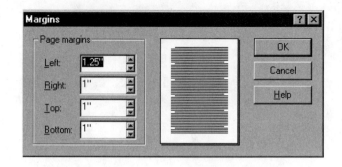

To change margins using the guidelines, position the mouse pointer on the left or right margin guideline. When the pointer changes to a left/right pointing arrow, drag the margin guideline to the desired position. As you drag the guideline, the margin measurements will display in a pop-up text box. To change margins for a block of text, select the text before you drag the margin guidelines.

- **Use the Margins dialog box.** This method allows for greater precision. To set margins in the dialog box, select Margins from the Format menu or click the Page Margins button on the Format Toolbar.

In the Margins dialog box which follows, enter the left and right margin amounts.

- **Use the Ruler Bar.** This method lets you see the effects of margin changes as you make them. Drag the left and/or right margin markers (the solid black part of the marker) to the new margin locations. As you drag the marker, note the margin position which displays in the lower right of the status bar.

- To display the Ruler Bar, select Toolbars/Ruler from the View menu and choose Ruler Bar.

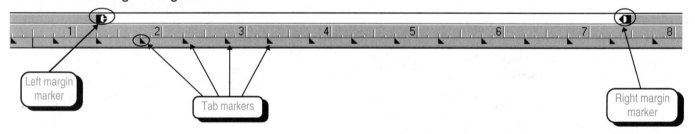

Set Tabs

- The Tab key indents a single line of text. Default tabs are set .5" apart. When the Tab key is pressed once, text will advance ½ inch; when the Tab key is pressed twice, text will advance one inch, etc.

- If, however, you desire text to advance .8" each time the Tab key is pressed, you can do so by changing the tab settings.

- When you change tab settings in a document, changes take effect from that point forward. If you wish to change tab settings in existing text, you must first select the text to be changed.

- Tabs may be changed on the Ruler Bar or in the Tab Set dialog box.

Set Tabs on the Ruler Bar

- Tab settings are displayed on the Ruler Bar as left-pointing triangles which, by default, are set .5" apart. Left-pointing triangles represent left-aligned tab settings.

There are four different tab types. Each tab type is represented by a triangle pointing in a different direction. Dots below the triangle indicate the addition of a dot leader.

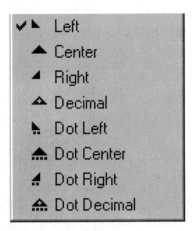

Note the effect each tab type has on text:

- **Left-Aligned Tab** Text moves to the right of the tab as you type.

- **Centered Tab** Text centers at the tab stop.

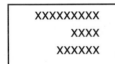

- **Right-Aligned Tab** Text moves to the *left* or backwards of the tab as you type.

```
xxxxxxxxx
     xxxx
   xxxxxx
```

- **Decimal-Aligned Tab** Text before the decimal point (or other designated alignment character) moves to the left of the tab. Text you type after the decimal point moves to the right of the tab. The decimals (or other align character) stay aligned.

```
123.65
 56.77
  4.6
```

- To set a new left-aligned tab, click anywhere on the Ruler Bar where a new tab is desired; a new tab marker is inserted. If you hold down the mouse button when you click the Ruler Bar, the status bar shows the position of the tab.

- To insert only one or two tab sets, you must first clear all the default tabs. To delete a tab setting, drag the tab marker(s) (triangle) off the Ruler Bar, or right-click the Ruler Bar and select Clear All Tabs.

- To set a right-aligned, centered, or decimal tab, you must first change the tab type. To do so, point to the Ruler Bar, right-click and select a tab type from the drop-down menu. After the tab type is selected, each click on the Ruler Bar will insert the tab type you have chosen. See keystrokes on page 51.

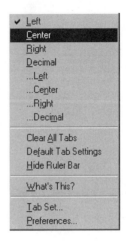

Set Tabs in the Dialog Box

- Tabs may also be set using the Tab Set dialog box. This method lets you set and clear tab positions and tab types in one operation. You cannot, however, see the result of your changes on text until all settings have been made.

- The Tab Set dialog box may be accessed by selecting Line, Tab Set from the Format menu or clicking the Tab Set button 📋 on the Format Toolbar.

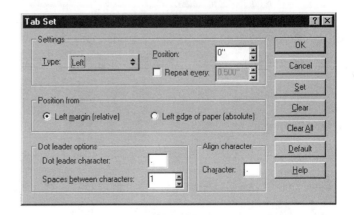

■ If you want to change the tab settings you inserted, click the icon in the left margin; a tab ruler will display showing you the tabs you set at that point in the document.

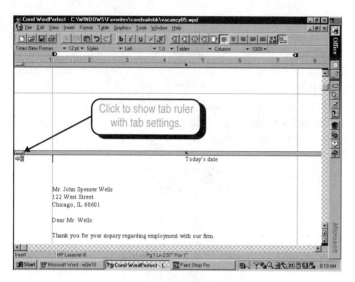

Relative Tabs vs. Absolute Tabs

■ When you set tabs, you can measure them from the left edge of the page (**absolute tabs**) or from the left margin (**relative tabs**). Default tab settings are *relative* to the left margin. The left edge of the page begins at zero (0) on the tab set ruler.

■ Relative and Absolute tabs are set on the Tab Set dialog box.

■ Clicking the Ruler Bar creates absolute tab settings.

■ The proofreaders' mark for changing uppercase letters to lowercase is: ╱

■ The proofreaders' mark for changing lowercase letters to uppercase is: ═══

In this exercise, you will edit a previously created letter using the features learned in this exercise.

EXERCISE DIRECTIONS

1. Start with a clear screen.

2. Display the Ruler Bar (if necessary).

3. Display the Format Toolbar.

4. Open ⊟VACANCY or ⊟10VACANC.

5. Set 1.5" left and right margins.

6. Clear all tabs. Set a left aligned tab stop at 4.5".

7. Make the indicated revisions.
    ✓   *Moving the date and closing to 4.5" makes this a modified-block letter.*

8. Insert a hard space between names, dates, and time.

9. Spell check.

10. Print one copy.

11. Close the file; save the changes.

12. Close the document window.

2.5"

Today's date) ——————————————→ 4.5"

Spenser

Mr. John Wells
122 West Street
Chicago, IL 60601

Dear Mr. Wells:

recent   *Quartz Industries. Inc.*
Thank you for your inquiry regarding employment with ~~our firm.~~

the various Quartz-affiliated companies, and
We have reviewed your qualifications with ~~several members of our firm.~~
We regret to report that we do not have an appropriate vacancy ~~at this time.~~

are, however, taking the liberty of   *of future*
We ~~will~~ retain your resume in our files in the event ~~that an~~ opening ~~occurs~~ in your field.
ing   *active*

Your interest in our organization is very much appreciated. *and* We hope to be able to offer you a
sincerely
position at ~~another time.~~ a later date.

Insert

Very truly yours,

4.5"

Christine Ford
~~PERSONNEL MANAGER~~

cf/yo

*You are, however, welcome to attend our open house
on Monday, January 23 at 5:00 p.m. where we can
talk informally about opportunities within our firm.*

KEYSTROKES

HARD SPACE

Ctrl + Space

1. Type first word.
2. Click **Format** .... `Alt`+`R`
3. Click **Line** .... `L`
4. Click **Other Codes** .... `O`
5. Click **Hard Space** .... `P`
6. Click **Insert** .... `Enter`
7. Type next word.

CONVERT CASE

1. Select/highlight text to be converted.
2. Click **Edit** .... `Alt`+`E`
3. Click **Convert Case** .... `V`
4. Click a convert option:
   - Lowercase .... `L`
   - Uppercase .... `U`
   - Initial Capitals .... `I`

SET MARGINS (LEFT/RIGHT, TOP/BOTTOM)

Ctrl + F8

1. Click Page Margins button on Format Toolbar.

   OR

   Drag guideline to desired margin position.

   OR

   a. Place insertion point where margin change will begin.
   b. Click **Format** .... `Alt`+`R`
   c. Click **Margins** .... `M`
2. Click appropriate text box to change desired margin:

   Left .... `Alt`+`L`

   Right .... `Alt`+`R`

   Top .... `Alt`+`T`

   Bottom .... `Alt`+`B`
3. Type margin amount.

   OR

   Click increment arrows to select margin amount.

4. Click **OK** .... `Enter`

   OR

Using Ruler bar For *Left/Right* Margin Change.

1. Display Ruler Bar:
   - Click **View** .... `Alt`+`V`
   - Click **Toolbars/Ruler** .... `T`
   - Click **Ruler** bar .... `↓`

   OR

   Press .... `Alt`+`Shift`+`F3`
2. Drag left and/or right margin markers to desired positions.

SET, CLEAR, OR DELETE TABS

Using the Ruler Bar

1. Display Ruler Bar (See above).
2. Point to a tab marker (triangle) on the Ruler Bar.
   - Click the *right* mouse button.
   - Select a tab type or Clear All Tabs.

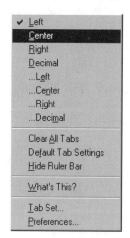

3. Click anywhere on Ruler Bar to set a new tab.

To delete a tab:

Drag the tab marker (triangle) off the Ruler bar.

Determine Relative and Absolute Margins

1. Click Tab Set button on Format Toolbar.

   OR

a. Click **Format** .... `Alt`+`R`
b. Click **Line** .... `L`
c. Click **Tab Set** .... `T`

   OR

   Double-Click a tab marker (triangle) on the Ruler Bar.
2. Click how tabs are to be measured (Position From):
3. Left margin (Relative) .... `Alt`+`M`

   OR

   Left edge of paper (Absolute) .... `Alt`+`E`

To clear desired tab setting:

1. Click **Tab Set** button on Format Toolbar .... `[icon]`
2. Click **Position** Text Box .... `Alt`+`P`
3. Type position of tab to be cleared ... *number*
4. Click **Clear** .... `Alt`+`C`

   OR

   Click **Clear All** to clear all tabs ... `Alt`+`A`

To set desired tab:

1. Click Tab Set button on Format Toolbar.
2. Click **Position** text box .... `Alt`+`P`
3. Type position of tab to set .... *number*
4. Click **Set** .... `Alt`+`S`

To set a tab type:

1. Click Tab Set button on Format Toolbar.
2. Click

   Type pop-up list ...... `Alt`+`T`, `↓``↑`
3. Select desired tab type.

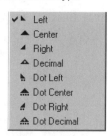

4. Click **Set** .... `Alt`+`S`
5. When tabs are set as desired, click **OK** .... `Enter`

Exercise

11

■ **Summary**

In this exercise, you will create a modified-block letter and edit it using the insert and delete procedures learned.

EXERCISE DIRECTIONS

1. Start with a clear screen.
2. Type and format a modified-block letter from the text shown in Part I, or open ▯11ABC and format a modified-block letter.
   ✓ *In a modified-block letter, the date and closing begin at 4.5".*
3. Clear all tabs; then set a tab stop at 4.5".
4. Set 1.5" left and right margins.
5. Make the indicated revisions shown in Part II.
   • Use Reveal Codes to combine the last two paragraphs.

6. Spell check.
7. Using the Document Properties feature, note the number of words in this document.
8. Preview your work.
9. Using the Convert Case feature, change Human Resources to uppercase.
10. Print one copy.
11. Save the file; name it ABC
12. Close the file.

PART I

Today's date Mr. Bill Demeo ABC Employment Agency 555 Kennedy Avenue Boston, MA 02210-2497 Dear Mr. Demeo: We now have opportunities available in our organization for qualified Partner Managers, Associate Managers and Shift Supervisors who are very interested in a career with a leader in the industry. ¶We offer an attractive salary, benefits, stock purchase plans and advancement opportunities. ¶If you have any individuals who you feel are qualified, send their resume to me. ¶We seek those who demonstrate customer service commitment and strong leadership ability. Some supervisory experience in a restaurant or a retail setting is important. Sincerely, Irene Zofran Director Human Resources iz/yo

PART II

Today's date Mr. Bill Demeo ABC Employment Agency 555 Kennedy Avenue Boston, MA 02210-2497

Dear Mr. Demeo: We now have *growth directed* opportunities available ~~in our organization~~ for qualified Partner

Managers, Associate Managers and Shift Supervisors who are ~~very~~ interested in a *fast-track* career with a leader ~~in~~ *n industry*

~~the industry~~. ¶We offer an attractive salary, *comprehensive* benefits, stock purchase plans and advancement *a comprehensive training program* *potential*

~~opportunities~~. ¶ If you have ~~any~~ *qualified* individuals ~~who you feel are qualified~~, send their resume to me. *or fax* ¶We

seek those who demonstrate *a passion for* customer service ~~commitment~~ *a genuine "can do" attitude* and strong leadership ability. Some

supervisory *or managerial* experience in a restaurant or a retail setting is important. Sincerely, Irene *Smith* Zofran Director

Human Resources iz/yo

Exercise 12

- **Center Line** ■ **Flush Right Line**
- **Vertical Centering (Center Current Page)** ■ **Justification**

NOTES

Center Line

- WordPerfect lets you center a single line of text between the left and right margins, on a tab, or in a column. Simply position the insertion point where you want the centering to begin, and either:

  • Select Line, Center from the Format menu.

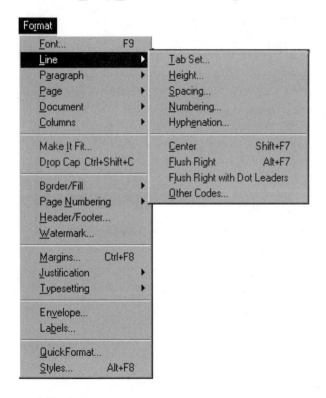

  • Click the *right* mouse button in the document window and select Center.

  • Press Shift + F7.

- Text may be centered before or after typing.

Flush Right Line

- The flush right feature aligns a single line or part of a line of text at the right margin. To flush right text, position the insertion point where you want the flush right to begin, and either:

  • Select Line, Flush Right from the Format menu.

  • Click the *right* mouse button in the document window and select Flush Right.

  • Press Alt + F7.

- Text may be right aligned before or after typing.

- To align a partial or full line of existing text at the right margin, make sure the line ends with a hard return.

Vertical Centering (Center Current Page)

- Text can also be centered vertically on a page (from top to bottom). If there are hard returns before or after the centered text, WordPerfect will include them in the vertical centering. Therefore, to vertically center text without additional blank lines, start the text at the top of the screen.

- Vertical centering may be accessed by selecting Page, Center from the Format menu.

Justification

- Justification should be used to affect blocks of text, not individual lines.

- WordPerfect applies left justification to your text by default.

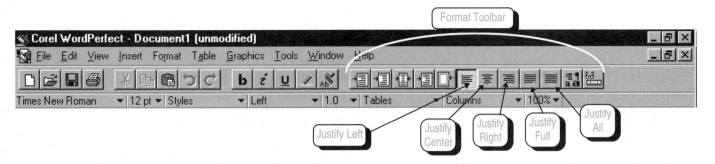

Format Toolbar

Justify Left · Justify Center · Justify Right · Justify Full · Justify All

- Justification lets you align all text that follows the justification code until another justification code is entered. WordPerfect provides five alignment options:

  - **Left** - all lines are even at the left margin but are ragged at the right margin (the default).

  - **Center** - all lines are centered between the margins.

    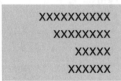

  - **Right** - all lines are ragged at the left margin and are even at the right margin.

    XXXXXXXXXX
    XXXXXXXX
    XXXXX
    XXXXXX

  - **Full** - all lines are even at the left and right margins, except for the last line of the paragraph.

    XXXXXXXXXXX
    XXXXXXXXXXX
    XXXXXXX

  - **All** - all lines are even at the left and right margins.

    XXXXXXXXXXXX
    XXXXXXXXXXXX
    XXXXXXXXXXXX
    XXXXXXXXXXXX

- Justification may be changed before or after typing.

- A justification option may be selected by

  - Clicking the Justification button on the Power Bar and selecting a justification option.

    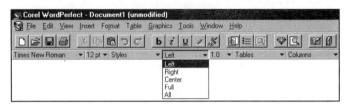

  - Clicking the desired justification button on the Format Toolbar, or

  - Clicking on a **QuickSpot** that appears to the left of the paragraph to be affected and selecting Justification and a justification option, or

    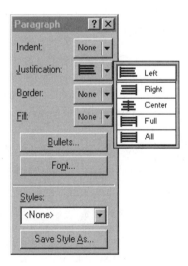

  - Selecting Justification, and then a justification option, from the Format Menu.

  CAUTION: When you change justification of existing text, all text following the code changes. Do not be alarmed. Insert another justification code to return your text as desired. To avoid this, select the text first, then apply an alignment choice.

In these exercises, you will create announcements using various alignment options.

EXERCISE DIRECTIONS

Part I

1. Begin the exercise at the top of a clear screen.

2. Display the Format Toolbar, if it is not currently on screen.

3. Use the default margins.

4. Center the current page vertically.

5. Create the announcement below as shown.

6. Preview your work.

7. Print one copy.

8. Save the exercise; name it JOIN.

9. Close the document window.

Part II

1. Begin a new exercise at the top of a clear screen.

2. Center the current page vertically.

3. Type each section of text shown in the exercise on the following page, changing the justification alignment appropriately.

4. Preview your document.

5. Print one copy.

6. Save the exercise; name it TIVOLI.

7. Close the document window.

PART I

MORITZ & CHASE

Is Pleased to Announce that the following Associates will become members of the firm on

January 3, 1998

DENVER	Steven M. Jones
NEW YORK	Arthur J. Williams
SAN FRANCISCO	Roberta W. Asher

and that the following Of Counsel will become members of the firm on

February 1, 1998

LONDON	Raymond T. Sedgewick
LOS ANGELES	Angela Tsacoumis

S W I N G I N G   J A Z Z   I N   W O N D E R F U L   C O P E N H A G E N

The Slukefter Jazz Club in Tivoli is the favorite haunt of jazz enthusiasts during the garden's open season. The jazz club is now ready to open its doors outside the Tivoli season, presenting a spectacular live swing-jazz program during the autumn and winter months. From October 5th and every weekend until December 28th the Slukefter Jazz Club will offer exciting listening and dancing to great jazz performed by the most outstanding musicians.

The October Program:

Friday 4
Jazzin Jacks, Sweden

Saturday 5
Jazzin Jacks, Sweden

Friday 11
Papa Bue's Viking Jazz Band

Friday 18
Fressors Big City Band

Saturday 19
Ricardo's Jazzmen

The Swinging Jazz
Produced by Slukefter Jazz Club
In Cooperation with the
Wonderful Copenhagen Convention & Visitors' Bureau

Sponsors:
Bijan Imports
and
Danisco Silversmiths
Copenhagen, Denmark

KEYSTROKES

CENTER LINE

Shift + F7

New Text

1. Place insertion point at beginning of line to center.
2. Click **Format**..........................`Alt`+`R`
3. Click **Line** ....`L`
4. Click **Center**............................`C`
5. Type text.
6. Press **Enter** ....`Enter`
   to return to left margin.

Existing Text

1. Position insertion point at the beginning of line to be centered.
2. Click *right* mouse button anywhere in document window.
3. Click **Center**............................`C`
4. Press the **End** key.
5. Press **Enter** ....`Enter`
   to return to left margin.

FLUSH RIGHT

Alt + F7

New Text

1. Place insertion point at beginning of text to flush right.
2. Click **Format**..........................`Alt`+`R`
3. Click **Line** ....`L`
4. Click **Flush Right**....................`F`
5. Type text.
6. Press **Enter** ....`Enter`
   to return to left margin.

Existing Text

1. Position insertion point at beginning of text to flush right.
2. Click *right* mouse button anywhere in document window.
3. Click **Flush Right**.........................`R`
4. Press the **End** key.
5. Press **Enter**...............................`Enter`
   to return to left margin.

CENTER PAGE (VERTICALLY CENTER)

1. Place insertion point anywhere on page.
2. Click **Format** ....`Alt`+`R`
3. Click **Page**...............................`P`
4. Click **Center**............................`C`
5. Select a page option:
   - Click **Current page** ....`P`
   - Click **Current and subsequent pages**...............................`S`
   - Click **Turn Centering Off** ....`T`
6. Click **OK** ....`Enter`

ALIGN OR JUSTIFY

Click **Align Text** button on Power Bar....................................`Left` ▼

OR

Click **Justification** button on Format Toolbar.......................`▤ ▥ ▦ ▧ ▨`

OR

1. Click **Format** ....`Alt`+`R`
2. Click **Justification**...........................`J`
3. Select a Justification option:
   - Click **Left**...............................`L`
   - Click **Right** ....`R`
   - Click **Center** ....`E`
   - **Full** ....`F`
   - **All** ....`A`

   OR
4. Click **QuickSpot**.
5. Click **Justification**.
6. Select a Justification option.

Exercise

13

■ **Font Faces** ■ **Font Style** ■ **Font Size**

NOTES

■ A **font** is a complete set of characters in a specific face, style, and size. Each set includes upper- and lowercase letters, numerals and punctuation. An example of a font that might be available to you in WordPerfect is: **Arial**.

■ A font face (often called **typeface** or just **font**) is the design of a character. Each design has a name and is intended to convey a specific feeling.

■ You should select typefaces that will make your document attractive and communicate its particular message. As a rule, use no more than two or three font faces in any one document.

Font Faces

■ There are basically three types of font faces: serif, sans serif, and script. A **serif** face has lines, curves, or edges extending from the ends of the letter: **T**, while a **sans serif** face is straight-edged: **T**, and **script** looks like handwriting: **7**

Serif Font Face:

Times New Roman

Sans Serif Font Face:

Arial

Script Font Face:

Brush Script MT

■ A serif font face is typically used for document text because it is more readable. Sans serif is often used for headlines or technical material. Script typefaces are used for formal invitations and announcements.

■ Font faces may be changed by selecting the desired font listed in the Font dialog box.

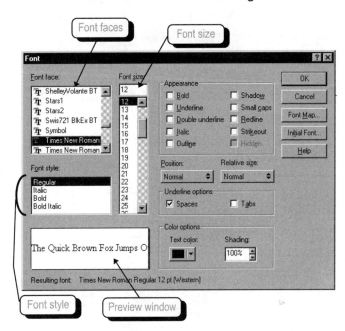

■ Font faces can also be changed by clicking the Font button on the Power Bar (which drops down a list of font choices).

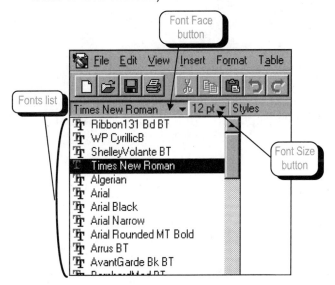

- The Font dialog box may be accessed by either:

  - Selecting <u>F</u>ont from the Fo<u>r</u>mat menu
  - Double clicking the Font Face or Font Size button on the Power Bar
  - Clicking the *right* mouse button anywhere in the document window and selecting Font.

- Clicking on a QuickSpot and clicking the Fo<u>n</u>t button.

- Clicking the QuickFonts button on the Power Bar displays a list of the last ten fonts you used in a document. If the QuickFonts button is not currently displayed, right-click the Power bar and select Edit, QuickFonts.

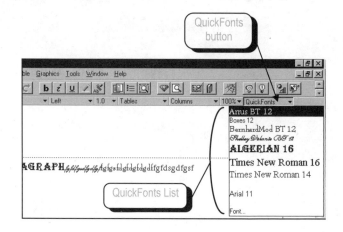

Font Style

- **Font style** refers to the slant and weight of letters, such as bold and italic.

Font Styles

Times New Roman Regular
Times New Roman Italic
Times New Roman Bold
Times New Roman Bold Italic

- Note the Font dialog box illustrated on the previous page. The Font Style box lists the styles or weights specially designed and available for the selected font. You may also apply attributes such as bold, italic, outline, and small cap through the Appearance panel of the Font dialog box. (This will be covered in the next exercise.)

Font Size

- **Font size** generally refers to the height of the font, usually measured in points. There are 72 points to an inch.

Bookman 8 point
Bookman 12 point
Bookman 18 point
Arial 20 point
Garamond 24 point

- Font size may be changed in the Font dialog box or by clicking the Font Size button on the Power Bar (which drops down a list of font sizes).

- In the Font dialog box, selected fonts are displayed in the Preview window at the lower left side and are described in the Resulting Font line.

- Font sizes may be increased or decreased in 2-point increments by selecting the text to be affected, then clicking the Font Up or Font Down buttons on the Design Tools Toolbar, as shown on the next page.

- You can change fonts *before* or *after* typing text.

- The fonts that are available to you depend on what you may have installed in your system and on your printer's capabilities.

Design Tools Toolbar

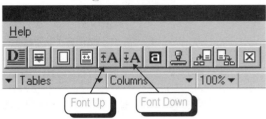

In this exercise, you will change the font faces, styles, and sizes of a previously created announcement.

EXERCISE DIRECTIONS

1. Start with a clear screen.

2. Open TIVOLI or open 13TIVOLI.

3. Display the Design Tools Toolbar.

4. Using the Font dialog box, make the font face, font size, and font style changes indicated on the exercise.

5. Preview your document.

6. Print one copy.

7. Close the file; save the changes.

KEYSTROKES

CHANGE FONT FACE, FONT SIZE, AND FONT STYLE

F9

—*USING FONT DIALOG BOX*—

1. Place insertion point where font change will begin (*before* typing).

   OR

   Select text to receive font change (*after* typing).

2. Follow one of the listed procedures to access the Font Dialog Box.

   - Click **Format**...................... Alt + R
   - Click **Font**................................... F

   OR

   - Click *right* mouse anywhere in the document window.
   - Select **Font**.

   OR

   - Double-click Font Face or Font Size button on Power Bar.

   OR

   - Click the QuickSpot.
   - Click **Font**.

   ✓ *In the Font dialog box, the currently selected font is displayed in Preview window and described in Resulting font line.*

   OR

1. Click **Font Face** button............... Times New Roman ▼ on Power Bar.

2. Click in **Font face** list............. Alt + F

3. Click desired font .... ↓

4. Click in **Font style** box........... Alt + O

5. Click desired style .... ↓

6. Click in **Font size** box .... Alt + S

7. Click desired size .... ↓

—*USING POWER BAR (FONT FACE AND FONT SIZE ONLY)*—

Place insertion point where font change will begin (*before* typing).

OR

Select text to receive font change (*after* typing).

To change font face:

1. Select desired font from list ...... ↓ ↑

To change font size:

1. Click Font size button .... 12 pt ▼

2. Select desired size from list .... ↓ ↑

S W I N G I N G   J A Z Z   I N
W O N D E R F U L   C O P E N H A G E N
} *Mistral*
24 pt

The Slukefter Jazz Club in Tivoli is the favorite haunt of jazz enthusiasts during the garden's open season.   The jazz club is now ready to open its doors outside the Tivoli season, presenting a spectacular live swing-jazz program during the autumn and winter months. From October 5th and every weekend until December 28th the Slukefter Jazz Club will offer exciting listening and dancing to great jazz performed by the most outstanding musicians.
} *Century gothic 11 pt*

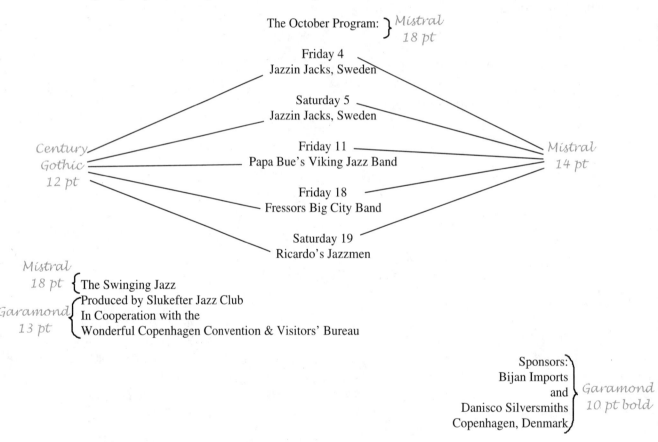

The October Program: } *Mistral 18 pt*

Friday 4
Jazzin Jacks, Sweden

Saturday 5
Jazzin Jacks, Sweden

Friday 11
Papa Bue's Viking Jazz Band

Friday 18
Fressors Big City Band

Saturday 19
Ricardo's Jazzmen

Century Gothic 12 pt

Mistral 14 pt

Mistral 18 pt {
The Swinging Jazz
Produced by Slukefter Jazz Club
In Cooperation with the
Wonderful Copenhagen Convention & Visitors' Bureau
}

Garamond 13 pt

Sponsors:
Bijan Imports
and
Danisco Silversmiths
Copenhagen, Denmark
} *Garamond 10 pt bold*

Exercise 14

■ Font Appearance

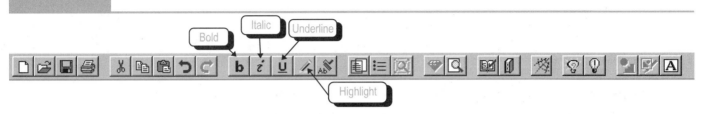

NOTES

Font Appearance

- **Bold**, underline, double underline, *italic*, and highlight are features used to emphasize or enhance text and are referred to as **appearance attributes**. These features work as on/off toggle switches. You must choose the command to turn on the feature; then choose the command to turn off the feature.

- Text may be emphasized before or after typing text.

- To emphasize text after typing, select the text to be affected, then click the style buttons on the WordPerfect 7 Toolbar.

  ✓ *There is no double underline option on the Toolbar. This option must be accessed from within the Font dialog box.*

- Or, you may access the Font dialog box and select the desired appearance style. There is no highlight option in the Font dialog box; you must use the highlight button on the Toolbar.

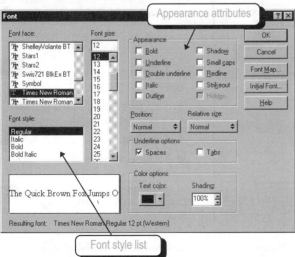

- Highlighted text will appear yellow (the default color) on the screen, but will appear gray when printed (unless you have a color printer). To change the highlight color, select Highlight, Change Color from the Tools menu.

- In addition to bold, underline, double underline, italic, and highlight, WordPerfect provides other effects. These include outline, shadow, small caps, redline, and strikeout.

- **Redline** and **strikeout** emphasis styles are usually used to indicate that text has been added, deleted, or moved, and are useful when comparing the current document with a different version of a document. Redline displays on screen in red but usually appears shaded, underlined or with a series of vertical bars (depending on your printer) when printed. Note examples below:

> Outline
>
> **shadow**
>
> SMALL CAPS
>
> ~~strikeout~~

- Like other appearance changes, these may be applied *before* or *after* typing text, and may be accessed from the Font dialog box.

- If your printer does not support italic, the printed copy will appear underlined. Some font appearances will not apply to certain font faces. For example, if you use outline or shadow on Courier, it simply appears bolded.

- As indicated in the previous exercise, font styles also add bold and italic to a font face, but not all font faces have these styles added. If bold and italic are unavailable in the Font Style

list box, they can be added as an appearance attribute.

✓ *In WordPerfect 7, the Outline attribute does not appear on the screen after it has been applied. However, the outline attribute will print if applied.*

In this exercise, you will create a menu using various text alignments and appearance attributes.

EXERCISE DIRECTIONS

1. Start with a clear screen.

2. Use the default margins.

3. Create the menu shown using the text alignments and font changes shown in the illustration.

   ✓ *If you do not have the indicated font, you may substitute another.*

4. Center the page.

5. Preview your document.

6. Print one copy.

7. Save the file; name it MENU.

8. Close the document window.

KEYSTROKES

APPEARANCE CHANGES

F9

Bold, Underline, Double Underline, Italic, Outline/Shadow/Small Caps/Redline/Strikeout

Place insertion point before text to receive appearance change (*before* typing).

OR

Select/highlight text to receive appearance change (*after* typing).

1. Click the desired font appearance button on the toolbar

   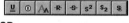

   OR

   a. Click For**m**at .... Alt + R
   b. Click **F**ont .... F

c. Click the desired font appearance options.

d. Click **OK** .... Enter

OR

a. Click *right* mouse button anywhere in document window.

b. Click **F**ont .... F

c. Click the desired font appearance options.

d. Click **OK** .... Enter

✓ *Highlight may only be selected from the toolbar.*

RETURN TO NORMAL OR TURN FEATURE OFF

1. Place insertion point where appearance change will end (*before* typing).

   OR

Select/highlight text to return to normal (*after* typing).

2. Click the desired font appearance button to deselect

   OR

   a. Click For**m**at .... Alt + R
   b. Click **F**ont .... F
   c. Click the desired appearance options to deselect then
   d. Click **OK** .... Enter

   OR

   e. Click *right* mouse button anywhere in document window.
   f. Click **F**ont .... F
   g. Click the desired font appearance options to deselect then
   h. Click **OK** .... Enter

Britannic Bold 26 pt {

The Maplewood Inn

Britannic Bold 12 pt italics {

**125 Maple Road
Arlington, VA 22207
703-555-4443**

Britannic Bold 18 pt double underline and highlight {

<u><u>BREAKFAST MENU</u></u>

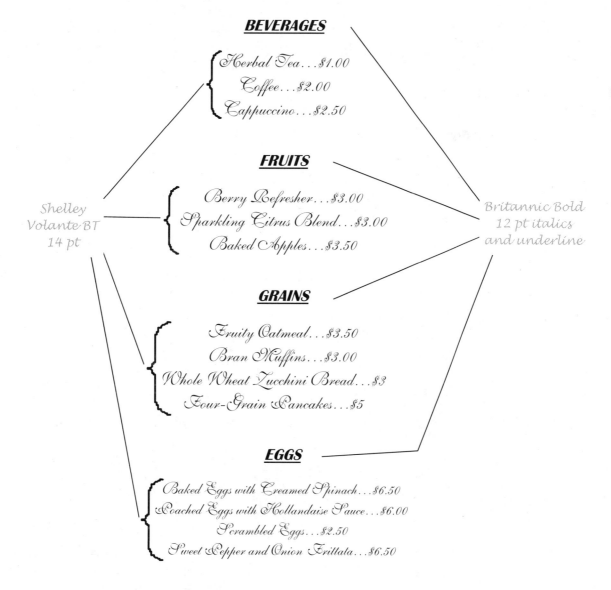

<u>*BEVERAGES*</u>

Herbal Tea...$1.00
Coffee...$2.00
Cappuccino...$2.50

<u>*FRUITS*</u>

Berry Refresher...$3.00
Sparkling Citrus Blend...$3.00
Baked Apples...$3.50

<u>*GRAINS*</u>

Fruity Oatmeal...$3.50
Bran Muffins...$3.00
Whole Wheat Zucchini Bread...$3
Four-Grain Pancakes...$5

<u>*EGGS*</u>

Baked Eggs with Creamed Spinach...$6.50
Poached Eggs with Hollandaise Sauce...$6.00
Scrambled Eggs...$2.50
Sweet Pepper and Onion Frittata...$6.50

Shelley Volante BT 14 pt

Britannic Bold 12 pt italics and underline

David Bratton, Proprietor } *Shelley Volante BT 16 pt*

Exercise 15

- ■ **Ornamental Fonts** ■ **Special Characters**
- ■ **Superscripts/Subscripts** ■ **Remove Font Appearance**

NOTES

Ornamental Fonts

■ **Wingdings, Monotype Sorts**, and **ZapfDingbats** are ornamental or symbol font face collections that are used to enhance a document. Below and to the right are samples from Wingdings and Monotype Sort font collections.

Wingdings Font Collection

Monotype Sorts Font Collection

■ The upper- and lowercase of each letter and character key provide different Wingdings and/or Monotype Sorts. To choose a Wingdings or a Monotype Sort face, select the font face and then press the corresponding keyboard letter or character shown in the chart.

Special Characters

- Another source of ornamental fonts is the special character set called **Iconic Symbols**.

- Special characters may be accessed by selecting Character from the Insert menu, or by pressing Ctrl + W. The following dialog box appears, with the most recently used character set selected. Each character has a number assigned to it. That number is displayed in the Number text box. These can be used to select a specific character.

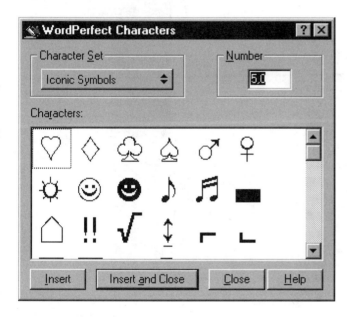

- Special character sets are also found as fonts. They can be accessed through the Font dialog box. Each set begins with WP.

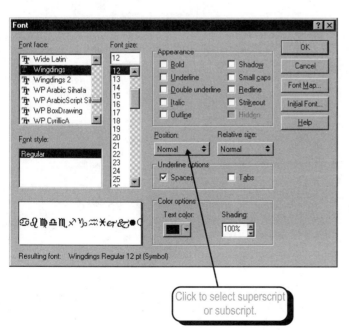

Click to select superscript or subscript.

- You may change the size of a symbol font face as you would any other character, by changing the point size.

- Ornamental characters can be used to:
  - Separate items on a page:

    > Wingdings
    > ❖◆❖◆
    > Graphics

  - Emphasize items on a list:

    > ✎dresses
    > ✎coats
    > ✎suits

  - Enhance a page:

    > 📖📖📖📖📖
    > BOOK SALE
    > 📖📖📖📖📖

  - Add an in-line graphic:

    > Save your document on 💾.

Superscripts/Subscripts

- **Superscripts** are characters that print slightly higher than the normal typing line; **subscripts** are characters that print slightly lower than the normal typing line. Note examples below:

  Superscript: A^3
  Subscript: H_2O

- Superscripts and subscripts may be accessed by clicking the Normal list arrow in the Position area of the Font dialog box, then selecting Superscript or Subscript.

Remove Font Appearance

- If you decide to remove the font appearance you applied to the text, select the text where the style is to be removed and repeat the procedures used to apply the appearance change. You can also remove font appearances by deleting the codes in Reveal Codes mode.

To delete a code in Reveal Codes mode:

- Click <u>V</u>iew, Reveal <u>C</u>odes.

- Use the mouse pointer to click on the code and press the Delete key, or

- Use the mouse pointer to drag the code out of the Reveal Codes window.

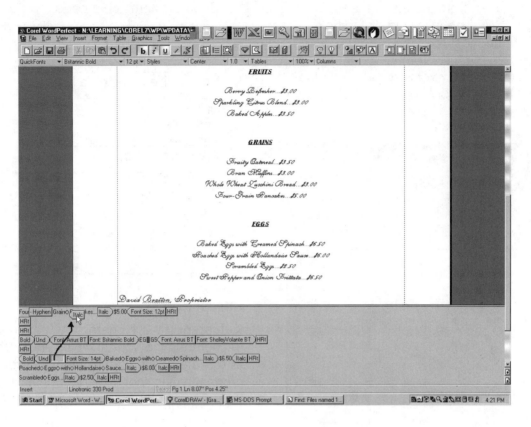

In this exercise, you will add special characters to a menu you created in a previous exercise, adjust alignment, and insert superscript and subscript characters.

EXERCISE DIRECTIONS

1. Start with a clear screen.

2. Open ⬛MENU or 🖫15MENU from the data disk.

3. Enhance the document with symbols from the Wingdings font collection and special characters as indicated.
   - Use any desired Wingdings or special characters.
   - Use a special character as the superscript after BREAKFAST MENU and preceding the inserted sentence: Breakfast is served from 7:00 a.m. to 11:00 a.m. daily.
   - Note the desired result.

4. Right align the last line, David Bratton, Proprietor.
   - ✓ *To change the alignment, click on the QuickSpot to the left of the line, select Justification and a right justification option.*

5. Preview your document.

6. Print one copy.

7. Using any desired method, remove the font appearances indicated in the exercise.

8. Print one copy.

9. Close the file; save the changes.

The Maplewood Inn

Insert Special Character 5,90

**125 Maple Road
Arlington, VA 22207
703-987-4443**

Insert Special Character 5,162
as a superscript in 18 pt

BREAKFAST MENU

BEVERAGES

Herbal Tea...$1.00
Coffee...$2.00
Cappuccino...$2.50

FRUITS

Berry Refresher...$3.00
Sparkling Citrus Blend...$3.00
Baked Apples...$3.50

Remove
single and
double
underlines.

Insert Centered
Wingdings
below each
section.

GRAINS

Fruity Oatmeal...$3.50
Bran Muffins...$3.00
Whole Wheat Zucchini Bread...$3.00
Four-Grain Pancakes...$5.00

EGGS

Baked Eggs with Creamed Spinach...$6.50
Poached Eggs with Hollandaise Sauce...$6.00
Scrambled Eggs...$2.50
Sweet Pepper and Onion Frittata...$6.50

David Bratton, Proprietor } Right align

Insert and center in
Britannic bold 9 pt

Insert special character
as superscript.

Breakfast is served from 7:00 a.m. to 11:00 a.m.

KEYSTROKES

ADD A SYMBOL FONT

F9

1. Position insertion point where symbol font will begin.
2. Click **Font** button on Power Bar.

   OR

   a. Click *right* mouse button anywhere in document window.
   b. Select **Font** .... `F`

   OR

   a. Click **Format** .... `Alt`+`R`
   b. Click **Font** .... `F`

3. In **Font Face** list, choose **Wingdings** or **Monotype Sorts** .... `↓``↑`
4. Press the keyboard letter or character for the desired symbol (see charts provided on previous pages).
5. To turn off symbol font, repeat step 2 and choose a different font.

INSERT SPECIAL CHARACTERS

Ctrl + W

1. Position insertion point to the left of where you wish to insert character.
2. Click **Insert** .... `Alt`+`I`
3. Click **Character** .... `C`
4. Click **Character Set** list box .... `Alt`+`S` to display character set list.
5. Click desired character set .... `↓``↑`
6. Click desired symbol.

   OR

   a. Click **Number** text box .... `Alt`+`N`
   b. Type number assigned to symbol.

7. Click **Insert** .... `Alt`+`I`
8. Click **Close** .... `Alt`+`C`

   OR

   Click **Insert and close** .... `Alt`+`A`

REMOVE FONT APPEARANCE

F9

1. Select/highlight text to change appearance or return to normal.
2. Click *right* mouse button anywhere in document window.
3. Select **Font** .... `F`
4. Click appearance change to remove.

   OR

   Reveal Codes .... `Alt`+`F3`

   OR

   a. Click **View** .... `Alt`+`V`
   b. Click **Reveal Codes** .... `C`

5. Drag code off screen.

Exercise 16

■ **Bullets and Numbers** ■ **Remove Bullets and Numbers**

WordPerfect 7 Toolbar

Insert Bullet

NOTES

Bullets and Numbers

■ A **bullet** is a dot or symbol used to highlight points of information or to itemize a list that does not need to be in any particular order.

- red
- blue
- green

■ Using the **Bullets and Numbers** feature, you can insert bullets automatically to create a bulleted list for each paragraph or item you type.

■ The Bullets and Numbers feature also allows you to create numbered paragraphs for items that need to be in a particular order. The numbers you insert increment automatically.

1. first
2. second
3. third

■ To create a bulleted list quickly, click the Insert Bullet button on the WordPerfect 7 Toolbar and, type your text. Press Enter after each line of text to create a new bullet.

✓ *To create a new bullet or number each time Enter is pressed, you must be sure that New Bullet or Number on Enter has been selected in the Bullets & Numbers dialog box.*

■ Or, you can create a QuickBullet by typing the following characters followed by a tab. A bulleted list is started. When you press Enter, the bulleted list continues. Type one of the following characters to produce the corresponding bullet:

> → ▸	* → •	^ → ◆	+ → ★
o → •	0 → ●	- → –	

■ To create numbers quickly, type the number one, followed by a period, followed by a tab (1. →). A numbered list is started. When you press Enter, the numbered list continues.

■ Or, you may access the Bullets and Numbers feature by selecting Bullets & Numbers from the Insert menu. In the Bullets & Numbers dialog box which follows, you may select the bullet or number style you desire.

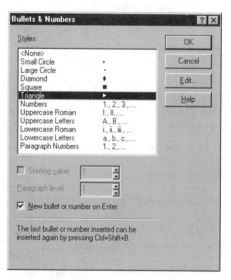

■ Once the bullet or number style is chosen, you may type your text. By selecting New Bullet or Number on Enter, the bullet or number is entered automatically each time the Enter key is pressed.

■ If you wish to insert bullets at a later point in the document, you can select the Insert Bullet button on the WordPerfect 7 Toolbar or press Ctrl + Shift + B. The bullet or number style you previously selected in the dialog box displays.

■ You can add bullets and numbers to existing text by clicking the QuickSpot to the left of the paragraph. Select <u>B</u>ullets from the Paragraph dialog box, then select the desired bullet or number style in the Bullets & Number dialog box.

Remove Bullets and Numbers

■ Bullets may also be removed by:

• Highlighting the list of bulleted items, selecting <u>B</u>ullets & <u>N</u>umbers from the <u>I</u>nsert menu and selecting <None> in the Bullets & Numbers dialog box, or

• Clicking the Quickspot to the left of the paragraph where the bullet/number is to be removed, clicking <u>B</u>ullets, then selecting <None> in the Bullets & Numbers dialog box, or

• Pressing the Backspace key at the point you wish the bullets or numbers to stop.

In this exercise, you will create a flyer using text alignments, enhancements, bullets, and numbers.

EXERCISE DIRECTIONS

1. Start with a clear screen.
2. Use the default margins.
3. Type the exercise as shown, using the appropriate alignments and enhancements. Use any desired bullet style for the bulleted items.
4. Enhance the document with any desired symbols from the Wingdings font collection.
5. Spell check.
6. Preview your document.
7. Vertically center the exercise.
8. Print one copy.
9. Save the file; name it COLORFUL.

KEYSTROKES

CREATE A BULLETED OR NUMBERED LIST

1. Place insertion point where bulleted or numbered list is to begin.
2. Click **Insert** .... `Alt` + `I`
3. Click **Bullets & Numbers** .... `N`
4. Click on a bullet choice .... `↓`
5. Click **OK** .... `Enter`
   OR
   Click **Ctrl + Shift + B** ..... `Ctrl` + `Shift` + `B`
   OR
   Click **Insert Bullet** button on WordPerfect 7 Toolbar.
   OR

Type one of the following characters followed by a tab to display the corresponding bullet.

> → ►	^ → ◆	* → •
0 → ●	- → —	0 → ●
+ → ★		

CHANGE BULLET OR NUMBER STYLE

1. Highlight bulleted or numbered list to be changed.
2. Click **Insert** .... `Alt` + `I`
3. Click **Bullets & Numbers** .... `N`
4. Click new desired bullet or number style.

To insert automatic bullet or number when Enter is pressed:

1. Click **New bullet or number on Enter** check box.
2. Click **OK** .... `Enter`

REMOVE BULLETS OR NUMBERS

1. Highlight list where bullets or numbers are to be removed.
2. Click **Insert** .... `Alt` + `I`
3. Click **Bullets and Numbers** .... `N`
4. Click **<None>**.
5. Click **OK** .... `Enter`
   OR
   Press the Backspace key to end bulleted or numbered list.

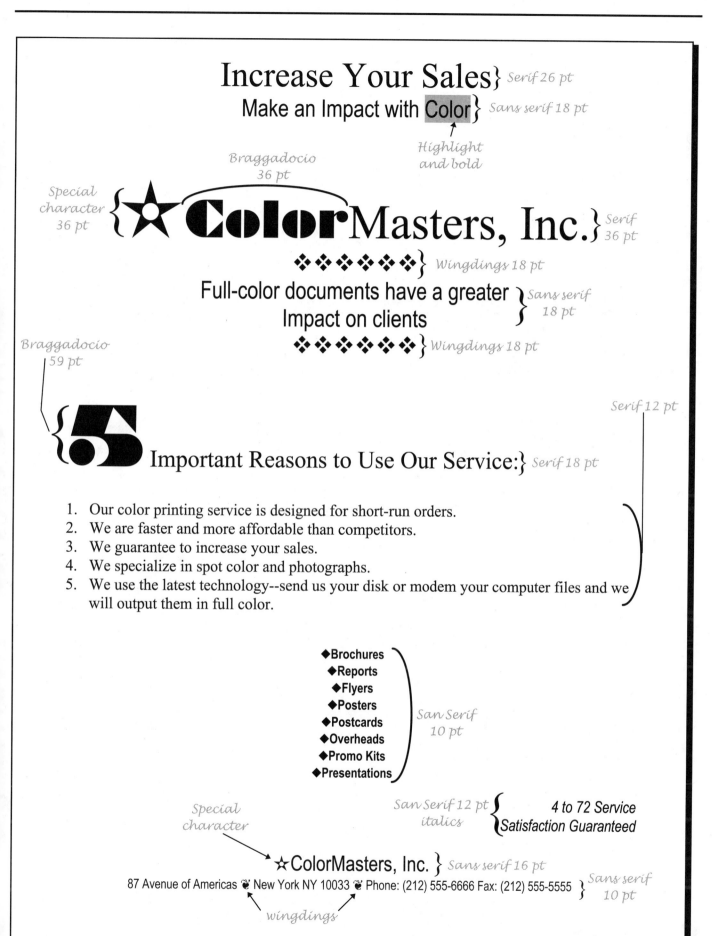

Increase Your Sales} *Serif 26 pt*

Make an Impact with Color } *Sans serif 18 pt*

↑ Highlight and bold

Braggadocio 36 pt

Special character 36 pt

{☆**Color**Masters, Inc.} *Serif 36 pt*

❖❖❖❖❖❖} *Wingdings 18 pt*

Full-color documents have a greater } *Sans serif 18 pt*
Impact on clients

❖❖❖❖❖❖} *Wingdings 18 pt*

Braggadocio 59 pt

Serif 12 pt

{**5** Important Reasons to Use Our Service:} *Serif 18 pt*

1. Our color printing service is designed for short-run orders.
2. We are faster and more affordable than competitors.
3. We guarantee to increase your sales.
4. We specialize in spot color and photographs.
5. We use the latest technology--send us your disk or modem your computer files and we will output them in full color.

◆Brochures
◆Reports
◆Flyers
◆Posters
◆Postcards
◆Overheads
◆Promo Kits
◆Presentations

San Serif 10 pt

Special character

San Serif 12 pt italics { **4 to 72 Service**
Satisfaction Guaranteed

☆ColorMasters, Inc. } *Sans serif 16 pt*

87 Avenue of Americas ❦ New York NY 10033 ❦ Phone: (212) 555-6666 Fax: (212) 555-5555 } *Sans serif 10 pt*

wingdings

Exercise

17

■ **Summary**

In this exercise, you will create an advertisement using the fonts, appearance changes, and text alignments learned in this lesson.

EXERCISE DIRECTIONS

1. Start with a clear screen.

2. Use the default margins.

3. Type the exercise shown on the following page using the fonts, styles, and sizes indicated. Use symbol fonts and special character as desired.

4. Center the page from top to bottom.

5. Preview your document.

6. Print one copy.

7. Remove the following:
   - All underline and double underlines.
   - Shadow text in the last line.
   - Highlight on the word Plus.
   - Bullets before each fish name.

8. Print one copy.

9. Save the file; name it FISH.

10. Close the document window.

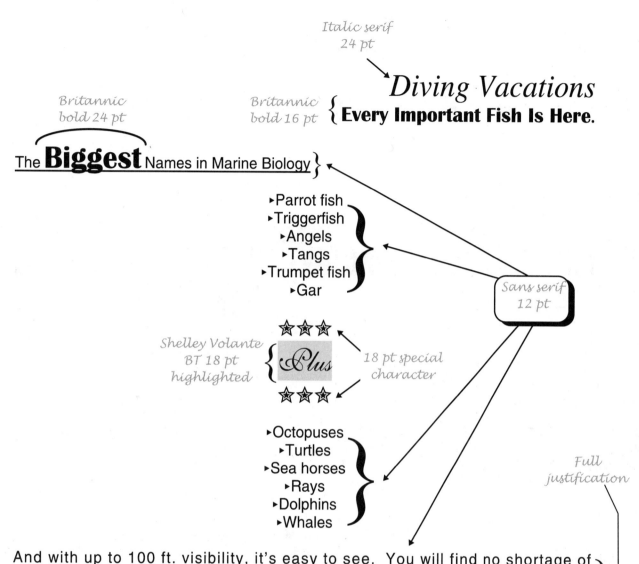

Italic serif 24 pt

Diving Vacriations

Britannic bold 16 pt

Every Important Fish Is Here.

Britannic bold 24 pt

The **Biggest** Names in Marine Biology }

- ▸Parrot fish
- ▸Triggerfish
- ▸Angels
- ▸Tangs
- ▸Trumpet fish
- ▸Gar

Sans serif 12 pt

★ ★ ★

Shelley Volante BT 18 pt highlighted

Plus

18 pt special character

★ ★ ★

- ▸Octopuses
- ▸Turtles
- ▸Sea horses
- ▸Rays
- ▸Dolphins
- ▸Whales

Full justification

And with up to 100 ft. visibility, it's easy to see. You will find no shortage of dive shops, run by professionals, who will make your stay more memorable than you can imagine. And when you surface, you'll find our islands as beautiful above as they are below.

The U. S. Virgin Islands}

Britannic bold

Special character 5,40

St. Croix ✈ St. John ✈ St. Thomas}

Shelley Volaute 20 pt

18 pt special character ★ ★ ★ ★ ★

Call Your Travel Agent or contact http://www.usi.net}

Serif, shadow italic 12 pt

Exercise 18

■ **Line Spacing** ■ **Indent Text**

NOTES

Line Spacing

■ Use line spacing to specify the spacing between lines of text. A line spacing change affects text from the insertion point forward. Line spacing may also be applied to selected text. If your line spacing is set for double, *two hard returns will result in four blank lines.*

■ The quickest way to change line spacing is to click the Line Spacing button on the Power Bar and select a line spacing amount.

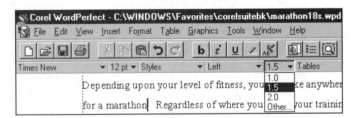

■ If you want to preview the effect of the line spacing change on your document or wish to use an exact measurement, set the line spacing amount in the Line Spacing dialog box. Select Line, Spacing from the Format menu.

Indent Text

■ The **Indent** feature moves a complete paragraph one tab stop to the right and sets a temporary left margin for the paragraph.

■ The **Double Indent** feature indents paragraph text one tab stop from both margins.

> This is an example of text which has an indented paragraph.
>
> > The Indent feature moves a complete paragraph one tab stop to the right and sets a temporary left margin for the paragraph.
>
> Note this example. Text is indented on left side only.

> This is an example of text which has a double-indented paragraph.
>
> > The Double Indent feature moves a complete paragraph one tab stop to the right and left of the margin.
>
> Note this example. Text is indented on the left and on the right.

■ Paragraphs may be indented *before* or *after* text is typed.

■ Text is indented to tab settings. Accessing the Indent feature once will indent text .5" to the right; accessing it twice will indent text 1", etc.

Format Toolbar

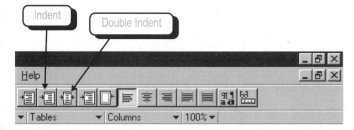

- The Indent mode is ended by pressing the Enter key.

- Before accessing the Indent feature, be sure to position the insertion point to the left of the first word in the paragraph to be indented.

- The Indent feature may be accessed in five ways:

1. By placing the insertion point to the immediate left of the paragraph to be affected and clicking the Indent or Double-Indent button on the Format Toolbar. This is the quickest way.

2. By clicking the QuickSpot to the left of the paragraph to be indented, clicking the Indent list arrow in the Paragraph dialog box and selecting Indent or Double Indent.

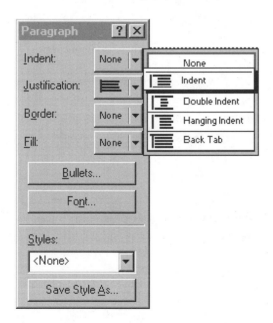

3. By selecting Paragraph from the Format menu, then selecting Indent or Double Indent from the resulting submenu.

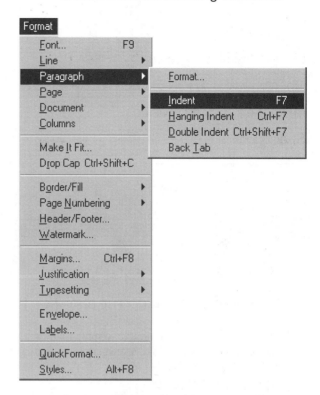

4. By clicking the *right* mouse button and selecting Indent. This process is used to indent text *from the left margin only*.

5. By pressing the F7 key to indent, or Ctrl + Shift + F7 to double indent.

- The proofreaders' mark for indenting is:] [

In this exercise, you will edit a previously created document and use the Indent features. See desired result on page 79.

EXERCISE DIRECTIONS

1. Start with a clear screen.
2. Open ⬛MARATHON or open ⬛18MARATH.
3. Make the indicated revisions.
4. Spell check.

5. Preview your document.
6. Print one copy.
7. Close the file; save the changes.

Double space

Regardless of where you are in your training program, if you follow these simple steps, you'll be well on your way to running a marathon.

SO YOU WANT TO RUN A MARATHON? *Center and set to 18 pt bold*

~~TWO MAJOR~~ STEPS TO GO THE DISTANCE *Center, convert case to initial caps*

↓ *3x*

It doesn't take a miracle to run a marathon. Going the distance can be easy. Depending upon your level of fitness, you can take anywhere from three months to a year to train for a marathon.

Training for Endurance
Endurance training is what is needed to build strength, speed and overall improved performance. The key is to run relaxed. While running, keep your wrists, hands and jaws loose. Keep your feet under your body and try to avoid leaning forward. *1"*

Training for Strength
Strength training builds power; it allows you to lengthen your stride and get more distance with every step. The best way to build strength is by running hills. *1"*

Training for Speed
Speed training puts finishing touches on your endurance and strength training and allows you to break personal records. Beware. Training for speed is the cause of most injuries and should only be considered after endurance and strength training. *1" ... 1"*

Stretching
Stretching warms up your muscles, improves the flow of blood and oxygen, increases your flexibility, improves your performance, and minimizes the risk of injury. *1" ... 1"*

Double indent 1"

SO YOU WANT TO RUN A MARATHON?

Steps to Go the Distance

It doesn't take a miracle to run a marathon. Going the distance can be easy. Depending upon your level of fitness, you can take anywhere from three months to a year to train for a marathon. Regardless of where you are in your training program, if you follow these simple steps, you'll be well on your way to running a marathon.

Training for Endurance

Endurance training is what is needed to build strength, speed and overall improved performance. The key is to run relaxed. While running, keep your wrists, hands and jaw loose. Keep your feet under your body and try to avoid leaning forward.

Training for Strength

Strength training builds power; it allows you to lengthen your stride and get more distance with every step. The best way to build strength is by running hills.

Training for Speed

Speed training puts finishing touches on your endurance and strength training and allows you to break personal records. Beware. Training for speed is the cause of most injuries and should only be considered **after** endurance and strength training.

Stretching

Stretching warms up your muscles, improves the flow of blood and oxygen, increases your flexibility, improves your performance, and minimizes the risk of injury.

KEYSTROKES

LINE SPACING

1. Place insertion point within paragraph where line spacing change will occur.

   OR

   Select multiple paragraphs to receive line spacing change.

2. Click **Line spacing** button....... `1.0 ▼` on the Power Bar.

3. Select line spacing amount.

OR

1. Place insertion point within paragraph where line spacing change will begin.

   OR

   Select text to receive line spacing change.

2. Click **Format** .... `Alt`+`R`

3. Click **Line**.................................... `L`

4. Click **Spacing**................................ `S`

5. Type desired amount in **Spacing** text box.

EXAMPLES:

1.5 = one and one half space
2 = double space
3 = triple space

OR

Click increment arrows to select a line spacing amount .... `↓` `↑`

6. Click **OK** .... `Enter`

INDENT/DOUBLE INDENT

F7/Ctrl + Shift +F7

1. Place insertion point where indentation should begin.

2. Click **Indent** or **Double Indent** button .... `▣` `▣` on Format Toolbar.

   —FOR LEFT INDENT ONLY—

1. Place insertion point where indentation should begin.

2. Click *right* mouse button.

3. Click **Indent**................................. `I`

   —FOR LEFT AND RIGHT INDENT—

1. Place insertion point where indentation should begin.

2. Click **Format**........................ `Alt`+`R`

3. Click **Paragraph** .... `A`

4. Click **Indent**................................. `I`

   OR

   Click **Double Indent** .... `D`

   ✓ *Repeat steps 1-3 until desired indentation is achieved.*

   OR

1. Click **QuickSpot** to the left of paragraph to receive indent.

2. Click **Indent** list arrow.

3. Select **Indent** or **Double Indent** option.

END INDENT MODE

Press **Enter**................................ `Enter`

Exercise

19

- ■ **Format a One-Page Report** ■ **Hanging Indent**
- ■ **First-Line Indent** ■ **Paragraph Spacing**

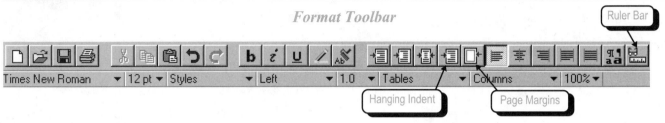

Format Toolbar

Ruler Bar

Hanging Indent   Page Margins

NOTES

Format a One-Page Report

■ A report or manuscript generally begins 2" from the top of the page and is prepared in double space. Each new paragraph begins .5" or 1" from the left margin (tab once). The title of a report is centered and keyed in all caps. A quadruple space follows the title.

■ Margins vary depending on how the report is bound. For an unbound report, use margins of 1" on the left and right (the default).

Hanging Indent

■ A **hanging indent** is created when all the lines in a paragraph are indented *except* the first line.

■ Note the effect of a hanging-indented paragraph. The second and succeeding lines of the paragraph indent to the first tab stop.

> This paragraph is an example of a "**hanging indent**." Note that all the lines in the paragraph are indented except the first line. This can be an effective way to emphasize paragraph text. *This paragraph style is commonly used for bibliographies.*

■ A hanging indent may be created in three ways:

1. By placing the insertion point to the left of the paragraph to be affected and clicking the Hanging Indent button on the Format Toolbar. This is the quickest way to accomplish this task.

2. By clicking the QuickSpot to the left of the paragraph to be indented, clicking the Indent list arrow in the Paragraph dialog box and selecting Hanging Indent.

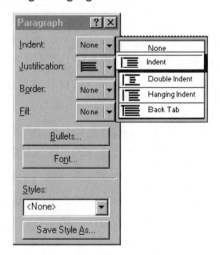

3. By selecting Paragraph, Hanging Indent from the Format menu.

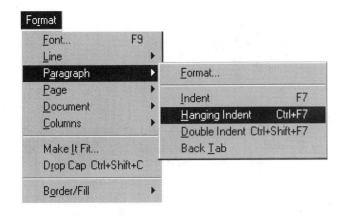

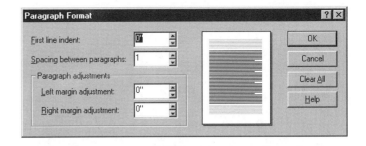

First-Line Indent

- A **first-line indent** lets you set the amount of space the first line of each paragraph indents. Each time you press Enter, the insertion point automatically begins the first line of a paragraph at the indented setting. This feature eliminates the need to use the Tab key to indent each new paragraph.

- First-line indents may be set by selecting Paragraph from the Format menu, then selecting Format from the submenu.

- In the Paragraph Format dialog box which follows, you may enter the amount you wish each paragraph to indent in the First line indent text box. **Paragraph Spacing** (adding space between paragraphs as you type your document) may also be adjusted in this dialog box by indicating the spacing amount in the Spacing between paragraphs text box.

- First-line indents may also be set by dragging the **first-line indent marker** (the top left triangle) *right* on the Ruler Bar to the desired first-line indent position. As the marker is being moved, the status bar displays the exact position of the marker. This method allows you to see the effect of your change as the marker is moved.

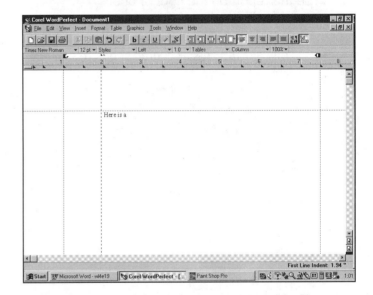

- To remove the first-line indent settings, select Paragraph, Format from the Format menu. In the Paragraph Format dialog box which follows, return the First-line indent setting to 0.

In this exercise, you will create a one-page report, setting first-line indents for some paragraphs and hanging indents for others. You will also gain more practice using the line spacing, margins, and font features.

EXERCISE DIRECTIONS

1. Start with a clear screen.

2. Access the Format Toolbar.

3. Click the Ruler Bar button on the Toolbar to display the Ruler Bar.

4. Click the Page Margins button on the Toolbar. Set 1.25" left and right margins and a .5" bottom margin.

5. Type the report on the right or open 🖫**19SURVIV**.

   - Begin the title on approximately Ln 2".
   - Use any desired special character before and after the title as shown.
   - Set title to a sans serif 14 point bold font.
   - Set body text to a serif 11 point font.
   - Set side headings to bold.

6. Set paragraph spacing to 1.75 for the document.

7. Set a 1" first-line indent and set line spacing to 1.5 for the *first two paragraphs only*. Use single spacing for the remainder of the document.

   ✓   *Remember, there is no need to tab each new paragraph. The first-line indent automatically advances text 1" when a new paragraph is created.*

8. Double indent the paragraphs shown 1" from the left and right margins.

9. Spell check.

10. Preview your document.

11. Print one copy.

12. Create hanging indents on the indented paragraphs.

13. Print one copy.

14. Save the file; name it SURVIVAL.

KEYSTROKES

HANGING INDENT

Ctrl + F7

1. Place insertion point at beginning of paragraph to be affected.

2. Click **Hanging Indent** button on Format Toolbar..........................🔳

OR

1. Place insertion point at beginning of paragraph to be affected.

2. Click **Format**..........................Alt + R

3. Click **Paragraph** ....A

4. Click **Hanging Indent** ....H

OR

1. Click **QuickSpot**.

2. Click **Indent**.

3. Click **Hanging Indent**.

To end Hanging Indent mode:

Press **Enter**..........................Enter

FIRST-LINE INDENT

1. Place insertion point anywhere within the paragraph to be affected.

2. Click **Format**..........................Alt + R

3. Click **Paragraph** ....A

4. Click **Format**..........................F

5. Click **First Line Indent**..........................Alt + F text box.

6. Enter first-line indent amount.

   OR

   Click increment arrows to select a first-line indent amount.

7. Click **OK**..........................Enter

—USING RULER BAR—

1. Place insertion point anywhere within the paragraph to be affected.

2. Drag first-line indent marker *right* to desired first-line indent position.

RETURN TO PREVIOUS SETTINGS

1. Place insertion point where reset adjustments should begin.

2. Click **Format**..........................Alt + R

3. Click **Paragraph** ....A

4. Click **Format**..........................F

5. Click **Clear All** ....Alt + A

6. Click **OK**..........................Enter

☎☎ SMALL BUSINESS SURVIVAL TIPS ☎☎

Change line spacing, paragraph indent and paragraph spacing

Owning a small business is an all-consuming experience. It requires the owner to constantly evaluate the business's potential and problems. All businesses experience problems. Accurate diagnosis of the severity and cause of the business problem is essential to resolving and preventing its recurrence.

How you go about diagnosing your business problems will depend on the nature of your business and the symptoms that are being experienced.

MOST COMMON FINANCIAL DIFFICULTIES

Return first-line indent to "0"

Create hanging indent

Expenses exceed revenues.

Overly rapid growth that outpaces a business's operating systems, the skills and abilities of its personnel, etc.

Poor management skills and business know-how among business owners and key management.

Failure to maximize a business's competitive strengths and to capitalize on its competitor's weaknesses.

ACTIONS TO CONSIDER

Create hanging indent

Evaluate all expenses including business-related travel or entertainment, subscriptions, the purchase of supplies, raw materials or equipment, insurance, the use of outside professionals, phone services, etc., to determine which can be reduced, delayed or eliminated.

Eliminate or discontinue products or services that are not making money. Do a careful analysis of this during each season of the year.

Reduce staff salaries and/or benefits. Do not do both at the same time; it can be very demoralizing.

Cut prices. This action alone can sometimes provide the cash a business needs to turn itself around.

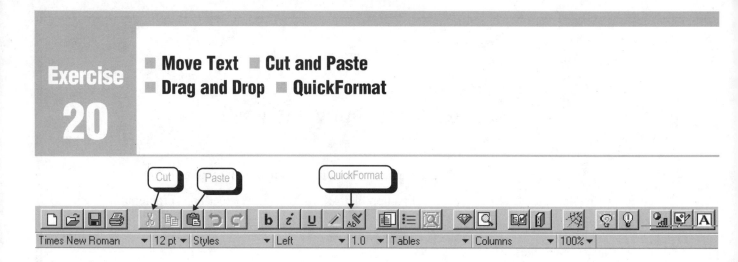

NOTES

Move Text

- WordPerfect provides two methods to move a block of text, a sentence, a paragraph, a page, or a column of text to another location in the same document or to another document. These methods are called cut and paste and drag and drop.

Cut and Paste

- The **cut** procedure allows you to "cut" or delete selected text from the screen and temporarily place it on the clipboard (temporary storage buffer). The **paste** procedure allows you to retrieve text from the clipboard and place it in a desired location in the document.

- There are several ways to cut and paste text. Note the keystrokes at the end of the exercise.

- Information remains on the clipboard until you cut or copy another selection (or until you exit Windows). Therefore, you can paste the same selection into many different locations, if desired.

Drag and Drop

- The **drag and drop** method of moving text allows you to move selected text using your mouse. This method is convenient for moving a word or several words from one location to another.

- Once text to be moved is selected, place the mouse pointer anywhere on the selected text, click and hold the *left* mouse button as you drag the highlighted text to the new location. The mouse pointer changes to a box with a dotted shadow to indicate that you are dragging text. When you reach the new location, release the mouse button to drop the text into place. Be sure to remove the selection highlight before pressing any key, so that you do not delete your newly moved text.

- If you move an indented or tabbed paragraph with formatting codes (double spacing, font changes, etc.), be sure the indent, tab and/or formatting code to the left of the text is moved along with the paragraph. To insure this, Reveal Codes and check that the insertion point is to the left of the code to move before selecting text.

- If text was not reinserted at the correct point, you can undo the action by selecting Edit, Undo. It is sometimes necessary to insert or delete spaces, returns, or tabs after completing a move.

- If you wish to move an indented or tabbed paragraph, be sure the indent or tab code to the left of the text is moved along with the paragraph. To insure this, reveal codes and check that the cursor is to the *left* of the code to be moved before selecting text.

- The proofreader's mark for moving is }⟶ or ◯⟶

QuickFormat

- The QuickFormat feature allows you to copy formatting, such as font face, style, and size, from one part of text to another.

- QuickFormat also allows you to **link** headings together so that when you make a format change to one heading, all the headings change and take on the same format. Linking is applied automatically when the Headings option is chosen. Linking is not available for individual words.

- QuickFormat can be accessed by highlighting the heading or text that contains the formatting you wish to copy, then selecting QuickFormat

from the Format menu or click the QuickFormat button on the Toolbar. In the QuickFormat dialog box which follows, you must indicate whether you wish to copy the format of Characters, or Headings.

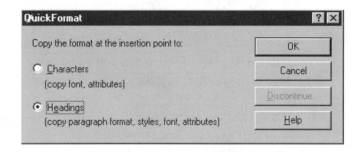

- After you click OK, a small paintbrush will appear on screen. Use the paintbrush to "paint" the formatting of the previously highlighted selection over an unformatted selection. Click the QuickFormat button again to turn the feature off. If you make an error while using QuickFormat, return to the QuickFormat dialog box and click the QuickFormat Discontinue button.

- Headings can be unlinked in the QuickFormat dialog box.

In this exercise, you will move paragraphs, then format them using the QuickFormat feature.

EXERCISE DIRECTIONS

1. Start with a clear screen.
2. Type the exercise exactly as shown in Illustration A or open 20TIPS.
   - Use the default margins.
   - Start on Ln 1".
   - Use special characters for the numbers preceding each paragraph.
   - ✓ *The numbers are out of order intentionally.*

To create Illustration B:

3. Set left margin to 2" and right margin to 1" at the top of the document.
4. Move the paragraphs in sequential numerical order by doing the following:
   - Use the drag and drop procedure for the first move.
   - Use the cut and paste procedure for the second move.
   - Use any desired procedure for the remaining moves.
5. Center the heading and set text to a sans serif 20 point bold font.

6. Press the Enter key once after each tip. Double indent text twice (1") below each tip.
7. Format the number 1 special character (①) to 20-point bold.
   - Using the QuickFormat feature, copy the Character formatting (point size change and bolding) to the remaining numbers.
8. Format the first tip (SLOW DOWN) to a sans serif 14 point font.
   - Using the QuickFormat feature, copy the Character formatting to the remaining tips.
9. Format the text below each tip to italics.
   - Using the QuickFormat feature, copy the Character formatting to the remaining text below each tip.
10. Center the current page.
11. Preview your document.
12. Print one copy.
13. Save the file; name it TIPS.

ILLUSTRATION A

SIX TIPS FOR THE WORKAHOLIC

①SLOW DOWN. Make a conscious effort to eat, talk, walk and drive more slowly. Give yourself extra time to get to appointments so you are not always rushing.

③DRAW THE LINE. When you are already overloaded and need more personal time, do not take on any other projects. You will be just causing yourself more stress.

②LEARN TO DELEGATE. Let others share the load--you don't have to do everything yourself. You will have more energy and the end result will be better for everyone.

⑥TAKE BREAKS. Take frequent work breaks: short walks or meditating for a few minutes can help you unwind and clear your head.

⑤CARE FOR YOURSELF. Eat properly, get enough sleep and exercise regularly. Do what you can so that you are healthy, both mentally and physically.

④CUT YOUR HOURS. Be organized, but do not let your schedule run your life. Also, try to limit yourself to working eight hours a day—and not a minute more.

ILLUSTRATION B

SIX TIPS FOR THE WORKAHOLIC

①SLOW DOWN.
> *Make a conscious effort to eat, talk, walk and drive more slowly. Give yourself extra time to get to appointments so you are not always rushing.*

②LEARN TO DELEGATE.
> *Let others share the load—you don't have to do everything yourself. You will have more energy and the end result will be better for everyone.*

③DRAW THE LINE.
> *When you are already overloaded and need more personal time, do not take on any other projects. You will be just causing yourself more stress.*

④CUT YOUR HOURS.
> *Be organized, but do not let your schedule run your life. Also, try to limit yourself to working eight hours a day—and not a minute more.*

⑤CARE FOR YOURSELF.
> *Eat properly, get enough sleep and exercise regularly. Do what you can so that you are healthy, both mentally and physically.*

⑥TAKE BREAKS.
> *Take frequent work breaks: short walks or meditating for a few minutes can help you unwind and clear your head.*

KEYSTROKES

MOVE

Ctrl + c, Ctrl + V

Cut and Paste

1. Select text to be moved (cut).
2. a. Click *right* mouse button.
   b. Click **Cut** .... `C`
   OR
   a. Click **Edit** .... `Alt`+`E`
   b. Click **Cut** .... `T`
   OR
   Click **Cut** button on Toolbar .... `✂`
3. Position insertion point where text is to be reinserted.
4. a. Click *right* mouse button.
   b. Click **Paste** .... `P`
   OR
   a. Click **Edit** .... `Alt`+`E`
   b. Click **Paste** .... `P`
   OR
   Click **Paste** button on Toolbar .... `📋`

Drag and Drop

1. Select text to be moved.
2. Position mouse pointer on selected text.
3. Click and hold left mouse button. (A shadowed box appears.)
4. Drag text to new location.
5. Release mouse button.

QUICKFORMAT

1. Format a character, word, or phrase with font face, style, or size you want copied to other text.
2. Select the text that has formatting to be copied.
3. Click **QuickFormat** button .... `Ab✓` on Toolbar.
   OR
   a. Click **Format** .... `Alt`+`R`
   b. Click **QuickFormat** .... `Q`
   OR
   a. Click *right* mouse button.
   b. Click **QuickFormat** .... `Q`

4. Click **Characters** .... `C`
   to format a character, word or phrase.
   OR
   Click **Headings** .... `E`
   to format an entire heading.

   ✓ *The mouse pointer changes to a paintbrush* `🖌`.

5. Drag the paintbrush over the text you wish to format.

   To turn off QuickFormat:
   - Repeat the procedure used in step 3.

UNLINK HEADINGS

1. Select a linked heading you wish to unlink.
2. Access the QuickFormat feature using any desired method.
3. Click on **Discontinue** .... `D`
   - Choose **Current** heading .... `C`
     to unlink the selected heading only.
   - Choose **All Associated** .... `A`
     headings to unlink all headings.
4. Click **OK** .... `Enter`

Exercise 21

■ **QuickFormat** ■ **Link Headings**

NOTES

QuickFormat

■ As noted in the previous exercise, the **QuickFormat** feature may be used to link headings together so that when you make a format change to one heading, all the headings change and take on the same format.

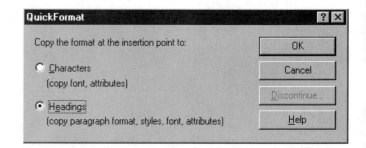

Link Headings

■ In order to **link headings**, you must first identify heading text by selecting (highlighting) the text that has the formatting you wish to copy. Then, click the QuickFormat button on the Toolbar. In the dialog box which follows, select H<u>e</u>adings.

■ When the mouse pointer becomes a paintbrush, drag it over any text you wish to link. Each word or phrase you "paint," receives a heading code. When you make a formatting change to text you identified as a heading, all heading text will take on the same format.

In this exercise, you will gain more practice moving text. You will also use the QuickFormat feature to link heading text and then make formatting changes to the linked text.

EXERCISE DIRECTIONS

1. Start with a clear screen.

2. Open ⬛MARATHON or ⬛21MARATH.

3. Insert new text as directed in the illustration.

4. Move the paragraphs as indicated. Use any procedure you desire to move the paragraphs.

   ✓ *Remember to include the bold codes in your selection before cutting the text.*

5. Using QuickFormat, identify the side headings as heading text. (Highlight the first heading, select QuickFormat button from the Toolbar, and paint each heading to identify it as heading text.)

6. Change the first side headings to a sans serif font (all side headings should change).

7. Preview your document.

8. Change one of the QuickFormat linked headings to 14 point italic (all side headings should change).

9. Full justify all text except the heading and subheading.

10. Print one copy.

11. Close the file; save the changes.

SO YOU WANT TO RUN A MARATHON?

Steps to Go the Distance

Here are some suggestions:

It doesn't take a miracle to run a marathon. Going the distance can be easy. Depending upon your level of fitness, you can take anywhere from three months to a year to train for a marathon. Regardless of where you are in your training program, if you follow these simple steps, you'll be well on your way to running a marathon.

Training for Endurance

Endurance training is what is needed to build strength, speed and overall improved performance. The key is to run relaxed. While running, keep your wrists, hands and jaw loose. Keep your feet under your body and try to avoid leaning forward.

Training for Strength

Strength training builds power; it allows you to lengthen your stride and get more distance with every step. The best way to build strength is by running hills.

Move as new ¶

Training for Speed

Speed training puts finishing touches on your endurance and strength training and allows you to break personal records. Beware. Training for speed is the cause of most injuries and should only be considered **after** endurance and strength training.

Stretching

Stretching warms up your muscles, improves the flow of blood and oxygen, increases your flexibility, improves your performance, and minimizes the risk of injury.

Insert

Nutrition

Good nutrition is an essential ingredient to any training program. Good eating will keep your body well-fueled, lean and strong for maximum race results.

Exercise

22

- ■ **Copy and Paste** ■ **Drag and Drop**

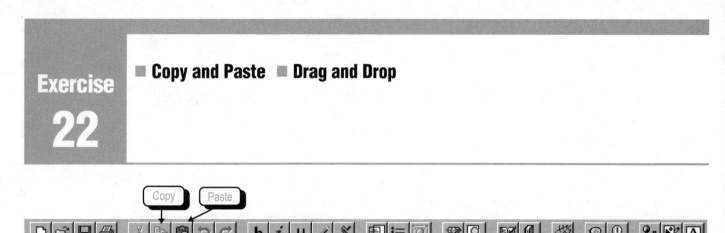

NOTES

- ■ **Copy and paste** and **drag and drop** are features that let you copy text from one location to another.

- ■ **Copying** leaves text in its original location while placing a duplicate in a different location in the same document or another document. (Copying text to another document will be covered in a later lesson.) In contrast, moving removes text from its original location and places it elsewhere.

Copy and Paste

- ■ The procedure for copying text is similar to the procedure for moving text. See keystrokes at the end of this exercise.

- ■ When text is copied, it remains on the screen while a copy of it is placed on the clipboard.

- ■ Text remains on the clipboard until you copy another selection (or until you exit Windows). Therefore, you can paste the same selection into many different locations, if desired.

- ■ Text is reinserted or retrieved from the clipboard at the insertion point. Therefore, place the insertion point to the *immediate left* of where the text is to be reinserted before following the paste procedures outlined in the keystrokes below.

Drag and Drop

- ■ Use the drag-and-drop copy method to copy selected text using your mouse.

- ■ Once text to be copied is selected, place the mouse pointer anywhere on the selected text, and *press the Ctrl key while dragging text to the new location* (a black shadowed box appears). Then drop a copy of the text into its new location by releasing the mouse button. Be sure to release the mouse button *before* releasing the Ctrl key.

- ■ As with the move feature, if text was not copied properly, you can undo it.

In this exercise, you will create a document and use the copy procedure as well as previously learned features. In addition, you will gain practice using the QuickFormat and Link Headings features.

EXERCISE DIRECTIONS

1. Start with a clear screen.

2. Open ☎TIPS or 🖥22TIPS.

3. Set the title to 25 point bold.

4. To link the side headings (the numbers and tips), use QuickFormat to identify the side headings and numbers as heading text. (In the previous exercise, this text was identified as character text.)

5. Using QuickFormat, change the first side heading and number to 18 point.
   - ✓ *All tips and numbers should change to the new format.*

6. Using the letter "s" and the Wingding font, create a line of diamonds to the right of the first tip.

7. Copy the line and paste it next to the remaining tips.

8. Type and center To Summarize: in a serif 14 point bold font as shown.

9. Copy each number and tip as shown.
   - Center align all summary tips.
   - Set font to serif 14 point.
   - ✓ *If necessary, change the bottom margin to .5" so the document fits on one page.*

10. Preview your document.

11. Print one copy.

12. Close the file; save the changes.

KEYSTROKES

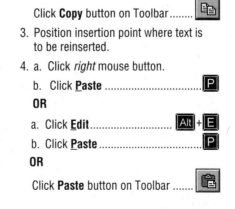

COPY AND PASTE

Ctrl + C, Ctrl + V

1. Select text to be copied.
2. a. Click *right* mouse button.
   b. Click **C<u>o</u>py** .... 〇
   OR
   a. Click **<u>E</u>dit** .... Alt + E
   b. Click **C<u>o</u>py** C
   OR

   Click **Copy** button on Toolbar .... 🖹
3. Position insertion point where text is to be reinserted.
4. a. Click *right* mouse button.
   b. Click **<u>P</u>aste** .... P
   OR
   a. Click **<u>E</u>dit** .... Alt + E
   b. Click **<u>P</u>aste** .... P
   OR

   Click **Paste** button on Toolbar .... 📋

DRAG AND DROP

1. Select text to be copied.
2. Position mouse pointer on selected text.
3. Press and hold **Ctrl** while clicking and holding left mouse button. (A black shadowed box appears.)
4. Drag text to new location.
5. Release mouse button.

SIX TIPS FOR THE WORKAHOLIC }

Set to 25 pt bold

①SLOW DOWN. ◆◆◆◆◆◆◆◆◆◆◆◆◆◆◆◆ }

Copy

Make a conscious effort to eat, talk, walk and drive more slowly. Give yourself extra time to get to appointments so you are not always rushing.

②LEARN TO DELEGATE.

Paste

Let others share the load—you don't have to do everything yourself. You will have more energy and the end result will be better for everyone.

③DRAW THE LINE.

When you are already overloaded and need more personal time, do not take on any other projects. You will be just causing yourself more stress.

Paste

④CUT YOUR HOURS.

Be organized, but do not let your schedule run your life. Also, try to limit yourself to working eight hours a day—and not a minute more.

Paste

⑤CARE FOR YOURSELF.

Eat properly, get enough sleep and exercise regularly. Do what you can so that you are healthy, both mentally and physically.

Paste

⑥TAKE BREAKS.

Take frequent work breaks: short walks or meditating for a few minutes can help you unwind and clear your head.

Copy

↓ *3x*

To Summarize:

↓ *2x*

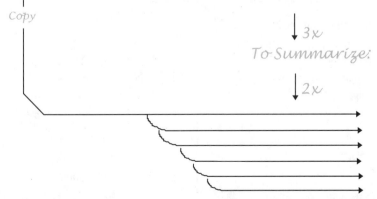

Exercise 23

■ **Make It Fit**   ■ **Thesaurus**

NOTES

Make It Fit

- The **Make It Fit** feature lets you shrink or expand a document to fill a desired number of pages.

- If, for example, your document fills 1¼ pages, but you would like it to fit on one page, the Make It Fit Expert automatically adjusts margins, font size, and/or line spacing so that the text will shrink to one page.

- You may return your document to the original number of pages by selecting Undo from the Edit menu.

- Make It Fit may be selected from the Format menu or by clicking the Make It Fit button on the WordPerfect 7 Toolbar. In the dialog box which follows, you must indicate how many pages you wish your document to fill. In addition, you must indicate which items you would like Make It Fit to adjust. If you do not want the margins affected, do not click the margin check boxes.

Thesaurus

- The **Thesaurus** feature enables you to select the right word when writing a document.

- The Thesaurus feature lists synonyms (words that have the same meaning) and antonyms (words that have the opposite meaning) for a selected word.

- The insertion point must be on the word you wish to look up before you access the feature.

- Thesaurus may be accessed by selecting Thesaurus from the Tools menu, or by pressing Alt + F1.

- In the dialog box shown on the next page, select the Thesaurus tab. The selected word is displayed in the Replace With text box along with a list of related words, synonyms, and antonyms for that word.

- To replace a word in your document with a word in the Thesaurus, click a related word or a synonym to insert it in the Replace With text box. Then click the Replace button.

- The Thesaurus feature replaces verbs with the same tense or form. For example, if you look up the word "inquiring," the replacement word would include "ing."

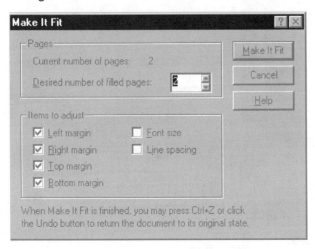

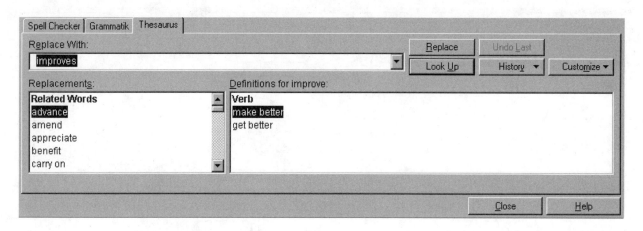

In this exercise, you will gain more practice copying text. In addition, you will use the Make It Fit feature to keep all text on one page and use the Thesaurus feature to substitute highlighted words.

EXERCISE DIRECTIONS

1. Start with a clear screen.

2. Open ⌨MARATHON or ⬜23MARATH.

3. Make the indicated revisions.

4. Copy and center the side headings below the last paragraph in the document (Remember these suggestions). Set the suggestions text to 12 point.

5. Change the first side heading (Nutrition) to no italics. (All side headings should change.)

6. Change the paragraph format below each side heading to a hanging indent.

7. Using the Thesaurus feature, substitute highlighted words.

8. Use the Make it Fit feature to shrink text to one page. You may include changes to any margins to make the document fit on one page.

9. Preview your document.

10. Print one copy.

11. Close the file; save the changes.

KEYSTROKES

MAKE IT FIT

1. Click **Make It Fit** button................. 🔍 on WordPerfect 7 Toolbar.

   OR

   a. Click **Format** .... Alt+R

   b Click **Make It Fit** I

2. Click **Desired Number of Filled Pages** text box .... D

3. Type number of pages you wish document to be .... *number*

   OR

   Click number of pages you wish document to be .... ↓ ↑

4. Click desired items to automatically adjust:

   • **Left Margin** .... Alt+L

   • **Right Margin**..................... Alt+R

   • **Top Margin** .... Alt+T

   • **Bottom Margin**.................. Alt+B

   • **Font Size** .... Alt+F

   • **Line Spacing**.................... Alt+I

5. Click **Make It Fit**.................... Enter

   To return document to its original state:

   Click **Undo** button on Toolbar.........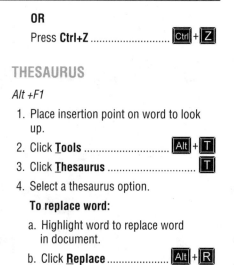

   OR

   a. Click **Edit**......................... Alt+E

   b. Click **Undo** .... U

   OR

   Press **Ctrl+Z** .... Ctrl+Z

THESAURUS

Alt +F1

1. Place insertion point on word to look up.

2. Click **Tools** .... Alt+T

3. Click **Thesaurus** .... T

4. Select a thesaurus option.

   To replace word:

   a. Highlight word to replace word in document.

   b. Click **Replace** .... Alt+R

SO YOU WANT TO RUN A MARATHON?

Steps to Go the Distance

It doesn't take a miracle to run a marathon. Going the distance can be easy. Depending upon your level of fitness, you can take anywhere from three months to a year to train for a marathon. Here are some suggestions:

Nutrition

Good nutrition is an essential ingredient to any training program. Good eating will keep your body well-fueled, lean and strong for maximum race results.

Stretching

Stretching warms up your muscles, improves the flow of blood and oxygen, increases your flexibility, improves your performance, and minimizes the risk of injury.

Training for Endurance

Endurance training is what is needed to build strength, speed and overall improved performance. While running, keep your wrists, hands and jaw loose. Keep your feet under your body and try to avoid leaning forward. The key is to run relaxed.

Copy

Training for Speed

Speed training puts finishing touches on your endurance and strength training and allows you to break personal records. Beware. Training for speed is the cause of most injuries and should only be considered **after** endurance and strength training.

Training for Strength

Strength training builds power; it allows you to lengthen your stride and get more distance with every step. The best way to build strength is by running hills.

suggestions

Regardless of where you are in your training program, if you follow these simple steps,

you'll be well on your way to running a marathon. *Remember these suggestions:*

2x

Corel WordPerfect 7 ■ Lesson 4 ■ Exercise 23   95

Exercise 24

■ Grammar Check (Grammatik)

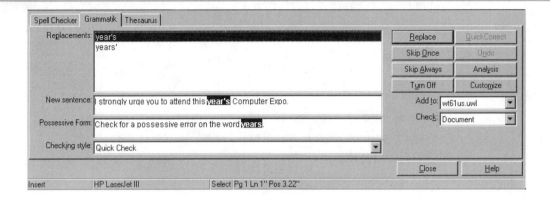

NOTES

Grammar Check (Grammatik)

- **Grammatik** is WordPerfect's grammar check feature that checks your document for errors in spelling, grammar usage, and punctuation. Style errors, including clichés, jargon, and wordiness, are generally not detected.

- Grammatik checks for errors based on the default writing style, Quick Check. Other writing-style options are available:
  - Very Strict
  - Formal Memo or Letter
  - Informal Memo or Letter
  - Technical or Scientific
  - Documentation or Speech
  - Student Composition
  - Advertising
  - Fiction

- When a writing style is selected, WordPerfect applies different grammar rules to detect different kinds of writing errors.

- Grammatik is accessed by selecting Grammatik from the Tools menu or by pressing Alt+Shift+F1. The following dialog box appears:

- When Grammatik detects an error, the window displays the following:

Replacements	Displays how to correct the error.
New Sentence	Displays the sentence correctly rewritten.
Third Window	Displays the grammar rule that was violated by the error.

- Grammatik also flags spelling errors.

  To respond to grammar and spelling errors, click the appropriate button:

Replace	Replaces the highlighted error with a new word.
Skip Once	Ignores the highlighted error for this occurrence only and advances to the next detected error.
Skip Always	Ignores the highlighted error for the entire document.
Add to	Adds a word to the selected spelling dictionary.
Turn Off	Disables checking for a particular rule.
Analysis	Offers various options to analyze your document. Analysis, Basic Counts displays a list of statistics about your document.
Undo	Reverses the last action.
Close	Closes Grammatik.

EXERCISE DIRECTIONS

1. Start with a clear screen.

2. Use the default margins.

3. Clear all tab stops. Set a tab stop at 4.5" from the left edge of the page.

4. Type the exercise exactly as shown in Illustration A, including the grammatical errors, or open ▣24MASON.

5. Set all text to a sans serif 12 point font.

6. Insert today's date, the inside address (use the address book to insert the address), and salutation as shown in Illustration B, beginning on approximately Ln 2".
   - Make the indicated revisions.
   - Type the paragraph at the bottom of the document as shown, and move it as indicated.

7. Set 2" left and right margins for the paragraphs containing event descriptions as shown in Illustration C.
   - Change the first event title to bold.
   - Use QuickFormat to copy the bold formatting to the other headings and link them as headings.

   - Change the first event description to italic.
   - Use QuickFormat to copy the italic formatting to the other descriptions and link them as headings.

8. Spell and grammar check. (Correct the possessive and agreement errors only.)

9. Use the thesaurus to replace the highlighted words.

10. Reformat the first event heading to a serif 14 point font. Reformat the event descriptions to serif. (All linked paragraphs should change to the new formatting.)

11. Use Make it Fit to keep text on one page. Adjust font size and top and bottom margins.

12. Preview your document.

13. Analyze the document to determine the number of words.

14. Print one copy.

15. Save the file; name it MASON.

KEYSTROKES

GRAMMAR CHECK

Alt+Shift+F1

1. Position insertion point at the beginning of document.
   - Click **Tools**........................ Alt + T
   - Click **Grammatik**........................ G

2. When an error is detected, click appropriate option:

   - **Replace** .... Alt + R
     to replace highlighted error with new word.
   - **Skip Once** .... Alt + O
     to ignore only this occurrence of highlighted error and advance.
   - **Skip Always** .... Alt + A
     to skip all occurrences of highlighted error.
   - **Add to** .... Alt + T
     to add word to Grammatik spelling dictionary.

   - **Undo**.................................. Alt + U
   - **Analysis**............................. Alt + Y
     to apply an analysis option.
   - **Close** .... Alt + C
     to close Grammatik.

   To change writing style:

   a. Click **Checking Styles** list
      arrow................................. Alt + I
   b. Choose desired checking style ... ↓ ↑
   c. Click **Close** .... Alt + C

ILLUSTRATION A

I strongly urge you to attend this years <u>Computer Expo</u>. In four days, you will pick up the latest computer news and discover new ways to put your computer to work—in the office, in the lab, in the studio, in the classroom or in your home.

If you are interested in attending, call *Derek Brennan* at 1-800-555-5555. He will preregister anyone who wish to attend. This will save you long lines at the show. The preregistration fee is $150.00. On-site registration will be an additional $25.00.

Here are some of the events you can look forward to:

Keynote Sessions.
These sessions will feature luminaries from the computer world who will offer you insights from industry.
Application Workshops.
Join a series of two-hour learning sessions which will provide guidelines, tips and "how-to's" on popular software packages.
Programmer/Developer Forums.
Veteran and novice computer users will discuss innovative advances and techniques.

Insert address using the address book

2
Today's date

Ms. Sharon Mason
{

Remove underline; set to italics

Dear Ms. Mason:

I strongly urge you to attend this years Computer Expo. In four days, you will pick up the latest computer news and discover new ways to put your computer to work—in the office, in the lab, in the studio, in the classroom or in your home.

es

If you are interested in attending, call *Derek Brennan* at 1-800-555-5555. He will preregister anyone who wish to attend. This will save you long lines at the show. The preregistration fee is $150.00. On-site registration will be an additional $25.00.

Here are some of the events you can look forward to:

Move

Keynote Sessions.
These sessions will feature luminaries from the computer world who will offer you insights from industry.

DS

Application Workshops.
Join a series of two-hour learning sessions which will provide guidelines, tips and "how-to's" on popular software packages.

DS

Programmer/Developer Forums.
Veteran and novice computer users will discuss innovative advances and techniques.

Move

Interest Group Meetings.
These sessions will include Education Workshops for teachers, resources and recommendations for the home office worker and ways to fully utilize your computer in a law office.

Sincerely,

John Mulligan
Expo Coordinator

ILLUSTRATION C - DESIRED RESULT

Today's date

Ms. Sharon Mason
60 Owens Walk
Albany, NY 12209

Dear Ms. Mason:

I strongly urge you to attend this year's *Computer Expo.* In four days, you will pick up the latest computer news and ascertain new ways to put your computer to work—in the office, in the lab, in the studio, in the classroom or in your home.

Here are some of the events you can look forward to:

Application Workshops.
Join a series of two-hour learning sessions which will provide guidelines, tips and "how-to's" on popular software packages

Keynote Sessions.
These sessions will feature celebrities from the computer world who will offer you insights from industry.

Interest Group Meetings.
These sessions will include Education Workshops for teachers, resources and recommendations for the home office worker, and ways to fully utilize your computer in a law office.

Programmer/Developer Forums.
Veteran and unseasoned computer users will discuss new advances and techniques.

If you are interested in attending, call *Derek Brennan* at 1-800-555-5555. He will preregister anyone who wishes to attend. This will save you long lines at the show. The preregistration fee is $150.00. On-site registration will be an additional $25.00.

Sincerely,

John Mulligan
Expo Coordinator

jm/yo

Exercise
25

■ **Find and Replace Text** ■ **Hyphenate Text**

NOTES

Find and Replace Text

■ The **Find and Replace** feature scans your document and searches for occurrences of specified words, phrases, or codes. Once the desired text or code is found, it can be edited or replaced.

■ Find and Replace may be accessed from the Edit menu. In the Find and Replace Text dialog box which displays, the word or phrase to be searched is typed in the Find text box; the replacement text or code is entered in the Replace with text box.

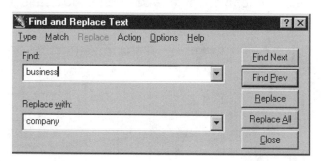

■ WordPerfect scans the document and stops at the first occurrence of the specified word or code. Click the appropriate button to continue your search:

Find Next	To stop at the next occurrence.
Find Prev	To search in a backward direction.
Replace	To confirm each replacement (with confirmation).
Replace All	To replace all occurrences without confirmation.

■ To search for text exactly in the case it was typed (uppercase, lowercase or initial caps), or a specific font, choose Case or Font from the Match menu. If, for example, you wanted to find the word HELP and you did not select the Case

option, both upper- and lowercase occurrences of the word would be found.

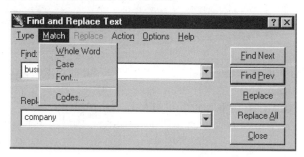

■ Use the Whole Word option to select whole words only. For example, if you were searching for the word *the*, and you did not select the Whole Word option, WordPerfect would flag words in which *the* was a part of the word, like *these*, *thesaurus*, *thesis*, etc.

■ Use the Codes option to find a code such as Bold On, Bold Off, Left Tab, etc.

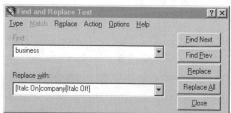

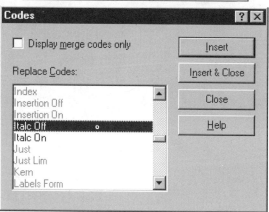

- The <u>W</u>ord Forms option in the <u>T</u>ype menu allows you to find and replace words based on the root form of the word. For example, if you select the <u>W</u>ord Forms option and you search for the word *call*, WordPerfect would find the words *call**s***, *call**ed***, *call**er***, and *call**ing*** as well.

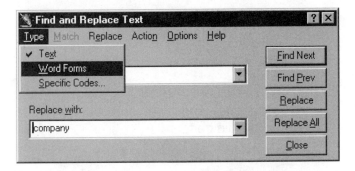

- Use the <u>S</u>pecific Codes option in the <u>T</u>ype menu to find a code that requires specific numbers or information, such as a margin code. For example, you could find a 1" left margin code and replace it with a 2" left margin code. Or you could find a Times New Roman font code and replace with an Arial font code.

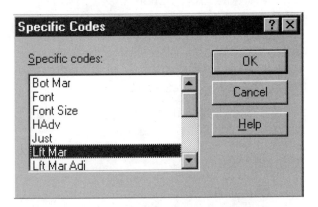

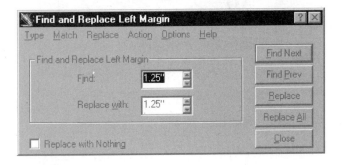

- WordPerfect searches in a forward direction. To search from the insertion point backward, click the Find <u>P</u>rev button.

Hyphenate Text

- Hyphenation produces a tighter right margin by dividing words that extend beyond the right margin rather than wrapping them to the next line. If text is full justified and hyphenated, the sentences have smaller gaps between words.

- By default, WordPerfect's hyphenation feature is set to off. In the *off* position, WordPerfect wraps any word extending beyond the right margin. When hyphenation is *on*, a word that starts before the left edge of the hyphenation zone and extends beyond the right edge of the zone will be hyphenated.

- Hyphenation may be accessed by selecting <u>L</u>ine, Hyphenation from the Format menu. In the Line Hyphenation dialog box which follows, you may change the width of the space a word must span before hyphenation divides it by changing the hyphenation zone. *Increase* the percentage of the zone to hyphenate *fewer* words; *decrease* to hyphenate *more* words.

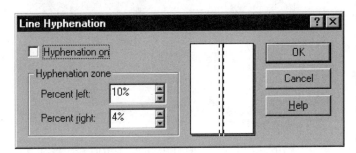

- To keep words such as sister-in-law or self-control together even if they span the hyphenation zone, type the word with a hard hyphen (Ctrl + -).

EXERCISE DIRECTIONS

1. Start with a clear screen.
2. Open ▧SURVIVAL or ▢25SURVIV.
3. Use the Find and Replace feature to place your insertion point on each of the following words in the document. Then use the Thesaurus feature to replace each word.
   - constantly
   - severity
   - Evaluate (first word in the first paragraph below ACTIONS TO CONSIDER).

4. Search for the word "business" and replace with "company" *except for the highlighted occurrences.*
5. Full justify the document.
6. Set the left hyphenation zone to 4%, and hyphenate the document.
7. Print one copy.
8. Close the file; save the changes.

☎☎ SMALL BUSINESS SURVIVAL TIPS ☎☎

Owning a small business is an all-consuming experience. It requires the owner to constantly evaluate the business's potential and problems. All businesses experience problems. Accurate diagnosis of the severity and cause of the business problem is essential to resolving and preventing its recurrence.

How you go about diagnosing your business problems will depend on the nature of your business and the symptoms that are being experienced.

MOST COMMON FINANCIAL DIFFICULTIES

Expenses exceed revenues.

Overly rapid growth that outpaces a business's operating systems, the skills and abilities of its personnel, etc.

Poor management skills and business know-how among business owners and key management.

Failure to maximize a business's competitive strengths and to capitalize on its competitor's weaknesses.

ACTIONS TO CONSIDER

Evaluate all expenses including business-related travel or entertainment, subscriptions, the purchase of supplies, raw materials or equipment, insurance, the use of outside professionals, phone services, etc., to determine which can be reduced, delayed or eliminated.

Eliminate or discontinue products or services that are not making money. Do a careful analysis of this during each season of the year.

Reduce staff salaries and/or benefits. Do not do both at the same time; it can be very demoralizing.

Cut prices. This action alone can sometimes provide the cash a business needs to turn itself around.

KEYSTROKES

FIND AND REPLACE TEXT/CODES

F2 then step 4

1. Place insertion point at top of document.
2. Click **Edit** .... `Alt` + `E`
3. Click **Find and Replace** .... `F`
4. Type text to be searched .... `Alt` + `I` in **Find** text box.
5. Type replacement text .... `Alt` + `W` in **Replace With** text box.

   To find specific text:
   a. Click **Match** .... `Alt` + `M`
   b. Click **Whole Word** .... `W`

      OR

      Click **Case** .... `C`

      OR

      Click **Font** .... `F`
   c. Type text information to be searched.

To find/replace codes:
a. Click **Match** .... `Alt` + `M`
b. Click **Codes** .... `O`
c. Click code to be searched/replaced .... `↓` `↑`
d. Click **Insert** .... `Alt` + `I` to insert each selected code.
e. Click **Insert & Close** .... `Alt` + `N` to return to Find and Replace Text dialog box.

To find/replace specific codes:
a. Click **Type** .... `Alt` + `T`
b. Click **Specific Codes** .... `S`
c. Click specific code to be searched .... `↓` `↑`
d. Click **OK** .... `Enter`
e. Select additional code information .... `Tab` , `↓` `↑`
6. Click **Find Next** .... `Alt` + `F` to search for each occurrence.
   • Click **Replace** .... `Alt` + `R`

   OR

   • Click **Replace All** .... `Alt` + `A`
7. Click **Close** .... `Alt` + `C`

HYPHENATION

1. Position insertion point where hyphenation is to begin.
2. Click **Format** .... `Alt` + `R`
3. Click **Line** .... `L`
4. Click **Hyphenation** .... `E`
5. Click **Hyphenation On** check box .... `Alt` + `O`

   To change hyphenation zone:
   a. Click **Percentage left** text box .... `Alt` + `L`
   b. Type a new left percentage.
   c. Click **Percentage right** .... `Alt` + `R` text box.
   d. Type a new right percentage.
6. Click **OK** .... `Enter`

Exercise 26

■ Outlines

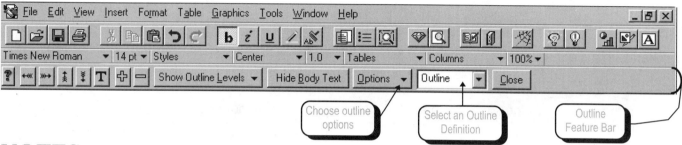

NOTES

Oulines

- An **outline** is used to organize information about a subject for the purpose of making a speech or writing a report.

- An outline contains many topics and subtopics, or levels. WordPerfect's Outline feature automatically formats each level of topic and subtopic differently.

- The Outline feature is accessed by selecting Outline from the Tools menu.

- An Outline Feature Bar displays, providing buttons for easy access to outline editing features.

- Outlines include several levels of information. A traditional outline, like the one illustrated on the right, uses Roman numerals to indicate the first outline levels (I, II, III, etc.), capital letters to indicate the second outline levels (A, B, C, etc.), and Arabic numerals to indicate the third outline levels (1, 2, 3, etc.). To view a document in traditional outline format, you must change the default Paragraph outline type to Outline by selecting Define Outline from the Options menu on the Feature Bar, or by clicking the drop-down arrow next to Paragraph and choosing Outline.

- When you begin typing the outline, symbols appear at the left of your screen, indicating non-outline text as well as the outline level of the text you type.

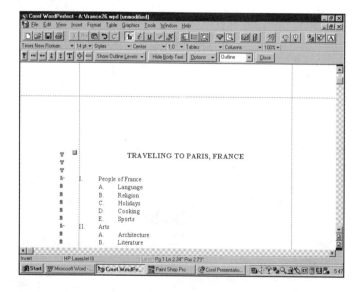

- A traditional outline may contain a title. If a title is desired, type the title, press Enter three times, then access the Outline feature.

- **To advance from one level to the next**, press the Tab key or click the right-pointing arrow on the Feature Bar.

- **If you make an error by advancing too far to the next level**, press Shift + Tab or click the left-pointing arrow on the Feature Bar.

- **To type non-outline text below the outline**, select <u>E</u>nd Outline from the <u>O</u>ptions drop-down menu on the Outline Feature Bar, and select <u>C</u>lose.

- Outlines created in WordPerfect may be imported into Presentations; outlines created in Presentations may be imported into a WordPerfect documents. Importing and exporting outline files will be covered in the Integration Chapter.

In this exercise, you will create a traditional outline.

EXERCISE DIRECTIONS

1. Start with a clear screen.

2. Set 1.5" left and right margins.

3. Begin the exercise at the top of the page (Ln 1").

4. Center the title; set the font to 14 point bold.

5. Create the outline shown on the following page using the Outline feature and the outline style.

6. Spell check.

7. Center the document vertically on the page.

8. Preview your document.

9. Print one copy.

10. Save the exercise; name it FRANCE.

KEYSTROKES

OUTLINE

1. Place insertion point where outline is to begin.
2. Click **Tools** .... `Alt`+`T`
3. Click **Outline** .... `O`
   - ✓ *The first outline level symbol and number of outline item you type appears.*

   To change outline style:
   a. Click **Options** .... `Shift`+`Alt`+`O` (on Outline Feature Bar).
   b. Click **Define Outline** .... `D`
   c. Select desired outline style .... `↓``↑`

d. Click **OK** .... `Enter`
   - ✓ *As you highlight a choice, a sample of the style appears in the Description area.*
   - ✓ *Select Outline for this exercise.*

To create outline:
   a. Keyboard text for first level.
   b. Press **Enter** .... `Enter`

To advance to next level:
   a. Press **Tab** .... `Tab`
   OR
   Click **right arrow** button .... `→` on Outline Feature Bar.

b. Keyboard text for next level.
c. Press **Enter** .... `Enter`
   To type text for next level:
   Repeat steps 5-7.
   To return to previous level:
   Press **Shift+Tab** .... `Shift`+`Tab`
   OR
   Click **left arrow** button .... `←` on Feature Bar.

To end outline:
   1. Click **Options** .... `Shift`+`Alt`+`O` (on Feature Bar).
   2. Click **End Outline** .... `E`

TRAVELING TO PARIS, FRANCE

I.   People of France
      A.   Language
      B.   Religion
      C.   Holidays
      D.   Cooking
      E.   Sports
II.   Arts
      A.   Architecture
      B.   Literature
      C.   Painting
III.   Tourist Attractions
      A.   Gardens, Squares and Parks
            1.   Latin Quarter
            2.   Tuileries
            3.   Champs-Elysées
      B.   Famous Buildings and Monuments
            1.   Eiffel Tower
            2.   Arc de Triomphe
            3.   Louvre Palace
            4.   Notre-Dame
      C.   Museums and Art Galleries
            1.   Louvre Museum
                  a.   Great Works of Art
                      (1)   Venus de Milo
                      (2)   Mona Lisa
                b.   Museum of Decorative Art
            2.   National Museum of Modern Art
IV.   Restaurants
V.   Hotels

Exercise 27

■ **Outline**

NOTES

Outline

■ In this exercise, you will prepare a letter which includes a paragraph outline. Paragraph outline style is the default.

■ A paragraph outline indicates the first levels as Arabic numbers, the second levels as lowercase letters, and the third levels as lowercase Roman numerals.

■ In order to center the outline within the letter in this exercise, it is necessary to change your left and right margins to 2". After completing the outline, you must change your margins back to the default of 1" on the left and right. Double space before and after the outline.

■ Be sure to end your outline before completing the letter.

In this exercise, you will create a letter with an outline.

EXERCISE DIRECTIONS

1. Start with a clear screen OR ⬜27CAREER.

2. Create the letter on the right as shown.
   • Set the font for the document to serif 11 point.
   • Start on Ln 1.36".
   • Use the default margins.

3. Create an address book entry for Ms. Joan Smith, 90 Trinity Place, New York, NY 10001. Use the address book to send this letter to Ms. Smith.

4. Set left and right margins to 2" after the first paragraph (before typing the outline).

5. After completing the outline:
   • End the Outline feature.
   • Reset the left and right margins to 1".

6. Spell check.

7. Find each occurrence of the word "talk" and replace it with "presentation."

8. Preview your document.

9. Print one copy.

10. Save the exercise; name it CAREER.

Today's date

Ms. Joan Smith
90 Trinity Place
New York, NY 10001

Dear Ms. Smith:

I would once again like to make a presentation to your classes on *Choosing and Planning a Career*. A brief outline of my planned talk appears below.

1. **CHOOSING AND PLANNING A CAREER**
   a. Discovering the World of Work
   b. Investigating Career Fields
      i. Medicine
      ii. Business
         (1) Marketing
         (2) Brokerage
         (3) Computer-related
            (a) Technician
            (b) Programmer
            (c) Data Entry Operator
         (4) Teaching
         (5) Engineering
2. **GETTING A JOB**
   a. Being Interviewed
      i. How to dress
      ii. What to say
   b. Writing a Resume

While I may not have enough time to include all the material in my talk, the outline will give you an overview of my topic. I look forward to addressing your classes on March 31.

Sincerely,

Janice Waller
Recruitment Representative

jw/yo

Exercise

28

■ **Summary**

In this exercise, you will create a flyer using the features learned in this lesson.

EXERCISE DIRECTIONS

1. Start with a clear screen.

2. Use the default margins.

3. Type the text as shown in Illustration A, or open ⬜27BROWN.

To create Illustration B (shown on page 112):

4. Set the title to a script 24 point bold font. Set the first word in the paragraph to a sans serif 14 point bold font; set the remaining paragraph text to italic.

5. Set the line spacing for the first paragraph (including the title) to 1.5.

6. Return the line spacing to 1.

7. Center and set the printing items to a bold decorative font as shown.

8. Set "Our Services Include" to italics.

9. Set the first Service title to a sans serif 14 point bold font (Complete Business Package).

10. Use QuickFormat to copy the formatting from the Complete Business Package title to the remaining Service titles.

11. Move the Services into alphabetical order.

12. Double indent the Services paragraphs (titles and descriptive text below) 1" from the left and right margins (double indent twice).

13. Center and set the company name and address in a sans serif font; set the name to 12 point and the address and phone number to 10 point.

14. Search for all occurrences of WILLIAM H. BROWN and change to WILLIAM BROWN.

15. Analyze the document to determine the number of words.

16. Find the word "quality" and use the Thesaurus feature to substitute the word.

17. Use Make It Fit to keep all text on one page (adjust top and bottom margins only).

18. Spell check.

19. Print one copy.

20. Save the exercise; name it BROWN.

Printing With a Personal Touch...
Whether you are creating a one-time special event or developing a long-term corporate identity program, it is important to demonstrate quality and professionalism in your printed materials. At WILLIAM H. BROWN, you will find a Special Services Center designed to handle your custom-printing needs. We have been in business for over 30 years. Our commitment to quality and service stands tall in a very competitive marketplace. Let WILLIAM H. BROWN help you with your personal printing needs for
Business Cards
Stationery
Invitations and Announcements
Rubber Stamps
Business Forms
Binders, Tabs, Folders
Signs, Banners, Name Plaques
Greeting Cards
Labels and Decals

Our Services Include:

COMPLETE BUSINESS PACKAGE
Create a corporate identity package including business cards, letterhead and envelopes.

SALES AND MERCHANDISING SUPPORT
Printed announcements, banners, flyers and brochures.

PRESENTATIONS AND MEETING MATERIALS
Customized imprints on three-ring binders, divider tabs and covers.

SPECIAL OCCASIONS
Invitations, matchbooks and napkins for weddings, anniversaries, graduations and other special events.

BUSINESS FORMS
Internal business forms, carbonless invoices, work orders, receipts, memos, request forms and more.

WILLIAM H. BROWN, INC.
122 West 28 Street
New York, NY 10033
(212) 444-4444

Printing With a Personal Touch...

Whether *you are creating a one-time special event or developing a long-term corporate identity program, it is important to demonstrate quality and professionalism in your printed materials. At WILLIAM BROWN, you will find a Special Services Center designed to handle your custom-printing needs. We have been in business for over 30 years. Our commitment to quality and service stands tall in a very competitive marketplace. Let WILLIAM BROWN help you with your personal printing needs for*

BUSINESS CARDS
STATIONERY
INVITATIONS AND ANNOUNCEMENTS
RUBBER STAMPS
BUSINESS FORMS
BINDERS, TABS, FOLDERS
SIGNS, BANNERS, NAME PLAQUES
GREETING CARDS
LABELS AND DECALS

Our Services Include:

BUSINESS FORMS
Internal business forms, carbonless invoices, work orders, receipts, memos, request forms and more.

COMPLETE BUSINESS PACKAGE
Create a corporate identity package including business cards, letterhead and envelopes.

PRESENTATIONS AND MEETING MATERIALS
Customized imprints on three-ring binders, divider tabs and covers.

SALES AND MERCHANDISING SUPPORT
Printed announcements, banners, flyers and brochures.

SPECIAL OCCASIONS
Invitations, matchbooks and napkins for weddings, anniversaries, graduations and other special events.

WILLIAM BROWN, INC.
122 West 28 Street
New York, NY 10033
(212) 444-4444

Exercise 29

■ **Hard vs. Soft Page Breaks** ■ **Second-Page Headings**
■ **Headers/Footers** ■ **Edit Headers/Footers** ■ **Page Numbers**

NOTES

Hard vs. Soft Page Breaks

- WordPerfect assumes you are working on an 8½" x 11" page. Since WordPerfect uses default 1" top and bottom margins, there are exactly 9" of vertical space on a standard page for entering text.

- Therefore, when text is entered beyond the bottom margin (the last line of the nine inches), it continues at the top margin of the next page. A solid horizontal line marks the page break.

- Once the insertion point is below the page break line, the Pg indicator on the status bar displays Pg 2 and the Ln indicator displays 1".

    ✓ *In Draft view, the hard page break is represented by a single line.*

- When WordPerfect ends the page, this is referred to as a **soft page break**.

- To end the page before the last line above the bottom margin, you can enter a **hard page break** by selecting Page Break from the Insert menu or by pressing Ctrl + Enter. Text can still be added above the page break, but the hard page break will always begin a new page.

- A hard page break may be deleted by moving the insertion point to the end of the page before the hard page break, and pressing Delete or revealing your codes and deleting the [HPg] code.

Second-Page Headings

- A multiple-page letter requires a heading on the second and succeeding pages. The heading should begin at 1" and include the name of the addressee (to whom the letter is going), the page number, and the date. To include a heading on the second and succeeding pages, a header may be created.

Headers/Footers

- A **header** is the same text appearing at the top of every page or every other page, while a **footer** is the same text appearing at the bottom of every page or every other page.

- After the desired header or footer text is typed once, the Headers/Footers feature will automatically insert it on every page or only on specified pages of your document.

- You can create two different headers (named A and B) and two different footers (also named A and B) any place in the document. You can have only two headers and two footers active on any given page.

- Headers/Footers may be created by selecting Header/Footer from the Format menu, selecting the header or footer type you wish to create from the Headers/Footers dialog box, and clicking Create.

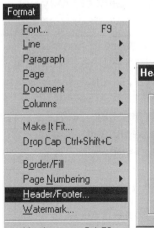

■ When you create a header or footer, the Header/Footer Feature Bar automatically displays and the insertion point displays inside the header or footer area, ready for you to keyboard header/footer text. This Feature Bar provides options for creating and editing headers and footers.

■ The header prints just below the top margin; the footer prints just above the bottom margin.

■ The distance between the text and header or footer may be changed. To do so, select Distance on the Header/Footer Feature Bar and make the desired adjustments.

■ Headers and footers display in **Page** or **Two Page** view.

■ If you plan to insert a header on the *left* side of your pages, insert page numbers on the top *right* side or bottom of your pages. Be sure that your header/footer text does not overlap or appear too close to the page number.

■ Headers, footers, and page numbers may be inserted after the document is typed.

■ If you want headers and footers to align with the body text, you must drag the header/footer boundaries to align with your margins. Or, you can set margins for the header or footer by positioning your insertion point inside the header or footer boundary and selecting Margins from the Format menu.

Edit Headers/Footers

■ To edit a header or footer, you may click inside the header or footer boundary or select Header/Footer, from the Format menu and the click Edit.

Page Numbers

■ Page numbers should be included on the second and succeeding pages of multiple-page documents. Page numbers may be included as part of header/footer text by selecting Number on the Header/Footer Feature Bar, or they may be placed in a document independent of the header/footer. Position the insertion point where you desire the page number before selecting the Number button on the Feature Bar. (Inserting page numbers independent of the header/footer will be covered in Exercise 30.)

■ Headers/footers and page numbers should *not* appear on the first page of a multiple-page document. Therefore, they must be suppressed on the first page by selecting Page, Suppress from the Format menu or by clicking the Suppress button on the Page Toolbar.

✓ *You may access the Page toolbar by right-clicking on the Toolbar and clicking Page.*

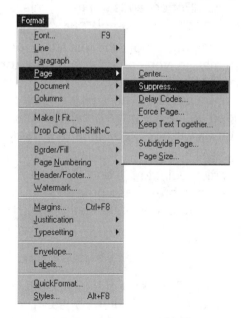

EXERCISE DIRECTIONS

1. Start with a clear screen.

2. Open ✉MASON or ⬜29MASON.

3. Display the Page Toolbar.

4. Change the font size to 12 point for all document text except side heading titles (which should remain 14 point).

5. Insert new text (shown in script) using the same font size and style as document text.

6. Create a header which includes the name of the addressee (Ms. Sharon Mason), the page number, and today's date in a sans serif 10 point font as shown; suppress the header on the first page.

7. Create a centered footer in a script font as shown. Set the font size to 35 points for the date and 18 points for the remaining footer text. Use any desired character between items as shown.

8. Spell check.

9. Preview the document.

10. Print one copy.

11. Close the file; save the changes.

KEYSTROKES

INSERT HARD PAGE BREAK

1. Place insertion point where new page is to begin.

2. Press **Ctrl + Enter** .... `Ctrl` + `Enter`

OR

1. Click **Insert** .... `Alt` + `I`

2. Click **Page Break** .... `P`

DELETE HARD PAGE BREAK

1. Place insertion point immediately after hard page break line.

2. Press **Backspace** .... `Backspace`

OR

1. Reveal Codes .... `Alt` + `F3`

2. Place insertion point on hard page break code (HPg).

3. Press **Delete** .... `Del`

   OR

   Drag code off the screen.

CREATE HEADERS/FOOTERS

1. Place insertion point on first page where you want new header/footer to appear.

2. Click **Format** .... `Alt` + `R`

3. Click **Header/Footer** .... `H`

4. Select **Header A** or **Header B** .... `A` or `B`

5. Click **Create** .... `C`

6. Type header/footer text.

To add a page number:

1. Position insertion point where number will appear.

2. Click **Number** .... `Shift` + `Alt` + `M` on Feature Bar.

3. Choose desired number from the drop-down list .... `↓` `↑`

To adjust distance between header/footer and document text:

1. Click **Distance** .... `Shift` + `Alt` + `D` on Feature Bar.

2. Type amount of space in text box.

OR

1. Click increment arrows.

2. Click **OK** .... `Enter`

SUPPRESS HEADER/FOOTER/PAGE NUMBER ON FIRST PAGE

1. Place insertion point on page where text is to be suppressed.

2. Click **Format** .... `Alt` + `R`

3. Click **Page** .... `P`

4. Click **Suppress** .... `U`

OR

1. Click **Suppress** button .... [icon] on Page Toolbar.

2. Click appropriate check box to suppress desired item.

3. Click **OK** .... `Enter`

EDIT HEADER/FOOTER

1. Place insertion point on first page where you want change to occur.

2. Click **Format** .... `Alt` + `R`

3. Click **Header/Footer** .... `H`

4. Choose which header or footer you wish to edit.

5. Click **Edit** .... `E`

6. Edit header/footer text.

CLOSE HEADER/FOOTER FEATURE BAR

Click Close .... `Shift` + `Alt` + `C` on Feature Bar.

Today's date

Ms. Sharon Mason
60 Owens Walk
Albany, NY 12209

Dear Ms. Mason:

I strongly urge you to attend this year's *Computer Expo.* In four days, you will pick up the latest computer news and ascertain new ways to put your computer to work—in the office, in the lab, in the studio, in the classroom or in your home.

Here are some of the events you can look forward to:

Application Workshops.
Join a series of two-hour learning sessions which will provide guidelines, tips and "how-to's" on popular software packages

Keynote Sessions.
These sessions will feature celebrities from the computer world who will offer you insights from industry.

Interest Group Meetings.
These sessions will include Education Workshops for teachers, resources and recommendations for the home office worker, and ways to fully utilize your computer in a law office.

Programmer/Developer Forums.
Veteran and unseasoned computer users will discuss new advances and techniques.

In addition, we have included numerous Internet workshops. There is one workshop that I think might be of particular interest to you, but it requires advance, early registration. "Selecting the Best Multimedia Web Browser" will explore the available web browsers t

1997 Computer Expo ☺ Los Angeles ☺ California

Ms. Sharon Mason
Page 2
Today's date

enable you to surf the multimedia section of the Internet. Unless you own the right
browser, you're missing all the noise, action and fun of the Internet. Other Internet
workshops include:

Multimedia Web Sites
Compressing Web Pages
Internet Law
New Internet Products

If you are interested in attending, call *Derek Brennan* at 1-800-555-5555. He will preregister anyone who wishes to attend. This will save you long lines at the show. The preregistration fee is $150.00. On-site registration will be an additional $25.00.

Sincerely,

John Mulligan
Expo Coordinator

jm/yo

1997 Computer Expo ☺ Los Angeles ☺ California

Exercise 30

- **Letters with Special Notations**
- **Bookmarks** ■ **Print Multiple Pages**

NOTES

Letters with Special Notations

- Letters may include special parts in addition to those learned thus far. The letter in this exercise contains a mailing notation, a subject line, and enclosure and copy notations.

- When a letter is sent by a special mail service such as Express Mail, Registered Mail, Federal Express, Certified Mail or by hand (via a messenger service), it is customary to include an appropriate notation on the letter. When a letter is faxed, a fax notation may also be included on the letter. This notation is placed a double space below the date and typed in all caps.

- The *subject* identifies or summarizes the body of the letter. It is typed a double space below the salutation. A double space follows it. It may be typed at the left margin or centered in modified-block style. "Subject" may be typed in all caps or in upper and lower case. "Re" (in reference to) is often used instead of "Subject."

- An *enclosure* or attachment notation is used to indicate that something else besides the letter is included in the envelope. The enclosure or attachment notation is typed a double space below the reference initials and may be typed in several ways (the number indicates how many items are enclosed in the envelope):

ENC.	Enclosure	Enclosures (2)
Enc.	Encls.	Attachment
Encl.	Encls (2)	Attachments (2)

- If copies of the document are sent to others, *a copy notation* is typed a double space below the enclosure/attachment notation (or the reference initials if there is no enclosure/attachment). A copy notation may be typed in several ways:

Copy to:	c:
Copy to	pc: (photocopy)

Bookmarks

- The **Bookmark** feature allows you to return quickly to a desired location in a document. This is a convenient feature if, for example, you are editing a large document and have to leave your work for a time. You may set a bookmark to keep your place. When you return to work, you can open your file, find the bookmark in your document and quickly return to the place you had marked. Or, you might not have all the information needed to complete your document. Setting bookmarks will enable you to return to those sections of the document which need development or information inserted.

- You can have several bookmarks in a single document; however, each bookmark must be named for identification. The bookmark name can be the first line of the paragraph or a one-word or character name.

- Your insertion point may be anywhere in the document when finding the bookmark.

- The Bookmark feature may be accessed by selecting Bookmark from the Insert menu.

Print Multiple Pages

- WordPerfect prints the full document by default. However, you can specify how much of the document you wish to print: current page, multiple pages, selected text, document summary, or document on disk.

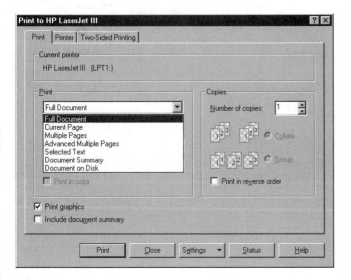

- When printing all pages in a multiple-page document, select Full Document option. The insertion point may be on any page in the document when selecting this option.

- To print selected pages (pages 2 and 3, pages 3-5, etc.), select the Multiple Pages option, then enter the page range you wish to print in the Page range text box.

- You may also print only odd pages, or even pages, or both.

- Click the Print in reverse order check box to print the document starting with the last page.

In this exercise, you will set several bookmarks as you create your document, find them when you have completed your document, and insert additional information at each bookmark location.

EXERCISE DIRECTIONS

1. Start with a clear screen.
2. Type the exercise on pages 120 and 121, or open ⊟30FILM.
3. Set left and right margins to 1.25".
4. Begin the letterhead on Ln 1" and the exercise on approximately Ln 2.5".
5. Create the letterhead in the point sizes shown in the exercise.
   - ✓ *To create the book symbol, type an ampersand (&), select it, and apply the Wingdings font.*
6. Use the Thesaurus feature to substitute the highlighted words.
7. Create a header which includes the name of the addressee, the page number, and today's date. Be sure to suppress the header on the first page.
8. Set bookmarks where indicated; name the first one INDENT1; the second, INDENT3; and the third, COPYTO.
9. Save the file as FILM. Do not close the document.
10. Go To the first bookmark, INDENT1. Insert the following sentence at the bookmark location:

Furthermore, they have captured the objects on film so true to life that anyone watching them is captivated.

11. Go To the second bookmark, INDENT3. Insert the following sentence as the third indented paragraph:

I will institute a program which will make schools throughout the country aware of their vocational potential.

12. Go To the third bookmark, COPYTO, and insert a copy notation to Tien Lee.
13. Full justify the document (except for the letterhead text).
14. Hyphenate the document. Set left hyphenation zone to 5%.
15. Insert a hard page break at the end of the first page as shown.
16. Spell check.
17. Preview your document.
18. Print one copy of the entire document and two copies of page 2.
19. Close the file; save the changes.

📖 EDUCATIONAL FILM LIBRARY

444 SAMARITAN AVENUE 📖 WASHINGTON, DC 40124   📖 301- 444-4444

Sans serif 32 point (Engravers Gothic Bt)

12 point

Today's date

REGISTERED MAIL

Ms. Michelle Ryan
Broward College
765 Southfield Road
Marietta, GA 30068

Dear Ms. Ryan:

Subject: **Educational Films for High Schools and Colleges**

Thank you for your interest in the films that we have available for high school and college students. We are pleased to send you the enclosed flyer which describes the films in detail. Also enclosed is an outline of those films that have recently been added to our collection since the publication of the flyer.

There have been many positive reactions to our films. Just three weeks ago, a group of educators, editors and vocational experts were invited to view the films at the annual Educators' Conference. Here are some of their comments:

We will be sure to send the films in time for you to preview them. Please be sure to list the date on which you wish to preview the film.

Mr. William R. Bondlow, Jr., president of the National Vocational Center in Washington, D.C. and editor-in-chief of *Science Careers*, said,

> I like the films very much. They are innovative and a great benefit to all those interested in the earth sciences as a professional career.

Create Bookmark (INDENT1)

Ms. Andra Burke, a well-known expert presently assigned to the United States Interior Department, praised the films by saying that,

Ms. Michelle Ryan
Page 2
Today's date

> They are a major educational advance in career placement, which will serve as a source of motivation for all future geologists.

A member of the National Education Center, Dr. Lawrence Pilgrim, also liked the films and said, ◄———— *Create Bookmark (INDENT3)*

These are just some of the responses we have had to our films. We know you will have a similar reaction.

We would very much like to send you the films that you would like during the summer session. It is important that your request be received immediately since the demand for the films is great, particularly during the summer sessions.

Cordially,

William Devane
Executive Vice President
Marketing Department

wd/yo
Enclosures (2)

Copy to: Robert Williams
             Nancy Jackson

◄———— *Create Bookmark (COPYTO)*

KEYSTROKES

SET BOOKMARK

1. Place insertion point where you want bookmark.
2. Click **Insert**........................... Alt + I
3. Click **Bookmark**............................. B
4. Click **Create** .... Alt + E
5. • Click in **Bookmark Name** text box.

   ✓ The **Bookmark Name** text box displays text following the insertion point.

   • Click **OK** .... Enter
     to accept text as bookmark name.

   OR

   • Type new bookmark name .... *name*
   • Click **OK** .... Enter

FIND BOOKMARK

1. Click **Insert**........................... Alt + I
2. Click **Bookmark**............................. B
3. Highlight name of bookmark to find.
4. Click **Go To**.......................... Alt + G

PRINT SELECTED PAGES

F5

1. Click **File** .... Alt + F
   Click **Print** .... P

   OR

   Click **Print** button on Power Bar .... 🖨
2. Click **Multiple Pages**...................... M
3. Click **Page range**.................. Alt + A
4. Type selected page(s).

   OR

   Click Increment arrows .... ↑ ↓
5. Click **Print** .... Enter

PRINT MULTIPLE PAGES

1. Click **File** .... Alt + F
   Click **Print**.................................... P

   OR

   Click **Print** button on Power Bar ....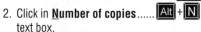
2. Click in **Number of copies**...... Alt + N
   text box.
3. Type desired number of copies to print.

   OR

   Click increment arrows .... ↑ ↓
4. Click a **Print** option: .... Alt + P
   and choose one of the following:

   • **Full Document** .... F
   • **Current Page** C
   • **Multiple Pages** .... M
   • **Document on Disk** .... D
5. Click **Print**................................. Enter

Exercise

31

■ **Footnotes** ■ **Endnotes**
■ **Edit a Footnote or Endnote** ■ **Widow and Orphan Lines**

NOTES

Footnotes

■ A **footnote** is used in a document to give information about the source of quoted material. The information includes: the author's name, the publication, the publication date, and the page number from which the quote was taken.

■ There are several footnoting styles. Traditional footnotes are printed at the bottom of a page. A separator line separates footnote text from the text on the page.

■ A reference number appears immediately after the quote in the text, and a corresponding footnote number or symbol appears at the bottom of the page.

■ The Footnote feature automatically inserts the reference number after the quote, inserts the separator line, numbers the footnote, and formats your page so that the footnote appears on the same page as the reference number. If you desire endnotes instead of footnotes, WordPerfect will change footnote information into endnotes and, if desired, back again to footnotes.

■ The actual note may be viewed in Page view if you scroll to the bottom of the page. To see how the page will format, select T<u>w</u>o Page from the <u>V</u>iew menu, or click the Magnification button on the Power Bar and select Full Page.

■ Footnotes may be inserted by selecting <u>F</u>ootnote, <u>C</u>reate from the <u>I</u>nsert menu.

■ In the Footnote screen which follows, the first footnote number appears, ready for you to type the first footnote.

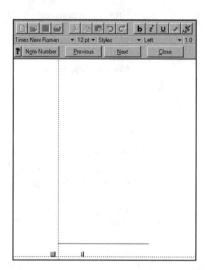

■ Footnotes and endnotes are printed using the Document Initial Font, which may be different from the font you selected for the body text. To change the footnote/endnote font to match the body text font, select <u>D</u>ocument, Initial <u>F</u>ont from the Fo<u>r</u>mat menu.

Endnotes

■ An **endnote** contains the same information as a footnote, but is printed at the end of a document or on a separate page and differs in format. Compare the endnote illustrations below with the footnotes shown in the exercise.

■ Endnotes at the End of a Document

Endnotes on a Separate Page

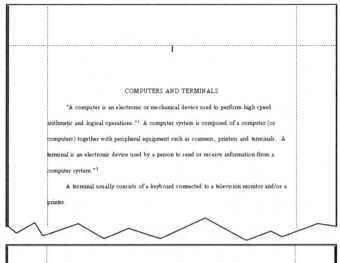

- When endnotes are created, they appear at the end of the document text. Each note number is indicated by an Arabic number and a period. You may space twice after the period or use the Indent button ⊞ before typing endnote text.

- To force endnotes onto a separate page, place the insertion point below the last line of document text and press Ctrl + Enter or click Insert, Page Break.

- Like footnotes, endnotes may be viewed in Page view if you scroll to the bottom of the page. To see how the page will format, select Two Page from the View menu, or click Page/Zoom Full button 🔍 on the WordPerfect 7 Toolbar.

- The Endnote feature may be accessed by selecting Endnote, Create from the Insert menu.

- To convert footnotes into endnotes or endnotes into footnotes, click the appropriate button on the Design Tools Toolbar.

  ✓ To switch Toolbars, point to Toolbar, right-click and select a new Toolbar.

Design Tools Toolbar

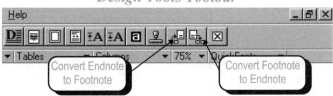

Edit a Footnote or Endnote

- If you need to make a correction to the footnote/endnote, you may return to the footnote window and edit the note. When you edit, add, or delete footnotes or endnotes, WordPerfect renumbers and reformats them as necessary.

- To edit a footnote or endnote, select Footnote or Endnote from the Insert menu and then click Edit. In the dialog box that follows, type the footnote or endnote number you want to edit in the Footnote or Endnote number text box and click OK. This will display the footnote or endnote screen and place your insertion point at the footnote or endnote to be edited.

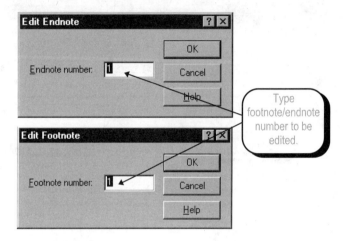

- To move to the previous or next note, click the Next or Previous button on the Footnote/Endnote Feature Bar. Click the Close button to return to your document when you have completed your edits.

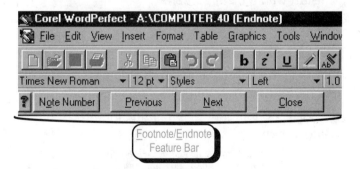

- You can edit the number style of a Footnote or Endnote in the text or in the note. In addition, you can change the line style or the amount of space before and/or after the line separating the footnotes from the text. To do so, select Footnote or Endnote from the Insert menu and then click <u>O</u>ptions. In the dialog box that follows, make the desired changes.

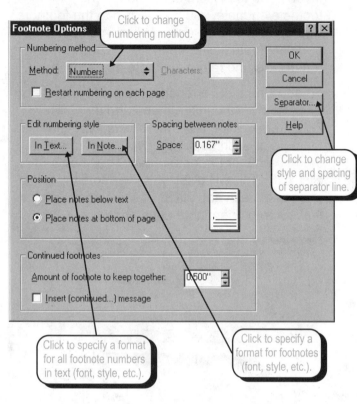

Widow and Orphan Lines

- A **widow** line occurs when the last line of a paragraph is printed by itself on the top of a page. An **orphan** line occurs when the first line of a paragraph appears by itself on the bottom of a page. Widow and orphan lines should be avoided.

- The <u>K</u>eep Text Together feature eliminates widows and orphans in a document and may be accessed by selecting <u>P</u>age, <u>K</u>eep Text Together from the For<u>m</u>at menu. In the Keep Text Together dialog box which follows, click the Widow/Orphan check box to turn on the feature.

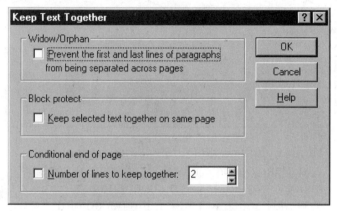

In this exercise, you will create a report with footnotes, then convert the footnotes into endnotes that appear on a separate page.

EXERCISE DIRECTIONS

1. Start with a clear screen.

2. Create the report shown on the following page, or open ⊟**31NEWLAN**. Create each footnote as it appears in the illustration.

3. Begin the exercise on approximately Ln 2".

4. Use a serif 12 point font for the document.

5. Set 1.25" left and right margins for the document.

   ✓ *If you want the header, footer, and/or footnotes to align with the body text, you must set margins for the document, not for the page. If you want the document font face, size, and style to apply to header or footer text, you must change the initial font settings. See keystrokes below to do so.*

6. Set line spacing to double after typing the title.

7. Create the following header using a serif 10 point italic font: COMING TO A NEW LAND. Include a right-aligned page number as part of the header. Suppress the header and page number on the first page.

8. Use widow and orphan protection.

9. Spell check.

10. Preview your document.

11. Edit the header to read, COMING TO AMERICA IN THE 19TH CENTURY.

12. Print one copy.

13. Save the file; name it NEWLAND.

14. Change the footnotes to endnotes.

15. Print one copy.

16. Save the file; name it NEWLAND1.

IMMIGRATION TO THE UNITED STATES
IN THE NINETEENTH CENTURY

The United States is sometimes called the "Nation of Immigrants" because it has received more immigrants than any other country in history. During the first one hundred years of US history, the nation had no immigration laws. Immigration began to climb during the 1830s. "Between 1830-1840, 44% of the immigrants came from Ireland, 30% came from Germany, 15% came from Great Britain, and the remainder came from other European countries."[1]

Most German immigrants settled in the middle western states of Ohio, Indiana, Illinois, Wisconsin and Missouri. With encouragement to move west from the Homestead Act of 1862, which offered public land free to immigrants who intended to become citizens, German immigrants comprised a large portion of the pioneers moving west. They were masterful farmers and they built prosperous farms.

The movement to America of millions of immigrants in the century after the 1820s was not simply a flight of impoverished peasants abandoning underdeveloped, backward regions for the riches and unlimited opportunities offered by the American economy. People did not move randomly to America but emanated from very specific regions at specific times in the nineteenth and twentieth centuries. "It is impossible to understand even the nature of American immigrant communities without appreciating the nature of the world these newcomers left."[2]

The rate of people leaving Ireland was extremely high in the late 1840s and early 1850s due to overpopulation and to the potato famine of 1846. "By 1850, there were almost one million Irish Catholics in the United States, especially clustered in New York and Massachusetts."[3]

Germans left their homeland due to severe depression, unemployment, political unrest, and the failure of the liberal revolutionary movement. It was not only the poor people who left their countries, but those in the middle and lower-middle levels of their social structures also left. "Those too poor could seldom afford to go, and the very wealthy had too much of a stake in the homelands to depart."[4]

Many immigrants came to America as a result of the lure of new land, in part, the result of the attraction of the frontier. America was in a very real sense the last frontier— a land of diverse peoples that, even under the worst conditions, maintained a way of life that permitted more freedom of belief and action than was held abroad. "While this perception was not entirely based in reality, it was the conviction that was often held in Europe and that became part of the ever-present American Dream."[5]

In the 1820s, Irish immigrants did most of the hard work in building the canals in the United States. In fact, Irish immigrants played a large role in building the Erie Canal. American contractors encouraged Irish immigrants to come to the United States to work on the roads, canals, and railroads, and manufacturers lured them into the new mills and factories.

---

[1]Lewis Paul Todd and Merle Curti, *Rise of the American Nation* (New York: Harcourt Brace Jovanovich, Inc., 1972), 297.

[2]John Bodner, *The Transplanted* (Bloomington: Indiana University Press, 1985), 54.

[3]E. Allen Richardson, *Strangers in This Land* (New York: The Pilgrim Press, 1988), 6.

[4]Richardson, 13.

[5]Richardson, 72.

KEYSTROKES

CHANGE DOCUMENT MARGINS

1. Click **Fo_r_mat**.................... Alt + R
2. Click **Document**.................... D
3. Click **Initial Codes Style**........ S
4. Click **Fo_r_mat**.................... Alt + R
   in **Styles Editor** dialog box.
5. Click **Margins**.................... M
6. Change left and right margins.
7. Click **OK**.................... Enter
8. Click **OK**.

CHANGE DOCUMENT FONT STYLE OR SIZE

1. Click **Fo_r_mat**.................... Alt + R
2. Click **Document**.................... D
3. Click **Initial Font**.................... F
4. Click desired option(s):
   • **Font face**.................... Alt + F
   • **Font size**.................... Alt + S
   • **Font style**.................... Alt + O
5. Click **OK**.................... Enter

FOOTNOTE

1. Type up to the first reference number.
   OR
   Place insertion point at the location of the first reference number.
2. Click **Insert**.................... Alt + I
3. Click **Footnote**.................... F
4. Click **Create**.................... C
   ✓ *The cursor moves tot he bottom of the screen displaying the separator line and the first assigned footnote number.*

5. Type footnote text.
6. Click **Close**.......... Shift + Alt + C
   to return to document.
   ✓ *The reference number is automatically inserted in the document.*

ENDNOTE

1. Type up to the first reference number.
   OR
   Place insertion point at the location of the first reference number.
2. Click **Insert**.................... Alt + I
3. Click **Endnote**.................... E
4. Click **Create**.................... C
   ✓ *The cursor moves to the bottom of the document and automatically assigns a reference number.*
5. Type endnote text.
6. Click **Close**.......... Shift + Alt + C
   to return to document.
7. Repeat steps 1-6 for each endnote.

PLACE ENDNOTES ON SEPARATE PAGE

1. Place insertion point at last line of text.
2. Press **Ctrl + Enter**.......... Ctrl + Enter
   OR
   • Click **Insert**.......... Alt + I
   • Click **Page Break**.......... P

EDIT FOOTNOTE OR ENDNOTE

1. Click **Insert**.................... Alt + I
2. Click **Footnote** or **Endnote**.... F or E
3. Click **Edit**.................... E
4. Type footnote or endnote number to edit.
5. Click **OK**.................... Enter
6. Make desired correction.
7. Click **Close**.......... Shift + Alt + C
   to return to document.

FOOTNOTE OR ENDNOTE OPTIONS

1. Click **Insert**.................... Alt + I
2. Click **Footnote** or **Endnote**.... F or E
3. Click **Options**.................... O
4. Make desired option changes.
5. Click **OK**.................... Enter

CONVERT FOOTNOTES TO ENDNOTES OR ENDNOTES TO FOOTNOTES

Click the appropriate button on the Design Tools Toolbar .... 🔲 or 🔲

SET WIDOW/ORPHAN PROTECT

1. Place insertion point on page where you want protection to begin.
2. Click **Fo_r_mat**.................... Alt + R
3. Click **Page**.................... P
4. Click **Keep Text Together**........ K
5. Click **Prevent the First and Last Lines of Paragraphs from Being Separated Across Pages** check box .... P
6. Click **OK**.................... Enter

Exercise

32

■ **Page Numbering Positions and Formats** ■ **File Stamp**

NOTES

Page Numbering Positions and Formats

■ As indicated in Exercise 29, page numbers can be included in a document independent of the header/footer text.

■ WordPerfect provides numerous page numbering position options and formats. To access **Page Numbering**, select Page Numbering, Select from the Format menu. In the Select Page Numbering Format dialog box which follows, you may select a page number position and page numbering format. The preview window displays your selection.

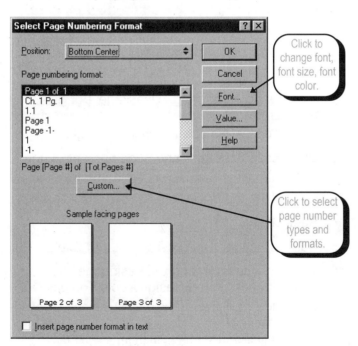

■ Page numbers may be positioned at the top or bottom, left, center, or right of the page and aligned left, center, right, inside, or outside. WordPerfect provides 15 different numbering styles. Numbering styles may be selected by clicking the desired page number format from the Page numbering format list box.

■ To create other combinations of page number types and formats other than those pre-formatted by WordPerfect, click the Custom button and choose a desired option.

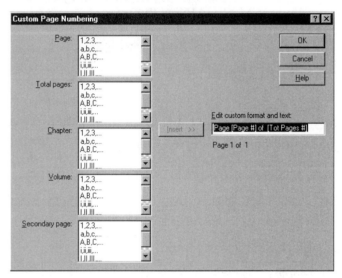

■ The page number you select appears in the default font. To change the page number font, click the Font button in the select Page Numbering Format dialog box, and select a new font style, size, or color.

File Stamp

■ The **File Stamp** feature allows you to insert the current filename in a document or within a header and/or footer.

■ To insert a filename, select Other, Filename (or Path and Filename) from the Insert menu. This method will insert the document filename (or path and filename) at the insertion point position.

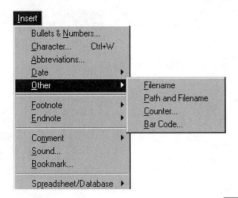

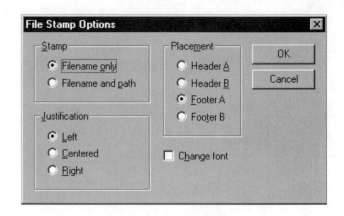

- Or, you may click the File Stamp button  on the Design Tools Toolbar. This method opens the File Stamp Options dialog box in which you can change the font size and style as well as indicate a Justification option for the filename. Using this method, the filename is displayed as a footer at the bottom left of the page.

File Stamp

- Including a filename and path on a document is a convenient way to later locate that file in the computer. In a letter, filenames are generally indicted below the typist's initials and should appear on the file copy only. In a report, filenames may be indicated as footer text at the bottom left or right of the document. It is recommended that the filenames which appear in a letter or a report use a font size which is smaller than the document text.

In this exercise, you will create a report with footnotes, a header, and a bottom centered page number. You will also insert the filename and path into your document. Remember to suppress the header and page number on the first page.

EXERCISE DIRECTIONS

1. Start with a clear screen.

2. Display the Design Tools Toolbar.

3. Create the report on the right, or open ⊟**32NET**.

4. Begin the exercise on approximately Ln 2".

5. Use a serif 13 point font for the document.

6. Set 1.5" left and right margins for the document.

7. Set the title to a 14 point bold font.

8. Set line spacing to 2.3".

   ✓ *While the exercise is shown in single space, you are to use 2.3 line spacing. Your printed document will result in two or three pages, depending on the selected font. Footnotes will appear on the same pages as reference numbers.*

9. Use widow/orphan protection.

10. Create the following right-aligned header using a script 14 point font: The Internet: What Is It?

11. Insert page numbering. Use Page 1 of 1 number format.
    - Position it at the bottom right of the page.

12. Suppress the header and page number on the first page.

13. Hyphenate the document.

14. Spell check.

15. Edit the header to read: The Internet Explained.

16. Insert the filename and path using the File Stamp button on the Design Tools Toolbar.
    - Position the filename and path at the bottom left of the document.
    - Size the filename and path to an 8 point font.
    - ✓ *The page number will now appear inside the footer along with the filename.*

17. Preview your document and print one copy.

18. Save the file; name it **NET**.

19. Close the document window.

THE INTERNET

The Internet, or "information superhighway" to which it is often referred, is a communications system that can be accessed by the public. It is used to access information about anything from the weather in Africa, to the latest Presidential address, to current movie reviews.

The Internet is a huge computer network; actually, it is the world's largest computer network. This network allows the computers that are connected to share information with each other. The information flows from one computer to another over electronic wires. This information can be letters (called *e-mail* on the Internet), reports, magazine articles, books, pictures, etc. Computers are even able to exchange music and videos over these electronic wires!

The Internet provides services. The two most frequently used services are e-mail and the World Wide Web.

E-mail is a system that allows messages to be sent from one computer to another. These messages might include sounds, pictures, spreadsheets, as well as software files. Before using e-mail, it is necessary that both correspondents have e-mail "addresses." An e-mail address has the same function as a home address—it allows mail to be appropriately delivered to the correct mailbox, and thus, the correct recipient. E-mail addresses usually contain three parts. The first part is the account name, the second part is the domain name, and the third part contains an extension which classifies the computer user's address as belonging to a company, government agency or a school. The domain name is "the address, or name, of the company, Internet service provider, or school that is giving the Internet access."[1] The account name and the domain name are separated by an "at" (@) symbol. A common e-mail address for Peter Clark at Tennessee State University, who gets his Internet service from the university, might be: pclark@tsu.edu. "Edu." represents an educational address.

The World Wide Web, or WWW, is the "fastest growing service on the Internet."[2] It is also the most visual and interesting service on the Internet. The WWW is made up of pages which are created by companies, individuals, schools, and government agencies around the world. Each page has an address and can be accessed by typing the exact address in an appropriate text box on the screen. Pages are also accessed by conducting a search of the pages on the WWW. This is done by using search engines, such as Lycos, Excite, Yahoo, and Infoseek. After entering the subject to be searched, the search engine provides topics relating to your inquiry. These topics are underlined and

---

[1]Samantha Blane, *Using E-mail* (New York: University Press, 1996), 25.

[2]Ned Peterson, *The Internet and Beyond* (New York City: Halpern Publishers, 1997), 3.

highlighted and can be accessed by clicking them. These underlined, highlighted words are known as *hypertext*--links to other pages relating to the search topic.

"Hypertext is text that is highlighted and/or underlined which, when clicked on with the left mouse button, will provide access to additional information that it describes."[3] "The World Wide Web is a system without boundaries. It has no capacity limit, either. Web pages are being added every minute of the day, all over the world."[4]

You might hear the term, "URL." This stands for Uniform Resource Locator, a formal name for "web address." A typical URL might be **http://www.vicinity.com.** This address provides a direct link to a particular Web page. So, instead of clicking hypertext links to get to a particular page, you can enter the URL-- the quick way to go to the source.

The Internet is an amazing information and communication source that has made the world a much smaller place. International communication has become as simple as the touch of a button, and visits to other countries have been made possible by viewing the vast number of photographs and videos that can be accessed on the Internet.

---

[3] Natasha Banks, *Understanding the Internet* (Los Angeles: CompuBooks, Inc., 1996), 104.

[4]Banks, 106.

KEYSTROKES

INSERT PAGE NUMBERS

1. Place insertion point at beginning of document or page.
2. Click **Format**..........................`Alt`+`R`
3. Click **Page Numbering**...................`N`
4. Click **Select**.................................`S`
5. Click **Position** list box............`Alt`+`P`
6. Click a page number position option:
   - **No Page numbering**...................`N`
   - **Top Left**......................................`L`
   - **Top Center**.................................`C`
   - **Top Right**...................................`R`
   - **Top Outside Alternating**............`O`
   - **Top Inside Alternating**...............`I`
   - **Bottom Left**...............................`B`
   - **Bottom Right**.............................`T`
   - **Bottom Outside Alternating**........`U`
   - **Bottom Inside Alternating**..........`S`

   To change numbering format:
   a. Select a numbering format option from the **Page numbering format** list box..............................`Alt`+`N`
   b. Click increment arrows ....`↓``↑`

   To change font:
   1. Click **Font** button ....`Alt`+`F`
   2. Select desired font.
   3. Click **OK** twice...............`Enter`, `Enter`

FILE STAMP

- Click **File Stamp** button on Design Tools Toolbar.............................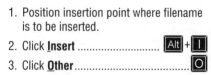
- Select desired option in **File Stamp Options** dialog box.

   OR
1. Position insertion point where filename is to be inserted.
2. Click **Insert** ....`Alt`+`I`
3. Click **Other**...................................`O`
4. Click **Filename** or **Path and Filename**............................`F`or `P`

Exercise 33

■ Move Text Using the GO TO Feature

NOTES

Move Text Using the GO TO Feature

■ The procedure for moving blocks of text from one page to another is the same as moving blocks of text on the same page. However, when moving text from one page to another, the **Go To** feature may be used to advance quickly to the page where the text is to be reinserted. Or, it may be used at any time to move the insertion point to a bookmark or a specific location in your document.

■ Go To may be accessed from the Edit main menu or by pressing Ctrl + G. In the Go To dialog box which follows, you may indicate what specific location in the document you wish to go to.

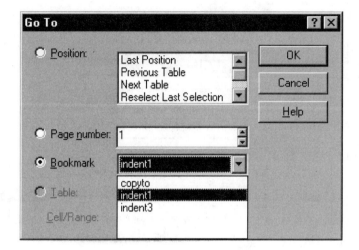

In this exercise, you will move paragraphs from one page to another using the Go To feature. You will also use Go To to return to a previous bookmark.

EXERCISE DIRECTIONS

Part I

1. Start with a clear screen.

2. Open ☐FILM or ☐33FILM.

3. Move the indicted paragraphs.

4. Use the Go To feature to return to the INDENT3 bookmark. Add the following sentence to the end of that paragraph:

   They make exploration come alive!

5. Make the remaining revisions.

6. Use widow/orphan protection.

7. Print one copy.

8. Close the file; save the changes.

Part II

1. Start with a clear screen.

2. Open ☐NEWLAND as shown on pages 133, 134, and 135 or open ☐33NEWLAN.

3. Set the title to a decorative font in 16-point bold.

4. Make the indicated revisions.

5. Full justify the document.

6. Using the Thesaurus, replace the highlighted words.

7. Insert the word "Page" and a space before the number in the header.

8. Set the first-line indent to .5" in the Document, Initial Codes style. (This will indent each paragraph 1" from the left margin.)

9. Print one copy.

10. Use Document Properties (File, Document, Properties, Information) to determine the number of words in the document.

11. Close the file; save the changes.

PART I

📖 EDUCATIONAL FILM LIBRARY

444 Samaritan Avenue 📖 Washington, DC 40124 📖 301-444-4444

Today's date

REGISTERED MAIL

Ms. Michelle Ryan
Broward College
765 Southfield Road
Marietta, GA 30068

Dear Ms. Ryan:

Subject: **Educational Films for High Schools and Colleges**

Thank you for your interest in the films that we have available for high school and college students. We are pleased to send you the enclosed flyer which describes the films in detail. Also enclosed is an outline of those films that have recently been added to our collection since the publication of the flyer.

There have been many positive reactions to our films. Just three weeks ago, a group of educators, editors and vocational experts were invited to view the films at the annual Educators' Conference. Here are some of their comments:

[A] We will be sure to send the films in time for you to preview them. Please be sure to list the date on which you wish to preview the film.

Mr. William R. Bondlow, Jr., president of the National Vocational Center in Washington, D.C. and editor-in-chief of *Science Careers*, said,

Move.

> I like the films very much. They are innovative and a great benefit to all those interested in the earth sciences as a professional career. Furthermore, they have captured the objects on film so true to life that anyone watching them is captivated.

Ms. Andra Burke, a well-known expert presently assigned to the United States Interior Department, praised the films by saying that,

Move.

Ms. Michelle Ryan
Page 2
Today's date

> They are a major educational advance in career placement, which will serve as a source of motivation for all future geologists.

A member of the National Education Center, Dr. Lawrence Pilgrim, also liked the films and said,

[B] I will institute a program which will make schools throughout the country aware of their vocational potential.

These are just some of the responses we have had to our films. We know you will have a similar reaction.

We would very much like to send you the films ~~that you would like~~ you desire ✓ during the summer session. It is important that your request be received immediately since the demand for the films is great, particularly during the summer sessions.

Cordially,

William Devane
Executive Vice President
Marketing Department

wd/yo
Enclosures (2)

Copy to: Robert Williams
            Nancy Jackson
            Tien Lee

IMMIGRATION TO THE UNITED STATES
IN THE NINETEENTH CENTURY

The United States is sometimes called the "Nation of Immigrants" because it has received more immigrants than any other country in history. During the first one hundred years of US history, the nation had no immigration laws. Immigration began to climb during the 1830s. "Between 1830-1840, 44% of the immigrants came from Ireland, 30% came from Germany, 15% came from Great Britain, and the remainder came from other European countries."[1]

Move to page 2.

[A] Most German immigrants settled in the middle western states of Ohio, Indiana, Illinois, Wisconsin and Missouri. With encouragement to move west from the Homestead Act of 1862, which offered public land free to immigrants who intended to become citizens, German immigrants comprised a large portion of the pioneers moving west. They were masterful farmers and they built prosperous farms.

The movement to America of millions of immigrants in the century after the 1820s was not simply a flight of impoverished peasants abandoning underdeveloped, backward regions for the riches and unlimited opportunities offered by the American economy. People did not move randomly to America but emanated from very specific regions at specific times in the nineteenth and twentieth centuries. "It is impossible to understand

---

[1]Lewis Paul Todd and Merle Curti, *Rise of the American Nation* (New York: Hartcourt Brace Jovanovich, Inc., 1972), 297.

even the nature of American immigrant communities without appreciating the nature of

the world these newcomers left."[2]

The rate of people leaving Ireland was extremely high in the late 1840s and early

1850s due to overpopulation and to the potato famine of 1846. "By 1850, there were

almost one million Irish Catholics in the United States, especially clustered in New York

and Massachusetts."[3]

Insert B ⟶ Germans left their homeland due to severe depression, unemployment, political

unrest, and the failure of the liberal revolutionary movement. It was not only the poor

people who left their countries, but those in the middle and lower-middle levels of their

social structures also left. "Those too poor could seldom afford to go, and the very

wealthy had too much of a stake in the homelands to depart."[4]

Insert A ⟶ Many immigrants came to America as a result of the lure of new land, in part, the

result of the attraction of the frontier. America was in a very real sense the last frontier—

a land of diverse peoples that, even under the worst conditions, maintained a way of life

that permitted more freedom of belief and action than was held abroad. "While this

perception was not entirely based in reality, it was the conviction that was often held in

Europe and that became part of the ever-present American Dream."[5]

---

[2]John Bodner, *The Transplanted* (Bloomington: Indiana University Press, 1985), 54.

[3]E. Allen Richardson, *Strangers in This Land* (New York: The Pilgrim Press, 1988), 6.

[4]Richardson, 13.

[5]Richardson, 72.

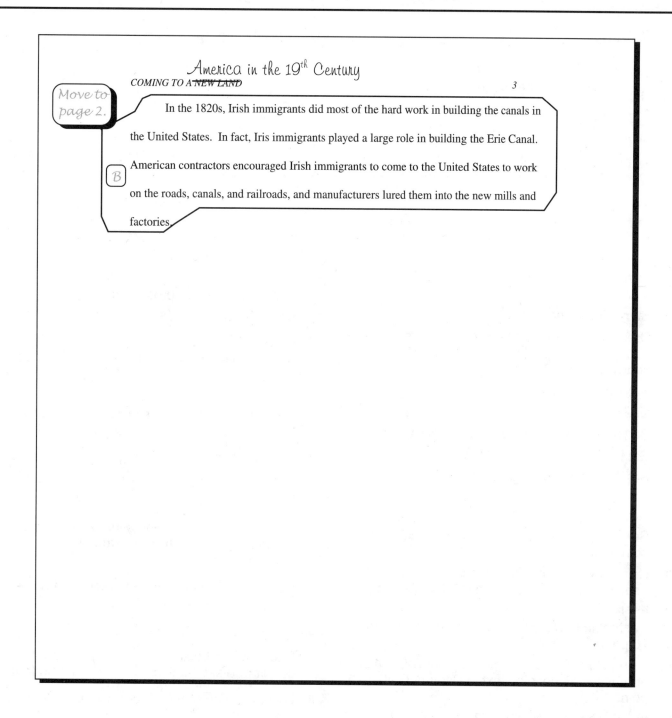

America in the 19th Century

COMING TO A NEW LAND   3

Move to page 2.

In the 1820s, Irish immigrants did most of the hard work in building the canals in the United States. In fact, Iris immigrants played a large role in building the Erie Canal.

B American contractors encouraged Irish immigrants to come to the United States to work on the roads, canals, and railroads, and manufacturers lured them into the new mills and factories.

KEYSTROKES

MOVE TEXT USING GO TO

1. Select text to be moved.
2. a. Click **Edit** .... Alt + E
   b. Click **Cut** .... T
   OR
   a. Click *right* mouse button.
   b. Click **Cut** C
3. Click **Edit** .... Alt + E

4. Click **Go To** .... G
5. Click in **Page number** .... Alt + N
   text box.
6. Type page number to go to.
   OR
   Click increment button to move to desired page number .... ↓ ↑
7. Click **OK** .... Enter

8. Place insertion point where text is to be reinserted.
9. a. Click **Edit** .... Alt + E
   b. Click **Paste** .... P
   OR
   a. Click *right* mouse button.
   b. Click **Paste** .... P

Exercise 34

■ Summary

In Parts I and II of this exercise, you will create a report with footnotes. The second report will be bound on the left. Therefore, you will need to place the footer and page number accordingly.

EXERCISE DIRECTIONS

Part I

1. Start with a clear screen.
2. Create the report on the following page, or open ▯34COLLEGE and format it with footnotes as shown.
3. Set 1.5" document margins.
4. Use the default font style and size.
5. Begin the exercise on approximately Ln 2".
6. Set the title to Arial Black 14 point.
7. Set the line spacing for the first and last paragraphs to 1.5.
8. Double-indent the site information as shown.
9. Set the first side heading to Century Gothic 14 point bold.
10. Using QuickFormat, format the remaining side headings as heading text in Century Gothic 14 point bold.
11. Set the first Web addresses to Century Gothic 10 point.
12. Using QuickFormat, format the remaining Web addresses as heading text in Century Gothic 10 point.
13. Insert the pencil symbol before the first side heading in 14 point.
14. Copy the pencil and paste so it precedes each side heading.
15. Insert a right-aligned header as shown in Arial Black 10 point italics. Suppress the header on page 1.
16. Insert a page number using the format shown at the bottom right of the page. Use Arial Black 10 point. Suppress the page number on page 1.
17. Hyphenate the document.
18. Use widow/orphan protection.
19. Spell check.
20. Print one copy.
21. Save the file; name it COLLEGE.

Part II

1. Create the document as shown on page 140, or open ▯34BRAZIL.
2. Set a 2" document left margin and a 1.5" document right margin.
3. Begin the exercise at approximately Ln 2".
4. Create a footer in a sans serif 12 point bold font which reads, BRAZIL: Investment Opportunities.
5. Include a page number in the top right corner of the second and succeeding page.
6. Set line spacing for double.
7. Use a serif 13 point font for the document; center and set the title to a 16 point bold font.
8. Use widow/orphan protection.
9. Edit the footer to read, BRAZIL.
10. Justify and hyphenate the document.
11. Use File Stamp to insert the filename as Footer B.
12. Spell check.
13. Preview your work.
14. Print one copy.
15. Save the file; name it BRAZIL.

PART I

RESEARCH COLLEGES ON THE WEB

Are you having trouble deciding where to go to college, let alone trying to figure out the best way to tackle the application process? Now there are hundreds of Web sites offering services and programs designed to help you make the best possible choices for your educational future. "These Web sites do more than give you information about particular colleges--they can provide answers to important questions about personal assessment, guidance, admission, financial aid, place-ment, curriculum, research and student services."[1] From there you can take virtual visits to campuses all around the world.

Here are some sites worth visiting:

✎Peterson's Education Center
(www.peterson.com)

Peterson's Education and Career Center is the online companion to its print counterpart: *Peterson's Guide to Four Year Colleges.* This Web site offers detailed information to colleges and universi-ties, graduate study programs, studying abroad, language study, careers and jobs, summer programs, financing your education, testing and assessment, continuing education, and even information on K-12 schools.

✎CollegeNet
(www.collegenet.com)

This Web site is inspired by the college CD-ROMs that are specifi-cally designed to offer similar information. "CollegeNet is interac-tive and profile-driven, and can help you research schools according to region and state, tuition costs, enrollment, degree programs, and

---

[1]Peter Jones, *Searching the Internet* (New York: Mullen Computer Publishing, 1996), 45.

Researching Colleges on the Web

more."[2] If you still have questions, you may be able to get specific answers by visiting this site's online discussion groups.

✎CollegeEdge
(www.collegeedge.com)

CollegeEdge is another online companion to the CD-ROM, College Edge Yearly Edition. This site is full of facts about colleges, fun facts, and links to high school pages where you can share stories or commiserate with fellow college-bound students.

✎FastWeb
(www.studentservices.com/fastweb/)

If you are looking for financial aid, this is a great place to start. As the name suggests, it's fast. "At this site, you can set up your own personal profile, then let FastWeb search the Web for matching sources of loan and scholarship sites suitable to your needs."[3]

✎Financial Aid Information
(www.finaid.org)

FinAid is the ultimate source presented by the National Association of Student Financial Aid Administrators. Here you will find all the information you need about tuition payment plans, grants, loans, scholarships and anything else related to financial aid.

✎Liberal Arts Schools
(www.liberalarts.org/choices_content.htm)

A good source of information for liberal arts colleges and universities, Liberal Arts Choices & Resources answers questions on where to find the leading liberal arts colleges, how to know what's best for you, how to get into the school of your choice, and more. "You can travel directly to the college Web site of your choice and cover

---

[2]Kiesha Lakes, "Top College Info Sites," *Internet World*, Vol. 3, No. 3 (March 1997), 12.

[3]Lakes, 13.

Page -2-

most (or all) of your bases in one virtual trip. In addition to providing useful tips for applicants, this site also gives an entire list of other Web sites worth browsing."[4]

College and University Home Pages

If you have already narrowed your choices down to a select group of colleges and universities, you can visit their online sites directly and learn specifics about admission, financial aid, academic departments, faculty, class schedules, student associations, athletics, on-campus networks, library sources, and more.

If you haven't done much online browsing, you can always find more sites with the help of search engines such as Yahoo, Excite, Pathfinder, InfoSeek, and AltaVista.

---

[4]Lakes, 14.

PART II

BRAZIL

Brazil is often viewed as the economic giant of the Third World. Its economy and territory are larger than the rest of South America's and its industry is the most advanced in the developing world. Brazilian foreign debt is also the Third World's largest. The problem of foreign debt has plagued the Latin American economies since the 1960s when foreign borrowing was the only way for Latin American nations to sustain economic growth. However, when international interest rates began to rise in the 1980s, the debt these nations accumulated became unmanageable. In Brazil, the debt crisis of the 1980s marked the decline of an economy that had flourished since 1967 when foreign borrowing enabled the nation to develop its own productive industries and lessen its dependence on foreign manufactured goods. "Similar to other Latin American nations, Brazilian overseas borrowing between 1967 and 1981 became a drain on the economy when international interest rates rose; by 1985, its excessive borrowing resulted in economic disaster, political dissension and protest, and the rise of an opposition government in Brazil."[1]

Throughout the beginning of the twentieth century, growth of the Brazilian economy remained dependent upon agricultural exports. The twentieth century witnessed a decline in the export of sugar from the northeast of Brazil and a rise in the export of coffee from the southeast of Brazil. This concentrated economic growth and political power in the developed southeast part of the nation, particularly in the states of Rio de Janeiro and Sao Paulo. "Industrial growth in this region progressed gradually and by 1919, domestic firms supplied over 70% of the local demand for industrial products and employed over 14% of the labor force."[2]

However, by the 1980s, Brazil accumulated massive foreign debt which ultimately caused the government to cut foreign spending and investment, drove interest rates so high that businesses could not borrow money for investment and expansion, and precipitated the bankruptcy of numerous companies, the unemployment of wage laborers, and growing social unrest. Between 1979 and 1982, the debt amassed by Brazilian banks increased from $7.7 billion to $16.1 billion. "By 1982, debt-service payments were equivalent to 91% of Brazil's merchandise exports, up from 51% in 1977."[3] In mid-1988, inflation in Brazil ran above 500% and the value of the foreign debt Brazil has to repay remains the largest in the Third World.

Brazil's financial situation is improving. "Currently, Brazil has been able to sustain a 5% economic growth rate and is encouraging expanded foreign investment. Inflation in Brazil has fallen to 1.5% a month while United States exports to Brazil jumped by 35% last year."[4]

Rising international trade which may culminate in a South American free trade zone, has enabled the Brazilian economy to flourish once again. Brazil's huge foreign debt, however, remains outstanding and continues to loom over its recent economic success.

---

[1]Jeffrey A. Frieden, *Debt, Development and Democracy: Modern Political Economy and Latin America, 1965-1985* (Princeton: Princeton University Press, 1991), 98.

[2]Frieden, 118.

[3]Frieden, 128.

[4]Barry Eichgreen and Peter H. Lindert, *The International Debt Crisis in Historical Perspective* (Cambridge, MA: The MIT Press, 1989), 130.

■ **Arrange Multiple Documents** ■ **Switch Among Open Documents**
■ **Closing Multiple Documents** ■ **Sizing Windows**
■ **Copy/Move Text from One Document to Another**

NOTES

- WordPerfect lets you open and work with up to nine documents at one time. This is a convenient feature for moving and/or copying text from one document to another.

- The area where you type your document is called the **document window**.

- You may open multiple files individually or all at once in the same operation. To open multiple files from the Open dialog box, hold down the Ctrl key as you select each of the desired files, then click Open.

- **Windowing** lets you view those documents as you work with them.

Arrange Multiple Documents

Cascaded Documents

- When you open more than one document window, you can decide how you want them arranged. One option is to **cascade** them. Cascaded windows overlap so that the title bar of each window is displayed.

- The **active window** is indicated by the shaded title bar. To change the active window, click the title bar of the desired window. The active window will display with the document. Note the illustration below of four cascaded documents.

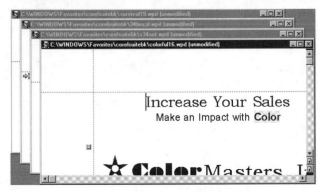

Tiled Documents

- Another arrangement option is to **tile** document windows. This allows you to view several documents at one time. Tiled windows are arranged on the screen with no overlapping.

- You may choose to tile your document horizontally or vertically. Vertically tiled documents are arranged side by side (Tile Side by Side) while horizontally tiled documents are tiled one below the other (Tile Top to Bottom). The active window is indicated by the shaded title bar. Note the illustrations below of documents tiled top to bottom and side by side.

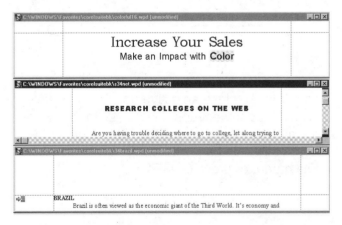

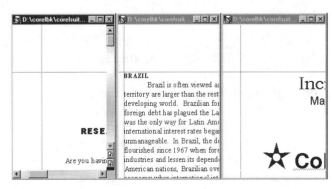

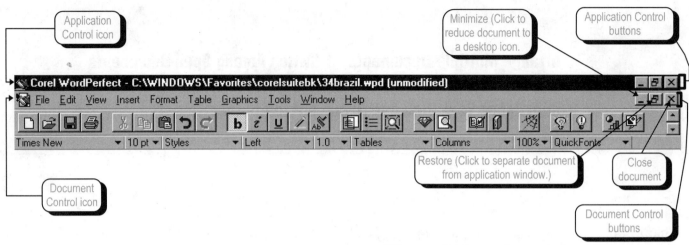

Switch Among Open Documents

- You can switch among document windows (whether they are currently displayed or not) by selecting the document you want to display from the Window menu. You may also press Ctrl+F6 to cycle through all open documents.

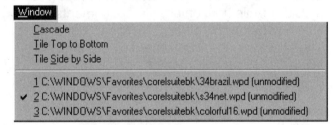

Closing Multiple Documents

- As you close each document, you can save its contents. To close an active document, double-click the document control icon 🔲 to the left of the title bar, or click the Close button ❌ to the right of the title bar, or select Close from the File menu, or press Ctrl+F4.

Sizing Windows

Maximizing a Window

- When you begin a new document, WordPerfect provides a full-screen or **maximized** window ready for you to begin typing. The icon and buttons in the WordPerfect title bar let you size and arrange WordPerfect in the Windows screen (application controls). The icon and buttons to the left and right of the Menu bar allow you to size and arrange the current document window (document controls).

- When a document is maximized (filling the full screen), the restore button 🔲 becomes active on the menu bar.

Separating the Document Window from the Application Window

- When you click the Restore button 🔲 in a maximized document window, your document separates from the application window. This allows you to view several documents at one time.

Minimizing a Window

- To minimize a document to an icon, click the Minimize document button 🔲 to the right of the document title bar. The document is reduced to a small rectangular icon at the bottom of the screen which displays the document name along with control buttons (Restoring, Maximizing, Closing).

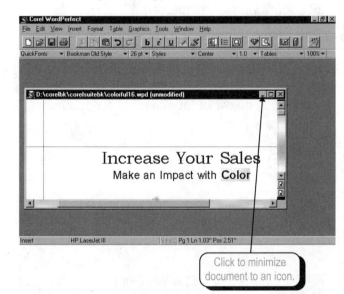

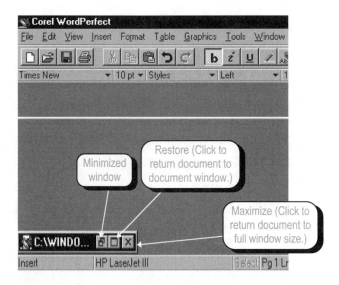

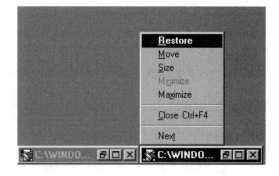

- To return the document to a separate document window, click the Restore button ⊡ (the Maximize button becomes a restore button), or click anywhere on the icon and a pop-up menu will display. Select Restore. To maximize the document to the full screen, click the Maximize button ⬜ or click the icon and select Maximize from the menu.

Copy/Move Text from One Document to Another

- The procedure for copying or moving text from one document to another is the same as copying/moving text within the same document.

- Opening multiple documents allows you to copy or move text easily from one document to another since you can actually see where the text is coming from and where it is going.

- When you have finished working in a document, close the file. Then tile or cascade the windows again to provide larger windows for the remaining documents.

In this exercise, you will open several documents and minimize and maximize them. In addition, you will practice different document arrangements. You will then copy text from one document to another.

EXERCISE DIRECTIONS

Part I

1. Open FRANCE or open 35FRANCE.
2. Click the Restore button to create a separate document window.
3. Click the Minimize button to reduce the document to an icon.
4. Click the Restore button to return the document to a separate document window.
5. Click the Maximize button to return the document to a full size window.
6. Open FILM or open 35FILM.
7. Open TIPS or open 35TIPS.
8. Cascade the documents.
9. Make FRANCE the active document.
10. Make FILM the active document.
11. Tile the documents side by side.
12. Maximize FRANCE (they will all maximize).
13. Tile the documents top to bottom.
14. Close each document window.

Part II

1. Start with a clear screen.
2. Type the letter on the right exactly as shown in Illustration A.
3. Use the default margins; begin the exercise on approximately Ln 2.5".
4. Use the default font size and style.
5. Save the file; name it WELLS.
   - ✓ *Note Illustration B.*
6. Open the last revision of MASON (if you completed it in Exercise 29) or open 35MASON.
7. Open NET (if you completed it in Exercise 32) or open 35NET.
8. Tile the documents top to bottom.

9. Maximize the WELLS document and create a footer; then, copy the footer in MASON to the footer area in WELLS.

10. Copy the indicated text in each document to WELLS.

    ✓   *You must copy text from an active document. When you are ready to insert the text, the new document must become the active document.*

    ✓   *Reveal codes before copying text selections B and C (as indicated on the Next page). Be sure to copy the center code that occurs prior to selection B and the margin begin and end codes within selection C.*

11. Close MASON and NET.

12. Maximize WELLS.

13. Make any necessary adjustments to the text. Avoid awkward paragraph breaks.

14. Insert a header which includes the addressee's name, page 2, and today's date on the second and succeeding pages.

15. Spell check.

16. Print one copy.

17. Close the file; save the changes.

ILLUSTRATION A

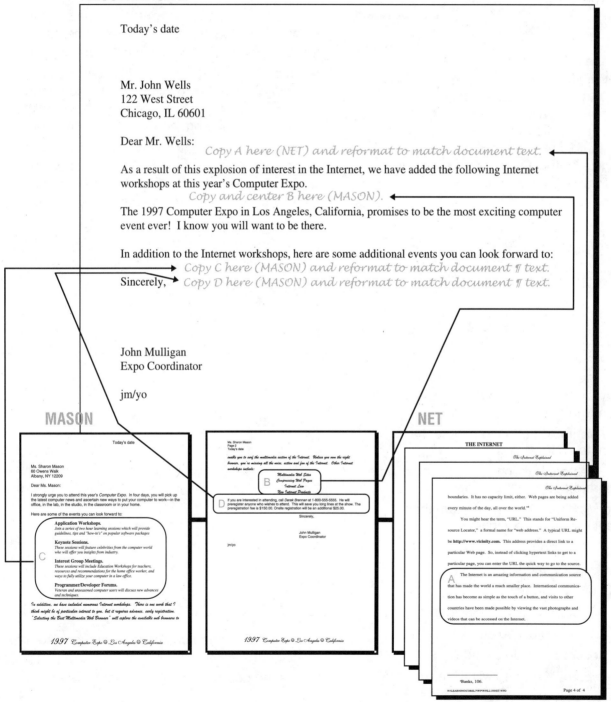

Today's date

Mr. John Wells
122 West Street
Chicago, IL 60601

Dear Mr. Wells:

The Internet is an amazing information and communication source that has made the world a
much smaller place. International communication has become as simple as the touch of a button,
and visits to other countries have been made possible by viewing the vast photographs and videos
that can be accessed on the Internet.

As a result of this explosion of interest in the Internet, we have added the following Internet workshops at
this year's Computer Expo.

Multimedia Web Sites
Compressing Web Pages
Internet Law
New Internet Products

The 1997 Computer Expo in Los Angeles, California, promises to
ever! I know you will want to be there.

In addition to the Internet workshops, here are some additional eve
forward.

1997 Computer Expo ☺ Los Ange

Mr. John Wells
Page 2
Today's date

Application Workshops.
*Join a series of two hour learning sessions which will provide
guidelines, tips and "how-to's" on popular software packages*

Keynote Sessions.
*These sessions will feature celebrities from the computer world
who will offer you insights from industry.*

Interest Group Meetings.
*These sessions will include Education Workshops for teachers,
resources and recommendations for the home office worker, and
ways to fully utilize your computer in a law office.*

Programmer/Developer Forums.
*Veteran and unseasoned computer users will discuss new
advances and techniques.*

If you are interested in attending, call *Derek Brennan* at 1-800-555-5555. He will preregister
anyone who wishes to attend. This will save you long lines at the show. The preregistration fee is
$150.00. Onsite registration will be an additional $25.00.

Sincerely,

John Mulligan
Expo Coordinator

jm/yo

1997 Computer Expo ☺ Los Angeles ☺ California

KEYSTROKES

OPEN MULTIPLE DOCUMENTS

Ctrl + O

1. Click **File** .... Alt + F
2. Click **Open** .... O

   OR

   Click **Open** button on Toolbar .... 🗁

3. Pressing the **Ctrl** key and click each file to be opened.

   OR

   To select consecutive files, click name of first file in group, use scroll bar/box as needed to bring last file of desired group into view, then **Shift + click** (press Shift while you click) name of that file.

4. Click **Open** .... Enter

CASCADE DOCUMENTS

1. Click **Window** .... Alt + W
2. Click **Cascade** C

TILE DOCUMENTS

1. Click **Window** .... Alt + W
2. Click **Tile Top to Button** .... T

   OR

   Click **Tile Side by Side** .... S

SWITCH AMONG OPEN DOCUMENTS

Click any visible portion of desired document.

   OR

1. Click **Window** .... Alt + W
2. Click desired document... *Document number*

OR

1. Next Document command ...... Ctrl + F6
2. Previous Document command .... Ctrl + Shift + F6

MOVE/COPY TEXT FROM ONE OPEN DOCUMENT TO ANOTHER

1. Open each file from which text is to be copied or moved. (See above)
2. Open a new file to receive the moved/copied text.

   ✓ *To make the Copy/Move procedure easier, tile the open documents.*

3. Click in the window *from* where text is to be moved/copied.
4. Highlight text to copy/move.

To copy text:

Ctrl + C

   a. Click **Edit** .... Alt + E
   b. Click **Copy** C

   OR

   Click **Copy** button .... 🗐
   on Toolbar.

To cut (move text):

Ctrl + X

   a. Click **Edit** .... Alt + E
   b. Click **Cut** .... T

   OR

   Click **Cut** button .... ✂
   on Toolbar.

5. Click in window *to* where text is to be moved/copied.

6. Position insertion point where text is to be inserted.

   Ctrl + V

   • Click **Edit** .... Alt + E
   • Click **Paste** .... P

   OR

   • Click **Paste** button .... 📋
     on Toolbar.

Exercise 36

■ Insert a File

NOTES

Insert a File

- When you insert a file into a document, the inserted file is made part of the current document window. This is quite different from opening a document. When you open a document, each new, opened document is layered over the previous one.

- The file which has been inserted will remain intact. You may insert it into another document when needed.

- A file may be inserted by selecting File from the Insert menu.

- In the Insert File dialog box which follows, you must select the drive and folder of the file you wish to insert. (Files may be accessed from the Insert dialog box using the same techniques used to open files in the Open dialog box. See Lesson 2, Exercise 6.)

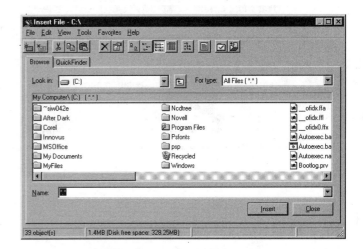

In this exercise, you will create a letter and insert a previously created file into it.

EXERCISE DIRECTIONS

1. Start with a clear screen.

2. Type the letter shown in Illustratration A in a serif 12 point font, or open ⊟36FRAN1.

3. Use the default left and right margins. Set .5" top and bottom margins.

4. Begin the letterhead at Ln 1".

5. Set the letterhead title to a decorative font in 18 point bold. Set the address and phone number information to the same descriptive font in 10 point.

6. Begin the date on approximately Ln 2".

7. Insert ⌂FRANCE (Illustration B) where indicated. Leave a double space before and after the insert.

   ✓ *After inserting the file, it may be necessary to return the left and right margins to 1" for the last paragraph.*

8. Create an appropriate page 2 header.

9. Spell check. Adjust page break if necessary to avoid awkward breaks.

10. Print one copy.

11. Close the file; name it FRANCE1.

ILLUSTRATION A

Deer Park University

787 Pineview Lane
North Sioux City, SD 57049

Phone: (605) 200-2000
Fax: (605) 200-3000

Today's date

Ms. Michele Petrie
6 West Street
New York, NY 10033

Dear Ms. Petrie:

We are planning a student exchange in March. We will be sending six students to Paris to study with Mr. Peter Moulin at the Elysée Français School.

I am developing a slide presentation about traveling to Paris, France, as a way of orientating them for their trip abroad. The following is an outline of the topics I will cover.

It would be helpful if you could provide me with some interesting web sites relating to these topics so my students can receive an even more exciting orientation.

Sincerely,

Carl Benton, Ph.D.
Foreign Language Department

cb/yo

Insert FRANCE file.

ILLUSTRATION B

TRAVELING TO PARIS, FRANCE

I.   People of France
    A.   Language
    B.   Religion
    C.   Holidays
    D.   Cooking
    E.   Sports
II.   Arts
    A.   Architecture
    B.   Literature
    C.   Painting
III. Tourist Attractions
    A.   Gardens, Squares and Parks
        1.   Latin Quarter
        2.   Tuileries
        3.   Champs Elysees
    B.   Famous Buildings and Monuments
        1.   Eiffel Tower
        2.   Arc de Triomphe
        3.   Louvre Palace
        4.   Notre Dame
    C.   Museums and Art Galleries
        1.   Louvre Museum
            a.   Great Works of Art
                (1)   Venus de Milo
                (2)   Mona Lisa
            b.   Museum of Decorative Art
        2.   National Museum of Modern Art
IV.   Restaurants
V.   Hotels

KEYSTROKES

INSERT FILE

1. Place the insertion point where you want file inserted.

2. Click **Insert** .... Alt + I

3. Click **File** I

4. Type or select name of document to insert .... ↑ ↓

5. Click **Insert** .... Enter

Exercise 37

■ Record a Macro

NOTES

■ A **macro** is a saved series of commands and keystrokes which may be *played* back at a later time.

■ Macros may be used to record repetitive phrases like the complimentary closing of a letter. When the phrase is needed, it is played back.

■ Or, a macro may be used to automate a particular task like changing margins and/or line spacing.

■ Rather than press many keys to access a feature, it is possible to *record* the process and play it back with fewer keystrokes.

■ To record a macro, select Macro, Record from the Tools menu, press Ctrl+F10, or click the Record button on the Macro Tools Toolbar.

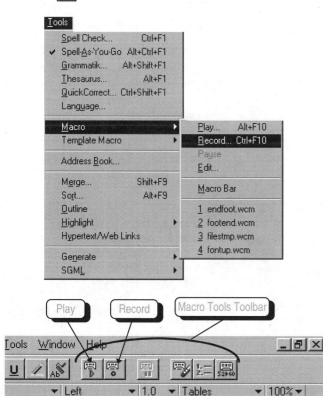

■ In the Record Macro dialog box which follows, type the name of your macro in the Name text box. Then, click Record.

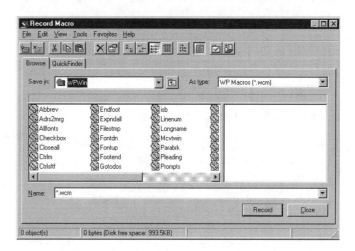

■ Unless you specify another location, WordPerfect automatically saves macros in the C:\COREL\OFFICE 7\MACROS\WPWIN directory and assigns a **.wcm** extension.

■ Record a macro carefully. When recording begins, the mouse pointer changes to a warning circle and Macro Record displays on the status bar. Any key or mouse action will then be recorded into the macro. Before ending your macro, always return to the default document font. Otherwise, the new text will take on the appearance of the macro font.

■ To stop recording, click the Stop Macro Play or Record button ■ on the Macro Bar. The Macro Feature Bar provides a quick way to access macro-related tasks.

✓ *The macro exercises in this text will not cover programming commands. (See your Corel Office Professional 7 documentation for macro programming command information.)*

In this exercise, you will create several macros. You will play them back in subsequent exercises.

EXERCISE DIRECTIONS

1. Start with a clear screen.

2. Access the Macro Tools Toolbar.

3. Create macro #1; name it P. Use a serif 12 point font and use italic and bold as shown in Illustration A. Insert a hard space (Ctrl + Spacebar) between the words.

   ✓ *If you are recording a macro with a font change, you must return the font back to the default font before you stop recording. Otherwise, any new text that you type will take on the appearance of the macro font.*

4. Close the document window.

5. Create macro #2; name it C. Use a script 14 point font. Insert a hard space between the words.

6. Close the document window.

7. Create macro #3; name it DT. Use a serif 12 point font and a bold sans serif 14 point font as shown.

8. Close the document window.

9. Create macro # 4; name it CL. Use a serif 12 point font.

10. Create macro # 5 (change margins); name it M.

11. Close the document window.

KEYSTROKES

RECORD A MACRO

Ctrl + F10, name macro, record it, Ctrl + F10

1. Click **Record** button .... 🖳
   on Macro Tools Toolbar.
   OR
   a. Click **Tools**........................ Alt + T
   b. Click **Macro** .... M
   c. Click **Record**............................. R

2. Type macro name.

3. Click **Record**.............................. Enter

4. Type keystrokes to be recorded.

   ✓ *If your macro contains all font appearance changes be sure to return the font the document default before ending the macro.*

To stop recording macro:

Click **Stop Record** button .... ■
on Macro Feature Bar.
OR
a. Click **Tools**........................ Alt + T
b. Click **Macro** .... M
c. Click **Record**............................. R

LLUSTRATION A

Macro #1: P

PsA Micro**Computer** Systems, Inc.

Macro #2: C

CompuTechnology Group, Inc.

Macro #3: DT

Document**Tech** *Pub*lishing Assistant

Macro #4: CL

Very truly yours,

David Altmann, Esq.

da/yo

Macro #5: M

1. Press Ctrl + F8.
2. Click Left margin up increment arrow and select 1.5".
3. Click Right margin up increment arrow and select 1.5".
4. Click OK.

Exercise

38

■ **Play a Macro**

NOTES

■ Once a macro has been recorded and saved, it can be *played* into your document whenever desired.

■ To play a macro, select Macro, Play from the Tools menu, press Alt + F10, or click the Play button 🖱 on the Macro Tools Toolbar.

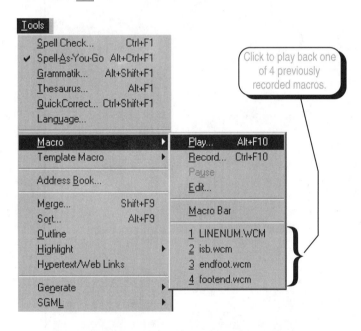

Click to play back one of 4 previously recorded macros.

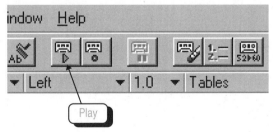

Play

■ In the Play Macro dialog box which follows, type the macro name to play in the Name text box. Or, select a macro from the filenames listed in the window. You will notice there are macros listed that you did not create. WordPerfect has provided you with numerous macros to automate a variety of tasks. To determine what each macro does, click the macro and note the displayed explanation at the bottom of the dialog box.

■ The last macro you recorded or played will be displayed on the Macro menu. You can select a macro to play back from the macros listed. *(See Illustration of drop-down menu.)*

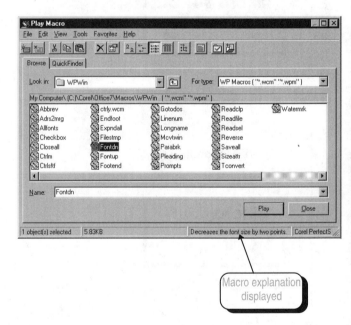

Macro explanation displayed

In Part I of this exercise, you will create a letter, and where indicated, play three macros you created earlier. You will also use WordPerfect's Filestamp (file stamp) macro to insert the filename in the document. (In a previous exercise, you inserted the document filename by clicking on the File stamp button on the Design Tools Toolbar. This is another way to access this feature.)

In Part II of this exercise, you will create a press release, a document that is prepared and sent to various newspapers and magazines announcing a new product of a company. Each time the product name appears, you will play one of the macros you created earlier. In addition, you will use WordPerfect's fontup.wcm macro (which automatically increases the font size two points) to increase the font size of the title.

EXERCISE DIRECTIONS

Part I

1. Start with a clear screen.

2. Create the letter shown in Illustration A.
   - ✓ You will note that this document contains a "re" line, which is commonly used in legal correspondence. "Re" means "in reference to" or "subject." Press the Enter key twice before and after typing the "re" line.

3. Use the default margins and font style and size.

4. Begin the exercise on approximately Ln 2".

5. Full justify the paragraphs.

6. Play the P, C and CL macros wherever they appear in the text.

7. Play the Filestmp macro. Insert the filename only (not the path) as a footer on the bottom left of the page.

8. Spell check.

9. Preview your document.

10. Print one copy.

11. Save the exercise; name it SETTLE.

12. Leave the document on the screen.

Part II

1. Start a new document.

2. Create the press release shown in Illustration B.

3. Use the default font style and size.

4. Play the M macro to set your margins.

5. Begin the exercise on approximately Ln 2". Use the Date Text feature to insert the current date.

6. Play the DT macro whenever Document**Tech** Pub*lishing Assistant* appears in the text.

7. Select (highlight) the two-line title. Play the fontup.wcm macro to increase the font size of the title.

8. Spell check.

9. Preview your document.

10. Print one copy.

11. Save the file; name it RELEASE.

12. Play the Closeall macro (to close both documents).

PART I – ILUSTRATION A

Today's date

Thomas Wolfe, Esq.
Wolfe, Escada & Yates
803 Park Avenue
New York, NY 10023

Dear Mr. Wolfe:

Re: [**Macro P**] vs.
ABC Manufacturing Company

I am enclosing a copy of the Bill of Sale that transfers all Gordon's assets to **[Macro P].**

In addition, you asked us to represent **[Macro C]** in their $200,000 payment to **[Macro P].** Because of this payment, **[Macro C]** became subrogated to the claim made by **[Macro P]**, and **[Macro P]** cannot settle this matter without the approval of **[Macro C].**

[Macro C] would also be entitled to recover some portion of any judgment recovered by **[Macro P]** in the above action. In order to get a settlement in this matter, we will need to obtain a release of ABC Manufacturing Company by **[Macro C]**.

Let's discuss this so that we can quickly settle this matter.

[Macro CL]

enclosure

PRESS RELEASE
For Immediate Release

For more information contact: Corine Cardoza

INTRODUCING the Document**Tech** *Pub*lishing Assistant

Cambridge, Massachusetts, March 7, 199-

The Document**Tech** *Pub*lishing Assistant is the first in a series of publishing products that put together three distinct technologies--digital scanning, laser imaging and xerograph--into one simplified publishing solution. The Document**Tech** *Pub*lishing Assistant provides high quality, low cost and quick turnaround. Document**Tech** *Pub*lishing Assistant eliminates complicated pre-press operations. It has a built-in scanner and quickly captures text, line art and photos, and converts them to digital masters.

Even booklet marking becomes easier. Document**Tech** *Pub*lishing Assistant has a signature booklet feature which will automatically turn out 11 x 17 or digest size (8.5 x 11) collated sets ready to be stitched, folded and trimmed. Document**Tech** *Pub*lishing Assistant prints an amazing 135 pages per minute and has a concurrent input/output capability. This means that while you are publishing one job, you'll be scanning, revising and readying others. Furthermore, Document**Tech** *Pub*lishing Assistant comes in a networked version.

KEYSTROKES

PLAY A MACRO

Alt + F10

1. Position insertion point where macro is to play.

2. Click **Play** button........................... [⏯]
   on Macro Tools Toolbar.

OR

a. Click **Tools** .... [Alt]+[T]

b. Click **Macro** .... [M]

c. Click **Play** .... [P]

3. Double-click desired macro to play.

OR

a. Type the macro name to play.

b. Click **Play** .... [Enter]

Exercise 39

■ **Summary**

In this exercise, you will record and play macros to create an advertisement.

EXERCISE DIRECTIONS

1. Create the following macro in a 12 point sans serif italic font; name it AD. Bold and capitalize the letters as shown. Return the font to the default before you stop recording.

   RideTheTrack ExerciSer

2. Close the document window.

3. Create the advertisement as shown below.

4. Begin on approximately Line 2".

5. Double indent the paragraphs as shown; use any desired symbol to precede each point.

6. Set the line spacing to 2 for the first and last all non-bulleted paragraphs.

7. Play the macros indicated.

8. Spell check.

9. Preview the document.

10. Print one copy.

11. Save the file; name it WORKOUT.

12. Close the document window.

**DISCOVER AN EXCITING NEW WAY TO
ACHIEVE WELLNESS OF BODY AND MIND**

[Macro M]

According to medical fitness experts, regular aerobic exercise is essential for achieving

all-around wellness. Aerobic exercise helps you prevent illness, feel better physically and

mentally, boost your energy level, and increase the years on your life. That's why you need

[Macro AD]. **[Macro AD]** will provide you with the following benefits:

✖ you can burn more fat than on other exercisers and burn up to
1,100 calories per hour!

✖ you can improve your cardiovascular fitness and lower your
overall cholesterol level.

✖ you'll feel more mentally alert, relaxed, positive and self-
confident.

With regular workouts on a **[Macro AD]**, you'll feel wonderful because you're doing

something positive for yourself.

Seven out of ten **[Macro AD]** owners use their machines an average of three times per

week.

Call your **[Macro AD]** representative today at 1-800-555-4444 to receive a FREE

video and brochure.

[Macro AD]

Exercise 40

■ **Columns** ■ **Newspaper Columns** ■ **Parallel Columns**

NOTES

Columns

■ The **Columns** feature allows text to flow from one column to another.

WordPerfect provides four column types:

- *newspaper columns,* in which text flows down one column to the bottom of a page then starts again at the top of the next column.

- *balanced newspaper columns*, in which text flows down one column to the bottom of a page then starts again at the top of the next column and is adjusted on the page so that the columns are equal in length.

- *parallel columns,* in which text moves across the columns.

- *parallel columns with block protect*, similar to parallel columns, except that if a column extends beyond a page break, the entire column is moved to the next page.

Regular Newspaper Columns

Newspaper columns allow text to flow from one column to another. This is an example of a regular newspaper column. When text reaches the bottom of one column, it automatically wraps to	the top of the next column. The gutter space is set by WordPerfect, but may be changed, as desired.

Balanced Newspaper Columns

This is an example of a **balanced newspaper column**. Each column is adjusted on the page so that they are equal in length. No matter how much text is typed the columns will always balance so that they are equal in length. As with	regular newspaper columns, the gutter space is set by WordPerfect, but may be changed as desired. Use this where you want as much text as possible to stay together in the section, like the top and bottom of a page.

Parallel Columns

Monday	Meeting with John Smith at 9:00 a.m.
Tuesday	Lunch appointment with Randy Grafco to discuss merger
Wednesday	Meeting with Sasha Mann at 10:30 a.m.

■ The Column feature is accessed by selecting Columns from the Format menu, then selecting Define.

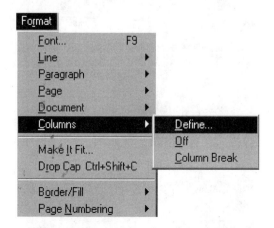

- In the Columns dialog box which follows, define the number of columns and the column type you desire. You may also adjust the spacing between columns, sometimes called the **gutter space**, and the width of each column. If you choose not to make any adjustments, the default settings will apply.

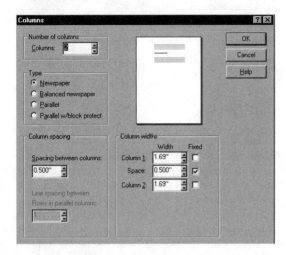

- After defining the columns and clicking OK, you have turned *on* the column feature. You must turn *off* the column feature when you have completed your columnar document if you plan to continue the document without columns.

- To include a vertical line between columns, select Border/Fill, Column from the Format menu. In the Column Border/Fill dialog box that follows, click the Border Tab, then click the vertical line between columns option Available border styles. You must scroll down to see this option.

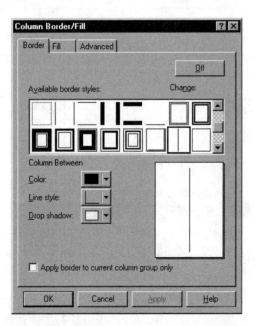

- Click the mouse in the desired column to move the insertion point quickly from column to column.

- Columns may be created *before* or *after* typing text.

Newspaper Columns

- Newspaper and balanced newspaper columns are particularly useful when creating newsletters, pamphlets, brochures, lists, or articles.

- You can retrieve text from a file into newspaper-style columns. When retrieving text from a file into columns, be sure your insertion point is within the column mode.

Parallel Columns

- Parallel columns are particularly useful when creating a list, script, itinerary, minutes of a meeting, or any document in which text is read horizontally.

- After text is entered in the first column, enter a hard column break (Ctrl + Enter) to force the insertion point to move to the next column. After text is entered in the second column, a hard column break must be entered to force the insertion point to the third column. A hard column break is also needed to move the insertion point back to the first column.

In Part I of this exercise, you will create a three-column newsletter using newspaper-style columns. In Part II of this exercise, you will create minutes of a meeting using parallel columns.

EXERCISE DIRECTIONS

Part I

1. Start with a clear screen.

2. Use the default margins.

3. Begin the exercise on Ln 1".

4. Set line spacing to 1.3.

5. Type the title, shown in Illustration A, on page 160 in a sans serif 18 point bold font as shown; press Enter three times.

6. Create the remainder of the newsletter shown in Illustration A (page 160), using a three-column, *regular* newspaper-style format. Use the default gutter space between columns.

7. Center (within the column) and set the headlines to a sans serif 14 point bold font.

8. Set column paragraph text to a serif 12 point font.

9. Insert a vertical line (border) between columns.

10. Full justify document text.

11. Spell check.

12. If necessary, adjust the bottom margin (drag the guide) to keep all text on one page.

13. Preview your document.

14. Print one copy.

15. Save the file; name it JOURNEY.

16. Close the document window.

Part II

1. Start with a clear screen.

2. Use the default margins.

3. Begin the exercise on approximately Ln 2".

4. Type the text shown in Illustration B on page 161.

5. Center the main heading in a sans serif 16 point bold italic font.
   - Use any desired special character before and after the heading as shown.
   - Center the minor headings in a sans serif 12 point italic font. Press the Enter key twice after the date.

6. Center four special characters to separate the date from the body text. Press the Enter key three times after the special characters.

7. Create a two-column, parallel style format.

8. Change the width of column one to 1.5". Change the width of column two to 4.5". Use the default distance between columns.

9. Set the side headings to a sans serif 12 point italic font. Set the body text to a serif 12 point font.

10. Spell check.

11. Preview your document (See desired result).

12. Print one copy.

13. Highlight the title; play the Font up macro to increase the font size two points.

14. Save the file; name it AGELESS.

15. Close the document window.

ILLUSTRATION A

AMERICAN TRAVELER

SMOKERS MEET NEW RESTRICTIONS DURING TRAVEL

Travelers should be aware of increased constraints on the ability to smoke in public places. About five years ago, smoking was prohibited on all domestic airline flights. The Dallas-Fort Worth Airport recently declared the entire passenger terminal off limits to smokers. Those wishing to smoke will now have to leave the airport premises to do so. Perhaps more far reaching is the law passed in Los Angeles which makes cigarette smoking illegal in restaurants. Violators face a $50 fine for the first offense, a $100 fine for the second offense within a year, and a $250 fine for every offense after that. Be cautious when traveling not to violate unexpected smoking laws!

CRUISING ON and BALLOONING OVER THE RHINE

Strasbourg, the capital of French Alsace, is a wonderful city to begin or end a cruise or a hot-air balloon ride. Its pink sandstone Cathedral and a well-preserved old town are enchanting attractions for vacationing tourists. The cost of a three-day cruise, including an afternoon hot-air balloon ride, two evening meals, two breakfasts, two luncheons and coffee and cakes will be approximately $567 a person. The view from the air and/or from the middle of the river is more dramatic than the glimpses of the same scenery that a passenger sees on the train ride along the river bank from Cologne to Frankfurt. For further information, contact your local travel agent and request the RHINE RIVER PACKAGE.

TRAVEL HIGHLIGHT OF THE SEASON: *THE GREEK ISLANDS*

There are over 3,000 islands which comprise "The Greek Islands." However, only 170 of these islands are inhabited, each with its own character and terrain. This summer, Sunshine Travel Network is offering special fares on cruises to many of these charming islands. A four-day cruise to Rhodes, Heraklion, Santorini, and Piraeus costs $799 per person. This package is definitely the buy of the season!

≈≈≈ *PERFECTION PLUS, INCORPORATED* ≈≈≈
MINUTES OF MEETING

March 29, 199-

≈ ≈ ≈ ≈

Present	Robin Jones, Quincy Garin, Zachary Malvo, Wendy Carley, Bill McKinley, Andrew Yang, Shirley DeChan.
Research	Mr. Malvo announced the development of a new product line. Several new chemical formulas were developed for a cream which will reduce skin wrinkling. The cream will be called **Ageless**.
Publicity	To launch this new product, Ms. Carley announced that promotions would be made at all the high-end New York department stores. Samples of the product will be given away at demonstration counters. Press releases will be sent to members of the press.
Advertising	The advertising budget was estimated at $5,223,000. Several advertising agencies were asked to submit presentations, and a decision will be made by the Advertising Committee as to which agency will represent this new line.
Sales	Mr. Garin, National Sales Manager, projected that sales could reach $10,000,000 the first year.
Adjournment	The meeting was adjourned at 4:00 p.m. Another meeting has been scheduled for Tuesday of next week to discuss future research and marketing of this new product.

KEYSTROKES

CREATE COLUMNS

1. Place insertion point where column is to begin.

OR

2. Select existing text to include in columns.

- Click **For̲mat**........................ `Alt`+`R`
- Click **C̲olumns** .... `C`
- Click **D̲efine**.............................. `D`

3. Click a Column type:

- **N̲ewspaper**........................ `Alt`+`N`
- **B̲alanced newspaper** .... `Alt`+`B`
- **P̲arallel** .... `Alt`+`P`
- **Parallel w/block protect** .... `Alt`+`A`

4. Change the following options as desired:

- Click **C̲olumns** .... `Alt`+`C`
- Type desired number of columns.

  OR

  Use increment arrows to choose desired number of columns... `↓`|`↑`

- Click **S̲pacing between columns** .... `Alt`+`S`
- Type desired distance.

5. Click **OK**.................................. `Enter`
   to force a new column.

To Force a New Column:

1. Click **For̲mat**......................... `Alt`+`R`
2. Click **C̲olumns** .... `C`
3. Click **C̲olumn Break**........................ `C`

OR

4. Position insertion point where new column is to begin.
5. Press **Ctrl + Enter**.............. `Ctrl`+`Enter`

INCLUDE VERTICAL LINE BETWEEN COLUMNS

1. Click **For̲mat**......................... `Alt`+`R`
2. Click **B̲order/Fill** .... `O`
3. Click **C̲olumn**............................. `C`
4. Select an **A̲vailable border style** .... `Alt`+`V`
5. Scroll down to vertical line option...................................... `↓`|`↑`
6. Click **OK**................................. `Enter`

TURN OFF COLUMNS

1. Place insertion point where column is to be turned off.
2. Click **For̲mat**........................ `Alt`+`R`
3. Click **C̲olumns** .... `C`
4. Click **O̲ff**.. `O`

MOVE INSERTION POINT FROM COLUMN TO COLUMN

Click in desired column.

CREATE COLUMNS WITH CUSTOM WIDTHS

1. Place insertion point where column is to begin.
2. Click **For̲mat**........................ `Alt`+`R`
3. Click **C̲olumns** .... `C`
4. Click **D̲efine**................................. `D`
5. Click **Column 1̲** text box .... `Alt`+`1`
6. Type desired width .... *number*
7. Click **Column 2̲** text box .... `Alt`+`2`
8. Type desired width .... *number*
9. Repeat procedure for each additional column .... `Tab`, *number*
10. Click **OK** .... `Enter`

Exercise 41

■ **Create a Table**   ■ **Move Within a Table**
■ **Enter Text in a Table**

NOTES

■ The **Table** feature allows you to organize information into columns and rows without using tabs or tab settings.

■ A table consists of **rows**, which run horizontally and are identified by number (1, 2, 3, etc.), and **columns**, which run vertically and are identified by letter (A, B, C, etc.). The rows and columns intersect to form empty boxes, called **cells**.

■ Note the example below of a table with three rows and four columns:

	Column A	Column B	Column C	Column D
Row 1				
Row 2				
Row 3				

■ Text, graphics, numbers, or formulas are entered into cells after you have defined the structure of your table—that is, how many columns and rows you require for your table. (Formulas will not be covered in this text.)

Create a Table

■ Select <u>C</u>reate from the <u>T</u>able menu. In the Create Table dialog box which follows, indicate the desired number of columns and rows.

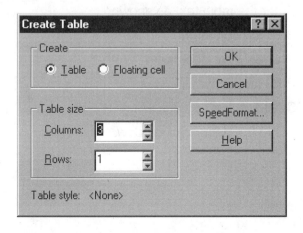

■ You can also create tables quickly by clicking the Tables button [Tables ▼] on the Power Bar, and dragging the mouse pointer to select the desired number of rows and columns. Double-clicking on the Tables button will bring you to the Create Table dialog box.

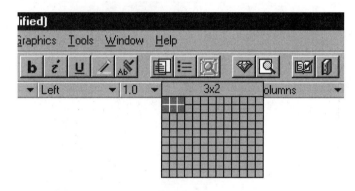

■ After the table is created, the **Tables Toolbar** automatically appears. The Tables Toolbar is convenient for accessing table-related tasks.

Tables Toolbar

■ The columns adjust automatically to fit between the left and right margins.

■ You can create a table with up to 64 columns and 32,767 rows.

Move Within a Table

■ The insertion point moves in a table the same way it moves in a document. You may use the mouse to click in the desired cell, or you may use keystrokes to move around the cells (*see keystrokes on following page*).

- If there is no text in a cell, the directional arrow keys move the insertion point from cell to cell; otherwise, they move the insertion point through text in the cell.

- When the insertion point is in a table cell, the status bar indicates the cell location by displaying the cell's column letter and row number.

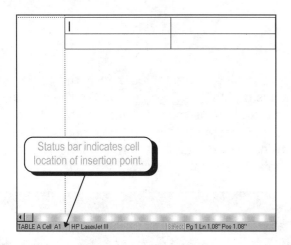

Enter Text in a Table

- As you enter text in a table cell, the cell expands downward to accommodate the text.

- Use the Tab key to advance the insertion point from one cell to the next, even at the end of the row.

- You can insert a tab within a cell by pressing Ctrl + Tab.

In Part I of this exercise, you will create a table using 4 columns and 5 rows. In Part II of this exercise, you will create another table using the same amount of columns and rows.

EXERCISE DIRECTIONS

Part I

1. Start with a clear screen.
2. Use the default margins.
3. Center the page.
4. Center the title as shown in Illustration A on page 165. Set the main title to a sans serif 14 point bold font. Set the second and third lines of the title to 12 point. Set the third line to italics. Return the font to serif 12 point. Press the Enter key three times.
5. Create the table as shown using 4 columns and 5 rows.
6. Enter the table text as shown. Bold the column headings.
7. Preview your document.
8. Print one copy.
9. Save the exercise; name it CRUISE.
10. Close the document window.

Part II

1. Start with a clear screen.
2. Use the default margins.
3. Center the page.
4. Center the title as shown in Illustration B on page 165. Set the title to a sans serif 14 point bold font. Return the font to serif 12 point. Press the Enter key three times.
5. Create the table as shown using 4 columns and 5 rows.
6. Enter the table text as shown.
7. Bold the column headings.
8. Preview your document.
9. Print one copy.
10. Save the file; name it SALARY.
11. Close the document window.

FESTIVAL TRAVEL ASSOCIATES

WORLD CRUISE SEGMENTS
SPRING 1998

DESTINATION	DEPARTS	NO. OF DAYS	COST
Panama Canal	March 6	13	$2,529
Trans Pacific	March 19	11	$4,399
Israel to New York	March 19	18	$5,299
Naples to New York	March 19	11	$3,499

ANALYSIS OF SALARY INCREASES

EMPLOYEE	SALARY 1996	SALARY 1997	% INCREASE
Johnson, James	45500.00	49000.00	7.69
Chassin, Matthew	32300.00	35000.00	8.36
Kahn, Amy	16500.00	17500.00	6.06
Ahmed, Jordan	18500.00	20000.00	8.11

KEYSTROKES

CREATE A TABLE

1. Position insertion point at left margin where you want table to appear.
2. Click **Table** button.... Tables ▼ on Power Bar.
3. Drag to select desired number of columns and rows.
4. Release mouse.

OR

1. Click **Table**.................... Alt + A
2. Click **Create** C
3. Click **Columns** text box .... Alt + C and type desired number of columns.

OR

Click increment buttons to select number of columns.................. ↓ ↑
4. Click **Rows** text box............... Alt + R and type desired number.

OR

Click increment buttons to select number of rows....................... ↓ ↑
5. Click **OK** .... Enter

ENTER TEXT IN TABLES

1. Click cell to receive text.
2. Type text.
3. Press **Tab**.................................... Tab to advance to next cell.

OR

Use the following insertion point movements:

TO MOVE:	PRESS:
One cell right	Tab
One cell left	Shift + Tab
One cell down	Alt + ↓
One cell up	Alt + ↑
First cell in row	Home , Home
Last cell in row	End , End
Top line of multi-line cell	Alt + Home
Bottom line of multi-line cell	Alt + End

Exercise

42

- Justification Within Table Cells ■ Insert and Delete Columns and Rows
- Change Column Width ■ Horizontal Positioning of a Table
- Table Lines and Borders ■ Inside and Outside Lines
- Individual Lines ■ Fills (Shading/Patterns) ■ SpeedFormat

NOTES

Justification Within Table Cells

- WordPerfect allows you to change the justification of text for a cell, column, or the entire table.

- You may left, center, right, full, all, or decimal align text either during the table creation process or afterward.

Justification Examples

Left	Decimal Align: .1
	10.0
	1000.00
Center	Full justify needs more than one line to show its effect.
Right	All justify also needs more than one line to show its effect.

- To align text in a table, place the insertion point in any cell, or select (highlight) several cells or columns, in which you wish to align text. Then, select Format from the Table menu, or click the Table Format button 🖳 on the Tables Toolbar, or click the Edit Table QuickSpot and select Format from the Tools dialog box (see next page).

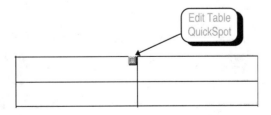

Edit Table QuickSpot

- In the Properties for Table Format dialog box which follows, click the Cell or Column Tab and choose a justification option from the Justification drop-down list box.

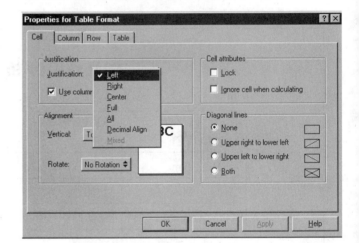

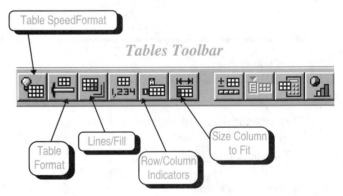

Table SpeedFormat

Tables Toolbar

Table Format

Lines/Fill

Row/Column Indicators

Size Column to Fit

- To easily identify column letters and row numbers, display them on screen by clicking the Row/Column Indicators button on the Tables Toolbar.

Insert and Delete Columns and Rows

- One or more rows and/or columns may be inserted or deleted in a table before or after the insertion point position.

- To insert a column or row, select Insert from the Table menu, or click the Edit Table QuickSpot and click Insert/Delete, then choose Insert.

- In the Insert Columns/Rows dialog box which follows, you must indicate if you wish to insert a column or a row, and if you wish to insert the column or row before or after the insertion point position.

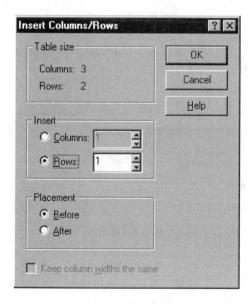

- To insert rows at the end of the table, position the insertion point in the last cell and press the Tab key.

- The text in the inserted column or row takes on the same formatting as the row or column of the insertion point.

- To delete a column or row, select Delete from Table menu or click the Edit Table QuickSpot and click Insert/Delete, then choose Delete. In the Delete dialog box which follows, you must indicate whether you wish to delete a column or row and the number of columns or rows to delete (if you did not highlight them first).

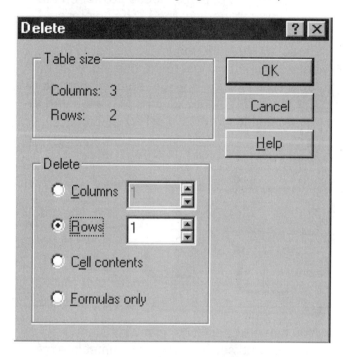

- The entire table may also be deleted by highlighting the entire table, selecting Delete from the Table menu, then selecting Entire Table.

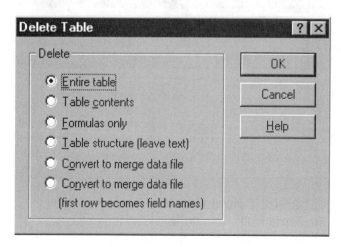

Change Column Width

- Column widths may be changed using a specific measurement or by dragging the vertical lines between columns to the desired width.

- To adjust column widths and see the immediate effect of the change on the table as it is being made, place the mouse pointer on a vertical line of the column to be sized. (To adjust table size, place mouse pointer on the far left or right vertical line.) The pointer's shape changes to a table sizing arrow ↔. Press and hold the mouse as you drag the dotted line left or right to the desired width or table size. As you drag the column's vertical line, the width of the columns to the left and to the right of the vertical line is displayed.

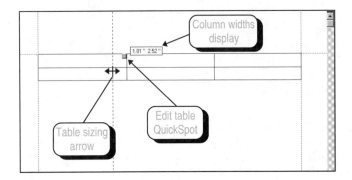

- You can also adjust column widths and margins and see the change's immediate effect by dragging the column margin markers on the Ruler Bar. (To display the Ruler Bar, press Alt + V, T, click Ruler Bar).

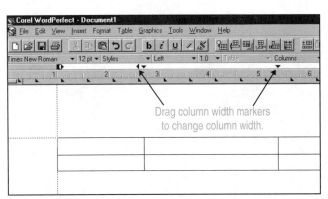

Drag column width markers to change column width.

- The **Size Column to Fit** feature allows you to automatically adjust the width of a cell or column to fit the width of the text. After highlighting the cell or column containing the widest text, click the Size Column to Fit button on the Tables Toolbar, or click the *right* mouse button and select Size Column to Fit.

- You may also adjust column widths and margins using a specific measurement in the Properties for Table Format dialog box.

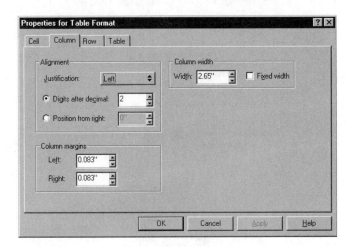

Horizontal Positioning of a Table

- WordPerfect sets column widths in a table to spread out evenly between the margins whether your table contains two or ten columns. When you change column width, WordPerfect keeps the same left margin. This means the table is no longer centered across the page.

- To horizontally center the table, click Table, Format, then click the Table tab in the Properties for Table Format dialog box. Select Center from the drop-down Table position options.

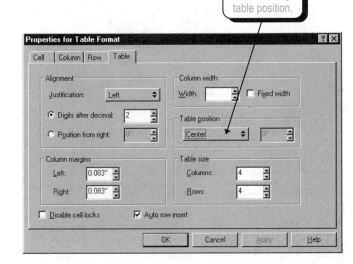

Click to change table position.

- You may also position the table to the left or right of the page, or a specific amount from the left edge of the page.

Table Lines and Borders

- A **table border** is a line (or lines) that surrounds a table. A **table line** divides the columns and rows to form the cells. By default, tables print with a single line around the outer edge (table border) and with single lines that divide columns and rows (table lines). Note the example below:

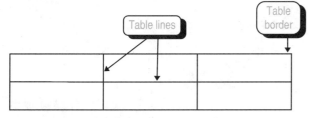

- WordPerfect lets you change the table border and table line style, and provides you with numerous line types.

Thick Border and Dashed Table Lines

- To change table lines and borders, place insertion point in the table, and click the Lines/Fill button ▦ on the Table Toolbar, or select Lines/Fill from the Table menu. Then, in the Properties for Table Lines/Fill dialog box, click the Table tab and select a table border from the Border drop-down palette and/or a line style from the Line drop-down palette. For each line and border type you select, you will see a sample in the Preview window.

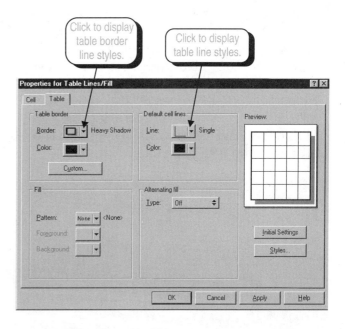

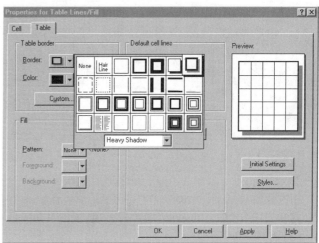

Inside and Outside Lines

- You may also change the line type of inside and outside lines. Lines that surround the selection are **outside lines**; lines within the selection are **inside lines**.

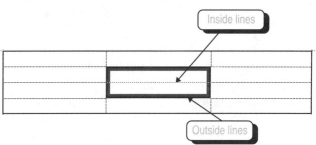

■ Inside and outside line styles may be changed by selecting the cells to affect, then selecting the Lines/Fill button from the Table Toolbar, or clicking the Edit Table QuickSpot and selecting a line style from the Tools dialog box. In the Properties for Table Lines/Fill dialog box which follows, select the Cell tab and select the Outside or Inside list arrow and choose a line style from the pop-up palette.

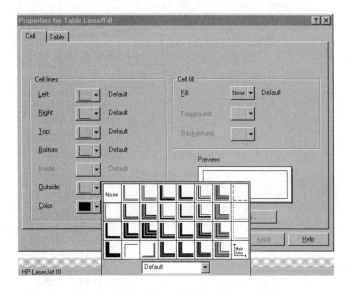

Individual Lines

■ Changing the line type of individual lines is an effective way of emphasizing data within a cell. Note the table below which uses different line styles in selected cells.

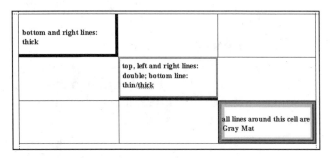

■ Individual line styles may be changed by placing the insertion point in the individual cell, or selecting a group of cells to affect. Then, in the Properties for Table Lines/Fill dialog box, click the specific line button (Left, Right, etc.) and choose a line style from the drop-down palette.

■ While color shading options are available for lines and borders, you need a color printer to output color.

Fills (Shading/Patterns)

■ The **Fill** feature lets you emphasize a cell, row, column, or group of cells by adding a pattern or shade.

■ Fills may also be changed in the Properties for Table Lines/Fill dialog box. Click the Fill button and choose a fill option from the drop-down palette.

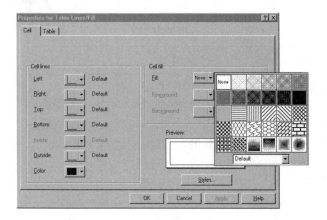

Using SpeedFormat

■ WordPerfect provides a quick way to enhance the appearance of tables through its **SpeedFormat** feature. One of WordPerfect's 40 predefined formatting styles can be applied to your table. SpeedFormat may be accessed by clicking the Table SpeedFormat button on the Tables Toolbar, or by selecting SpeedFormat from the Table menu. In the Table SpeedFormat dialog box which follows, available styles are listed on the left, and a preview window displays the selected style.

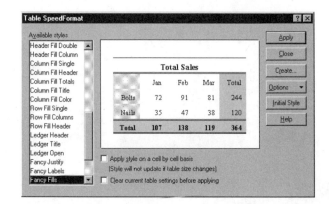

In Parts I and II of this exercise, you will insert columns and rows as well as adjust column widths of tables you created previously. You will enhance your table using various line styles.

EXERCISE DIRECTIONS

Part I

1. Start with a clear screen.

2. Open ▣SALARY or ▣42SALARY.

3. Display the column and row indicators. (Your insertion point must be within the table structure to access this feature.)

4. Insert two rows and one column and enter text as shown in Illustration A on page 172.

5. Delete the Amy Kahn row.

6. Center-align all column headings.

7. Center-align Years of Service column text.

8. Decimal-align numerical text in columns C, D, and E.

9. Use the Size-Column-to-Fit feature to adjust column widths in all columns.

10. Horizontally position the table on the page.

11. Use the Lines/Fill feature to edit the table as shown in Illustration B on page 172:
    - Select the Table tab. Apply a shadow table border.
    - Apply a dashed line style for cell lines.
    - Select the Cell tab. Highlight the column headings and apply a 5% fill.

12. Preview your document.

13. Print one copy.

14. Close the file; save the changes.

Part II

1. Start with a clear screen.

2. Open ▣CRUISE or ▣42CRUISE as shown on page 173.

3. Set top and bottom margins to .5".

4. Display the column and row indicators.

5. Insert one column after DESTINATION and enter the text as shown in Illustration C on page 173.

   ✓ *Once the new column is inserted, Column A becomes shorter and truncates the text in that column. Do not be concerned. You will adjust column widths in a later step.*

6. Insert one row at the end of the table and enter the text as shown.

7. Set column A width to 1.38"; set column B width to 1.31".

8. Use Size Column to Fit feature to size columns C, D, and E.

9. Center-align all column headings as well as text in Columns D and E.

10. Reposition the table to center on the page.

11. Using the SpeedFormat feature, apply the Header Fill Column Style to your table as shown in Illustration D on page 174.

12. Preview your document.

13. Print one copy.

14. Close the file; save the changes.

PART I – ILLUSTRATION A

ANALYSIS OF SALARY INCREASES

Insert one column.

Delete row.

Insert two rows.

EMPLOYEE	Years of Service	SALARY 1996	SALARY 1997	% INCREASE
Johnson, James	5	45500.00	49000.00	7.69
Chassin, Matthew	3	32300.00	35000.00	8.36
Kahn, Amy		16500.00	17500.00	6.06
Ahmed, Jordan	1	18500.00	20000.00	8.11
Zano, Anthony	8	18500.00	20000.00	8.11
Lee, Kim	4	254000.00	27000.00	6.30

ILLUSTRATION B

ANALYSIS OF SALARY INCREASES

EMPLOYEE	YEARS OF SERVICE	SALARY 1996	SALARY 1997	% INCREASE
Johnson, James	5	45500.00	49000.00	7.69
Chassin, Matthew	3	32300.00	35000.00	8.36
Ahmed, Jordan	1	18500.00	20000.00	8.11
Zano, Anthony	8	38000.00	41500.00	9.21
Lee, Kim	4	25400.00	27000.00	6.30

PART II – ILLUSTRATION C

FESTIVAL TRAVEL ASSOCIATES

WORLD CRUISE SEGMENTS
SPRING 1998

Insert column.

DESTIN ATION	PORTS	DEPARTS	NO. OF DAYS	COST
Panama Canal	New York, Cartegen a, Panama Canal, Acapulco	March 6	13	$2,529
Trans-Pacific	Los Angeles, Ensenada, Kona, Honolulu, Fiji, Auckland	March 19	11	$4,399
Israel to New York	Haifa, Kusadasi, Istanbul, Athens, Naples, Cannes, New York	March 19	18	$5,299
Naples to New York	Naples, Cannes, Lisbon, Southham pton, New York	March 19	11	$3,499
Trans-Atlantic	Fort Lauderdal e, Madiera, Lisbon, Gibralter, Genoa	April 6	15	$2,599

Insert row.

ILLUSTRATION D

FESTIVAL TRAVEL ASSOCIATES

WORLD CRUISE SEGMENTS
SPRING 1998

DESTINATION	PORTS	DEPARTS	NO. OF DAYS	COST
Panama Canal	New York, Cartegena, Panama Canal, Acapulco	March 6	13	$2,529
Transpacific	Los Angeles, Ensenada, Kona, Honolulu, Fiji, Auckland	March 19	11	$4,399
Israel to New York	Haifa, Kusadasi, Istanbul, Athens, Naples, Cannes, New York	March 19	18	$5,299
Naples to New York	Naples, Cannes, Lisbon, Southhampton, New York	March 19	11	$3,499
Transatlantic	Fort Lauderdale, Madiera, Lisbon, Gibralter, Genoa	April 6	15	2,599

KEYSTROKES

ALIGN TEXT WITHIN CELLS, COLUMNS, OR TABLE

1. Place insertion point in table.
   OR
   Select cell(s) or column(s) to receive alignment change.
2. Click *right* mouse button.
   - Click **F**o**rmat** .... `O`
   OR
   Click Edit Table Quickspot.
   - Click **F**o**rmat** .... `M`
   OR
   Click **Table Format** button .... 🖮
   on Tables Toolbar.
3. Select desired tab:
   - **Cell**
   - **Column**
   - **Table**
4. Click **J**ustification list box ...... `Alt`+`J`
5. Click desired justification (alignment) option:
   - **Left** .... `L`
   - **R**ight .... `R`
   - **C**enter .... `C`
   - **F**ull .... `F`
   - **A**ll .... `A`
   - **D**ecimal align .... `D`
6. Click **OK** .... `Enter`

DISPLAY COLUMN LETTERS AND ROW NUMBERS

Click **Row/Column Indicator** button ...... 🖩
on Tables Toolbar.

INSERT ROWS/COLUMNS

1. Place insertion point inside table before or after where desired insertion is to occur.
2. Click **T**able .... `Alt`+`A`
   - Click **I**nsert .... `I`
   OR
   a. Click *right* mouse button.
   b. Click **I**nsert .... `I`
   OR
   a. Click **Edit Table QuickSpot**.
   b. Click **Insert/Delete** list arrow .. `Alt`+`D`
   c. Click **I**nsert .... `Alt`+`↓`, `I`
3. Click button of item to insert:
   - **Columns** .... `Alt`+`C`
   - **Rows** .... `Alt`+`R`
4. Type number of columns or rows to be inserted.
   OR
   - Click increment arrows to desired number .... `↓`+`↑`
5. Click desired **Placement** button:
   - **Before** .... `Alt`+`B`

   - **After** .... `Alt`+`A`
6. Click **OK** .... `Enter`

DELETE ROWS/COLUMNS

1. Place insertion point in column or row to delete.
   OR
   Select columns or rows to delete.
2. Click **T**able .... `Alt`+`A`
   - Click **D**elete .... `D`
   OR
   a. Click *right* mouse button.
   b. Click **D**elete .... `D`
   OR
   a. Click **Edit Table QuickSpot**.
   b. Click **Insert/Delete** list arrow .. `Alt`+`D`
   c. Click **D**elete .... `Alt`+`↓`, `D`
3. Click button of item to be deleted:
   - **Columns** .... `Alt`+`C`
   - **Rows** .... `Alt`+`R`
4. Type number of columns or rows to delete.
   OR
   - Click increment arrows to desired number .... `↓`+`↑`
5. Click **OK** .... `Enter`

DELETE TABLE OR CELL CONTENTS

1. Select entire table.
2. Click **Table** .... `Alt`+`A`
3. Click **Delete** .... `D`
4. Click a delete option:
   - **Entire table** .... `E`
   - **Table contents** .... `C`
   - **Formulas only** .... `F`
   - **Table structure (leave text)** .... `I`
5. Click **OK** .... `Enter`

CHANGE COLUMN WIDTHS OR MARGINS

To see immediate changes:

1. Place mouse pointer on a vertical line separating the column until it changes to a table sizing arrow .... ↔
2. Drag sizing arrow left or right to desired width.

OR

1. Place insertion point in the table.
2. Display Ruler bar .... `Alt`+`Shift`+`F3`
3. Drag markers and guides to change the table.

OR

1. Place insertion point in cell containing longest text.
2. Click *right* mouse button.
3. Click **Size Column to Fit** .... `Z`

   OR

   Click **Size Column to Fit** button ..... `▦` on Tables Toolbar.

OR

1. Click **Edit Table QuickSpot**.
2. Click **Adjust Columns** list arrow .... `Alt`+`A`
3. Click **Size Column to Fit** .... `Alt`+`↓`, `S`

To set specific settings:

1. Place insertion point in column to format.

   OR

   - Select several columns to format.
2. Click **Table** .... `Alt`+`A`
3. Click **Format** .... `O`
4. Select **Column** tab.

To set column margins:

a. Click in **Column margins Left** text box .... `Alt`+`F`
b. Type a left column margin amount .... *number*

   OR

   Click increment arrows to desired number .... `↓` `↑`

---

c. Click in **Column margins Right** text box .... `Alt`+`I`
d. Type a right column margin amount .... *number*

   OR

   Click increment arrows to desired number .... `↓` `↑`

To set column widths:

a. Click in **Column Width** text box .... `Alt`+`T`
b. Type a column width amount.............................. *number*

   OR

   Click increment arrows to desired number .... `↓` `↑`

To keep width of current column same, regardless of changes to other columns:

- Click **Fixed width** .... `Alt`+`X`

To retain all adjustments made to column widths and/or margins:

- Click **OK** .... `Enter`

HORIZONTALLY POSITION TABLE ON PAGE

1. Place insertion point in table.
2. Click **Table Format** button on Tables Toolbar .... `▦`

   OR

   a. Click *right* mouse button.
   b. Select **Format** .... `O`

   OR

   a. Click **Table** .... `Alt`+`A`
   b. Click **Format** .... `O`
3. Click **Table** tab.
4. Click **Table position** list box .. `Alt`+`P`
5. Select desired position:
   - **Left** .... `L`
   - **Right** .... `R`
   - **Center** .... `C`
   - **Full** .... `F`
   - **From Left Edge** .... `E`
     - Type amount from left edge . *number*

   OR

   Click increment arrows to desired number .... `↓` `↑`
6. Click **OK** .... `Enter`

TABLE LINES AND BORDERS

1. Place insertion point in table.
2. Click **Table** .... `Alt`+`A`

- Click **Lines/Fill** .... `L`

   OR

   - Click **Lines/Fill** button on Table Toolbar .... `▦`
3. Click on **Table** tab.
4. Click on **Line** style button .... `Alt`+`L`
   - Click line style drop-down arrow.
5. Click desired line style from drop-down palette .... `↓` `↑`
6. Click on **Border** style button ... `Alt`+`B`
   - Click border style drop-down arrow.
7. Click desired border style from drop-down palette .... `↓` `↑`
8. Click **OK** .... `Enter`

INSIDE/OUTSIDE AND INDIVIDUAL LINES

1. Select cells to affect.

   OR

   - Place insertion point in cell to affect.
2. Click **Table** .... `Alt`+`A`
   - Click **Lines/Fill** .... `L`

   OR

   - Click **Lines/Fill** button on Table Toolbar .... `▦`

   OR

   - Click **Edit Table QuickSpot**.
3. Click **Cell** tab (if necessary).
4. Click line to affect:
   - **Left** .... `L`
   - **Right** .... `R`
   - **Top** .... `T`
   - **Bottom** .... `B`
   - **Inside** .... `I`
   - **Outside** .... `O`
   ✓ When changing all sides of a single cell, the Inside option will have no effect.
5. Click desired line style from drop-down palette.
6. Click **OK** .... `Enter`

FILLS AND PATTERNS

1. Follow steps 1-4, above.
2. Click **Fill** .... `F`
3. Click desired fill style from drop-down palette.
4. Click **OK** .... `Enter`

   OR

   If you clicked a QuickSpot, simply click the Close button `X` to Exit the Tools dialog box.

■ **The Merge Process** ■ **Create a Data File** ■ **Create a Form File**
■ **Merge the Form and Data Files** ■ **Merge Selected Records**
■ **Merge with Conditions** ■ **Prepare Envelopes While Merging**

NOTES

The Merge Process

■ The **Merge** feature allows you to mass produce letters, envelopes, mailing labels, and other documents so they appear to be personalized.

■ The merge exercises in this lesson illustrate the mail merge feature using typical letters. However, other document types may be merged, such as reports or catalogs.

■ The merge process combines the form file with a data source file to produce a merged document.

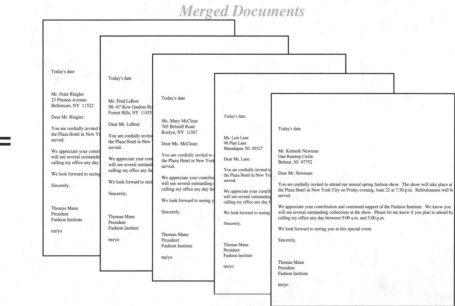

Form File

Today's date

FIELD(TITLE) FIELD(FIRST) FIELD(LAST)
FIELD(ADDRESS)
FIELD(CITY), FIELD(ST) FIELD(ZIP)

Dear FIELD(TITLE) FIELD(LAST):

You are cordially invited to attend our annual spring fashion show. The show will take place at the Plaza Hotel in New York City on Friday evening, June 22 at 7:30 p.m. Refreshments will be served.

We appreciate your contribution and continued support of the Fashion Institute. We know you will see several outstanding collections at the show. Please let me know if you plan to attend by calling my office any day between 9:00 a.m. and 5:00 p.m.

We look forward to seeing you at this special event.

Sincerely,

Thomas Mann
President
Fashion Institute

tm/yo

Data File

TITLE	FIRST	LAST	ADDRESS	CITY	ST	ZIP
Mr.	Peter	Ringler	23 Preston Avenue	Bellemore	NY	11522
Mr.	Fred	LeBost	98--67 Kew Gardens Road	Forest Hills	NY	11455
Ms.	Mary	McClean	765 Belmill Road	Roslyn	NY	11567
Ms.	Lois	Lane	98 Pine Lane	Manalapan	NJ	05527
Mr.	Kenneth	Newman	One Raintop Circle	Belmar	NJ	07752

Merged Documents

- The same data source document may then be used to produce the envelopes and/or labels, thus making it unnecessary to type the name and address list a second time.

- There are three steps in the mail merge process:

  1. Create the data source file that contains the variable information (actual names and addresses of those receiving the letter).

  2. Create a form file that contains the text that will not change and codes where variable information will be inserted (see illustration on previous page).

  3. Merge the form and data source files to create individual, personalized letters.

  ✓ *Before creating the data source file, you should create a rough copy of the form file you wish to send. This will help you determine what variables will be included in your letter. Then you can create and insert the proper merge codes in your data source file.*

Create a Data File

- The data source file contains the inside address and salutations of the people receiving the letter.

- A data file may contain many records. A **record** is a collection of related information about one person. The information in each record is divided into fields. When data is arranged in a table format, the fields are the columns of specific information. Records are the table rows.

- To create a data file, select Merge from the Tools menu. In the Merge dialog box that displays, click Place records in a table to organize your data into columns and rows (this format makes it easier to check the data file for accuracy), and then select Data File.

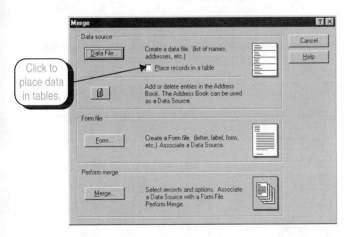

- If you have information in the current document, you are prompted to indicate whether you want to use the current document or open a new one.

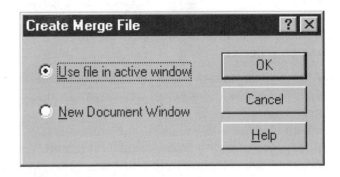

- The Create Data File dialog box appears. The field names are entered by typing the name of the field in the Name a field text box, then clicking Add. Each field is named for what will eventually be inserted into that location. For example, the first field in the inside address is named *title*, the second is named *first*, the third is named *last*, the fourth is named *address*, the fifth is named *city*, the sixth is named *state*, and the seventh is named *zip*.

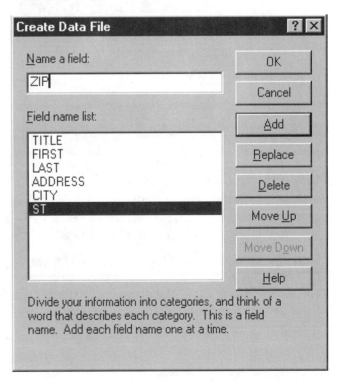

■ It is not necessary to enter variable information more than once where fields are used more than once. For example, in a typical letter, a person's last name is used in the inside address and the salutation. WordPerfect will insert the information that relates to LAST during the merge process.

■ After all field names are entered and you click OK, you can add the actual data (names and addresses) in the Quick Data Entry dialog box which follows. After entering the names and addresses of all the fields for the first record, click the New Record button and repeat the procedure for each person to receive a letter.

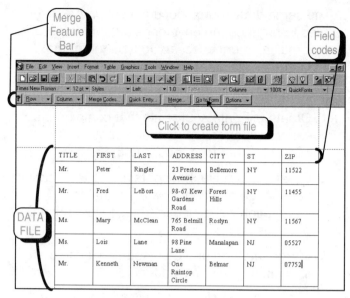

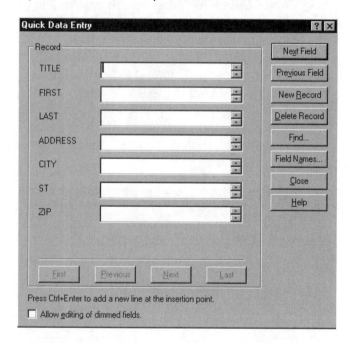

■ When all names and addresses have been entered, click the Close button and you will be prompted to save the data file. WordPerfect inserts the file extension **.dat** to saved data files.

■ Note the following illustration of records entered in a data file table format and the Merge Feature Bar which is automatically displayed. The Merge Feature Bar provides a quick way to access merge-related tasks.

■ Note, too, that no comma is inserted after the city since it will be inserted in the form file.

Create a Form File

■ The form file contains information that does not change. All formatting, punctuation, margins, spacing, etc., as well as graphics and paper size information, should be included in the form file.

■ A field code (that was created in the data source file) is inserted where variable information will be placed. Note the form letter below.

- To create a form letter file after creating the data file, click the Go To Form button on the Merge Feature Bar, and click the Create button in the Associate dialog box.

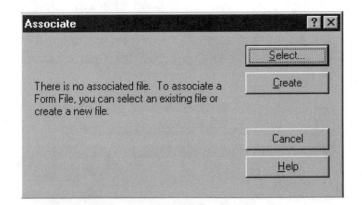

- Begin your letter by typing until you reach the first field location (first variable).

- Click the Insert Field button on the Merge Feature Bar and select an appropriate field name from the list. The field name will be inserted in your letter as a code. Repeat this procedure for each variable in your letter, and insert the appropriate field code from the drop-down list. Create spaces between field codes as you would if you were typing actual text. When the letter is completed, save it. WordPerfect inserts the file extension **.frm** to saved form letters.

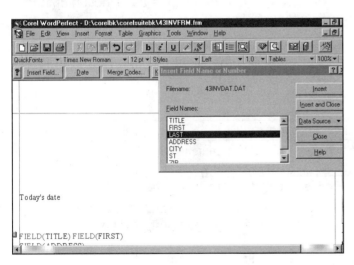

Merge the Form and Data Files

- Once the form and data files have been created, they may be merged to create a third document. The final, merged third document will appear as separate pages, each page representing a record. This document may be saved under its own filename. Saving the merged third document under its own filename is particularly helpful if you wish to edit individual pages of the document. For example, a postscript (PS) or special mailing notation might be added to selected letters.

- To merge the form and data files, click the Merge button on the Merge Feature bar.

- In the Perform Merge dialog box which follows, enter the filenames of the Form file and Data source file you wish to merge. The default Output merges the files to a new document window, showing you the merge on the screen and allowing you to save it as a third document. If you wish to change the output, click the Output button and make another selection.

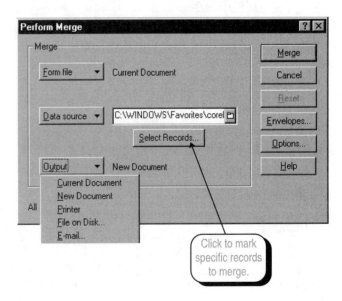

Merge Selected Records

- It is possible to merge selected records rather than all the records contained in the data file by marking them at the beginning of the merge process.

■ To mark specific records to merge, click the Mark records button in the Select Records dialog box. This produces a list of records in the Record list window with a check box next to each record. Click the check box to indicate the records you wish to merge.

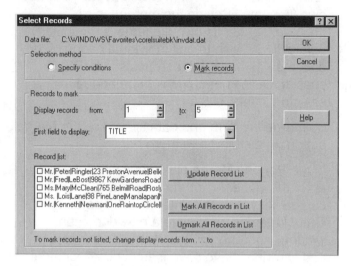

Merge with Conditions

■ In addition to merging specific records, you can define conditions that data records must meet to be included in the merge. For example, you might want to merge only those letters in a specific zip code or job title. Or, you might want to merge letters for only those individuals who owe more than $200 and live in New Jersey.

■ To define conditions for a merge, click the Specify conditions button in the Select Records dialog box.

■ A table displays with four rows which represent conditions and three columns which represent fields. To select a field to enter a condition, click the list button below the field column. For example, if you wanted to send letters to only those in a particular zip code, you would select ZIP from the drop-down list and enter the zip code you want selected in the Cond 1 text box.

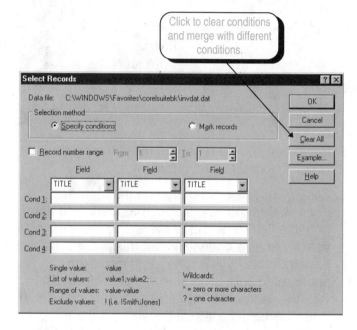

Click to clear conditions and merge with different conditions.

■ A record is selected for merge if it meets any one of the conditions you define as selection criteria. See table below.

■ Before merging again with different conditions, you must click the Clear All button in the Select Records dialog box.

Criteria	Records that will be Selected	Examples
Single value	All records in which the selected field matches the value.	NJ
List of values	All records in which the selected field matches one of the values.	NJ;NY
Range of values	All records in which the selected field is within the range of values.	NJ-NY
Excluded values	All records in which the selected field does not match the value.	!NY
Zero or more characters wildcard	All records in which the selected field is a possible match of the wildcard value.	New*
One-character wildcard	All records in which the selected field is a possible match of the wildcard value.	1008?

Prepare Envelopes While Merging

- WordPerfect makes it possible for you to create envelopes while merging a letter or other form file. (Creating envelopes and labels independent of a merge will be covered in Exercise 49.)

- After specifying the form and data filenames to merge in the Perform Merge dialog box, click the Envelopes button.

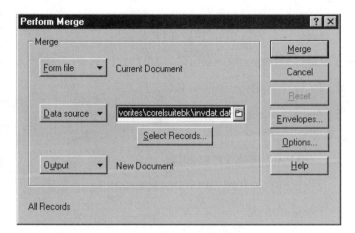

- In the Envelope dialog box which follows, specify the envelope size you require in the Envelope definitions text box, or select one from the drop-down list.

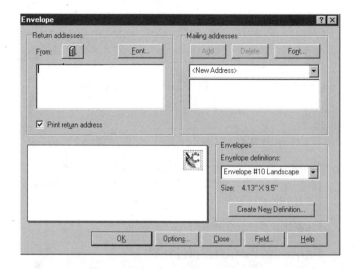

- Then, enter the fields in the Mailing addresses window that will be needed for the envelopes. That is, include only the fields used in the inside address. Click the field button and select a field to be inserted on the envelope, then click the Insert and Close button. Be sure to create spaces after each field as you would if you were typing actual names and addresses.

- The merged envelopes follow the last merged letter. After your letters have printed, be sure your printer is loaded with the necessary envelopes.

In Part I of this exercise, you will create and merge form and data source files. In Part II of this exercise, you will create form and data source files and merge selected records.

EXERCISE DIRECTIONS

Part I

1. Start with a clear screen.

2. Create a data file from the records shown in Illustration A on page 183. Format the data file as a table.

3. Use the default margins.

4. Begin the exercise on Ln 1".

5. Save the file; name it INVDAT.

6. Create the form letter file as shown in Illustration B inserting appropriate merge fields as shown.

7. Use the default margins.

8. Begin the exercise on approximately Ln 2.5".

9. Spell check.

10. Save the file; name it INVFRM.

11. Merge the form file with the data file to a new document.

12. Save the merged letters under a new filename: INVFI.

13. Close the document window.

Part II

1. Create the data file from the records shown in Illustration C on page 184. Format the data file as a table.

2. Use the default margins.

3. Begin the exercise on Ln 1".

4. Save the file; name it DUEDAT.

5. Create the form letter file as shown in Illustration D.

6. Use the default margins.

7. Begin the exercise on approximately Ln 2.5".

8. Spell check.

9. Save the file; name it DUEFRM.

10. Merge the form file with the data file to a new document.

11. Define the following criteria for the merge: merge and print letters for only those individuals who live in New Jersey and owe more than $200.

   HINT: In the ST field, enter the single value NJ; in the AMOUNT field, enter single value >200.

12. Print the full document (one copy of each merged letter).

13. Prepare an envelope for each letter in the merge.

14. Save the merged letters under a new filename: DUEFI.

15. Close the document window.

TITLE	FIRST	LAST	ADDRESS	CITY	ST	ZIP
Mr.	Peter	Ringler	23 Preston Avenue	Bellemore	NY	11522
Mr.	Fred	LeBost	98--67 Kew Gardens Road	Forest Hills	NY	11455
Ms.	Mary	McClean	765 Belmill Road	Roslyn	NY	11567
Ms.	Lois	Lane	98 Pine Lane	Manalapan	NJ	05527
Mr.	Kenneth	Newman	One Raintop Circle	Belmar	NJ	07752

ILLUSTRATION B

Today's date

FIELD(TITLE) FIELD(FIRST) FIELD(LAST)
FIELD(ADDRESS)
FIELD(CITY), FIELD(ST) FIELD(ZIP)

Dear FIELD(TITLE) FIELD(LAST):

You are cordially invited to attend our annual spring fashion show. The show will take place at the Plaza Hotel in New York City on Friday evening, June 22 at 7:30 p.m. Refreshments will be served.

We appreciate your contribution and continued support of the Fashion Institute. We know you will see several outstanding collections at the show. Please let me know if you plan to attend by calling my office any day between 9:00 a.m. and 5:00 p.m.

We look forward to seeing you at this special event.

Sincerely,

Thomas Mann
President
Fashion Institute

tm/yo

PART II

ILLUSTRATION C

TITLE	FIRST	LAST	ADDRESS	CITY	ST	ZIP	AMOUNT	DATE
Mr.	Johnathan	Price	One Gracie Terrace	New York	NY	10022	255.55	April 18
Ms.	Vanessa	Jackson	48 Endor Avenue	Brooklyn	NY	11221	256.98	March 1
Mr.	Kenneth	Hall	3 Windsor Drive	West Long Branch	NJ	07764	450.50	March 15
Mr.	Glenn	Babbin	187 Beach 147 Street	Queens	NY	11694	128.86	Februrary 28
Ms.	Stephanie	Eaton	137 Brighton Avenue	Perth Amboy	NJ	08861	615.75	February 15
Ms.	Shirley	Kee	876 Ocean Parkway	Seaside	NJ	07765	449.08	April 15

ILLUSTRATION D

Today's date

FIELD(TITLE) FIELD(FIRST) FIELD(LAST)
FIELD(ADDRESS)
FIELD(CITY), FIELD(ST) FIELD(ZIP)

Dear FIELD(TITLE) FIELD(LAST):

Just a brief reminder, FIELD(TITLE) FIELD(LAST), that your account is now past due. As you can see from the enclosed statement, you still have an outstanding balance of FIELD(AMOUNT). This balance was due on FIELD(DATE).

We need your cooperation so that we can continue to give you the service we have provided you for many years.

Please mail your remittance for FIELD(AMOUNT) today, so we are not forced to send your account to our collection agency.

Cordially,

Brenda Nadia
Collection Manager

bn/yo
Enclosure

KEYSTROKES

CREATE A DATA FILE

Shift + F9

1. Click **Tools** .... `Alt`+`T`
2. Click **Merge** .... `E`
3. Click **Place records**
   in a table .... `P`
4. Click **Data File** .... `D`
5. Click **Use file in active**
   window .... `U`

   ✓ *This screen will not appear if you open a clear screen when the merge command is accessed.*

   OR

   Click **New Document Window** .... `N`
   if necessary.
6. Click **OK** .... `Enter`
7. Click **Name a field** text box.... `Alt`+`N`
8. Type a first field name.

   EXAMPLE: TITLE
9. Click **Add** .... `Alt`+`A` or `Enter`
10. Repeat steps 8 and 9 for each field name used in form file.
11. Click **OK** .... `Enter`

    ✓ *The Quick Data Entry dialog box appears.*

To enter data:

a. Type data for first field in **Quick Data Entry** dialog box.
b. Click **Next Field** ..... `Alt`+`X` or `Enter`
c. Repeat steps a-b for each field to receive data.

After all fields are entered:

d. Click **New Record** `Alt`+`R` or `Enter`
e. Repeat steps a-d for each record.
f. Click **Close** .... `Alt`+`C`
g. Save the file .... `Enter`

   ✓ *Save this file as usual.*

CREATE A FORM FILE

1. Click **Go To Form** .... `Alt`+`Shift`+`G`
   on Merge Feature Bar.
2. Click **Create** .... `Alt`+`C`
3. Type first field location.
4. Click **Insert Field** .... `Alt`+`Shift`+`I`
   on Feature Bar.
5. Click on
   Field Name to Insert ... `Alt`+`f`, `↓`↑`
6. Click **Insert** .... `Alt`+`I`
7. Type next field location.

8. Type remainder of document.
9. Click **Close** .... `Alt`+`C`

   ✓ *Save this file as usual.*

MERGE FORM AND DATA FILES

1. Click **Merge** .... `Alt`+`Shift`+`M`
   on Merge Feature Bar.
2. Click **Form File** .... `Alt`+`F`
   drop-down list.
3. Enter name of **Form file** (or click on file arrow or drop-down list arrow to browse for file .... `Alt`+`F`, `↓`
4. Enter name of **Data source** (or click on file icon or drop-down list arrow to browse for file) .... `Alt`+`D`, `↓`
5. Change output, as desired... (*see below*)
6. Select records, as desired ... (*see below*)
7. Click **Merge** .... `Enter`

To change output:

a. Choose **Output** File
   text box .... `Alt`+`U`, `↓`
   - **Current Document** .... `C`
   - **New Document** .... `N`
   - **Printer** .... `P`
   - **File on Disk** .... `F`
   - **E-mail** .... `E`

To merge selected records:

a. Click **Select Records** .... `Alt`+`S`
b. Click **Mark Records** .... `Alt`+`A`
c. Click check box of each record you wish to merge .. `Alt`+`L`, `↑` or `↓`
d. Click **OK** .... `Enter`

MERGE WITH CONDITIONS

1. Click **Specify conditions** in **Select Records** dialog box .... `Alt`+`S`
2. Click **Field** text box .... `Alt`+`F`
   in first column.
3. Click **Field** list arrow and select a field on which you will set a condition .... `↓`↑`
4. Click **Cond 1** text box .... `Alt`+`1`
   Keyboard selection criteria.
5. Type selection criteria.
6. Select another field .... `Tab`
   on which to set a condition.

OR

Click on the **Cond 2** row .... `Alt`+`2`
to add another condition to the first field.
7. Click **Field** list arrow .... `Alt`+`E`, `↓`
   and select a field on which you will set a condition.
8. Type selection criteria.
9. Repeat steps 6-8 to select another field to set conditions or to add conditions to a field which has been selected.
10. Click **OK** .... `Enter`

CREATE ENVELOPES WHILE MERGING

1. Click **Tools** .... `Alt`+`T`
2. Click **Merge** .... `E`
3. Click **Merge** .... `M`
4. Enter name of **Form file** (or click on file arrow or drop-down list arrow icon to browse for file .... `Alt`+`F`, `↓`
5. Enter name of **Data source** (or click on file icon or drop-down list arrow to browse for file) .... `Alt`+`D`, `↓`
6. Set **Output file** .... `Alt`+`U`, `↓`, `N`
   as New Document.
7. Click **Envelopes** .... `Alt`+`E`
   The Envelope dialog box appears.
8. Select an envelope size from **Envelope Definitions** ..... `Alt`+`V`, `↓`
   (use your printer's default).
9. Click **Mailing Addresses** text box.
10. Click **Field** .... `Alt`+`I`

Data file's Field Name list appears.

11. Select first field name needed for address.
12. Click **Insert and Close** .... `Alt`+`N`
13. Repeat steps 10-12 for each field of mailing address.
14. Set desired **Return Address** criteria:
    - For no Return Address, deselect **Print return address** .... `Alt`+`U`
    - To include Return Address, select **Print return address** .... `Alt`+`U`

    AND
    - Type desired address in **Return addresses** text box.
15. Click **OK** .... `Enter`
    to return to **Perform Merge** box.
16. Click **Merge** .... `Alt`+`M`, `Enter`
    to perform merge.

Exercise 44

■ **Summary**

In this exercise, you will create a four-column tabular document in which the first and second columns are left aligned, the third is right aligned, and the fourth is decimal aligned.

EXERCISE DIRECTIONS

1. Create a form file and data file from the information on the right.

2. Format the form file using any letter style. Begin the letter approximately 2.5" from the top of the page.

3. Use the default margins and a serif 12-point font for the document.

4. Spell check the document.

5. Save the data file; name it BUYD.

6. Create the data file using a table file format.

7. Save the form file; name it BUYF.

8. Merge the form and data files to a new document.
   - Define the following criteria for your merge: merge and print letters for companies located in Texas or California (TX;CA).

9. Print the full document (one copy of each merged letter).

10. Save the merged letters under a new document name: BUYFI.

11. Close the document window.

Today's date

FIELD(TITLE) FIELD(FIRST) FIELD(LAST)
FIELD(ADDRESS)
FIELD(CITY), FIELD(ST) FIELD(ZIP)

Dear FIELD(TITLE) FIELD(LAST):

We received your order for FIELD(QUAN) FIELD(SOFTPKG) software packages. We will process it immediately. To expedite the order, we are arranging to have the software shipped directly from our warehouse in FIELD(CITY).

The cost of the software packages totals $FIELD(AMOUNT). We would appreciate payment as soon as you receive your order.

Thank you, FIELD(TITLE) FIELD(LAST), for your confidence in our company. I know you will be satisfied.

Sincerely,

Yolanda Reeves
Sales Manager

yr/yo

+

DATA FILE

TITLE	FIRST	LAST	ADDRESS	CITY	ST	ZIP	QUAN	SOFTPKG	AMOUNT
Mr.	Jason	Lochner	65 Linden Boulevard	Houston	TX	77069	two	Microsoft Office	810.76
Ms.	Rose	Zaffarano	645 Hammond Drive	Los Angeles	CA	90210	three	Excel	1,221.98
Ms.	Valerie	Vetri	70 Klondike Avenue	Cleveland	OH	44199	four	PageMaker	1,235.85
Mr.	Deepa	Lakani	87 Rockhill Road	San Diego	CA	90211	three	Corel Office 7	800.00
Ms.	Diane	Nordquist	43-98 Sela Drive	Dallas	TX	76767	two	MS Word 7	555.87

Exercise

45

■ **Create a Graphics Image**   ■ **Create a Text Box**

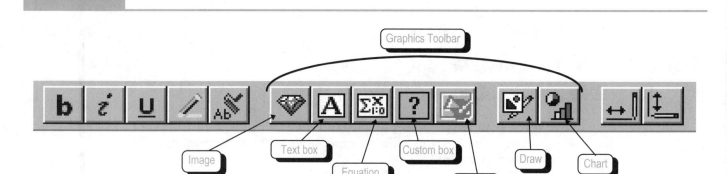

NOTES

Create a Graphics Image

■ **Graphics** are design elements, such as pictures (art), charts, and lines, used to make a visual statement. The ability to combine graphics and text enables you to create documents such as letterheads, newsletters, brochures, and flyers in which pictures contribute to the effectiveness of the message.

■ WordPerfect places each graphic image in a "box" without a border, which is called a **graphics image box**. A graphics box can contain an image, text, or an equation. (Equations will not be covered in this text.) Note the illustration below. The box on the left contains a graphic; the box on the right contains text. The "box" around the graphic is invisible because, by default, there is no box border.

■ WordPerfect provides hundreds of graphic image files from which to choose. Some are drawings (called **QuickArt** and/or **vector graphics**) while others are pictures (called **bit mapped images**). These files include QuickArt, pictures, backgrounds, borders, and textures. Note the example below of a drawn image vs. a picture image.

■ By default, these files are saved in the c:\corel\office7\graphics directory.

■ Graphics may be accessed by selecting <u>I</u>mage from the <u>G</u>raphics menu, or by clicking the Image button [◈] on the Graphics Toolbar.

- Double-click on a folder and graphic images relating to that folder display. Select the desired image and click Insert.

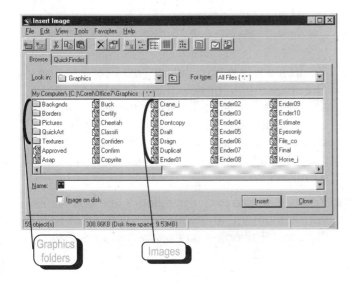

- You can also preview an image prior to inserting into a document. From the Insert Image dialog box, click View, Preview and then Content (to display the entire contents of the image) or Page View (to display it as it will appear on the page). Click once on the image you wish to preview. A thumbnail view will display in the preview window to the right.

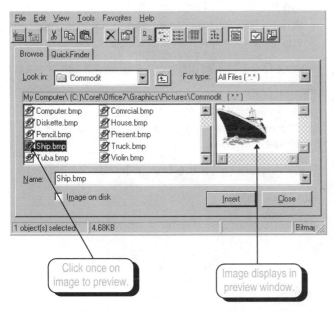

- When a graphic appears on screen, it displays with sizing handles. A QuickSpot also appears, giving you access to the most commonly used graphics editing features.

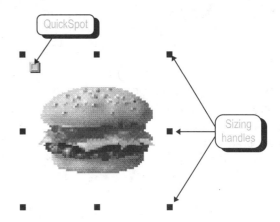

- When the graphics figure first appears, it is aligned at the left margin and presized by WordPerfect. The default size of the graphic varies, depending on the graphic selected.

- You may also create a graphic using the Drag to Create option on the Graphics menu. This feature allows you to draw the graphics box directly on your document before you select and insert the image, thus giving you control over the graphic's size and location.

- Select Drag to Create from the Graphics menu (a check mark appears next to the menu item).

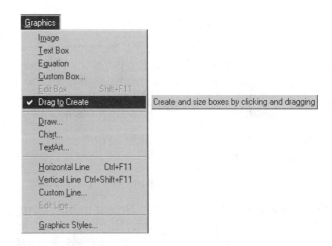

- Then, select Image from the Graphics menu. A special pointer appears. Position the pointer where you want the upper left corner of the box to begin and drag diagonally to the desired position for the lower right corner of the box. Then, release the mouse button. The Insert Image dialog box automatically appears for you to select the image you want inserted into the box.

- Once activated, the Drag to Create option remains selected until you deselect it. Reselect Drag to Create from the Graphics menu to deselect it.

- You can reduce, enlarge, stretch, move, or delete the graphic when the sizing handles are displayed. The sizing handles indicate that the graphic is selected and in Edit mode. You will learn to edit a graphic in the next exercise.

Create a Text Box

- A **text box** is typically used for setting off special text such as tables, charts, sidebars, and callouts. WordPerfect automatically applies a thick top and bottom border to a text box.

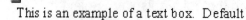

This is an example of a text box. Default border options are "thick" for top and bottom and none for the sides.

- To create a text box, select <u>T</u>ext Box from the Graphics menu, or select the Text Box button [A] on the Graphics Toolbar. When the text box first appears, it is aligned at the right margin and presized by WordPerfect. Like the graphic box, it appears with sizing handles and a QuickSpot.

- You can resize and reposition a text box within your document, and you can edit the text within the box. Editing a text box will be covered in Exercise 46.

In this exercise, you will import two graphics using the default position and size and one graphic using the Drag to Create option. In addition, you will create a text box, using the default position and size.

EXERCISE DIRECTIONS

1. Start with a clear screen.

2. With the insertion point at the top of your screen, import the MONKEY graphic. (Select Image from the Graphics menu, and from the Look In box select Corel/Office7/Graphics/QuickArt/Premium/Outdoors/Animals/Monkey.)

3. Click anywhere off the image to deselect it (remove handles).

4. Press the Enter key 10 times.

5. Import the TREE graphic. (Select Image from the Graphics menu, Pictures/Nature/Tree.)

6. Click anywhere off the image to deselect it.

7. Press the Enter key 10 times.

8. Create a text box and enter the following text using the default font:
   - What a beautiful day to sit beneath a tree and enjoy the wonderful surroundings.

9. Select Drag to Create from the Graphics menu.

10. Drag to create a graphics box to the right of the other graphics and insert the CLOUD image (Pictures/Nature/Cloud) as shown in the exercise.

11. Click anywhere off the image to deselect it.

12. Print one copy.

13. Save the exercise; name it RELAX.

What a beautiful day to sit beneath a tree and enjoy the wonderful surroundings.

KEYSTROKES

IMPORT A GRAPHIC

F11

1. Click **Image** button on Graphics Toolbar .... 💎

    OR

    a. Click **Graphics** .... `Alt` + `G`

    b. Click **Image** .... `M`

2. Select the **Graphics** folder. (Look in Corel/Office7/Graphics.)

3. Double-click the desired graphics folder.

4. Click once on desired graphic file and click **Insert** .... `Enter`

    OR

    Double click on desired graphic file.

DRAG TO CREATE

1. Click **Graphics** .... `Alt` + `G`

2. Click **Drag to Create** .... `O`

3. Click **Graphics** .... `Alt` + `G`

    ✓ *You will see a check next to Drag to Create which means the feature is selected.*

4. Click **Image** .... `M`

5. Drag cursor to define area to receive graphic.

6. Select image to be inserted.

DESELECT DRAG TO CREATE

1. Click **Graphics** .... `Alt` + `G`

2. Click **Drag to Create** .... `O`

CREATE A TEXT BOX

Alt + F11

1. Click **Text Box** button Graphics Toolbar .... `A`

    OR

    a. Place insertion point where you want text box (vertically on the page).

    b. Click **Graphics** .... `Alt` + `G`

    c. Click **Text Box** .... `T`

    ✓ *A text box appears with active insertion point.*

2. Type text into box.

3. Click anywhere off the text box.

4. Select image to be inserted.

Exercise

46

- ■ **Select a Graphics Box or a Text Box**
- ■ **Size a Graphics Box or a Text Box**
- ■ **Position (Move) a Graphics Box or Text Box**
- ■ **Delete a Graphics Box or Text Box**
- ■ **Copy a Graphics Box or a Text Box** ■ **Rotate a Text box**

NOTES

■ As noted in the previous exercise, a graphics box or text box appears with sizing handles after it is imported. To remove the sizing handles, click anywhere off the graphic.

Select a Graphics Box or a Text Box

■ The sizing handles must be displayed to edit the graphics box or text box; that is, to delete, copy or change its size or position.

■ Clicking on a box will select it, thus displaying the sizing handles.

Size a Graphics Box or a Text Box

■ To size a graphics or text box using the mouse, point to one of the sizing handles. When the pointer becomes a double-headed arrow ↔, you may change the size or shape of the image by dragging the sizing handle.

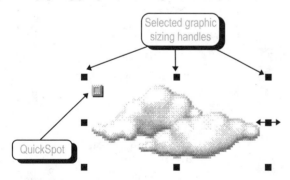

■ When any one of the four corner handles are dragged on a graphics box or text box, the size of the entire image changes, but the proportions are retained. When any one of the four middle handles are dragged, only the height or the width changes, thus changing the proportions or scale of the image and giving it a different appearance.

■ WordPerfect provides a Graphics Toolbar which contains buttons to make working with graphics more convenient. To access the Graphics Toolbar, point to the current Toolbar, right-click and select Graphics.

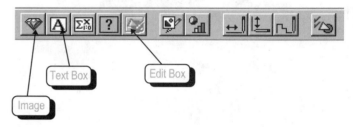

■ The size of an image box or text box may also be adjusted by a specific amount. Select the image and click on the QuickSpot, or select Edit Box from the Graphics menu to access the Edit Box dialog box.

- Select the Size button in the Edit Box dialog box and enter the desired width and height by typing the values in the text boxes. Choose Full to fill the page with the image, or choose Maintain proportions to create a proportioned image.

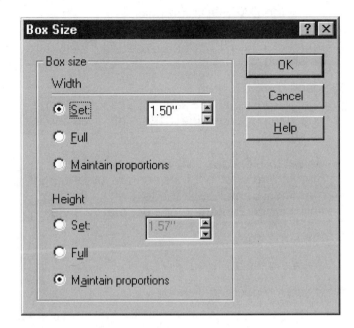

Position (Move) a Graphics Box or Text Box

- To position a graphics or text box using the mouse, point, click and hold down the mouse button within the selected box. When the pointer becomes a **four-headed arrow** ✛, drag the box to the desired location. Or, you may click the Position button in the Edit Box dialog box and specify the desired Horizontal or Vertical position in the Box Position dialog box.

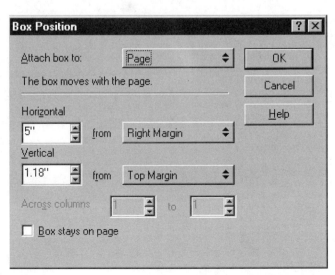

Delete a Graphics Box or a Text Box

- To delete a graphics or text box, select the box to display the sizing handles, and press the Delete key or click the Cut button ✂ on the Toolbar.

Copy a Graphics Box or a Text Box

- To copy a graphics or text box, select the box, and select Copy from the Edit menu or click the Copy button 📋 on the Toolbar. Position the insertion point where the copied box should appear. Then, select Paste from the Edit menu or click the Paste button 📋 on the Toolbar.

Rotate a Text Box

- The text box may be rotated counterclockwise in 90-degree increments by selecting Content from the Edit Box dialog box and selecting a rotation amount in the Box Content dialog box which follows.

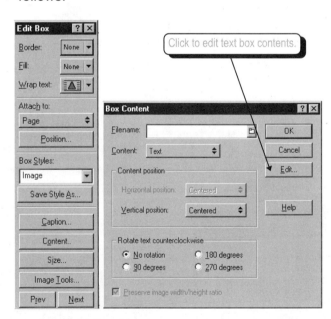

- To edit the text within the box, select Edit from the Box Content dialog box. You can then change the alignment, font size or style of the text using the methods learned previously.

In this exercise, you will edit the graphics inserted in the previous exercise to create a scene.

EXERCISE DIRECTIONS

✓   *It will be helpful to view the page in full view while working through the exercise (View, Zoom, Full Page).*

1. Open RELAX.

2. Select the tree graphic. Size it to 5" wide x 6" high, and position it on the left bottom so the tree trunk rests on the bottom margin, as shown.

3. Select the monkey graphic, and move it beneath the tree. Reduce the size proportionally (by stretching a corner handle) so that the monkey fits better under the tree.

4. Select the cloud graphic, and move it above the tree. Stretch it (by dragging the handles) so that it covers the tree area.

5. Insert the DAFFODIL graphic (QuickArt/Premium/Outdoors/Flowers/Daffodil), and size it to .75" wide x .75" high. Position it as shown.

6. Insert the SUN graphic (QuickArt/Premium/Seasonal/Seasons/Sun), and size it to 1.5" wide x 1.5" high. Position it as shown.

7. Select the text box. Move it below the top margin and stretch it between the left and right margins. Center-align the text within the box, and change the font to any decorative style.

8. Print one copy.

9. Save the file as RELAXING.

10. Close the document window.

WHAT A BEAUTIFUL DAY TO SIT BENEATH A TREE AND ENJOY THE WONDERFUL SURROUNDINGS.

KEYSTROKES

DISPLAY GRAPHICS TOOLBAR

1. Point to current Toolbar with mouse.
2. Right-click.
3. Select **Graphics**.

SELECT A GRAPHICS BOX OR TEXT BOX

Shift+F11

Click graphic.
OR
1. Click **Graphics** .... `Alt` + `G`
2. Click **Edit Box** .... `E`
OR
Click QuickSpot.
OR
Click **Edit Box** button on Graphics Toolbar .... 🖾

DELETE A GRAPHICS BOX

Ctrl + X

1. Select graphic to delete (see above).
2. Press **Delete** key .... `Del`
OR
3. Click Cut button on Toolbar .... ✂️

POSITION A GRAPHICS BOX

Select graphic and drag to desired position using the mouse.
OR
1. Select the graphic (see above).
2. Open **Edit Box** dialog box by clicking **Edit Box** button on Graphics Toolbar .... 🖾
OR
Click **QuickSpot**.
3. Click **Position** .... `P`
To position horizontally:
a. Click **Horizontal** .... `Alt` + `Z`
b. Type desired horizontal measurement.

c. Click **horizontal from** list box to select from where graphic placement should be measured .... `Alt` + `F`, `↓`
d. Click a placement option:
- **Left Edge of Page** .... `L`
- **Left Margin** .... `M`
- **Right Margin** .... `R`
- **Center of Margins** .... `C`
- **Left Column** .... `L`
- **Right Column** .... `R`
- **Centered in Columns** .... `C`

To position vertically:
a. Click **Vertical** .... `Alt` + `V`
b. Type desired vertical measurement.

c. Click **vertical from** list to select from where graphic placement should be measured ... `Alt` + `R`, `↓`
d. Click a placement option:
- **Top of Page** .... `T`
- **Top Margin** .... `M`
- **Bottom Margin** .... `B`
- **Center of Margins** .... `C`
4. Click **OK** .... `Enter`

SIZE A GRAPHICS BOX

1. Select the graphic (see above).
2. Drag the sizing handles to desired box size.
OR
1. Select the graphic.
2. Open **Edit Box** dialog box by clicking **Edit Box** button on Graphics Toolbar .... 🖾
OR
Click **QuickSpot**.
3. Click **Size** .... `I`
To set height and width:
a. Click **Set Width** .... `Alt` + `S`
b. Type desired width.
c. Click **Set Height** text box .... `Alt` + `E`
d. Type desired height.

To have graphic fill page:
- Click **Full** for **Width** and **Height** .... `Alt` + `F`, `Alt` + `U`
4. Click **OK** .... `Enter`

COPY A GRAPHICS BOX

Ctrl + C, Ctrl + V

1. Select the graphic.
2. Click **Edit** .... `Alt` + `E`
3. Click **Copy** .... `C`
4. Click location on page where copied graphic should appear.
5. Click **Edit** .... `Alt` + `E`
6. Click **Paste** .... `P`

ROTATE TEXT BOX

1. Select a text box to rotate.
2. Click **Edit Box** button on the Graphics Toolbar .... 🖾
OR
Click **QuickSpot**.
3. Click **Size** .... `I`
4. Click **Width: Maintain proportions** .... `Alt` + `M`
5. Click **Height: Maintain proportions** .... `Alt` + `A`
6. Click **OK** .... `Enter`
7. Click **Content** .... `O`
8. Select desired degree of rotation:
- **No Rotation** .... `N`
- **90 Degrees** .... `9`
- **180 Degrees** .... `1`
- **270 Degrees** .... `2`
9. Click **OK** .... `Enter`
10. Close Edit Box by clicking anywhere on the screen.

Exercise 47

■ **Text Wrap Options** ■ **Captions** ■ **TextArt**

NOTES

Text Wrap Options

■ WordPerfect provides you with several options for wrapping text around a graphics box or text box. You can control the type and position of the text wrap. Note the **text wrap options** illustrated below:

Contour/Right Side

Contour Both Sides

Neither Side

No Wrap

Square/Largest side

Square/Left Side

Square/Right Side

Square Both Sides

Contour/Largest Side

Contour/Left Side

■ To select text wrap options, insert the graphic into text, select it, and click the QuickSpot or click the Edit Box button on the Graphics Toolbar. In the Edit Box dialog box which follows, click the arrow next to the Wrap text option and select a wrapping style.

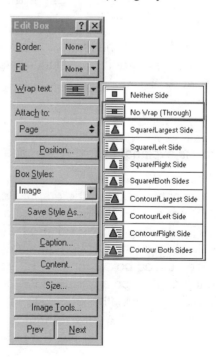

■ The Contour Both Sides wrapping option flows text in a silhouette pattern up to and around the image.

■ The No Wrap (Through) option allows the text to overlay the graphic. When working with border graphics, you must use the No wrap option if you want the text to appear inside the border.

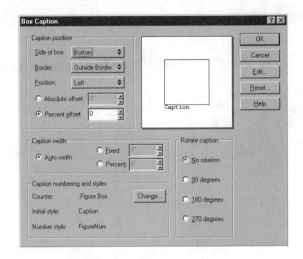

■ Click the Edit button to type a caption. The Caption Editor appears with a box or figure number already entered and the insertion point in place for you to type the caption. Normal editing and formatting features apply here. For instance, to delete the figure number, press the Backspace key.

TextArt

■ WordPerfect's **TextArt** feature can create striking text effects for special uses, such as flyer headlines or logos. Waves, pennants, circles, and crescents are among the included effects.

■ To access TextArt, select TextArt from the Graphics menu. The TextArt program enables you to create an image which will then be imported into the current document.

■ At the TextArt screen, you can enter up to 58 characters on one, two, or three lines, or you can select text to be used for TextArt then access the TextArt feature.

■ When using text wrap, carefully proofread the text that flows around the graphic. You may need to adjust the graphic position to avoid awkward word breaks.

Captions

■ A **caption** is explanatory text that appears below a graphic.

■ To create a caption, select the graphic, click on the QuickSpot or click the Edit Box button on the Graphics Toolbar 🖾. In the Edit Box dialog box which follows, click the Caption button. In the Box Caption dialog box which follows, you can position the caption on any side of the box. By default, the caption width matches the graphic width, but you may set your own width. You may rotate the caption to appear along any side of the box.

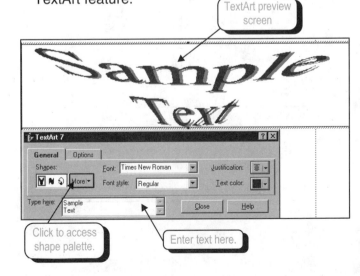

- Once the text to be used for TextArt has been identified, select a font, font style, justification, and capitalization style. Select a TextArt shape from the palette of shapes. You may also change the text color and choose numerous design enhancements. For the image itself, you may set a rotation degree, width, and height. These options may be accessed by clicking the appropriate button or selecting it from the menu.

- The TextArt image is placed in a graphics box which can then be positioned and sized like any other graphics box on the page.

In this exercise, you will enhance a previously created document by adding TextArt and graphics (with and without captions).

EXERCISE DIRECTIONS

Part I

1. Open ☐BROWN or ☐47BROWN.

2. Display the Graphics Toolbar.

3. Select the heading, Printing with a Personal Touch, and create a wave TextArt design as shown in Illustration A. Choose any desired script font.
   - Size the text art graphic so your document stays on one page.

4. Insert the DOCUMENT graphic (Pictures/Business/Document) as shown:
   - Use the default size.
   - Select the No Wrap option.

5. Insert the CLIPNOTE graphic (Quickart/Premium/Business/Supplies/Clipnote) as shown:
   - Size it to .75" wide x .75" high.
   - Position it in the right corner as shown.
   - Add a centered caption using the default font as shown.
   - Copy the graphic.
   - Position the copy in the left corner as shown.

6. Print one copy.

7. Close the file; save the changes.

Part II

1. Start with a clear screen.

2. Use the default margins.

3. Insert the BD_drvin border graphic (Borders/Bd_drvin). Size the border width and height to Full.

4. Select the No Wrap option.

5. Center the text as shown using the font sizes and styles indicated in Illustration B.

6. Preview the document.

7. Print one copy.

8. Save the file; name it NEWFILM.

Printing with a Personal Touch...

Whether *you are creating a one-time special event or developing a long-term corporate identity program, it is important to demonstrate quality and professionalism in your printed materials. At WILLIAM BROWN, you will find a Special Services Center, designed to handle your custom printing needs. We have been in business for over 30 years. Our commitment to quality and service stands tall in a very competitive marketplace. Let WILLIAM BROWN help you with your personal printing needs for*

BUSINESS CARDS
STATIONERY
INVITATIONS AND ANNOUNCEMENTS
RUBBER STAMPS
BUSINESS FORMS
BINDERS, TABS FOLDERS
SIGNS, BANNERS, NAME PLAQUES
GREETING CARDS
LABELS AND DECALS

Our Services include:

BUSINESS FORMS

Internal business forms, carbonless invoices, work orders, receipts, memos, request forms and more.

COMPLETE BUSINESS PACKAGE

Create a corporate identity package including business cards, letterhead and envelopes.

PRESENTATIONS AND MEETING MATERIALS

Customized imprints on three-ring binders, divider tabs and covers.

SALES AND MERCHANDISING SUPPORT

Printed announcements, banners, flyers and brochures.

SPECIAL OCCASIONS

Invitations, matchbooks and napkins for weddings, anniversaries, graduations and other special events.

WILLIAM
BROWN

WILLIAM BROWN, INC.
122 West 28 Street
New York, NY 10033
(212) 444-4444

WILLIAM
BROWN

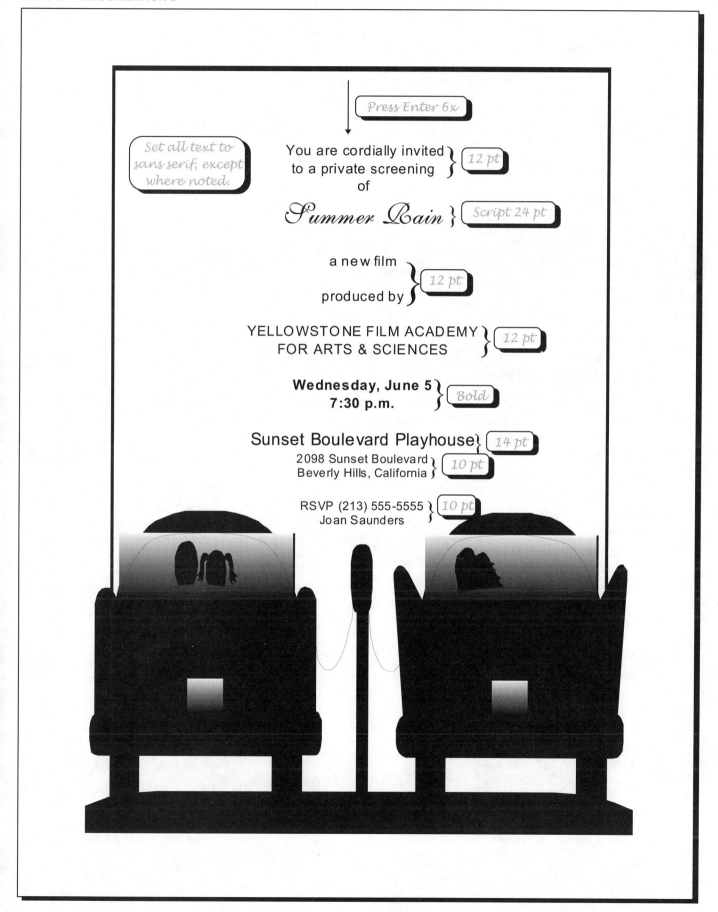

KEYSTROKES

WRAP TEXT

1. Select graphic.
2. Click **Edit Box** button on Graphics Toolbar..
3. Click **Wrap text**..................... `Alt`+`W`
4. Click the drop-down arrow.
5. Select a Wrapping option: .... `↓` `↑`
   - **Neither Side**
   - **No Wrap (Through)**
   - **Square/Largest Side**
   - **Square/Right Side**
   - **Square/Both Sides**
   - **Contour/Largest Side**
   - **Contour/Left Side**
   - **Contour/Right Side**
   - **Contour/Both Sides**

ADD A CAPTION

1. Select graphic.
2. Click **Edit Box** button on Graphics Toolbar..
3. Click **Caption**......................... `Alt`+`C`
4. Click **Edit**.............................. `Alt`+`E`
5. Backspace to delete the figure number.
6. Type and format caption text.
7. Click anywhere outside the graphic.

REMOVE A CAPTION

1. Select graphic.
2. Click **Edit Box** button on Graphics Toolbar..
3. Click **Caption**......................... `Alt`+`C`
4. Click **Reset**............................ `Alt`+`R`
5. Click **OK** at warning box .... `Enter`
6. Click **OK**............................... `Enter`

CREATE A TEXTART IMAGE

1. Place insertion point where you want to insert the image.
2. Click **Graphics**...................... `Alt`+`G`
3. Click **TextArt**................................ `X`
4. Click in text box and enter desired text.
5. Click **Font** list arrow .... `Alt`+`F` and select desired font.
6. Click **Font style** list arrow....... `Alt`+`S` and select desired style, if applicable.
7. Click desired shape on **Shape** palette .... `Alt`+`A`, `←` `→`

To make optional changes:

a. Click the **Options** tab in the TextArt 7 dialog box.
b. Click **Pattern**..................... `Alt`+`P`
c. Click **Shadow**..................... `Alt`+`S`
d. Click **Insert Character** .... `Alt`+`I`
e. Click **Outline** .... `Alt`+`O` to select outline color and thickness.

To rotate text box:

a. Click **Rotation** button (on the Options tab).
b. Click in TextArt text box and drag on a rotation handle in desired direction.

To return to your document:

a. Click **Close** to exit the TextArt 7 dialog box.......................... `Alt`+`C`
b. Click anywhere outside the text image.

Exercise

48

- **Watermark** ■ **Horizontal and Vertical Lines**
- **Drop Capital** ■ **Reverse Text**

NOTES

Watermark

- A **watermark** is a lightened graphics image or text that prints in the background, behind the printed text. A watermark can appear on every page of your document or on selected pages. You can also create two watermarks that will appear on alternating pages.

- WordPerfect provides a **Design Tools Toolbar** which contains buttons to make working with special effects more convenient. To display the Design Tools Toolbar, right-click the Toolbar and select Design Tools.

Design Tools Toolbar

- A watermark may be accessed by selecting Watermark from the Format menu or by clicking the Watermark button 🔲 on the Design Tools Toolbar.

- When the watermark window appears (it is blank), you can insert a graphic image, a file, or typed text. You can edit text content, apply font changes and use most editing features within the watermark window. A **Watermark Feature Bar** appears at the top of the watermark window.

- If you choose to insert a graphics image as a watermark, select the Image button on the Watermark Feature Bar.

- To adjust the shading of a watermark image or watermark text, select the Shading button on the Watermark Feature Bar. This can be done before or after the graphic image is selected, or it

may be done by editing the watermark after it is in the document window.

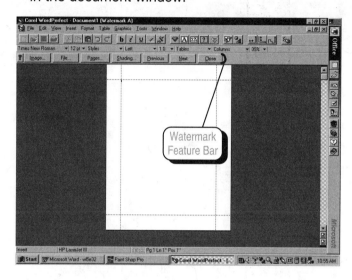

- Page borders, along with any of the other graphic images, may be used as watermarks.

Horizontal and Vertical Lines

- You can use the **Horizontal and Vertical Lines** feature to insert horizontal and vertical lines in your document. Lines are used to create designs, to separate parts of a document, or to draw attention to a particular place.

- You may adjust the position, length, and thickness of the lines. You may select decorative line styles such as triple, thick-thin, and dashed.

- Lines may be inserted by selecting Horizontal Line or Vertical Line from the Graphics menu. WordPerfect automatically inserts a full line (a single line that extends from the left to the right margin, or a single line that extends from the top to the bottom margin) at the insertion point position.

- To create a specified line thickness, size, or style, you may create a custom line. Or you may select an existing line (Note that handles appear), then select Edit Li<u>ne</u> from the <u>G</u>raphics menu.

- In the Edit Graphics Line dialog box which appears, you may specify the horizontal position and length of the line.

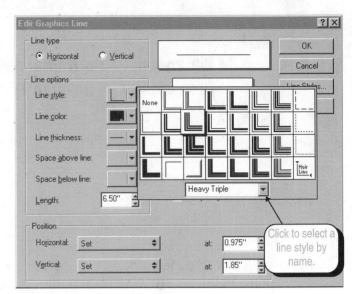

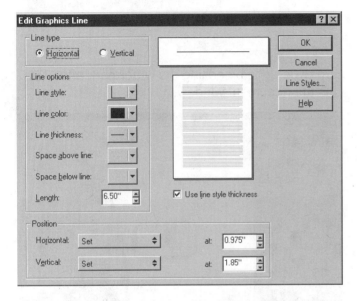

- You may determine the amount of spacing to leave blank above and/or below a horizontal line by selecting the Space <u>a</u>bove/<u>b</u>elow line list arrow(s) and choosing a spacing amount.

- You may also specify the thickness of the line by selecting the Line <u>t</u>hickness list arrow and choosing a line thickness, or you may enter a measurement in the text box.

- You may select a Line <u>s</u>tyle by sight or by name. When you click the Line <u>s</u>tyle list arrow, a palette of defined styles displays. Select a desired line style from the palette or click the Line <u>s</u>tyle name list arrow and select a line style by name.

- To move, size, or change the thickness of a line with the mouse, click to select it, then drag it to a new position. Or, you may drag one of the sizing handles to enlarge or reduce its width and/or length.

Drop Capital

- A **drop capital** is an enlarged capital letter that drops below the first line of body text. It is usually the first letter of a paragraph. It is often used to draw the reader's attention to chapter beginnings, section headings, and main body text.

> Drop capitals are large, decorative letters often used to mark the beginning of a document, section or chapter. Drop caps are set to a much larger font than the text, and often span the height of three or four lines.

- Drop caps may be created before or after typing a new paragraph. To apply a drop capital to text before it is typed, click the Drop Cap button 🄳 on the Design Tools Toolbar, or select D<u>r</u>op Cap from the Fo<u>r</u>mat menu and type the first few words of the paragraph. To apply a drop capital to existing text, position the insertion point anywhere in the first paragraph, click the Drop Cap button on the Design Tools Toolbar, or select D<u>r</u>op Cap from the Fo<u>r</u>mat menu.

- After accessing the Drop Cap feature, a **Drop Cap Feature Bar** appears, giving you options to edit your drop capital. You may select a different predefined drop cap style or you can customize the drop capital by changing the font style, height and position, or you may wish to add a border around it.

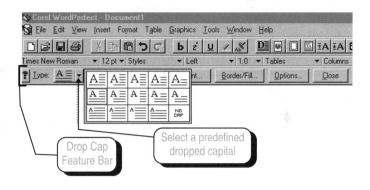

Drop Cap Feature Bar

Select a predefined dropped capital

Reverse Text

- **Reverse text** is text that appears white against a dark background. Black letters on a white background are converted to white (or colored) letters on a black background.

REVERSE TEXT

- To reverse text, click the Reverse Text button on the Design Tools Toolbar, or select Macro from the Tools menu and choose reverse.wcm. (The reverse.wcm macro automates the process of

reversing text.) In the Reverse Text Options dialog box which follows, choose a text color and fill style/color option.

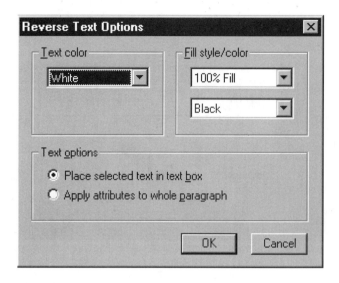

- WordPerfect places text which has been reversed in a graphics box. If you click on the reversed text, handles appear. The graphics box may then be edited like any other graphics or text box.

In this exercise, you will enhance a previously created document using drop capitals, horizontal and vertical lines, and reverse text.

EXERCISE DIRECTIONS

Part I

1. Open ☞TIVOLI or ☐48TIVOLI.
2. Insert the SAXOPHONE graphic (QuickArt/Premium/Symbols/Instruments/Saxopone) as a watermark image.
3. Create a drop capital on the first letter in the paragraph (as shown on the right using any desired drop-cap style.
4. Create reverse text for The October Program as shown in Illustration A.
5. Create a horizontal line below the title using a thick double line style.
6. Print one copy.
7. Preview the document. Make any adjustments necessary to keep the document on one page.
8. Close the file; save the changes.

Part II

1. Open ☞SURVIVAL or ☐48SURVIV.
2. Delete the title and the blank space above the first line of text.

3. Re-create the title as shown in Illustration B using any desired TextArt design. Position the TextArt at the top margin.
4. Change the line spacing for the first two paragraphs to single.
5. Change the font size to 12 point. Change the font style to sans serif.
6. Create a drop capital on the first letter in the first paragraph as shown.
7. Create reverse text on the side headings as shown.
8. Insert the PEN PUSH graphic (QuickArt/Premium/Cartoons/White Collar/Pen Push) as a watermark image. Lighten the graphic image. (Select Edit in the Watermark dialog box, click Shading; change image shading amount to 10%.)
9. Make any necessary adjustments to keep text on one page.
10. Preview the document.
11. Print one copy.
12. Save the document as SURVIVAL2; close the file.

S W I N G I N G   J A Z Z   I N
W O N D E R F U L   C O P E N H A G E N

The Slukefter Jazz Club in Tivoli is the favorite haunt of jazz enthusiasts during the garden's open season. The jazz club is now also to open its doors outside the Tivoli season, presenting a spectacular live-swing-jazz program during the autumn and winter months. From October 5th and every weekend until December 28th the Slukefter Jazz Club will offer exciting listening and dancing to great jazz performed by the most outstanding musicians.

The October Program:

Friday 4
Jazzin Jacks, Sweden

Saturday 5
Jazzin Jacks, Sweden

Friday 11
Papa Bue's Viking Jazz Band

Friday 18
Fressors Big City Band

Saturday 19
Ricardo's Jazzmen

The Swinging Jazz
Produced by Slukefter Jazz Club
In Cooperation with the
Wonderful Copenhagen Convention & Visitors' Bureau

Sponsors:
Bijan Imports
and
Danisco Silversmiths
Copenhagen, Denmark

Small Business Survivial Tips

Owning a small company is an all-consuming experience. It requires the owner to continually evaluate the business's potential and problems. All businesses experience problems. Accurate diagnosis of the intensity and cause of the company problem is essential to resolving and preventing its recurrence.

How you go about diagnosing your business problems will depend on the nature of your company and the symptoms that are being experienced.

MOST COMMON FINANCIAL DIFFICULTIES

Expenses exceed revenues.

Overly rapid growth that outpaces a company's operating systems, the skills and abilities of its personnel, etc.

Poor management skills and company know-how among company owners and key management.

Failure to maximize a company's competitive strengths and to capitalize on its competitor's weaknesses.

ACTIONS TO CONSIDER

Analyze all expenses including company-related travel or entertainment, subscriptions, the purchase of supplies, raw materials or equipment, insurance, the use of outside professionals, phone services, etc., to determine which can be reduced, delayed or eliminated.

Eliminate or discontinue products or services that are not making money. Do a careful analysis of this during each season of the year.

Reduce staff salaries and/or benefits. Do not do both at the same time; it can be very demoralizing.

Cut prices. This action alone can sometimes provide the cash a company needs to turn itself around.

KEYSTROKES

CREATE A WATERMARK

1. If in Draft view:
   a. Click **View** .... `Alt`+`V`
   b. Click **Page** .... `P`

   OR

   a. Click **View** .... `Alt`+`V`
   b. Click **Two Page** .... `W`

2. Click **Format** .... `Alt`+`R`
3. Click **Watermark** .... `W`
4. Click **Watermark A** .... `A`

   OR

   Click **Watermark B** .... `B`

5. Click **Create** .... `C`

   ✓ *Watermark Feature bar and Watermark window appear.*

6. Click **Pages** on Watermark
   Feature bar .... `Alt`+`Shift`+`A`
7. Make desired option placement:
   - **Odd Pages** .... `Alt`+`O`
   - **Even Pages** .... `Alt`+`E`
   - **Every Page** .... `Alt`+`V`
8. Click **Image** on Watermark
   Feature bar .... `Alt`+`Shift`+`M`
9. Select image to be inserted.
10. Click **Insert** .... `Enter`

   To change shading:
   a. Click **Shading** .... `Alt`+`Shift`+`S`
   b. Click **Text shading** .... `Alt`+`T`
   c. Type desired shade amount or click
      increment arrows .... `↓`/`↑`
   d. Click **Image shading** .... `Alt`+`I`
   e. Type desired shade amount or click
      increment arrows .... `↓`/`↑`
   f. Click **OK** .... `Enter`

11. Click **Close** on Watermark Feature
    bar .... `Alt`+`Shift`+`C`
12. Type document text as desired.

CREATE DEFAULT VERTICAL OR HORIZONTAL LINE

Ctrl + F11

1. Place insertion point at desired vertical
   line position.
2. Click **Graphics** .... `Alt`+`G`
3. Click **Vertical Line** .... `V`

   OR

   Click **Horizontal Line** .... `H`

CREATE A CUSTOM VERTICAL OR HORIZONTAL LINE

1. Follow steps 1-2, above.
2. Click **Custom Line** .... `L`
3. Click **Vertical** .... `Alt`+`V`

   OR

   Click **Horizontal** .... `Alt`+`O`

4. Select one or more of the following
   options:
   a. Click **Line style** button .... `Alt`+`S`
      - Click drop-down arrow ...... `↓`/`↑`
   b. Click **Line color** .... `Alt`+`C`
      - Click drop-down arrow ...... `↓`/`↑`
   c. Click **Line thickness** .... `Alt`+`T`
      button.
      - Click drop-down arrow ...... `↓`/`↑`
   d. Click **Length** .... `Alt`+`L`, `↓`/`↑`
      text box

   Custom vertical options:
   a. Click **Horizontal** pop-up
      list .... `Alt`+`R`
      - Click a position option .... `↓`/`↑`
   b. Click **Vertical** pop-up
      list .... `Alt`+`E`
      - Click a position option .... `↓`/`↑`
   c. From Line options,
      click **Border offset** button ... `Alt`+`B`
      - Click drop-down arrow .... `↓`/`↑`

   Custom horizontal options:
   a. Click **Horizontal** pop-up
      list .... `Alt`+`R`
      - Click a position option .... `↓`/`↑`
   b. Click **Vertical** pop-up list .... `Alt`+`E`
      - Click a position option .... `↓`/`↑`

   c. From Line options, enter desired
      spacing option:
      - **Space above line** .... `Alt`+`A`
        Click drop-down arrow .... `↓`/`↑`
      - **Space below line** .... `Alt`+`B`
        Click drop-down arrow .... `↓`/`↑`

5. Click **OK** .... `Enter`

DROP CAPITAL

1. Place insertion point at beginning of
   paragraph to receive drop cap.

   OR

   Begin typing a new paragraph.

2. Click **Drop Cap** button
   on Design Tools Toolbar .... `D`

3. Click **Close** button .... `Close`

   OR

   a. Click **Format** .... `Alt`+`R`
   b. Click **Drop Cap** .... `R`

To Edit a drop cap, select appropriate buttons on the Drop Cap Feature bar:

   a. Click **Type** button and select desired
      drop cap type.......................... `A≡▼`
   b. Click **Position** button and click
      desired drop cap position ..... `Position ▼`
   c. Click **Font** button and select a
      desired font .... `Font...`
   d. Click **Border/Fill** button and select
      desired border/fill. .... `Border/Fill...`

REVERSE TEXT

1. Type text to reverse, using desired
   font.

   OR

   Select text to reverse.

2. Click **Reverse Text** button on Design
   Tools Toolbar .... `a`

   OR

   a. Click **Tools** .... `Alt`+`T`
   b. Click **Macros** .... `M`
   c. Click **Play** .... `P`
   d. Type REVERSE.WCM.
   e. Click **Play** .... `Enter`

3. Select desired
   Text color .... `Alt`+`T`, `↓`/`↑`

4. Click **OK** .... `Enter`

Exercise

49

■ **Templates** ■ **Create Envelopes and Labels**

NOTES

Templates

■ A **template** is a skeleton document that may contain formatting, graphics, and/or text. It may be used to create documents that are used over and over again.

■ Using WordPerfect's predesigned templates, you can create documents such as newsletters, menus, faxes, letters and resumes (as well as other documents).

■ To use a template to create a document, select New from the File menu. The Select New Document dialog box displays.

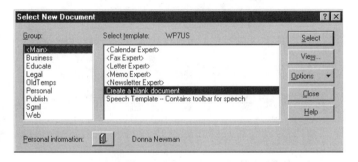

■ Templates are located within a group (or category). Select the group type. Templates relating to that group display in the Select template window to the right of the Group items. In the <Main> group, you will note templates for commonly used documents – a calendar, fax, letter, memo, and newsletter. Each of these templates include the word "Expert" next to the template name. The Expert option walks you through the steps for creating and/or sending a document.

■ When you access Memo Expert, for example, the following Memo Expert dialog box appears:

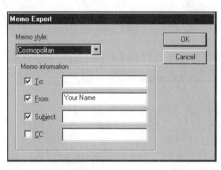

■ The **Memo Expert** provides four template styles: Cosmopolitan (the default), Contemporary, Traditional, and Elegant. Each template style is designed to communicate a different feeling— indicated by its name. To change the default, click the list arrow and select another style. Enter the appropriate information in the text boxes, and if you want a copy notation to be included on the memo, click the CC box and enter the person's name who will receive a copy. After clicking OK, Expert will create the memo heading, including today's date. You can then type the body of your memo.

■ When you select the **Letter Expert** template, a Letter Expert dialog box displays.

■ You may modify each element of the letter by clicking the Select element to modify list arrow and choosing an element to modify. If you select Closing, for example, you will be given a choice of the type of Complimentary closing you desire (Sincerely, Very truly yours, etc.), and whether you want Writer's initials, Typist's initials and/or Enclosures included. Click the desired check box and enter the appropriate initials or number of enclosures in the appropriate text box.

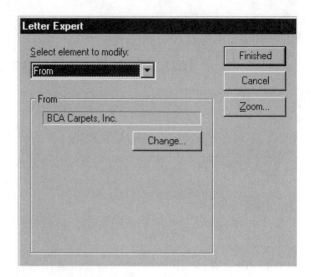

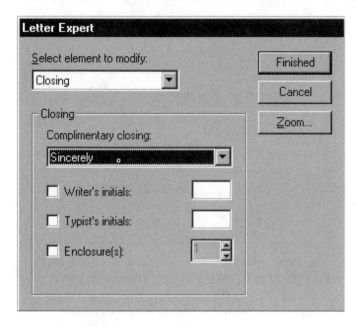

■ To add a letterhead design, click the **Appearance** element option. You will be given several letterhead design choices.

■ The letterhead will be created based on the address book entry displayed when you select the **From** element option in the Letter Expert dialog box. Be sure the address book entry contains a display name (and title, if desired) as well as an organization name and address if you wish the organization name and address to be used in the letterhead and the display name to be used in the signature line. To change the address book information, click the Change button and either add a new address, or choose and edit an existing one.

■ When all elements have been modified, click the Finished button. A document window displays for you to enter the body text of your letter. The date is pulled from the computer's memory and is automatically inserted in the proper location on the letter.

■ When your letter is complete, you can prepare an envelope. With the letter onscreen, select Envelope from the Format menu. WordPerfect automatically retrieves the mailing address into the Mailing Address window.

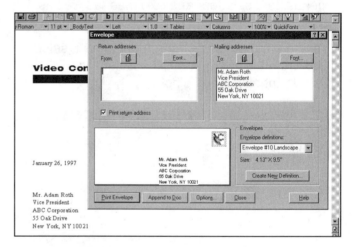

■ If you desire a return address, you may type it in the Return addresses window.

■ Clicking the Append to Doc button inserts the envelope file at the end of your document so you can print it at a later time (it will be saved as part of your document file).

■ The Print Envelope button allows you to print your envelope without appending it to the document.

Envelopes

■ Envelopes can also be created independent of templates or merging.

■ To create an envelope, select Envelope from the Format menu.

- In the Envelope dialog box which follows, select an envelope size from the Envelope definitions drop-down list.

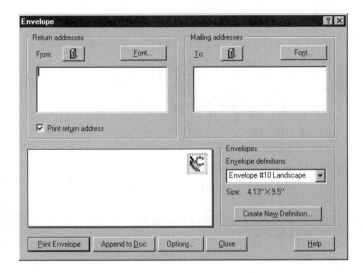

- As with letter templates, if a document is on screen (in the current document window), WordPerfect automatically retrieves its mailing address into the mailing address window.

- You may also type a return address in the Return addresses window. To ensure that the return address is printed, the Print return address check box must be selected.

- To change the appearance of the return or mailing address text, you may select a desired font face and font size by selecting the appropriate Font button.

- Depending on the capabilities of your printer, the envelope definition will specify landscape or portrait, which is the way the font prints on the envelope.

- As indicated earlier, clicking the Append to Doc button inserts the envelope file at the end of your document and the Print Envelope button allows you to print your envelope without appending it to the document.

- Once the envelope is addressed, the template may be saved and used again.

Labels

- The **Label** feature allows you to create mailing labels, file folder labels, or diskette labels.

- Labels may be printed on label sheets or rolls.

- Labels may be accessed by selecting Labels from the Format main menu.

- In the Labels dialog box which follows, you may select the type of label on which you will be working from the predefined Labels list.

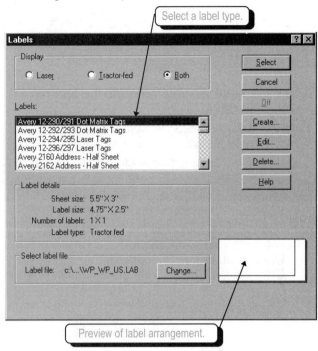

Select a label type.

Preview of label arrangement.

- For each label type you highlight, information about the label and sheet size displays in the Label details area of the dialog box, and an illustration of the label arrangement displays in the preview window.

- Once the label format has been specified, the first blank label displays ready for you to start keyboarding text. Once the label is filled, a new label appears.

- If you do not enter enough text to fill a label, press Ctrl + Enter to end the text you are keyboarding and display a new label.

- The status bar reports each new label as a new page. WordPerfect calls these **logical pages**, as opposed to the **physical page**, or sheet, to which the labels are physically attached.

- To see the labels as they will be arranged when you print, select Page or Two Page from the View menu.

- When you are ready to print, load your printer with the proper size and type of label paper you specified, and then print. When you print a single page, the entire physical page is printed.

In Part I of this exercise, you will create a letter using Letter Expert and prepare an envelope. In Part II of this exercise, you will create a memo using the Memo Expert and create several file labels.

EXERCISE DIRECTIONS

Part I

1. Start with a clear screen.

2. Use the Letter Expert to create the letter in Illustration A:
   - Select the Appearance element to modify; choose a full-block, contemporary-style letter.
   - Select the Closing element to modify; choose Sincerely as the closing and include the writer's initials (your own) and an enclosure notation.
   - Select the From element to modify; click the Change button and add the following personal entry into your address book:

Display Name:	Your Own
Organization:	Video Conferencing Centers
	2323 Image Street
	Baldwin, NY 11543
	(516) 555-5555
	Fax: (516) 555-0000

   - Select this new entry into the letter.
   - Select the To element to modify and use the inside address and the salutation from the illustration.

3. Click the Finished button to insert all the elements.

4. Type the letter text as shown.

   ✓ *Press Enter once at the end of each paragraph. The paragraph format is set to add 1.75" spacing between paragraphs.*

5. Spell check.

6. Create an envelope. Do not include the return address. Use a number 10 Landscape envelope, if available.

7. Print one copy of the letter and the envelope.

8. Save the file; name it VIDEO.

9. Close the document window.

Part II

1. Start with a clear screen.

2. Use the Memo Expert to create the memo in Illustration B:
   - Use any desired memo style.
   - Enter the following information:

To:	Janice Smith
From:	Your Name
Subject:	New Product Announcement
CC:	Michael Perez

3. Print one copy.

4. Save the file; name it ANNOUNCE.

5. Close the document window.

6. Create the following three file labels; use Avery 5066 File Folder-Red as your label type:

   Research Department
   January - March

   MicroForm
   January - March

   InterOffice Memorandums
   January - March

7. Print one copy of the page.

   ✓ *If you have the label type specified, insert a sheet of labels and print. Otherwise, print on letter size paper.*

8. Save the file; name it LABEL.

Video Conferencing Centers

2323 Image Street
Baldwin, NY 11543
(516) 555-5555
Fax: (516) 555-0000

January 26, 1997

Mr. Adam Roth
Vice President
ABC Corporation
55 Oak Drive
New York, NY 10021

Dear Mr. Roth:

Thank you for your interest in our new video-conferencing service centers.

Now there's a way to have a face-to-face meeting with business associates or relatives across the country without the time and expense of travel. At our video conferencing center, it is easier and more affordable than ever. You can see and talk to people thousands of miles away without leaving town.

The enclosed brochure will give you all the details you need to book and plan a video conference, including a cost breakdown.

If you have any further questions that the brochure cannot answer, please do not hesitate to phone me at 1-800-555-5555.

Sincerely,

Your Name
Manager

YO
Enclosure

ILLUSTRATION B

interoffice
M E M O R A N D U M

To:	Janice Smith
From:	Your name
Subject:	New Product Announcement
Date:	May 12, 1997
CC:	Michael Perez

As you know, we will be announcing a new product into the Canadian market in the third quarter of this year.

At our next regional sales meeting on May 26, we will discuss how this product might affect the various market segments. Since John Yule cannot attend, I would appreciate it if you would represent him.

Call me if you need additional information.

KEYSTROKES

ACCESS TEMPLATES

1. Click **File** .... `Alt`+`F`
2. Click **New** .... `N`
   To fill in Personal Information:
   a. Click **Personal Information** button .... `Alt`+`P`
   b. Choose an address book entry.
   c. Click **Select** .... `Enter`
3. Click **Group** .... `Alt`+`G`
4. Select desired group .... `↓` `↑`
5. **Select template** .... `Alt`+`T`
6. Select a desired template .... `↓` `↑`
7. Click **Select** .... `Alt`+`S`
8. Type prompted information:
   - Select elements to modify.
   - Change address book information if needed.
9. Click **Finished** .... `Enter`
10. Type document body text.

CREATE AN ENVELOPE

–FROM MAIN MENU–

1. Click **Format** .... `Alt`+`R`
2. Click **Envelope** .... `V`

3. Click **Envelope definitions** ..... `Alt`+`V`
4. Select definition from drop-down list .... `↓` `↑`
5. Click **To** .... `Alt`+`T`
6. Type address in **Mailing addresses** window.
   ✓ *If a document containing an inside address is on screen, the mailing address will automatically be retrieved into the Mailing addresses window.*
7. Click **From** .... `Alt`+`R`
8. Type return address in **Return addresses** window.
   To print return address:
   a. Click **Print return address** check box .... `Alt`+`U`
   b. Select printing option:
   - **Append to Doc** .... `Alt`+`D`
   OR
   - **Print Envelope** .... `Alt`+`P`

CREATE LABELS

1. Click **Format** .... `Alt`+`R`

2. Click **Labels** .... `B`
3. Select a label type:
   - **Laser** .... `Alt`+`R`
   - **Tractor-fed** .... `Alt`+`T`
   - **Both** .... `Alt`+`B`
4. Click **Labels** box .... `Alt`+`L`
5. Highlight label type .... `↓` `↑`
6. Click **Select** .... `Alt`+`S`
7. Type address for first label.
   If label text does not fill label:
   Press **Ctrl + Enter** .... `Ctrl`+`Enter`
   Use the following keystrokes when typing labels.

TO:	PRESS:
- End text you are typing on current label and move to next label.	`Ctrl`+`Enter`
- End a line of text within a label	`Enter`

8. Type next address.
9. Repeat steps 7-8 for each additional address.
10. Load labels into printer.
11. Print as a normal document.

Exercise 50

■ Summary

In Part I of this exercise, you will use the features learned in this lesson to enhance a newsletter created earlier. In Part II of this exercise, you will use the Newsletter Template to create another newsletter.

EXERCISE DIRECTIONS

Part I

1. Open ▨JOURNEY or ▨50JOURNE.

To create Illustration A on page 216:

2. Change the nameplate to any desired TextArt design. (Highlight the nameplate, then select TextArt from the Graphics menu.)
   - Use a sans serif font.
   - Size it to 2" wide x 1" high and place it as shown.

3. Import the World1graphic (Graphics/QuickArt/Premium/World/World/World1), and place as shown.

4. Create a .013" thick full horizontal line and place it below the nameplate.

5. Center the dateline information as shown using a sans serif 10-point font. Use any desired special character between dateline information.

6. Change the line spacing to single for document text.

7. Create drop initial capitals for the paragraphs shown.

8. Set the headlines to reverse (text will align left).

9. Create a light 10% paragraph fill around Greek Island text. Left align the headline.

10. Enter the following text into a text box in a sans serif 10-point bold italic font:

    Travel Trivia: Q: What city is said to take its name from the Huron word meaning "Meeting Place of the Waters?" A: Toronto
    - Use a triple border around the text box. Use the mouse to size it to approximately 1.75" wide x 2.5" high, and place it as shown.

11. Import any desired graphic below the Cruising On and Ballooning Over the Rhine information.

12. Use the Make it Fit feature to keep all text on one page, if necessary. You may adjust top and bottom margins.

13. Preview your document.

14. Close the file; save the changes.

Part II

1. Start with a clear screen.

2. Access the Newsletter Expert template.

3. Use the text shown in Part I to create a new newsletter.

4. Insert any desired graphics or other elements to enhance the newsletter.

5. Save the file; name it Journey1.

6. Close the document window.

ILLUSTRATION A

AMERICAN TRAVELER

Volume 3, Number 3 ☼ A Publication of Carls Travel Network ☼ Summer 1997

SMOKERS MEET NEW RESTRICTIONS DURING TRAVEL

Travelers should be aware of increased constraints on the ability to smoke in public places. About five years ago, smoking was prohibited on all domestic airline flights. The Dallas-Fort Worth Airport recently declared the entire passenger terminal off

---

Travel Trivia:

Q: **What city is said to take its name from a Huron word meaning "Meeting Place of the Waters?"**

A: **Toronto.**

---

limits to smokers. Those wishing to smoke will now have to leave the airport premises to do so. Perhaps more far reaching is the law passed in Los Angeles which makes cigarette smoking illegal in restaurants. Violators face a $50 fine for the first offense, a $100 fine for the

second offense within a year, and a $250 fine for every offense after that. Be cautious when traveling not to violate unexpected smoking laws!

CRUISING ON and BALLOONING OVER THE RHINE

Stasbourg, the capital of French Alsace, is a wonderful city to begin or end a cruise or a hot-air balloon ride. Its pink sandstone Cathedral and a well-preserved old town are enchanting attractions for vacationing tourists. The cost of a three-day cruise, including

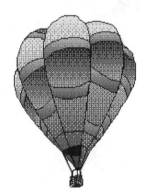

an afternoon hot-air balloon ride, two evening meals, two breakfasts, two luncheons and coffee and cakes will be approximately $567 a person. The view from the

air and/or from the middle of the river is more dramatic than the glimpse of the same scenery that a passenger sees on the train ride along the river bank from Cologne to Frankfurt. For further information, contact your local travel agent and request the RHINE RIVER PACKAGE.

TRAVEL HIGHLIGHT OF THE SEASON: *THE GREEK ISLANDS*

There are over 3,000 islands which comprise "The Greek Islands." However, only 170 of these islands are inhabited, each with its own character and terrain. This summer, Sunshine Travel Network is offering special fares on cruises to many of these charming islands. A four-day cruise to Rhodes, Heraklion, Santorini, and Piraeus costs $799 per person. This package is definitely the buy of the season!

Quattro Pro 7

Exercise 1

- Start Quattro Pro ■ The Quattro Pro Window
- Quattro Pro Menu and Toolbars
- Explore the Notebook Using the Mouse and Keyboard

NOTES

Start Quattro Pro

■ Quattro Pro like the other programs in the Corel Office 7 Professional package, may be started from the Windows 95 Taskbar, or by using DAD (See Corel Office Basics, Exercise 1):

- Click Start on the Windows Taskbar, highlight Programs, select Corel Office 7, and then select Corel Quattro Pro 7.

- Click the Corel Quattro Pro icon 🔲 on the **Desktop Application Director (DAD)** on the Windows 95 taskbar.

The Quattro Pro Window

■ The Corel Quattro Pro 7 screen displays when the program is first started. (*See Illustration A.*)

Illustration A

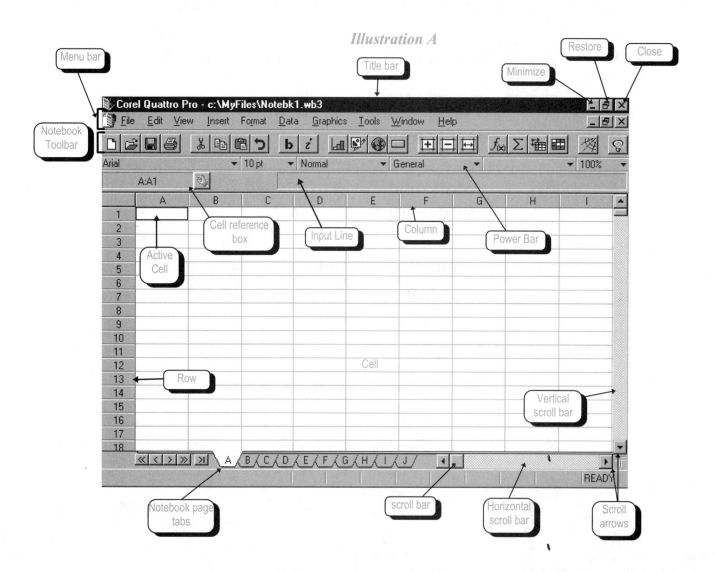

- The default notebook displays at least ten pages, lettered A through J, that contain rows and columns made up of cells. Some screens will display more notebook tabs.

- The active cell is the cell that is ready to receive data or a command. You can change the active cell in a notebook by using the mouse or keyboard.

- When you change the active cell, the cell reference box, located on the left side of the input line, shows the new cell reference. The cell reference identifies the location of the active cell in the notebook page by the column and row headings.

  ✓ *Note the location of the cell reference on the Input line displaying the address of the active cell.*

Quattro Pro Menu and Toolbars

- As shown in Illustration A, the default Quattro Pro window contains the menu bar, Notebook Toolbar, Power Bar and Input line. The first ten buttons are similar to those discussed in the WordPerfect section of this text, while the other buttons and bars are specific to Quattro Pro. There are eleven toolbars available in Quattro Pro that may be displayed as needed.

Explore the Notebook Using the Mouse and Keyboard

- The **notebook** window displays a limited portion of the notebook page. It is possible to view other portions of the page by **scrolling** to the desired location. You can scroll to different areas on a page by using the mouse or keyboard. Scrolling does not change the active cell.

- There are 256 columns and 8192 rows in a notebook page. Although ten notebook pages are visible, there are actually 256 pages available in a notebook. The pages are lettered up through IV.

  ✓ *Note the illustrations of the outer edges of a notebook page in Illustration B.*

Illustration B

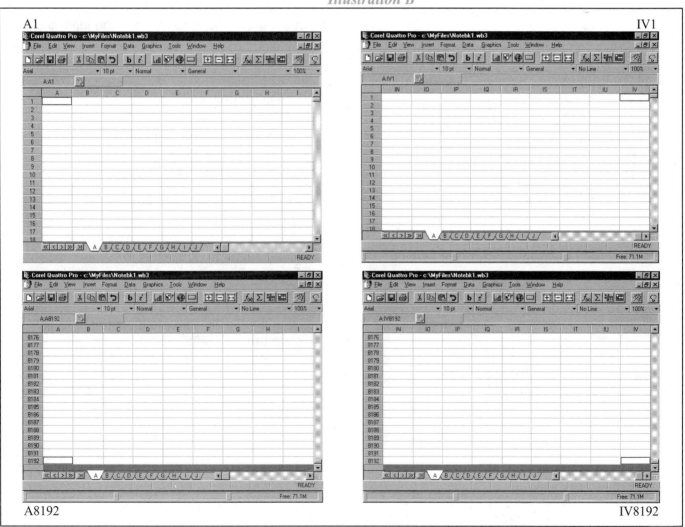

■ You can also change the active cell in a notebook page by selecting the <u>G</u>o To command on the <u>E</u>dit menu or by pressing F5.

✓   *Note the Go To dialog box that appears when Go To is selected or F5 is pressed.*

Go To Dialog Box

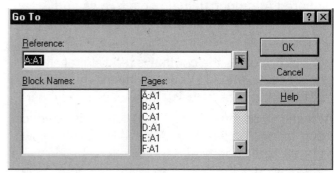

In this exercise, you will use the scroll bars as well as the menu bar and the Go To command to move around the notebook.

EXERCISE DIRECTIONS

1. Click cell E5 to make it active.
    ✓   *Note the cell reference in the cell reference box.*

2. Press the left arrow key until cell C5 is selected.
    ✓   *Note the cell reference in the cell reference box.*

3. Select cell C9.
    ✓   *Note the cell reference in the cell reference box.*

4. Use the arrow keys to select the following cells:

    *   A6
    *   R19
    *   B14
    *   AA45
    *   G2
    *   J33
    *   H20
    *   A1

5. Click the down scroll arrow on the vertical scroll bar.
    ✓   *Note the notebook page moves down by one row.*

6. Click the right scroll arrow on the horizontal scroll bar.
    ✓   *Note the notebook page moves right by one column.*

7. Click the scroll bar below the scroll box on the vertical scroll bar.
    ✓   *Note the notebook page moves down by one screen.*

8. Click the scroll bar to the right of the scroll box on the horizontal scroll bar.
    ✓   *Note the notebook page moves right by one screen.*

9. Drag the horizontal scroll box all the way to the right on the scroll bar.
    ✓   *Note how the view of the notebook page has changed.*

10. Drag the vertical scroll box all the way down on the scroll bar.
    ✓   *Note how the view of the notebook page has changed.*

11. Use the scroll bars to move to the following parts of the notebook page:

    *   Down one screen
    *   Up one screen
    *   Right one screen
    *   Left one screen
    *   Lower left of notebook page
    *   Top right of notebook page
    *   Bottom right of notebook page

12. Select Edit on the menu bar.

13. Select Go To.

14. Type A10 in the Reference text box.

15. Click OK.
    ✓   *Note the active cell is A10.*

16. Using the Go To command, change the active cell to the following:

    *   AB105
    *   BG200
    *   K965
    *   A1 (Home)

KEYSTROKES

CHANGE ACTIVE CELL USING THE KEYBOARD

To Move:	Press:
One cell right	→
One cell left	←
One cell down	↓
One cell up	↑
One screen up	Page Up
One screen down	Page Down
One screen right (Ctrl+right arrow)	Ctrl + →
One screen left (Ctrl+left arrow)	Ctrl + ←
First cell in current row (End+left arrow)	End + ←
Last cell in current row (End+right arrow)	End + →
First cell in notebook page (Home)	Home

CHANGE ACTIVE CELL USING THE MOUSE

Click desired cell.

✓ *If desired cell is not in view, use the scroll bars to move area of notebook page containing cell into view, then click the cell.*

SCROLL USING THE MOUSE

The vertical scroll bar is located on the right side of the notebook window. The horizontal scroll is located on the bottom of the notebook window.

To scroll one column left or right:

Click left or right scroll arrow.

To scroll one row up or down:

Click up or down scroll arrow.

To scroll one screen up or down:

Click vertical scroll bar above or below the scroll box.

To scroll one screen right or left:

Click horizontal scroll bar to right or left of the scroll box.

To scroll to the beginning columns:

Drag horizontal scroll box to the extreme left of the scroll bar.

To scroll to the beginning rows:

Drag vertical scroll box to the top of the scroll bar.

To scroll quickly to an area in a notebook page:

Drag scroll box to desired position on the scroll bar.

✓ *The limits of the scrolling area will depend on the location of data in the notebook page.*

To scroll quickly to the last row where data was entered:

Press Ctrl and drag vertical scroll box to the bottom of the scroll bar.

CHANGE ACTIVE CELL USING GO TO

F5

1. Click **Edit** .... Alt + E
2. Click **Go To** .... G
3. Type cell reference .... *cell reference* in **Reference** text box.
4. Click **OK** .... Enter

Exercise 2

■ **Enter Labels** ■ **Make Simple Corrections**
■ **Save and Close a Notebook** ■ **Exit Quattro Pro**

NOTES

Enter Labels

■ The **status** of a cell is determined by the first character entered.

■ When an alphabetical character or a symbol (` ~ ! % ^ & * _ \ | [ ] { } ; : ' " < > , ?) is entered as the first character in a cell, the cell contains a **label**.

■ By default, each cell is approximately eight (8) characters wide; however, it is possible to view an entered label that is longer than the cell width if the cell to the right is blank.

■ As a label is being entered, it appears on the Input line.

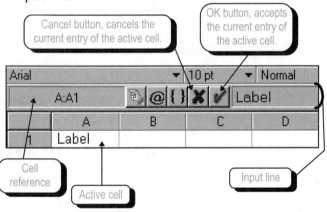

It is entered in the cell after you do one of the following:

- Press an arrow key
- Click another cell
- Click the OK button 🖱 on the Input line
- Press Enter

■ The contents of a label will automatically align to the left of the cell, making it a left-justified entry.

Make Simple Corrections

■ Before data is entered, the Backspace key may be used to correct an error. To delete the entire entry, press the Escape key or click the Cancel button 🗙 on the input line. After text is entered, a correction may be typed directly over the existing text.

Save and Close a Notebook

■ As with text files, each notebook should be saved on a removable disk or on a hard drive for future recall and must be given a name for identification. A saved notebook is called a **file**.

■ Prior to Windows 95, filenames were limited to eight characters. Now filenames may be more descriptive, since the limit for the name, drive and path is 255 characters. When you save a file, Quattro Pro automatically adds a period and a filename extension (**.wb3**) to the end of the filename. Because Quattro Pro identifies file types by their extension, you should not type the filename extension.

■ A notebook must be saved before closing, or all current or updated entries will be lost. Notebooks should be saved often as you work, so that your most current work is not lost if a problem occurs. If you attempt to close a notebook or exit Quattro Pro before saving, you will be asked if you want to save the changes.

✓ *If you make a mistake and want to begin again, you may choose to close the notebook without saving it.*

- A notebook may be saved by clicking the Save button 🖫 on the Toolbar or by selecting Save from the File menu. The dialog box that appears allows you to name the path, folder, and file.

Save File Dialog Box

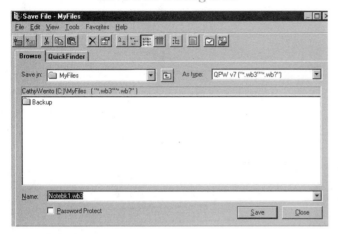

Exit Quattro Pro

- After all open files have been saved and closed, you can exit the application. Select Exit from the File menu. If prompted, Click Yes to save any additional changes. Click No if you wish to save the document without the most recent changes.

In this exercise, you will begin to create a notebook page for the Neighborhood Superette by entering labels. Numeric data will be entered in a later exercise.

EXERCISE DIRECTIONS

1. Go to cell B2.

2. Type your name while looking at the input line.
   ✓ *Note the Cancel and Enter buttons to the left of the input area.*

3. Cancel the entry by pressing the Escape key or by clicking the Cancel button 🗙.

4. Create the notebook page below.

5. Enter the labels in the exact cell locations shown in the illustration.

6. Correct errors using the Backspace key or strikeover method.

7. Save the notebook; name it CASH.

8. Close the notebook.

A	A	B	C	D	E	F	G	H	I	J
1			NEIGHBORHOOD SUPERETTE							
2			DAILY CASH RECEIPTS							
3										
4	DATE:									
5										
6	CODE	DEPARTMENT	SALES	TAX	TOTAL	% OF TOTAL				
7	A	DAIRY								
8	B	PRODUCE								
9	C	MEAT & FISH								
10	D	GROCERIES								
11	E	GROCERIES-TAX								
12	F	BEAUTY AIDS								
13	G	HOUSEWARES								

KEYSTROKES

ENTER A LABEL

✓   *Labels are left-aligned and cannot be calculated.*

1. Click cell .... *cell*
   to receive label.

2. Type label text .... *label text*

3. Press any **arrow key** .... [⬆⬇⬅➡]
   to enter label and move to next cell.

   OR

   Click **OK** button .... [✔]
   on the Input line.

   OR

   Press Enter.

 SAVE A NEW NOTEBOOK

1. Click **File** .... [Alt]+[F]

2. Click **Save As** .... [A]

   To select a drive:

   a. Click **Save in** .... [Alt]+[I]

   b. Select desired drive
      letter................................. [⬇],[⬆]

To select a directory:

Double-click directory
name in Directories box .. [Tab],[Tab],[⬇]

3. Double-click **Name** .... [Alt]+[N]

4. Type filename .... *filename*

5. Click **Save** .... [Enter]

CLOSE A NOTEBOOK

1. Click **File** .... [Alt]+[F]

2. Click **Close** .... [C]

   **If a Save Changes in Notebook
   message appears:**

   Click **Yes** .... [Y]
   to save changes to the notebook.

   ✓   *If you have not previously saved
       the notebook, the Save As dialog
       box appears. (See SAVE A NEW
       NOTEBOOK, left.)*

   OR

   Click **No** .... [N]
   to close without saving the changes.

 EXIT QUATTRO PRO

Alt + F4

1. Click **File** .... [Alt]+[F]

2. Click **Exit** .... [X]

   **If a Save Changes in Notebook
   message appears:**

   Click **Yes** .... [Y]

   ✓   *If you have not previously saved
       the notebook, the Save As dialog
       box appears. (See SAVE A NEW
       NOTEBOOK, left.)*

   OR

   Click **No** .... [N]
   to close without saving the changes.

Exercise 3

- **Numeric Labels and Values** ■ **Label Alignment**
- **Repeat Labels**

NOTES

Numeric Labels and Values

- When a number or a symbol (+-.@#=$) is entered as the first character in a cell, the cell contains a **value**.

- A value is entered after you do one of the following:

  - Press Enter

  - Click another cell

  - Press an arrow key

  - Click the OK button ✔ on the input line

- If a value is longer than the cell, Quattro Pro displays the number in scientific notation, or asterisks (********) appear in the cell. In either case, the column width must be reset. (*Setting column width will be covered in Exercise 11.*)

- A **numeric label** is a number that will not be used in a calculation. Examples of numeric labels are social security numbers or identification numbers. To indicate that such numbers are to be treated as labels and not values, it is necessary to begin the entry with one of the following label prefixes:

  - an apostrophe (') to left-align the numbers

  - double-quotes (") to right-align the numbers

  - a carat (^) to center-align the numbers

- Label prefixes are not displayed on the notebook page but are shown on the Input line, as illustrated below:

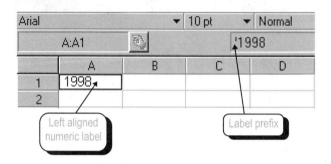

- Left aligned numeric label
- Label prefix

Label Alignment

- A value automatically aligns to the right of the cell, making it a right-justified entry, and a label automatically aligns to the left of the cell. Since labels are left-justified and values are right-justified in a cell, column titles (which are labels) will not appear centered over numeric data. When necessary, alignment may be adjusted. For example, column title labels above numeric data may be centered or right-aligned to improve the appearance of the notebook page. Note the illustration of how data is aligned in cells.

	A	B	C	D	E	F
1	Text	◄	default label alignment - left justified			
2	Text	◄	centered label			
3	Text	◄	right justified label			
4	123	◄	default value alignment - right justified			
5	123	◄	left justified numeric label			
6	123	◄	centered value			

■ Label alignment may be adjusted by following any of the three methods outlined below:

- Enter a label prefix in a cell (as mentioned above).

- Select the cells to be aligned and choose an alignment option on the Power Bar *(see illustration below)*.

- Select the cells to be aligned and choose <u>B</u>lock from the Fo<u>r</u>mat menu. Then click the Alignment tab and choose the desired horizontal and vertical alignment options.

Repeat Labels

■ If you wish to repeat data across an entire cell, you can use the repeat label prefix (\) before typing the character. For example, if you wish to repeat a $ across a cell, type \$ and the dollar sign will repeat to fill the cell.

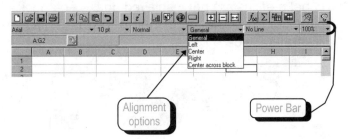

In this exercise, you will create a payroll for employees of the Jerome Insurance Agency. Gross Pay refers to total salary earned before taxes; Federal With. Tax refers to the amount withheld for Federal Taxes. Soc. Sec. Tax and Medicare Tax refers to the amount deducted for these benefits. Net Pay refers to salary received after taxes are deducted.

EXERCISE DIRECTIONS

1. Create the notebook page below.

2. Enter the labels in the exact cell locations shown in the illustration.

   ✓ *Enter the time card numbers as numeric labels, not as values.*

3. Correct any errors.

4. Right-align the Hourly Rate and Hours Worked column headings.

5. Enter the company logo JI as a repeat label in cells A1 and I1.

6. Save the notebook; name it **PAY**.

7. Close the notebook.

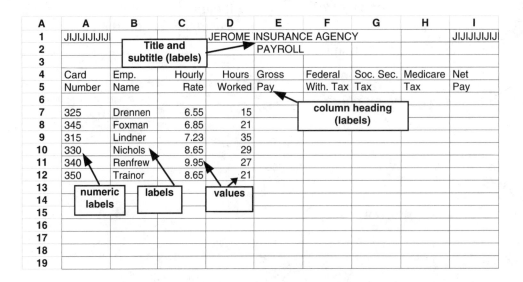

	A	B	C	D	E	F	G	H	I
1	JIJIJIJIJIJI			JEROME	INSURANCE	AGENCY			JIJIJIJIJIJI
2		Title and			PAYROLL				
3		subtitle (labels)							
4	Card	Emp.	Hourly	Hours	Gross	Federal	Soc. Sec.	Medicare	Net
5	Number	Name	Rate	Worked	Pay	With. Tax	Tax	Tax	Pay
6									
7	325	Drennen	6.55	15		column heading			
8	345	Foxman	6.85	21		(labels)			
9	315	Lindner	7.23	35					
10	330	Nichols	8.65	29					
11	340	Renfrew	9.95	27					
12	350	Trainor	8.65	21					
13		numeric	labels	values					
14		labels							
15									
16									
17									
18									
19									

KEYSTROKES

ENTER A NUMERIC LABEL

✓ *Numbers entered as numeric labels cannot be calculated.*

1. Click cell.. *cell* to receive numeric label.

2. Press ", ^, or '
   (label prefix)............. ⬛ or ⬛ or ⬛

3. Type number........................... *number*

4. Press arrow key .... ⬛

REPEAT LABEL

✓ *Data can be repeated to fill a cell.*

1. Type \... ⬛

2. Type data to repeat .... *data*

3. Press **Enter** .... ⬛

ENTER A VALUE

✓ *Numbers entered as values are right-aligned and can be calculated.*

1. Click cell.. *cell* to receive value.

2. Type number........................... *number*

✓ *Begin entry with a number from zero to nine or a decimal point. Precede a negative number with a minus sign (-), or enclose it within parentheses().*

3. Press **Enter** .... ⬛

✓ *If Quattro Pro displays asterisks (********) or the number in scientific notation, the column is not wide enough to display the value. Quattro Pro stores the value in the cell but cannot display it. To see the entry, adjust the column width.*

SELECT (HIGHLIGHT) A RANGE OF CELLS USING THE MOUSE

1. Point to interior of first cell to select.

2. Drag through adjacent cells until desired cells are highlighted.

SELECT (HIGHLIGHT) A RANGE OF CELLS USING THE KEYBOARD

1. Press arrow keys .... ⬛

2. Press **Shift** + arrow keys ..... ⬛+⬛ until adjacent cells to select are highlighted.

ALIGN LABELS USING THE POWER BAR

1. Select cell(s) containing label(s)............................... ⬛+⬛

2. Click the **Align** button on the **Power Bar**.

3. Click **General, Left, Center, Right,** or **Center across block** .... ⬛ ⬛

Exercise

4

Summary

EXERCISE DIRECTIONS

1. Mr. Abrams, the teacher of English 852, would like you to prepare a notebook for quiz marks for the Spring 199- term.

2. First, include the appropriate data in a three-line notebook page title.

3. Using the data below, create a notebook page.
CLASS:

TERM:

TEACHER:

4. Leave a blank column (column C) between NAME and QUIZ 1. Enter ID as numeric labels. Right-align column labels for quiz marks.

5. Save and close the notebook; name it MARK.

ID	NAME		QUIZ 1	QUIZ 2	QUIZ 3
2314	Bronte, C.		85	80	90
5432	Carson, R.		35	55	68
2311	Fromm, E.		72	76	85
3454	Hardy, T.		55	42	67
5413	Hemingway, E.		64	68	69
5487	Melville, H.		83	87	86
2379	Miller, A.		98	96	97
5438	Poe, E.		76	79	81
2390	Steinbeck, J.		90	87	95
5498	Wouk, H.		100	96	98

Exercise

5

■ **Use Formulas**

NOTES

Use Formulas

- A **formula** is an instruction to calculate a number and may include actual numbers or cell addresses.

- A formula is entered in the cell where the answer should appear. As you type the formula, it appears in the cell and on the Input line. After a formula is entered, the answer is displayed in the cell, and the formula is displayed on the Input line.

- A formula must begin with a period, plus, minus, open parenthesis, at symbol, dollar sign, or equal sign (.+-(@$=). Generally, the plus sign is used since it is on the numeric keypad. There should be no spaces between mathematical operators and cell references. If you include extraneous spaces, Quattro Pro will delete them when you click the OK button ✔ to enter the formula.

- **Cell references** and **mathematical operators** are used to develop formulas. The cell reference can be typed or inserted into a formula. For example, the formula +C3+C5+C7 results in the addition of the values in these cell locations. Therefore, any change to the values in these cell locations causes the answer to change automatically.

- The standard mathematical operators used in formulas are:

    + Addition   - Subtraction
    * Multiplication   / Division
    ^ Exponentiation

- It is important to consider the order of mathematical operations when preparing formulas. Operations enclosed in parentheses have the highest priority and are executed first; exponential calculations are executed second. Multiplication and division operations have the next priority and are completed before any addition and subtraction operations.

- All operations are executed from left to right in the order of appearance. For example, in the formula +A1*(B1+C1), B1+C1 is calculated before the multiplication is performed. If the parentheses were omitted, A1*B1 would be calculated first and C1 would be added to that answer. Each procedure results in a different outcome.

- Multiplication and division formulas may result in answers with decimal places. These numbers can be rounded off using a formatting feature. (*See Format Data, Exercise 6.*)

- When using a percentage as a numeric factor in a formula, you can enter it either with a decimal or with the percent symbol. For example, you may enter either .45 or 45% to indicate 45 percent in a formula.

A notebook will be used to calculate markup and sales tax on items in the Good Samaritan Hospital Gift Shop.   MARKUP refers to the amount added to the cost of goods to determine the selling price; in this case, it will be calculated at 40%. The SALES TAX percentage for this exercise will be 6% and, as illustrated, the percent has been changed to .06 in the formula.

EXERCISE DIRECTIONS

1. Create the notebook page below.

2. Enter the labels and values in the exact cell locations shown in the illustration. The ITEM numbers should be entered as numeric labels.

3. Enter the formula, as illustrated, in the MARKUP column to calculate a 40% markup. Note that after the formula is entered, the answer appears in the cell and the formula is visible on the Input line.

4. Enter formulas in the MARKUP column for the remaining items using the appropriate cell addresses.

5. Enter the formula to calculate the first SELLING PRICE, which is COST plus MARKUP.

6. Enter the formula to calculate SALES TAX at 6% of the SELLING PRICE.

7. Enter the formula to calculate TOTAL PRICE, which is SELLING PRICE+SALES TAX.

8. Complete the formulas for the remaining items using the appropriate cell addresses for each formula.

9. Check formula entries for accuracy.

10. Save and close the notebook; name it COST.

A	A	B	C	D	E	F
1		GOOD SAMARITAN HOSPITAL GIFT SHOP				
2						
3				SELLING	SALES	TOTAL
4	ITEM	COST	MARKUP	PRICE	TAX	PRICE
5	345	6	+B5*.40	+B5+C5	+D5*.06	+D5+E5
6	436	10				
7	543	14				
8						
9						

KEYSTROKES

ENTER A FORMULA USING MATHEMATICAL OPERATORS

1. Click cell......................................
    to receive formula.

2. Press + ... ➕

3. Type formula........................... *formula*
    using cell references and mathematical operators.

Example: +A1*(B2+B10)/2

✔ *You can select cells instead of typing references to tell the notebook page which cells you wish the formula to reference.*

To insert cell references by selecting cells:

a. Click formula where cell references will be inserted.

b. Type preceding operator.

c. Select each cell(s) you want formula to reference.

d. Type desired operator or parenthesis.

e. Repeat steps above as needed.

f. Press **Enter** ....

Exercise

6

- ■ **Open Files** ■ **Save Files**
- ■ **Format Data** ■ **Use Blocks**

NOTES

Open Files

- ■ Notebooks that have been saved and closed must be opened using the same drive designation and filename used during the saving process. The Open File dialog box contains a drop-down list with the drives or folders and a box containing a list of the files in that directory. In addition to opening a previously saved file, you may preview it, search for the file, or list details or properties about the file. Note the illustration of the Open File dialog box below.

Open Dialog Box

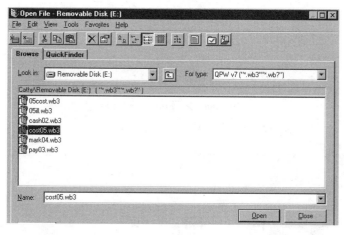

- ■ When the File menu is accessed, a list of the last ten files used is provided at the bottom of the menu. Clicking the filename of one of these recently used files is a quick way to open a file.

- ■ A newly opened notebook becomes the active notebook and hides any other open notebooks. Open notebooks can be made active by selecting the file from the Window menu.

Save Files

- ■ When you resave a workbook using the Save command from the File menu, the new version of the file overwrites the previous version.

- ■ Use the Save As command from the File menu, or press F3, to change the filename. This is the easiest way to save both the original file and the revised one as separate notebooks. Simply give the revised file a new name.

Format Data

- ■ You can change the appearance of data to make it more attractive and readable by formatting it. Some available number formats are normal, currency, percent, date, or comma. Note the illustration of the number format button on the Power Bar.

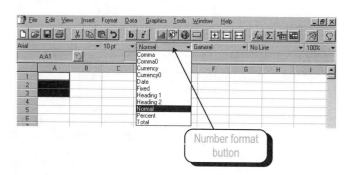

Number format button

■ The following formats may be used for formatting number values:

Normal Displays numbers without added decimal places or as entered.

Fixed Displays numbers with two decimal places.

Currency0 Displays numbers with dollar signs and no decimal places.

Currency Displays numbers with dollar signs and two decimal places.

✓ *Other formats will be introduced in later exercises.*

Use Blocks

■ A **block** is a defined area or range in a notebook. For example, the cells F4, F5, and F6 can be indicated as **F4:F6**; **A1:G2** indicates all the cells in columns A through G in rows one and two. You can format data in a column or row by selecting the block of cells containing the data to format.

■ Cell contents may be formatted before or after data is entered.

■ As noted in Exercise 3, label text is left-aligned while values are right-aligned in a cell. The alignment button on the Power Bar may be used to align a column heading in a single cell or all the column titles in a selected range.

In this exercise, you will add data to the COST notebook and format money columns and column titles. In addition, the file will be saved using the Save and Save As options.

EXERCISE DIRECTIONS

1. Open ▭COST or ▭06COST.

2. Select the block of data in cells B3:F4.

3. Right-align column titles using the alignment button on the Power Bar.

4. Enter the new item data.

5. Enter formulas to complete the information for the new data.

6. Select the block of data in cells B5:F10.

7. Format the data for Fixed using the number format button on the Power Bar.

8. Select the data in cells F5:F10.

9. Format the data for Currency using the number format button on the Power Bar.

10. Save/overwrite the notebook file.

11. Format cells F5:F10 for Fixed using the number format button on the Power Bar.

✓ *The change in step 11 is saved in the COST2 file.*

12. Save the notebook as COST2.

13. Close the notebook.

A	A	B	C	D	E	F	G	H	I
1		GOOD SAMARITAN HOSPITAL GIFT SHOP							
2									
3				SELLING	SALES	TOTAL	← Block		
4	ITEM	COST	MARKUP	PRICE	TAX	PRICE			
5	345	6	3	9	0.45	9.45			
6	436	10	5	15	0.75	15.75			
7	543	14	7	21	1.05	22.05	← Block B5:F10		
8	582	5.25							
9	498	3.75							
10	765	7.25							

KEYSTROKES

OPEN A NOTEBOOK FILE

1. Click **Open** button .... 🖾
   on Toolbar.
   OR
   a. Click **File** .... Alt + F
   b. Click **Open** .... O

   To select a drive:

   a. Click **Look in** .... Alt + L
   b. Select desired drive letter .... ↓

*Files in current directory of selected drive
appear in window.*

   To list files of a different type:

   a. Click **For type:** .... Alt + Y
   b. Click file type to list .... ↓

*Only files of specified type appear in
window.*

   ✓   *Use this option to change the
       kinds of files displayed in the Open
       window. For example, if you
       wanted to open a Lotus file into
       notebook page, you would select
       the 1-2-3 v4/v5("*.wk") item in the
       drop-down list.*

2. Click file to open in Open window.
   OR
   a. Select File **Name** list box... Alt + N
   b. Select file to open .... ↓
3. Click **OK** .... Enter

RESAVE/OVERWRITE A NOTEBOOK FILE

   Click **Save** button .... 🖫
   on Toolbar.
   OR
1. Click **File** menu .... Alt + F
2. Click **Save** .... S

SAVE AS

Saves and names the active notebook.

1. Click **File** .... Alt + F
2. Click **Save As** .... A

   To select a drive:

   a. Click **Save in:** .... Alt + I
   b. Select desired drive letter .... ↓

   To select a directory:

   a. Double-click directory name
      in Save window .... Tab + ↓
   b. Double-click in **Name:** .... Alt + N
   c. Type filename .... *filename*

SELECT (HIGHLIGHT) A BLOCK OF CELLS USING THE MOUSE

   ✓   *A block of cells is two or more
       cells. Cells in a selected block are
       highlighted and the active cell
       within the selection is white.*

To select a range of adjacent cells:

1. Point to interior of first cell to select.
2. Drag through adjacent cells until
   desired cells are highlighted.

To select entire row or column:

 Click row heading or column heading to
 select.

To select adjacent rows or columns:

1. Point to first row heading or column
   heading to select.
2. Drag through adjacent headings until
   desired rows or columns are
   highlighted.

SELECT (HIGHLIGHT) A BLOCK OF CELLS USING THE KEYBOARD

To select a block of adjacent cells:

1. Press arrow keys .... ⇆
   until first cell to select is highlighted.

2. Press **Shift** + arrow keys ..... Shift + ⇆

To select entire row containing active cell:

Press **End + Shift + Right**
arrow .... End + Shift + →

To select entire column containing active cell:

Press **End + Shift + Down**
arrow .... End + Shift + ↓

To select adjacent rows:

1. Press arrow keys to select first cell in
   first row.

2. Press and hold **End + Shift**... End + Shift
   then press **Down arrow** .... ↓
   to highlight first row.

3. Still pressing **End + Shift**, press **Up** or
   Down arrow .... ↑ , ↓
   to highlight adjacent rows.

FORMAT NUMBERS USING THE POWER BAR

Applies commonly used number formats.

1. Select cells to format (see above).
2. Click **Number format button** on the
   Power Bar.
3. Select a style .... ↑ ↓

Exercise

7

■ **Copy Data** ■ **Print a Notebook Page**

NOTES

Copy Data

■ Formulas may be copied:

- Horizontally or vertically
- To another cell or range of cells
- To another notebook page or notebook

■ When a formula is copied, the cell references change relative to their new location. To copy data, select the cell to be copied, click the Copy button 🗐 on the Toolbar, select the block or cell to receive the data, and click the Paste button 🗐 on the Toolbar. The Edit, Copy and Edit, Paste commands on the menu bar may also be used.

Print a Notebook Page

■ The notebook, selected notebook page(s), or a the selected range of data may be printed using the Print command on the File menu. You can also use the Print button 🖨 on the Toolbar if you wish to print the current page. When you access the Print command, Quattro Pro allows you to select various print options. You can preview the print output by selecting the Print Preview button in the Spreadsheet Print dialog box or by selecting Print Preview from the File menu.

Spreadsheet Print Dialog Box

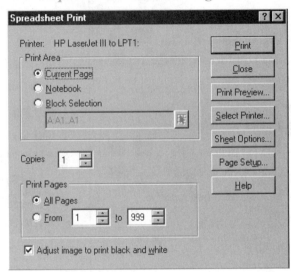

■ Quattro Pro uses the default page size (usually 8½" x 11") of the current printer. The page size settings can be accessed by clicking the Page Setup button. The top and bottom default page margins are set at .33" and the right and left default page margins are set at 0.40". The margin page settings can be accessed by clicking the Print Margins tab from the Spreadsheet Page Setup dialog box.

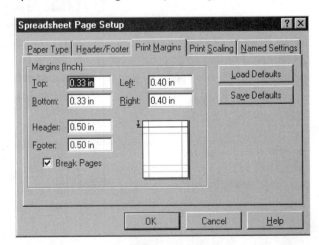

You will complete the Jerome Insurance Agency payroll by entering formulas to calculate the taxes and net pay. Federal Withholding Taxes are normally determined using a table where the tax varies according to your salary and number of exemptions; however, we will use a percentage rate for this problem. The payroll will be printed using the Print command.

EXERCISE DIRECTIONS

1. Open ▨PAY or ▭07PAY.

   ✓ *If you are using the data disk, you should make the disk read-only to preserve the data files. Instructions will be given to save the file as a new file.*

2. Enter a formula to calculate Gross Pay for the first employee.

   *Hint: Hours * Rate*

3. Copy the Gross Pay formula for each employee.

4. Enter a formula to calculate Federal Withholding Tax at 20%.

   *Hint: Gross Pay * 20%*

5. Copy the Federal With. Tax formula for each employee.

6. Enter a formula to compute Social Security Tax at 6.2%.

7. Copy the Soc. Sec. Tax formula for each employee.

8. Enter a formula to compute Medicare Tax at 1.45%.

9. Copy the Medicare Tax formula for each employee.

10. Enter a formula to calculate Net Pay.

    Hint: Deduct all taxes from the gross pay.

11. Copy the Net Pay formula for each employee.

12. Format columns E, F, G, H, and I for two decimal places using the Format, Block, Fixed option.

13. Center all column labels.

14. Print one copy of the notebook page using default settings for paper and margins.

15. Close and save the notebook, or *save as* PAY.

    ✓ *If you are using the PAY file you created previously, you are asked to save changes to update the file before closing the notebook. If you are using the data disk, you must use the Save As command to create a new PAY file since the data file should be kept on a read-only disk.*

A	A	B	C	D	E	F	G	H	I
1	JIJIJIJIJIJI			JEROME INSURANCE AGENCY					JIJIJIJIJIJI
2				PAYROLL					
3									
4	Card	Emp.	Hourly	Hours	Gross	Federal	Soc. Sec.	Medicare	Net
5	Number	Name	Rate	Worked	Pay	With. Tax	Tax	Tax	Pay
6									
7	325	Drennen	6.55	15					
8	345	Foxman	6.85	21					
9	315	Lindner	7.23	35					
10	330	Nichols	8.65	29					
11	340	Renfrew	9.95	27					
12	350	Trainor	8.65	21					
13									
14									
15									
16									
17									

KEYSTROKES

COPY AND PASTE

Ctrl + C, Ctrl + V

Copies the data once and overwrites existing data in the destination cells.

1. Select cell(s) to copy.
2. Click **Copy** button ....
   OR
   a. Click **Edit** .... Alt + E
   b. Click **Copy** C
3. Select destination cell(s).

   ✓ *Select an area the same size as the area to copy, or select the upper left cell in the destination cell range. The destination can be in the same notebook page, another sheet, or another notebook.*

4. Click **Paste** button ....
   OR
   a. Click **Edit** .... Alt + E
   b. Click **Paste** .... P

PRINT A NOTEBOOK PAGE

Prints notebook page data using the current page settings.

   ✓ *When printing a notebook page, Quattro Pro will print only the print area, if you defined it.*

Click **Print** button ....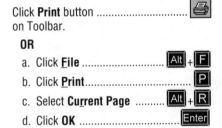
on Toolbar.
   OR
   a. Click **File** .... Alt + F
   b. Click **Print**.................................. P
   c. Select **Current Page** .... Alt + R
   d. Click **OK** .... Enter

<table>
<tr><td>**Exercise**
8</td><td>■ **Copy Formulas (Absolute and Relative Reference)**
■ **Format Data (Percents, Fonts, and Font Size)**</td></tr>
</table>

NOTES

Copy Formulas (Absolute and Relative Reference)

■ In some cases, a value in a formula must remain constant when copied to other locations. This is referred to as an **absolute reference**. To identify a cell as an absolute value, a dollar sign ($) must precede the column and row references for that cell. For example, in the formula +D7/$D$15, the reference to D15 is an absolute reference. The dollar signs may be typed with the cell reference or you may press F4 to enter the dollar signs after the cell address is entered.

■ In this example, we must divide each department's sales by the total to find each department's percentage of total sales. Therefore, the total sales amount, D15, is a constant value in each line's formula and should be an absolute reference. When this formula is copied, the total sales remains constant in every formula.

Format Data (Percents, Fonts, and Font Size)

■ Formatting may be used to change decimal answers into a percentage format.

■ Quattro Pro lets you apply desktop publishing features to create a more attractive screen view and printout. Your monitor and printer, however, must be able to support these features.

■ Notebook page enhancements such as changing the font and font size can be accomplished using the Power Bar. Note the illustration of the Power Bar with the font button selected:

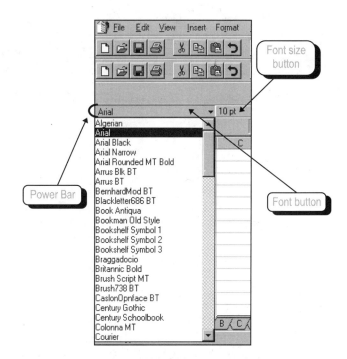

■ A **font** is a set of characters that share a design style and name. Since Windows TrueType fonts are scalable, a single TrueType font can be set to a variety of sizes. The current font name is displayed on the Font button
Arial ▼, and the current font size is displayed on the Font size button
10 pt ▼ on the Power Bar.

■ The **font size** is an attribute that sets the height of characters in a scalable font. This size is measured in points. A point is 1/72 of an inch. When the size of a font is changed, Quattro Pro automatically adjusts the row height but does not adjust the column width.

- The easiest way to apply a new font or font size is to select the cells to format and then select the font or font size via the Font or Font size buttons on the Power Bar.

- When a font and font size are selected, Quattro Pro immediately formats the text in the selected cells.

- You can change the font or font size for only those characters you select while editing a cell.

In this exercise, you will complete the Daily Cash Receipts report for March 14 for the Neighborhood Superette by calculating sales, tax, and total sales. To analyze departmental sales, the owner requests an analysis showing each department's percentage of total sales before taxes.

EXERCISE DIRECTIONS

1. Open 🖫CASH or 🖫08CASH.

2. Enter sales data and the date of the report, as shown.

3. Enter a formula to calculate a 5% TAX on GROCERIES-TAX, which represents the total sales of taxable groceries.

4. Copy the TAX formula for the BEAUTY AIDS and HOUSEWARES departments.

5. Enter a formula to determine TOTAL for the DAIRY department.
   Hint: *Sales + Tax.*

6. Copy the TOTAL formula for each department.

7. Enter the label TOTALS in cell A15.

8. Enter a formula in cell D15 to calculate TOTALS for the SALES column.

9. Copy the TOTALS formula to cells E15 and F15.

10. Enter the formula to find the % OF TOTAL using an absolute reference as illustrated.

11. Copy the % OF TOTAL formula for each department.

12. Copy the TOTALS formula to find the total of the % OF TOTAL column.

13. Use the format block commands to format the money columns (D, E, and F) for fixed with two decimal places.

14. Use the format block commands to format the % OF TOTAL column for percents with two decimal places.

15. Center column A, D, E, and F labels.

16. Make the font changes indicated below:
    - Main title: Arial 16 point
    - Secondary title: Arial 14 point
    - Column titles: Arial 12 point
    - Data in rows: MS Sans Serif 10 point
    - TOTALS row: Arial 10 point
    - ✓   *If your system does not have these fonts, choose a font that best matches the illustration.*

17. Print one copy of the notebook page.

18. Close and save the notebook, or *save as* CASH.

A	A	B	C	D	E	F	G	H	I	J
1			NEIGHBORHOOD SUPERETTE							
2			DAILY CASH RECEIPTS							
3										
4	DATE:	*March 14, 199-*								
5										
6	CODE	DEPARTMENT		SALES	TAX	TOTAL	% OF TOTAL			
7	A	DAIRY		*355.67*			+D7/$D$15			
8	B	PRODUCE		*149.55*						
9	C	MEAT & FISH		*815.54*						
10	D	GROCERIES		*556.98*						
11	E	GROCERIES-TAX		*436.92*						
12	F	BEAUTY AIDS		*386.65*						
13	G	HOUSEWARES		*315.66*						
14										
15	TOTALS									

KEYSTROKES

ENTER FORMULAS FOR ABSOLUTE CONDITIONS

1. Select cell to receive formula.
2. Press + ... **+**
3. Type formula............................*formula* using absolute references and mathematical operators.

   Example of a formula using absolute references: +$A$1*($B$2+$B$10)/2

   ✓ *You can select cells instead of typing absolute references to tell Quattro Pro which cells you wish the formula to reference.*

To insert cell references by selecting cells:

a. Click formula where cell reference will be inserted.

   ✓ *If necessary, type preceding operator or parenthesis.*

b. Select cell(s) you want formula to reference. Reference appears in formula.

c. Press **F4**.............................. **F4** until absolute reference appears.

d. Type desired operator or parenthesis.

e. Repeat steps a-d as needed.

4. Press **Enter** .... **Enter**

CHANGE FONT USING THE FONT BOX

1. Select cells or characters in cells to format.

2. Click **Font** drop-down arrow on Power Bar.

3. Select desired font ....

CHANGE FONT SIZE USING THE FONT SIZE BOX

1. Select cells or characters in cells to format.

2. Complete one of the following procedures:

   a. Click **Font size** button... `10 pt ▼` drop-down arrow on Power Bar.

   b. Select a number in list..........

   OR

   a. Click **Font size** button..... `10 pt ▼` on Power bar.

   b. Enter desired number............*number*

3. Press **Enter** .... **Enter**

Exercise

9

■ **Summary**

The New England Soup Company would like to prepare a report listing the number of employees in each of their plants. They would also like to determine the percent of total employees in each plant.

EXERCISE DIRECTIONS

1. Create an appropriate title for your notebook page.

2. Enter a listing of each PLANT and the NO. OF EMPS. as listed below:

   ✓   *Allow columns A and B for PLANT list.*

PLANT		NO. OF EMPS.
Connecticut		167
Maine		50
Massachusetts		182
New Hampshire		95
Rhode Island		130
Vermont		125

3. Skip one line below the list, enter the label TOTAL, and find the TOTAL number of employers.

4. Add a column % OF TOTAL.

5. Find what percent each plant's staff is of the total.

6. Format % OF TOTAL column for two-place percents.

7. Right-align column titles over numeric data.

8. Use font and font size changes to enhance the spreadsheet.

9. Print one copy of the notebook page.

10. Save the notebook; name it PLANTS.

Exercise 10

- ■ **Use Functions** ■ **Formula Composer**
- ■ **Quick Sum**

NOTES

Use Functions

- ■ A **function** is a built-in formula that performs a special calculation automatically. For example, the @SUM function can be used with a range of cells to add all values in the specified range. To add the values in A4, A5, and A6, for example, the function would appear in the formula as follows: @SUM(A4..A6)

- ■ Functions appear in formulas in the following order: first the function name (in either uppercase or lowercase), followed by an open parenthesis; then the number, cell, or range of cells to be affected, followed by a closed parenthesis.

- ■ A function may be used by itself, or it may be combined with other functions.

- ■ Quattro Pro provides functions that are used for statistical and financial analysis or for database operations:

@AVG()	Averages values in a range of cells.
@COUNT()	Counts all the non-blank cells in a range. Cells containing values as well as labels are counted.
@MAX()	Indicates the highest value in a range of cells.
@MIN()	Indicates the lowest value in a range of cells.
@SUM()	Adds all values in a range of cells.

- ■ The data you must supply to complete the functions are called **arguments**. For example, in @MAX(A1..A5) the range of cells A1 to A5 is the argument.

- ■ You can type or insert functions into formulas. If you are typing a function and you wish to start the formula with a function, first type an "at" sign (@). You can also insert a function by clicking Insert, Function which will display the Functions dialog box. You can also use the Formula Composer. (As illustrated on the following page.) In either case, the @ sign is automatically entered as part of the assistance provided by Quattro Pro.

Insert Function Dialog Box

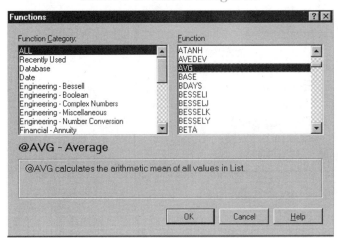

Formula Composer

■ The Formula Composer button $f_{(x)}$, located on the Toolbar, lets you insert functions into formulas by selecting the function from a list. It evaluates the formula as you enter it to determine proper syntax. When you press the @ button, located on the input line, the **Functions** dialog box displays, as illustrated on the previous page.

Formula Composer Dialog Box

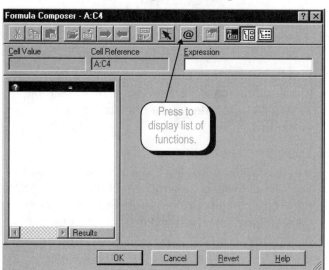

Quick Sum

■ Quattro Pro provides a quick method to enter the @SUM function. After entering the data to be added, move to the next cell and click the Sigma button Σ on the Toolbar. The formula then automatically displays on the Input line and the answer appears in the cell.

You will be adding more items to the COST notebook and summarizing the information using SUM, AVG, MAX, and MIN functions. Functions will be entered using the keyboard, Formula Composer, and Quick Sum.

EXERCISE DIRECTIONS

1. Open COST or 10COST.
2. Enter new data as shown in the illustration.
3. Copy the formulas from the MARKUP, SELLING PRICE, SALES TAX, and TOTAL PRICE columns in the block C10:F10 to the block C11:F13.
4. Enter summary labels in column A, as indicated.
5. Enter a SUM function formula to total the COST column.
6. Use the Sigma button on the Toolbar to total the MARKUP column. Copy the formula across to the remaining columns.
7. Enter an AVG function formula to average the Cost column. Copy the formula to the remaining columns.
8. Use the Formula Composer to enter the COUNT function as follows:

- Place the cursor in B16 and click the Formula Composer button.
- Click the @ function button.
- Select COUNT from the Function list and click OK.
- Click in the area between the parentheses in the function formula.
- Click the Point to Cell or Block button and select the COST data in B5:B13.
- Press Enter twice.

9. Copy the COUNT function across to the remaining columns.
10. Enter MAX and MIN functions with the keyboard or using the Formula Composer. Copy formulas to the remaining columns.
11. Format summary data money amounts for fixed with two decimal places. Format the Total Price summary data for currency.
12. Print one copy of the notebook.
13. Close and save the notebook, or *save as* COST.

A	A	B	C	D	E	F
1		GOOD SAMARITAN HOSPITAL GIFT SHOP				
2						
3				SELLING	SALES	TOTAL
4	ITEM	COST	MARKUP	PRICE	TAX	PRICE
5	345	6.00	3.00	9.00	0.45	$9.45
6	436	10.00	5.00	15.00	0.75	$15.75
7	543	14.00	7.00	21.00	1.05	$22.05
8	582	5.25	2.63	7.88	0.39	$8.27
9	498	3.25	1.63	4.88	0.24	$5.12
10	765	7.25	3.63	10.88	0.54	$11.42
11	897	3.75				
12	755	5.15				
13	347	2.95				
14	TOTALS					➤
15	AVG.					➤
16	COUNT					➤
17	HIGHEST					➤
18	LOWEST					➤

KEYSTROKES

INSERT A FUNCTION USING KEYBOARD

1. Type @ .... @
2. Type function name .... *function name*
3. Type open parenthesis .... (
4. Type arguments or block ...... *arguments*
5. Type close parenthesis ....)

INSERT A FUNCTION USING MENU

1. Click cell .... *cell* to contain formula.
2. Click **Insert** .... Alt + I
3. Click **Function** .... U
4. Follow steps 4-9 below.

INSERT A FUNCTION USING FORMULA COMPOSER

1. Click cell .... *cell* to contain formula.
   OR

a. Double-click cell containing formula.
b. Click formula where function will be inserted.

2. Click **Formula Composer** button ..... $f_{(x)}$ on Toolbar.
   OR
a. Click **Tools** menu .... Alt + T
b. Click **Formula Composer** .... F
   OR
   Press **Ctrl + F2** .... Ctrl + F2

3. Click @ button .... @
4. Select a category in **Function Category** list .... Alt + C
5. Select a function in **Function** list .... Alt + F
6. Click **OK** .... Enter
7. Type arguments and data. Depending on the function, enter the following kinds of data:
   - Numbers (constants) – type numbers (integers, fractions,

   mixed numbers, negative numbers) as you would in a cell.
   - References – type or insert cell references.
   - Named references or formulas – type or insert named references or formulas.
   OR
a. Click **Point** button ....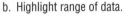
b. Highlight range of data.
c. Press **Enter**.

8. Repeat step 7, as needed.
9. Click **OK** .... Enter
   ✓ *Quattro Pro will inform you if you have entered incorrect arguments.*

USE QUICK SUM

1. Enter data to be added.
2. Place cursor in answer location. (The cell below or to the right of the data.)
3. Click **Sigma** button .... Σ

<table>
<tr><td>Exercise
11</td><td>■ **Change Column Width**
■ **Create a Series** ■ **Comma Format**</td></tr>
</table>

NOTES

Change Column Width

- It is sometimes desirable to change (widen or narrow) the column widths so text or values can fit or have a better appearance. Only the width of an entire column or a group of columns may be changed, not the width of a single cell. You can select a column (or range of columns) and then use the QuickFit button ⊞ on the Toolbar. The column width will adjust automatically to fit the longest current entry.

- You can also use the mouse to manually drag a column to a desired width. Simply place the mouse between two columns. When the cursor changes to a crosshair ◄►, drag the column to the desired width.

- All notebook pages in a notebook are set for a **standard column width** (default setting). The default setting represents the number of characters displayed in a cell using the standard font. Column width may be changed by selecting Block from the Format menu and then clicking on the Column Width tab. Note the default column setting. Auto Width sets the column to fit the widest entry. Another way to quickly set the column to fit the widest entry is to select QuickFit from the Format menu.

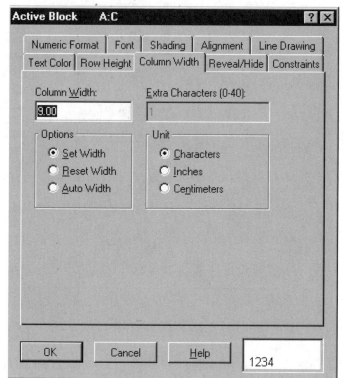

- When you enter long labels, the text flows into the next column if the cell to the right is empty. If the next cell is not empty, text that exceeds the column width is covered by the data in the cell to the right.

- Quattro Pro displays numeric data that exceeds the column width by filling the cell with asterisks (********), by displaying the number in scientific notation, or by hiding the numeric data–depending on which number type has been selected.

Create a Series

■ You can use the Fill command on the Data menu to quickly enter sequential values in a range of cells. You can enter sequential numbers, dates, or times in any increment (e.g., 2, 4, 6, 8 or 5, 10, 15, 20 or January, February, March, April). In addition, you can define a pattern of entries to fill a block by using the Data, Define Fill Series selection. Note the illustration of the Data Fill dialog box used to set a sequential range of numbers beginning with 316. The ending value need not be set if you select the range before opening this dialog box.

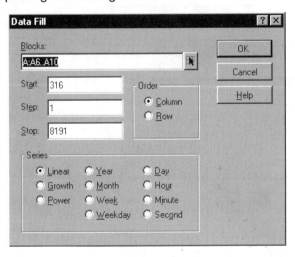

Comma Format

■ To make large numbers more readable, formatting may be used to include commas. To do so, highlight the block of cells, columns or rows to receive the comma format and click Format, Block. Click on the Numeric Format tab, click the Comma option and then enter the number of desired decimal places.

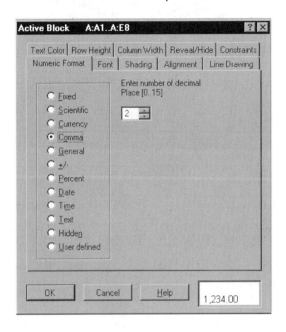

You will create a notebook page for Atlantis Auto Sales showing employees' quarterly SALES and COMMISSIONS earned. Each employee receives a 2% commission on sales.

EXERCISE DIRECTIONS

1. Create the notebook as shown on the following page or open ▭11AUTO.

2. Set column widths as follows:
   - Column A: 4
   - Column B: 15

3. Use the QuickFit button ⊞ on the Notebook Toolbar for column E, and as needed throughout this exercise.

4. Select the block for EMP. NO. in cells A6:A10. Use the Fill option on the Data menu. Enter employee numbers starting with 316 and incrementing by 1.

5. Copy BASE SALARY to the remaining employees.
   ✓ *All employees have the same base salary.*

6. Enter a formula to find COMMISSIONS for the first employee. The commission rate is 2% of sales. Copy the formula to the remaining employees.

7. Enter a formula to find 1ST QTR. EARNINGS for the first employee by adding BASE SALARY and COMMISSIONS for the quarter. Copy the formula to the remaining employees.

8. Enter formulas using functions to find TOTALS, AVERAGES, HIGHEST, and LOWEST values. Copy the formulas to each column.

9. Center column title labels.

10. Format numeric data to include commas and two decimal places.

11. Save the notebook; name it AUTO.

12. Print one copy.

13. Close the notebook.

A	A	B	C	D	E	F
1			ATLANTIS AUTO SALES			
2			QUARTERLY SALES AND SALARY REPORT			
3						
4	EMP.		BASE	1ST QTR,		1ST QTR.
5	NO.	NAME	SALARY	SALES	COMMISSIONS	EARNINGS
6	316	Mario Bumpa	1500.00	342,567.77		
7	317	Charles Fender		432,567.86		
8	318	Phil Muffler		564,343.43		
9	319	Harriet Hood		654,544.44		
10	320	Terry Trunk		432,445.66		
11						
12		TOTALS				
13		AVERAGES				
14		HIGHEST				
15		LOWEST				

KEYSTROKES

CHANGE COLUMN WIDTHS USING THE MENU

1. Select any cell(s) in column(s) to change.
2. Press **F12** .... `F12`

   OR

   Click **Format** .... `Alt`+`R`

   Click **Block** .... `B`
3. Click **Column Width** tab .... `Ctrl`+`Tab`
4. Type number (0-299) .... *number* in **Column Width** text box.

   ✓ *Number represents number of characters that can be displayed in cell using the standard font. You can change the units of measure by selecting **Inches** or **Centimeters** from the **unit** group.*
5. Click **OK** .... `Enter`

CHANGE COLUMN WIDTHS USING THE MOUSE

Change One Column Width

1. Point to right border of column heading to size.

   Pointer becomes a .... `◄►`
2. Drag `◄►` left or right.

Change Several Column Widths

1. Select columns to size.
2. Point to right border of any selected column heading. Pointer becomes left and right arrows.
3. Drag `◄►` left or right.

SET COLUMN WIDTH TO FIT LONGEST ENTRY

1. Select column to size.
2. Click .... `↔`

   OR

   Click **Format** .... `Alt`+`R`

   Click **QuickFit** .... `Q`

   ✓ *You can also choose **Auto Width** in the **Format**, **Block**, **Column Width** dialog box.*

CREATE A SERIES OF NUMBERS, DATES, OR TIMES USING THE MENU

1. Select cell(s) containing cells to fill.
2. Click **Data** .... `Alt`+`D`
3. Click **Fill** .... `F`

To enter starting value:

   a. Click **Start** .... `Alt`+`A`
   b. Enter start value .... *start value*

To change proposed step value:

   a. Click **Step** .... `Alt`+`E`
   b. Type step value .... *number* in **Step** text box.

To change proposed direction of series:

   Select desired **Order** in option:

   • **Rows** .... `Alt`+`R`
   • **Columns** .... `Alt`+`C`

To change proposed series type:

   Select desired **Series** option:

   • **Linear** .... `Alt`+`L` to increase/decrease each value in series by number in **Step** value text box.

   • **Growth** .... `Alt`+`G` to multiply each value in series by number in **Step** value text box.

   • **Power** .... `Alt`+`P` to increase each value in series exponentially.

   • You may also choose **Year**, **Month**, **Week**, **Weekday**, **Day**, **Hour**, **Minute Second**.

To set stop value for series:

   ✓ *Type a stop value if you want series to end at a specific number.*

   a. Click **Stop** .... `Alt`+`S`
   b. Type stop value .... *number*
4. Click **OK** .... `Enter`

FORMAT DATA FOR COMMAS

Press **F12** .... `F12`

OR

1. Click **Format** .... `Alt`+`R`
2. Click **Block** .... `B`

OR

1. Right-click.
2. Select **Block Properties**.
3. Select **Numeric Format** tab ... `Ctrl`+`Tab`
4. Click **Comma** .... `O`
5. Click **Enter number of decimal Place** .... `Shift`+`Tab`
6. Use arrows or enter number ...... `↓` `↑`
7. Click **OK** .... `Enter`

Exercise 12

- **Print Options** ■ **Edit Data**
- **Documentation Notes**

NOTES

Print Options

■ When the **Print** command is accessed, the Spreedsheet Print dialog box allows you to select various print options. Note the illustration of the Spreedsheet Print dialog box below.

Spreedsheet Print Dialog Box

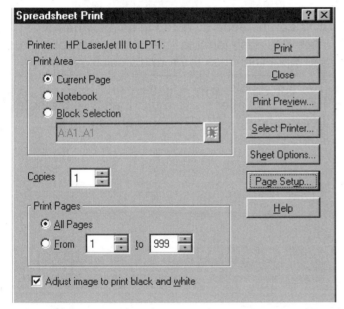

Paper Type Tab on Spreadsheet Page Setup Dialog Box

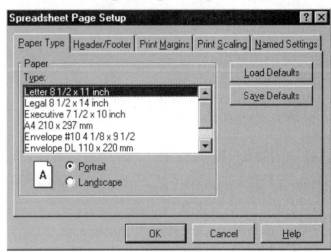

Print Scaling Tab on Spreadsheet Page Setup Dialog Box

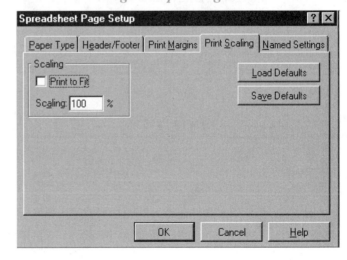

■ The **Page Setup** button, in the Spreedsheet Print dialog box, is used to access page setting options. Note the illustrations of the Paper Type and Print Scaling tabs of the Spreadsheet Page Setup dialog box. The other setting tabs are for Header/Footer, Print Margins, and Named Settings.

■ When you select the Sheet Options button from the Speedsheet Print dialog box, you can set various print options for the Notebook sheet, such as gridlines, and row and column headings as shown in the Spreadsheet Print Options box below.

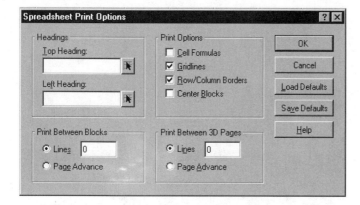

■ In the Spreadsheet Print dialog box you can also select the Print Preview button to review, on screen, the output your settings will yield.

Edit Data

■ Data may be changed either before or after it has been entered in a cell.

■ Before data is entered, the Backspace key may be used to correct a keystroke.

■ To clear a cell's content before it is entered:

• Press the Escape key, or

• Click the Cancel button [✖] on the Input line.

■ After data is entered, there are several methods of correction:

• Replace the entire entry with new data.

• Edit part of an entry by enabling cell editing.

• Erase a single cell entry.

• Erase a range of cell entries.

■ You can enable cell editing by pressing F2 or by double-clicking the cell. The cursor will then appear at the end of the entry and the data will appear on the Input line. Entries can be erased by selecting the data and then clicking Edit, Clear.

Documentation Notes

■ When a notebook is created by one person and later used by others, it is beneficial to document or explain the formulas used to create the report. This can be done by entering an explanatory note with each formula. The note will display on the Input line when the formula cell is selected.

■ To enter a note, type a semi-colon (;) immediately after the formula, then type the note. For example: +C7*D7; Hours times rate per hour.

In this exercise, you will complete the payroll for the Jerome Insurance Agency for the week ending February 6, 199-. You will then copy the entire notebook page to a new location and edit entries to create another payroll for the week ending February 13, 199-. Documentation notes will be added to several formulas.

EXERCISE DIRECTIONS

1. Open ⌨PAY or ⌨12PAY.

2. Clear the PAYROLL label from the subtitle.

3. Enter a new subtitle in column D: PAYROLL FOR THE WEEK ENDING 2/6/9-

4. Enter the new row labels at the bottom of the notebook, as indicated.

5. Find Totals and Averages for columns from Gross Pay to Net Pay.

6. Format Totals and Averages for two decimal places.

7. Enter documentation notes in the formulas listed by enabling cell editing, adding a semi-colon and adding the notes shown below:
   E7: Hours worked times hourly pay.
   F7: Used 20% of Gross Pay.
   G7: Used 6.2% of Gross Pay.
   H7: Used 1.45% of Gross Pay.

8. Copy the block of data that represents the entire payroll, as shown, to A17 on the notebook page.

   ✓ *When copying a block, it is only necessary to specify the first position as the destination block.*

   – ON THE BOTTOM PAYROLL –

9. Edit the title to read:

   PAYROLL FOR THE WEEK ENDING 2/13/9-

10. Edit the HOURS WORKED as follows:

    | Drennen | 22 |
    | Foxman | 25 |
    | Lindner | 37 |
    | Nichols | 25 |
    | Renfrew | 26 |
    | Trainor | 35 |

11. Preview the printout of this file.

12. Print one copy of the February 13 payroll.

13. Close and save the notebook, or *save as* PAY.

A	A	B	C	D	E	F	G	H	I	J	K
1	JIJIJIJIJIJ			JEROME INSURANCE AGENCY					JIJIJIJIJIJ		
2				*PAYROLL FOR THE WEEK ENDING 2/6/9-*							
3											
4	Card	Emp.	Hourly	Hours	Gross	Federal	Soc. Sec.	Medicare	Net		
5	Number	Name	Rate	Worked	Pay	With. Tax	Tax	Tax	Pay		
6											
7	325	Drennen	6.55	15	98.25	19.65	6.09	1.42	71.08		
8	345	Foxman	6.85	21	143.85	28.77	8.92	2.09	104.08	Copy block	
9	315	Lindner	7.23	35	253.05	50.61	15.69	3.67	183.08	A2:I15 to A17	
10	330	Nichols	8.65	29	250.85	50.17	15.55	3.64	181.49		
11	340	Renfrew	9.95	27	268.65	53.73	16.66	3.90	194.37		
12	350	Trainor	8.65	21	181.65	36.33	11.26	2.63	131.42		
13											
14	*Totals*										
15	*Averages*										
16		copy									
17											
18											
19											

KEYSTROKES

EDIT CELL CONTENTS AFTER IT IS ENTERED (ENABLE CELL EDITING)

1. Double-click cell to edit.

   OR

   a. Select cell to edit .... [⬍⬌]
   b. Press **F2** .... [F2]

   An insertion point appears in the active cell and these buttons appear on the formula bar:

   [✖] *Cancel button – cancels changes made in cell.*

   [✔] *OK button – accepts changes made in cell.*

2. Click desired data position in cell or in formula bar.

3. Type new data .... *data*

   OR

   Press **Backspace** .... [Backspace]
   to delete character left of insertion point.

   OR

   Press **Delete** .... [Del]
   to delete character left of insertion point.

   To accept changes:

   Press **Enter** .... [Enter]

   OR

   Click **OK** button .... [✔]
   on the formula bar.

   To cancel changes:

   Press **Escape** .... [Esc]

   OR

   Click **Cancel** button .... [✖]
   on the formula bar.

EDIT CELL CONTENTS WHILE TYPING

To delete character to the left of insertion point:

Press **Backspace** .... [Backspace]

To cancel all characters:

Press **Escape** .... [Esc]

ERASE CONTENTS OF CELL OR RANGE

1. Select cell or range containing contents to erase.

2. Press **Delete** .... [Del]

   OR

   Click **Edit** .... [Alt]+[E]
   Click **Clear** .... [E]

PRINT PREVIEW

1. Click **Print** button on Standard Toolbar .... [🖶]

2. Click **Print Preview** .... [Alt]+[V]

   OR

   a. Click **File** .... [Alt]+[F]
   b. Click **Print Preview** .... [V]

   – FROM PREVIEW WINDOW –

   To view next page:

   Click **Next Page** button .... [▶]

   To view previous page:

   Click **Previous Page** button .... [◀]

   To view a magnified portion of the page:

   Left-click area of page to magnify.

   OR

a. Click **Increase Zoom** button .... [🔍+]

   OR

   Click **Reduce Zoom** button .... [🔍−]

b. Right-click any area of page to return to full page view.

3. Click [✖] to exit Print Preview.

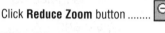 PRINT RANGE OF CELLS

Prints data in range using the current page settings.

✓   *When printing a range, this procedure will override a print area, if you defined one.*

1. Select range of cells to print.
2. Click **File** menu .... [Alt]+[F]
3. Click **Print**.................................... [P]
4. Click **Block Selection** .... [B]
5. Click **Print**............................ [Alt]+[P]

SET PRINT OPTIONS FOR WORKSHEET

1. Click **File** menu .... [Alt]+[F]
2. Click **Print** .... [P]
3. Click **Page Setup** .... [Alt]+[U]
4. Select desired tab .... [Ctrl]+[Tab]

   OR

   Choose from the following:
   - **Paper Type** .... [Alt]+[P]
   - **Header/Footer** .... [Alt]+[E]
   - **Print Margins** .... [Alt]+[M]
   - **Print Scaling** .... [Alt]+[S]
   - **Named Settings** .... [Alt]+[N]

1. Select desired setting .... [Tab]
2. Enter setting or use list box .... [⬍]
3. Click **OK**................................... [Enter]

Exercise 13

- ■ **Page Setup**
- ■ **Block Properties**

NOTES

Page Setup

■ Quattro Pro uses the default page size (usually 8 ½"x11") of the current printer. To change the page size, select <u>P</u>rint from the <u>F</u>ile menu, click the Page Set<u>u</u>p button, and select the <u>P</u>aper Type tab. Use the following Page Setup options to control the print output for the selected page size.

■ <u>P</u>aper Type options include:

- **Type:** The size of paper on which to print the notebook page.

- **Orientation:** P<u>o</u>rtrait prints the notebook page vertically on the paper. Lan<u>d</u>scape prints the notebook page horizontally on the paper.

Page Setup Dialog Box With Paper Type Tab Selected

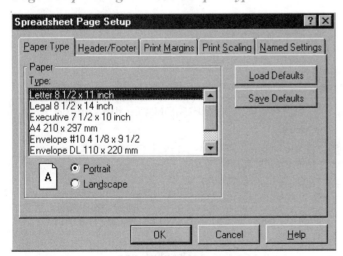

■ H<u>e</u>ader/Footer options include:

- **Head<u>e</u>r:** Text to be printed at the top of each notebook page.

- **Footer:** Text to be printed at the bottom of each notebook page.

- **H<u>e</u>ader Font:** Sets the font for the header text.

- **F<u>o</u>oter Font:** Sets the font for the footer text.

■ Print <u>M</u>argins options include:

- **<u>T</u>op, <u>B</u>ottom, <u>L</u>eft, <u>R</u>ight:** Sets the size for a notebook page's top, bottom, left, and right margins.

- **He<u>a</u>der, F<u>o</u>oter:** Sets margins for the header and footer area of a notebook page.

- **Break Pages:** Configures Quattro Pro to break pages when a line count is reached.

Page Setup Dialog Box With Print Margins Tab Selected

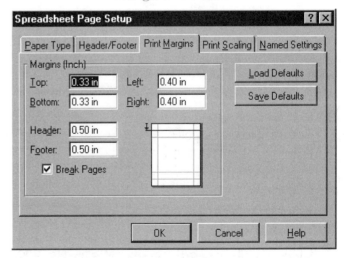

■ Print <u>S</u>caling options include:

- **Print to F<u>i</u>t:** Prints notebook so that it fits on as few pages as possible.

- **Scaling:** Sets percentage (1-1000) to increase or decrease size of data printed on a page. Margins don't change.

■ And, finally, the <u>N</u>amed Settings options include:

- **New Set:** Type the name for a new print setting.

- **<u>A</u>dd:** Adds the setting to the list.

- **<u>U</u>se:** Uses the selected named print setting.

- **Updat<u>e</u>:** Replaces the settings stored under the selected name with the current print settings.

- **<u>D</u>elete:** Deletes the selected named setting.

Block Properties

■ You may apply several formatting options at once when you format text or values by using the **Block Properties Active Block** dialog box. To access the Active Block dialog box, select the block of cells you wish to format, and then choose one of the following methods:

- Select <u>B</u>lock from the Fo<u>r</u>mat menu

- Right-click (on the block of cells) and choose Block Properties

- Press F12

■ Note in the illustration below, that although the Numeric Format tab is currently displayed, the box also contains nine other tabs which contain block formatting options. Settings for column widths, data alignment, font, color, and numeric formats can be set all at once for a block of data using this dialog box.

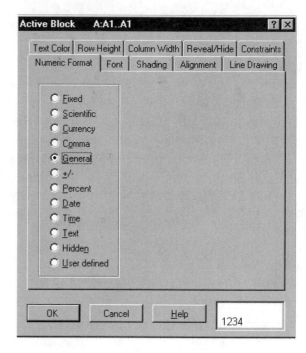

In this exercise, you will add data to the Atlantis Auto Sales and Salary report, set column widths, and use block properties and page setup commands.

EXERCISE DIRECTIONS

1. Open ⛭AUTO or 🖫13AUTO.
2. Edit the second line of the title. Add: JANUARY-JUNE.
3. Replace 1ST QTR. with JAN-MAR.
4. Use Block Properties to change column widths as follows:
   - Select columns G, H, and I.
   - Change width to 14.
5. Copy column titles SALES, COMMISSIONS, and EARNINGS to columns G, H, and I. Insert the label APR-JUN over SALES in column G.
6. Center all column headings.
7. Enter new sales data in column G.
8. Copy the COMMISSIONS formula for the first employee in column E to column H.
9. Copy the COMMISSIONS formula down for each employee.

10. Enter the label 2ND QTR. over EARNINGS in column I.
11. Enter a formula in column I to compute BASE SALARY + COMMISSIONS for the second quarter.
12. Copy the BASE SALARY + COMMISSIONS formula down for each employee.
13. Find TOTALS, AVERAGES, HIGHEST, and LOWEST for the second quarter. (Copy formulas using one copy command.)
14. Use Block Properties to format numeric data for commas and two decimal places.
15. Use Page Setup to change the scale setting to fit the notebook page on one page.
16. Check your scale setting using Print Preview.
17. Print one copy.
18. Close and save the notebook, or *save as* AUTO.

A	A	B	C	D	E	F	G	H	I	J
1			ATLANTIS AUTO SALES							
2			QUARTERLY SALES AND SALARY REPORT			←	*JANUARY-JUNE*			
3			*JAN-MAR*					14		
4	EMP.		BASE	1ST QTR.		1ST QTR.				
5	NO.	NAME	SALARY	SALES	COMMISSIONS	EARNINGS				
6	316	Mario Bumpa	1500.00	342,567.77	6,851.36	8,351.36	*356,789.43*			
7	317	Charles Fender	1500.00	432,567.86	8,651.36	10,151.36	*478,987.03*			
8	318	Phil Muffler	1500.00	564,343.43	11,286.87	12,786.87	*421,767.89*			
9	319	Harriet Hood	1500.00	654,544.44	13,090.89	14,590.89	*611,435.78*			
10	320	Terry Trunk	1500.00	432,445.66	8,648.91	10,148.91	*489,090.87*			
11										
12		TOTALS	7500	2,426,469.16	48,529.38	56,029.38				
13		AVERAGES	1500	485,293.83	9,705.88	11,205.88				
14		HIGHEST	1500	654,544.44	13,090.89	14,590.89				
15		LOWEST	1500	342,567.77	6,851.36	8,351.36				

KEYSTROKES

CHANGE SCALE OF PRINTED DATA

1. Click **File** .... Alt + F
2. Click **Print** .... P
3. Click **Page Setup** .... U
4. Select **Print Scaling** .... Alt + S

   To reduce or enlarge data on printed sheet:

   Type percentage (1-100).... Tab + *number*

   To Print to Fit on one page:

   Click **Print to Fit** .... Alt + I
5. Click **OK** .... Enter

USE BLOCK PROPERTIES TO FORMAT DATA

1. Press **F12** F12

   OR

   Click **Format** .... Alt + R

   Click **Block** .... B

   OR

   Right-click.

   Select **Block Properties**.
2. Select appropriate tab .... Ctrl + Tab
   from the following:
   - Numeric Format
   - Font
   - Shading
   - Alignment
   - Line Drawing
   - Text Color
   - Row Height
   - Column Width
   - Reveal/Hide
   - Constraints
3. Use list boxes and/or buttons to set options.
4. Click **OK** .... Enter

<table>
<tr><td>Exercise
14</td><td>■ **Page Breaks** ■ **Bold** ■ **Headers and Footers**</td></tr>
</table>

NOTES

Page Breaks

- Before printing, you may set hard page breaks and add headers and footers.

- Quattro Pro inserts soft page breaks based on the current paper size, scaling, and margin settings. You can override the automatic page breaks by inserting hard page breaks in your notebook page. When you click Insert, Page Break, Quattro Pro stops printing on the current page and starts printing on the top of a new page. Hard page breaks are denoted by two colons (::) in the first column of a row.

- You can remove soft page breaks by choosing Print from the File menu, clicking the Page Setup button and deselecting the Break Pages check box in the Print Margins dialog box. Hard page breaks may be removed by deleting the two colons that indicate the hard page break.

Bold

- Labels or values may be emphasized by bolding the characters. Select the text and press the Bold button **b** on the Notebook Toolbar.

Headers and Footers

- Headers and footers are used when you want to repeat the same information at the top (header) or bottom (footer) of every page.

- Headers/footers are limited to a single line of text. You can specify different fonts for headers and footers.

- The following table lists special characters you can use to format header and footer text.

Code	Description
|	(vertical bar) Determines the position of the text: left-aligned, right-aligned, or centered.
#d	Enters the current date in the Short Date International format. (02/06)
#D	Enters the current date in the Long Date International format. (02/06/98)
#ds	Enters the current date in Short Date format. (20-Feb)
#Ds	Enters the current date in Long Date format. (20-Feb-98)
#t	Enters the current time in Long Time International format. (18:47)
#ts	Enters the current time in Short Time format. (06:47PM)
#Ts	Enters the current time in Long Time format. (06:48:49PM)
#p	Enters the current page number.
#P	Enters the number of pages in the document.
#f	Enters just the name of the notebook being printed (EXPENSE.WB2).
#F	Enters the name and path of the notebook being printed (C:\DATA\EXPENSE.WB2).
#n	Prints the remainder of the header or footer on a second line.
#	(number sign) Enters the current page number. Use for compatibility with Quattro Pro for DOS.
@	Enters the current date (per your computer's calendar). Use for compatibility with Quattro Pro for DOS.

✓ *If you want a # or @ character to appear in your header or footer without being treated as a header or footer code, type a backslash (\) character before the # or @.*

- Header and Footer information can be added and edited by selecting the Header/Footer tab on the Spreadsheet Page Setup dialog box. Note the illustration of the text settings provided in the Header/Footer tab and compare it with the illustration of the headers and footers that result from those settings. The vertical bar is used to separate left-aligned, centered, or right-aligned data. For example, If you wish to display only a centered filename, you would enter: |#f| as illustrated in the Footer below.

Spreadsheet Page Setup Dialog Box, Header/Footer Tab

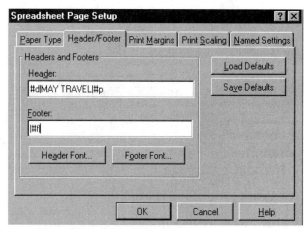

Header

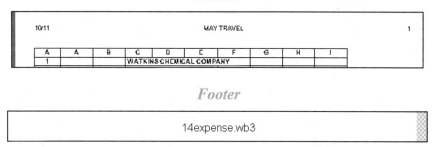

Footer

14expense.wb3

In this exercise, you will create a travel expense report for one of the engineers at the Watkins Chemical Company. The May travel report will include two trips, each printed on a separate page with a header and footer.

EXERCISE DIRECTIONS

1. Create the top notebook page shown on the next page, or open 🖫14EXPENS.

   ✓ *Enter the days of the month as numeric labels. Bold headings as illustrated.*

2. Set column C width to 7.

3. Use block properties to format block D12:I37 for fixed number format.

4. Find Mileage reimbursement at $.29 per mile in cell D14.

5. Find for TRANSPORTATION EXPENSES:
   - TOTAL - find the horizontal total for the Airplane row, columns D-H, excluding column C, the MILES column.
   - Copy the formula down for all Transportation items.
   - TOTAL TRANSPORTATION: find the total of column D from row 12 down.
   - Copy the formula across for all columns of data.

6. Find for DAILY EXPENSES:
   - Copy TOTALS formula down for all rows of data.

- TOTAL DAILY EXPENSES: enter a formula to total the DAILY EXPENSES items.

7. Copy formula for all columns.

8. Find TOTAL EXPENSES by adding TOTAL TRANSPORTATION and TOTAL DAILY EXPENSES.

9. Copy the formula for all columns.

10. Copy the entire top notebook page to cell A40.

11. Create a page break at cell A39.

12. Edit the DESTINATION, PURPOSE, DATES, and all EXPENSES to display the data for the next trip, as indicated.

13. Print the file to fit columns to the page with the following header/footer specifications: (*See dialog box illustration above.*)
    - Header: left-justified date, centered title that reads MAY TRAVEL, right-justified page number.
    - Footer: centered file name.

14. Close and save the notebook file; name it EXPENSE.

A	A	B	C	D	E	F	G	H	I
1			WATKINS CHEMICAL COMPANY						
2			EXPENSE REPORT						
3									
4	NAME:		Rudy Montana						
5	DESTINATION:		Petrolia, PA						
6	PURPOSE:		Technical Assistance						
7	DATES:		5/12-5/15/9-						
8									
9			MILES	@ $.29	1	2	3	4	TOTALS
10		DATES:			5/12	5/13	5/14	5/15	
11	TRANSPORTATION:								
12	Airplane								
13	Car Expenses:								
14		Miles	356						
15		Tolls			6.50		1.25	6.50	
16		Parking			10.50				
17		Rental							
18	Taxi					8.25			
19	Train								
20	Other								
21									
22	TOTAL TRANSPORTATION								
23									
24	DAILY EXPENSES:								
25	Hotel				65.00	65.00	65.00	65.00	
26	Meals				62.75	54.78	25.98	75.76	
27	Telephone, Fax, etc.				12.66	14.65	32.65	5.45	
28	Copy Services					5.75	10.65		
29	Entertainment						124.86		
30	Fees, etc.								
31	Tips				10.00	11.00	22.00	12.00	
32	Other								
33									
34	TOTAL DAILY EXPENSES								
35									
36	TOTAL EXPENSES								
37									
38									
39	::		Page break						
40									
41			WATKINS CHEMICAL COMPANY						
42			EXPENSE REPORT						
43									
44	NAME:		Rudy Montana						
45	DESTINATION:		Los Angeles, CA						
46	PURPOSE:		Technical Assistance						
47	DATES:		5/25-5/28/9-						
48									
49			MILES	@ $.29	1	2	3	4	TOTALS
50		DATES:			5/25	5/26	5/27	5/28	
51	TRANSPORTATION:								
52	Airplane				554.85				
53	Car Expenses:								
54		Miles							
55		Tolls			2.50	1.25	1.25	2.50	
56		Parking				22.00	12.00		
57		Rental			45.00	45.00	45.00	45.00	
58	Taxi								
59	Train								
60	Other								
61									
62	TOTAL TRANSPORTATION								
63									
64	DAILY EXPENSES:								
65	Hotel				92.00	92.00	92.00	92.00	
66	Meals				75.43	56.79	81.54	25.76	
67	Telephone, Fax, etc.				10.87	24.35	19.86	6.87	
68	Copy Services								
69	Entertainment					165.54			
70	Fees, etc.								
71	Tips				22.00	35.00	21.00	19.00	
72	Other								
73									
74	TOTAL DAILY EXPENSES								
75									
76	TOTAL EXPENSES								

KEYSTROKES

INSERT HARD PAGE BREAKS

✓ *After you insert a hard page break, Quattro Pro adjusts the soft page breaks that follow it.*

1. Select row where new page will start.
2. Click **Insert**............................ `Alt` + `I`
3. Click **Page Break** .... `P`

REMOVE HARD PAGE BREAKS

✓ *After you remove a hard page break, Quattro Pro adjusts the soft page breaks that follow it.*

1. Select the cell containing the page break.
2. Click **Delete** .... `Del`

DISABLE SOFT PAGE BREAKS

1. Click **File**................................ `Alt` + `F`
2. Click **Print** .... `P`
3. Click **Page Setup** .... `U`
4. Click **Print Margins** .... `Alt` + `M`
5. Disable the **Break Pages** option .... `Alt` + `A`
6. Click **OK** .... `Enter`

SET HEADER AND FOOTER OPTIONS

Adds text or special codes to top or bottom of each page.

1. Click **File** .... `Alt` + `F`
2. Click **Print** .... `P`
3. Click **Page Setup** .... `U`
4. Select **Header/Footer** tab .... `Alt` + `E`
5. Type header/footer text.
6. Place insertion point where code will appear.
7. Type desired code:
   | Moves text to next alignment position–left, center, or right.
   #p Inserts current page number.
   #P Inserts total number of pages in document.
   #d Inserts current date in short format.
   #t Inserts current time.
   #f Inserts the name of the notebook.

CHANGE HEADER/FOOTER FONT

To change the header/footer font:

1. Follow steps 1-4 (under Set Header and Footer Options).
2. Click **Header Font** .... `Alt` + `A`
   OR
   Click **Footer Font** .... `Alt` + `O`
3. Click **Typeface** .... `Alt` + `T`
4. Select a typeface .... `↓` `↑`
5. Click **Point Size**........ `Alt` + `P`, `↓` `↑`
6. Select desired font options.
7. Click **OK** .... `Enter`

Exercise

15

- ■ **Print Preview**
- ■ **Top and Left Headings**

Print Preview Toolbar

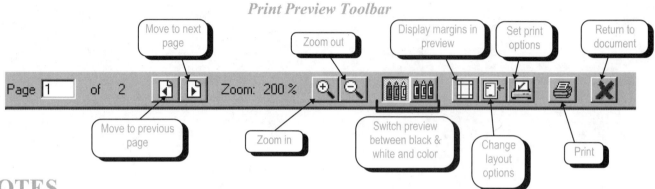

NOTES

Print Preview

- ■ When working with multiple pages or when making print settings, it is advisable to preview your report prior to printing by selecting Print Preview from the File menu. The Print Preview Toolbar, illustrated above, allows you to advance through multiple pages in the report, zoom in or out for a better view, switch between color and black and white output views, change the layout, set print options, print, or simply return to the notebook.

Top and Left Headings

- ■ As a print option, you may print **top and left headings** which come from rows and columns in the notebook. Notebook headings may be useful when:
  - Printing a range that is too wide or too long to fit on one page. Headings will then display on the remaining pages to clarify the data.
  - Printing part of a columnar series of data that does not have column or row headings immediately adjacent to the column of data you wish to print.
- ■ The top or left headings you select from the notebook:

- Should not be included in the print range when you have already assigned a heading to a part of a columnar series.

- Will appear only on the pages that follow the page containing the heading data (when an extra wide or extra long notebook page is set up as the print range).

- ■ Top and left headings are set by selecting Print from the File menu, clicking on the Sheet Options button, and inputting the top or left ranges to indicate which rows or columns you want repeated on every page of the printed notebook.

- ■ Note that the Spreadsheet Print Options dialog box below also shows the Gridlines and Row/Column Borders options selected. These settings are used to produce the notebooks illustrated on the following page.

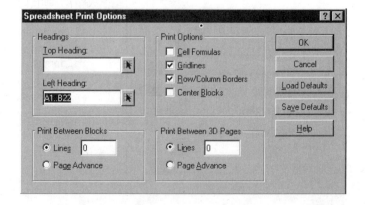

✓ *Note the illustrations below. They show the first and second pages of a notebook page that is too wide for one page (using 100% sizing). Since left headings were set for column A, both pages show the labels contained in that column.*

Page 1

A	A	B	C	D	E	F	G	H
1			LOPEZ INSURANCE AGENCY					
2			COMPARATIVE INCOME STATEMENT					
3			FOR THE MONTHS ENDED 199-					
4								
5			JANUARY	FEBRUARY	MARCH	APRIL	MAY	JUNE
6	INCOME:							
7	Commissions		10,212.32	11,212.22	13,453.88	12,546.87	12,965.33	13,221.77
8	Consultations		3,245.65	2,843.23	3,565.89	3,867.22	3,144.55	3,256.87
9	Total Income		13,457.97	14,055.45	17,019.77	16,414.09	16,109.88	16,478.64
10								
11	EXPENSES:							
12	Advertising		125.00	125.00	145.00	155.00	125.00	165.00
13	Rent		1,500.00	1,500.00	1,500.00	1,500.00	1,500.00	1,500.00
14	Salaries		9,576.88	9,576.88	9,978.65	10,434.34	9,576.88	9,576.88
15	Payroll Taxes		954.54	954.54	992.15	995.43	954.54	954.54
16	Supplies		215.00	123.00	333.00	245.00	189.00	209.00
17	Utilities		278.65	286.75	276.56	289.87	277.43	298.76
18	Other		136.76	35.45	43.56	115.64	132.65	165.33
19	Total Expenses		12,786.83	12,601.62	13,268.92	13,735.28	12,755.50	12,869.51
20								
21	NET INCOME		671.14	1,453.83	3,750.85	2,678.81	3,354.38	3,609.13

Left heading

Page 2

A	A	I	J
1			
2			
3			
4			
5		TOTALS	AVERAGES
6	INCOME:		
7	Commissions	73,612.39	12,268.73
8	Consultations	19,923.41	3,320.57
9	Total Income	93,535.80	15,589.30
10			
11	EXPENSES:		
12	Advertising	840.00	140.00
13	Rent	9,000.00	1,500.00
14	Salaries	58,720.51	9,786.75
15	Payroll Taxes	5,805.74	967.62
16	Supplies	1,314.00	219.00
17	Utilities	1,708.02	284.67
18	Other	629.39	104.90
19	Total Expenses	78,017.66	13,002.94
20			
21	NET INCOME	15,518.14	2,586.36

Left heading

KEYSTROKES

SET REPEATING PRINT TITLES FOR NOTEBOOK PAGE

Sets titles to print on current and subsequent pages.

1. Click **File** .... `Alt`+`F`
2. Click **Print** .... `P`
3. Select **Sheet Options** .... `Alt`+`E`

   To set columns as repeating print headings:

   a. Choose **Left heading**. .... `Alt`+`F`

   b. Select columns in notebook page.

   OR

   Type column reference.

   ✓ *Columns must be adjacent. To remove print titles, delete the reference.*

   To set rows as repeating print titles:

   a. Click **Top heading** .... `Alt`+`T`

   b. Select rows in notebook page.

   OR

   Type row reference.

   ✓ *Rows must be adjacent. To remove print titles, delete the reference.*

4. Click **OK** .... `Enter`
5. Click **Close** .... `Alt`+`C`
   to return to Notebook Page.

   OR

   Click **Print** .... `Alt`+`P`
   to print notebook page using current settings.

In this exercise, you will create a comparative income statement for the Lopez Insurance Agency. To print data for only the last three months, it is necessary to set a left heading for the labels in the first column.

EXERCISE DIRECTIONS

1. Create the notebook page as illustrated, or open 🖫15INCOME.

2. Set column widths as follows:

   Column A:　　　18

   Column B:　　　5

   Column C-J:　　12

3. Format the entire data block for commas with two decimal places.

4. Find for each month:
   - Total Income
   - Total Expenses
   - NET INCOME　(Income-Expenses)

5. Find for each item in the income statement:
   - TOTALS
   - AVERAGES

6. Center all column headings.

7. Select Print from the File menu and click Sheet Options. Set column A as a left heading.

8. Create a header that includes the page number and total pages centered on the page.

9. Set the print range for the entire notebook page and be sure that scaling is set to 100% of normal size. Preview both pages of the notebook page.
   - ✓　*Page one will show column A with JANUARY through JUNE data. Page two will show column A with TOTALS through AVERAGES data, as illustrated.*

10. Print one copy of the two-page report.

11. Change columns C-J back to the standard width.

12. Print one copy of the April-June data with column titles:
   - Highlight the April-June columns. Enter commands to print the selection.
   - Preview the print selection. (The column border was set previously.)
   - ✓　*The April-June data will be shown with the column titles in column A.*
   - Print the selection.

13. Save the notebook file; name it INCOME.

14. Close the notebook.

	A	B	C	D	E	F	G	H	I	J
1			COMPARATIVE INCOME STATEMENT							
2			FOR THE MONTHS ENDED 199-							
3	18	5	12	12	12	12	12	12	12	12
4			JANUARY	FEBRUARY	MARCH	APRIL	MAY	JUNE	TOTALS	AVERAGES
5	INCOME:									
6	Commissions		10,212.32	11,212.22	13,453.88	12,546.87	12,965.33	13,221.77		
7	Consultations		3,245.65	2,843.23	3,565.89	3,867.22	3,144.55	3,256.87		
8	Total Income									
9										
10	EXPENSES:									
11	Advertising		125.00	125.00	145.00	155.00	125.00	165.00		
12	Rent		1,500.00	1,500.00	1,500.00	1,500.00	1,500.00	1,500.00		
13	Salaries		9,576.88	9,576.88	9,978.65	10,434.34	9,576.88	9,576.88		
14	Payroll Taxes		954.54	954.54	992.15	995.43	954.54	954.54		
15	Supplies		215.00	123.00	333.00	245.00	189.00	209.00		
16	Utilities		278.65	286.75	276.56	289.87	277.43	298.76		
17	Other		136.76	35.45	43.56	115.64	132.65	165.33		
18	Total Expenses									
19										
20	NET INCOME									
21										
22										
23										
24										

Exercise 16

■ **Summary**

Mr. Abrams would like to continue to add grades to his notebook and average the grades. He has administered three major examinations this term for his English 852 class.

EXERCISE DIRECTIONS

1. Open ⌨MARK or ⬚16MARK.

2. Add the column headings as indicated in the illustration. Adjust column widths as necessary.

3. Enter the grades for tests 1, 2, and 3.
   ✓ *A Blank cell indicates that the student was absent for the test.*

4. Find for each student:
   - QUIZ AVERAGE
   - TEST AVERAGE

5. Enter summary labels at the bottom of the notebook as illustrated.

6. Find for each test:
   - NO. OF PAPERS
   - CLASS AVERAGE
   - HIGHEST GRADE
   - LOWEST GRADE

7. Format all averages to one decimal place.

8. Center all column titles.

9. Create a series to number students consecutively beginning with 1 in the STUDENT NUMBER column.

10. Print one copy in landscape orientation so that it fits on one page.

11. Close and save the file; name it MARK.

A	A	B	C	D	E	F	G	H	I	J	K	L
1	CLASS:		ENG 852									
2	TERM:		SPRING 199-									
3	TEACHER:		MR. ABRAMS									
4							*QUIZ*				*TEST*	*STUDENT*
5	ID	NAME		QUIZ 1	QUIZ 2	QUIZ 3	*AVERAGE*	TEST 1	TEST 2	TEST 3	*AVERAGE*	*NUMBER*
6												
7	2314	Bronte, C.		85	80	90		83	86	92		1
8	5432	Carson, R.		35	55	68		40	59	65		
9	2311	Fromm, E.		72	76	85		72	83	86		
10	3454	Hardy, T.		55	42	67		35	49	62		
11	5413	Hemingway, E.		64	68	69		68	74	69		
12	5487	Melville, H.		83	87	86		85	93	88		
13	2379	Miller, A.		98	96	97		95	93	98		
14	5438	Poe, E.		76	79	81		79	85	82		
15	2390	Steinbeck, J.		90	87	95		95	80			
16	5498	Wouk, H.		100	96	98		95	97	99		
17												
18	*NO. OF PAPERS*											
19	*CLASS AVERAGE*											
20	*HIGHEST GRADE*											
21	*LOWEST GRADE*											

Exercise

17

- ■ **Insert and Delete Columns and Rows**
- ■ **Move (Cut/Paste and Drag/Drop)** ■ **Copy (Drag/Drop)**

NOTES

Insert and Delete Columns and Rows

- ■ It is recommended that you save the notebook *before* you insert, delete, move, or copy data so you can retrieve the original notebook page in the event of an error. Inserting, deleting, moving, or copying data can affect formulas and data. Be sure formulas are correct after an insert, delete, move, or copy operation.

- ■ Columns and/or rows may be inserted or deleted to change the structure of a notebook page. Inserting a column or row creates a blank area. Existing columns or rows shift to allow for the newly created space. To insert columns or rows, select Block from the Insert menu and complete the dialog box, illustrated below. The Span options allow you to set whole or partial columns, rows, or pages. Or you can use the Insert Block button ⊞ on the Notebook Toolbar.

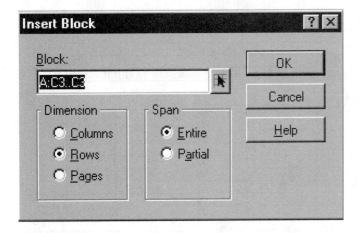

- ■ When a column or row is deleted, all data in that column or row is eliminated. Remaining columns or rows shift to fill in the space left by the deletion. To delete a column or row, select the

row or column and select either Delete, Row or Delete, Column from the Edit menu, or use the Delete Block button ⊟ on the Notebook Toolbar. The button will display a Delete Block dialog box that is similar to the Insert Block dialog box illustrated at the bottom left.

Move (Cut/Paste and Drag/Drop)

- ■ When you move data, the data is removed from one location and inserted into another. You may choose to overwrite existing data or insert the data and shift existing data in the direction that you specify. The Cut (Ctrl+X) ✂ and Paste (Ctrl+V) 📋 commands are on the Edit menu and may be activated using either the keyboard or Toolbar. These commands may also be activated by also right-clicking the active cell. Moving data can also be accomplished by selecting the range and dragging it to the paste location (known as **drag and drop**). The mouse pointer will change to a hand during the drag and drop procedure.

- ■ The format of data will be moved along with the data itself.

Copy (Drag/Drop)

- ■ Data may also be copied by using the drag and drop method. To copy a range of cells, select the block of cells, press the Ctrl key, and when the mouse pointer changes to a hand, click and drag the block of cells to its new location then release the mouse.

- ■ The format of the data will be copied along with the data itself.

In this exercise, you will insert, delete, and move columns and rows to include additional information in the Jerome Insurance Agency payroll notebook page. In addition, a new payroll notebook page will be created below the existing one for the new pay period.

EXERCISE DIRECTIONS

1. Open ✑PAY or ☐17PAY.

2. Make the following changes on the *top* payroll as shown in the illustration below:
   - Insert a new column A.
   - Move the data in the Emp. Name column to column A.
   - Set column width for column C to 11 and enter the label Soc. Sec. No. as the column title.
   - Enter social security numbers as follows:

Drennen	069-65-4532
Foxman	123-75-7623
Lindner	107-53-6754
Nichols	103-87-5698
Renfrew	127-78-0045
Trainor	043-67-7600

   - Copy the Soc. Sec. No. column title and data from the 2/6/9- payroll to the 2/13/9- payroll.
   - Copy the entire 2/13/9- payroll, including the title, to a new location below the existing notebook page.

3. Make the following changes on the bottom payroll only:
   - Edit the title to read:
     FOR THE WEEK ENDING 2/20/9-
   - Delete the row containing data for Foxman.
   - Insert a row where necessary to maintain alphabetical order for a new employee named Polla.
     Enter the following information for Polla:

Card Number:	355
Soc. Sec. No.:	146-93-0069
Hourly Rate:	$8.25

   - Edit the HOURS WORKED as follows:

Drennen	22
Lindner	33
Nichols	21
Polla	16
Renfrew	18
Trainor	28

   - Copy payroll formulas to complete Polla's data.

4. Format numeric and text data where necessary.

5. Print one copy to fit on a page.

6. Close and save the notebook file, or *save as* PAY.

A	A	B	C	D	E	F	G	H	I
1	JIJIJIJIJIJI			JEROME INSURANCE AGENCY					JIJIJIJIJIJI
2	← Insert new column A			PAYROLL FOR THE WEEK ENDING 2/6/9-					
3									
4	Card	Emp.	Hourly	Hours	Gross	Federal	Soc. Sec.	Medicare	Net
5	Number	Name	Rate	Worked	Pay	With. Tax	Tax	Tax	Pay
6									
7	325	Drennen	6.55	15	98.25	19.65	6.09	1.42	71.08
8	345	Foxman	6.85	21	143.85	28.77	8.92	2.09	104.08
9	315	Lindner	7.23	35	253.05	50.61	15.69	3.67	183.08
10	330	Nichols	8.65	29	250.85	50.17	15.55	3.64	181.49
11	340	Renfrew	9.95	27	268.65	53.73	16.66	3.90	194.37
12	350	Trainor	8.65	21	181.65	36.33	11.26	2.63	131.42
13									
14	Totals	Move column B data			1196.30	239.26	74.17	17.35	865.52
15	Averages	to the new column.			219.61	43.92	13.62	3.18	158.89
16									
17				PAYROLL FOR THE WEEK ENDING 2/13/9-					
18									
19	Card	Emp.	Hourly	Hours	Gross	Federal	Soc. Sec.	Medicare	Net
20	Number	Name	Rate	Worked	Pay	With. Tax	Tax	Tax	Pay
21									
22	325	Drennen	6.55	22	144.1	28.82	8.93	2.09	104.26
23	345	Foxman	6.85	25	171.25	34.25	10.62	2.48	123.90
24	315	Lindner	7.23	37	267.51	53.50	16.59	3.88	193.54
25	330	Nichols	8.65	25	216.25	43.25	13.41	3.14	156.46
26	340	Renfrew	9.95	26	258.7	51.74	16.04	3.75	187.17
27	350	Trainor	8.65	35	302.75	60.55	18.77	4.39	219.04
28									
29	Totals				1360.56	272.11	84.35	19.73	984.37
30	Averages				243.29	48.66	15.08	3.53	176.02

KEYSTROKES

INSERT COLUMNS/ROWS

Inserts blank columns or rows and shifts existing columns or rows to make room for the insertion.

1. Select as many adjacent columns or rows as you want to add to notebook page.

   ✓ *Be sure to select the entire column or row. New columns will be placed to the left of the highlighted columns. New rows will be placed above the highlighted rows.*

2. Click **Insert** .... Alt + I
3. Click **Block** .... Alt + B
4. Choose **Columns** .... Alt + C
   OR
   Choose **Rows** .... Alt + R

DELETE COLUMNS/ROWS

Deletes columns or rows and the data they contain. Existing columns or rows shift to fill in the space left by the deletion.

1. Select column(s) or row(s) to delete.

   ✓ *Be sure to select the entire column or row. When deleting more than one row or column, select adjacent columns or rows.*

2. Click **Edit** .... Alt + E
3. Click **Delete** .... D
4. Choose **Columns** .... Alt + C
   OR
   Choose **Rows** .... Alt + R

 MOVE (CUT/PASTE) USING THE MENU

Moves data in a cell, or a range of cells, to another area.

1. Select cell or range to move.
2. Click **Edit** menu .... Alt + E
3. Click **Cut** .... T
4. Select cell or range to receive data.

   ✓ *You only have to specify the top left cell. The destination range can be in another notebook or notebook page.*

5. Click **Edit** .... Alt + E
6. Click **Paste** .... P

 MOVE (DRAG AND DROP)

Moves data in a cell, or a range of cells, to another area.

1. Select cell or range to cut.
2. Hold down left mouse button and move mouse pointer to edge of range.

Pointer becomes a hand.

1. Move to new location.
2. Release mouse button.

 COPY (DRAG AND DROP)

Copies data in a cell, or range of cells, to another area.

1. Select cell or range to copy.
2. Hold down left mouse button and move mouse pointer to edge of range.

Pointer becomes a hand.

   To copy and overwrite existing data in destination cells:

   a. Press **Ctrl** and drag .... Ctrl +*drag* border outline to new location.
   b. Release the key, then mouse button.

Exercise

18

- ■ **Copy and Paste Special**
- ■ **Transpose Data**

NOTES

Copy and Paste Special

- ■ **Paste Special** is a feature that gives you added control during the pasting process once data has been copied. As shown in the illustration of the Paste Special dialog box to the right, you can select which features in a block will be pasted, i.e. Formula Cells, Label Cells, Number Cells, or Properties. The following options are also available: Avoid Pasting Blanks, Transpose Rows and Columns, and Paste Formulas as Values. In this exercise, we will use the Transpose feature in the Paste Special dialog box.

Transpose Data

- ■ Use the **Transpose** feature to copy and rearrange data so that data in rows can be copied to columns and vice versa. Data can be transposed by copying the data and then choosing Paste Special from the Edit menu and clicking the Transpose Rows and Columns option. Note the illustration of the Paste Special dialog box and the illustration of transposed data. The labels in column B, when transposed, are pasted to row 5.

Paste Special Dialog Box

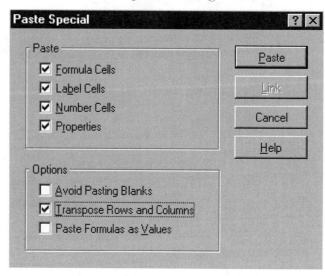

Transposed Data

	B	C	D	E	F
	JAN.				
	FEB.				
	MAR.	⟶	JAN.	FEB.	MAR.

- ■ Note the following precautions when transposing data:

  - Choose an area outside the selected range in which to copy the transposed data; otherwise, the data will become garbled.

  - If you are transposing values that are the result of formulas, you must select the Paste Formulas as Values option in the Paste Special dialog box, since the formulas will not work in their new locations.

In this exercise, you will insert a new expense item in the Lopez Insurance Agency notebook. In addition, you will use transposed data from the Income Statement to prepare an income statement analysis.

EXERCISE DIRECTIONS

1. Open ▨INCOME or ▤18INCOME.

2. Delete column B.

3. Set column widths for column B through column H to 12.

4. To include a monthly interest expense of $25:
   - Insert a row between Utilities and Other.
   - Enter the label: Interest.
   - Enter $25 for each month.
   - Copy the TOTALS and AVERAGES formulas for the interest line.
   - Format the interest line for two decimal places.

5. Enter new title and column labels below the existing notebook page, as illustrated on the following page.

6. Center column labels.

7. Transpose the column titles JANUARY through JUNE, including TOTALS and excluding AVERAGES, to become row titles in column A in the range A30:A36.

8. Transpose Total Income data for JANUARY through JUNE, including TOTALS and excluding AVERAGES, to become row data for column B in the range B30:B36.
   - ✓ *Be sure to select the Paste Formulas as Values option when transposing.*

9. Transpose Total Expenses data for JANUARY through JUNE, including TOTALS and excluding AVERAGES, to become row data for column D in the range D30:D36.
   - ✓ *Be sure to select the Paste Formulas as Values option when transposing.*

10. Transpose NET INCOME data for JANUARY through JUNE, including TOTALS and excluding AVERAGES, to become row data for column F in the range F30:F36.
    - ✓ *Be sure to select the Paste Formulas as Values option when transposing.*

11. Enter formulas in the % OF TOTAL columns to find what percent each item is of the six month total for each item.
    - *Hint: Use an absolute reference for the TOTAL in the formulas.*

12. Format % OF TOTAL columns for percentage with one decimal place.

13. Print one copy to fit on a page. (Remove sheet option to print column titles, set previously.)

14. Close and save the notebook file, or *save as* INCOME.

KEYSTROKES

TRANSPOSE DATA

Copies and transposes data from horizontal to vertical arrangement and vice versa.

1. Select range to transpose.

2. Click **E**dit .... `Alt`+`E`

3. Click **C**opy .... `C`

4. Click upper-left cell .... `⬆⬇⬅➡`
   to receive transposed data.

5. Click **E**dit .... `Alt`+`E`

6. Click Paste **S**pecial .... `S`

7. Click **T**ranspose Rows and
   Columns .... `Alt`+`T`

If formulas are to be transposed:

Click Paste Formulas
as **V**alues .... `Alt`+`V`

8. Click **OK** .... `Enter`

Delete column B

Transpose

Insert row.

A	A	B	C	D	E	F	G	H	I	J	K	L
1			LOPEZ INSURANCE AGENCY									
2			COMPARATIVE INCOME STATEMENT									
3			FOR THE MONTHS ENDED 199-									
4												
5			JANUARY	FEBRUARY	MARCH	APRIL	MAY	JUNE	TOTALS	AVERAGES		
6	INCOME:											
7	Commissions		10,212.32	11,212.22	13,453.88	12,546.87	12,965.33	13,221.77	73,612.39	12,268.73		
8	Consultations		3,245.65	2,843.23	3,565.89	3,867.22	3,144.55	3,256.87	19,923.41	3,320.57		
9	Total Income		13,457.97	14,055.45	17,019.77	16,414.09	16,109.88	16,478.64	93,535.80	15,589.30		
10												
11	EXPENSES:											
12	Advertising		125.00	125.00	145.00	155.00	125.00	165.00	840.00	140.00		
13	Rent		1,500.00	1,500.00	1,500.00	1,500.00	1,500.00	1,500.00	9,000.00	1,500.00		
14	Salaries		9,576.88	9,576.88	9,978.65	10,434.34	9,576.88	9,576.88	58,720.51	9,786.75		
15	Payroll Taxes		954.54	954.54	992.15	995.43	954.54	954.54	5,805.74	967.62		
16	Supplies		215.00	123.00	333.00	245.00	189.00	209.00	1,314.00	219.00		
17	Utilities		278.65	286.75	276.56	289.87	277.43	298.76	1,708.02	284.67		
18	Other		136.76	35.45	43.56	115.64	132.65	165.33	629.39	104.90		
19	Total Expenses		12,786.83	12,601.62	13,268.92	13,735.28	12,755.50	12,869.51	78,017.66	13,002.94		
20												
21	NET INCOME		671.14	1,453.83	3,750.85	2,678.81	3,354.38	3,609.13	15,518.14	2,586.36		
22												
23												
24												
25			*INCOME STATEMENT ANALYSIS*									
26			*LOPEZ INSURANCE AGENCY*									
27												
28			*TOTAL*	*% OF*	*TOTAL*	*% OF*	*NET*	*% OF*				
29	*MONTH*		*INCOME*	*TOTAL*	*EXPENSES*	*TOTAL*	*INCOME*	*TOTAL*				
30												
31												
32												
33												
34												
35												
36												
37												
38												

Exercise

19

- **Lock Titles**
- **Copy and Paste Special**

NOTES

Lock Titles

- Quattro Pro provides two methods for working with large notebook pages: locking titles to keep them in view and splitting the window into panes that can be scrolled.

- To keep headings or titles in view at the left or top edge of the notebook page when scrolling, it is necessary to hold, or lock, them in place. To lock row or column titles, place your cursor in the row or column after the titles area, then select Locked Titles from the View menu.

- You can view different sections of a large notebook page at one time by splitting the screen into separate panes. Each pane can be used to access information from different parts of the document. For example, you may wish to compare data at the top of your notebook with the data at the bottom. Splitting the window into separate panes allows you to see both sections.

- When you split a window vertically, the panes move together when you scroll up or down, but they move independently when you scroll left and right.

- When you split a window horizontally, the panes move together when you scroll left or right, but they move independently when you scroll up and down.

- A notebook can be divided into panes using the pane splitter button, which is located in the lower right corner of the notebook, or by selecting Split Windows from the View menu. The Pane Splitter button and the Split Windows dialog box are illustrated below and at the top of the next column, with an example of a vertically split screen view.

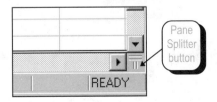

Split Window Dialog Box

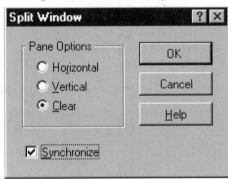

Vertically Split Screen

	A			K	L	M
3			3			
4			4			
5			5	JULY	AUGUST	SEPTEMBER
6	INCOME:		6			
7	Commissions		7	13211.65	12764.21	12994.21
8	Consultations		8	3054.32	2954.32	3356.76
9	Total Income		9	16,265.97	15,718.53	16,350.97
10			10			
11	EXPENSES:		11			

- When you lock a split notebook page, the top and/or left panes lock when you scroll through the notebook page.

Copy and Paste Special

- New notebooks can be created to store new or extracted data.

- Use the Copy and Paste Special commands to copy part of a notebook page into another notebook. The dialog box that appears depends on the type of data copied to the clipboard.

- If you want to paste the results of formulas, mark the Paste Formulas as Values check box in the Paste Special dialog box. If you want to paste the formulas themselves, leave the check box blank.

- When working with more than one notebook at a time, you can use the Window menu to select the notebook you want to activate.

In this exercise, you will divide the Lopez Insurance Agency data into quarterly information by inserting and deleting columns. Because inserting or deleting columns from the top portion of the notebook page will affect the bottom portion, you will extract the bottom portion of the notebook page, save it to another file, and delete it from the original. The top portion of the notebook page will then be expanded and edited.

EXERCISE DIRECTIONS

1. Open ☐INCOME or ☐19INCOME.

2. Use the Copy and Paste Special commands to extract the Income Statement Analysis portion of the notebook page to a new notebook:
   - Copy Income Statement Analysis portion of notebook.
   - Open new notebook.
   - Click cell A1.
   - Paste Special, using Paste Formulas as Values option.
   - Save the new notebook file; name it ANALYSIS.

3. Switch to the INCOME notebook.

4. Delete the Income Statement Analysis portion from the INCOME notebook page.

5. Insert a column between MARCH and APRIL and enter the column titles:
   1ST QTR.
   TOTALS

6. Find 1ST QTR. TOTALS. Format the new column for two decimal places and adjust column width as necessary.

7. Copy the formula to the remaining items. Format the new column for two decimal places.

8. Insert a column between JUNE and TOTALS and enter the column title:
   2ND QTR.
   TOTALS

9. Copy the formulas for 1ST QTR. TOTALS to the column for 2ND QTR. TOTALS.

10. Edit column title TOTALS to read:
    HALF-YEAR
    TOTALS

11. Delete the AVERAGES column.

12. Edit the formula in the HALF-YEAR TOTALS column to add 1ST QTR. TOTALS and 2ND QTR. TOTALS.

13. Lock titles in column A.

14. Enter third quarter data indicated below beginning in the next available column of your notebook page.

	JULY	AUGUST	SEPTEMBER
Commissions	13211.65	12764.21	12994.21
Consultations	3054.32	2954.32	3356.76
Advertising	150.00	145.00	135.00
Rent	1500.00	1500.00	1500.00
Salaries	9321.78	9321.78	9576.88
Payroll Taxes	930.34	930.34	954.54
Supplies	165.00	183.00	210.00
Utilities	296.65	299.67	269.87
Interest	25.00	25.00	25.00
Other	107.54	95.65	120.65

15. Copy and edit formulas, where necessary, to complete the notebook page.

16. Find 3RD QTR. TOTALS.

17. Copy the formula to the remaining items.

18. Center all column heading labels.

19. Format numeric data for two decimal places.

20. Print one copy of INCOME in landscape orientation to fit on a page.

21. Close and save the notebook; name it INCOME.

22. In the ANALYSIS notebook: format and align data as needed.

23. Print one copy.

24. Close and save the notebook; name it ANALYSIS.

LOPEZ INSURANCE AGENCY
COMPARATIVE INCOME STATEMENT
FOR THE MONTHS ENDED 199-

Insert Column: 1ST QTR TOTALS
Insert Column: 2ND QTR TOTALS
Delete column.

	JANUARY	FEBRUARY	MARCH	APRIL	MAY	JUNE	HALF-YEAR TOTALS	AVERAGES	JULY	AUGUST
INCOME:										
Commissions	10,212.32	11,212.22	13,453.88	12,546.87	12,965.33	13,221.77	73,612.39	12,268.73	13211.65	12764.21
Consultations	3,245.65	2,843.23	3,565.89	3,867.22	3,144.55	3,256.87	19,923.41	3,320.57	3054.32	2954.32
Total Income	13,457.97	14,055.45	17,019.77	16,414.09	16,109.88	16,478.64	93,535.80	15,589.30		
EXPENSES:										
Advertising	125.00	125.00	145.00	155.00	125.00	165.00	840.00	140.00	150.00	145.00
Rent	1,500.00	1,500.00	1,500.00	1,500.00	1,500.00	1,500.00	9,000.00	1,500.00	1500.00	1500.00
Salaries	9,576.88	9,576.88	9,978.65	10,434.34	9,576.88	9,576.88	58,720.51	9,786.75	9321.78	9321.78
Payroll Taxes	954.54	954.54	992.15	995.43	954.54	954.54	5,805.74	967.62	930.34	930.34
Supplies	215.00	123.00	333.00	245.00	189.00	209.00	1,314.00	219.00	165.00	183.00
Utilities	278.65	286.75	276.56	289.87	277.43	298.76	1,708.02	284.67	296.65	299.67
Interest	25.00	25.00	25.00	25.00	25.00	25.00	150.00	25.00	25.00	25.00
Other	136.76	35.45	43.56	115.64	132.65	165.33	629.39	104.90	107.54	95.65
Total Expenses	12,811.83	12,626.62	13,293.92	13,760.28	12,780.50	12,894.51	78,167.66	13,027.94		
NET INCOME	646.14	1,428.83	3,725.85	2,653.81	3,329.38	3,584.13	15,368.14	2,561.36		

Extract to new notebook: ANALYSIS

INCOME STATEMENT ANALYSIS
LOPEZ INSURANCE AGENCY

MONTH	TOTAL INCOME	% OF TOTAL	TOTAL EXPENSES	% OF TOTAL	NET INCOME	% OF TOTAL
JANUARY	13,457.97	14.4%	12,811.83	16.4%	646.14	4.2%
FEBRUARY	14,055.45	15.0%	12,626.62	16.2%	1,428.83	9.3%
MARCH	17,019.77	18.2%	13,293.92	17.0%	3,725.85	24.2%
APRIL	16,414.09	17.5%	13,760.28	17.6%	2,653.81	17.3%
MAY	16,109.88	17.2%	12,780.50	16.4%	3,329.38	21.7%
JUNE	16,478.64	17.6%	12,894.51	16.5%	3,584.13	23.3%
TOTALS	93,535.80	100.0%	78,167.66	100.0%	15,368.14	100.0%

KEYSTROKES

COPY AND PASTE SPECIAL (EXTRACT DATA)

Copies a portion of the current notebook page to a new notebook.

1. Copy range to extract to the clipboard:
   a. Select range of notebook page to extract.
   b. Click **Edit**.........................**Alt**+**E**
   c. Click **Copy**.................................**C**
2. Open a new notebook:
   a. Click **File**.........................**Alt**+**F**
   b. Click **New**...................................**N**
3. Use Paste Special command:
   a. Click **Edit**.........................**Alt**+**E**
   b. Click **Paste Special**.....................**S**
   c. Click **Paste Formulas as Values**..................**Alt**+**V**
      to copy data as it appears in cells (results of formulas).
   d. Click **Paste**................................**P**
4. Save and name the new notebook.
   a. Click **File**.........................**Alt**+**F**
   b. Click **Save As**............................**A**
   c. Type new filename .... *filename*
   d. Click **Save**.......................**Alt**+**S**

CREATE NEW NOTEBOOK

Opens a new notebook based on the default template.

Click New Notebook button on the Standard toolbar................................**▯**

OR

1. Click **File**...............................**Alt**+**F**
2. Click **New**...................................**N**

SELECT NOTEBOOK

✓ *When more than one notebook is open, the notebook you want to access may be hidden or reduced to an icon. In order to use a hidden or reduced notebook, follow one of the listed methods.*

Click anywhere on notebook window.

OR

Double click on a Notebook icon.

OR

a. Click **Window** menu ....**Alt**+**W**
b. Select name of notebook.............**↓**
   near bottom of the menu.

SPLIT NOTEBOOK PAGE INTO PANES USING SPLIT BOXES

Provides simultaneous scrolling of up to two panes. You can lock panes (see right) to prevent top, left, or both panes from scrolling.

1. Click **View** ....**Alt**+**V**
2. Click **Split Window**........................**W**
3. Select options.

OR

1. Point to the **Split View** button on the scroll bar.

   Pointer becomes a ←|→

2. Drag pointer along scroll bar until split bar is in desired position.

REMOVE SPLIT BARS

Point to **Split View** button on the scroll bar.

Drag split bar to the top, bottom, left, or right.

OR

a. Click **View** ....**Alt**+**V**
b. Click **Split Window**.....................**W**
c. Click **Clear**..................................**C**
d. Click **OK**...............................**Enter**

ADJUST NOTEBOOK PAGE PANES

1. Point to **Split View** button ▯ on the scroll bar.

   Pointer becomes a ←|→

2. Drag pointer along scroll bar until split bar is in desired position.

MOVE BETWEEN NOTEBOOK PAGE PANES

Click desired pane.

OR

Press **F6** **F6**
until active cell is in desired pane.

LOCK TITLES

Locks top and/or left pane when scrolling.

1. Click **View** ....**Alt**+**V**
2. Click **Locked Titles** ....**L**
3. Click the desired lock option.
4. Click **OK** ....**Enter**

UNLOCK TITLES

1. Click **View** ....**Alt**+**V**
2. Click **Locked Titles** ....**L**
3. Click **Clear** ....**Alt**+**C**
4. Click **OK** ....**Enter**

Exercise

20

■ **Notebook Pages** ■ **Print Notebook**

NOTES

Notebook Pages

■ By default, each new notebook contains 256 notebook pages labeled A through IV. Sheet tabs show the names of the sheets (*see illustration below*).

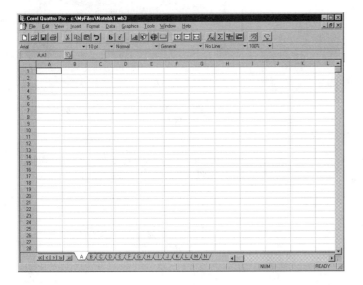

■ Quattro Pro lets you work with pages by right-clicking the page tab, which activates the Active Page dialog box. For example, you can set page display, name, colors, protection, default cell widths, and the zoom factor. Note the illustration of the Active Page dialog box below. These features let you modify your notebook pages to fit your work objectives. To rename a tab quickly, you can double-click the Name tab and enter the new name.

Active Page Dialog Box

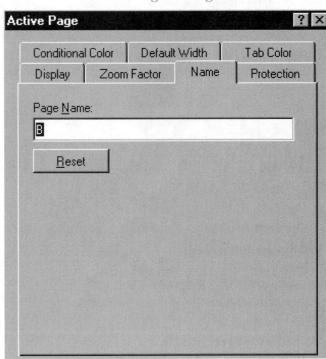

■ Quattro Pro provides tab scrolling controls at the lower left of the notebook window. You can click these buttons to move the page tab display.

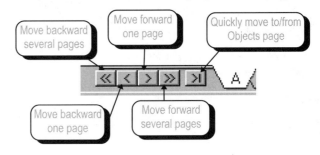

- You can insert new pages by selecting <u>B</u>lock from the <u>I</u>nsert menu and choosing the <u>P</u>ages option.

- You can select multiple pages, which is called **grouping**, to work on several sheets simultaneously. Select each of the pages while holding down the Shift key, then select <u>G</u>roup Name from the <u>I</u>nsert menu to name and define the group.

- Once pages are grouped, Group Mode must be enabled in order to view and make changes to the pages as a group. Select <u>G</u>roup Mode from the <u>V</u>iew menu and a check will appear next to the command indicating that it is active. Selected page tabs will then appear with an underline connecting the grouped pages, as illustrated below.

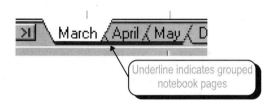

Underline indicates grouped notebook pages

- Formats changed on one page will now affect all grouped pages. To make formatting changes to individual pages in the group, you must first deselect <u>G</u>roup Mode from the <u>V</u>iew menu to disable the command. If you wish to enter data through all pages at once, you must enter the text using Ctrl + Enter while in group mode.

Print Notebook

- You can tell Quattro Pro to print all the pages in your notebook by selecting <u>F</u>ile, <u>P</u>rint and choosing the <u>N</u>otebook option in the Spreadsheet Print dialog box. Or, you can click the Page Set<u>u</u>p button (in the Spreadsheet Print dialog box), select the Print <u>S</u>caling tab and choose Print to F<u>i</u>t to fit the entire document on as few pages as possible. Or, select Sc<u>a</u>ling to manually adjust the desired print size.

In this exercise, you will create a payroll template for future use. To do this, you will delete unnecessary sheet tabs, insert and rename sheet tabs, and work with grouped sheets to edit data on more than one notebook page at a time.

EXERCISE DIRECTIONS

1. Open ⌨PAY or 🖫20PAY.

2. Resave the notebook file as PAYFORM.

3. Click page tab labeled B to select it.
   - ✓ *Note that page B is empty.*

4. Select Page A.

5. Use tab scrolling buttons to scroll to last page.

6. Select Page A, double-click and rename the page February.

7. Insert a page using Insert, Block, Pages, and name it March.

8. Move the March page to the right of the February page.

9. Select and double-click page C, rename it April.

10. Select the February page. To make payrolls uniform:
    - Foxman has left our employment; delete the Foxman rows in the top two payrolls.
    - Copy the Polla information from the last payroll to the first two payrolls in the correct order.
    - Edit the titles in each week's payroll to read:
      FOR THE WEEK ENDING
    - ✓ *Delete the dates.*

11. Select all the data on the FEBRUARY page and copy it to the clipboard.
    - HINT: *You can click the Select All button (the top left corner of the worksheet) to select the entire notebook page.*

12. Paste the worksheet to cell A1 on the March and April pages.

13. Select the February page.

14. Click cell A1 to deselect the range.

15. Select all the pages in the notebook (February through April):
    - Select the sheets while the Shift key is down.
    - Click Insert, Group Name, and name the range FebApr.
    - Check that Group Mode is selected on the View menu.

16. WHILE ALL PAGES ARE GROUPED

    a. Use Edit, Clear Values to clear the data in the cells containing the hours worked for each employee in each payroll week. (Do not delete the column.) This will result in zeros for payroll data.

    b. Deselect View, Group Mode.

    c. Check that each page contains identical data.

    d. Set each notebook page to fit on one page when printed.
    - ✓ *You cannot set print page options for a group.*

17. Print the entire notebook.

18. Close and save the notebook file.

A	A	B	C	D	E	F	G	H	I	J	K	L	M
1		JIJIJIJIJIJ				JEROME INSURANCE AGENCY				JIJIJIJIJIJ			
2						PAYROLL FOR THE WEEK ENDING 2/6/9							
3													
4	Emp.	Card	Soc. Sec.	Hourly	Hours	Gross	Federal	Soc. Sec.	Medicare	Net	Copy A1:J46 to March		
5	Name	Number	No.	Rate	Worked	Pay	With. Tax	Tax	Tax	Pay	and April pages.		
6													
7	Drennen	325	069-65-4532	6.55	15	98.25	19.65	6.09	1.42	71.08			
8	Foxman	345	123-75-7623	6.85	21	143.85	28.77	8.92	2.09	104.08	Delete row		
9	Lindner	315	107-53-6754	7.23	35	253.05	50.61	15.69	3.67	183.08			
10	Nichols	330	103-87-5698	8.65	29	250.85	50.17	15.55	3.64	181.49			
11	Renfrew	340	127-78-0045	9.95	27	268.65	53.73	16.66	3.90	194.37			
12	Trainor	350	043-67-7600	8.65	21	181.65	36.33	11.26	2.63	131.42			
13													
14		Totals				1196.30	239.26	74.17	17.35	865.52			
15		Averages				219.61	43.92	13.62	3.18	158.89			
16													
17						PAYROLL FOR THE WEEK ENDING 2/13							
18													
19	Emp.	Card	Soc. Sec.	Hourly	Hours	Gross	Federal	Soc. Sec.	Medicare	Net			
20	Name	Number	No.	Rate	Worked	Pay	With. Tax	Tax	Tax	Pay			
21													
22	Drennen	325	069-65-4532	6.55	22	144.1	28.82	8.93	2.09	104.26			
23	Foxman	345	123-75-7623	6.85	25	171.25	34.25	10.62	2.48	123.90	Delete row		
24	Lindner	315	107-53-6754	7.23	37	267.51	53.50	16.59	3.88	193.54			
25	Nichols	330	103-87-5698	8.65	25	216.25	43.25	13.41	3.14	156.46			
26	Renfrew	340	127-78-0045	9.95	26	258.7	51.74	16.04	3.75	187.17			
27	Trainor	350	043-67-7600	8.65	35	302.75	60.55	18.77	4.39	219.04			
28													
29		Totals				1360.56	272.11	84.35	19.73	984.37			
30		Averages				243.29	48.66	15.08	3.53	176.02			
31													
32						PAYROLL FOR THE WEEK ENDING 2/20/9							
33													
34	Emp.	Card	Soc. Sec.	Hourly	Hours	Gross	Federal	Soc. Sec.	Medicare	Net			
35	Name	Number	No.	Rate	Worked	Pay	With. Tax	Tax	Tax	Pay			
36													
37	Drennen	325	069-65-4532	6.55	22	144.10	28.82	8.93	2.09	104.26			
38	Lindner	315	107-53-6754	7.23	33	238.59	47.72	14.79	3.46	172.62			
39	Nichols	330	103-87-5698	8.65	21	181.65	36.33	11.26	2.63	131.42			
40	Polla	355	146-93-0069	8.25	16	132.00	26.40	8.18	1.91	95.50			
41	Renfrew	340	127-78-0045	9.95	18	179.10	35.82	11.10	2.60	129.58			
42	Trainor	350	043-67-7600	8.65	28	242.20	48.44	15.02	3.51	175.23			
43													
44		Totals				1117.64	223.53	69.29	16.21	808.61			
45		Averages				186.27	37.25	11.55	2.70	134.77			
46													
47													
48													
49													
50													
51													
52													
53													
54													

KEYSTROKES

SELECT PAGES

Select One Page

1. If necessary, click tab scrolling controls to scroll .. `« ‹ › » ›| A ⁄` a hidden page tab into view.
2. Click desired page tab.

Select Multiple Pages

1. Click the first page tab in the selection.
2. Press the **Shift** key, then click the last page in the selection.

Select (Group) Consecutive Pages

✓ *IMPORTANT: When you group pages, formatting applied to one page is duplicated on all pages in the group.*

1. If necessary, click tab scrolling controls to scroll .... `« ‹ › » ›| A ⁄` a hidden page tab into view.
2. Click first page tab to select.
3. If necessary, click tab scrolling controls to scroll ... `« ‹ › » ›| A ⁄` a hidden page tab into view.
4. Press **Shift** and click...................... `Shift` last page tab to select.

Black line appears under tabs.

5. Click **I**nsert........................... `Alt`+`I`
6. Click **G**roup Name .... `G`
7. Type name of group .... *name*
8. Click **OK**................................ `Enter`
9. Click **V**iew .... `Alt`+`V`
10. Click **G**roup Mode .... `G`

Blue line appears under group.

To deactivate group mode:

Alt + F5

1. Click **V**iew .... `Alt`+`V`
2. Click **G**roup Mode .... `G`

DELETE PAGES

Delete One Page

1. Click page tab to delete.
2. Click **E**dit.............................. `Alt`+`E`
3. Click Se**l**ect All.............................. `L`
4. Click **E**dit.............................. `Alt`+`E`
5. Click **D**elete Page(s) .... `D`

Delete Multiple Pages

1. Click the first page tab.
2. Press **Shift** and click..................... `Shift` last page tab to select.
3. Follow steps 2-5 above.

RENAME A SHEET

1. Double-click page tab to rename.
2. Type new name ....*name*
3. Press **Enter** .... `Enter`
   OR
   a. Right-click page tab.
   b. Select **Name**.
   c. Type new name ....*name*
   d. Click **OK**................................ `Enter`

INSERT PAGES

Insert One Notebook Page

1. Click page tab of the page you want to follow the new page.
2. Click **I**nsert........................... `Alt`+`I`
3. Click **B**lock .... `B`
4. Click **P**ages .... `Alt`+`P`
5. Click **OK**................................. `Enter`

Quattro Pro inserts sheet and makes the new page active.

Insert Multiple Notebook Pages

1. Highlight as many sheets as you wish to insert.
2. Click **I**nsert .... `Alt`+`I`
3. Click **B**lock .... `B`
4. Click **P**ages .... `Alt`+`P`
5. Click **OK**................................. `Enter`

Quattro Pro inserts sheets and makes the last new page active.

MOVE SHEETS WITHIN A NOTEBOOK

Move One Sheet

Drag page tab to desired sheet tab position.

Move Multiple Sheets

1. Select pages to move.
2. Drag selected page tabs to desired sheet tab position.

 ## PRINT NOTEBOOK

Prints notebook page data using the current page settings.

1. Click **F**ile menu .... `Alt`+`F`
2. Click **P**rint.............................. `P`
3. Click **N**otebook............................. `N`
4. Click **P**rint................................ `P`

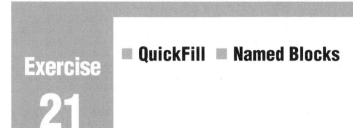

Exercise

21

■ **QuickFill** ■ **Named Blocks**

NOTES

QuickFill

■ The **QuickFill** feature is used to enter a series of labels or values in columns, rows, or on tabs. The Quick Fill dialog box, illustrated below, will appear when you click the Quick Fill button ▦ on the Notebook Toolbar.

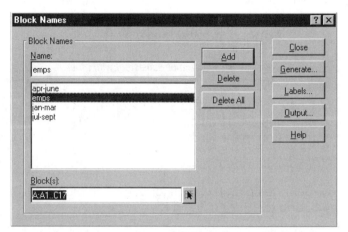

■ Naming blocks makes formulas easy to read and understand and makes printing and combining blocks easier to accomplish. For example, when you define a print area you can type the name of a block (such as EMPS), rather than typing the cell reference (such as A1:C17). You should keep block names short and descriptive.

■ Block names may contain up to 64 characters and may consist of letters, numbers, underscores (_), backslashes (\), periods (.), and question marks (?), as well as other special characters.

Named Blocks

■ Quattro Pro allows you to assign a name to a cell or block of cells rather than use the cell reference for identification. To assign a name to a block select Block Names from the Insert menu or press Ctrl+F3. The Block Names dialog box, illustrated at the top right, is then used to define the name of the block.

■ A list of the named blocks you create and their corresponding cell references can be inserted on the notebook page by selecting the Output button in the Block Names dialog box.

■ A named block can be modified by changing the block or the name.

In this exercise, you will include third-quarter sales commission data for Atlantis Auto Sales as well as add named blocks in the report for printing and for later use in combining files.

EXERCISE DIRECTIONS

1. Open ⬛AUTO or ⬛21AUTO.

2. Edit the title to read:
   QUARTERLY SALES AND SALARY REPORT – JANUARY– SEPTEMBER

3. Insert a row at the bottom of the list to include a new employee hired on July 1. Employee Number, 321; Name, Walter Wiper; Base Salary, $1500.

   ✓ *Format base salary to be consistent with other formatting.*

4. Copy column headings from columns G-I to columns J-L. Edit column headings as indicated in the illustration.

5. Lock columns A-C for vertical titles.

6. Change column widths to 12 for columns J and L and to 15 for column K.

7. Enter July-Sept sales data as indicated in the illustration or as listed below:

Mario Bumpa	343,657.99
Charles Fender	465,879.09
Phil Muffler	432,657.91
Harriet Hood	602,435.76
Terry Trunk	497,987.34
Walter Wiper	210,456.77

8. Format all data to be consistent with notebook formats.

9. Copy the COMMISSIONS formulas to the new column.

10. Find JULY-SEPT SALARY using BASE SALARY + COMMISSIONS.

11. Copy the formula to the remaining employees.

12. Clear the lock.

13. Edit the formulas for TOTALS, AVERAGES, HIGHEST, and LOWEST in the BASE SALARY column to include the new employee data.

14. Copy the edited formulas to all columns.

15. Create the following named blocks:

EMPS	A1:C17
JAN_MAR	F1:F17
APR_JUNE	I1:I17
JUL_SEPT	L1:L17

16. Print one copy of the block EMPS.

17. Beginning at cell B19, insert list of named blocks by using the Insert, Block Names, Output command.

18. Close and save the notebook file, or *save as* AUTO.

ATLANTIS AUTO SALES
QUARTERLY SALES AND SALARY REPORT - JANUARY - SEPTEMBER

EMP. NO.	NAME	BASE SALARY	JAN-MAR SALES	COMMISSIONS	1ST QTR. EARNINGS	APR-JUNE SALES	COMMISSIONS	2ND QTR. EARNINGS	JULY-SEPT. SALES	COMMISSIONS	3RD QTR. EARNINGS
316	Mario Bumpa	1500.00	342,567.77	6,851.36	8,351.36	356,789.43	7,135.79	8,635.79	343,657.99		
317	Charles Fender	1500.00	432,567.86	8,651.36	10,151.36	478,987.03	9,579.74	11,079.74	465,879.09		
318	Phil Muffler	1500.00	564,343.43	11,286.87	12,786.87	421,767.89	8,435.36	9,935.36	432,657.91		
319	Harriet Hood	1500.00	654,544.44	13,090.89	14,590.89	611,435.78	12,228.72	13,728.72	602,435.76		
320	Terry Trunk	1500.00	432,445.66	8,648.91	10,148.91	489,090.87	9,781.82	11,281.82	497,987.34		
321	*Walter Wiper*	*1500.00*							210,456.77		
	TOTALS	7500.00	2,426,469.16	48,529.38	56,029.38	2,358,071.00	47,161.42	54,661.42			
	AVERAGES	1500.00	485,293.83	9,705.88	11,205.88	471,614.20	9,432.28	10,932.28			
	HIGHEST	1500.00	654,544.44	13,090.89	14,590.89	611,435.78	12,228.72	13,728.72			
	LOWEST	1500.00	342,567.77	6,851.36	8,351.36	356,789.43	7,135.79	8,635.79			

Edit formulas

KEYSTROKES

NAME/MODIFY A BLOCK USING THE MENU

1. Select block to be named.
2. Click **Insert**......................`Alt`+`I`
3. Click **Block Names** ....`N`
4. Type name for block......................*name* in **Name** text box.
5. Click **Add** ....`Alt`+`A`

   To delete a name:

   a. Click name to delete ....`Tab`,`↓` in list box.
   b. Click **Delete**.......................`Alt`+`D`
   c. Click **Close**.

   To change a name:

   a. Click name to change ....`Tab`,`↓` in list box.
   b. Select name in **Name** edit box.
   c. Type new name for block.

---

d. Click **Add** ....`Alt`+`A`
e. Click old name to delete in list box.
f. Click **Delete** ....`Alt`+`D`

To change reference a name refers to:

a. Click name ....`Tab`,`↓` to edit in list box.
b. Drag through existing reference ...`Tab` in Blocks text box.
c. Select cells in notebook page to reference.

   OR

   Type new reference.............*reference*
6. Click **Close**............................`Alt`+`C`

SELECT A NAMED BLOCK

1. Press **F5** ....`F5`
2. Select name in
   Block Names list...........`Alt`+`B`,`↓`
3. Click **OK** ....`Enter`

INSERT LIST OF NAMED BLOCKS

Inserts a list of named blocks and their corresponding references in current notebook page.

1. Select upper-left cell in block to receive list.
2. Click **Insert**..........................`Alt`+`I`
3. Click **Block Names** ....`N`
4. Click **Output** ....`Alt`+`O`
5. Click **OK**...................................`Enter`
6. Click **Close** ....`C`

   ✓   *Quattro Pro includes page names.*

PRINT NAMED BLOCK

1. Select named block.
2. Click **File** menu ....`Alt`+`F`
3. Click **Print**......................................`P`
4. Click **Block Selection** ....`Alt`+`B`
5. Click **Print**.............`Alt`+`P`, or `Enter`

Exercise 22

■ **Templates** ■ **Quick Templates** ■ **Quick Tasks**
■ **Arrange Notebooks**

Quick Template Toolbar

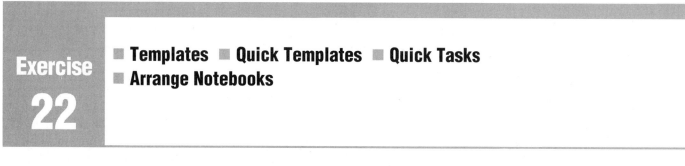

Load and display sample data

Highlight data-entry cells

Clear data-entry

Display Help Page for active Quick Template

Current Version: -Empty-

NOTES

Templates

■ When you need to create more than one notebook that will contain similar formatting, data and formulas, you can save a model notebook with the desired formats and formulas and use it as a template. Saving a Quattro Pro document into the **\Corel\Office7\Template** directory automatically turns it into a template file. When you open a template file, Quattro Pro opens a copy of it and leaves the original file intact so you can use it again. When data is added to this type of notebook, it is saved under a new name to preserve the original file.

Quick Templates

■ Quattro Pro provides thirty quick template formats that you can use or modify for your own purposes. In addition, there are order forms for additional templates included in each file. When a **Quick Template** is selected, the model notebook displays with preset formats and formulas. In addition, a Quick Template Toolbar displays. Note the illustration of the Quick Template Toolbar above, and the Job Estimate Quick Template on page 283.

QuickTasks

■ Additional spreadsheet templates are provided by Corel Office 7 in QuickTasks, which is a tool that can be accessed by clicking the DAD Corel QuickTask button. Model notebooks with instructions are provided for financial applications, as illustrated in the QuickTasks dialog box below.

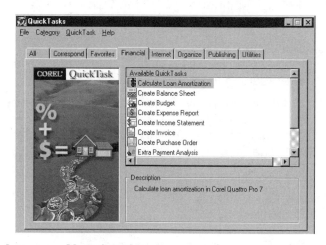

Arrange Notebooks

■ When working with a number of open files, you may want to use the Cascade or Tile options available on the Window menu. These options allow you to position the notebook windows so that they are all visible at once, allowing you to quickly move from one notebook to another.

In this exercise you will explore the Quick Templates that are available in Quattro Pro. You will customize the Job Estimate template for your firm, Dribbler Plumbing, and prepare two job estimates. The estimates will be arranged on the screen so that both are viewed simultaneously.

EXERCISE DIRECTIONS

1. Use the File menu to open the New file dialog box.

2. Click Create From Quick Template.

3. Click each template name and note the explanation for each template.

4. Select the Personal Net Worth template.

5. Select the Sample Data button 🖥 on the Quick Template Toolbar to insert sample data.

6. Scroll to view the notebook and note the Net Worth.

7. Change the Cash In Bank amount to $10,000.00. Note the change in Net Worth.

8. Remove all data with the Clear Data button 🗐 on the Quick Template Toolbar.

9. Close the template and answer No to prompts to remove the toolbar and save the file.

10. Click File, New, create From Quick Template.

11. Select the Job Estimate template.

12. Turn the highlight on the data areas by clicking the Highlight button 💡 on the Quick Template Toolbar.

13. Select the Template Help button ❓ to view the Help screen for this template. Close the screen after reading the notes.

14. Enter the company name and address below by selecting the Company Name line, entering the data, and using the down arrow to move to the next line.

    Dribbler Plumbing
    432 Piper Street
    Bergenfield, NJ 07621   201-555-4320

15. Scroll down and enter your name on the Prepared By line at the bottom of the form.

16. Enter @TODAY on the date line to use the current system date.

17. Save this form as a template for Dribbler Plumbing, name it DPJOBEST.

18. Open the DPJOBEST template and enter the data as follows:

    To:
    Mrs. John Leakey
    325 Dogwood Street
    Bergenfield, NJ 07621

    Job Description:
    Install new 1¼" return piping. Flush boiler. Add boiler cleaner.

Itemized Estimate:	AMOUNT
Materials	$110.25
Labor	285.00

    ✓   *The total will automatically calculate.*

19. Save the notebook as LEAKEY.

20. Print one copy.

21. Open the DPJOBEST template again and enter the data as follows:

    To:
    Mr. Sam Wrench
    54 Water Street
    Bergenfield, NJ 07621

    Job Description:
    Install kitchen sink and compactor.

Itemized Estimate:	AMOUNT
Sink	$255
Compactor	125
Labor	400

22. Save the notebook as WRENCH.

23. Use the Window, Cascade command to view the notebooks.

24. Select the LEAKEY notebook.

25. Select the Tile option from the Window menu to view both notebooks.

26. Select the WRENCH notebook.

27. Close both files.

Dribbler Plumbing

432 Piper Street
Bergenfield, NJ 07621   201-555-4320

JOB ESTIMATE

TO:
Mr. Sam Wrench
54 Water Street
Bergenfield, NJ 07621

JOB DESCRIPTION
Install kitchen sink and compactor.

ITEMIZED ESTIMATE: TIME AND MATERIALS	AMOUNT
Sink	$255.00
Compactor	125.00
Labor	400.00
TOTAL ESTIMATED JOB COST	$780.00

This is an estimate only, not a contract. This estimate is for completing the job described above, based on our evaluation. It does not include unforeseen price increases or additional labor and materials which may be required should problems arise.

Your Name	12/13/96
PREPARED BY	DATE

KEYSTROKES

CREATE A TEMPLATE NOTEBOOK

Saves and names the active notebook as a template file.

1. Create a model notebook to be saved as a template.

2. Click **File** .... `Alt`+`F`
3. Click **Save As** .... `A`
4. Change directories to \COREL\OFFICE7\TEMPLATE.
5. Double-click in **Name** .... `Alt`+`N`
6. Type filename .... *filename*

7. Click **Save** .... `Alt`+`S` or `Enter`

ARRANGE NOTEBOOK WINDOWS

1. Click **Window** .... `Alt`+`W`
2. Click **Cascade** or **Tile** .... `C` or `T`

Exercise

23

- **3-D Formulas** ■ **Notebook Pages**
- **Duplicate Notebook Views**

NOTES

3-D Formulas

- You can use references to values that exist in any page or range of pages in a notebook. These references are called 3-D references because you are summarizing data through the pages rather than on one page.

  ✓ *Note the illustration of a 3-D reference on the following page.*

- Quattro Pro uses a colon (:) to separate a page name from cell references, and two periods (..) between notebook page names to indicate a range of notebook pages. Quotation marks are used if the notebook page name contains a space. In addition, the name of a group can be used in a 3-D formula if you want all the pages in a group to be included in the formula. You can type a 3-D reference in a formula, or you can insert it by selecting the desired cells in the notebook page while typing or editing a formula. Note the illustrations below and on the next page showing examples of 3-D formulas.

To refer to:	3D reference examples:
Cells in a **different notebook page** (range A1:D1 on Sales 96)	"Sales 96":A1..D1
Cells in **range of notebook pages** (ranges A1..D3, on page C through page E)	C..E:A1..D3 or C:A1..E:D3
Cells in a **group of pages** (cells E7..E9 in the group, FebApr)	FebApr:E7..E9

Notebook Pages

- You should consider copying a page when you need to create multiple pages that contain similar or identical data arrangements. You can use the page tabs to copy pages and the data they contain by selecting the tab, pressing Ctrl and dragging the page to a new location. The page (March) will then display as a copy (March_2).

Duplicate Notebook Views

- You can create duplicate views of the active notebook by selecting New View from the Window menu. This allows you to view different pages of the same notebook simultaneously.

- Consider the following when working with duplicate notebook views:

  - Quattro Pro places the new notebook view in front of the active notebook window. Therefore, if the active notebook is maximized, you will not be able to see the new notebook.

  - Duplicate notebook views are indicated in the title bar which shows the notebook name followed by a colon and a number. For example, NOTEBK1:1

  - Your system memory determines the number of duplicate views you can have open at one time.

  - Closing a duplicate view will not close the notebook.

  - You can add or edit data in the original or duplicate view.

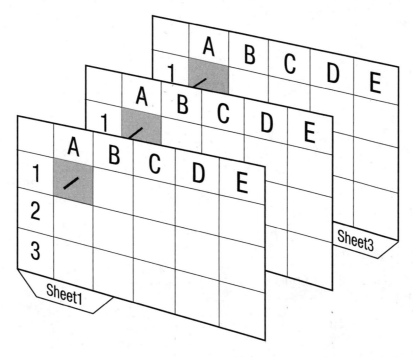

Example: *Using 3-D references to add the values in A1 in a range of sheets.*
@SUM(A..C:A1) or
@SUM(A:A1..C:C1)

KEYSTROKES

COPY PAGES WITHIN A NOTEBOOK

✓ *Quattro Pro will rename pages that you copy.*

Copy One Page by Dragging

Press **Ctrl** and drag page tab to copy to desired page tab position.

Copy Multiple Pages by Dragging

1. Select pages to copy.
2. Press **Ctrl** and drag selected page tabs to desired page tab position.

INSERT 3-D REFERENCE IN FORMULA

1. If necessary, type or edit formula.
2. Place insertion point in formula where reference will be inserted.
3. Select page containing cell(s) to reference.

✓ *When you click a page tab, its name appears in the formula bar.*

4. Select cell(s) to reference.

✓ *When you select the cell(s), the complete 3-D reference appears in the formula bar.*

To enter a 3-D reference for a range of notebook pages:

Press **Shift** and click last notebook page tab to reference.

5. Type or insert remaining parts of formula.
6. Press **Enter** .... Enter

TYPE A 3-D REFERENCE IN FORMULA

1. If necessary, type or edit formula.
2. Place insertion point in formula where reference will be typed.
3. Type the page name.............*page name*

To type a 3-D reference for a range of notebook pages:

a. Type two periods.........................(..)
b. Type last page name in range.

4. Press colon ....(:)
5. Type cell reference or range.

✓ *EXAMPLES: A..C:A1..C1 or "Total Sales":A1..A5*

OPEN A DUPLICATE NOTEBOOK WINDOW

Creates a new view for active notebook window.

1. Click **Window**........................ Alt + W
2. Click **New View**.............................. N

CLOSE A DUPLICATE NOTEBOOK WINDOW

Click Close **button** .... ✕

In this exercise, you will add a summary page to the PAYFORM file and enter formulas containing 3-D references to the February, March, and April notebook pages. You will also open a duplicate notebook window so you can view the Totals notebook page while you change test values in the February notebook page.

EXERCISE DIRECTIONS

1. Open ⌨PAYFORM or ⬚23PAYFOR.

2. Copy the March page to a new page, to the right of the original.

3. Rename March_2 page; name it Totals.

4. Move the Totals tab to the right of April by dragging the tab into place.

5. Use the Insert, Group Name command to select a previously named group, FebApr, and check that View, Group Mode is activated.

6. Select February and, while notebook pages are grouped, enter test values in the HOURS WORKED columns for each employee as shown:
   - On the first payroll, enter 10 hours for Drennan, using Ctrl+Enter to input the number.
   - Copy 10 for all employees for the first payroll week.
   - On the second payroll, enter 20 hours for Drennan, again using Ctrl+Enter to input the number.
   - Copy 20 for all employees for the second payroll week.
   - On the third payroll, enter 30 hours for Drennan, using the same method to input the number.
   - Copy 30 for all employees for the second payroll week.

7. Turn View mode off, deselect grouped pages and check that test values have been entered on each month's notebook page.

8. Select cell E7 in the Totals notebook page and enter a 3-D formula that adds the values in cell E7 in the February, March, and April notebook page.

   HINT: The completed formula would read: +February:E7+March:E7+April:E7, if the formula cells are selected using the mouse. Or, you can type @SUM(February..April:E7) or @Sum(febapr:E7), and 30 (the sum of the test values) should appear in the cell.

9. Copy the formula for each employee in the first week of the payroll.

10. Enter a 3-D formula on the Totals page to add the values in E23 on all sheets.

11. Copy the formula for all employees on the last two payrolls.

12. Open a duplicate notebook window and arrange them in a tiled fashion. Note the names of the windows.

13. Both notebooks should be on the Totals page with A1 in the top left corner. Select one notebook and move to the February page.

14. On the February notebook page, change the HOURS WORKED test values in the first payroll week to 50 for each employee.
    ✓   Note that the Totals notebook page in the duplicate window shows updated values.

15. Change the HOURS WORKED test values back to 10.

16. Close the duplicate notebook window.

17. Select the Totals notebook page and set it to fit on one page when printed.

18. Print the Totals notebook page.

19. Select View, Group Mode to group February, March, and April pages.

20. Select the February notebook page and delete all test values in HOURS WORKED.

21. Deselect Group Mode and check that test values have been deleted on each month's notebook page and that Totals page shows zeros in the HOURS WORKED column.

22. Save PAYFORM as a template file.

23. Close the notebook file.

Exercise 24

■ Summary

Mr. Abrams administered two additional exams plus a final examination to his class. He needs to revise the notebook page he prepared earlier to include the new test data and two new students. In addition, Mr. Abrams' supervisor has requested a separate notebook page showing student names and final exam averages.

EXERCISE DIRECTIONS

✓ *You may lock row labels when it is helpful to facilitate data entry.*

1. Open ▱MARK or ▱24MARK.

2. Insert rows in alphabetical sequence for two students who have been transferred in from another class. Enter the information below, as shown in the illustration on the following page, and extend the quiz and test average formulas for the new rows.

   5162 Cather, W. quizzes 78, 84 tests 81, 89 Adm. 5/1
   3465 Wharton, E. quizzes 69, 72 tests 75, 70 Adm. 5/1

3. Insert two new columns after TEST 3, as shown, for TEST 4 and TEST 5.

4. Enter TEST 4 and TEST 5 data, leaving blanks for absentees, from the list below.

   ✓ *The Final Exam data will be entered in step 7 of this exercise.*

	TEST 4	TEST 5	FINAL EXAM
Bronte, C.	88	89	90
Carson, R.	54	69	60
Cather, W.	72	75	81
Fromm, E.	81	79	76
Hardy, T.		52	55
Hemingway, E.	70	75	70
Melville, H.	90	91	88
Miller, A.	95	92	93
Poe, E.	72	82	75
Steinbeck, J.	84	86	84
Wharton, E.	67	71	65
Wouk, H.	99	97	97

5. Edit the formulas in the TEST AVERAGE column to include the new test data and to create averages for the new students.

6. Delete the STUDENT NUMBER column.

7. Create a new column after TEST AVERAGE for FINAL EXAM. Enter the grades shown in the FINAL EXAM column at bottom left in the new column.

8. Create a new column for FINAL AVERAGE after the FINAL EXAM column.

9. Find the FINAL AVERAGE for each student if the Quiz Average and Final Exam are each worth 25% of the final average and the Test Average is worth 50% of the Final Average.

   HINT: *@AVG(Quiz Average, Test Average, Test Average, Final Exam) Use commas to separate cell addresses.*

10. Format test averages to one decimal place and center all new column headings.

11. Check the accuracy of the summary formulas for NUMBER OF PAPERS, CLASS AVERAGE, HIGHEST GRADE, and LOWEST GRADE, and copy them for the new columns of data.

12. Save the notebook file, or *save as* MARK.

13. Print one copy in landscape orientation to fit on one page.

14. Using the Copy and Paste Special feature, copy columns A:C and the FINAL AVERAGE column to a separate notebook. Use the Paste Formulas as Values option for FINAL AVERAGE data.

15. Save the new file; name it MARKSUM.

16. Print one copy of MARKSUM.

17. Close the notebook files.

Annotations on the spreadsheet:
- **Insert two new columns.** (between QUIZ 3/AVERAGE and TEST AVERAGE areas)
- **Insert two new columns.** (near column M)
- **Insert two rows.**
- **Delete column.** (pointing to STUDENT NUMBER column)
- *Adm. 5/1* (rows for Cather, W. and Wharton, E)

Row	A	B	C	D QUIZ 1	E QUIZ 2	F QUIZ 3	G QUIZ AVERAGE	H TEST 1	I TEST 2	J TEST 3	K TEST AVERAGE	L STUDENT NUMBER	M
1	CLASS:		ENG 852										
2	TERM:		SPRING 199-										
3	TEACHER:		MR. ABRAMS										
4							QUIZ				TEST	STUDENT	
5	ID	NAME		QUIZ 1	QUIZ 2	QUIZ 3	AVERAGE	TEST 1	TEST 2	TEST 3	AVERAGE	NUMBER	
6													
7	2314	Bronte, C.		85	80	90	85.0	83	86	92	87.0	1	
8	5432	Carson, R.		35	55	68	52.7		59	65	62.0	2	
9	*5162*	*Cather, W.*			78	84			81	89	80.3	3	*Adm. 5/1*
10	2311	Fromm, E.		72	76	85	77.7	72	83	86	80.3	3	
11	3454	Hardy, T.		55	42	67	54.7	35		62	48.5	4	
12	5413	Hemingway. E.		64	68	69	67.0	68	74	69	70.3	5	
13	5487	Melville, H.		83	87	86	85.3	85	93	88	88.7	6	
14	2379	Miller, A.		98	96	97	97.0	95	93	94	94.0	7	
15	5438	Poe, E.		76	79	81	78.7	79	85	82	82.0	8	
16	2390	Steinbeck, J.		90	87	95	90.7	95	80	92	89.0	9	
17	*3465*	*Wharton, E*			69	72			75	70			*Adm. 5/1*
18	5498	Wouk, H.		100	96	98	98.0	95	97	99	97.0	10	
19													
20		NO. OF PAPERS		10	12	12	10	9	11	11	10		
21		CLASS AVERAGE		75.8	76.1	82.7	78.7	78.6	82.4	81.3	79.9		
22		HIGHEST GRADE		100	96	98	98	95	97	99	97		
23		LOWEST GRADE		35	42	67	53	35	59	62	49		

Exercise 25

■ **Insert an IF function**

NOTES

Insert an IF Function

■ An **IF statement** is a logical function which sets up a conditional statement to test data. The truth or falsity of the condition will determine the results of the statement.

The format for an IF statement is:

@IF(Condition, True Expression, False Expression)

■ Using this formula, if the condition is true, the function results in True Expression; if the condition is false, the function results in False Expression.

■ For example, in this exercise, the teacher uses an IF statement to determine the final grade based on the final average and a passing grade of 65. Therefore, an IF statement can be used to test whether the final average is greater than 64.9. If so, then the student passes and the word PASS is entered in the function location. If the condition is false, the word FAIL is entered in the function location.

✓ Note the breakdown of one of the IF statement formulas used in this problem. Since PASS and FAIL are text, you must enclose them in quotation marks (").

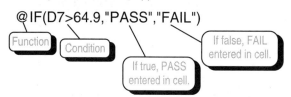

■ IF statements may use conditional operators as listed below:

=	Equals	<=	Less than or equal to
>	Greater than	>=	Greater than or equal to
<	Less than	&	Used for connecting text (concatenation)
<>	Not equal to		

✓ IF statements may be used in combination with OR, AND, and NOT statements to evaluate complex conditions.

KEYSTROKES

INSERT AN IF FUNCTION USING FORMULA COMPOSER

✓ You can also type a function to insert it.

1. Click cell.

2. Click **Formula Composer** button f_{∞} on toolbar.

3. Click @ button in Expression group.

4. Select **Function Category** list ..... `Alt`+`C`

5. Select **Logical** .... `↓` `↑`

6. Select **Function** list .... `Alt`+`F`

7. Select **IF** function .... `↓` `↑`

8. Click **OK** .... `Enter`

9. Click **Condition** box .... `Alt`+`O`

10. Type condition.

✓ You can click cells in notebook page to insert cell references.

11. Click **TrueExpr** box .... `Alt`+`T`

12. Type the argument if condition is true.

13. Click **FalseExpr** box .... `Alt`+`F`

14. Type the argument if condition is false.

15. Click **OK** .... `Enter`

In this exercise, you will use an IF statement to calculate the FINAL GRADE and CREDITS GRANTED for Mr. Abrams' class based on a 65% passing grade.

EXERCISE DIRECTIONS

1. Open ✒MARKSUM or 💾25MARKSU.

2. Insert the following columns after FINAL AVERAGES and center the headings:

   FINAL   CREDITS
   GRADE   GRANTED

3. Enter an IF statement for the first student in the FINAL GRADE column that will produce the word PASS if the final average is greater than 64.9, and FAIL if it is not.

4. Copy the formula to the other students.

5. Enter an IF statement for the first student in the CREDITS GRANTED column that will produce the number three if the final average is greater than 64.9, and zero if it is not.

6. Copy the formula to the other students.

7. Center all new entries.

8. Delete the row containing Number of Papers.

9. Print one copy of the notebook page.

10. Close and save the notebook file, or *save as* MARKSUM.

A	A	B	C	D	E	F	G	H	I
1	CLASS:		ENG 852						
2	TERM:		SPRING 199-						
3	TEACHER:		MR. ABRAMS						
4				FINAL	*FINAL*	*CREDITS*			
5	ID	NAME		AVERAGE	*GRADE*	*GRANTED*			
6									
7	2314	Bronte, C.		87.6					
8	5432	Carson, R.		59.0					
9	5162	Cather, W.		80.1					
10	2311	Fromm, E.		78.5					
11	3454	Hardy, T.		52.2					
12	5413	Hemingway, E.		69.9					
13	5487	Melville, H.		88.0					
14	2379	Miller, A.		94.4					
15	5438	Poe, E.		78.4					
16	2390	Steinbeck, J.		87.4					
17	3465	Wharton, E		69.3					
18	5498	Wouk, H.		97.5					
19								DELETE	
20		NO. OF PAPERS		12.0				ROW	
21		CLASS AVERAGE		78.5					
22		HIGHEST GRADE		97.5					
23		LOWEST GRADE		52.2					
24									
25									
26									
27									
28									

Exercise

26

■ **IF Functions** ■ **Hide Data**

NOTES

IF Functions

■ An **IF** statement may be created to perform one calculation if the condition is true and perform another calculation if the condition is false. For example, if sales are over $50,000, multiply the sales by 3% commission, otherwise multiply sales by 2%.

■ When creating a condition using the greater than operator (>), make sure to use the correct value. If you are looking for all values of 5 or over, you should use >4.9 or >=5, not >5.

• A condition may test the presence of specific text entries. As discussed in the previous exercise, any text in an IF function should be enclosed in quotation marks.

For example: @IF(D7="M",4,5) If the data is M, then enter 4, otherwise enter 5.

Hide Data

■ Data that should not be viewed by all users of a notebook or data that is not necessary for a report may be **hidden**.

■ To hide rows or columns, select a cell in the row or column to be hidden and then select <u>B</u>lock from the <u>F</u>ormat menu, click the Reveal/Hide tab, and select the <u>R</u>ows or <u>C</u>olumns and H<u>i</u>de options.

■ This Hide operation can be reversed by selecting the columns or rows on both sides of the hidden area, returning to the Reveal/Hide tab and selecting the Re<u>v</u>eal option.

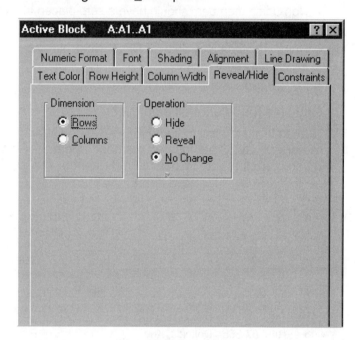

■ You can use the mouse to reveal a single row or column by placing the mouse pointer slightly to the right of the hidden column's border and dragging it to the right.

■ To view all hidden column and rows at once, click <u>E</u>dit, Se<u>l</u>ect All, then click Fo<u>r</u>mat, <u>B</u>lock and select the Re<u>v</u>eal option. (This is the easiest way to reveal row 1 or column A when they are hidden.)

In this exercise, Strong Equipment Manufacturing Co. is preparing a notebook to calculate miscellaneous payroll deductions for its employees. Union dues, insurance, and locker and uniforms charges will be calculated based on union or non-union membership.

EXERCISE DIRECTIONS

1. Create the worksheet below or open 📄26EMP.WB3.

2. Center data and column headings in the NUMBER INSURED, U/N and M/F columns.

3. Center S.S.NO. and NAME column headings.

4. Right-align the remaining column headings and adjust column width as necessary.

5. Use an IF function to find the UNION DUES.
   - Union and non-union members are noted with U or N.
   - Non-union members should have a zero placed in the Union Dues column.
   - Union members pay dues of $5 per week plus $2 for each insured member.

   *Hint: IF data equals "U", 5+NUMBER INSURED*2,0.*

6. Copy the formula for all employees.

7. Use an IF statement to find INSURANCE. Union members pay $3 per insured member, and non-union members pay $7 per insured member.

8. Copy the formula to all employees.

9. Use an IF statement to find LOCKER + UNIFORMS deduction. Males pay $4 per week and females pay $5 per week due to variations in uniforms and locker facilities.

   Hint: If M/F data is "M", then $4, otherwise $5.

10. Copy the formula to all employees.

11. Find the TOTAL MISC. DEDUCTIONS.

12. Find the TOTALS for the columns indicated in the illustration.

13. Format all money data to two decimal places.

14. Bold titles, column headings, and TOTALS line.

15. Insert a blank column in column A.

16. Hide the Social Security Number (S.S.NO.) column.

17. Print one copy of the worksheet.

18. Reveal the S.S.NO. column.

19. Close and save the workbook file; name it EMP.

A	A	B	C	D	E	F	G	H	I	J
1			STRONG EQUIPMENT MANUFACTURING CO.							
2			MISCELLANEOUS PAYROLL DEDUCTIONS							
3				TREMONT PLANT						
4										
5			NUMBER			UNION		LOCKER +	TOTAL MISC.	
6	S. S. NO.	NAME	INSURED	U/N	M/F	DUES	INSURANCE	UNIFORMS	DEDUCTIONS	
7	054-65-4532	Biceps, Martin	2	U	M					
8	087-87-5654	Deltoids, Kay	3	U	F					
9	127-87-0980	Heavy, Pat	1	N	F					
10	354-65-6543	Muscle, Gary	3	U	M					
11	234-76-5788	Quadis, Wendy	4	U	F					
12	107-87-9944	Strong, Sam	2	N	M					
13	103-54-3433	Triceps, Bob	4	U	M					
14										
15		TOTALS								

KEYSTROKES

REVEAL/HIDE COLUMNS OR ROWS

1. Select a cell in the column or row to be hidden, or select the area around data to be revealed.

2. Click **Format** .... `Alt`+`R`

3. Click **Block** .... `B`

4. Select **Reveal/Hide** tab .... `Ctrl`+`Tab`

5. Click **Hide** .... `I`

   or **Reveal** .... `R`

6. Click **Rows** .... `R`

   or **Columns** .... `C`

7. Click **OK** .... `Enter`

Exercise 27	■ **Enter a Date as Numerical Data** ■ **Format Numerical Dates**

NOTES

Enter Date as Numerical Data

■ As previously noted, dates can be entered as label data, but when there is a need to add or subtract dates, they must be entered as numerical data.

■ Quattro Pro recognizes the appropriate number format based on the way you enter data. For example, if you enter 25%, the entry is recognized as a value with the percent format. This also applies to dates.

Format Numerical Dates

■ If you enter a date in one of the standard formats, Quattro Pro automatically recognizes the entry as a numerical date value or serial value.

✓ *To view a serial value for a date, enter the date in number format.*

■ Illustrated below are some of the standard date formats that Quattro Pro recognizes as numerical date values. Notice the serial value for a date and time is expressed as a decimal number. When you subtract one date value from another, Quattro Pro subtracts the serial values of the numbers and displays the result. In the Quattro Pro date system, the date December 30, 1899, is represented by the serial value 0.

Formats	Date	Example Entries	Serial values
mm/dd/yy	January 1, 1900	1/1/00	1
dd-mmm-yy	February 23, 1997	23-Feb-97	35484
dd-mmm	July 25, 1997	25-Jul	35636
mmm-yy	July 1, 1997	Jul-97	35612

In this exercise, the Sportsmania Supply Company is creating a workbook to determine the due date of invoices, the due date for cash discounts, the discounts, and the amounts paid as determined by the date paid. The Net Terms refer to the number of days given to pay the invoice in full. The Discount Terms reflect the number of days within which payment must be made to earn the discount.

EXERCISE DIRECTIONS

1. Create the notebook page as shown on the next page, or open ⬚27PAYABL.

2. Complete the following steps:
   • Center all column headings.
   • Center data in the NET TERMS, DISCOUNT TERMS, and DISCOUNT RATE.
   • Format titles and column headings for bold.
   • Enter dates as values with MM/DD/YY format (no label prefix).
   • Adjust column width as necessary.

3. Find DUE DATE:
   HINT: *INVOICE DATE+NET TERMS*
   ✓   *This formula adds the serial value of a date with a number and the result is a serial value.*

4. Format the date serial number for Long Date International format, MM/DD/YY.

5. Find the DISCOUNT DATE.

   HINT: INVOICE DATE+DISCOUNT TERMS

6. Format the date serial number for Long International format.

7. Find the DISCOUNT: Use an IF statement to determine if a discount has been earned.

   HINT: If the date paid is earlier (less than) than the discount date, then multiply the amount of the invoice by the discount rate, otherwise enter a zero.

8. Format DISCOUNT for two decimal places.

9. Find AMOUNT PAID.

   HINT: AMOUNT-DISCOUNT.

10. Format AMOUNT PAID for two decimal places.

11. Find totals for the AMOUNT, DISCOUNT, and AMOUNT PAID columns.

12. Format totals for two decimal places.

13. Create a block name that includes the entire notebook page. Name it PRINTALL.

14. Print one copy of the block PRINTALL, using landscape orientation to fit on one page.

15. Save and close the file; name it PAYABLE.

A	A	B	C	D	E	F	G	H	I	J	K	L
1			SPORTSMANIA SUPPLY COMPANY									
2			ACCOUNTS PAYABLE									
3												
4		INVOICE		NET	DUE	DISCOUNT	DISCOUNT	DISCOUNT	DATE			AMOUNT
5	INVOICE #	DATE	VENDOR	TERMS	DATE	TERMS	RATE	DATE	PAID	AMOUNT	DISCOUNT	PAID
6	2341	02/03/97	Sneaker Corp.	30		20	2%		02/21/97	1400.50		
7	M453	02/04/97	Uniforms Unlimited	90		30	3%		03/05/97	997.45		
8	6454	02/05/97	Carson Glove Co.	60		20	2%		04/04/97	875.98		
9	87578J	02/05/97	O'Neill Sports, Inc.	120		30	2%		03/06/97	1650.89		
10	BJ54765	02/07/97	Yankee Supplies Co	45		10	1%		03/24/97	1245.87		
11	M6575	02/08/97	Zenon Jackets, Inc.	90		20	3%		02/27/97	988.12		
12	C56465	02/10/97	JJV Equipment Co.	30		10	1%		02/18/97	450.67		
13												
14	TOTALS											
15												
16												
17												
18												

KEYSTROKES

ENTER DATE AS NUMERICAL DATA

✓ *Dates entered as numerical data are right-aligned and can be calculated.*

1. Select cell to receive date.

   To enter a specific date:

   Type date .... *date in valid format*

   You may use the following formats:

   - **mm/dd/yy** .... (e.g. 6/24/94)
   - **dd-mmm** .... (e.g. 24-Jun)
   - **dd-mmm-yy** .... (e.g. 24-Jun-94)
   - **mmm-yy** .... (e.g. Jun-94)

2. Press **Enter** .... `Enter`

   ✓ *If Quattro Pro displays number signs (######), the column is not wide enough to display the date. To see the entry, double-click the right border of the column heading.*

FORMAT NUMERICAL DATES

1. Select cells containing numerical dates to format.

2. Press **F12** .... `F12`

   OR

   a. Click **Format** .... `Alt`+`R`

   b. Click **Block** .... `B`

   OR

   a. Right-click cells.

   b. Click **Block Properties**.

3. Click **Numeric Format** tab.

4. Select **Date** .... `Alt`+`D`

5. Select desired format... `↓`, `Shift`+`Tab`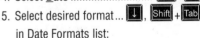

   in Date Formats list:

   - DD-MMM-YY
   - DD-MMM
   - MMM-YY
   - Long Date Intl. (mm/dd/yy)
   - Short Date Intl. (mm/dd)

6. Click **OK** .... `Enter`

Exercise

28

- ■ **SpeedFormat**
- ■ **Shading and Text Colors**

NOTES

SpeedFormat

- ■ Quattro Pro provides built-in formats which can be applied to a block of data. These formats are called **SpeedFormats** and include number formats, fonts, borders, patterns, colors, alignments, row heights, and column widths. They give the notebook page a professional, organized appearance.

- ■ Select SpeedFormat, from the Format menu or click the SpeedFormat button ▦ to display a dialog box with a selection of table formats that may be applied to a range of data. (*See the illustration below.*) SpeedFormats may be customized by creating your own format and then clicking the Add button to include it on the SpeedFormat list of options.

Shading and Text Colors

- ■ Custom formats may be set using the Active Block dialog box, which is accessed by selecting Block from the Format menu. The Shading tab in the dialog box provides a palette of colors that can be used to color the background of a selected cell or block. The Color 1 and Color 2 palettes are used to blend or mix colors. For example, if you select red in Color 1 and yellow in Color 2, those colors will be at either end of the Blend spectrum that appears below. Shades that transition between those colors will appear in the middle. You can then select orange, a blend of red and yellow, from the middle of the spectrum. Note the illustration of the Shading tab below.

SpeedFormat Dialog Box

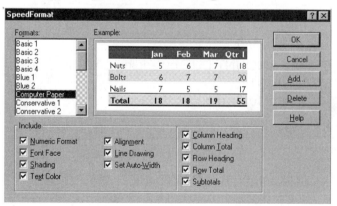

Shading Tab

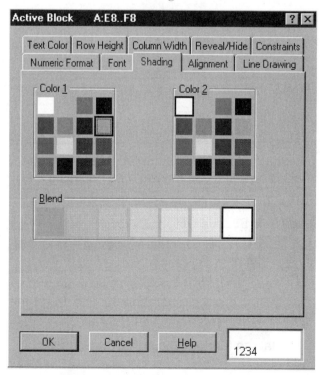

■ The Text Color tab in the Active Block dialog box is used to color the text in a selected cell. Text colors are limited to the palette illustrated.

■ While a block is selected, you may set all the format options at once using the various tabs in the Active Block dialog box. If you will be reusing a format, it may be saved as a SpeedFormat option.

Text Color Tab

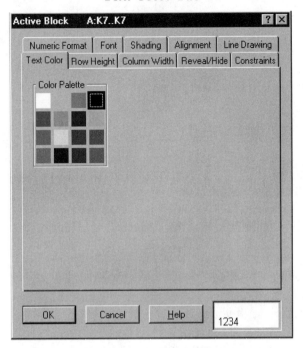

In this exercise, the Tennis and Racquet Center is determining the number of days each account has been unpaid as of March 10, 1997. Customers are given terms of ten to thirty days to pay the bills. A late fee of 1% is charged on unpaid amounts that are outstanding for more than thirty days past their due date. (Accounts Receivable are records for customers who owe money to a company. Aging of accounts receivable is done to determine how many days the customers' payments are overdue.)

EXERCISE DIRECTIONS

1. Create the notebook page as illustrated, or open 🖫28ACCREC.

2. Find the DUE DATE.
    Hint: *INVOICE DATE+TERMS*

    Format the serial value for DD-MMM-YY date format. Adjust column width as necessary.

3. Find the DAYS UNPAID.
    Hint: *DATE-DUE DATE*

    ✓   *The reference to the date in C4 should be an absolute reference.*

4. Find the LATE FEE. Use an IF statement. If the days unpaid are greater than 30, find 1% of the amount, otherwise enter zero.

    Format the fee for fixed with two decimal places.

5. Find AMOUNT DUE by adding LATE FEE and AMOUNT.
    Format for two decimal places.

6. Copy the formulas to the remaining invoices.

7. Total and format all money columns.

8. Select the range A1:I3 and use the Format, Block dialog box to set the Shading to navy, the Text color to white, and the Font to bold.

9. With the block still selected, add this format to SpeedFormat by clicking Format, SpeedFormat, Add. Name this format Navy. Click OK.

10. Select the range A5:I6 and use Format, SpeedFormat, Navy to format the column headings.

11. Select the range A7:I17, select Format, SpeedFormat and view all the choices provided in the dialog box.

   ✓ *As you highlight each table format, an example of the style appears in the Sample box.*

12. Select Grey 3 and deselect the Numeric Format and the Column Heading features since the heading and the numbers have been formatted. Click OK.

13. Adjust column widths as necessary.

14. Print one copy so that it all fits on one page.

15. Save and close the file; name it **ACCREC**.

A	A	B	C	D	E	F	G	H	I
1			TENNIS AND RACQUET CENTER						
2			AGING OF ACCOUNTS RECEIVABLE						
3									
4	DATE:		03/01/97						
5	INVOICE	INVOICE			DUE	DAYS			AMOUNT
6	DATE	NO.	CUSTOMER	TERMS	DATE	UNPAID	AMOUNT	LATE FEE	DUE
7	01/03/97	54332	Thomas Racket	20			156.75		
8	01/05/97	54355	Sally String	10			65.98		
9	01/07/97	54410	Larry Love	30			234.76		
10	01/12/97	54554	Fred Forty	20			167.87		
11	01/13/97	54570	Al Advantage	30			325.87		
12	01/15/97	54600	Nell Nett	30			187.65		
13	01/18/97	54715	Thomas Racket	20			345.55		
14	01/20/97	54790	Sam Serve	20			132.98		
15	01/22/97	54817	Sally String	10			49.89		
16	01/24/97	54910	Bakk Handd	20			55.75		
17									
18			Totals						

KEYSTROKES

APPLY SPEEDFORMAT

1. Select range of data to be formatted.

2. Click the **SpeedFormat** button .... 🔳
   OR
   a. Click **Format** .... `Alt`+`R`
   b. Click **SpeedFormat** .... `F`

3. Select desired format.

4. Click **OK** .... `Enter`

ADD FORMAT TO SPEEDFORMAT

1. Select formatted range of data to be added to list.

2. Click the **SpeedFormat** button .... 🔳
   OR
   a. Click **Format** .... `Alt`+`R`
   b. Click **SpeedFormat** .... `F`

3. Click **Add** .... `Alt`+`A`

4. Enter format name.

5. Click **OK** .... `Enter`

APPLY COLOR TO CELL FOREGROUND

1. Select object or range of cells.

2. Right-click cells.

3. Choose **Block Properties**.

4. Click **Shading** .... `Alt`+`Tab`

5. Select or create the color you want.

6. Click **OK** .... `Enter`

APPLY COLOR TO TEXT

1. Select range of data.

2. Right-click cells.

3. Click **Block Properties**.

4. Click **Text color** .... `Alt`+`Tab`

5. Select color.

6. Click **OK** .... `Enter`

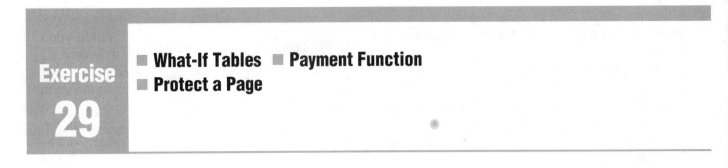

Exercise

29

- **What-If Tables** ■ **Payment Function**
- **Protect a Page**

NOTES

What-If Tables

- A **What-If table** is used to answer a question based on one or two factors that might influence the outcome. What-if tables are created by selecting the <u>N</u>umeric Tools, and then <u>W</u>hat-If from the <u>T</u>ools menu as illustrated below.

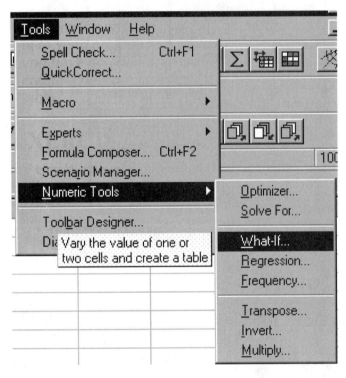

- The table created in a what-if problem enables you to find the best solution to a problem by presenting a range of solutions based on one or two **variables**. A what-if table evaluates a series of possible answers using input values you supply. The first row and left-most column of the table are call **substitution values**. The values that are in the first row and column are called **input values** and are listed at the bottom of the notebook.

- For example, if you want to purchase a home and can only afford to spend $1,000 per month on your mortgage payment, you might want to determine the maximum mortgage amount you can afford to borrow and the number of years for which you should apply. A what-if table should be created showing the mortgage payments for various loan amounts and loan payment periods. Then you can determine what you can afford.

- When you use the what-if table command, Quattro Pro uses the formula in the upper-left corner of the table to calculate the substitution values. What-if tables that require two sets of substitution values (a row and a column) are called **two-variable what-if tables**. Note the illustration of the What-If dialog box.

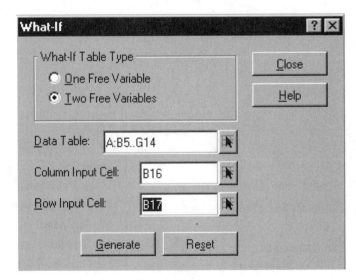

- The format of a two-variable what-if table must meet the following criteria:

  - The column and row input values that the formula will use must be outside the table.

- The formula must be in the top-left cell of the table range and must refer to the column and row input values.

- The substitution values for the table must be arranged in the first row and column of the table as shown in Illustration A.

Illustration A

	A	B	C	D	E	F	G	H
1		**FRANK AND MARIE REISER**						
2	formula cell	**MORTGAGE PAYMENT TABLE AT 9%**					what-if data table range	
3								
4					TERM IN YEARS			
5		=PMT(B16,.09/12,B17*12)	10	15	20	25	30	
6	PRINCIPAL	$100,000.00						
7		$105,000.00						
8		$110,000.00						
9		$115,000.00						
10		$120,000.00						
11		$125,000.00						
12		$130,000.00						
13		$135,000.00						
14								
15	*Input cells*							
16	*column:*	100000	input column and row cells					
17	*row:*	10						

- To create the table values, select the what-if table range (which includes the formula), then indicate the row and column input cells (the cells that contain the column and row input values), and then click Generate to create the table.

Payment Function

- The **PMT (payment) function** can be applied to calculate a loan payment amount using principal, interest rate, and number of payment periods. The PMT function uses the following format and contains three parts, as defined below.

The arguments for the PMT function are:

@PMT	(Pv, Rate, Nper)
Pv	Present value – total amount that a series of future payments is worth now (for example, the principal or amount of the loan).
Rate	Interest rate per period (for example, interest/12 represents the interest per month).
Nper	Number of payment periods (for example, term*12 months).

✓ *The rate and the number of payment periods (nper) must be expressed in the same manner. For example, if you are calculating a monthly payment at a % annual rate of interest for 25 years, you must enter .09/12 as the rate and 25*12 to get the number of monthly payment periods (nper).*

Protect a Page

- It is possible to protect, or **lock**, an entire notebook page, individual cells, or a range of cells from accidental changes or unauthorized use. When a notebook page is protected, the message "Protected Cell or Block" will appear when you try to change the contents of a locked cell.

- To protect a document, click Format, Page, click the Protection tab and then click Enable Cell Locking.

Format Page Protection Dialog Box

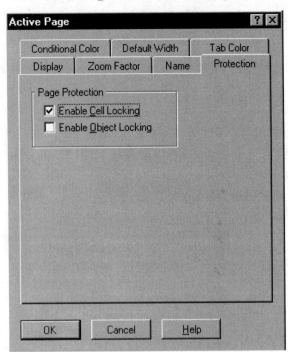

Format Block Constraints Tab

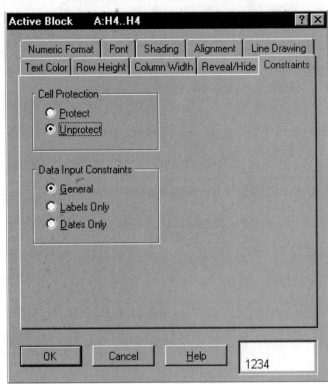

- When a notebook is protected, by default, all cells are protected and data entry is disabled.

- To enable certain cells to receive data in a protected notebook page, you must **unlock** those individual cells. To unlock a cell or block of cell, select the block, click Format, Block, click the Constraints tab and click the Protect option button.

IMPORTANT: If you set a password when protecting a notebook page and you forget the password, you will not be able to make changes to the notebook page.

In this exercise, you will create a mortgage payment table for Frank and Marie Reiser to determine payment amounts at 9% for various principal amounts and numbers of years. The table will be formatted using SpeedFormat, and the notebook page will be protected.

EXERCISE DIRECTIONS

1. Create the notebook page below, or open ⊟29LOAN.

2. Find in B5 the monthly mortgage payment for $100,000 at 9% for 10 years using the locations of the input cell data for principal and term.

   HINT: @PMT (pv, rate, nper)

   @PMT(B16, .09/12, B17*12)

   ✓   *The formula must reference the input values in cells B16 and B17. These input values will not affect the computed values in the table. Note that to determine monthly payments, the rate and nper values have been adjusted by a factor of 12.*

3. Create a two-variable what-if table by completing the What-If dialog box. Click Generate.

4. Select the table data beginning in row 5 and use the Legal Pad SpeedFormat. Deselect Column Headings and Number Format.

5. Select the top four rows of the notebook and format the block for light yellow to match the table.

6. Save the file; name it LOAN.

7. Print one copy.

   ❷ Based on the data in the table, what would be the highest principal you can borrow with a payment of approximately $1,000 a month?

8. Use the Format, Page, Protection tab to enable cell locking feature.

9. Use the Format, Block, Constraints tab to unprotect the top three rows of the notebook.

10. Go to cell C8, F11, and G13 and try to edit the data.

    ✓   *A protection message should appear.*

11. Go to the third row of the title and enter, March 1997.

    ✓   *Since this area was unprotected, you can change these cells.*

12. Save and close the file; name it LOAN.

A	A	B	C	D	E	F	G
1		FRANK AND MARIE REISER					
2		MORTGAGE PAYMENT TABLE AT 9%					
3							
4					TERM IN YEARS		
5			10	15	20	25	30
6	PRINCIPAL	$100,000.00					
7		$105,000.00					
8		$110,000.00					
9		$115,000.00					
10		$120,000.00					
11		$125,000.00					
12		$130,000.00					
13		$135,000.00					
14							
15	*Input cells*						
16	*column:*	100000					
17	*row:*	10					

KEYSTROKES

TWO-VARIABLE WHAT-IF TABLES

What-if tables generate values that change depending on one or two values in a formula. For example, a two-variable input table displays the results of changing two values in a formula.

The row input cell is used to indicate an initial input value to which the formula will refer.

The column input cell is used to indicate an initial input value to which the formula will also refer.

Although instructions listed below are for a two-variable what-if table, you could also create a one-variable what-if table that would find answers for a single row or column of substitution values.

CREATE A TWO-VARIABLE WHAT-IF TABLE

1. Select cells outside the table you will be using to serve as row and column input cells.
2. Enter initial value .... *number* in row input cell.
3. Enter initial value .... *number* in column input cell.
4. Enter series of substitution...... *numbers* values in a column.
5. Enter series of substitution...... *numbers* values in a row.
   - ✔ *The first value in row and column will contain the formula.*
6. Click upper-left cell........................... `⟷` in table.
7. Type formula .... *formula*
   - ✔ *Formula must refer to row and column input cells.*
8. Select all cells in what-if table range.
   - ✔ *Select cells containing formula substitution values and cells where results will be displayed.*
9. Click **Tools** .... `Alt`+`T`
10. Click **Numeric Tools** .... `N`
11. Click **What If** .... `W`
12. Click **Two Free Variables** ..... `Alt`+`T`

13. Select What-If table range using the mouse, or select **Data Table** .. `Alt`+`D` and type range of cells.
14. Select **Column Input Cell** .... `Alt`+`E`
15. Select **Row Input Cell**............. `Alt`+`R`
    OR
    Type cell references for entire table, column input and row input cells.
16. Click **Generate** .... `Alt`+`G`
17. Click **Close** .... `Alt`+`C`

USE THE PMT FUNCTION

Applies the PMT function to find the monthly payment for a principal for a specific number of years.

1. Click cell where answer should appear.
2. Click `f₍ₓ₎` on toolbar.
3. Click `@`.
4. Click **Financial-Annuity** in Function Category list.
5. Click **PMT** in Function List.
6. Click **OK**............................. `Enter`
7. Click **Monthly Payment** option.
8. Click **Pv** and enter value.......... `Alt`+`V`
   - ✔ *The principal is the amount of the loan. You can type the amount or type the cell reference containing the amount.*
9. Click **Rate** and enter value ...... `Alt`+`A`
   - ✔ *The rate is a percentage. You can type the percentage or type the cell reference containing the percentage.*
10. Click **Nper** and enter value...... `Alt`+`N`
    - ✔ *Nper is the number of years. You can type the number or type the cell reference containing the number.*
11. Click **OK**.................................... `Enter`

PROTECT A PAGE (ENABLE CELL LOCK)

Prevents changes to locked cells, graphic objects, embedded charts in a notebook page, or chart items in a chart page.

1. Click **Format** .... `Alt`+`R`
2. Click **Page**.................................... `P`
3. Click **Protection** tab .... `Ctrl`+`Tab`
4. Click **Enable Cell Locking**............... `C`
5. Click **OK**.................................... `Enter`

   To password protect page:
   a. Right-click notebook title bar when document window is not maximized.
   b. Select **Active Notebook Properties**.
   c. Click **Password Level** tab.
   d. Choose a password protection level (**None**, **Low**, **Medium**, or **High**) ..... `↓`/`↑`
   e. Click **OK** .... `Enter`
   f. Type the **Password**.
   g. Click **OK** .... `Enter`
   h. Verify the password by retyping it.
   i. Click **OK** .... `Enter`

UNPROTECT A PAGE

1. Right-click page tab to unprotect.
2. Click the **Protection** tab .... `Ctrl`+`Tab`
3. Clear the **Enable Cell Locking** or **Enable Object Locking** check boxes.
   If page is password protected:
   a. Right-click on notebook title bar.
   b. Select **Active Notebook Properties**.
   c. Click **Password Level**.
   d. Click **None**.
   e. Click **OK**.

LOCK/UNLOCK CELLS IN A NOTEBOOK PAGE

- ✔ *By default, all cells and objects in a notebook page are locked.*

1. Select block to unlock or lock.
2. Click **Format** .... `Alt`+`R`
3. Click **Block** .... `B`
4. Select **Constraints** tab .... `Ctrl`+`Tab`
5. Click **Unprotect**............................. `U`
   or **Protect** .... `P`

Exercise

30

■ **Summary**

In this exercise, you will create a notebook for Sonoma Chemical Supplies, Inc. to analyze its sales and commissions for the month and quarter. The staff receives a base salary of $1,500 per month plus a 1.5% commission on all sales.

There is a bonus incentive plan as follows:
Under $40,000   no bonus
$40,000 - up   1% additional commission on sales of $40,000 or more.

EXERCISE DIRECTIONS

1. Create the worksheet as illustrated or open ▢30COMM.

2. Find COMMISSION. The commission is 1.5% of sales.

3. Format the commission for two decimal places and copy the formula for all sales.

4. Find BONUS. Enter an IF function that does the following:
   IF (SALES are greater than or equal to 40000, (Sales-40000)*.01, otherwise, zero.)

5. Format the bonus for two decimal places and copy the formula for all sales.

6. Enter the salary data as shown on the illustration. Format for two decimal places.

7. Find the MONTHLY EARNINGS by totaling the COMMISSION, BONUS, and SALARY columns.

8. Format the monthly earnings for two decimal places and copy the formula for all sales.

9. Find the summary TOTALS.

10. Enter an IF function to enter a note for those who sold less than $30,000 to "See Mr. Microbe" or a "-" for the others.

11. Rename page A to JANUARY.

12. Copy the worksheet three times before page B.

13. Rename the copies FEBRUARY, MARCH, and FIRST QUARTER.

14. Change the third line of the headings to reflect the month on the FEBRUARY and MARCH sheets.

15. Enter the data listed below on the new sheets:

SALES STAFF	FEBRUARY SALES	MARCH SALES
Alumina, Vera	29,921.22	32,134.67
Bismuth, William	28,321.32	35,435.89
Carben, Charles	18,545.77	21,457.87
Kaolin, Robert	51,567.54	60,986.98
Lactulose, Larry	32,598.09	27,876.97
Pectin, Perry	35,325.78	43,254.54
Sulfa, Sally	55,896.95	62,453.88
Tinny, Tom	51,548.45	58,956.76

16. On the FIRST QUARTER sheet, change the third line of the heading to state:

    FIRST QUARTER SUMMARY

17. Delete all Notes text and numeric data except for TOTALS formulas.

18. Enter a three-dimensional formula to summarize the JANUARY, FEBRUARY, and MARCH sheet data in the SALES column for Vera Alumina.

19. Copy the formula down and across for all numeric columns.

20. In the Notes column, enter an IF function that will print "Congratulations on a great quarter." for SALES over $165,000, and no message "-" for sales under that amount.

21. Print one copy of the workbook.

22. Save and close the workbook; name it COMM.

Sheet1	A	B	C	D	E	F	G	H	I
1			SONOMA CHEMICAL SUPPLIES, INC.						
2			SALES AND COMMISSION REPORT						
3			JANUARY 199-						
4							MONTHLY		
5	SALES STAFF		SALES	COMMISSION	BONUS	SALARY	EARNINGS		NOTE:
6	Alumina, Vera		28,765.98			1500			
7	Bismuth, William		34,443.44			1500			
8	Carben, Charles		19,564.33			1500			
9	Kaolin, Robert		54,454.43			1500			
10	Lactulose, Larry		26,876.09			1500			
11	Pectin, Perry		42,646.45			1500			
12	Sulfa, Sally		64,534.45			1500			
13	Tinny, Tom		56,465.77			1500			
14									
15	TOTALS								

Exercise 31

- Create Charts ■ Change Chart Types
- Select and Size Inserted Charts ■ Enable Graph Editing

NOTES

Create Charts

- **Charts** present and compare data in a graphic format and are always linked to the data that they plot. When you change data in the plotted area of a notebook page, the data and visual graphics in the linked chart also change. A chart may be created by selecting New Chart from the Graphics menu, or by using the Floating Chart button on the Notebook Toolbar.

- To create a graph using the Notebook Toolbar, you must first select the data, then click the Floating Chart button [icon], and then place it on the notebook page. Here are some guidelines for selecting data to chart.

  - The selection should be rectangular.

  - The selection should not contain blank columns or rows.

- The selection determines the orientation (in columns or rows) of the data series. However, orientation may be changed as desired.

- Typically, a chart or graph will contain the following elements:

Chart data	Values the chart represents.
Series labels	Labels identifying the charted values. These labels appear in the chart legend, which identifies each data series.
Category labels	Labels identifying each data series shown on the x or y-axis.

✓ *Note the illustration of a labeled column graph showing arrows parts of a graph.*

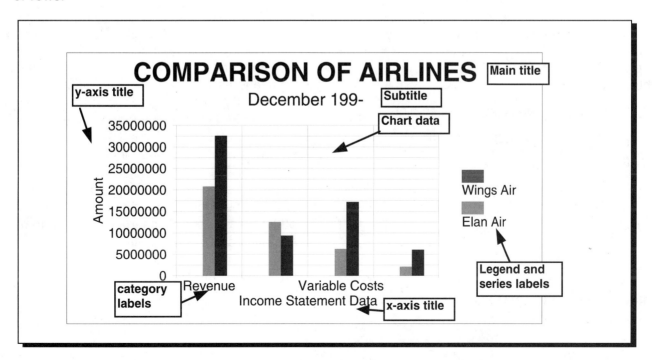

■ The illustration below shows two selections that would result in different charts. Both selections are rectangular. The second selection is for a pie chart and contains only one value range. If you wish to select the labels and the data for Elan Air for a pie chart, you would hide column C or the Wings Air data, or move the data to a new area on the notebook as illustrated.

A	A	B	C	D	E	F	G	H
1	COMPARISON OF AIRLINE REVENUES							
2								
3		Wings Air	Elan Air					
4	Revenue	20,800,000	32,604,000		Fixed Cos	9,360,000		
5	Fixed Costs	12,480,000	9,360,000		Variable C	17,160,000		
6	Variable Costs	6,240,000	17,160,000		Net Profit	6,084,000		
7	Net Profit	2,080,000	6,084,000					
8								
9								
10			1st selection (of			2nd selection (a copy of		
11			data for Wings Air			data for Elan Air only)		
12			and Elan Air) results			results in a Pie chart.		
13			in a Column chart.					
14								
15								

■ Most charts (excluding pie charts) also typically contain the following:

y-axis	Represents the vertical scale. Scale values are entered automatically, based on the values being graphed.
x-axis	Represents the horizontal scale and typically the data series categories.
x-axis title	Describes the x-axis (horizontal) data. *(See Income Statement Data Chart in the illustration on the previous page.)*
y-axis title	Describes the y-axis (vertical) data. *(Amount in the illustration on the previous page.)*

■ To create a chart using the Floating Chart button:

1. Select the notebook page data to plot.

2. Click the Floating Chart button 📊 on the Notebook Toolbar.

3. Double-click within the notebook, or click once and drag to indicate desired size and position.

■ These steps will create a floating graph on the notebook page. A copy of the chart will also appear as an icon on the **Objects** page, the last page of the notebook. Charts may be copied, moved, or edited from the Objects page or from the notebook page.

Change Chart Types

■ Quattro Pro provides many chart types. In this exercise we will discuss and explore three chart types: Column, line, and pie *(illustrated on page 309)*

- Column or bar charts compare individual or sets of values. The height of each bar is proportional to its corresponding value in the notebook page.
- Line charts are especially useful when plotting trends, since lines connect points of data and show changes over time effectively.
- Pie charts are circular charts used to show the relationship of each value in a data range to the entire data range. The size of each wedge represents the percentage each value contributes to the total.

■ Only one numerical data range may be used in a pie chart. The data in that range is represented as pie slices. The data range must be adjacent to the data labels when using the Floating Chart button to create a pie chart. Therefore, it may sometimes be necessary to copy the labels and values to another section of the notebook in order to plot the chart.

Pie charts may be formatted to indicate the percentage each piece of the pie represents of the whole.

■ Charts can be copied and then edited to produce a different chart type that uses the same notebook page data.

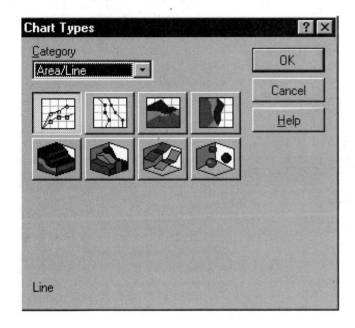

Select and Size Inserted Charts

■ You can click an inserted chart once to format it as an object, or to size, move, and copy it. The selected object will display a border outline with handles. Drag the border to size the chart or use the mouse to drag and drop or move the object. A chart may be copied using the Edit menu or Toolbar buttons.

Enable Chart Editing

■ To edit a chart, double-click the graph you want to change on the Objects page or on the notebook page. The chart will display in a dotted border and a chart menu will appear on the menu bar. Use the Chart menu to edit items on the graph.

■ When charts are created using the Floating Chart button, titles are not included. The chart may be edited to include the titles by selecting the Titles from the Charts menu and completing the Chart Titles dialog box as illustrated below.

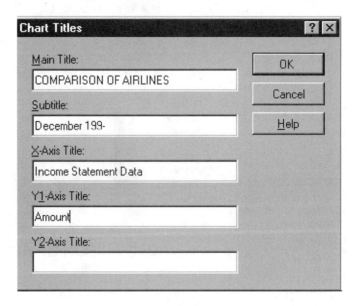

■ All chart items, such as legends and titles, can be changed and enhanced by clicking on them and making changes through the Chart menu. When you right-click a chart item, Quattro Pro displays a shortcut menu containing relevant commands, as illustrated below.

Right-Click Menu for Chart Items

■ After editing is complete, return to the notebook by using the Windows menu, or by clicking on the Notebook page.

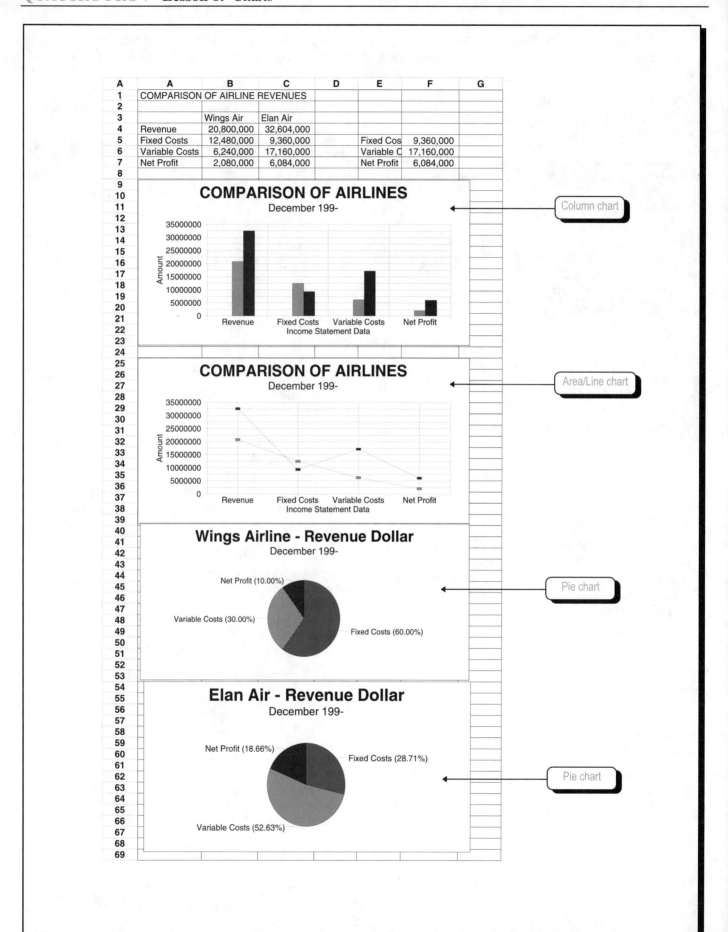

A	A	B	C	D	E	F	G
1	COMPARISON OF AIRLINE REVENUES						
2							
3		Wings Air	Elan Air				
4	Revenue	20,800,000	32,604,000				
5	Fixed Costs	12,480,000	9,360,000		Fixed Cos	9,360,000	
6	Variable Costs	6,240,000	17,160,000		Variable C	17,160,000	
7	Net Profit	2,080,000	6,084,000		Net Profit	6,084,000	
8							

COMPARISON OF AIRLINES

December 199-

Column chart

COMPARISON OF AIRLINES

December 199-

Area/Line chart

Wings Airline - Revenue Dollar

December 199-

Net Profit (10.00%)
Variable Costs (30.00%)
Fixed Costs (60.00%)

Pie chart

Elan Air - Revenue Dollar

December 199-

Net Profit (18.66%)
Fixed Costs (28.71%)
Variable Costs (52.63%)

Pie chart

In this exercise, you will use an airline comparison worksheet to prepare and modify several charts presenting the data graphically.

EXERCISE DIRECTIONS

1. Create the worksheet as illustrated below or open ☐31FLY. (Make only one copy of the worksheet.)

A	A	B	C
1	COMPARISON OF AIRLINE REVENUES		
2			
3		Wings Air	Elan Air
4	Revenue	20,800,000	32,604,000
5	Fixed Costs	12,480,000	9,360,000
6	Variable Costs	6,240,000	17,160,000
7	Net Profit	2,080,000	6,084,000

2. Use the Floating Chart button to create a floating column chart in the notebook, selecting data as highlighted in the illustration, comparing Wing and Elan airlines.

   ✓ *When selecting notebook data to chart, the selection area must be rectangular and a blank cell should be included in the selection. The selection of a blank cell helps Quattro Pro correctly identify the category and data series labels.*

   • Place chart in the range A9:G23. (A column chart, with legends but without titles, will appear.)

3. Enable chart editing by double-clicking the chart. Right-click the chart to open the shortcut menu and choose Titles. Insert the following information:

   Main title: COMPARISON OF AIRLINES
   Subtitle: December 199-
   X-axis title: Income Statement Data
   Y-axis title: Amount

4. Return to the notebook by using the Window menu.

5. Click on the chart once and copy the chart to A25.

6. Double-click the chart in A25 to enable chart editing. Change the chart type to an Area/Line chart, by selecting Type/Layout from the Chart menu. Select the first line chart in the category options.

7. To create a pie chart for Wings Air:
   • Select labels and values for Wings Air for Fixed Costs, Variable Costs, and Net Profit.
   • Place the chart in the range A40:G54.

8. Edit the pie chart and insert a chart title: Wings Airlines - Revenue Dollar

9. In the notebook, change Fixed Costs to Fixed Expenses.
   ✓ *Linked text changes in chart labels.*

10. Change the label back to Fixed Costs.

11. Edit the pie chart and add a second line to the chart title to read:
    December 199-

12. Create a pie chart of Fixed Costs, Variable Costs, and Net Profit labels and data for Elan Air:
    • Copy the labels for Fixed Costs, Variable Costs, and Net Profit to E5.
    • Copy the data for Elan Air to F5.
    • Place the pie chart in the range A55:G69.
    • Add a chart title: Elan Airlines - Revenue Dollar, and a subtitle, December 199-.

13. If necessary, move and size charts to align them.

14. Set notebook to fit on one page.

15. Use Print Preview to view and print the notebook.

16. Move to the last page of the notebook, the Objects page, by using Move to Objects Page button ▶| at the bottom of the window.

17. Double-click on one of the charts.

18. Close chart using ☒ button at the top right of screen.

19. Return to the notebook and to page A by using the Return from Objects Page button |◀.

20. Save and close the workbook file; name it FLY.

KEYSTROKES

USE TOOLBAR TO CREATE A GRAPH

1. Select cells containing data to plot.
2. Click **Chart** button .... [📊]
3. Select size and location on notebook. (Chart appears on notebook page and also on objects page as an icon.)
4. Edit chart to add titles or to change chart type.

ENABLE CHART EDITING

Double-click chart.

CHANGE GRAPH TYPE

✓ *Available types depend upon the selected general graph type.*

In chart edit mode:

1. Click **Chart**............................ [Alt]+[C]
2. Click **Type/Layout** .... [Y]
3. Select **Category**.................... [↓],[Enter]
4. Select type............................ [Tab]+[→]
5. Click **OK**.................................. [Enter]

ADD TITLES TO CHART

In chart edit mode:

1. Click **Chart**............................... [Alt]+[C]
2. Click **Titles** .... [T]
3. Click **Main Title** .... [Alt]+[M]
4. Enter title.
5. Click **Subtitle** .... [Alt]+[S]
6. Enter title.
7. Click **X-Axis Title**................... [Alt]+[X]
8. Enter title.
9. Click **Y1-Axis Title**................. [Alt]+[1]
10. Enter title.
11. Click **Y2-Axis Title**................ [Alt]+[2]
12. Enter title.
13. Click **OK**...................................... [Enter]

SELECT CHART AS AN OBJECT

When chart is selected as an object, it can be sized, moved, or copied.

Click anywhere on inserted graph.

Handles (black squares) appear on graph border.

SIZE INSERTED CHARTS

1. Select graph.
2. Point to handle on side of border to size.
   ✓ *To size object proportionally, point to corner handle.*

To size object without constraints:

Drag border outline until desired size is obtained.

Exercise

32

■ **Use Graphics Menu to Create Charts** ■ **Change Chart Subtype**
■ **Stacked Bar Charts** ■ **Line-Bar Charts** ■ **Change Legend Positions**

NOTES

Use Graphics Menu to Create Charts

■ As mentioned in the previous exercise, charts may be created by selecting the area to be charted and then selecting Underline{N}ew Chart from the Graphics menu. A new chart dialog box will appear with the **series** tab in view, indicating the data series information for the area you have selected.

New Chart Dialog Box - Series Tab

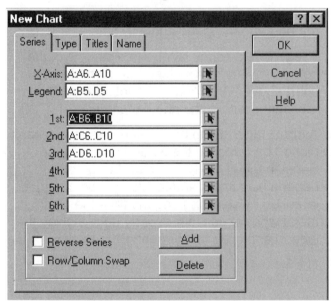

■ You can also use these commands to select the data series individually to complete the series information. This is necessary if you are using data that is separated by blank or non-relevant data.

■ The New Chart dialog box also contains the Type, Titles, and Name tabs which you can complete as you create the chart. (Note the Type and Title dialog boxes illustrated in Exercise 31.) The Name tab allows you to give the chart a name other than Chart1, Chart2, etc. Note the illustration of the Name tab below.

New Chart Dialog Box - Name Tab

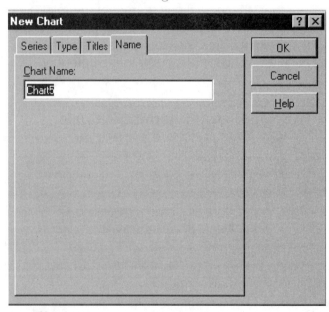

■ When you use the New Chart option to create a chart, the chart is placed on the Objects page, the last page in the notebook. You can place the chart on any notebook page by copying it or by selecting Insert Chart from the Graphics menu.

Change Chart Subtype

■ When you create a chart, you want to select a chart type and format that will best present the notebook page data. Notebook page data may be charted using one of the following chart types, each of which has subtypes: Area/Line, Bar, Stacked Bar, Pie, Specialty, Text.

■ Chart **subtypes**, such as the three dimensional variation, offer additional options to standard chart types. Once you select a chart type, the subtypes display graphically for selection.

Stacked Bar Charts

■ The **stacked bar chart** is an example of one chart type category that offers several subtypes. This chart type is often used to show the total effect of several sets of data. For example, in the illustration below, each bar has two sections, which represent sales for 1995 and 1996. Together, these sections represent the total sales for the region for the two years. The chart illustrated is called the Rotated 2-D Stacked Bar, which is the second subtype in the category.

Rotated 2-D Stacked Bar Chart

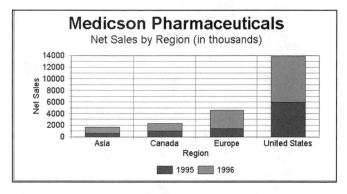

Line-Bar Charts

■ The **Line-Bar**, or combination chart, is a subtype in the Bar category that lets you plot the data using lines and bars to present a clear comparison. For example, in the illustration below, a line is used to plot the 1995 data and bar to plot the 1996 data.

Line-Bar Chart

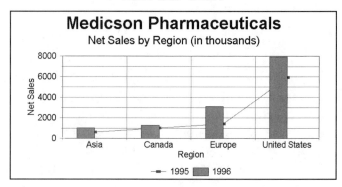

Change Legend Positions

■ Any part of a chart may be edited by selecting the part and using the right-click menu.

■ A legend is a series label with a sample of the color or style of the series. For example, in the chart above, 1995 and 1996 data are shown in the legend with a line and bar sample.

■ A **chart legend** can be created when the data is plotted by selecting the legend range on the Series page of the New Chart dialog box. Legend placement and labels may be changed or edited by selecting Legend from the Chart menu while in edit mode, or by right-clicking the legend and changing Legend Properties.

EXERCISE DIRECTIONS

1. Create the notebook as illustrated below or open ⬜32PHARM.
   - ✓ *Enter the years as numeric labels.*

A	A	B	C	D
1	MEDICSON PHARMACEUTICALS			
2	Net Sales by Geographic Segment			
3	In thousands			
4		1995	1996	
5	Asia	613	1,044	
6	Canada	1,022	1,292	
7	Europe	1,423	3,111	
8	United States	5,906	7,929	
9				
10				
11				

2. To create a stacked bar graph:
   - Select graph data, A4:C8.
   - Select, New Chart from the Graphics menu.
   - ✓ *Note that the Series page has been completed using your data selection.*
   - Select the Type tab.
   - Select the Stacked Bar category.
   - Select the second subtype, Rotated 2-D Stacked Bar.
   - Select the Titles tab.
   - Enter titles as follows:
     Main Title: Medicson Pharmaceuticals
     Subtitle: Net Sales by Region (in thousands)
     X-Axis Title: Region
     Y-Axis Title: Net Sales
   - Select the Name tab.
   - Name the chart Stackbar.
   - Click OK.

3. Switch back to the notebook using the Window menu.

4. Move to the Objects page and copy the Stackbar icon.

5. Return to Page A and paste the chart in A10:J31.

6. Double-click to edit the chart. Right-click on the chart legend. Change legend properties so that the legend appears on the bottom of the chart.

7. Copy the Stacked Bar chart to A33.

8. Enable chart editing and change the type to the Bar category, Line-Bar subtype.

9. Create a pie chart showing 1996 sales as follows:
   - Select, New Chart from the Graphics menu.
   - Type in the X-Axis block A5..A8, or use the [⬉] to select the block.
   - Type in the 1st Series block C5..C8, or use the [⬉] to select the block.
   - Select the Titles page and enter the following titles:
     Medicson Pharmaceuticals
     1996 Regional Sales
   - Select the Name page and name the graph Pie.
   - Click OK.

10. Copy the pie chart and paste it in to the block A56:G74.

11. Use the Toolbar to create a line chart for the 1995 and 1996 data, place it in A75, and size it to match the other charts.

12. Select the chart as an object and delete the chart.

13. Set the notebook to print on one page.

14. Preview the notebook page.

15. Print the notebook page.

16. Close and save the notebook file, or *save as* PHARM.

KEYSTROKES

USE MENU TO CREATE A CHART

1. Select data to be graphed.
2. Click **Graphics**........................ `Alt`+`G`
3. Click **New Chart**............................. `N`
4. On series page, if series data is not correct, reselect data for each series using [▨] button.
5. Click **Type** tab........................ `Ctrl`+`Tab`
6. Click **Category**...................... `↓`, `Enter`
7. Select a subtype .... `Tab`, `→`
8. Select **Titles** page.................. `Ctrl`+`Tab`
9. Click **Main Title**...................... `Alt`+`M`
10. Type main title.
11. Click **Subtitle** .... `Alt`+`S`
12. Type subtitle.
13. Click **X-Axis Title** .... `Alt`+`X`
14. Type X-Axis title.
15. Click **Y1-Axis Title** .... `Alt`+`1`
16. Type Y1-Axis Title.
17. Select **Name** page................. `Ctrl`+`Tab`
18. Type chart name.
19. Click **OK** .... `Enter`

SELECT CHART ITEMS

Select chart items (such as the legend or a data series) prior to selecting commands to change the item in some way.

✓ *Quattro Pro marks the currently selected graph item with squares and displays its name in the name box.*

Enable graph editing.

- To select next or previous class of graph items:

  Press Tab or Shift Tab.

- To select a specific item with the mouse:

  Click graph item.

- To select a data series:

  Click any data marker in data series.

- To select a data marker:

  1. Click any data marker in data series.
  2. Click data marker in selected series.

- To select the graph area:

  Click any blank area outside plot area.

- To select the plot area:

  Click any blank area inside plot area.

- To select the legend:

✓ *Legend items are the legend entry and key.*

  Click legend.

- To deselect a selected graph item:

  Press **Escape**............................. `Esc`

DELETE AN INSERTED CHART

1. Select inserted graph as an object.
2. Press **Delete**.
3. Answer **Yes** if you want to delete the graph from the Objects page as well.

POSITION LEGEND IN CHART

1. Enable chart editing.
2. Right-click legend.
3. Select **Legend Properties**.
4. Select **Legend Position**.
5. Select desired position:
   - None
   - Bottom
   - Right
6. Click **OK**.

Exercise

33

■ **Change Chart Font** ■ **Explode Pie Chart Slice**
■ **Print Charts** ■ **Print Inserted Chart**

NOTES

Change Chart Font

■ Due to size or appearance constraints, you may wish to change the font size of text labels. Remember, any object on a chart may be formatted once you are in chart edit mode. From within Chart Edit mode, choose Selected Object from the Format menu. Or, right click the object and select the Properties item from the menu that appears.

■ For example, to change the font size of a chart title, enable chart editing, select the chart title, right-click the object, then select Chart Title Properties. You can set alignment, text font, text settings, box settings, and fill settings for the chart title. The properties dialog box will provide the settings pages that are appropriate for the object selected. Note the illustration of the dialog box that appears when a Chart Title Properties, Format, or Selected Object is selected.

Chart Title Properties Dialog Box

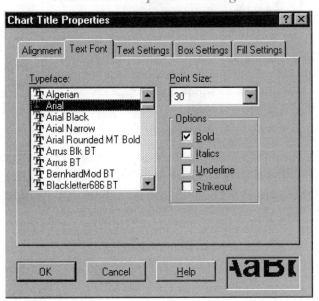

Explode Pie Chart Slice

■ To highlight one aspect of pie chart data, you may wish to explode a slice of the pie. This can be done by selecting the segment in chart edit mode and using the Properties dialog box. The dialog box that appears contains an Explode Pie page that can be used to make the setting. Note the illustration of the setting and the resulting pie chart below.

Pie Chart Dialog Box - Explode Slice Tab

Pie Chart with Exploded Slice

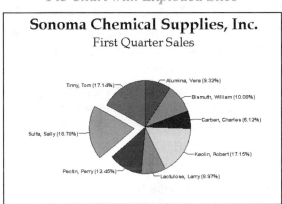

Print Charts

■ Charts can be printed with the notebook page or as separate pages. You can select an inserted graph to print it apart from the notebook page.

■ You can use Print Preview to see how a notebook page or graph will print.

From Print Preview, you can also:

- View the Previous or Next page when more than one page will be printed.

- Change the page margins by dragging the guide lines that appear when you select the Margin button .

- Zoom in or out to view the chart , .

- Change from color to black and white view .

- Add headers or footers to the printout .

- Print the graph or notebook page .

Print Inserted Chart

■ When printing a selected inserted chart or a chart page, you can change the page orientation from the Page tab in the Page Setup dialog box.

■ If your computer equipment includes a color monitor, the chart components will be shown in different colors. When you print the charts on a black and white printer, the colored text and lines are printed in black; the colored areas are printed in different shades of gray; and the background color is ignored.

In this exercise, you will create a pie chart for an existing notebook. The pie chart fonts will be changed and one slice will be exploded for emphasis. The chart will be printed on a separate page and the notebook will be printed with all the charts.

EXERCISE DIRECTIONS

1. Open COMM or 33COMM.

2. Move to the First Quarter page.

3. Create a pie chart using the menu to display the sales for each employee:
   - Use A6:A13 for the X-Axis.
   - Use C6:C13 for the 1st Series.
   - Set type for pie chart.
   - Set titles as follows:
     - Main Title: Sonoma Chemical Supplies, Inc.
     - Subtitle: Sales

4. Return to the notebook and copy the chart from the Objects page to A17:H35 on Page A.

5. Enable chart editing and select the chart title.

6. Change the font to Book Antiqua and the font size to 30 by selecting Chart Title Properties from the right-click shortcut menu.

7. Select the chart subtitle.

8. Change the subtitle to First Quarter Sales and change the font to Book Antiqua.

9. Select any X-axis label, right-click and select Pie Chart Properties.

10. Set text font to Arial, 10 point, bold.

11. Select the Sally Sulfa data slice and set properties to explode the slice.

12. Return to the notebook and select the chart as an object.

13. Print Preview and print the chart page.

14. Create a bar chart using the following series settings by selecting or entering the blocks:
    - X-Axis: January:A6:A13
    - January: A6:A13
    - Legend: January:C3, February:C3, March:C3
    - 1st Series: January:C6:C13
    - 2nd Series: February:C6:C13
    - 3rd Series: March:C6:C13

15. Set titles:
    - Main Title: Sonoma Chemical Supplies, Inc.
    - Subtitle: First Quarter Sales
    - X-Axis: Staff
    - Y-Axis: Amount

16. Return to the notebook and copy the chart from the objects page to A37:H56.

17. Enable chart editing and select the appropriate objects to make the following changes:
    - Chart main title to Book Antiqua, 30 point, bold
    - Chart subtitle to Book, Antiqua.

- Move legend to bottom of chart and set text to Arial, 10 point.
  - X and Y axis text to 12 point.
  - X and Y axis titles to 12 point.
18. Return to the notebook and set notebook and charts to fit on one page.

19. Print preview.

20. Change orientation to landscape using the Page Setup button.

21. Print preview and change margins to center the data on the page.

22. Print one copy of the notebook and charts.

23. Close and save the notebook file, or *save as* COMM.

FIRST QUARTER	A	B	C	D	E	F	G	H	I
1			SONOMA CHEMICAL SUPPLIES, INC.						
2			SALES AND COMMISSION REPORT						
3			FIRST QUARTER SUMMARY						
4							MONTHLY		
5	SALES STAFF		SALES	COMMISSION	BONUS	SALARY	EARNINGS		NOTE:
6	Alumina, Vera		90,821.87	1,362.33	0.00	4,500.00	7,224.66		-
7	Bismuth, William		98,200.65	1,473.01	0.00	4,500.00	7,446.02		-
8	Carben, Charles		59,567.97	893.52	0.00	4,500.00	6,287.04		-
9	Kaolin, Robert		167,008.95	2,505.13	470.09	4,500.00	9,980.36		Congratulations on a great quarter.
10	Lactulose, Larry		87,351.15	1,310.27	0.00	4,500.00	7,120.53		-
11	Pectin, Perry		121,226.77	1,818.40	59.01	4,500.00	8,195.81		-
12	Sulfa, Sally		182,885.28	2,743.28	628.85	4,500.00	10,615.41		Congratulations on a great quarter.
13	Tinny, Tom		166,970.98	2,504.56	469.71	4,500.00	9,978.84		Congratulations on a great quarter.
14									
15	TOTALS		974,033.62	14,610.50	1,627.66	36,000.00	66,848.67		

KEYSTROKES

CHANGE CHART FONTS

1. Enable chart editing. (Double-click chart.)
2. Select text object.
3. Right-click object.
4. Select **Properties**.
5. Select **Text Font** tab.
6. Select **Typeface** .... `Alt`+`T`
7. Select font................................`↓`
8. Select **Point Size**.................. `Alt`+`P`
9. Select size ....`↓`
10. Select **Options** ....`Tab`
11. Click **OK**....................................`Enter`

EXPLODE PIE SLICE

1. Enable chart editing. (Double-click chart.)
2. Select slice to be exploded.

3. Right-click object.
4. Select **Pie Chart Properties**.
5. Select **Explode Slice** tab.
6. Select **Explode** .... `Alt`+`X`
7. Click **OK** .... `Enter`

PRINT GRAPHS

Print graph page or inserted graph as part of the notebook page.

1. Select notebook page or graph page containing graph to print.
2. Follow steps to PRINT A NOTEBOOK PAGE, Lesson 2, Exercise 7.

PRINT INSERTED GRAPH SEPARATELY

1. Enable graph editing for graph to print.

2. Follow steps to PRINT A NOTEBOOK PAGE, Lesson 2, Exercise 7.

SET PAGE ORIENTATION OF PRINTED PAGE

– FROM PRINT DIALOG BOX –

1. Click **File**.............................. `Alt`+`F`
2. Click **Print** ....`P`
3. Click **Page Setup** button .... `Alt`+`U`
4. Click **Paper Type** tab............. `Alt`+`P`
5. Click **Type** .... `Alt`+`Y`
6. Click **Portrait**....................... `Alt`+`O`
   OR
   Click **Landscape** .... `Alt`+`D`
7. Click **OK** to return to page or Print Preview ....`Enter`

Exercise

34

■ **Summary**

You have been asked to analyze employment trends in the state of Virginia using data from the 1980 and 1990 census reports. You will create a notebook page using the data below and create several graphs as directed.

Employment in Selected Industries

	1980	1990	Change
Agriculture, etc.	24,447	40,161	64.3%
Mfg., nondurable	414,416	347,224	-16.2%
Mfg., durable	405,728	306,212	-24.5%
Finance, real estate	231,953	346,037	49.2%

EXERCISE DIRECTIONS

1. Create a notebook page using the data above, or open ⊟34VADATA.

2. Format labels and values appropriately and set column widths where needed.

3. Create a horizontal bar chart comparing 1980 and 1990 trends and place it below the data.

4. Include appropriate titles and legends.

5. Change typeface and point size, if necessary.

6. Using the same data and titles above, create line and line-bar charts below the bar chart.

7. Create a pie chart of 1990 data. Explode the section of the pie representing the largest employment area in the state.

8. Include appropriate titles and data labels.

9. Change typeface and point size, if necessary.

10. Use Edit, Cut and then Edit, Paste to move each chart to a separate page in the notebook.

   ✓   *Do not delete the source charts on the objects page.*

11. Rename each page containing a chart as follows:

   BAR CHART

   LINE CHART

   LINEBAR CHART

   PIE CHART

12. Rename Page A; name it DATA.

13. Print the pie and line bar charts on separate pages.

14. Close and save the notebook file, name it VADATA.

Paradox 7

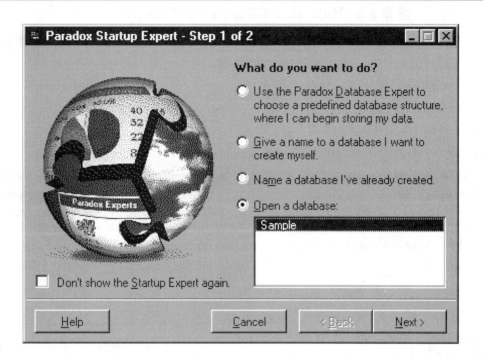

DATABASE BASICS

> ■ **What is Paradox?** ■ **What is a Database?**
> ■ **What is a Database Management System?**
> ■ **What are Database Objects?**
> ■ **How is a Paradox Database Organized?**
> ■ **What are Paradox Tables?** ■ **How are Paradox Tables Related?**

Database Basics

NOTES

What is Paradox?

■ Borland Paradox 7 is the **database management system** in the Corel Office Professional 7 package. To understand what a database management system is and what it can do, you need to study the database basics information that follows.

What is a Database?

■ A **database** is an organized collection of facts about a particular subject. An address book or a library's card catalog is a database; an office filing cabinet can also contain a database.

■ Examples of manual databases are illustrated below. To use and maintain them requires manual labor and a lot of time. Suppose you have two hundred people listed in your address book. To update the telephone number and address of a friend who just moved to Boise, you must page through the book, locate the entry, and make the change.

Examples of Manual Database Records

Name
Address
City   St   Zip
Telephone

Address Book Entry

Call Number
Author
Title
Subject

Card Catalog Entry

■ A **Paradox database** is the electronic equivalent of a manual database. It lets you organize the facts and provides a way for you to maintain the data electronically. To update the telephone number of a friend who moved to Boise, you simply call up the friend's entry and make the change.

What is a Database Management System?

■ If all you gained from an electronic database were ease of data update and maintenance, you would probably think it worth the trouble. But Paradox is a database management system that provides a great many other functions besides data maintenance.

■ A database management system provides functions to store, search, filter, query, and report on the data in the database. For example, suppose you wish to find all books about political science. To do this manually, you must read the card catalog entries and write down those with a subject of political science. Such a manual search could be quite time-consuming. With an automated database management system like Paradox, however, you can locate all the political science books with its search function and a few simple keystrokes.

What are Database Objects?

■ To help you use your database efficiently, modern database management systems, like Paradox, provide **database objects**. Database objects are the tools you need to store, maintain, search, analyze, and report on the data in your database.

- In the Paradox exercises, you will learn about the four database objects listed below.

Table	Data is automatically formatted into a table or spreadsheet format. Each column provides specific information about a specific aspect of the database (such as name, phone number, store number, etc.). Each row in a table represents one record in the database.
Form	A format that displays one record (one row from a table) at a time. Forms are used to enter or update data. A form can be designed and customized to contain all data base fields or only those you wish to display.
Query	A structured way to tell Paradox to retrieve data that meets certain criteria from one or more database tables. For example, a query may request that Paradox retrieve data on all printers sold within the last six months.
Report	A formatted way to display information retrieved from the database. A report formats and analyzes data that you specify.

How is a Paradox Database Organized?

- The Paradox database management system lets you maintain several related database objects that are displayed in the Project Viewer for the Working Directory. The Project Viewer contains tabs for each object. You can select each tab to display lists of the named objects of that type.

Paradox Project Viewer

- Using Paradox, you organize the data itself into separate electronic storage containers called **tables**. Each table contains data about a particular part of the entire subject.

Consider a company that sells computer hardware and software. The company database may contain one table that identifies customers, another that describes its hardware products, a third that tracks software, a fourth that maintains data about the sales force, and a fifth that tracks sales. These tables, along with others perhaps, form the database. By organizing its data into an electronic database of a number of tables, the company replaces filing cabinets with their electronic equivalent.

What are Paradox Tables?

- A Paradox table is a group of rows and columns. Each row contains one **record**. A record is a set of details about a specific item. For example, one record in a company's hardware inventory table will contain details on one of its NEC printers, giving a product identifier, the manufacturer, model number, cost, and purchase date. When data processing people ask about the "NEC printer record," they want to know the details in the table row where the printer is described.

- Each column in the table represents a **field**, headed by a **field name**. Each row in the column contains specific data called the **field contents**. The field contains a detail. For example, the field MANUFACTURER in one of the hardware records would contain the entry NEC to identify the manufacturer of a piece of equipment. When data processing people ask, "What's in the manufacturer field?", they are asking about the field contents of the field name "manufacturer."

How are Paradox Tables Related?

- When designing a database, you should provide at least one field in each Paradox table that is repeated from table to table. This field relates the tables to each other so that you can create queries from all the tables in the database. The field should be unique and not contain duplicate entries. In a library database, an obvious candidate for a field common to all tables is a book's call number. A company that has many stores can create one table that contains generalized information for each store (Stores) and other tables that contain information about Inventory, Hardware, and Software. These tables can then be related to the Stores table by use of a Store identifier such as the Branch field.

Exercise 1

- ■ **Database Basics** ■ **Plan the Database** ■ **Startup Expert**
- ■ **Project Viewer** ■ **Create a Table** ■ **Table Field Types**
- ■ **Key Field** ■ **Save a Table**

NOTES

Database Basics

- ■ Paradox is a **relational database management system**. A **database** is a collection of information (**data**) organized into one or more tables. In a **relational database**, two or more tables have data in common which relates, or links, them together. They are usually stored in the same directory, referred to as the **working directory**. Each table stores data pertaining to a specific aspect or category of the information being organized.

- ■ For example, a corporation that has many stores can create one table that contains generalized information for each store (like the name, location, etc.) and a second table that contains a listing of computer equipment in each store. These tables would both be stored in the same directory (the working directory) and would be related by data, such as a branch name common

to both tables. Each table would contain information about a specific aspect of the company, but when related or connected in a database, the tables would provide a more complete picture of the corporation.

- ■ A Paradox database is like a filing cabinet of *related* information in which each drawer, or table, contains a specific aspect of that information. Using the previous example, one drawer in the filing cabinet would have generalized store information and another drawer would have information about the computer equipment in each store.

- ■ Each drawer, or table, in the filing cabinet contains individual "index cards" called **records**. Each record contains information about one item, for example, one type or brand of computer equipment. A group of records makes up a table, and a group of tables make up a database.

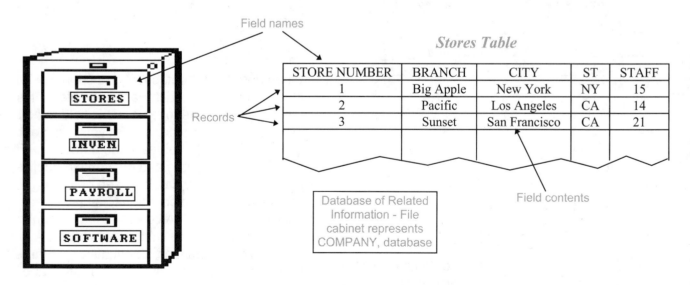

Stores Table

STORE NUMBER	BRANCH	CITY	ST	STAFF
1	Big Apple	New York	NY	15
2	Pacific	Los Angeles	CA	14
3	Sunset	San Francisco	CA	21

Field names

Records

Field contents

Database of Related Information - File cabinet represents COMPANY, database

- Each record contains categories of information about the item. Each category is referred to as a **field**. There are two parts to a field: the **field name** and the **field contents**. Note the illustration of a record from the STORES table, below, providing information about one store with fields for Store Number, Branch, City, ST, Sales, Eve and Staff.

Branch:	Big Apple
City:	New York
ST:	NY
Sales:	789,300.00
Eve:	YES
Staff:	20.00

Plan the database

- Before creating a database, you should plan the fields you want to include in each table–that is, what type of information the database should contain and how you wish to organize it. Plan your database on paper first by writing the field names that would best identify the information entered as field contents. If you want to access information simultaneously from two or more tables, you should have these tables share common field names and contents. The planning and development phase is very important. Within a corporation, this expertise is generally provided by database consultants. You can also develop your database in stages and link tables for optimum results throughout the development process, as we will in this text.

- It is often advisable to organize data into its smallest units for the greatest flexibility. For example, using field names of FIRST and LAST gives you more options than using NAME for the entire name.

Startup Expert

- To start Paradox, click Start on the Windows Taskbar, click Corel Office 7, then click Paradox 7. Or, you can click the Paradox button [✔] on the Desktop Application Director (DAD). When you first open Paradox, the **Startup Expert** screen appears, as illustrated above right.

✓ The Startup Expert screen will not appear if the **Don't Show the Startup Expert again** option has been selected.

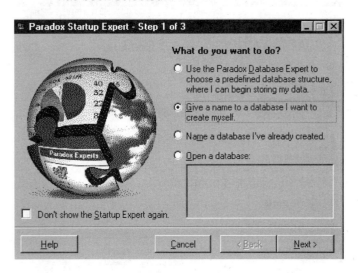

From the Startup Expert preliminary screen you can:

- Use the Database Expert, which contains predefined databases you may use for your data.
- Give a name to a database you wish to create yourself.
- Name a database you have already created.
- Open an existing database.

Successive screens prompt you according to the option you have chosen. In this exercise, we will be exploring an existing database and naming a new database.

Project Viewer

- Behind the Startup Expert, you will see the **Project Viewer**. This tool provides a view of all the objects in a database. **Database objects** can be tables, forms, queries, reports, etc. The illustration on the next page shows the Project Viewer screen for the SAMPLE database. The Tables object is selected and a list of tables in the database appears. This screen, showing the tables within the database, is like the illustration of the file drawers in a file cabinet. Note that all table files have a **.db** extension, the default extension for all Paradox tables.

Project Viewer

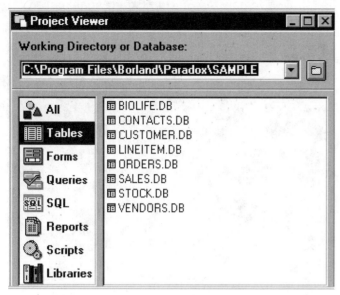

Create Paradox 7 Table

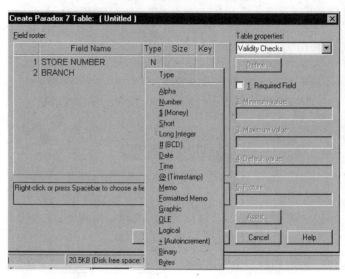

Create a Table

- A table may be created using the **Table Expert**, which can be launched from the Startup Expert, or by clicking Tools, Experts, selecting Table and then clicking the Run Expert button. The Table Expert provides table templates that can be customized for your own purposes.

- You can also create a table on your own by clicking File, New, then Table. When the Create Table dialog box appears, click OK to create a Paradox 7 table. You will then be presented with the Create Paradox 7 Table dialog box for creating the Field roster. The **Field roster** defines the field names, types, sizes, and whether or not a field is a key field. (Key fields are discussed on the next page.) After the field name is entered, you must enter the field type and size. Note the illustration above right of the Create Paradox 7 Table dialog box with the drop-down list displayed for field type.

Table Field Types

- The most common field type is **Alpha**, which consists of alphanumeric text. The list of data types is displayed by right-clicking the Type field or by pressing the spacebar while the cursor is in the Type column of the Field Roster. (The size allowed for each field type is listed in the table on the following page, along with the symbol you can use to select that field type.)

- When naming a field consider the following naming rules:

  - The maximum length of a field name is 25 characters.

  - A field name cannot start with a blank space (unless it is enclosed in quotation marks), but it can contain blank spaces.

  - Each field name in a table must be unique.

  - A field name should not contain certain characters if you plan to use the table in a query. These characters are the comma (,), pipes (|), and exclamation point (!).

Symbol	Size	Type
A	1-255	Alpha
N	N/A	Number (can contain only numbers)
$	N/A	Money
S	N/A	Short
I	N/A	Long Integer
#	0-32	BCD
D	N/A	Date
T	N/A	Time
@	N/A	Timestamp
M	1-240	Memo (Can be any length. The assigned size tells Paradox how much of the memo will be stored in the table. Anything over the specified size is stored in the .MB file.)
F	0-240	Formatted Memo (Lets you format text including typeface, style, color, and size.)
G	0-240	Graphic (Lets you store a graphic image in the field. Graphics are not saved with the table, but are stored in separate files.)
O	0-240	OLE
L	N/A	Logical
+	N/A	AutoIncrement
B	0-240	Binary
Y	1-255	Bytes

Key Field

- Although it is possible to create tables without it, a **key** should be created for every table in a database because:

- It ensures that each record will be unique.
- The table is sorted by the key field.
- It enables keyed tables to be linked together.
- It provides a means to ensure the accuracy of linked data.
- It expedites querying, searching and locating data.

- If the key is to be defined with one field, it must be a field with unique values. An EMPLOYEE ID field would be appropriate since each employee would have a unique ID. Since it is not possible to key all tables with one unique field, Paradox allows multiple-field, or composite, keys. Multiple-field keys will not be discussed in this text.

- The key for a table must be at the beginning of the Field roster. If the key consists of only one field, it must be the first field in the Field roster.

Save a Table

- After defining the fields in the Field roster, a table must be named and saved by clicking on the Save As button in the Create Paradox 7 Table dialog box, or by clicking File, Save As. The table will be stored in the directory that has been set as the default directory. All related files should be saved in this directory, thereby making them readily available for opening, editing and linking. If you want the database files to be private or separated into groups, you need to create separate working directories using Windows Explorer. This will be discussed later in the text.

The Kitchen Korner has opened numerous branches throughout the United States during the last several months. In order to keep track of the branches and the cities in which the branches are located, you have been asked to create a database to organize information relating to these stores. In this exercise, you will explore the Sample database and Expert screens, view completed tables, and create the first table for Kitchen Korner.

EXERCISE DIRECTIONS

1. Start Paradox 7 using the Start button on the Taskbar or the DAD Paradox icon ✔.

2. Select Sample in the Open a Database box. Click Next. Click Do It.

3. In the Project Viewer, click Tables, Forms, Queries, and Reports and note the files that have been created in each object category. (No files are stored in the Queries category.)

4. Click on the Tables icon and double-click on the CUSTOMER.DB table.

5. Use the scroll bar to view the records in the CUSTOMER table.

6. Close the table using the Close button ☒ and view several other tables. Notice that all the tables present groups of information about one aspect of a business.

7. Close the Project Viewer.

8. Select File, New, then Table.

9. Click OK in the Create Table dialog box.

10. Create a table using the information provided in steps a-i and in the table above right:

Field Name	Type	Size	Key
Branch	A	16	*
Store Number	N		
City	A	13	
ST	A	2	
Staff	N		

a. Type the field name.
b. Press Tab.
c. Right-click on Type and select the desired field type.
d. Press Tab.
e. Enter the field size. (The number type does not allow a field size.)
f. Define the Branch field as a key field by double-clicking in the Key column or pressing the spacebar.
g. Press Tab.
h. Repeat steps a-f until the table is complete.
i. Save the table; name it STORES.

✓   *By default, the STORES table will be saved in the ProgramFiles\Borland\Paradox\Sample directory. Select a different drive and/or directory if you wish to save it in another location.*

11. Close the STORES Field roster box.

KEYSTROKES

CREATE NEW TABLE

1. Click **File** .... Alt + F
2. Click **New** .... N
3. Click **Table** .... T
4. Click **OK** .... Enter
5. Define a field name.
6. Press **Tab** .... Tab
7. Right-click to display Type list.
   OR
   Press **Spacebar** .... Space

8. Select type .... ↓ ↑
   or press underscored letter for type
9. Press **Tab** .... Tab
10. Define a field size.
11. Press **Tab** .... Tab
12. Repeat steps 5-11 until table is complete.
13. Save the table.

SAVE TABLE

—From the Create Paradox 7 Table Dialog Box—
1. Click **Save As** .... Alt + A

2. Click **Save in** .... Alt + I
3. Select directory .... ↓
4. Click **File Name** .... Alt + N
5. Type table name.
6. Click the **Display Table** option .... Alt + B
7. Click **Save** .... Alt + S

✓ *The table will be left open if the **Display table** option is checked.*

Exercise 2	■ **Create Working Directories** ■ **Create and Save a Database Table**

NOTES

Create Working Directories

■ In Paradox, each table is saved as a separate file in the current directory, referred to as the **working directory**. However, if you are creating tables for separate companies, or unrelated departments that will not be used together, you should create a separate working directory with a database name for each group of tables.

■ New directories should be created outside of Paradox using Windows Explorer. Directions for this task will be included in the exercise. For the purposes of this text, it is advisable that you use one directory for data and subdivide it with subdirectories for each database scenario. If you were working for one firm, however, all tables and database objects would most likely remain in one directory.

■ You can set the new working directory by selecting Working Directory from the File menu. Once the directory settings are made, you can change working directories with the Working Directory or Database drop-down list within the Project Viewer. You can open the Project Viewer by clicking the Project Viewer button 🔲 on the Global Toolbar, or by selecting Project Viewer from the Tools menu.

Create and Save a Database Table

■ Tables are designed to store information regarding different components of your business. Therefore one database, made up of tables and other objects (to be discussed later in this text), may contain all the related data for a company. For example, in Exercise 1 you created a table for STORES which contained information about each branch. You will now create a table for INVENTORY, listing computer equipment purchased for each store. In order to correlate information between tables, the tables should have data in common, such as the branch name.

■ Some of the field types that do not allow entry of a field size are the Date, Time, Number, and $ data types.

> *In order to keep track of equipment purchased by Kitchen Korner, your employer has asked you to create an inventory table for your corporation database. You will set up a separate working directory for Kitchen Korner, called CORP.*

EXERCISE DIRECTIONS

1. Create a directory for the Kitchen Korner database using Windows Explorer:
    a. Click Start.
    b. Click Programs.
    c. Click Windows Explorer.
    d. Click the drive that contains the STORES data from Exercise 1.
    e. Double click the directory where the STORES data is stored and note the Stores.db and Stores.PX files. (If you selected the default location, the path will be: Program Files\Borland\Paradox\Sample.)
    f. In the Paradox folder, click File, New, Folder.
    g. On the New folder type over "New folder" with the name "DATA."
    h. In the Data folder, click file, new, folder.
    i. On the New Folder, type over "New Folder" with the new name "CORP."
    j. Move the Stores.db and Stores.PX files from its location into the CORP database directory using drag and drop.
    k. Close Windows Explorer.

2. Change the working directory to CORP:
    a. Start Paradox.
    b. Click File, Working Directory from the Paradox menu.
    c. Enter the path to the new directory, which should be the old directory with the \CORP subdirectory added. For example, c:\Program Files\Borland\paradox\data\corp or a:\corp.
    d. Click OK.

3. Open Project Viewer using the Project Viewer button on the Global Toolbar. Note the new working directory \CORP, which includes the STORES table.

4. Create a new table using the field data listed below. (Do not create a key field.)
    ✓   *In this table, Branch cannot be a key field since it may contain several occurrences of the same branch. You will remember that key field data items must be unique.*

Field Name	Type	Size
Branch	A	16
Item	A	15
Mfg	A	8
Model	A	15
Cost	$	
Purdate	Date	
Wty	A	1

5. Save the table; name it HARDWARE.
    ✓   *If you added an eighth field by mistake, Paradox will not let you save the table without entering more field data. To eliminate a field that was added in error, click on the previous field number.*

6. Close the table.

7. Open the Project Viewer and click on Tables. Note the Stores and Hardware tables.

8. Click on the Working Directory or Database drop-down list arrow and note the available directories.

9. Close the Project Viewer.

KEYSTROKES

Exercise 3

- **Open a Table** ■ **Enter Records** ■ **Correct Entries**
- **Change Table Column Width**

NOTES

Open a Table

- A saved table can be opened, for viewing or editing, by highlighting and double-clicking the desired table name in Project Viewer. In addition, you can right-click on a table name and choose <u>V</u>iew data or select <u>O</u>pen from the <u>F</u>ile menu and click <u>T</u>able.

- Tables have two modes of operation, View or Edit mode. You can switch to Edit mode by pressing F9, by clicking the Edit Data button ⎙ on the Toolbar or by selecting <u>E</u>dit Mode from the T<u>a</u>ble menu. If you wish to add or change data, you must be in Edit mode. A row and column format, similar to a spreadsheet, is displayed with the previously entered field names as the column headings. The table view gives you an efficient way to work with more than one record on the same screen. In this view, as illustrated below, each row will contain the data of a single record.

Paradox Table

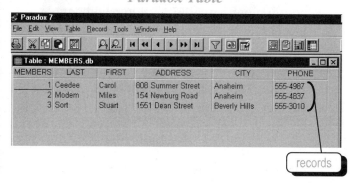

records

Enter Records

- To enter records in the table, type the data below each field name as you would in a spreadsheet. Use the Tab key or cursor arrows to advance from field to field. To advance to the next (record) row, click in the new row, or use the Tab key or the direction-arrow keys. When you leave a record, your data will automatically be saved in the table.

- It is recommended that field data be entered in upper- and lowercase so that it may be used in word processed files. Field headings may be entered in uppercase to distinguish them from field data.

- Data entered into a table is automatically saved when you close the table or switch back to View mode.

- Once records have been added to a table, you can use the navigation buttons on the Standard Toolbar, as illustrated below, to scroll through the records.

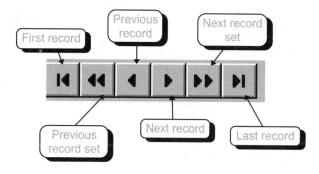

- You may use Control + D (duplicate) to copy an entry from the record above to the active record. Or, you may use the Copy or Cut and Paste options to quickly enter repetitive data. You can copy either one cell entry or an entire record. To select an entire row or record after it has been entered, double-click the shaded area to the left of the first field in the row record number area. You may wish to select a row if it is to be deleted.

Correct Entries

- Use the Backspace key to correct an error made while typing an entry. If you have already advanced to another field, you can return to the field that needs correction by clicking in the field, pressing Shift+Tab, or by using the direction arrow keys on the keyboard. Retype the entry, and then move to another field. You can also edit field contents in Field view by clicking the Field View button 🔲 on the Standard Toolbar, pressing F2 or Ctrl + F, or by selecting Field View from the View menu.

Change Table Column Width

- You may find that the default column width for a field is not appropriate for your entries, and/or that the table is too wide to fit on one screen. Column size can be changed at any time by clicking and holding the mouse on the right column border and dragging it to size. The stored field size is *not* affected by the column display size.

You are the president of CUG, a computer users' group in California. One of your responsibilities is to send announcements and annual reports to the members. To make your mailings easier, you have decided to create a table for your computer group's members. In this exercise, you will create a new directory and a table. You will save the table, add members' names, and close the table.

EXERCISE DIRECTIONS

1. Use Windows Explorer to create a subdirectory for the new table and database in your data folder.

   - Name the directory CUG and close Windows Explorer.
   - In Paradox, change the working directory to CUG.

2. Create a table using the field names and sizes indicated below.

3. Use the Alpha field type for all fields. Do not set a key field.

Field Names	Size
Last	10
First	8
Address	20
City	15
Phone	13

4. Save the table; name it MEMBERS.

5. Open the MEMBERS table.

6. Switch to Edit mode by pressing F9.

7. From the illustration at the top of the next page, enter the information for each member into your table. Use Control+D to repeat field entries, such as Anaheim, to save time.

8. Use the mouse to adjust column widths to accommodate the longest entry in each field.

9. Using the Toolbar navigation buttons, click on the First Record, Next Record and Last Record buttons and observe their functions.

10. Proofread and correct any errors.

11. Close the MEMBERS table.

12. Save view properties, if prompted, by clicking the Yes button.

CUG MEMBERSHIP LIST

LAST	FIRST	ADDRESS	CITY	PHONE
Ceedee	Carol	808 Summer Street	Anaheim	(213) 555-4987
Modem	Miles	154 Newburg Road	Anaheim	(213) 555-4837
Sort	Stuart	1551 Dean Street	Beverly Hills	(213) 555-3010
Monitor	Michael	17 Pine Street	Beverly Hills	(213) 555-9275
Mouse	Trina	3954 Wood Avenue	Anaheim	(213) 555-7283
Icon	Sheila	417 Specific Court	Anaheim	(213) 555-7284
Wave	Bette	1584 F. Street	North Hollywood	(213) 555-9174
Midi	Carl	1956 Park Avenue	North Hollywood	(213) 555-5192
Graphic	John	P.O. Box 2333	North Hollywood	(213) 555-8129
Disk	Amy	237 Albee Street	North Hollywood	(213) 555-8917

KEYSTROKES

OPEN TABLE WITH THE MOUSE

1. Click **Project Viewer** icon .... 🗂
2. Click **Tables**.
3. Double-click on the desired table.

OPEN TABLE WITH THE MENU

1. Click **File** .... `Alt`+`F`
2. Click **Open** .... `O`
3. Click **Table** .... `T`
4. Click desired file or enter filename.
5. Click **Open** .... `Alt`+`O`

CHANGE TABLE COLUMN WIDTH

Click right border of the field and drag border to desired size.

EDIT DATA

Before moving to the next/previous field, data may be edited by backspacing and correcting the entry.

After data is entered:

1. Move to the field:

   Press **Tab** .... `Tab`

   OR

   Press **Shift + Tab** .... `Shift`+`Tab`

   OR

   Click on the field.

2. Press **F9** .... `F9`
   to go into Edit mode.

   OR

   Click Edit Data button .... 📝

   OR

a. Click **Table** .... `Alt`+`A`
b. Click **Edit Data** .... `E`
3. Make corrections.
4. Press **Enter** .... `Enter`
   to save changes to field.

EDIT FIELD CONTENTS

In table Edit mode:

   Click Edit Field button .... `ab`

   OR

   Press **F2** .... `F2`

   OR

   Press **Ctrl + F** .... `Ctrl`+`F`

   OR

1. Click **View** .... `Alt`+`V`
2. Click **Field View** .... `F`

Exercise **4**	■ **Edit Data** ■ **Use Project Viewer**		

NOTES

Edit Data

■ As discussed in Exercise 3, you may correct errors during data entry or after the record or table is complete. After data is entered, use Tab, Shift + Tab, the direction arrow keys on the keyboard, or the mouse to go to the field to be corrected. There is no need to perform a Save command when entering or editing information in Edit mode, since records are automatically saved when a table is closed or when you switch back to View mode.

■ You can navigate around the table using the Toolbar buttons, as discussed in Exercise 3, or you can use keyboard shortcuts.

Ctrl + D	Copy an Entry
Home	Move to first field in a record
End	Move to last field in a record
Esc	Undo a field edit (prior to exiting the field)

Use Project Viewer

■ If you are working in one table and wish to open a different table or database object, you may use Project Viewer to do so. To open Project Viewer, click Tools, Project Viewer, or click the Project Viewer button 🔲, or use the Window menu if Project Viewer was open. If several tables or objects are open and you wish to move among them, you may use the Window menu to switch to the object you wish to display.

In this exercise, you will enter records into the STORES and HARDWARE tables. You will make several edits, as directed, and save the tables.

EXERCISE DIRECTIONS

1. Open Project Viewer and switch to the \CORP working directory.

2. Open 📄STORES.DB or 📄04STORES.DB.

3. Switch to Edit mode (F9) and enter the data listed to the right:

4. Move to the Sunset branch record and change the STAFF from 24 to 21 by re-entering the data.

5. Move to the Wheatland branch record and change KA to KS.

6. Close the table.

BRANCH	STORE NUMBER	CITY	ST	STAFF
Astro Center	7	Houston	TX	8
Bean Town	6	Boston	MA	16
Big Apple	1	New York	NY	15
Lakeview	4	Chicago	IL	15
Oceanview	10	Providence	RI	6
Pacific	2	Los Angeles	CA	14
Peach Tree	5	Atlanta	GA	9
Sunset	3	San Francisco	CA	24
Twin Cities	8	St. Paul	MN	7
Wheatland	9	Topeka	KA	12

7. Open ⏛HARDWARE.DB or ▯04HARDWARE.DB.

8. Switch to Edit mode and enter the data below. Use Ctrl+D for repetitive entries.

9. Use the Toolbar to move to the previous record until you reach the Wilson Hard Drive for the Sunset store.

10. Change the purchase date for the Wilson Hard Drive to 7/10/96.

11. Close the table.

BRANCH	ITEM	MFG	MODEL	COST	PUR. DATE	WTY
Big Apple	Computer	GBM	PC220	$1248.50	6/5/96	Y
Big Apple	Printer	GBM	ColorJet II	$335.00	6/8/96	Y
Sunset	Computer	GBM	Notepad 500C	$2199.00	6/10/96	Y
Pacific	Computer	GBM	Notepad 600	$1399.00	6/15/96	Y
Pacific	Hard Drive	Barton	LPS80 220MB	$199.00	6/20/96	Y
Sunset	Hard Drive	Wilson	CFS4 330MB	$250.00	6/10/96	N
Pacific	Printer	BP	Laserjet	$1479.00	7/15/96	N
Bean Town	Computer	Debb	Notebook 586	$1889.00	1/10/97	Y

KEYSTROKES

DATA ENTRY SHORTCUTS

1. Move to first field in the record .. `Home`
2. Move to last field in the record .... `End`
3. Move to first field in the table ... `Ctrl`+`Home`
4. Move to last field in the table .... `Ctrl`+`End`
5. Duplicate information from field in record above selected field ...... `Ctrl`+`D`
6. Undo a field edit..... `Esc` or `Alt`+`Backspace`
7. Enter current date in date field .. `Space` (once each for month, day, year)

OPEN PROJECT VIEWER

Project Viewer allows you to view all database objects. It filters the contents of the current working directory into categories, such as tables, forms, etc., and displays only those objects appropriate to the currently selected icon in the left panel.

1. Click **Tools** .... `Alt`+`T`
2. Click **Project Viewer** .... `P`

If Project Viewer is open but not visible:

1. Click **Window** .... `Alt`+`W`
2. Select **Project Viewer** .... `↓`, `Enter`

From a Table:

Click **Project Viewer** button ....

Exercise

5

- Create a Form from an Existing Table ■ Enter Records
- Design Form View ■ Move Between Views

NOTES

Create a Form from an Existing Table

- You may view or enter data in a database in either a table or a form. A **table** displays the data in a column and row format, similar to a spreadsheet grid. Each row is a record and each column is a field.

- A **form** is another database object which allows you to display your records one at a time, as they would be on index cards in a file drawer. Forms let you see a full screen view of the data that is in one row of a table.

- The Quick Form button  on the Toolbar automatically creates a Form view of the fields and data in an open table. The navigation buttons on the Toolbar can be used to scroll through the records in a table in either Table view or Form view.

- The illustration of an enhanced form below is in Edit mode as indicated by the (Data Entry) notation on the title bar. Note that Paradox uses **.fsl** as the extension for a saved form file.

![Form : memform.fsl [Data Entry] — LAST: Ceedee, FIRST: Carol, ADDRESS: 808 Summer Street, CITY: Anaheim, PHONE: (213)555-4987]

- You can create several forms for one table. Forms simply offer you different ways of viewing information that is stored in a table. For example, the sales division of a company may only need viewing access to its customer's Name, Address and Phone number data, whereas accounts receivable may need access to sales information. A separate form may be created for each group's viewing needs and saved as its own .fsl file.

Enter Records

- It is easy to enter records in table view, but many companies use forms for data entry. Data may be entered in Form view using Toolbar buttons and keyboard shortcuts, just as you would enter data in Table view. The data you enter in a form is actually stored in the Table. You must be in Edit mode to enter data, and you must use the Next Record button ▶ (or press Page Down) to move to the next record. Note the illustration of the Toolbar on the next page when a form is active. You will note that you can move between View Data, Form Design and Table Views from the Toolbar. Insert or Page Down can be pressed at any time in Edit mode to insert a new, blank record.

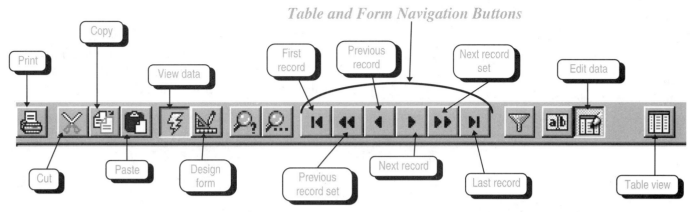

Table and Form Navigation Buttons

Design Form View

■ You can only make changes to a form or save a form while in **Form Design mode**. You can switch to Form Design by clicking the **Design Form** button ☒ on the Toolbar, by pressing F8, or by selecting Design Form from the Form menu. Note the illustration of Form Design mode below.

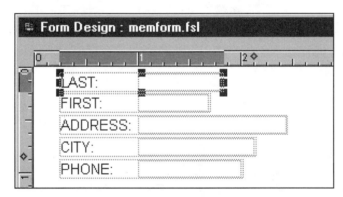

■ In Form Design mode, you can change a selected field item's properties, such as font type, size, color, style or alignment. To make a change to an object on a form, click on the object while in Form Design. Handles will appear around the object. Right-click and select Properties to display a dialog box with tabs for every type of property setting. For example, if you want to color the background of a field, you would select the General tab and click the desired color.

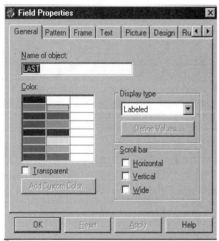

■ If you wish to format only the data area font, color, alignment, etc. (and not the field name area), you must double-click on the desired data area. When handles appear, right-click and select Properties to display the EditRegion Properties dialog box.

✓ *Making font changes may result in a need to reset the item's size.*

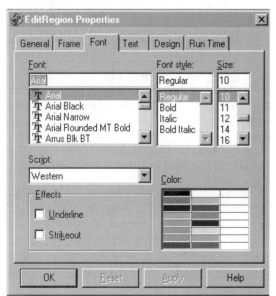

■ If you discover that the Form view data areas need adjusting, you must return to Form Design mode to make changes. To resize a field, first click on the item, then click and hold down the left mouse button on one of the handles, and drag in the desired direction. You can also move each field on the screen to redesign the layout of the form.

Move Between Views

■ You can move between Form view, Design view, and Table view using the buttons on the Toolbar, or by using the <u>W</u>indow menu. The <u>W</u>indow menu will display all opened database objects.

The California Users Group has added more members and would like to create a form for data entry. The form will be enhanced in Design view and saved in the CUG database.

EXERCISE DIRECTIONS

1. Open Project Viewer and switch your working directory to \CUG.

2. Open 📧MEMBERS or 🗔05MEMBER.

3. Switch to Edit mode (F9). Move to the last record (Ctrl+End). Press Tab and enter the first three records into the MEMBERS table:

LAST	FIRST	ADDRESS	CITY	PHONE
Zip	Drew	15 Imperial Way	Beverly Hills	(213) 555-9888
Sistem	Sally	27 Ocean Avenue	Anaheim	(213) 555-7777
Wyndow	Walter	188 Riverside Drive	Culver City	(213) 555-7655
Coller	Jenny	879 Beverly Drive	Beverly Hills	(213) 555-6676
Cable	Cleo	666 Santa Ana Drive	Culver City	(213) 555-9988
Matricks	Martin	90 Rodeo Drive	Beverly Hills	(213) 555-2222

4. Click the Quick Form button on the Toolbar to create a Form view of the table.

5. Scroll through all the records using the Toolbar navigation buttons or by pressing Page Up or Page Down.

6. Move to the last field on the last record. (Use Ctrl+End, End.)

7. Click the Next button to display a blank form.

8. Add the last three records from the list above into the quick form.

9. Move to the next blank record.

10. Click the Design Form button on the Toolbar, or press F8, to go into Form Design mode.

11. Change the font of the LAST field edit region:

   - Double-click on the LAST field to select the edit region (the box inside the box).
   - Right-click on the selected edit region, then choose Properties.
   - Click the Font tab in the EditRegion Properties dialog box.
   - Change the font size to 12 point, and the font style to bold.
   - Click OK.

12. Set the FIRST field edit region to 12 point bold as well.

13. Color the LAST field gray:

   - Click once on the LAST field to select the entire field entry.
   - Right-click on the LAST field, choose Properties.
   - Click the General tab in the Field Properties dialog box.
   - Change the color to light gray.

14. Repeat this change for the FIRST field.

15. Select each field and move them so that there is some space between each field.

16. Save the form and name it MEMFORM.

17. Click the View Data button 🔯 on the Toolbar to return to View mode.

18. Switch to Table view, using the Table view button or the Windows menu.

19. Check that the three new records have been added to the table.

20. Close all database objects.

KEYSTROKES

CREATE FORM VIEW FOR TABLE

1. Open table.
2. Click the **Quick Form** button .... 🔲 on the Toolbar.

ENTER DATA IN FORM VIEW

1. Press **F9** .... F9 for Edit mode.
2. Click **Insert** button on the keyboard to add next record .... Ins

   OR

   Click **Next Record** button .... ▶ on Toolbar.

   Press **Page Down** .... Page Down
3. Type data in first field.
4. Press Tab .... Tab
5. Repeat steps 2-4 until complete.

SWITCH TO FORM DESIGN

From Form view:

   Click **Form Design** button .... 📐

   OR

   Press **F8** F8

   OR

   a. Click **Form** .... Alt + M
   b. Click **Design Form** .... D

SWITCH TO FORM VIEW

From Form Design mode:

   Click **View Data** button .... 🔯

   OR

   Press **F8** F8

   OR

   Click **Form** .... Alt + M

Click **View Data** V

From Table view:

Click **Quick Form** button .... 🔲
on the Toolbar.

CHANGE FORM DESIGN

To change entire field:

   - Click field to be changed.

   OR

To change only the edit region:

1. Double-click on edit region of field.
2. Right-click.
3. Click **Properties**.
4. Select appropriate tab.
5. Change desired settings.
6. Click **OK** .... Enter

Exercise 6

■ **Summary**

At Kitchen Korner, you are the staff member responsible for ordering and evaluating software products used at company stores. To keep track of the types of software ordered, their prices, and where they are stored, you have been asked to set up a new table and form for the CORP database.

EXERCISE DIRECTIONS

1. Open Project Viewer and switch your working directory to \CORP.
2. Create a new table using the field data listed below:

NAME	DATA TYPE	SIZE
Branch	Alpha	16
Title	Alpha	11
Type	Alpha	17
Price	$	
Purdate	Date	
Stored	Alpha	4

3. Save the table; name it SOFTWARE.
4. View the SOFTWARE table.
5. Click the Quick Form button on the Toolbar.
6. Switch to Form Design mode.
7. Select the BRANCH field object. Change color to light gray.
8. Select the BRANCH edit region. Make the following changes: font size - 12 point.; font style - bold; text alignment - center.
9. Make the data area larger to accommodate the new font size, if necessary.
10. Select each field, starting with the last field, and move each one down to allow more space between fields. Keep the fields aligned on the left.
11. Switch to Form view. Note the results of your enhancements.
12. Check for any design adjustments that must be made; make these adjustments in Form Design mode.
13. Save the form as SOFTFORM.FSL in Form Design.
14. Switch to Form view and go into Edit mode by pressing F9.
15. Enter the software data listed below:
16. Switch to the SOFTWARE table to verify data. Make any corrections.
17. Close the table, form and Project Viewer.

Branch	Software Title	Type	Price	Purchase Date	Stored
Sunset	Word-O	Word Processing	499.85	6/12/96	D230
Big Apple	Micro Words	Word Processing	459.80	6/14/96	C330
Pacific	Word-O-D	Word Processing	499.85	7/18/96	B235
Lakeview	Word-O-2	Word Processing	499.85	7/20/96	A135
Lakeview	Tulip5	Spreadsheet	594.20	8/21/96	A138
Big Apple	Exceller	Spreadsheet	475.50	8/21/96	C338
Bean Town	BBS	Communications	111.50	9/15/96	D230
Wheatland	Officemate	Integrated	479.95	9/15/96	B238
Sunset	Harwood	Graphics	299.95	1/30/97	D230
Lakeview	Pagemaker	Desktop	399.40	2/15/97	A114

Exercise 7

- **Modify a Table or Form** ■ **Add, Delete, or Move a Field in a Table**
- **Add, Delete, or Move a Field in a Form**

NOTES

Modify a Table or Form

- Fields may be added, moved, or deleted in a table or a form. When you add a field to an existing table or form, it is not automatically added to the other views of this record.

- For tables, all structural changes must be made in the Restructure Paradox Table dialog box. You must be certain that no forms or tables that use this data are running when structural changes are being made. You can open an existing table by double-clicking it in the Project Viewer. Then open the Restructure Table dialog box by pressing the Restructure button ▦.

- Structural changes in a form must be made in Design view. Enter Design mode by double-clicking the form in the Project Viewer, and then clicking the Design Form button ▦ on the Toolbar.

Add, Delete, or Move a Field in a Table

- In the Restructure Paradox 4 Table dialog box, as illustrated above right, you can create space for a new field by clicking where you want to insert the new field, then pressing the Insert key. To delete a field, simply click on the field, and then press Ctrl+Delete. You will be asked to confirm the deletion, and when you agree, the field will be deleted and the remaining data will reposition itself. To move a field most efficiently, you should drag it to its new position.

Restructure Paradox 4 Table

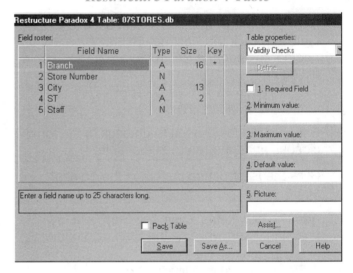

Add, Delete, or Move a Field in a Form

- If a field is added in a table, it is not automatically added to the form. A new field may be added to a form directly by clicking the Field button ▦ on the Toolbar in Form Design mode. A set of screens will display that will enable you to define the field, its contents and its format, as well as establish if the data is independent of a table or connected to a field in a specific table.

- You can include a new field added to a table into a form by clicking the Quick Form button on the Toolbar and recreating the form. When the new form is saved, using the same name, it will overwrite the old one.

Your manager at Kitchen Korner has asked you to add two more fields to your STORES table. She realized that sales data and whether or not a branch has evening hours should have been included.

EXERCISE DIRECTIONS

1. Open Project Viewer and switch to the \CORP database.

2. Open ▦STORES or ▯07STORES.

3. Click Quick Form on the Toolbar to create a form for this table.

4. Switch to Design view and save the form as STOREFORM.

5. Use the Window menu to switch back to the table and click the Restructure button on the Toolbar to open the Restructure Paradox Table dialog box.

   ✓   *Paradox will not let you restructure the table while the related form is open.*

6. Use the Windows menu to go back to the form, close it, and then return to the table.

7. Click the Restructure button on the Toolbar again.

8. Add two new fields above the Staff field, by pressing Insert while on the Staff field name:
   SALES (Type - Number)
   EVE (Type - Alphanumeric; Size - 3)

9. Delete the STORE NUMBER field.

10. Save the changes you made, confirm the deletion, and return to the table.

11. From the list below, enter the information for each branch:

BRANCH	SALES	EVE
Astro Center	541,000	NO
Bean Town	682,450	YES
Big Apple	789,300	YES
Lakeview	755,420	NO
Oceanview	433,443	YES
Pacific	685,400	NO
Peach Tree	457,800	YES
Sunset	876,988	NO
Twin Cities	235,420	YES
Wheatland	352,415	YES

12. Use Quick Form to create a related form for this table.

13. Scroll through the form to locate the Lakeview form.

14. Print this record.

15. Close the table.

KEYSTROKES

ADD FIELD

1. In Table view, click **Restructure** button............... 🖾 on the Toolbar.
2. Click the field directly below where you want to add the new field.
3. Press **Insert**............................... Ins

DELETE FIELD

1. In Table view, click **Restructure** button............... 🖾 on the Toolbar.
2. Select field to delete.
3. Press **Ctrl+Delete**............... Ctrl + Del

MOVE FIELD

1. In Table view, click **Restructure** button............... 🖾 on the Toolbar.
2. Click the field selector (the number to left of field name).
3. Click and drag field selector to new position.

Exercise 8

■ **Validity Checks** ■ **Print** ■ **Print in Landscape**

NOTES

Validity Checks

■ Once a table is created, employees will enter new records as necessary. To ensure that data is accurate, it is possible to establish rules or validity checks for fields to verify that data meets certain requirements. The Validity Checks feature is available in the Create Paradox Table and the Restructure Paradox 4 Table dialog boxes. Note that the validity checks option is selected in the Table properties drop-down list in the Restructure Paradox 4 Table dialog box, below.

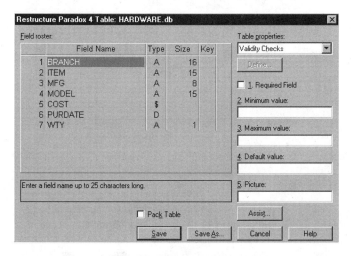

■ The Restructure Paradox 4 Table dialog box has two main sections: the Field roster and the Table properties sections. Use the F4 key to move from the Field Roster to the Table Properties section and the Shift+Tab or Alt+F to return.

■ Paradox provides five types of validity checks:

• **Required field:** If this is selected, the field cannot be left blank.

• **Minimum value:** You can specify a minimum numeric value for the field, and then the entry must be equal to or greater than this amount.

• **Maximum value:** You can specify a maximum numeric value for this field, and then the entry must be equal to or less than this amount.

• **Default value:** You can specify a default value for the field which will be used if data is not entered.

• **Picture:** A picture is a pattern of characters that defines what a user can type into a field during editing or data entry, or in response to a prompt. Therefore a picture check restricts the type of information that can be entered.

■ If you try to enter data into a form or table (while in Edit mode) that does not meet the requirements of any preset validity checks, you will not be allowed to move to the next field. An error message will appear on the status bar at the bottom of the screen explaining the problem.

■ When a table is saved, Validity Checks are saved in a file with the table's name and the .VAL file extension. You will be asked if the validity checks should be enforced on existing data when saving the new structure.

Print

■ You can get a printout of current screen data in either Table view or Form view. To print the current screen data, either choose the Print option from the File menu, or click the Print button on the Toolbar. The dialog box that appears gives you the ability to choose the print range, number of copies, and overflow handling options. Note the Print File dialog box, on the next page.

Print File Dialog Box

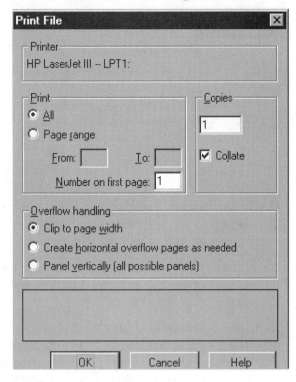

Print in Landscape

■ If you are printing a table that is wide, you should use landscape mode for a better view of the data. You can specify landscape mode by clicking File, Printer Setup. Select your printer

and click Modify Printer Setup. On the Properties screen for a HP LaserJet III illustrated below, you will note the Orientation and Paper size settings along with tabs for other setup features.

✓ *Setup options may vary, depending on what type of printer you are using.*

Printer Properties Dialog Box

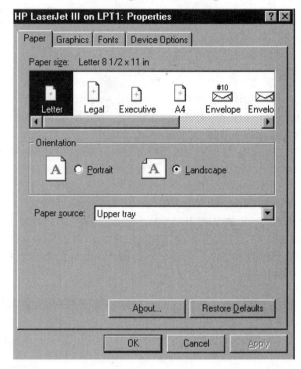

Kitchen Korner stores will be adding validity checks and additional data to its tables. Tables and forms will be printed.

EXERCISE DIRECTIONS

Part I

1. Open Project Viewer and switch your working directory to \CORP.

2. Open ▧HARDWARE or ▧08HARDWA.

3. Click the Restructure button on the Toolbar to open the Restructure Paradox 4 Table dialog box.

4. Move to each field, as listed at the right, and set the validity checks indicated. Use F4 to move to the Table Properties section and Shift+Tab to return to the Field Roster.

5. When finished, click Save to save the settings. Confirm the restructure at the warning screen.

✓ *If you make an error, you can open the Restructure box, correct the error and save the settings again. If you need to delete the file with these settings to clear an error, you can find the file using Windows Explorer. The file will be named Hardware.val.*

FIELD	VALIDITY CHECK
Item	Required Field
Mfg.	Required Field
Model	Required Field
Cost	Minimum: 100 (Items less than $100 would be considered supplies.)
Purdate	Required Field
Wty	Picture: {Y,N} (Yes or No in the indicated format.)

Part II

6. From Table view, switch to Edit mode.

7. Enter the data listed below:

BRANCH	ITEM	MFG.	MODEL	COST	PURDATE	WTY
Lakeview	Computer	Debb	P200	2507.52	1/12/97	Y
Lakeview	Printer	Jokidota	BJ800	355.00	1/12/97	Y
Astro Center	Computer	Pancard	PE166	2095.54	1/25/97	Y
Astro Center	Zip Drive	Howell	Z100	169.95	1/25/97	N

Part III

8. Attempt to enter the data below, some of which contains errors or omissions, and note the messages that appear at the bottom of the screen. Use the corrected information listed under the incorrect data to complete the entries.

9. Print a copy of the table in landscape orientation.

10. Use the Quick Form button to create a form from this table.

11. In Form Design mode, select the BRANCH field and set the following properties:

    Color: light gray
    Font: 12 point, bold
    Alignment: Center

12. Move the fields so that they are separated from one another.

13. Save the form as HARDFORM.

14. Click the View Data Toolbar button.

15. Move through the records and locate the computer purchased on 6/15/96.

16. Print a copy of that record in portrait orientation.

17. Close the form and table.

	BRANCH	ITEM	MFG.	MODEL	COST	PURDATE	WTY
Entry	Twin Cities	Computer	Pancard		2095.54	1/29/97	Y
Correction				PE166			
Entry	Twin Cities	Printer	BP	LaserJet	13.03	1/29/97	U
Correction					1303.00		Y

KEYSTROKES

PRINT DATA IN TABLE

1. Open table to print.
2. Click **File** .... `Alt`+`F`
3. Click **Print** .... `P`
4. Click **Print** section to select:... `Alt`+`P`
   - **All** .... `Alt`+`A`
   - **Page range** .... `Alt`+`R`
   - **From** .... `F`
   - **To** .... `Alt`+`T`

5. Click **Copies** text box............. `Alt`+`C`
   and type desired number of copies.
6. Click **OK** .... `Enter`

PRINT DATA IN FORM

1. View form to print
2. Click **File** .... `Alt`+`F`
3. Click **Print** .... `P`
4. Click **Copies** text box............. `Alt`+`C`
   and type desired number of copies.
5. Click **OK** .... `Enter`

SETUP LANDSCAPE MODE

1. Click **File** .... `Alt`+`F`
2. Click **Printer Setup** .... `R`
3. Select **Printers** .... `Alt`+`P`, `↓`
4. Click **Modify Printer Setup** ..... `Alt`+`M`
5. Click **Landscape** .... `Alt`+`L`
6. Click **OK** .... `Enter`

Exercise 9

- **Edit a Record** ■ **Add a Record**
- **Delete a Record** ■ **Radio Buttons**

NOTES

Edit a Record

- To change data that has already been entered in a field, highlight the existing data and retype the new data. This may be done in either Table or Form view. You may also double-click on the section of the data that needs revising, or press F2 or Ctrl + F, and make the needed changes.

- To delete the contents of a field, select the data then press the Delete key, Backspace, or select the Delete option from the Edit menu.

Add a Record

- Records may be added in either Table or Form view by pressing Enter on the last field of the last record, or by pressing Insert anywhere in the table.

Delete a Record

- Records may be deleted in either Table or Form view by pressing Ctrl + Delete. Paradox will renumber the records when a record is added or deleted.

Radio Buttons

- In some cases, data in a field is a choice from a list of specific entries. For example, you can list specified items that can be charged to club members, (such as dues, newsletters, publications, etc.) and then use radio buttons on a form to select the item instead of typing it. Each value for the field is listed with a button beside it, to provide a quick way to enter data. Note the illustration of radio button to the right.

Radio Button Field for a Form

- Radio buttons are created in Form Design mode by right-clicking the field and opening the Properties dialog box. On the General tab, as illustrated below, select Radio Buttons in the Display type drop-down list and click Define Values to enter the values to be used for this field.

Field Properties Dialog Box

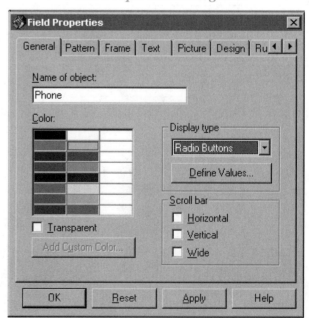

- In the Define List dialog box (illustrated below), you can enter each item in the Item box, press the Enter key and the item will move to the Item list. The dialog box provides buttons to modify and remove items. Item names can be sorted into alphabetical order, making data entry easier, or you can change the order of items manually.

- Once you have created the Radio Buttons field for the form, you may wish to label the radio buttons section with a field name. This can be done in Form Design view by clicking the text tool button abl on the Toolbar and entering the field label in a position above the radio buttons. Note the illustration of the Form Design for CHGFORM with a new label placed above the radio button field.

Form with Radio Button Field

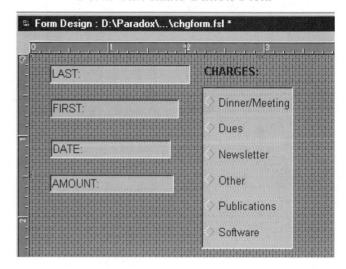

The California Users Group will be adding a new table to its database for the charges that members incur. A form will be created for the data, and a field will be formatted to display radio buttons. The Field will be labeled in Form Design mode using the text tool. Data will be added to tables and forms. In addition, you will discover several errors in the records that need to be edited.

EXERCISE DIRECTIONS

Part I

1. Open Project Viewer and switch your working directory to \CUG.

2. Create a new table, using the fields and table properties indicated below:

3. Save the table; name it CHARGES.

4. View the table.

FIELD	TYPE	SIZE	VALIDITY CHECKS
Last	Alpha	10	Required Field
First	Alpha	8	
Date	Date		Required Field
Amount	Number		Required Field
Charge	Alpha	15	Required Field

Part II

5. Click the Toolbar Quick Form button to create a form for this table.

6. Switch to Form Design mode.

7. Select the Charge field and right-click to select Properties.

8. Change the Display type to Radio Buttons and click Define Values.

9. Key the following items into the item box and press the Enter key after each item:
   Dues
   Newsletter
   Dinner/Meeting
   Publications
   Software
   Other

10. Click Sort List to sort the list into alphabetical order. Click OK to close the Define List dialog box, then click OK again to close the Field Properties dialog box.

11. In the Form Design window, use the Text Tool button to add the label, CHARGES. Set the label text for bold style.

12. Adjust placement of the label so that it is above the radio buttons, if necessary.

13. Save the form as CHGFORM.

14. Click View Data button.

15. Enter the following data into the form in Edit mode using the radio buttons for the Charge field data.

LAST	FIRST	DATE	AMOUNT	CHARGE
Sort	Stuart	11/15/96	$59.95	Software
Monitor	Michael	11/16/96	$15.00	Newsletter
Graphic	John	11/18/96	$35.00	Publications
Wave	Bette	11/19/96	$25.00	Dues
Disk	Amy	11/20/96	$10.00	Other

Part III

16. Switch to Project Viewer.

17. Open MEMBERS or 09MEMBER.

18. Add the new members listed below to the end of the MEMBERS table in Edit mode.

19. Cleo Cable has asked to be removed from our club listings. Check the Charges table to note if she has charged any items. If not, delete her record from the MEMBERS table.

LAST	FIRST	ADDRESS	CITY	PHONE
Boot	Barry	6 Terminal Drive	North Hollywood	(213) 555-1122
Web	Warren	15 Design Road	Anaheim	(213) 555-5454
Bugg	Barbara	345 Systems Street	Culver City	(213) 555-9191
Chipp	Charley	231 Board Avenue	Beverly Hills	(213) 555-7171

Part IV

20. Use the Window menu to switch to CHGFORM. Add the following data: (Use navigation buttons to add a new form.)

LAST	FIRST	DATE	AMOUNT	CHARGE
Zip	Drew	11/22/96	$30.00	Dinner/Meeting
Wyndow	Walter	11/22/96	$30.00	Dinner/Meeting

21. Switch to the CHARGES table.

22. Print the table.

23. Close the tables and form.

KEYSTROKES

EDIT DATA

Paradox automatically saves changes to fields when you move to the next record.

If you are entering data into a field that has validity checks, you cannot move from that field until the validity check requirement is met.

1. In Edit mode, place insertion point in field to change.

   OR

   Click and drag to select field contents.

2. Type desired new value.

DELETE RECORD

In Edit mode:

1. Scroll to the record to be deleted.

2. Press **Ctrl + Delete** .... `Ctrl`+`Del`

SET FORM RADIO BUTTON FIELD

In Design Form mode:

1. Select the field to be displayed with radio buttons.

2. Right-click and select **P**roperties .... `R`

3. Click **Display type** .... `Alt`+`Y`

4. Select **Radio Buttons** .... `↓`
   on drop-down list.

5. Click **Define Values** ......

6. Click **Item** ....

7. Enter first item/value for field.

8. Press **Enter** .... `Enter`

9. Repeat steps 7-8 until list is complete.

10. To sort list; click **Sort List** .....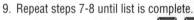

11. Click **OK** .... `Enter`

12. Click **OK** .... `Enter`
    to close Field Properties box.

Exercise 10

■ Enhance Form Design

NOTES

Enhance Form Design

■ Many companies use forms as their main method of data entry or for viewing records. Forms can be enhanced to make data attractive and easier to read. Note the illustration of a form with background color, field frames, field color, and font changes.

Form View

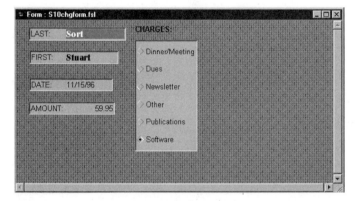

Page Properties Dialog Box

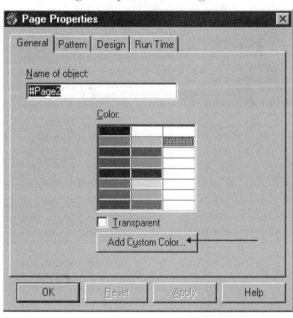

■ You can change the background color or pattern of a form by selecting the background while in Form Design mode, right-clicking and selecting Properties. The Page Properties dialog box will display on the General tab. As you will note in the illustration to the right, colors are available for selection along with an Add Custom Color button.

■ To create a custom color, click on a blank color box and then click Add Custom Color. Colors may be customized for field areas and form backgrounds using the Custom Color dialog box (illustrated on the right), by sliding the Red, Green, and Blue bars to create a custom color.

Custom Color Dialog Box

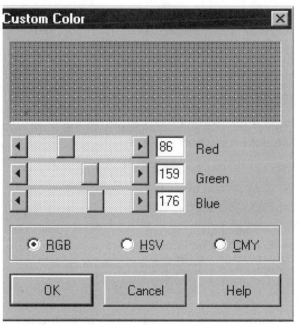

■ **Frames** can be used to highlight fields on a form. You can select the frame tab from the Field Properties dialog box and choose from various colors, line styles, and line thickness options. Note the illustration of the Frame tab of the Field Properties dialog box below.

Frame Tab - Field Properties Dialog Box

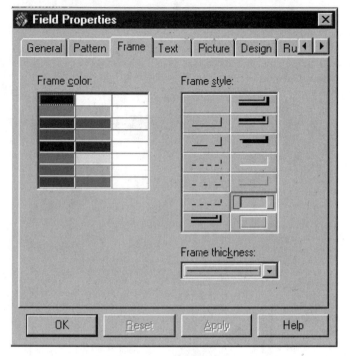

■ If you wish to enhance several items on a form, using the same Properties settings, press the Shift key and select each item. Right-click and select Properties.

✓ *You can also hold the Shift key and drag a box around the items to be selected and enhanced.*

The California Users Group has decided to enhance its forms. In addition, data will be added to the MEMBERS and CHARGES tables, and corrections to will be made to existing data.

EXERCISE DIRECTIONS

1. Open Project Viewer and switch your working directory to \CUG.

2. Open ≣CHGFORM or ▯10CHGFOR.

3. Switch to Form Design mode.

4. Right-click on the background of the form and select Properties.

5. To set a custom color background:
   • Click on one of the blank color locations.
   • Click Add Custom Color.
   • Click and slide Red bar to 86 (or type 86).
   • Click and slide Green bar to 159 (or type 159).
   • Click and slide Blue bar to 176 (or type 176). (Or create any background color you wish.)
   • Click OK.

6. Select each field and change the color to light gray. Add the indented frame style (right column, frame six).

7. Move the fields so that they are spaced as shown in the Form View illustration on page 347.

8. Select the edit region (data area) for the Last and First name fields and change the font to Britannic Bold, Regular, 12 point.

9. Save the changes in the form design.

10. In Edit mode, enter the new charges as indicated in the table below:

LAST	FIRST	DATE	CHARGE	AMOUNT
Boot	Barry	12/1/96	Dues	$25.00
Web	Warren	12/2/96	Dues	$25.00
Web	Warren	12/2/96	Newsletter	$15.00
Bugg	Barbara	12/3/96	Dues	$25.00
Coller	Jenny	12/3/96	Publications	$50.00
Chipp	Charley	12/3/96	Dues	$25.00

11. Close the form and switch to Project Viewer.

12. Open the ▨CHARGES table and check your data entry.

13. Close the table.

14. Open ▨MEMFORM or ▨10MEMFORM.

15. Enhance this form, in Form Design mode, using the same frame and data format, but creating a different background color.

16. Save the changes.

17. Switch to Form view and scroll through records to make the following changes in Edit mode:
    - Drew Zip has moved to 23 Hillside Street in Beverly Hills and has kept the same telephone number.
    - Martin Matricks has changed his telephone number from 555-2222 to 555-2651.

18. Print a copy of the Drew Zip record.

19. Close all database objects.

KEYSTROKES

CHANGE FORM BACKGROUND COLOR

In Form Design mode:

1. Right-click on the form background.
2. Select **P**roperties .... [R]
3. Select **C**olor on the **General** tab .... [Alt]+[C], [↔]

   OR

   Select a custom color:
   - Click one of the blank color locations .... [→]
   - Click **Add C**ustom Color ..... [Alt]+[U]
   - Move slides of each color bar until desired color is obtained.

4. Click **OK** .... [Enter] to save custom color.
5. Click **OK** .... [Enter]

ADD FRAME TO FIELD

In Form Design mode:

1. Right-click on the field.
2. Select **P**roperties .... [R]
3. Select **Frame** tab.
4. Select **Frame s**tyle .... [Alt]+[S], [↓][↑]
5. Click **OK** .... [Enter]

SELECT MULTIPLE FORM ITEMS TO ADJUST OR DESIGN

Hold **Shift** and drag box .... [Shift] + *drag* around objects to be selected.

OR

1. Select first item.
2. Press and hold **Shift** key .... [Shift]
3. Select next item.
4. Repeat as necessary.

Exercise

11

■ **Summary**

In an earlier exercise, you created an inventory table called HARDWARE for Kitchen Korner's computer inventory and you began to make entries. In this exercise, you will add new fields to the table and enter new information into the database. A form will be created and enhanced, and data will be added using the form. In addition, you will be adding new branches to the STORES table and editing existing records.

EXERCISE DIRECTIONS

Part I

1. Open Project Viewer and switch your working directory to \CORP.

2. Open the ⬛HARDWARE or ⬛11HARDWA.

3. Restructure the table to add two alpha fields at the end of the existing table:
   ASSIGNED TO (Alpha - 15)
   SERIAL # (Alpha - 7)

4. Save the new structure.

5. Add the new field data listed below.

   ✓ *You should maximize the table window or scroll to view all fields in this table.*

BRANCH	ITEM	MFG	MODEL	COST	PUR. DATE	WTY	ASSIGNED TO	SERIAL #
Big Apple	Computer	GBM	PC220	$1248.50	6/5//96	Y	Accounting	651198
Big Apple	Printer	GBM	ExecJetII	$335.00	6/8/96	Y	Accounting	55211
Sunset	Computer	GBM	Notepad 500C	$2199.00	6/10/96	Y	Accounting	AB2059
Pacific	Computer	GBM	Notepad 600	$1399.00	6/15/96	Y	Accounting	671150
Pacific	Hard Drive	Barton	LPS80 220 MB	$199.00	6/20/96	Y	Accounting	54219
Sunset	Hard Drive	Wilson	CFS4 300MB	$250.00	7/10/96	N	Purchasing	12345
Pacific	Printer	BP	LaserJet	$1479.00	7/15/96	N	Accounting	88842
Bean Town	Computer	Debb	Notebook 586	$1889.00	1/10/97	Y	Shipping	1145A
Lakeview	Computer	Debb	P200	$2507.52	1/12/97	Y	Accounting	765498
Lakeview	Printer	Jokidota	BJ800	$355.00	1/12/97	Y	Accounting	43567
Astro Center	Computer	Pancard	PE166	$2095.54	1/25/97	Y	Purchasing	VC2342
Astro Center	Zip Drive	Howell	Z100	$169.95	1/25/97	N	Purchasing	324222
Twin Cities	Computer	Pancard	PE166	$2095.54	1/29/97	Y	Accounting	BV3452
Twin Cities	Printer	BP	LaserJet	$1303.00	1/29/97	Y	Accounting	1213H

Part II

6. Create a Quick Form from this table.

7. In Form Design mode, enhance the form by changing font size, field placement, and background color.

8. Add a Radio Button for the Assigned To field. Use the following to define field values:
   - Accounting
   - Purchasing
   - Shipping
   - MIS
   - Sales
   - Administration
   - Other

9. Sort the items.

10. Use the Text Tool to add a label above the radio buttons. Use ASSIGNED TO: as the label and set it for bold. Move the label in place above the radio buttons.

11. Save the form; name it HARDFORM, replacing the previous form with the same name.

12. In Edit mode, add the records listed below.

BRANCH	ITEM	MFG	MODEL	COST	PUR. DATE	WTY	ASSIGNED TO	SERIAL #
Wheatland	Printer	NIC	FGE/3V	$539.00	2/3/97	N	Purchasing	87098
Sunset	Printer	BP	Deskjet	$429.00	2/5/97	Y	Accounting	99911
Pacific	Printer	BP	Deskjet	$429.00	2/6/97	Y	Purchasing	22230
Wheatland	Computer	Canton	Notebook	$2436.00	2/10/97	Y	MIS	98763

Part III

13. Switch to the HARDWARE table. Make the following edits:
   - The correct cost of the GBM PC220 purchased on 6/5/96 was $1348.50; make the correction.
   - The Barton hard drive is not under warranty; make the correction.
   - The GBM ColorJettII Printer purchased on 6/8/96 is no longer in use; delete the record from the table.

14. Print one copy of the table in landscape mode.

15. Close the table and form.

Part IV

16. Open ⬛STORES or ⬛11STORES.

17. Add the new branches to the table as listed below:

BRANCH	CITY	ST	SALES	EVE	STAFF
Liberty	Philadelphia	PA	423,150	YES	19
Seal City Center	Anchorage	AK	185,420	NO	9
Central States	San Diego	CA	144,524	NO	14
Federal Plaza	Washington	DC	245,860	NO	11
Desert View Mall	Phoenix	AZ	189,252	YES	8
Rocky Mountain	Denver	CO	102,563	YES	9
Southland	Mobile	AL	104,566	NO	7
River View Plaza	Atlanta	GA	215,400	NO	6
Dixieland	Atlanta	GA	352,622	YES	14
Iron City Plaza	Cleveland	OH	543,233	NO	13

18. There have been changes in the number of employees in the following branches. Make these changes in the table:

Big Apple	20
Wheatland	11
Astro Center	12
Peach Tree	16
Sunset	13

19. The Oceanview branch closed; delete the record.

20. Print the table in landscape mode.

21. Close all database objects.

Exercise 12

■ **Locate Values** ■ **Use Wildcards**
■ **Locate and Replace Data**

NOTES

Locate Values

■ The **Record** menu in Table and Form views contains commands which assist in locating records. You may wish to find a specific record for editing or informational purposes. After opening a table in either Table or Form view, select Locate, Value from the Record menu, or press Ctrl+Z, or click the Locate Field Value button 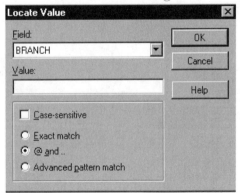 on the Toolbar to display the Locate Values dialog box (illustrated below).

Locate Value Dialog Box

■ After entering the value you wish to locate in the Value box, set the Locate Value conditions:

• **Field** - Indicates the field from which you want to search. By default, it lists the field that currently contains the cursor. Click the drop-down arrow to select another field to search.

• **Case-sensitive** - Select to match capitalization as typed, or if not selected, search will ignore case of entry.

• **Exact match** - Check Exact match if you do not want to treat pattern characters as wildcards.

• **@ and ..** - Wildcards. @ stands for any character, and .. stands for any number of characters, including none.

• **Advanced Pattern match** - Check Advanced pattern match if you want to use an extended list of wildcards in your search. (Click the Help button for the extended list of wildcards.)

■ When all the appropriate conditions have been set, click OK to begin the search. The first record, containing the search value, is presented with the search value highlighted. You can now view or edit the located record.

■ To search for another record that contains the same data, select Record, Locate Next or click the Locate Next button, or press Ctrl+A to move to the next occurrence. Either the next matching record is presented, or a message that the search value was not found displays on the status bar.

Use Wildcards

■ A **wildcard operator** is a symbol used in a search value to substitute for unknown characters. There are two wildcard operators that broaden the locate command, the ellipsis (..) and the "at" symbol (@).

■ The ellipsis (..) is used to indicate an unknown group of characters. For example; if you were searching for a particular name but were certain of only the first two letters, you would indicate the search value as *Br...* This will find all records in which the last name begins with *Br*.

■ The at symbol (@) is used to substitute for an unknown single character. If you were searching for a particular name but were uncertain of some characters in the spelling, the search value could be entered as, for example, *Br@wn* or *Br@w@* or *B@@wn*. This would find records with any letter in the @ wildcard operator location.

Locate and Replace Data

- You may determine that you wish to locate all occurences of a specific value and replace it with another value. In this case, you should use the Locate and Replace feature. This feature is available in Edit mode of a Form or Table. Select Locate, and Replace from the Record menu, or press Shift+Ctrl+Z, to open the dialog box (illustrated below). Enter the Field, Value, and Replace with value in the dialog box.

- The settings for the Find and Replace dialog box are the same as those for the Locate Value dialog box. These settings will locate and replace values as specified, stopping at each occurrence of the value and allowing you to determine if it should be replaced. Note the illustration of the Found a Match dialog box that appears for each occurrence of the value. You may elect to change all occurences without viewing each one.

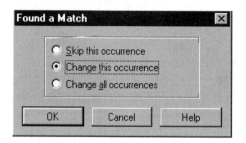

CUG, your computer users' group, has decided to add a field to its MEMBERS table. In addition, several new members have joined CUG and you have been notified that several members' records need to be updated. After updating the records, you will be in a better position to generate membership information.

EXERCISE DIRECTIONS

Part I

1. Open Project Viewer and switch your working directory to \CUG.

2. Open ⊟12MEMBER or ⊠MEMBERS.

3. Use the Restructure feature to add two new fields to the table as follows:
   - Insert after the CITY field: ZIP (Alpha – 5)
     Hint: Press Insert while on the PHONE field.
   - Insert after the PHONE field: PROF. (Alpha – 15)
   - Save the changes.

4. Add the new information to the records of the present members as listed below:
   ✓ *For easier data entry, you might temporarily move the PROF field next to the ZIP field. Return it after data is entered.*

LAST	FIRST	ZIP	PROF
Ceedee	Carol	92803	Student
Modem	Miles	92803	Accountant
Sort	Stuart	90210	Lawyer
Monitor	Michael	90210	Teacher
Mouse	Trina	92803	Student
Icon	Sheila	92803	Chiropractor
Wave	Bette	91615	Lawyer
Midi	Carl	91615	Banker
Graphic	John	91615	Student
Disk	Amy	91615	Orthopedist
Zip	Drew	90210	Teacher
Sistem	Sally	92803	Editor
Wyndow	Walter	90311	Accountant
Coller	Jenny	90210	Banker
Matricks	Martin	90210	Student
Boot	Barry	91615	Lawyer
Web	Warren	92803	Manager
Bugg	Barbara	90311	Teacher
Chipp	Charley	90210	Manager

Part II

5. Use Quick Form to create an updated form for the table.

6. In Form Design Mode, change the background and field colors, and add field frames.

LAST	FIRST	ADDRESS	CITY	ZIP	PHONE	PROF.
Folder	Fred	45 Anita Street	Anaheim	92803	(213) 555-7199	Sales
Graphiks	Gene	231 Fifth Street	Culver City	90311	(213) 555-0091	Insurance
Image	Iggy	79 Sunny Drive	Beverly Hills	90210	(213) 555-1009	Student

Part III

9. Switch to Table view. Using Record, Locate, Value, search the database for the answers to the following questions. Make note of the answers.
   - Which members live in Anaheim? (CITY field)
   - Which members live in Beverly Hills? (CITY field)
   - Which members are Lawyers? (PROF. field)
   - How many members are Students? (PROF. field)
   - What is Trina Mouse's profession? (LAST field)

10. Switch to MEMFORM, in Edit view. Locate the record for Michael Monitor.
    Make the following changes to his record:
    - His new address is 32 Oak Street.
    - His new phone number is (213) 555-8750.

7. Save the form as MEMFORM, replacing the original form.

8. Add the following new members at the end of the records in Form view:

11. Locate the record for Bette Wave.
    Make the following changes to her record:
    - Her new name is Bette Wave-Sim.
    - Her new address is 1745 River Street, located in North Hollywood, 91615.
    - Her new phone number is (213) 555-8520.

12. Locate the record for Sheila Icon. Change her phone number to (213) 555-7255.

13. Locate and replace all occurrences of the value Lawyer with Attorney in the PROF. field.

14. Close the MEMBERS table and MEMFORM.

KEYSTROKES

LOCATE VALUES

Ctrl+Z

In Form or Table view:

1. Click **Locate Field Value** button...... 🔎
   OR
   a. Click **Record**...................... Alt + R
   b. Click **Locate**............................. C
   c. **Value**.. V
2. Select **Field**.................... Alt + F , ↓
3. Enter **Value**................. Alt + V , *value*
4. Set options as desired:
   - **Case sensitive**.................. Alt + C
   - **Exact match**...................... Alt + E
   - **@ and**.............................. Alt + A
   - **Advanced pattern match**.... Alt + P
5. Click **OK**............................ Enter

   Value will be located, or a status bar message will appear, noting that the value was not found.

6. To locate next occurrence of the value:
   Ctrl+A
   a. Click **Record**...................... Alt + R
   b. Click **Locate Next**........................ T
   OR
   Click **Locate Next** button................. 🔎

LOCATE AND REPLACE DATA

Shift+Ctrl+Z

In Form or Table Edit mode only:

1. Click **Record**.......................... Alt + R
2. Click **Locate**................................ C
3. Click **and Replace**........................ R
4. Select **Field**.................... Alt + F , ↓
5. Enter **Value**................. Alt + V , *value*
   to be located.
6. Enter **Replace with**
   value............................ Alt + W , *value*

7. Set options as desired:
   - **Case sensitive**.................. Alt + C
   - **Exact match**...................... Alt + E
   - **@ and**.............................. Alt + A
   - **Advanced pattern match**... Alt + P
8. Click **OK**............................ Enter

   If a match is found the Found a Match dialog box will appear; if not a status bar message will appear, noting that the value was not found.

In the Found a Match dialog box:

1. Select desired action:
   - **Skip this occurrence**......... Alt + S
   - **Change this occurrence**.... Alt + T
   - **Change all occurrences**.... Alt + A
2. Click **OK**............................ Enter

Exercise

13

■ **Sort Records**   ■ **Multiple Sorts**

NOTES

Sort Records

■ The order in which records are entered is frequently not appropriate for locating and updating records. Sorting allows you to rearrange the information so that you can look at it in different ways.

■ Sorting a collection of records can provide the following:

• Data arranged in alphabetical or numerical order.

• Data arranged by size (largest to smallest or smallest to largest).

• Data arranged into groups (for example; all people who live in Washington).

• A method to find duplicate entries.

■ Records are best sorted in Table view. To sort data in Table view, select Sort from the <u>T</u>able menu, or when in Table or Form view you can use <u>T</u>ools, <u>U</u>tilities, <u>S</u>ort. Paradox will not allow you to sort a table if it is also open in Form view. You must close the form first. When you select the Sort command, the Sort Table dialog box will appear. All the fields in the table are listed so that you can add the desired fields to the sort order list.

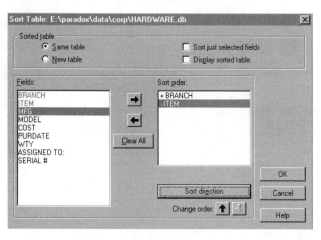

■ The dialog box provides choices as to how the table should be sorted, under the Sorted <u>t</u>able heading:

• **<u>S</u>ame table:** Overwrites the existing order of the table. (Not available for keyed tables.)

• **<u>N</u>ew table:** Creates a new table that you can name, while preserving the original table.

• **Sort just selected fields:** Sorts only the selected fields but all the fields are displayed.

• **Dis<u>p</u>lay sorted table:** If you are sorting to a new table, this selection displays the table after it is sorted.

■ To add a field to the sort order list on the Sort Table dialog box, select the field from the list and click the right arrow button ➡. A field may be removed from the sort order list by selecting the field and clicking the left arrow button ⬅.

■ Tables can be sorted in either ascending or descending order. **Ascending order** goes in alphabetical order from A to Z, or in numerical order from lowest to highest. Dates are sorted from the oldest to the most recent date and time from the earliest to the latest. **Descending order** is the opposite. The Sort dir<u>e</u>ction button will change the order of the selected field. A plus sign (see BRANCH in the illustration) means ascending sort, and a minus sign (see ITEM in the illustration) means descending sort.

Multiple Sorts

■ Several fields (columns) of data may be sorted at one time, and each fields's sort order can be set independently to provide a sort on multiple criteria. The order of the fields listed in the Sort order box may be changed by selecting the field and clicking one of the Change order arrow buttons to move it either up or down in the list.

> *Your company manager at Kitchen Korner has requested lists of information from the HARDWARE table that requires sorting records. In this exercise, you will sort records on one or more fields and create new tables with sorted data.*

EXERCISE DIRECTIONS

1. Open Project Viewer and switch your working directory to \CORP.

2. Open ⌨HARDWARE or 🖫13HARDWA.

3. Use Table, Sort to sort the table in the following way:
   - In ascending order (+) by BRANCH.
   - In ascending (+) order by ITEM.
   - In descending (-) order by COST.

4. Select the Same table option in the Sorted Table section of the dialog box.

5. Click OK to sort.

6. Print a copy of this sort in landscape mode.

7. Sort the table in the following way:
   - In ascending order by ITEM.
   - In ascending order by MFG.
   - In ascending order by BRANCH.

8. Select the New table option (name the table HINVENTORY). Also, select Display sorted table.

9. Print a copy of this sort in landscape mode.

10. Close the table.

11. Switch to Project Viewer and open ⌨HARDFORM or 🖫13HARDFO.

12. Use Tools, Utilities, Sort. Open the HARDWARE table, and sort in ascending order by PURDATE. Select the Same table option.
    - ✓ *You will not be able to complete the sort since the table selected relates to the open form.*

13. Close the form.

14. Switch to Project Viewer and open ⌨SOFTFORM or 🖫13SOFTFO.

15. Use Tools, Utilities, Sort. Open the HARDWARE table, and sort as listed below:
    - In ascending order by PURDATE.
    - In ascending order by BRANCH.
    - In descending order by COST.

    Select the Same table and Display sorted table options.
    - ✓ *Since you were sorting a table that was not in use by an open form, the commands will sort the table.*

16. Print a copy of this sort in landscape mode.

17. Close the form and tables.

KEYSTROKES

SORT RECORDS IN TABLE VIEW

1. Click **Table** .... Alt + A
2. Click **Sort** .... S
3. Select **Sorted table** options:... Alt + T
   - **Same table** .... S
   - **New table** .... N
   - **Sort just selected fields** .... Tab , Space
   - **Display sorted table** .... P
4. Select **Fields** .... Alt + F
5. Click desired field .... ↑ ↓
6. Click right arrow .... →
   to list fields in **Sort order** box.

7. Repeat steps 4-6, as desired.

To change sort direction:

7. Select field in **Sort order** box ..... Alt + O , ↑ ↓
8. Click **Sort direction** .... Alt + E

To change order of sort:

9. Select field .... Alt + O , ↑ ↓
   in **Sort order** box.
10. Click Change order up or down arrow .... ↑ ↓
11. Click **OK** .... Enter

SORT RECORDS IN FORM OR TABLE VIEW

- ✓ *The form view of the table to be sorted cannot be in use when sorting in Table view.*

1. Click **Tools** .... Alt + T
2. Click **Utilities** .... U
3. Click **Sort** .... S
4. Select table to be sorted.
5. Click **OK** .... Enter
6. Follow steps in SORT RECORDS IN A TABLE.

Exercise

14

■ **Filter Fields** ■ **Filter Tables**

NOTES

Filter Fields

■ Sometimes the most efficient way to get information from a table is to isolate, or filter out, only those records that satisfy a specific set of conditions. You can also use filters to view and edit records which meet your criteria and whose fields are arranged in a different order from how they are stored in the table.

■ Records may be filtered using the Field Filter or Filter Tables dialog boxes. To filter fields, right-click a field in a table (or a field object on a form) and select Filter. The Field Filter dialog box will appear requesting the value to be filtered from the selected field. The illustrated setting will filter only those records with a value of Sunset in the Branch field. Filters are case-sensitive, therefore enter the value exactly as it should appear in the table. After filtering, a table can be edited, sorted or printed.

Field Filter Dialog Box

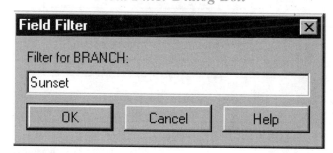

■ To reverse the filter and display all records, right-click the field, click Filter, and remove the value setting.

Filter Tables

■ If you wish to set filter data based on conditions, you must use the Filter Tables dialog box. When you click Table, Filter in a table, or Form, Filter in a form, the Filter Table dialog box will appear as illustrated below.

Filter Tables Dialog Box

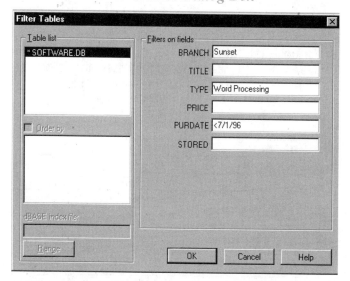

■ In the Filter Tables dialog box, the Table list will display the table being filtered. The Filters on fields section lists the fields in the table and conditions for the filter. Notice in the illustration that the less than sign (<) is being used to indicate a date earlier than 7/1/96. The conditions set in the illustration will result in all records that represent Word Processing software from the Sunset branch purchased before 7/1/96.

■ To remove a filter and display all the records, you must re-open the Filter Tables dialog box and clear the filter settings.

In this exercise, you will add data to the SOFTWARE table and use field and table filters to answer questions about the data in several tables or forms in the CORP database.

EXERCISE DIRECTIONS

1. Open Project Viewer and switch your working directory to \CORP.
2. Open 🖳SOFTFORM or 🖳14SOFTFO.
3. In Form Design mode, enhance the form by changing the background color, and setting field color and frame options.
4. Create a Radio Button field for TYPE using the following field values:
   - Communications
   - Spreadsheet
   - Desktop
   - Integrated
   - Graphics
   - Word Processing
   - Database
   - Other
5. Sort the list.
6. Arrange fields to allow spaces between items. Save the form as SOFTFORM, replacing the original layout.
7. Add the new data listed in the table below to Form view in Edit mode.
8. Use Project Viewer to switch to the 🖳SOFTWARE or open 🖳14SOFTWA.
9. Check that data was entered correctly.
10. Use the Field Filter method to answer the following questions, removing the filter between questions:
    HINT: Right-click the field, select Filter, enter desired value, click OK.

a. How many copies of Graphics software do we have? (TYPE field)
b. Which branches have copies of Trenta? (TITLE field)
c. Which software packages do we have in all branches for Desktop publishing? (TYPE field)
d. What was purchased on 9/15/96? (DATE field)
e. What software is in the Lakeview branch? (BRANCH field)

11. Use the Field Filter to find the item purchased for the Wheatland branch.
12. Edit the PURDATE field and change the date of purchase to 2/15/97.
13. Use the Filter Tables dialog box to find the answers to the following questions, clearing conditions between filters:
    HINT: Click Table, Filter and enter conditions for appropriate fields.

a. Which word processing software titles were purchased before 8/31/96?
b. Which word processing software titles cost less than $300.00?
c. What spreadsheet software titles do we have that cost less than $500?

14. Clear all filters.
15. Close the form and table.

BRANCH	TITLE	TYPE	PRICE	PURDATE	STORED
Peach Tree	BBS	Communications	99.50	11/2/96	A15
Peach Tree	WordEX	Word Processing	259.42	11/5/96	A15
Astro Center	WordEX	Word Processing	259.42	11/15/96	B110
Twin Cities	Trenta	Spreadsheet	202.55	1/30/97	A101
Twin Cities	Harwood	Graphics	287.49	1/30/97	A101
Pacific	Trenta	Spreadsheet	202.55	2/10/97	B235
Bean Town	Word-O	Word Processing	389.95	2/12/97	D230
Pacific	PublishDesk	Desktop	289.95	2/15/97	A135
Sunset	Tulip7	Spreadsheet	389.95	2/16/97	D230

KEYSTROKES

USE FIELD FILTER

In a table:
1. Right-click on field to be filtered.
2. Select **Filter**.
3. Enter value .... *value* to be filtered
4. Click **OK** .... Enter

USE TABLE FILTER

From a Form:
1. Click **Form** .... Alt + M
2. Click **Filter** .... F
3. Select table to filter.
4. Click **Filters on fields** ..... Alt + F , ↓ Select fields to be filtered.
5. Enter filter condition .... *condition*
6. Click **OK** .... Enter

From a Table:
1. Click **Table** .... Alt + A
2. Click **Filter** .... F
3. Click **Table list** .... ↓ and select table, if necessary.
4. Click **Filters on fields** ..... Alt + F , ↓ Select fields to be filtered.
5. Enter filter condition.
6. Click **OK** .... Enter

Exercise 15

■ **Filter Tables**

NOTES

Filter Tables

■ The Filter Tables dialog box discussed in Exercise 14 is used when you have multiple criteria to be defined. You can use comparison operators to narrow, or limit, the resulting record set of a filter. The conditional operators are:

=	Is equal to (The default symbol can be omitted.)
<	Is less than
<=	Is less than or equal to
>	Is greater than
>=	Is greater than or equal to
<>	Is not equal to

■ The ellipsis (..), the wildcard operator discussed in Exercise 12, may also be used with filter conditions. For example, if you wanted to filter out only those members whose last names begin with C, you would enter C.. in the Last name field in the Filters on fields section of the Filter Tables dialog box. To clear a filter, remove the criterion settings.

■ If you have a filtered set of records you can filter it again for records that meet additional filter conditions.

In this exercise, you will add a new table for RECEIPTS to the CUG database. Field filters and table filters with comparison operators will be used to edit and answer questions about the records.

EXERCISE DIRECTIONS

Part I

1. Open Project Viewer and switch your working directory to /CUG.

2. Create a new table using the following field structure.

FIELD NAME	TYPE	SIZE	VALIDITY CHECKS
Last	Alpha	10	Required field
First	Alpha	8	Required field
Date	Date		Required field
Check#	Alpha	5	
Amount	Number		Required field

3. Save the table and name it RECEIPTS.

Part II

4. Open the RECEIPTS table.

5. Enter the data from the list of receipts below.

LAST	FIRST	DATE	CHECK#	AMOUNT
Monitor	Michael	12/5/96	605	15.00
Wave	Bette	12/10/96	1851	25.00
Sort	Stuart	12/11/96	3421	59.95
Zip	Drew	12/18/96	324	30.00
Wyndow	Walter	12/29/96	2345	30.00
Graphic	John	12/30/96	1689	35.00
Web	Warren	1/5/97	8769	25.00
Coller	Jenny	1/8/97	6542	50.00

Part III

6. Open Project Viewer and open ▦MEMBERS or ▦15MEMBER.

7. Use the Filter Tables dialog box to answer the following questions:

   ✓ *Clear the filter between questions.*

   a. Which member, whose last name begins with a C, is a banker?

   b. Which members live in Beverly Hills and are teachers?

8. Filter on Anaheim in the City field.

9. Edit all area codes from (213) to (818). Clear the filter.

10. Filter on North Hollywood in the City field.

11. Edit all area codes from (213) to (817). Clear the filter.

12. Filter on Culver City in the City field.

    ✓ *Since Culver City contains the name of the field, Paradox will return an empty table. You must enclose "Culver City" in quotes.*

13. Edit all area codes from (213) to (214). Clear the filter.

Part IV

14. Open Project Viewer and open ▦CHGFORM or ▦15CHGFOR.

15. Add the data below:

LAST	FIRST	DATE	AMOUNT	CHARGE
Folder	Fred	12/8/96	Dues	25.00
Graphiks	Gene	12/10/96	Dues	25.00
Image	Iggy	12/12/96	Dues	25.00
Image	Iggy	12/12/96	Dinner/ Meeting	30.00
Boot	Barry	12/15/96	Dinner/ Meeting	30.00

16. Open ▦CHARGES or ▦15CHARGE.

17. Use Table Filter to answer the following questions:

    a. What types of charges were greater than $25.00?

    ✓ *Do not clear the filter before answering the next question.*

    b. Which of these charges were made after 12/1/96?

    ✓ *This is subset of a subset.*

18. Print these records.

19. Clear the filters and close all tables and forms.

**Exercise
16**

■ **Summary**

Part I

The owner of Sassy's Sports Togs, a local sports togs manufacturer, has hired you to create an inventory system for her company. The clothing is arranged by style number, type of garment, color, size, and date of manufacture. The firm specializes in carrying a full range of sizes from Petite to Extra Large. In this exercise, you will create a table to keep track of the number of garments on hand. You will then search the table when customers call about availability of stock or when information is needed for production.

EXERCISE DIRECTIONS

1. Use Windows Explorer to create a new subdirectory for the new database:
   • Name the directory SPORTS. Close Windows Explorer.
   • In Paradox, change the working directory to \SPORTS.
2. From the information listed below, create a table with a suitable structure:
   • Use the column headings as field names.
   • Determine field properties from the information shown in the fields. (Inventory values are numeric.)
   • Set the Style, Type, Color, and Datemfg fields as required fields.
3. Save the table as INVEN.
4. Open the table.
5. Create a Quick Form from the table.
6. Enhance the form as desired.
7. Set the Type field for radio buttons and define the following items:
   • Jacket
   • Crew Top
   • T-Shirt
   • Pants
   • Shorts
8. Sort the values and save the form as INVFORM.
9. Enter the data provided in the table below in either Form or Table view.
10. Locate the following information on the table:
    a. What color is style number T1327?
    b. What color Jackets do we have in stock?
    c. What are the style numbers for blue items?
11. Use locate and replace to change the color Blue to Navy.
12. Close the table and form.

STYLE	TYPE	COLOR	P	S	M	L	XL	DATEMFG
J2354	Jacket	Black	4	4	2	4	2	10/18/96
C3276	Crew Top	White	5	6	6	4	3	10/19/96
P4532	Pants	Tan	2	12	12	4	4	10/20/96
S7823	Shorts	Blue	4	15	16	3	14	10/21/96
T1327	T-Shirt	Green	12	17	34	12	12	10/22/96
P4653	Pants	Black	5	7	4	34	12	10/23/96
C3654	Crew Top	Black	3	6	8	8	8	10/28/96
J2543	Jacket	White	3	3	5	5	5	10/29/96
S7932	Shorts	Black	5	4	4	6	8	10/30/96
T1421	T-Shirt	White	10	15	15	14	18	10/31/96
P4821	Pants	Blue	13	32	30	26	30	11/6/96
C3911	Crew Top	Blue	23	32	26	36	32	11/12/96
S7214	Shorts	Blue	3	6	33	23	17	11/18/96
P4276	Pants	White	12	18	20	18	16	11/21/96
J2399	Jacket	Blue	17	21	26	21	18	11/25/96

Part II

> *Sally Jogger, your boss at Sassy's Sports Boutique, has asked you to enter additional data into the computer inventory you created earlier, (INVEN). In addition, she would like you to add a new field and then provide lists from sorted or filtered data to respond to various questions*

EXERCISE DIRECTIONS

1. Open Project Viewer and switch your working directory to \SPORTS.

2. Open ▤INVEN or ▯16BINVEN.

3. Restructure INVEN to add the PRICE numeric field after the COLOR field.

4. Add the highlighted information to the Price field as indicated for existing data, and add the new data listed below.

STYLE	TYPE	COLOR	PRICE	P	S	M	L	XL	DATEMFG
J2354	Jacket	Black	35.50	4	4	2	4	2	10/18/96
C3276	Crew Top	White	15.75	5	6	6	4	3	10/19/96
P4532	Pants	Tan	21.75	2	12	12	4	4	10/20/96
S7823	Shorts	Navy	13.65	4	15	16	3	14	10/21/96
T1327	T-Shirt	Green	10.25	12	17	34	12	12	10/22/96
P4653	Pants	Black	22.75	5	7	4	34	12	10/23/96
C3654	Crew Top	Black	15.25	3	6	8	8	8	10/28/96
J2543	Jacket	White	34.25	3	3	5	5	5	10/29/96
S7932	Shorts	Black	12.75	5	4	4	6	8	10/30/96
T1421	T-Shirt	White	10.50	10	15	15	14	18	10/31/96
P4821	Pants	Navy	21.50	13	32	30	26	30	11/6/96
C3911	Crew Top	Navy	14.75	23	32	26	36	32	11/12/96
S7214	Shorts	Navy	13.15	3	6	33	23	17	11/18/96
P4276	Pants	White	22.35	12	18	20	18	16	11/21/96
J2399	Jacket	Blue	32.25	17	21	26	21	18	11/25/96
C3276	Crew Top	Green	15.75	9	10	15	20	25	11/27/96
T1421	T-Shirt	Red	10.50	8	12	15	22	30	11/29/96
S7823	Shorts	Red	13.65	8	10	12	18	20	12/1/96
P4276	Pants	Navy	22.35	10	12	15	18	22	12/3/96
J2543	Jackets	Black	34.25	8	8	8	8	10	12/5/96
C3911	Crew Top	Red	14.75	8	8	10	12	16	12/6/96
C3654	Crew Top	Red	15.25	10	10	15	20	25	12/9/96
T1327	T-Shirt	Navy	10.25	12	15	15	20	23	12/12/96
S7214	Shorts	Black	13.15	5	8	10	12	10	12/14/96
P4532	Pants	Green	21.75	10	15	15	20	20	12/16/96

5. The following item is no longer in stock. Delete the record.
   - P4532 Tan Pants

6. Sort the records in each of the following ways and answer the questions:

   a. In ascending order by COLOR and ascending order by PRICE within each color:
      - What is the lowest priced style for a black jacket?

   b. In ascending order by TYPE and descending order by PRICE:
      - How much is the most expensive crew top?

   c. In ascending order by COLOR, in ascending order by TYPE, and ascending order by STYLE:
      - Which colors do we have stock in at this time? Which color is most prevalent?

7. Print a copy of the last sort in landscape mode.

8. Use table or field filters to answer the following questions:

   a. Which Shorts styles and colors are presently in stock?

   b. Which styles and types are White and have more than ten items in Large and Extra Large?

   c. What is the style number for a Petite Navy Crew Top of which five or more are in stock?

   d. Which items are black and were manufactured before 10/25/97?

9. Print one copy of the last filtered list in landscape mode.

10. Remove all filters and print one copy of the table in landscape orientation.

11. Close the table.

Exercise

17

■ **Create a Query** ■ **Save a Query**

NOTES

Create a Query

■ A **query** can utilize advanced techniques to isolate a group of records, determine which fields to include and in what order, calculate data, and use data from more than one table. Queries are used to create datasets that answer a question. They can be saved, printed, and used as the basis for a form or report.

■ A query is created by selecting New, Query from the File menu or by right-clicking the Queries icon in Project Viewer and selecting New. The Select File dialog box displays, as illustrated below, and lists the database tables in the current working directory that may be used for the query. You can also open tables from a different directory, if desired. The directory can be changed and the desired database selected. Select the tables to be included in the query and click Open.

Select File Dialog Box

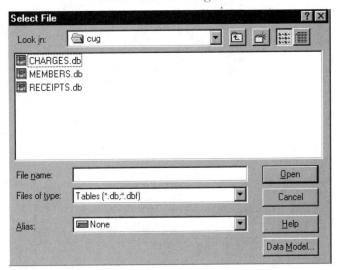

■ After the table(s) are selected and the Select File dialog box is closed, the Query form appears in a window.

■ Paradox uses a method called **query by example** (QBE) to ask questions about the data. You give Paradox an example of the result you want, and Paradox gives you the result in a temporary table named Answer in your PRIVATE directory.

Query Form

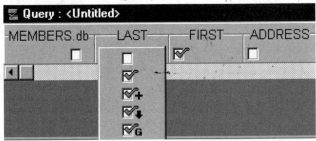

■ On the Query form, there is a check box under each field, and also under the table name which can be checked to include all the fields in the query. When you right-click the check box, you see the different types of checks you can use. You check the boxes under the fields to tell Paradox which fields to include in the Answer table by either clicking with the mouse or by pressing F6 or Shift+F6.

■ The checks are used as follows:

☑ **Check:** shows all unique values for a field in ascending order.

☑+ **CheckPlus:** shows all values in a field, including duplicates, without sorting, as they appeared in the table. A Check Plus will override any Check or CheckDescending selections.

CheckDescending: shows unique values sorted in descending order.

GroupBy: specifies a group of records to use in a query. This field will not appear in the answer table.

An empty check box clears any check.

- To see the results of your Query Design, use the Run option from the Query menu, press F8, or click the Run Query button ⚡ on the Toolbar. In the query design shown above we checked the LAST, FIRST, PHONE, and PROF. fields. The sorted answer table appears below.

Answer Table

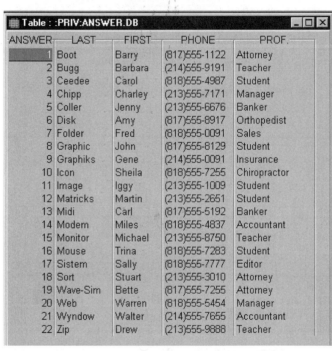

- If you wish to select records with a specific item in a field, you can enter the criterion in the space after the check box. The box will expand to fit the criterion. You can use comparison operators (< > >= etc.), or merely enter the item you wish to select from the field. The criterion must be in the same case and spelled exactly the same as the data in the table to filter correctly. Notice, in the illustration below, that the Charge field has a criterion of Dues, but it is not checked. This will result in an Answer table with LAST, FIRST, and DATE fields only for records with Dues in the CHARGES field.

Query Form

Save a Query

- Save the query by either selecting Save, or Save As from the File menu, or Close without saving. Query names can contain a maximum of 64 characters including spaces. The query design will be saved using the name you specify with a **.qbe** extension.

The California Users Group would like to query its data and develop answer sets to be used for telephoning members or calling segments of the membership list. The query form window will be used with various criteria and checks to query the table.

EXERCISE DIRECTIONS

1. Open Project Viewer and switch your working directory to \CUG.

2. From Project Viewer, right-click on Queries, then click New.

3. In the Select File dialog box, open MEMBERS.db or 17MEMBER.db, then choose OK.

4. Check the LAST, FIRST, PHONE, and PROF. fields to tell Paradox to display only those fields in the Answer table.

5. Click the Run Query button on the Toolbar to see the results in the Answer Table. Notice the table is sorted by the data in the LAST field (Last name).

6. Print a copy of the list of members and their telephone numbers.

7. Close the Answer table.

8. Modify the query to tell Paradox to list only students in the Answer table. Leave the check in the field and type Student in the PROF. field.

9. Run the query.

10. Examine the Answer table, then close it.

11. Save the query as STUDENT.qbe. Close the query.

12. Define a new query for the MEMBERS table, which selects the Last, First, and Phone fields for members who live in Anaheim. Do not include the City field in the Answer table.

    Hint: *Enter Anaheim in the City field but do not check the field.*

13. Run the query. Print a copy of the answer table. Close the table.

14. Save the query as ANAHEIM.qbe. Close the query.

15. Define a new query on the 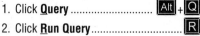CHARGES.db table or 17CHARGES.db.

16. Select the fields with appropriate checks to display all records in the DATE, AMOUNT and CHARGE fields, sorted so that the DATE and AMOUNT fields display in descending order.

17. Run the query. Print a copy of the answer table. Close the table.

18. Modify the query as follows:

    • Produce a listing of LAST, FIRST, and DATE fields only for Dues charges.

    • The CHARGE and AMOUNT fields should not be displayed.

19. Run the query. View and close the table.

20. Save the query as DUES.qbe.

21. Close all tables and queries.

KEYSTROKES

CREATE A QUERY

1. From Project Viewer:

   a. Select and right-click **Queries**.

   b. Click **New** .... N

   OR

   From menu:

   a. Click **File** .... Alt + F

   b. Click **New** .... N

   c. Click **Query** .... Q

2. In Select File dialog box, Select table(s) to be included. (Hold **Ctrl** key to select more than one table.)

3. In Query Form window, Check fields to be included in the query.

4. To set specific query selections, Right-click check box and make selection (or press **Shift+F6** to cycle through options):

   ☑ **Check** shows all unique values for that field in ascending order.

   ☑+ **CheckPlus** shows all values in a field without sorting, as they appeared in the table. A CheckPlus will override any Check or CheckDescending selections.

   ☑↓ **CheckDescending** shows unique values sorted in descending order.

   ☑G **GroupBy** specifies a group of records to use in a query. This field will not appear in the answer table.

   An empty check box clears any check.

5. To enter field values:

   a. Click in field to right of check box.

   b. Type value.

RUN QUERY

F8

If Query is open:

Click Run Query button ....

OR

1. Click **Query** .... Alt + Q

2. Click **Run Query** .... R

SAVE QUERY

1. Click **File** .... Alt + F

2. Click **Save** .... S

   OR

   Click **Save As** (if new) .... A

3. Enter filename.

4. Click **OK** .... Enter

OPEN QUERY

1. Click on **Queries** icon in Project Viewer.

2. Right-click on name of query.

3. Select **Run Query** .... R

   OR

   Double-click name of query.

Exercise 18

■ **Open a Query** ■ **Rename a Query** ■ **Field Checks**
■ **Change Field Names** ■ **Query Properties**

NOTES

Open a Query

■ To open an existing query, click Queries in Project Viewer and double-click the query you wish to open, then select <u>O</u>pen Query. Or, click <u>F</u>ile, <u>O</u>pen, Query. Or, click the Open Query button 📖 on the Toolbar. A query may be opened, changed and resaved, or saved as a new query.

Rename a Query

■ If you wish to rename a query, right-click the query in the Queries section of Project Viewer, select <u>R</u>ename and enter the new query name. Note the illustration below of the menu that appears when a query name is right-clicked. You can use this menu to run, open, copy, delete, or rename a query.

Query Quick Menu

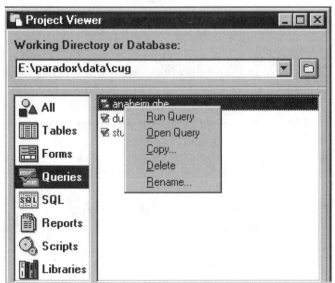

Field Checks

■ You can clear a check in a query by clicking on the check, or by pressing F6. If you wish to select or remove all the checks in a table, click on the check box at the left edge of the query form, underneath the table name.

Change Field Names

■ When you check fields to be part of an answer table, the field names in the answer table are taken from the original table. If you wish to change the name of a field in the answer table (for printing purposes, for example), you can indicate the new name in the query. In the field you wish to change in the answer table, enter AS followed by the new field name. See the illustration below, where the City field will appear AS Store Location. This setting will not change the field name in the table, however.

Query Form

Query Properties

■ If you wish to view the answer table with a different layout, you may move columns to rearrange data. You may also sort fields to present information as desired. With a query open, click <u>Q</u>uery, <u>P</u>roperties to display the Query Properties dialog box. The Structure tab, illustrated on the following page, allows you to rearrange fields in the answer table. The field order determines the emphasis of the sort order in the answer table. For example, you might want to place the ST field first for a listing of stores by state.

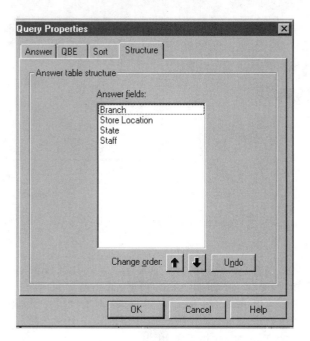

illustration of the Sort tab of the Query Properties dialog box below:

- You can set sort properties, or review settings made with check marks, by selecting the Sort tab of the Query Properties dialog box. Note the

Your manager at Kitchen Korner has many questions about the branch stores and their computer hardware. You can provide the answers using queries.

EXERCISE DIRECTIONS

1. Open Project Viewer and switch your working directory to \CORP.

2. Create a new query, using the STORES.db table or 18STORES.db, to develop a listing of stores with evening hours sorted by state:

   a. Select all fields, by clicking the table name box.

   b. Enter settings to change field names as follows:

   c. City field   AS Store Location

   d. ST field   AS State

   e. Enter a criteria to display only stores with evening hours.

      HINT: In Eve field, enter Yes.

   f. Open the Query Properties dialog box. Select the Sort tab and double-click on the ST field in the Fields list box.

   g. Run the query.

3. Print a copy of this table. Close the Answer table.

4. Save the query as EVEHOURS.qbe.

5. Create a new query to locate stores that have sales less than $350,000, using the STORES table. *Do not use dollar ($) or comma (,) symbols in the SALES criteria area.*

   The query should include the Branch, City, Sales and Staff fields.

6. Run the query and print a copy of the answer table.

7. Close the table and save the query design as Poor Performers.

8. Close the query design. Rename the Poor Performers query, Sales Under $350K.

9. Open the appropriate query, or create a new one, to answer each of the following questions.

 ✓   *Do not save the queries you create to answer these questions.*

   a. What stores are located in Atlanta?
   b. Which stores have sold more than $400,000 worth of merchandise?
   c. Which stores have sold more than $400,000 and are open evenings?
   d. Which stores have sold more than $400,000 and have more than 14 employees?
   e. What stores are located in CA (California)?

10. Clear the query design.

11. Query ⌨HARDWARE.db or 🖫18HARDWA.db to display a list of computers:

   a. Include BRANCH, MFG., MODEL, COST, PURDATE, and WTY.
   b. Do not display the ITEM field, but enter a criterion for Computer items.
   c. Change field names as follows:
      • PURDATE field name to DATE OF PURCHASE.
      • MFG. field name to MANUFACTURER.
   d. Run the query and adjust column width, as necessary.

12. Print the table and then close the answer table.

13. Save the query as COMPINVENTORY.

14. Close all database objects.

KEYSTROKES

OPEN QUERY

In Project Viewer:

   a. Click **Queries**.
   b. Right-click name of query.
   c. Select **Open Query**.
   OR
   Double-click query to open.

From the Toolbar:

• Click **Open Query** button...................... 🖳

RENAME QUERY

In Project Viewer:

1. Click **Queries**.
2. Right-click query to rename.
3. Select **Rename** .... R
4. Enter new query name.
5. Click **Rename** .... Enter

SET SORT AND TABLE STRUCTURE QUERY PROPERTIES

In a Query Form window:

1. Click **Query**........................... Alt + Q
2. Click **Properties** .... P
3. Select desired tab................. Ctrl + Tab
4. Sort tab:
   a. Click **Answer fields** .... Alt + F
   b. Select field........................ ↓
   c. Click right arrow.
   d. Add fields to **Sort order** as desired.

To Change order of sort:

   a. Select field in **Sort order** list box.
   b. Click **Change order**............. Alt + R
   c. Click up or down arrow.
   d. Click **OK**........................ Enter
5. Structure tab:
   a. Click **Answer fields**............ Alt + F
   b. Select field........................ ↓
      in **Fields** list box
   c. Click **Change order**............ Alt + R
   d. Click up or down arrow.
   e. Click **OK**......................... Enter

Exercise 19

- **Create Queries Using Two Tables**
- **Summary Operators**

NOTES

Create Queries Using Two Tables

- You may wish to combine data from two tables into one answer table. When you query more than one table, you must join the tables by a common field. You can then select fields from each table as desired. The joined fields are fields in each table that contain the same information. For example, the BRANCH field that appears in the STORES and HARDWARE tables can be used to join these two tables.

- When you create a query, you can add additional tables to the query design by clicking the Add Table button ▦ on the Toolbar, by selecting Add table from the Edit menu, or by selecting multiple tables in the Select File dialog box. The new table will be added to the design.

- The joined fields do not have to have the same field name, but the field types must be compatible. You can join up to 24 tables in a single query. The joining of fields is called **creating an example element**. To join fields, click the Join Tables button ▦ and then click in the appropriate field of each table to be joined. Paradox will enter an example element (highlighted with a different color) to join the tables, as illustrated below:

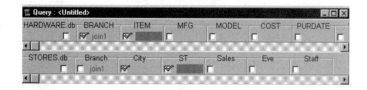

- Once you join the tables, you can select fields and set criteria and properties, as with a single-table query.

Summary Operators

- You can do simple and complex calculations with data by using summary operators. A **summary operator** performs a calculation on a group of records. For example, in the query illustrated below, you are calculating the total price of each type of software. The field you wish to group, TYPE, is checked and CALC SUM is entered in PRICE, the field to be totaled. The answer table illustrated shows each type of software and the total price paid for each group. You can use AVERAGE, MAX, MIN, and COUNT in the same manner. Paradox creates a new column for the calculation result and names it Sum of PRICE by default. You can change this name by following the summary operator with "AS (desired new field name)."

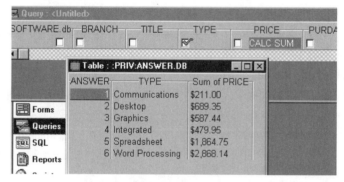

- If you do not group data by checking a field, but enter a summary operator instead, you will display the AVERAGE, MAX, MIN, SUM, or COUNT for all the records. In the case of the COUNT operator, if you wish to count all records you must enter CALC COUNT ALL in order to count all records including duplicates; otherwise, you will get a count of unique records.

- You may enter summary operators in upper- or lowercase letters.

In this exercise, you will create a query that combines data from two tables and print the results. In addition, you will use summary operators to develop totals and averages for our software inventory.

EXERCISE DIRECTIONS

1. Open Project Viewer and switch your working directory \CORP.
2. Create a new query using the STORES.db table or 19STORES.db.
3. Click the Add Table button and add the HARDWARE.db table or 19HARDWA.db.
4. The query result should be a list of computers owned by branches, which includes the city and state location of the branch:
   a. Use Join Tables button to join the tables on the Branch field.
   b. Check the CITY, ST, MODEL, COST, PURDATE, ASSIGNED TO, SERIAL # fields.
   c. Change field names as follows:
   d. PURDATE AS Date of Purchase
      ST AS State
   e. In the Item field, set a criterion for Computer.
   f. Use Query Properties to place State in the first position on the Structure tab.
   g. Run the query.
   h. Adjust column width, as necessary.
5. Set to print in landscape mode, and print one copy of the answer table.
6. Close the answer table and save the query as COMPBYSTATE.
7. Close the query.
8. Create a new query using the SOFTWARE.db table or 19SOFTWA.db.
9. The query result should summarize the types of software and total paid for each type of software.
   a. Check Type field.

b. Enter summary operator, CALC SUM, in the Price column. (Do not check the column.)
   ✓ To rename the field in the Answer table, type CALC SUM AS Total Cost.
   c. Run the query.
   d. Adjust column width, as necessary.
10. Print answer table.
11. Close the answer table.
12. Save the query as SOFTWARE TYPES.
13. Change the summary operator to CALC AVERAGE, CALC MAX, CALC MIN, or CALC COUNT, and run the query to answer the following questions:
   a. What is the average cost of Word Processing software?
   b. What is the average cost of Desktop Publishing software?
   c. What is the highest price we paid for Word Processing software?
   d. What is the lowest price we paid for Word Processing software?
   e. How many total spreadsheet software packages do we have?
14. Close the answer table.
15. Modify the query design to find the total value of all software.
   HINT: Do not check the Item field.
   What is the total value of all our software?
16. Close the answer table and query without saving changes.
17. Close all database objects.

KEYSTROKES

ADD ADDITIIONAL TABLE TO QUERY

In Query Form window:

1. Click **Add Table** button ....
2. Select **Table**.
3. Click **Open**.
   OR
   Double-click table name.

JOIN TABLES FOR QUERY

In Query design:

1. Click **Join Table** button ....
2. Click field in first table.
3. Click similar field in second table.

ENTER SUMMARY OPERATORS

In Query Form window:

1. Check field to group.
2. Enter
   CALC SUM
   CALC AVERAGE
   CALC MIN
   CALC COUNT
   in field to be calculated.

Exercise

20

■ **Summary**

> *Sassy's Sports Boutique will be adding a SALES table to its database. You will use queries to answer questions about the data in both tables, and you will use summary operators to gather information about inventory and sales.*

EXERCISE DIRECTIONS

Part I

1. Open Project Viewer and switch your working directory to \SPORTS.

2. Create a new table with the fields and data as listed below. Make the STYLE field a required field and set the size fields to be numeric. Save the table as SALES.

DATE	STYLE	P	S	M	L	XL	CUSTOMER
10/30/96	C3654	3	6	8	8	8	JRZ145
10/30/96	S7214	3	6	8	8	8	JRZ145
10/31/96	T1327	5	10	10	10	10	RKD456
10/31/96	C3276	5	6	6	4	3	RKD456
11/1/96	T1421	5	10	10	10	12	TYD695
11/1/96	S7932	5	4	4	6	8	TYD695

Part II

3. Create a new query using the INVEN.db table or 20INVEN.db.
   a. Use the STYLE, COLOR, P, S, M, L, XL, and PRICE fields.
   b. Enter a criterion in the Type field for Jacket.
   c. Change STYLE to STYLE NO.
   d. Run the query.
   e. Adjust column widths, if necessary.

4. Print one copy of the answer table.

5. Close the answer table and save the query as JACKETSMFD.

Part III

6. Create queries to answer the questions below. Do not save the queries or the answer tables.
   a. How many Red Crew Tops do we have in XL in all styles?
   b. How many Navy Shorts do we have in XL and L in all styles?
   c. What types of items do we carry in Red that cost less than $14.00?
   d. In which style do we have the highest number of Petite Shorts?
   e. In which style do we have the highest number of XL Crew Tops?
   f. In which style do we have the highest number of M Red items?
   g. What are the styles of Petite T-Shirts that are available?
   h. In which style number do we have the most Green Medium items?
   i. Which style Crew Top has the lowest number of P items on hand?
   j. What is the highest Jacket price?

7. Create a new query to determine the type, price, size, and colors of items sold, using the INVEN table or 20INVEN.
   a. Add a table to the query. Add the SALES table.
   b. Join the Style fields in both tables.
   c. Check the Type, Color, Price fields in the INVEN table.
   d. Check the P, S, M, L, XL, Customer fields in the SALES table.
   e. Change Customer to Customer No.
   f. Run the query.
   g. Adjust column widths, if necessary.

8. Print a copy in landscape.

9. Save the query as SALETYPE.

10. Close all database objects

Exercise 21

■ **Reports** ■ **Create Reports with Report Expert** ■ **Modify a Report**
■ **Save a Report** ■ **Print a Report**

NOTES

Reports

■ **Reports** allow you to customize the way you present or print data. You can sort and group records, calculate totals, and layout your data in many different ways. Reports can be based on tables, forms, or queries.

■ Reports can include:

- Report headers and footers.
- Page headers and footers.
- Summary statistics.
- Objects imported from other sources (such as graphics).

■ You can design a report from scratch in the Report Design window (see the illustration below), which looks and behaves very much like the Form Design window, or you can let Paradox design a report for you by using the Report Expert. Once the report is designed, it can be modified in Report Design mode.

Report Design Mode

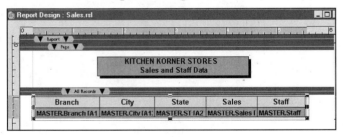

Create Reports with Report Expert

■ To begin creating a report with the Report Expert:

1. Right-click on the Reports icon in the Project Viewer, and select <u>N</u>ew.

2. Select Report <u>E</u>xpert.

3. Respond to a series of questions on eight screens to select:

- How many tables to include.
- How many records per page (table or form layout).
- Which table(s) to include (tables or queries can be included).
- Which fields to display.
- The report output (page size, printer and orientation).
- Which style sheet is to be used for the report.
- Whether to include a title, page numbers, headers, footers, etc.
- The name of the report, and whether you want to run the report, print it, or open it in Report Design mode for modification.

■ Click <u>D</u>o it! on the final Report Export screen and a report is generated. Note the illustration of a report below.

Example of a Report

KITCHEN KORNER STORES Sales and Staff Data				
Branch	City	State	Sales	Staff
Big Apple	New York	NY	789,300.00	20.00
Pacific	Los Angeles	CA	685,400.00	14.00
Sunset	San Francisco	CA	876,988.00	13.00
Lakeview	Chicago	IL	755,420.00	15.00
Peach Tree	Atlanta	GA	457,800.00	16.00
Bean Town	Boston	MA	682,450.00	16.00
Astro Center	Houston	TX	541,000.00	12.00

■ You can also access the Report Expert by clicking the Experts button ⚲ , while in Table or Form view, selecting Report from the Paradox Experts dialog box that appears, and then clicking the <u>R</u>un Expert button. Note the illustration of the Paradox Expert dialog box below.

Paradox Experts Dialog Box

Modify a Report

■ You can modify the layout of a report by switching to Report Design mode. Click the Design Report button 📉 on the Toolbar while the report is running.

■ You may want to move items to adjust alignment of titles and column headings. To move a report detail item, click and hold down the mouse button within the item's boundary, and drag the item to the desired position. The rulers at the top and left side of the screen can be used to help position the item.

■ You can view changes to the report at any time by clicking the Run Report button on the Toolbar 🗲 .

Save a Report

■ Reports are saved and named by selecting the <u>S</u>ave (if new) or Save <u>A</u>s option from the <u>F</u>ile menu, while in Report Design mode. Or, you may name the report on the last screen of the Report Expert. Click the Reports icon in Project Viewer to display a list of saved reports. Your new report will appear here with an **.RSL** extension.

Print a Report

■ You can print an open report by selecting <u>P</u>rint from the <u>F</u>ile menu, or by clicking the Print button on the Toolbar. You may have to change the printer setup to landscape mode, even if you specified landscape in Report Expert, since the default orientation is determined by the printer setup feature.

EXERCISE DIRECTIONS

1. Open Project Viewer and switch your working directory to \CORP.

2. Right-click Reports and select New.

3. Click on Report Expert.

4. In step 1 of the Report Expert, choose Data from one table, then click Next.

5. In step 2, select Multiple records per page, with the data displayed in a table, then click Next.

6. In step 3, select STORES.DB or open 21STORES.DB, then click Next.

7. In step 4, select Branch, City, ST, Sales and Staff fields, then click Next.

8. In step 5, accept defaults to print to printer on letter paper in portrait orientation, then click Next.

9. In step 6, select the Ocean Objects style, then click Next.

10. In step 7, click the Title Text box and enter KITCHEN KORNER STORES, Sales and Staff Data, as the title, then click Next.

11. In step 8, name the report SALES. Leave the default setting to Run the report and show you the data onscreen selection. Click Do it!

12. Click the Report Design button to view the report design.

13. Select the title text box and move it so that it begins at the 1½ inch mark on the horizontal ruler.

14. Click in the title text box after the word STORES, and press Enter to move Sales and Staff Data to a new line.

    ✓ *You may have to click several times on this text box to select it.*

15. Select the column title ST and change it to State.

16. Save the report design.

17. Click the Run Report button on the Toolbar.

18. Print the report.

19. Close the report.

KEYSTROKES

OPEN REPORT EXPERT

From Project Viewer:

1. Right-click **Reports**.
2. Click **New** .... N
3. Click **Report Expert** .... E

From Table or Form view:

1. Click **Experts** Button .... [icon]
2. Click Report .... [↓]
3. Click **Run Expert** .... Alt + R

CREATE REPORT WITH REPORT EXPERT

1. Follow one of the steps above to open Report Export.
2. Step 1:
   - Click **Data from one table** .. Alt + O
   OR
   Click **Data from two tables** .... Alt + T
   - Click **Next** .... Alt + N
3. Step 2:
   - Click **one record per page** .. Alt + O
     with the data displayed in a list.
   OR
   Select **Multiple records** .... Alt + M
   per page, with the data displayed in a table.
   OR
   Click **Next** .... Alt + N
   to select one record per page.
4. Step 3:
   - Select table or query .... [↓]
     to use for report.
   - Click **Next** .... Alt + N

5. Step 4:
   - Select **Available fields** .... Alt + A , [↓] [↑]
   - To display each field, click .... [>]
   - To select all fields, click .... [>>]
   - Click **Next** .... Alt + N
6. Step 5:
   - Select Target Output:
   Video Screen .... Alt + I
   OR
   Printer .... Alt + R
   - Select **Available page sizes** . Alt + S , [↓]
   - Select page size .... [↓]
   - Select **Available printers** ...... Alt + V , [↓]
   - Select printer .... [↓]
   - Click **Next** .... Alt + N
7. Step 6:
   - Select style sheet .... [↓]
   - Click **Next** .... Alt + N
8. Step 7:
   - If desired, click **Title text** .... Alt + X
   - Enter title .... [↓] , *title*
   - If desired,
     click **Page Numbers** tab ..... Alt + P
   - Click **None** .... Alt + O
   OR
   Page N .... Alt + G
   OR
   Page N of M .... Alt + M
   - If desired,
     click **Date/Time** tab .... Alt + D
   - Click **Display date** .... Alt + A
   OR
   Click **Display time** .... Alt + Y
   - Click **Next** .... Alt + N
   ✓ *These choices also have an option for L, C or R for placement in the header or footer.*

9. Step 8:
   - Enter report name.... Alt + T , *name*
   - Click **Run the report and show you the data onscreen** .... Alt + U
   OR
   Click **Print the Report** .... Alt + P
   OR
   Click **Open the report in a design window so you can modify it** .... Alt + O
   - Click **Do it!** .... Alt + D

SWITCH TO REPORT DESIGN

While running a report:

Click Design button .... [icon]

SWITCH TO RUN REPORT

While designing a report:

Click Run Report button .... [icon]

MODIFY REPORT

In Report Design window:

1. Click on design item (eg. text box, table frame, etc.).
2. Drag to desired position.

SAVE REPORT

In Report Design window:

1. Click **File** .... Alt + F
2. Click **Save As** .... A
3. Name report.
4. Click **Save** .... Enter

PRINT REPORT

1. Click **File** .... Alt + F
2. Click **Print** .... P
3. Click **OK** .... Enter

Exercise

22

- ■ **Modify a Report** ■ **Change Object Properties**
- ■ **Header and Footer Settings**

NOTES

Modify A Report

- ■ The Report Export simplifies the process of creating basic reports. However, the results may sometimes yield unwanted items, exclude desired items, or provide insufficient formatting. To solve these problems, all aspects of a report can be changed in the Report Design window.

- ■ The Report Design window consists of bands that represent the parts of a report. The parts of a report are the Report, Page, and Record bands, as illustrated below. Every band has a top and bottom (header and footer). The Group band, an optional band, will be discussed in Exercise 23. To change the size of a band, click on the boundary line to first select the band. You will know it is selected when it changes color. Move the mouse toward the top of the selected

band until you see a double-headed arrow, click on the resizing handles, then drag up or down. You may have to repeat this adjustment a number of times.

- ■ The items or objects on a report may be edited by clicking on the object to select it and then making the necessary changes. For example, if you wish to change a field name heading for a report, you can select it and edit the text to become the column heading you desire. To delete an object, click on it, and when the resizing handles appear, press the Del key. If the column headings of a report are changed, the size of the report frame may have to be adjusted to fit all the fields in the report. Select the last field and use the sizing handles to adjust the size of the report frame.

Report Design Window

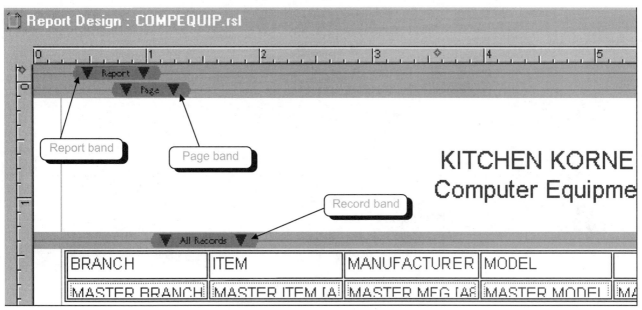

Change Object Properties

■ To change an object's font, font size, alignment, color, border, or shading, you must right-click the object and select Properties. The Properties dialog box, with tabs appropriate to the object selected, will appear. Note, for example, the illustration of the Text Properties dialog box that appears when a page header text object is right-clicked.

Text Properties Dialog Box

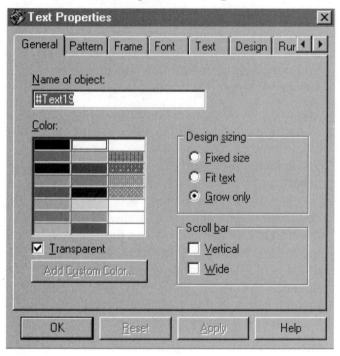

■ If you wish to change the properties of a group of objects at once; select the first object and hold down the Shift key while selecting the other items. Right-click and set the desired properties. All selected objects will receive the selected properties.

Header and Footer Settings

■ On step 7 of the Report Expert, you may set headers and footers that include the title, page numbers, and date and/or time stamp(s). Use the Page Numbers and Date/Time tabs to place page numbers, or the date and/or time, in a specific location on the header or footer. Note the illustration below of the Step 7 screen.

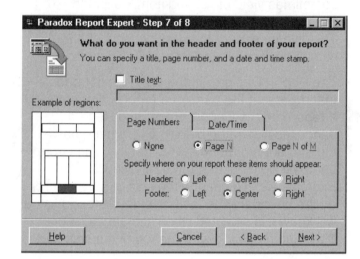

KEYSTROKES

CHANGE OBJECT PROPERTIES
In Report Design:
1. Right-click item to be changed.
2. Select **Properties**............................ R
3. Select appropriate tab.
4. Make desired changes.
5. Click **OK**.................................... Enter

EXERCISE DIRECTIONS

1. Open Project Viewer and switch your working directory to \CORP.

2. Right-click Reports, and then choose New.

3. Create a new report using the Report Expert as follows:
   a. Select data from one table and show multiple``ecords per page.
   b. Select HARDWARE.DB as the table for the report, or use 22HARDWA.DB.
   c. Do not display the WTY. field.
   d. Set the target output for the printer in landscape mode.
   e. Select the Framed Objects style sheet.
   f. Title the report KITCHEN KORNER STORES.
   g. Name the report, COMPEQUIP.
   h. Click Do it!

4. Switch to Report Design window.

5. Change Record Headers:
   MFG. to MANUFACTURER
   PURDATE to PURCHASED

6. Check the last field and adjust the size of the table frame, if necessary, to fit the whole field on the report.

7. Add the subtitle, Computer Equipment Inventory, to the title text box.

8. Select the title text box. Change properties of the title font size to 16 point.

9. Adjust the title text box so that the title and subtitle fit on two lines.

10. Move the title box so that the left edge of the box is lined up with the three inch mark on the horizontal ruler.

11. Select the text for each column heading (except Cost) by pressing the Shift key between selections. Right-click and set Alignment to Left on the Text tab of the Text Properties dialog box.

12. Right-align the text for the Cost column heading.

13. Save the report design.

14. Run the report.

15. Change the printer setup to landscape mode and print the report.

16. Create a new report using the SOFTWARE.DB as the table for the report, or use 22SOFTWA.DB. Show multiple records per page, display all fields, print in landscape mode, select the Shaded objects style, and title the report, KITCHEN KORNER STORES, Software Inventory. Set the date to display at the center of the footer, and name the report SOFTINVEN.

17. Change PURDATE column heading to PURCHASED.

18. Adjust the size of the table frame to fit the last field.

19. Set the title text box font to 16 point, and adjust it to display as a two-line title.

20. Center the title over the records.

21. Align column heading text to match data alignment.

22. Set format of Price field for Windows $ on the Format tab of the Properties dialog box.

23. Select all the shaded areas on the report and change the color property to light blue.

24. Save the report design.

25. Run the report.

26. Print a copy in landscape mode.

27. Close all database objects.

Exercise

23

■ **Add Group Band**   ■ **Add Summary Field**

NOTES

Add Group Band

■ As illustrated in Exercise 22, a report is divided into bands – the Report, Page, and Record bands. In the previous two exercises, reports were produced that listed the data as it appeared in the table. By grouping records and adding summary data you can make the report information more useful. For example, if you were producing a list of members, it might be beneficial to group the members by city to determine the number of members in each location.

■ To add a group band, click <u>R</u>eport, Add Group <u>B</u>and, or click the Add Group Band button 🔳 on the Toolbar, in Report Design mode. The Define Group dialog box, illustrated right, appears.

Define Group Dialog Box

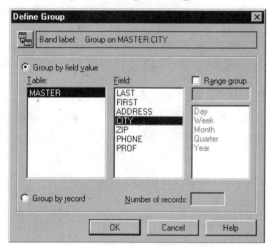

■ To produce a membership list by city, you would select CITY as the group field. A new group band will be added to the report design with the City field added to the band, as shown in the second illustration. When a field is added to a group band, it is not automatically removed from the record band. The CITY field must be deleted from the record area to eliminate duplication of data.

Report Design Window

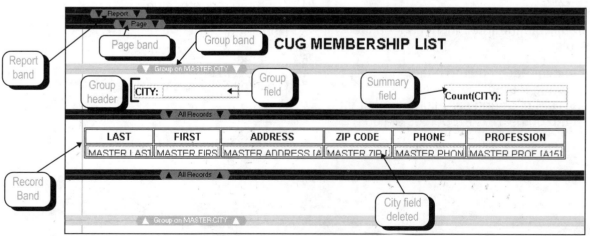

Add Summary Field

■ To further improve the report, you can add a subtotal or summary field for the group to the design. You can add a field to a group band by first clicking the Field Tool button 🔲 and then clicking in the new group band. When you add a field, the Paradox Field Expert will open (if Experts are enabled) to assist you in defining the field. To define the field on your own, cancel the Field Expert and right-click the new field. Then, select Define Field to open the Define Field Object dialog box. Select the field to be summarized and the desired summary operator from the respective drop-down lists. The Define Field Object dialog box and an example of the grouped report is illustrated below.

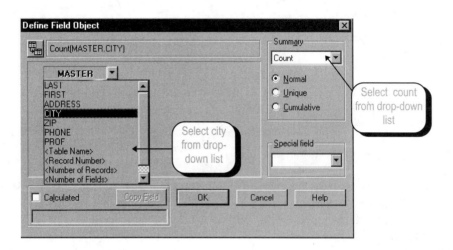

KEYSTROKES

ADD GROUP BAND

In Report Design mode:

1. Click **Report** .... Alt + R
2. Click **Add Group Band** .... B
3. Select **Field** .... Alt + F , ↓
4. Click **OK** .... Enter

    OR

    Click **Add Group Band** button on the
    Toolbar .... ⬚

ADD FIELD

In Report Design:

1. Click **Field Tool** button .... 🔲
2. Click and drag on report to place new field.

DEFINE FIELD OBJECT

1. Right-click field to be defined.
2. Select field from drop-down list.

To summarize a field:

1. Click **Summary** .... Alt + A
2. Select summary operator .... ↓
3. Select summary specification:
    • **Normal** .... Alt + N
    • **Unique** .... Alt + U
    • **Cumulative** .... Alt + C
4. Click **OK** .... Enter
5. Click **OK** .... Enter

> *In this exercise, you must create two reports for the California Users Group that will require the grouping and summarizing of report data.*

EXERCISE DIRECTIONS

Part I

1. Open Project Viewer and switch your working directory to \CUG.

2. Right-click Reports, and then choose New.

3. Create a new report using the Report Expert as follows:
   a. Select data from one table and display to show multiple records per page.
   b. Select 📁MEMBERS.DB as the table for the report, or use 💾23MEMBER.DB.
   c. Display all fields.
   d. Set the target output for the printer in landscape mode.
   e. Select the Bold text objects style sheet.
   f. Title the report CUG MEMBERSHIP LIST and set Page N of M to appear in the footer on the right.
   g. Name the report, LIST.
   h. Create the report.

4. Switch to Report Design mode, if you did not select opening the report into a design window.

5. Change column headings:
   ZIP to   ZIP CODE
   PROF. to   PROFESSION

6. Extend width of report table frame to fit all fields.

7. Select Report, Add Group Band from the menu, or click the Add Group Band button and group the members by CITY.

8. Select and delete the CITY field and header. Move fields together to eliminate the blank column.

9. Add a summary field to count the number of members in each city:

   a. Click the Field Tool button, and then click on the right side of the group band.
   b. Cancel the Field Expert screen.
   c. Right-click the new field and select Define Field.
   d. Select CITY from the drop-down list for the table.
   e. Select Count from the Summary drop-down list.
   f. Click OK.

10. Format the title text to 16 point font.

11. Adjust size of title text box, and center it over the report.

12. Save the report design.

13. Run the report and print in landscape mode.

Part II

14. Create a new report using the 📁CHARGES.DB table for the report, or use 💾23CHARGE.DB.
    - Show multiple records per page.
    - Display all fields
    - Print in portrait mode
    - Select the Shaded objects style sheet
    - Title the report, CUG CHARGES, Month Ended 12/15/96.
    - Set Page N to display at the center of the footer. Name the report CHG1215.

15. Switch to Report Design mode.

16. Add a group band to group the data by the CHARGE field.

17. Delete the CHARGE field from the record band.

18. Use the Field tool to add a field to the group band.

19. Define the field as a summary field to Sum the AMOUNT field.

20. Set the title box font to 14 points.

21. Modify the size of the title box so that the title becomes a two-line title. Delete the comma.

22. Set format of the AMOUNT field to Windows $ on the Format tab of the Field Properties dialog box.

23. Make any alignment settings as needed.

24. Save the report design.

25. Run and print the report.

26. Close all database objects.

Exercise 24

■ Summary

You have been hired by the Human Resources Department of Cutler College. One of your first jobs is to help organize information about the faculty. Once the information is organized, you will be asked to update and modify it, as well as create several reports requested by the college President.

This summary exercise will review and apply all concepts learned throughout the Paradox 7 sections of this book.

EXERCISE DIRECTIONS

Create and Save a Table:

1. Create a new directory using Window Explorer; name it COLLEGE.

2. Change your working directory to \COLLEGE.

3. Create a table using the field names and properties indicated below:

FIELD NAME	TYPE	SIZE	VALIDITY CHECK
TITLE	Alpha	3	
LAST	Alpha	10	
FIRST	Alpha	8	
DEPT	Alpha	4	Required field
BUDGET	Number		
BLDG	Alpha	1	
NO OF CLASSES	Number		
START	Date		
TENURE	Alpha	1	

4. Save the table; name it STAFF.

5. Switch to Table view.

Enter Records:

6. Use Quick Form to create a form for the table.

7. In Form Design mode, change the BLDG field to display as a radio button display for the BLDG field. Enter M or A as the item values to represent the Main or Annex buildings. Sort values.

   a. Add a text label, BUILDING, above the radio buttons in bold.

   b. Enhance the form design by:

   c. Adding a background color.

   d. Changing the field object color to light gray.

   e. Moving the items for better appearance.

8. Save the form as STAFFORM.

9. Enter the records listed in the table on the following page.

10. Switch to Table view and print one copy.

11. Close all database objects if you do not have time to complete the next segment. Otherwise, move to next step.

TITLE	LAST	FIRST	DEPT	BUDGET	BLDG	NO OF CLASSES	START	TENURE
Dr.	Martinez	Jose	Eng	200	M	5	9/16/88	Y
Ms.	Roberts	Diana	Eng	250	M	4	9/18/88	Y
Dr.	Harris	Sally	Eng	250	M	5	9/16/95	Y
Mr.	Bergen	Paul	Math	150	A	3	9/14/86	N
Mr.	Price	Robert	Sci	200	A	3	9/14/88	N
Mr.	Creighton	Matthew	Math	120	A	2	1/10/90	N
Ms.	Bryson	Jaime	PE	120	M	3	9/15/90	N
Ms.	Chang	Julie	Sci	160	M	4	9/15/88	Y
Ms.	Brewster	Donna	Hist	200	A	5	2/1/91	Y
Mr.	Anderson	Harvey	Hist	200	A	5	1/10/89	N
Dr.	Brown	Donald	Lang	140	M	3	2/1/89	Y
Mr.	Martinelli	William	Sci	120	A	2	9/16/90	N
Dr.	Zhan	Rafu	Sci	200	M	5	9/9/86	Y
Ms.	Browning	Paula	Eng	150	A	4	9/10/96	Y
Dr.	Ng	Tom	Lang	180	M	3	9/11/96	N
Mr.	Greene	Ralph	Math	140	A	5	2/5/92	N
Ms.	Linn	Sarah	Bus	180	A	4	2/3/91	N
Mr.	Fernandez	Ricardo	Bus	180	A	3	1/20/91	N
Dr.	Kramer	Mel	Bus	200	A	5	2/10/93	Y
Mr.	Grosso	Lenny	PE	140	M	2	9/13/95	Y

Modify the Table/Add Records:

12. Open the **STAFF** table in the COLLEGE directory.

13. To keep track of faculty members' years of teaching experience, restructure the table and add one new field, EXP, with a Short field type (whole number) format.

14. From the list on the following page, enter the experience information into the table.

TITLE	LAST	FIRST	DEPT	BUDGET	BLDG	NO OF CLASSES	START	TENURE	EXP
Dr.	Martinez	Jose	Eng	200	M	5	9/16/88	Y	15
Ms.	Roberts	Diana	Eng	250	M	4	9/18/88	Y	12
Dr.	Harris	Sally	Eng	250	M	5	9/16/95	Y	13
Mr.	Bergen	Paul	Math	150	A	3	9/14/86	N	14
Mr.	Price	Robert	Sci	200	A	3	9/14/88	N	18
Mr.	Creighton	Matthew	Math	120	A	2	1/10/90	N	10
Ms.	Bryson	Jaime	PE	120	M	3	9/15/90	N	9
Ms.	Chang	Julie	Sci	160	M	4	9/15/88	Y	13
Ms.	Brewster	Donna	Hist	200	A	5	2/1/91	Y	8
Mr.	Anderson	Harvey	Hist	200	A	5	1/10/89	N	12
Dr.	Brown	Donald	Lang	140	M	3	2/1/89	Y	10
Mr.	Martinelli	William	Sci	120	A	2	9/16/90	N	16
Dr.	Zhan	Rafu	Sci	200	M	5	9/9/86	Y	15
Ms.	Browning	Paula	Eng	150	A	4	9/10/96	Y	15
Dr.	Ng	Tom	Lang	180	M	3	9/11/96	N	10
Mr.	Greene	Ralph	Math	140	A	5	2/5/92	N	8
Ms.	Linn	Sarah	Bus	180	A	4	2/3/91	N	9
Mr.	Fernandez	Ricardo	Bus	180	A	3	1/20/91	N	9
Dr.	Kramer	Mel	Bus	200	A	5	2/10/93	Y	7
Mr.	Grosso	Lenny	PE	140	M	2	9/13/95	Y	11

15. Several teachers' records were left out of the table. Add the following records.

TITLE	LAST	FIRST	DEPT	BUDGET	BLDG	NO OF CLASSES	START	TENURE	EXP
Dr.	Hochman	Pamela	Sci	200	M	5	9/9/90	Y	17
Mr.	Tracey	Charles	Sci	140	A	3	2/10/89	N	13
Ms.	Godiva	Kayli	PE	160	A	4	2/10/92	Y	16
Mr.	Bertinelli	Thomas	Lang	150	A	3	9/10/96	N	8
Dr.	Hawkins	Joyce	Math	200	A	5	2/10/83	Y	16

Sort and Search the Table:

16. Sort the table in ascending order by LAST NAME.

17. Print a copy of this list.

18. Sort the table by department and last name in ascending order, and sort start by date in descending order.

19. Print a copy of this list.

20. Select Locate, Value from the Record menu, or click the Locate Field Value button, to search the database for the answers to the following questions:

   a. Which teachers work in the English Department?

   b. In which building does Ralph Greene work?

21. Locate and Replace all Hist Dept entries and change to S.S.

22. Using Table, Filter to search the table, find the answers to each of the following questions:

   a. Which teachers work in the main building and have more than 10 years experience?

   b. Which English teachers hold a doctoral degree?

   c. Which Math teachers work in the Annex and have a supply budget of at least $140?

23. Create a query for teachers who work in the M (Main) Building sorted by Dept:

   - Include the fields listed: DEPT, TITLE, LAST, FIRST, and TENURE.
   - Set Query Properties to structure the query in the field order listed above.
   - Set a criterion in the Bldg field for M.
   - Save the query; name it MAIN BUILDING STAFF.

24. Run the query.

25. Print the Answer table.

26. Create and save a query to list those teaching in the Annex who have four or more classes:

   - Include the fields listed: TITLE, LAST, FIRST, NO OF CLASSES, and DEPT.
   - Set Query Properties to structure the query in the field order listed above.
   - Set criteria to select Annex teachers who teach four or more classes.
   - Save the query as ANNEX.

27. Run the query.

28. Print the Answer table.

Prepare Reports:

Report I:

29. Create a new report with the Report Expert and respond as follows:

   a. Use one table with multiple records per page.
   b. Use the STAFF table.
   c. Display all fields.
   d. Set the target output for the printer in landscape mode.
   e. Select the Shaded objects style sheet.
   f. Title the report Cutler College Staff, and set Page N of M to appear in the center of the footer.
   g. Name the report LIST.

30. Switch to Report Design and add the subtitle By Department.

31. Set title font to 16 points and adjust the size of the title text box, if necessary.

32. Add a group band to group the report by DEPT.

33. Delete the DEPT field from the Record band.

34. Use the Field tool to add a field to the group band.

35. Define the field to count the number of staff in each department.

36. Make any adjustments necessary to make the report more attractive.

37. Save the report.

38. Print one copy in landscape mode.

Report II:

39. Create a new report with the Report Expert and respond as follows:
   a. Use one table and create a report in Table mode.
   b. Use the STAFF table.
   c. Select fields: LAST, BUDGET, and BLDG.
   d. Set the target output for the printer.
   e. Select the Shaded objects style sheet.
   f. Title the report Cutler College Department Budgets, and set Page N of M as a centered footer.
   g. Name the report BUDGET.

40. Switch to Report Design and set title to 14 point font. Adjust the size of the title box so that the title is on one line.

41. Add a group band and group the report by DEPT.

42. Use the Field tool to add a field to the group band.

43. Define the field to sum the BUDGET field.

44. Make any adjustments necessary to make the report more attractive.

45. Save the report.

46. Print one copy.

47. Close all open windows.

Corel Presentations 7

Lesson 1: Create, Save, and Print a Slide Show

Lesson 2: Edit and Enhance Slides

Lesson 3: Work with Slide Shows

<table>
<tr><td rowspan="4">**Exercise**
1</td><td>■ **About Corel Presentations 7** ■ **Start Corel Presentations 7**</td></tr>
<tr><td>■ **Create a Presentation** ■ **The Corel Presentations 7 Window**</td></tr>
<tr><td>■ **Add Text to Slides** ■ **Add Slides to a Slide Show**</td></tr>
<tr><td>■ **Save a Slide Show** ■ **Close a File/Exit Presentations**</td></tr>
</table>

NOTES

About Corel Presentations 7

■ **Corel Presentations 7** is the presentation component of Corel Office Professional 7 that lets you create slide shows.

■ A **presentation**, also known as a slide show, is a collection of slides related to the same topic which may be shown while an oral report is given to help summarize data and emphasize report highlights. From the presentation slides, you can prepare handouts for the audience, speaker notes for use during the presentation, and/or outlines to provide an overview of the presentation. In addition, you can use slides to create a table of contents, overhead transparencies, and/or 35 mm slides of your presentation.

■ Slides may include text, drawings, charts, outlines, and/or graphics.

■ Outlines created in WordPerfect or data created in Paradox or Quattro Pro may be imported into a Presentations slide. (*See Integration Section, Exercise 7.*)

Start Corel Presentations 7

■ To start Presentations, click the Corel Presentations 7 icon on the Desktop Application Director (DAD).

DAD

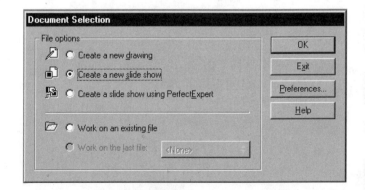

■ Or, you may click the Start button on the Windows 95 Taskbar, highlight Corel Office 7, then click to select Corel Presentations 7.

■ After launching Corel Presentations 7, the Document Selection dialog box appears which presents options to Create a new drawing, Create a new slide show, Create a slide show using PerfectExpert, or Work on an existing file.

Create a Presentation

- The **Create a new slide show** option allows you to build your own unique presentation from slides that contain the standard default formats and layouts.

- After selecting Create a new slide show and clicking OK, the New Slide Show dialog box appears.

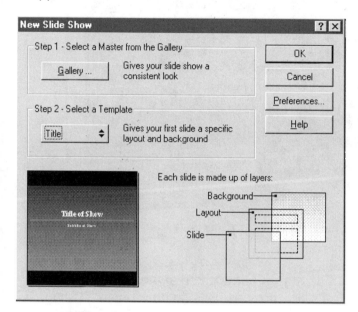

- A slide consists of the following three layers:

1. The **Background Layer**, which contains designs and colors that give the slide an appealing look.

2. The **Layout Layer**, which contains placeholders that determine the position and format of text or objects on the slide.

3. The **Slide Layer**, where drawings, QuickArt, and other items are inserted.

- To create a presentation, you need to make two choices—you must select a background and you must decide on the template (the layout of placeholders). To select a background for your slide, click the **Gallery** button. A gallery of master background choices displays.

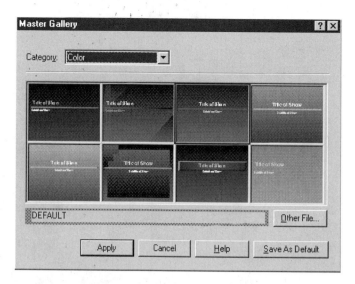

- To select a template, click the Select a Template list, and choose an option.

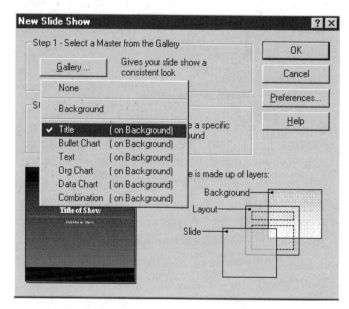

- The template option generally follows the natural progression of a presentation. You start with a Title slide template (the default) and move to more complex layouts using outlines.

  - After applying the background and the template and clicking OK, the Corel Presentations 7 window appears.

The Corel Presentations 7 Window

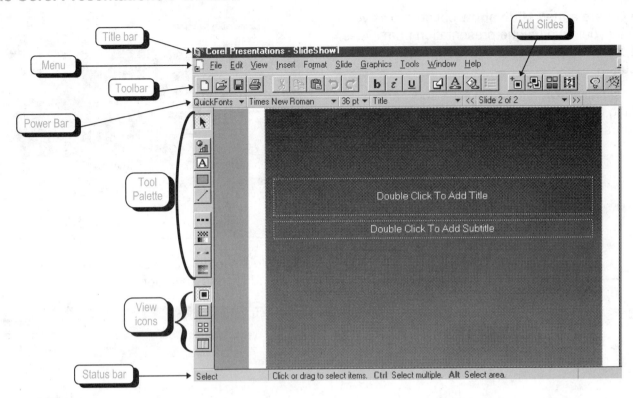

- Corel Presentations 7 places the title *SlideShow1 (unmodified)* in the **title bar** of each slide show you create. After the slide show is saved, the filename appears in the Title bar.

- The **Toolbar** contains buttons to give you quick access to features you use most often. These buttons work like other Toolbar buttons in the Corel Office Suite.

- The **Power Bar**, located below the Toolbar, contains drop-down buttons which make basic formatting changes to text more efficient.

- The **Tool Palette**, located down the left side of the screen, contains some of the most common tools used to add drawings to slides.

- **View icons**, located at the bottom of the Drawing Toolbar, control the number of slides Presentations will display as well as the display layout. (*Views will be covered in Exercise 2.)*

- The **status bar**, located at the bottom of the screen, provides hints on drawing and editing. The name of the currently selected Drawing Toolbar button is indicated in this location.

Add Text to Slides

- Corel Presentations 7 displays a slide containing **placeholders** (an empty box or boxes) which identify the placement and location of text on the slide. Each placeholder contains directions to help you complete the slide.

- **Title and subtitle placeholders** contain the format for title and subtitle text, while **text placeholders** include the format and design for bulleted lists.

- To type text into a placeholder, double-click inside the placeholder and type the desired text. WordPerfect has preset the font style and size. However, you may change these attributes at a later time. To insert text into the next placeholder on a slide, press the down arrow key or double-click the next placeholder.

Add Slides to a Slide Show

- To add a new slide to the slide show, click the Add Slides button on the Toolbar. In the Add Slides dialog box that follows, choose the number of slides to add and the template to use for the new slides. Click the <u>T</u>emplate drop-down list and select Bullet Chart as the template type.

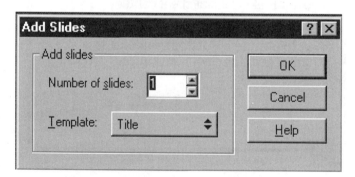

- The Bullet Chart template lets you format bulleted lists. A bulleted list format typically follows the Title slide.

- Six different bullet levels are available. Pressing the Tab key indents text and produces sub-levels of bulleted items. Corel Presentations 7 displays the first three sub-levels with a different bullet as well as reducing the text size for each new level. Press Shift + Tab to return to the previous bullet level.

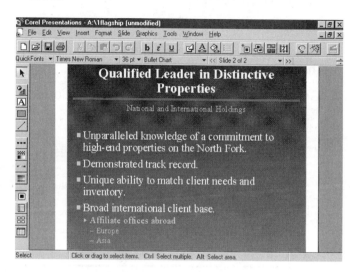

- Corel Presentations 7 places the new slide immediately after the slide that is displayed or selected when you create the new slide.

Save a Slide Show

- Slide shows are saved using the same procedures used to save WordPerfect documents and Quattro Pro spreadsheets.

- Corel Presentations 7 automatically adds a .SHW extension to slide shows saved for the first time.

Close a File/Exit Presentations

- Presentations 7 follows the same procedures for closing a slide show file and exiting as those used in the WordPerfect and Quattro Pro application tools.

- If the slide show you are working on has been modified or has not yet been saved, you will be prompted to save it.

In this exercise, you will create a new slide show containing title and bullet chart slides and save the presentation.

EXERCISE DIRECTIONS

1. Start Corel Presentations 7 using the Windows 95 Taskbar.

2. Create a new slide show.

3. Accept the default master and Title template for the first slide.

4. Create the title slide as shown in Illustration A.

5. Click the Add Slides button on the Toolbar.

   - Change the template to Bullet Chart for the second slide.
   - Type the bullet chart as shown in Illustration A.

6. Save the presentation; name it KIT.

7. Close the slide show.

8. Create a new slide show.

9. Use the default Title slide template for the first slide.

10. Type the title slide information as shown in Illustration B.

11. Add the bullet chart template for the second slide, and type the information shown in Illustration B.

12. Save the presentation; name it FLAGSHIP.

13. Close the slide show.

ILLUSTRATION A

CREATIVE SALES

Sales Meeting
January 8, 1997

SALES KITS

- Tool for making initial client contact
- A support system for sales rep
- Way to provide clients with material to make an informal decision about buying your product

FLAGSHIP REALTY

Pamela DeStefano, President

Qualified Leader in Distinctive Properties

National and International Holdings

- Unparalleled knowledge of and a commitment to high-end properties on the North Fork.
- Demonstrated track record.
- Unique ability to match client needs and inventory.
- Broad international client base.
  ‣ Affiliate offices abroad
    – Europe
    – Asia

KEYSTROKES

START PRESENTATIONS

Click the DAD **Corel Presentations 7** icon .... 🔳

OR

1. Click **Start** .... Ctrl + Esc
2. Highlight Corel Office 7.
3. Click **Corel Presentations 7**.

CREATE NEW SLIDE SHOW

1. Click **File** .... Alt + F
2. Click **New** .... N
3. Select **Create a new slide show** .... Alt + S
4. To choose a slide background, click Step 1, **Gallery** .... Alt + G
   a. Select background from displayed defaults.
   OR
   • Click Category drop-down list .... Alt + Y
   • Select new category .... ↓ ↑
   • Click on a background choice ..... Tab , ↕↔
   b. Click **Apply** .... Enter

5. To change the template format, click step 2, drop-down list and select the desired template .... Tab , ↓ ↑
6. Click **OK** .... Enter

ADD NEW SLIDE

Click **Add Slides** button on Toolbar .... 🔳

OR

1. Click **Slide** .... Alt + S
2. Click **Add Slides** .... A
3. Enter the number of slides ..... Alt + S in **Number of slides** text box.
4. To change template format, click **Template** .... Alt + T
5. Select a Template format .... ↓ ↑
6. Click **OK** .... Enter

ADD TEXT TO PLACEHOLDERS

1. Double-click desired placeholder.
2. Type text; press **Enter** to move to a new line .... Enter
3. Press **down arrow** to move to next text object .... ↓

SAVE PRESENTATION

Ctrl + S

Click **Save** button on Toolbar .... 🔳

OR

1. Click **File** .... Alt + F
2. Click **Save** .... S
3. Type the slide show name in the **Filename** text box.
4. Select alternate drive and directory, if desired.
5. Click **OK** .... Enter

EXIT COREL PRESENTATIONS 7

Alt + F4

Click **Program Close** button X

OR

1. Click **File** .... Alt + F
2. Click **Exit** X

Exercise

2

- Open a Slide Show ■ Slide Views ■ Move from Slide to Slide
- Spell Check ■ Print a Presentation

NOTES

Open a Slide Show

■ Slide shows may be opened by selecting Work on an existing file or Work on the last file in the Document Selection dialog box, or by using the same procedures to open documents in other Corel Office 7 applications.

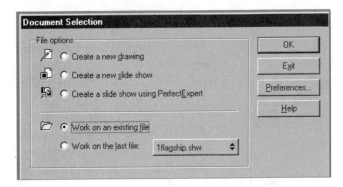

■ If you select Work on an existing file, the Open File dialog box displays for you to indicate the filename you wish to open. To open a slide show file you recently saved, click the list button next to the Work on the last file option, and choose from one of the listed slide shows.

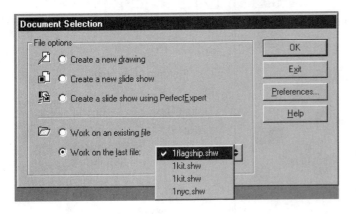

Slide Views

■ Corel Presentations 7 allows you to view your slide show in four different ways:

- **Slide Editor view**, the default, allows you to see a single slide on screen. You may edit or modify a slide in this view.

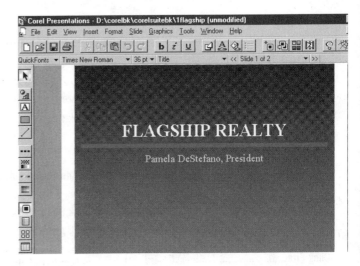

- **Outliner view** displays slide text on a notebook page layout to give an overview of the content of a presentation. Use this view to organize a presentation. *(This view will be detailed in Exercise 5.)*

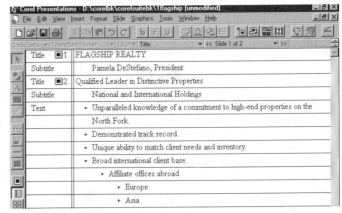

- **Slide Sorter view** allows you to see miniature copies of your slides on screen so that you can see the flow of the presentation. Use this view to move, copy, and delete slides. *(Moving, copying, and deleting slides will be detailed in Exercise 4.)*

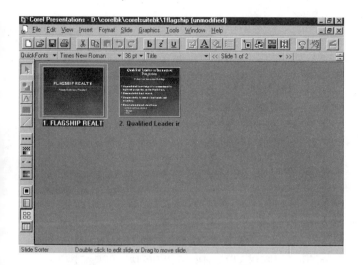

- **Slide List view** allows you to display a summary of each slide with transition, advance, and other slide options.

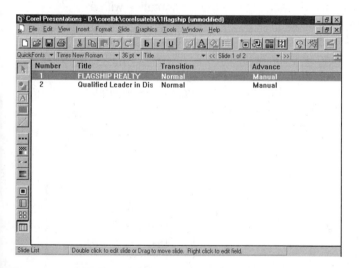

- Views may be changed by clicking the appropriate view icon on the bottom of the Drawing Toolbar or by selecting the desired view from the View menu.

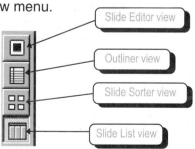

Move from Slide to Slide

- When there are a number of slides included in a slide show, you will find it necessary to move from slide to slide to edit, enhance, or view slide information. Corel Presentations 7 offers a variety of ways to select and display slides in Slide view:

  - Press the PgDn key to display the next slide or the PgUp key to display the previous slide.

  - Click the ⟨⟨ or ⟩⟩ buttons on the Power Bar.

  - Click the Slide Select button Slide 1 of 2 ▼ on the Power Bar, then choose the desired slide.

Spell Check

- Slide text may be spell checked by selecting Outliner view then selecting Spell Check from the Tools menu or by clicking the right mouse button and selecting Spell Check. (The spell check procedures are the same as those used in the other Corel Office 7 applications.)

Print a Presentation

- Slides in your presentation may be used as an on-screen Slide show or to create transparencies, audience notes, speaker note, handouts, or an outline. When you select Print from the File menu, Corel Presentations 7 lets you choose different print options in the Print dialog box for the type of output you want.

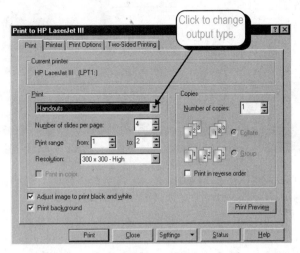

- The default selection (Full Document) in the Print window prints all slides. Other options include:

Print Option	Description
Slides	Prints all or a specific range of slides.
Current View	Prints only what is shown on your screen. For example, if zoom settings are set to 200%, the Current View option prints only the portion of the slide displayed in the window.
Slide List	Prints the title and options used for each slide in a slide show.
Handouts	Prints a thumbnail sketch of each slide in the presentation.
Speaker Notes	Prints a thumbnail sketch of each slide in the presentation with a space for notes on each slide.
Audience Notes	Prints a thumbnail sketch of each slide but adds lines below each slide to make notetaking easier.
Adjust Image to Print Black and White	Adapts color slides to print black and white. Use this option if you plan to use your slides as overhead transparencies or if you have a printer that only prints in black and white.
Print Background	Prints the master layer of slides.

- Note the illustrations below and on the next page of the Speaker Notes, Audience Notes and Handouts options. When you select any one of these print options, you may indicate how many thumbnail sketches you want printed on a page. The fewer thumbnails per page, the larger each image will display.

Audience Notes

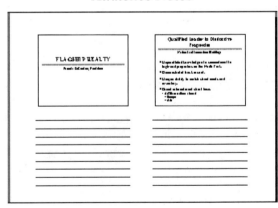

Speaker Notes

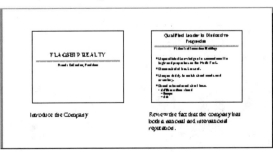

Handouts

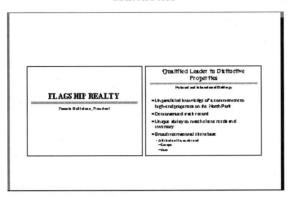

■ You can also click the Print button 🖨 on the Toolbar. When you use this technique, you bypass the Print window and send the print command directly to the printer. Presentations automatically prints information using the settings last selected in the Print window.

In this exercise, you will add new slides to a previously created presentation. You will then use different slide views to see the flow of your presentation.

EXERCISE DIRECTIONS

1. Start Presentations.

2. Select Work on an existing file.
   ✓ *If a Corel Presentations 7 slide show is already running, select File, Open to open a slide show.*

3. Open 📁FLAGSHIP.

4. Display slide 2 by clicking the ▶▶ button on the Power Bar.

5. Display slide 1 by clicking the ◀◀ button on the Power Bar.

6. Add a new Bullet Chart slide using the following information:
   ✓ *The new slide will be inserted after slide 1. You will move it into a desired order in a later exercise.*

   ┌───┐
   │ SERVICES INCLUDE   │
   │   │
   │ • Private financial evaluation   │
   │ • Mortgage payment table constructed for each │
   │   buyer   │
   │ • Property tour videos   │
   │ • Internet access for international sales and │
   │   listings   │
   └───┘

7. Switch to Slide Sorter view.

8. Switch back to Slide Editor view.

9. In the Print dialog box, change Print selection to Handouts, then change the Number of slides per page to three. Print one copy in black and white.

10. Close the file; save the changes.

11. Open 📁KIT.

12. Display slide 2 using the PgDn key.

13. Display slide 1 using the PgUp key.

14. Add a new Bullet Chart slide using the following information:

   ┌───┐
   │ CORPORATE IDENTITY   │
   │   │
   │ • Prepare a well-thought out logo and corporate │
   │   image   │
   │ • Use logo on all company-related materials │
   │   -correspondence   │
   │   -invoices   │
   │   -price sheets   │
   └───┘

15. Switch to Slide Sorter view.

16. Switch to Outliner view.

17. Spell check.

18. Print one copy.

19. In the Print dialog box, change Print selection to Handouts, then change Number of slides per page to three. Print one copy in black and white.

20. Close the file; save the changes.

KEYSTROKES

OPEN PRESENTATION

1. Click the DAD **Corel Presentations 7** icon .... ▣
2. Select **Work on an existing file** in the Document Selection dialog box and:
    - Type slide show name in **Name** text box.

   OR

   Double-click desired slide show from those listed.

   OR

   Click **Work on the last file** and click list arrow in Document Selection dialog box.
    - Select file from drop-down list.
3. Click **OK** .... Enter

If a slide show is open and you wish to open another:

1. Click **File** .... Alt + F
2. Click **Open** .... O
3. Type slide show name in **Name** text box.

   OR

    - Double-click desired slide shown from those listed.
4. Click **OK** .... Enter

SWITCH VIEWS

1. Click **View** .... Alt + V
2. Click a desired view:
    - **Slide Editor** .... E
    - **Outliner** .... O
    - **Slide Sorter** .... S
    - **Slide List** L

   OR

   Click desired view button:
    - **Slide Editor** .... ▣
    - **Outliner** .... ▤
    - **Slide Sorter** .... ▦
    - **Slide List** .... ▥

MOVE FROM SLIDE TO SLIDE

1. Press **PgUp** or **PgDn** ...... [Page Up] or [Page Down] to display previous or next slide.

   OR

    - Click **Next Slide** [>>] or **Previous Slide** [<<] button on Power Bar.

   OR

    - Click **Slide Select** button on Power Bar .... [Slide 1 of 3 ▼]
    - Select desired slide.

SPELL CHECK

   ✓ *The Spell-As-You-Go feature is inactive in this application.*

Ctrl + F1

1. Switch to Outliner view.
2. Click **Tools** .... Alt + T
3. Click **Spell Check** .... S

PRINT A PRESENTATION

Ctrl + P

Click **Print** button on Toolbar .... 🖨
OR
1. Click **File** .... Alt + F
2. Click **Print** .... P
3. Select desired options.
4. Click **OK** .... Enter

<table>
<tr><td>

Exercise

3

</td><td>

■ **Add QuickArt Graphics to Slides** ■ **Use Undo**
■ **Change the Slide's Template**
■ **Change the Slide's Master Background**

</td></tr>
</table>

NOTES

Add QuickArt Graphics to Slides

■ **Graphics** on slides help capture the audience's attention during the slide show. Graphics may be added to a slide by clicking the Chart or Graphics tool on the Tool Palette then selecting the Retrieve a QuickArt graphic button.

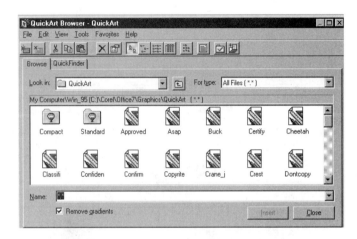

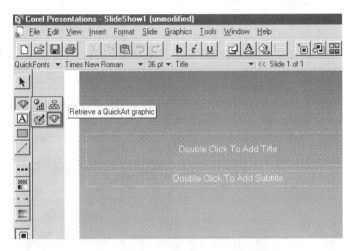

■ Or, a graphic may be added to a slide by selecting QuickArt from the Insert menu. After accessing QuickArt using either procedure, the mouse pointer changes to a hand holding a box. As you drag the mouse, the box size becomes larger. Size the box to the desired size of the graphic. When you release the mouse button, the QuickArt Graphics Browser dialog box opens for you to select the desired graphic. The selected graphic is then inserted into the box.

■ The QuickArt graphics in Corel Presentations 7 are the same as those found in Corel WordPerfect 7.

■ Once the graphic is inserted, it appears with handles. When handles appear, you can size the graphic as you did with WordPerfect graphics. Simply drag a top or bottom middle handle to change the height, drag a left or right middle handle to change the width, drag a corner handle to size the graphic proportionally.

■ You can move the graphic by displaying the handles and then placing the pointer within the graphic (not a handle). Next, click and hold the left mouse button while dragging the graphic to a desired location.

Use Undo

- Like other Corel Office 7 applications, the Undo feature reverses the most recent action. Undo is available only in Slide Editor view.

Change the Slide's Template

- The layout or template of a slide may be changed at any time. If you have graphics or other objects on the slide when changing the layout, they will not be lost – they will be rearranged.

- Use Slide Editor view when changing a slide's layout or template.

- To change the template for a slide, click the Templates button on the Power Bar, then choose the desired template.

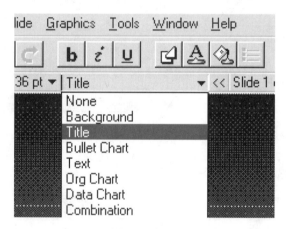

Change the Slide's Master Background

- In Exercise 1 you learned to choose a background from those in the Master Gallery. Corel Presentations 7 also provides a Background Gallery with other background choices. The Background Gallery dialog box contains backgrounds with border lines and one or two images. The images are found within categories. For example, if you want a background to contain a finance-related image, you will find them within the Finance category.

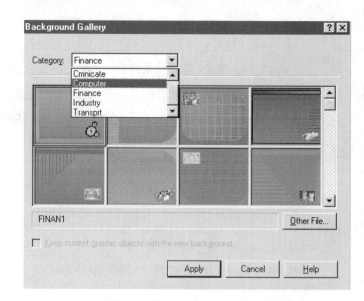

- To change the master background for a slide, select Background Layer from the Slide menu. You will note that Backgrounds appears as a new menu item. Select Background Gallery (or Master Gallery, if you desire) from the Backgrounds menu.

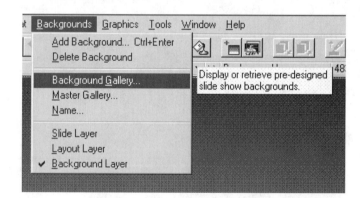

- In the Background Gallery dialog box that follows, select a desired background. To view other backgrounds within other categories, click the button next to the Category text box, select a desired background, and click Apply. To return to the slide layer, select Slide Layer from the Backgrounds menu.

EXERCISE DIRECTIONS

Part I

1. Open 🖮FLAGSHIP.SHW.

2. Add a Bullet Chart slide.

3. Enter the bullet chart information shown in Illustration A on page 402.

4. Insert a relevant QuickArt graphic in the approximate size shown.

5. Add another new Bullet Chart slide.

6. Enter the bullet chart information shown in Illustration B.

7. Insert one or more relevant QuickArt graphic(s) in the approximate size(s) shown.

8. Switch to Slide Sorter view.

9. Switch back to Slide Editor view.

10. Change the background to EXECUTIV found in the Business Category of the Master Gallery.

11. Switch to Outliner view.

12. Spell check.

13. In the Print dialog box, change Print selection to Handouts and change number of slides per page to 6.

14. Print one copy in Black and White.

15. Close the file; save the changes.

Part II

1. Open 🖮KIT.SHW.

2. Add a new Bullet Chart slide.

3. Enter the bullet chart information shown in Illustration C on page 402.

4. Insert a relevant QuickArt graphic in the approximate size shown.

5. Add another new Bullet Chart slide.

6. Enter the bullet chart information shown in Illustration D.

7. Insert a relevant QuickArt graphic in the approximate size shown.

8. Switch to Slide Sorter view.

9. Switch back to Slide Editor view.

10. Spell check.

11. Change the background to FINAN10 found in the Finance category of the Background Gallery.

12. In the Print dialog box, change the Print selection to Handouts and the number of slides per page to six.

13. Print one copy in Black and White.

14. Close the file; save the changes.

ILLUSTRATION A

PROPERTY TYPES

- Homes of Distinction
- Commercial Properties
- Residential Townhouses
- Exclusive Agent for Pineview Estates

ILLUSTRATION B

OUR SALES FORCE

- 85 Professional Salespeople
- 50% are members of Flagship's Private Brokerage Council
  - Designation
  - Awarded to sales agents who handled sales over $1 million.

ILLUSTRATION C

WHY USE IT?

- Builds corporate identity
- Provides numerous sales materials
  - Brochures
  - Product Catalog
  - Presentation Materials

ILLUSTRATION D

SALES MATERIALS

- The same logo on all materials
- The same paper
- The same typefaces
- Business cards, letterheads, brochures, catalogs, presentation materials

KEYSTROKES

INSERT A GRAPHIC

1. Click **Insert** .... `Alt` + `I`
2. Click **QuickArt** .... `Q`
3. Drag mouse to desired graphic size, and release mouse button.
4. Double-click **Compact** or **Standard Folder**.
5. Double-click desired category folders.
6. Select desired graphic.
7. Click **Insert** .... `Enter`

CHANGE MASTER BACKGROUND

1. Click **Slide** .... `Alt` + `S`
2. Click **Background Layer** .... `B`
3. Click **Backgrounds** .... `Alt` + `B`
4. Click **Background Gallery** .... `B` or `M` or **Master Gallery**.
5. Click **Category** drop-down list button .... `Alt` + `Y`
6. Select desired category .... `↓` `↑`
7. Select desired background.
8. Click **Apply** .... `Enter`

CHANGE TEMPLATE

Click **Template** button on Power Bar ....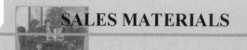

- Select desired template.

OR

a. Click **Slide** .... `Alt` + `S`
b. Click **Apply Template** .... `T`

Exercise
4

- ■ **Move, Copy, and Delete Slides**
- ■ **Slide Sorter View**
- ■ **Return to Slide Editor View**

NOTES

Move, Copy, and Delete Slides

- ■ Each slide in a slide show is part of the entire presentation. Slides may be moved, copied, or deleted within the slide show.

- ■ You should save a slide show before moving, copying, or deleting slides to prevent loss of data.

Slide Sorter View

- ■ You may move, copy, or delete slides from all views using menu commands or cut/copy and paste procedures. However, it is easier and more efficient to perform these tasks in **Slide Sorter view** since all slides are displayed in miniature. In this view, you can easily see the flow of the entire slide show.

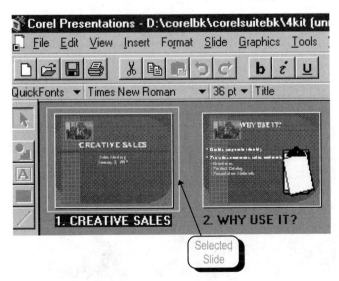

Selected Slide

- ■ To move, copy, or delete a slide in Slide Sorter view, click the Slide Sorter view button on the Tool Palette, or select Slide Sorter from the View menu.

- ■ Select the slide to be moved, copied, or deleted. (Selected slides are outlined with a color border.) You can select slides using one of several techniques:

  - Click the desired slide.

  - Press the insertion point arrow keys until a border outlines the desired slide.

  - To select multiple slides, press and hold down the Shift key as you click each slide. Selecting multiple slides allows you to move, copy, or delete them as a group. You cannot undo changes made in Slide Sorter view.

- ■ The easiest way to move a slide in Slide Sorter view is to select it and drag it to a new location. When the slide is being moved, the mouse pointer changes to a slide with a diagonal arrow, and a vertical bar identifies the new position of the slide (as indicated in the illustration below). When the vertical bar is in the position where you want to place the slide, release the mouse button.

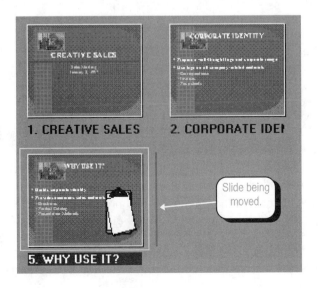

Slide being moved.

- To copy a slide, press the Ctrl key as you drag the slide to a new location.

- To delete a slide, select the slide and press the Delete key, or select <u>D</u>elete Slide(s) from the <u>S</u>lide menu.

Return to Slide Editor View

- Since you cannot edit slide contents in Slide Sorter view, you will need to return to Slide

Editor view to make changes and adjust text. You can return to Slide Editor view using one of the following techniques:

- Double-click a slide in Slide Sorter view.

- Select the slide and click the Slide Editor view button on the Tool Palette.

- Select the desired slide and select Slide <u>E</u>ditor from the <u>V</u>iew menu.

In this exercise, you will insert several slides into an existing slide show, then move them into a different order.

EXERCISE DIRECTIONS

1. Open KIT.

2. Create a new slide using the Bullet Chart template.

3. Enter the information shown in Illustration A.

4. Create a new slide using the Bullet Chart template.

5. Enter the information shown in Illustration B.

6. Create a new slide using the Bullet Chart template.

7. Enter the information shown in Illustration C, on page 405 and insert a relevant graphic.

8. Switch to Slide Sorter view.

9. Move the slides into the order shown in Illustration D on pages 405 and 406.

10. Delete the slide entitled CORPORATE IDENTITY.

11. Display slide 1.

12. Change the date of the meeting to June 8, 1997.

13. Switch to Slide Editor view.

14. Change the background to ARROWS found in the Business category of the Master Gallery.

15. Print one copy as Handouts with 8 slides per page in black and white.

16. Spell check.

17. Close the file; save the changes.

ILLUSTRATION A

THE SALES BROCHURE

- Similar to marketing brochure
  - Contains creative headlines
  - Contains Attractive graphics
- Should possess the same visual elements of your corporate identity
- Result should be company and product exposure

ILLUSTRATION B

THE PRODUCT CATALOG

- Contains more specific information about company products
- May include prices and discount offers
- May be sent through mail to prospective clients
- More effective when handed out personally on a sales call or visit to set up a sales call
- Use simple drawings or photos to show product line

ILLUSTRATION C

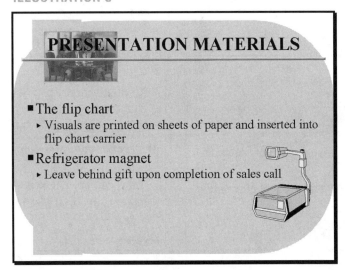

CREATIVE SALES

Sales Meeting
June 8, 1997

1

WHY USE IT?

- Builds corporate identity
- Provides numerous sales materials
  - ‣ Brochures
  - ‣ Product Catalog
  - ‣ Presentation Materials

2

SALES KITS

- Tool for making initial client contact
- A support system for sales rep
- Way to provide clients with material to make an informal decision about buying your product

3

SALES MATERIALS

- The same logo on all materials
- The same paper
- The same typefaces
- Business cards, letterheads, brochures, catalogs, presentation materials

4

◀◀◀◀◀◀
THE SALES BROCHURE

- Similar to marketing brochure
  - ▸ Contain creative headlines
  - ▸ Contain attractive graphics
- Should possess the same visual elements of your corporate identity
- Result should be company and product exposure

▶▶▶▶▶▶

5

◀◀◀◀◀◀
THE PRODUCT CATALOG

- Contains more specific information about company products
- May include prices and discount offers
- May be sent through mail to prospective clients
- More effective when handed out personally on a sales call or visit to set up a sales call
- Use simple drawings or photos to show product line

▶▶▶▶▶▶

6

◀◀◀◀◀◀
PRESENTATION MATERIALS

- The flip chart
  - ▸ Visuals are printed on sheets of paper and inserted into flip chart carrier
- Refrigerator magnet
  - ▸ Leave behind gift upon completion of sales call

▶▶▶▶▶▶

7

KEYSTROKES

MOVE SLIDES

1. From Slide Sorter view, select slide to move.
2. Drag slide to new location.
   OR
   - Click **Edit** ....
   - Click **Cut** .... T
   - Move insertion point to new slide location.
   - Click **Edit** .... Alt + E
   - Click **Paste** .... P

COPY SLIDES

1. From Slide Sorter view, select slide to copy.
2. Press **Ctrl** while dragging slide to new location.

DELETE SLIDES

1. From Slide Sorter view, select slide to delete.
2. Press **Delete** key .... Del
   OR
1. Click **Slide** .... Alt + S

2. Click **Delete Slide(s)** .... D
3. Click **Yes** or **No** .... Y or N
   OR
   a. Click **Edit** .... Alt + E
   b. Click **Clear** .... A
   c. Click **Slide #** .... Alt + L
      to clear current slide only.
   OR
   Click **Slide show** ....
   to delete all slides in a slide show.

Exercise 5

■ **Outliner View** ■ **Add Slides in Outliner View**

NOTES

Outliner View

■ Outliner view displays slide text as titles and subtitles in an outline format to give an overview of the contents of a slide show. This view is usually used to organize a slide show.

■ Outliner view may be used before creating text on slides to organize your thoughts in an outline format. Or, you may create your presentation on slides first, then switch to Outliner view to see the flow of your slide show in an outline format. It can also serve as a Table of Contents to distribute to your audience.

■ Note the illustration below of the KIT slide show displayed in Outliner view. A slide icon, a number, and a text placeholder mark each slide on the left. Slide text is shown on the right.

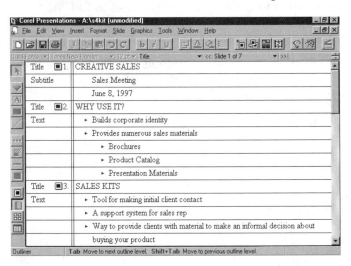

■ Graphics and objects do not appear in Outliner view.

■ To display Outliner view, click the Outliner View button on the Tool Palette, or select <u>O</u>utliner from the <u>V</u>iew menu.

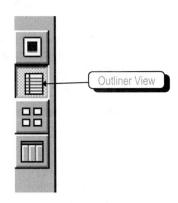

■ You can change to Outliner view after creating a slide show, or you can create an entire presentation in Outliner view. Once you change views, the outline will convert to a series of slides.

■ In Outliner view, press Ctrl + Enter to create a new slide, use the Tab key to promote the outline to the next level, and use Shift+Tab to demote the outline to the previous level. As you promote or demote outline levels, Presentations 7 changes the placeholder type for the level from Title to Subtitle to Text (Bullet Chart).

■ You cannot print in Outliner view.

■ As indicated in an earlier lesson, you can spell check in Outliner view.

Add Slides in Outliner View

■ The same procedures may be used to add slides in Outliner view that you used to add slides in Slide Editor view:

• Click Add Slides button on the Toolbar.

• Select <u>S</u>lide, <u>A</u>dd Slides from the menus.

■ Press Enter after typing the slide title.

In this exercise, you will create a slide show in Outliner view. After creating the slide show, you will move slides, add a new slide, and print the slide show.

EXERCISE DIRECTIONS

1. Create a new slide show.
2. Select a Title template as the first slide.
3. Use the default Master background.
4. Switch to Outliner view.
5. Enter the following titles and subtitles to create your outline.
   - ✓ *In the outline below, numbered items represent Titles, indented items represent Subtitles, and bulleted items represent Text.*

   1. Smartfood, Inc.
      "Eat Well and Stay Trim"
      - ✓ *Change template to Bullet Chart.*
   2. Smartfood Products
      - Frozen dinners
      - Cakes and cookies
      - Crackers
      - Ice cream
      - Soft drinks
   3. Smartfood's Success...
      - People are eating healthier to reduce body fat.
      - People want low-fat, low-calorie foods that taste great!
   4. International Expansion--Where and When?
      - Paris, 6 months
      - Milan, 8 months
      - London, 12 months
      - Madrid, 18 months
      - Sydney, 20 months
      - Hong Kong, 24 months

6. Spell check.
7. Switch to Slide Sorter view.
8. Move slide 4 to become slide 3.
9. Switch to Slide Editor view and display slide 2.
10. Insert a relevant graphic.
    - ✓ *You may insert more than one graphic, if you wish to create an interesting effect.*
11. Change the background to BRUSH found in the 35mm Category of the Master Gallery.
12. Switch to Outliner view.
13. Insert a new bullet chart slide after slide 3 that reads:

U.S. Markets
• East-New York
• North-Illinois
• West-California
• South-Florida

14. Switch to Slide Editor view.
15. Insert a relevant graphic (or graphics) on this new slide.
16. Switch to Slide Sorter view, then to Outliner view.
17. Spell check.
18. Print one copy as Handouts with 5 slides per page in black and white.
19. Save the file; name it FOOD.
20. Close the window.

KEYSTROKES

SWITCH TO OUTLINER VIEW

Click **Outliner View** button .... 🔲
on the Tool Palette.
OR
1. Click **View** .... Alt + V
2. Click **Outliner** .... O

ADD SLIDES IN OUTLINER VIEW

1. Position insertion point at the end of the last line in the outline.
2. Press **Ctrl + Enter**.

ADD TEXT IN OUTLINER VIEW

Press **Tab** .... Tab
to indent or add subtitles
and text (bullet) items.

   - ✓ *To add a bulleted item under the Title line, press **Enter** and then press **Tab**.*

OR

Press **Shift+Tab** to go back one level.

Exercise 6

■ **Insert a Graph** ■ **Create a Table**

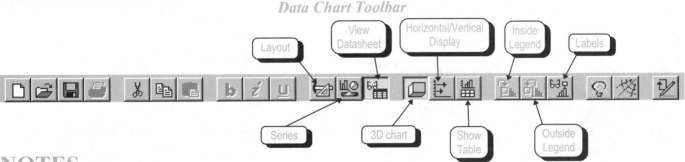

Data Chart Toolbar

NOTES

Insert a Graph

■ Thus far, you have been working with Title and Bullet Chart templates. Corel Presentations 7 provides other templates to help display data. The Data Chart template allows you to create a graph on a slide. You can also import graphs that have been created in Quattro Pro. *(See Integration Chapter to import a Quattro Pro chart and workbook data.)*

■ To insert a graph, click the Add Slides button 🔲 on the Toolbar, and select Data Chart as the Template.

✓ *A combination template has four placeholders: title, subtitle, bullet chart on the left, and data chart on the right.*

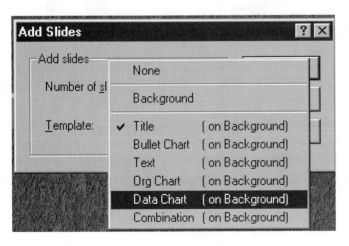

■ On the data chart slide which follows, double-click in the placeholder as directed.

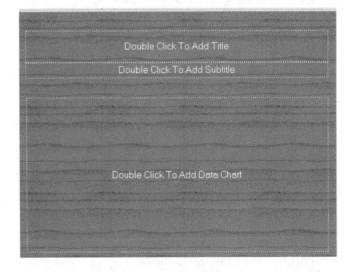

■ This will open the Data Chart Gallery for you to choose a desired Chart type. The default Chart type is Bar (Vert). Select a desired chart type from the Chart type list, then choose one of the display options.

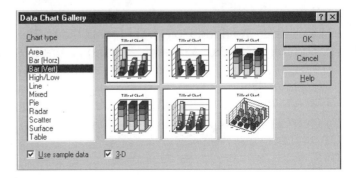

■ A datasheet table then displays along with a Data Chart Toolbar. Enter the data you wish to chart (and delete the sample data) as you did in Quattro Pro. The graph will reflect the new data. Click the View Datasheet button on the Toolbar to hide the datasheet. To see the datasheet table again, click the View Datasheet button again.

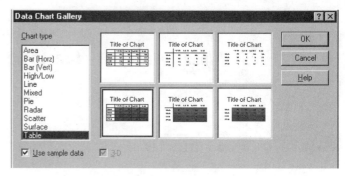

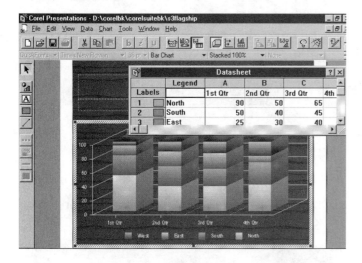

■ You may enhance your graph with data labels. **Data labels** let you indicate the exact value of each data point. Click the Labels button on the Charting Toolbar.

■ To add a **legend**, click data chart placeholder, then select Legend from the Chart menu. Make the desired choices in the Legend Properties dialog box.

■ You may also display the data table along with the graph by clicking the Show Table button on the Toolbar.

■ To add a chart to a slide that does not have a chart placeholder, select Data Chart from the Insert menu. Then, click on the slide or drag to create an area for the chart to be inserted (similar to inserting a graphic).

Create a Table

■ A table may be added to Corel Presentations 7 using the same procedures used to add a graph. To create a table, select Data Chart as the slide template. Double-click the data chart placeholder. In the Data Chart Gallery dialog box which follows, select Table as the Chart type.

■ You may then choose from the table layouts which display.

■ In the Datasheet dialog box which follows, enter your data in place of the sample data.

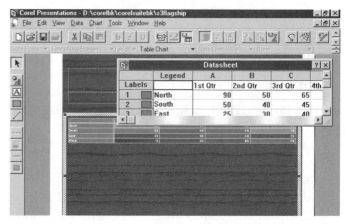

■ The font size may appear small. To change font attributes, click the Layout button on the Charting Toolbar. In the Table Properties dialog box which follows, click the Font tab and make the desired changes.

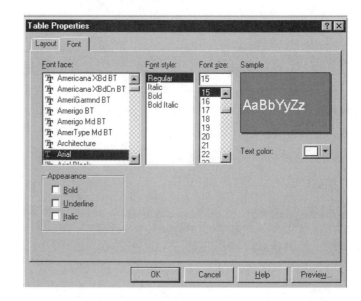

In this exercise, you will insert a graph slide and a table slide into a previously created presentation.

EXERCISE DIRECTIONS

1. Open ☐FLAGSHIP or ☐6FLAGSHIP.

2. Add a new Data Chart slide.

3. Enter the slide title and subtitle shown in Illustration A.

4. Create a vertical bar chart using the format shown in the illustration.

5. Delete the data from the datasheet and enter the new data shown below:

	1994	1995	1996	1997
Townhouses	20	40	85	88
Comm. Prop.	8	12	24	31
Houses	45	44	87	91

6. Display all labels.

7. Switch to Slide Sorter view.

8. Move the new graph slide to become slide 4.

9. Switch to Slide Editor view.

10. Display slide 3 (OUR SALES FORCE). Change the graphic(s).

11. Add a new Data Chart slide after slide 4 and select Table as the Chart type. Use any desired table layout.

12. Create the Slide title table data shown in Illustration B.

13. Change the font size for table text to 30 point.

14. Switch to Slide Sorter view. Check your slide order with those shown in Illustration C. Make any necessary adjustments.

15. Print one copy as Handouts with 6 slides per page in Black and White.

16. Close the file; save the changes.

ILLUSTRATION A

Successful Sales Techniques=Increased Sales

Commercial Property and House Unit Sales Over Four Years

ILLUSTRATION B

Sample Inventory

TYPE	RMS	BATHS	PRICE	FEATURES
Country Est	7	4	$1,300,000	pool, spa
Townhouse	8	3	$500,000	fml dng rm
Colonial Est	10	5	$1,585,000	waterfront

ILLUSTRATION C

FLAGSHIP REALTY

Pamela DeStefano, President

1

PROPERTY TYPES

- Homes of Distinction
- Commercial Properties
- Residential Townhouses
- Exclusive Agent for Pineview Estates

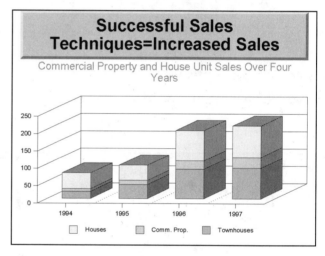

2

OUR SALES FORCE

- 85 Professional Salespeople
- 50% are members of Flagship's Private Brokerage Council
  - Designation
  - Awarded to sales agents who handled sales over $1 million.

3

Successful Sales Techniques=Increased Sales

Commercial Property and House Unit Sales Over Four Years

4

Sample Inventory

TYPE	RMS	BATHS	PRICE	FEATURES
Country Est	7	4	$1,300,000	pool, spa
Townhouse	8	3	$500,000	fml dng rm
Colonial Est	10	5	$1,585,000	waterfront

5

Services Include

- Private financial evaluation
- Mortgage payment table constructed for each buyer
- Property tour videos
- Internet access for international sales and listings

6

ILLUSTRATION C *(continued)*

Qualified Leader in Distinctive Properties

National and International Holdings

- Unparalleled knowledge of and a commitment to high-end properties on the North Fork.
- Demonstrated track record.
- Unique ability to match client needs and inventory.
- Broad international client base.
  - ▸ Affiliate offices abroad
    - – Europe
    - – Asia

7

KEYSTROKES

CREATE A GRAPH ON A SLIDE

1. Click **Add Slides** button .... 🔲
   on the Toolbar.
   OR
   - Click **Slide**........................ `Alt`+`S`
   - Click **Add Slides**........................ `A`
2. Click **Template** list box .... `Alt`+`T`
   - Select **Data Chart**.
   - Click **OK** .... `Enter`
3. Double-click placeholder.
4. Highlight to select desired **Chart type** .... `Alt`+`C`
   - Click to select desired chart layout.
5. Click **OK** .... `Enter`

6. Enter the data you wish to chart in the datasheet.
   To delete data in a datasheet:
   a. Click to select Chart.
   b. Click **View Datasheet** button on Toolbar....................................... 🔳
   c. Click **Edit** .... `Alt`+`E`
   d. Click **Select All**........................... `S`
      to select data.
   e. Press **Delete** key .... `Del`
   f. Click **Data**............................. `D`
   g. Click **OK**................................. `Enter`
   h. Click the **View Datasheet** button on Toolbar to hide the datasheet ...... 🔳
   i. Click outside the graph to return to Corel Presentations 7 slide.

CREATE A TABLE

1. Follow steps 1-3 on the left.
2. Highlight to select **Table** .... `Alt`+`C`
   as **Chart type**.
   - Click to select desired table layout.
3. Click **OK**................................... `Enter`
4. Type text in cells.
5. Press **Tab** to advance to next cell.
   OR
   Press **Shift + Tab**................. `Shift`+`Tab`
   to move to the previous cell.
6. Click on slide to insert table and return to Corel Presentations 7 slide.

ADD GRAPH OR TABLE TO AN EXISTING SLIDE

1. Click **Insert** .... `Alt`+`I`
2. Click **Data Chart** .... `A`
3. Drag mouse to desired size and release.

Exercise

7

■ **Insert an Organization Chart on a Slide**

NOTES

Insert an Organization Chart on a Slide

■ An **Organization Chart** is used to illustrate a company's hierarchy or structure.

■ Organization charts may also be used to show the flow of a project or a family tree.

■ Corel Presentations 7 contains an organization chart template to help display organization chart data.

■ To create an organization chart, select the Org Chart template. If you are inserting a slide to an existing presentation, click the Add Slides button 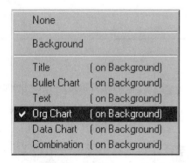 on the Toolbar, then select Org Chart as the template.

None	
Background	
Title	(on Background)
Bullet Chart	(on Background)
Text	(on Background)
✓ Org Chart	(on Background)
Data Chart	(on Background)
Combination	(on Background)

■ On the organization chart slide which follows, double-click in the placeholder as directed.

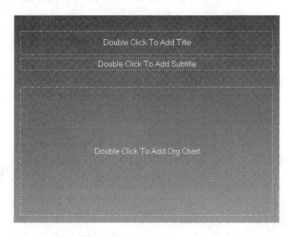

■ By default, nine boxes display. (You will note, too, that new menu items appear). You can attach additional boxes to existing boxes, and rearrange boxes. You can format each box with different fonts, font sizes, fill colors, and borders, as well as align text left, center, or right within the box.

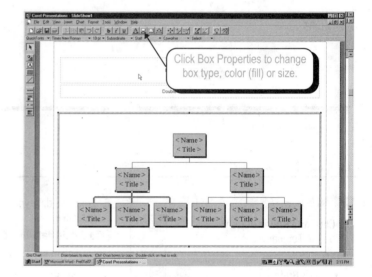

Click Box Properties to change box type, color (fill) or size.

■ You may insert boxes in order to change the organizational structure. There are four box types; each one attaches to existing boxes differently:

• A Subordinate attaches below another box because a subordinate is below another position in the chain of command.

• A Co-worker attaches to the left or right of another box because a co-worker is a position of equal authority.

• A Manager attaches above another box because a manager is a position of higher authority.

• Staff does not attach to another box; it comes off another position.

- To add a new box, click an existing box to which you wish to add a new box. Then, select the box type from the Insert menu.

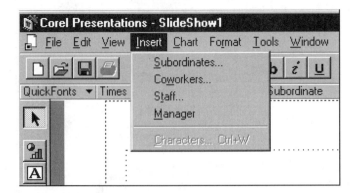

- The number of lines you can enter in a box is dependent on font size and number of other boxes in the organization chart. You can type text continually; the box expands as you type. Press Enter to start a new line. Double-click the box placeholder and type the desired text to be added.

- To change the box type, color (fill), or size, click the box to be affected, then click the Box Properties button ▣ on the Toolbar. In the Box Properties dialog box which follows, select the desired tab and make the desired changes.

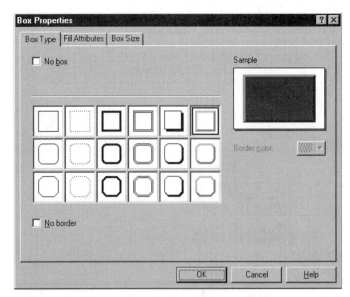

- To delete a box, click the box, then press the Delete key.

- To finish the chart, click anywhere outside the Organization Chart.

In this exercise, you will insert an organization chart slide and a graph slide to a previously created slide show. See desired result on pages 416 and 417.

EXERCISE DIRECTIONS

1. Open ▦FOOD or 🖫7FOOD.

2. Add a new Org Chart slide.

3. Enter the slide title and subtitle as shown in Illustration A on page 416.

4. Add two subordinate boxes; one to Barney Kind and the other to Bob Vestry. Include the information shown. Delete two boxes on the third level.

5. Change the second level of boxes to blue, the third level to green, and the fourth level to brown.
   ✓ *Hold the Shift key while clicking the mouse to select multiple boxes.*

6. Switch to Slide Sorter view.

7. Move the new slide to become slide 4.

8. Switch to Slide Editor view.

9. Add a new Combination slide.

10. Select Pie Chart as the Chart type and select the default format. Enter the slide title and subtitle and bullet text as shown in Illustration B on page 416. Delete the data from the datasheet and enter the following new data:

Paris	Milan	London	Madrid	Sydney	Hong Kong
400	600	800	300	300	900

   ✓ *Enter the cities in the Legend column as well as the Labels 1 column. Enter the data in the Pie 1 column.*

11. Switch to Slide Sorter view.

12. Move the combination slide to become Slide 6.

13. Print one copy as Handouts with 6 slides per page in black and white.

14. Close the file; save the changes.

ILLUSTRATION A

ILLUSTRATION B

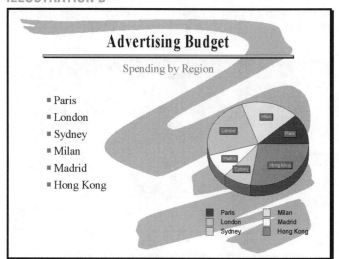

DESIRED RESULT

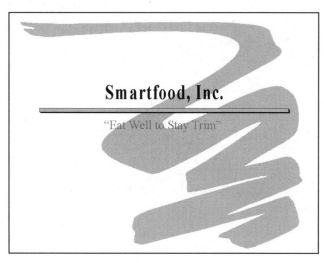

1

2

3

4

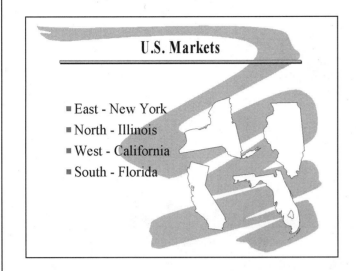

5

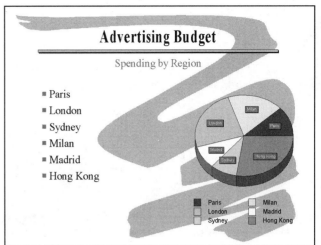

6

Smartfood's Success...

- People want low-fat, low-calorie foods that taste great

7

KEYSTROKES

CREATE AN ORGANIZATION CHART

1. Click **Add Slides** button .... [+🔲]
   on Toolbar.
   OR
   a. Click **Slide**........................ [Alt]+[S]
   b. Click **Add Slides**....................... [S]
2. Click **Template** list box .... [Alt]+[T]
   - Select **Org Chart**.................. [↓][↑]
   - Click **OK** .... [Enter]
3. Double-click placeholder.

4. Double-click each box to enter text.
   OR
   To add boxes:
   a. Click box to select it.
   b. Click **Insert**..................... [Alt]+[I]
   c. Click desired box type:
      - **Subordinate**............................ [S]
      - **Coworker** .... [W]
      - **Staff**...................................... [T]
      - **Manager**................................. [M]

5. Click outside organization chart to return to slide.

To change box properties (fill, box type and size):
   - Click **Box Properties** button........ [🖥]
     on Toolbar.
   - Make desired changes.
   - Click **OK** .... [Enter]

Exercise

8

■ **Summary**

In this exercise, you will create a presentation in Outliner View. You will move the slides, change the master for the show, and print the slide show.

EXERCISE DIRECTIONS

1. Create a new slide show.

2. Select a Title template as the first slide.

3. Use the default Master background.

4. Switch to Outliner view and create the outline shown in Illustration A on page 419.

5. Switch the template to Bullet Chart beginning with slide 2.

6. Switch to Slide Editor view.

7. Display slide 1.

8. Change the background to FOREST found in the Nature category of the Master Gallery.

9. Switch to Slide Sorter view.

10. Move slide 5 to become slide 4.

11. Select slide 3 and change the template to Title.

12. Select slide 6 and change the template to Title.

13. Display slide 8 and insert a relevant graphic.

14. Insert a new Bullet Chart slide after slide 4 (Rising Exports) that reads:

> Political Stability
> - Current Leadership
> - Free Elections

15. Switch to Outliner view.

16. Spell check.

17. Switch to Slide Editor view.

18. Add a new Org Chart slide, and enter the text as shown in Illustration B on page 419. Delete/Add boxes as necessary.

19. Switch to Slide Sorter view.

20. Move the new Org Chart slide to become slide 10.

21. Display slide 3. Insert a relevant graphic.

22. Print one copy as Handouts with six slides per page in black and white.

23. Save the file; name it BRAZIL.

24. Close the slide show window.

I.   BRAZIL
        A.   Investment Opportunities
II.   Brief History of the Brazilian Economy
        A.   Debt crisis in the 1980s
                1.   Increased foreign borrowing
                2.   Rising international interest rates
        B.   Recent recovery of the economy
        C.   Research Department's report on the history of the economy
III.   Why is the Brazilian Economy Ready for Foreign Investment?
IV.   Undervaluation
        A.   Specific stocks
        B.   Government debt
V.   Rising Exports
        A.   To the U.S.
        B.   To Europe
        C.   To Latin America
VI.   Overview of Possible Investments
VII.   Stocks in Specific Industries
        A.   Coffee
        B.   Steel
        C.   Chemical
VIII.   Bonds
        A.   Short term
        B.   Long term
IX.   Conclusion
        A.   Reasons to Invest through Simpson Investment Advisors, Inc.
                1.   Rate of return on investments
                2.   Global trading
                3.   Highly trained professionals
        B.   To Summarize...

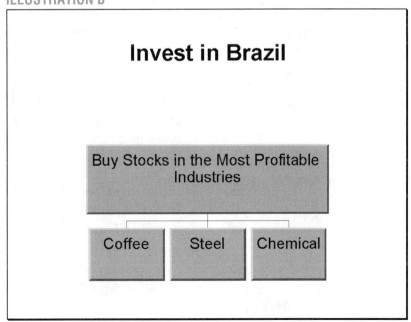

Exercise 9

- Select Text Align Text
- Change Text Appearance Copy and Move Text on a Slide
- Move and Size Placeholders

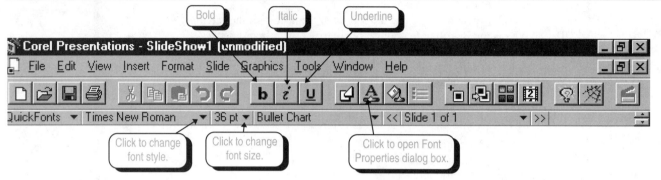

NOTES

Select Text

- In order to edit text on a slide, you must be in edit mode. To do so, double-click the text you wish to edit. The placeholder will then display with sizing handles, and the insertion point will change to an I-beam – ready for you to select the text you wish to edit. The same techniques for selecting text in WordPerfect 7 apply in Presentations 7:

  - Double-click to select a word.

  - Position the insertion point before the first word to select, hold down the Shift key and click at the end of the text you wish to select in order to highlight several words or a sentence.

  - Click and drag the mouse to highlight text.

- Text may be edited in Slide Editor or Outliner views; text *may not* be edited in Slide Sorter view.

- Some edits affect individual slides, and others affect all slides in a slide show. Changes affecting all slides in a slide show will be covered in Exercise 10.

Align Text

- Corel Presentations 7 lets you left, right, or center justify text in a placeholder on individual slides or for all slides in the slide show. To change alignment, select Justification from the Format menu, then choose Left, Right, or Center. You can also change justification using the following keystrokes:

  - Left: Ctrl+L

  - Right: Ctrl+R

  - Center: Ctrl+E

- Use Slide Editor view to change text alignment because text formatting is displayed in this view.

Change Text Appearance

- Corel Presentations 7 allows you to change the text's font face, style, size, appearance (bold, underline, italic), and color using the same techniques learned in WordPerfect. To do so, select (highlight) the text you want to change and click an appropriate button on the Toolbar or Power Bar.

  - To apply more than one change to text, select Font from the Format menu, or click the Font button 🅰 on the Toolbar.

- In the Font Properties dialog box which follows, select the Font tab and make the desired changes.

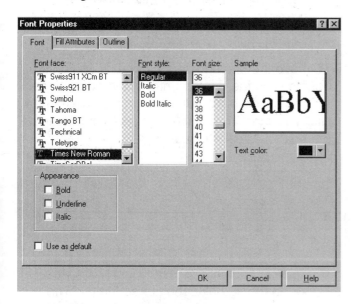

- To change the text color, click the Text color button and choose a desired font color from the displayed palette.

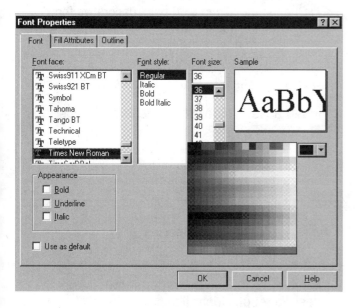

■ You can also change the outline color and/or style, as well as the fill pattern of text. For example, you can create a yellow font with a blue outline. Or you can create a white font with a patterned fill. Be careful because some combinations make text difficult to read, though others can create interesting text effects.

- To change the text outline color, style or fill, select the Fill Attributes and/or Outline tab. In the dialog boxes which follow, make the desired selections.

■ Remember, to receive a format change, text must first be selected.

Copy and Move Text on a Slide

■ You can use the same methods to cut, copy, paste, and drag and drop text in Presentations 7 that you used in WordPerfect 7.

■ You can move text only in Slide Editor or Outliner views. It is more efficient however to use Outliner view when moving or copying text since all text can be viewed on screen at the same time.

■ Use cut/copy and paste techniques to copy text to more than one new location or to copy text to a different presentation. Use the drag and drop technique in Outliner view to move or copy text to a new location or to rearrange bulleted items.

■ To move or copy an entire slide in Outliner view, point to the slide icon, then click and hold down the mouse button which will highlight all the items on the slide. Drag the highlighted text to the desired point of insertion. (You will see a horizontal red line positioned where you want to insert the text.) Release the mouse button and your text will drop into place. To move a bulleted item, point to the bullet you wish to move. When a double-headed arrow appears, click and hold down the mouse button to highlight the text, then drag it to the desired location. Again, you will see a horizontal red line positioned where you want to insert the text. Release the mouse button and your text will drop into place.

Move and Size Placeholders

■ Placeholders can be moved, sized and deleted.

■ To move, size or delete a placeholder, you must first display handles (to put the placeholder into edit mode).

■ Double-click the text to display handles and a placeholder box. You can then size the placeholder as you did when working with graphics: Drag a top or bottom middle handle to change the vertical size (height); drag a left or right middle handle to change the horizontal size (width); drag a corner handle to size the placeholder proportionally. When you size a placeholder, the text within it will adjust to the new borders.

✓ *If you click the placeholder once, Corel Presentations 7 displays handles without a placeholder box. Sizing the box in this mode will change the size of the text as well as the box. To change only the size of the box, you must double-click the text so that both handles and the placeholder box appears.*

■ To move the placeholder box and its contents, double-click the text (to enter edit mode), place the pointer on the border (not on a handle), then click and hold the mouse button while dragging the box to a desired location.

In this exercise, you will insert an organization chart and a graph slide to a previously created slide show. In addition, you will manipulate placeholders and change the size and color of text on slides. Check your changes with the desired result shown on page 424.

EXERCISE DIRECTIONS

1. Open ☐KIT or ☐9KIT.

2. Add a new Org Chart slide, and enter text in 28 point as shown in Illustration A on page 423. Delete/Add boxes as necessary.
   - Color the title red.
   - Add a Coworker box to include the information shown.

3. Add a new Data Chart slide using the default format as shown in Illustration B. (Stacked 100% bar chart.)
   - Delete the data from the datasheet and enter the new data shown below.
   - Sales Before and After Using Creative Kits.

	Great Foods	Harly Hotel	Venus Graphics
Before	100	485	195
After	200	555	305

   ✓ *Since you will not need all the columns and rows in the datasheet, highlight the row and/or column you do not need and select Exclude Row/Col from the Data menu.*

4. Change titles in all slides, except the Title slide, to upper- and lower-case.

5. Display Slide 1.

6. Shorten the title placeholder so the text wraps to two lines, and move the title to the top left of the slide as shown in the desired result illustrated on page 424.
   - Left align the title text.
   - Change the title to a 60-point decorative font.
   - Shorten the subtitle placeholder, and move it to the bottom right of the slide.
   - Right-align subtitle text.

7. Switch to Outliner view.

8. Insert a New Slide after slide 6 that reads:
   Creative Sales Kits provide….
   - Sales Brochures
   - Business Cards
   - Letterheads
   - Brochures
   - Catalogs
   - Presentation Materials

9. Switch to Slide Sorter view.

10. Move the slides in the order shown in the desired result illustration.

11. Switch to Slide Editor view.

12. Print one copy as Handouts with six slides per page in black and white.

13. Close the file; save the changes.

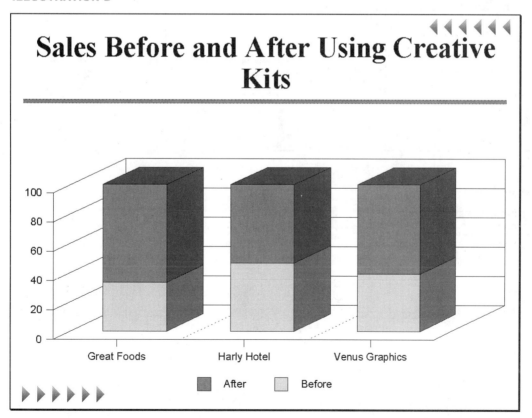

DESIRED RESULT

1

◄◄◄◄◄

CREATIVE SALES

Sales Meeting
June 8, 1997

▶▶▶▶▶▶

2

◄◄◄◄◄

Why Use It?

- Builds corporate identity
- Provides numerous sales materials
  - Brochures
  - Product Catalog
  - Presentation Materials

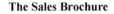

▶▶▶▶▶▶

3

◄◄◄◄◄

Sales Kits

- Tool for making initial client contact
- A support system for sales rep
- Way to provide clients with material to make an informed decision about buying your product

▶▶▶▶▶▶

4

◄◄◄◄◄

Sales Materials

- The same logo on all materials
- The same paper
- The same typefaces
- Business cards, letterheads, brochures, catalogs, presentation materials

▶▶▶▶▶▶

5

◄◄◄◄◄

The Sales Brochure

- Similar to marketing brochure
  - Contain creative headlines
  - Contain attractive graphics
- Should possess the same visual elements of your corporate identity
- Result should be company and product exposure

▶▶▶▶▶▶

6

◄◄◄◄◄

The Product Catalog

- Contains more specific information about company products
- May include prices and discount offers
- May be sent through mail to prospective clients
- More effective when handed out personally on a sales call or visit to set up a sales call
- Use simple drawings or photos to show product line

▶▶▶▶▶▶

7

◄◄◄◄◄

Creative Sales Kits provide...

- Sales Brochures
- Business Cards
- Letterheads
- Brochures
- Catalogs
- Presentation Materials

▶▶▶▶▶▶

8

◄◄◄◄◄

Presentation Materials

- The flip chart
  - Visuals are printed on sheets of paper and inserted into flip chart carrier
- Refrigerator magnet
  - Leave-behind gift upon completion of sales call

▶▶▶▶▶▶

9

◄◄◄◄◄

Sales Before and After Using Creative Kits

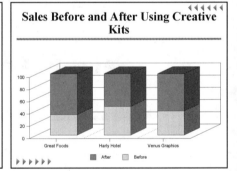

Great Foods   Harly Hotel   Venus Graphics

■ After   ■ Before

▶▶▶▶▶▶

10

◄◄◄◄◄

Our Company's Strength is Our Organization

Creative Sales, Inc.

David Warren
President

Pamela Brice
Vice President

Junior Medina
Vice President

Barry James
Vice President

Karen Akers
Manager

Donald Greeny
Manager

Bryan Mathis
Manager

Kevin Waren
Sales

Mary Carley
Sales

Crist Kabala
Sales

▶▶▶▶▶▶

KEYSTROKES

CHANGE FONT

F9

1. Select text to change.

2. Click **Font** button on
   Power Bar .... `Times New Roman  ▼`

   OR

1. Click **Format** .... `Alt`+`R`

2. Click **Font**............................... `F`

3. Select desired font and options..... `↓` `↑`

4. Click **OK** .... `Enter`

CHANGE FONT SIZE

F9

1. Select text to change.

2. Click **Font Size** drop-down list
   on Power Bar .... `36 pt ▼`

   • Select desired font size.

   OR

   • Click **Format**...................... `Alt`+`R`

   • Click **Font**................................. `F`

3. Select desired font size .... `↓` `↑`

4. Click **OK** .... `Enter`

CHANGE EMPHASIS (BOLD, ITALIC, SHADOW, UNDERLINE, COLOR)

1. Select text to affect.

2. Click desired attribute
   button on Toolbar .... `b` `i` `U`

   OR

   • Click **Format**...................... `Alt`+`R`

   • Click **Font** .... `F`

3. Select desired options .... `↓` `↑`

4. Click **OK** .... `Enter`

EDIT PLACEHOLDERS

To display handles:

• Click once on text to display handles
  and placeholders box.

• Double-click inside the text
  placeholder box to display placeholder.

To move:

1. Display handles.

2. Position mouse pointer on border (not
   on a handle).

3. Hold down left mouse button and drag
   text to new location.

4. Release mouse button.

To copy:

1. Display handles.

2. Position mouse pointer on border (not
   on a handle).

3. Press **Ctrl** and position mouse pointer
   on border (not on a handle).

4. Hold down mouse button and drag
   text to new location.

5. Release mouse button.

To size:

1. Display handles.

2. Position mouse pointer on a top or
   bottom middle handle to change
   height, a left or right handle to change
   width, or a corner handle to change
   size proportionately.

3. Drag the handle until the placeholder is
   the desired size.

To delete:

1. Display handles.

2. Press **Delete**.

■ **Customize the Slide Background**
■ **Customize the Template** ■ **Customize Bullet Chart Slides**

NOTES

Customize the Slide Background

■ In the previous exercise, you learned to make editing changes on individual slides. You can, however, edit one slide and have the changes appear on all slides in a slide show.

■ To change the background color, add clip art or a logo and have it affect all slides in a slide show, you must make the changes to the slide's **Background Layer**. To insert a graphic, for example, select Background Layer from the Slide menu. Select QuickArt from Insert menu and position the image on the slide as desired. Then, select Slide Layer from the Background menu to return to the slide layer. The graphic will appear on all slides in your slide show, regardless of the template type (Bullet Chart, Data Chart, etc.).

Customize the Template

■ To change the font style, font size, color, and/or position of text or placeholders so that they affect all the slides of a particular template (Title, Bullet Chart, Data Chart), you must make changes to the template's Layout Layer. For example, if you wish to change the layout of a Bullet Chart slide, display a bullet chart slide, then select Layout Layer from the Slide menu and make any desired changes. If you right-align the title placeholder in a Bullet Chart slide, all Bullet Chart slides in the active slide show will display right-aligned placeholder text. If you change the title text color to red on a Data Chart slide, it will affect the text color on all Data Chart slides. Use the same procedures to edit text as you did in the previous exercise, but remember, any change you make to the template will affect all slides.

■ Text formatted on separate slides override changes made on the layout layer.

■ After making the desired changes on the Background or Layout Layers, return to Slide Layer and view each slide in the slide show to see its effects. You may need to make adjustments to the Background or Layout layer after seeing the effects on individual slides.

Customize Bullet Chart Slides

■ Bullet Chart slides contain several parts which can be modified. You can change the appearance and spacing of the text and the bullets, as well as the box around the bulleted text. (The default displays no box around the bulleted text.)

• To make modifications to bullet chart slides, click on the bullet placeholder, then select Bullet Chart Properties from the Format menu. In the Bullet Chart Properties dialog box which follows, select the Fonts tab to make font changes to bulleted text.

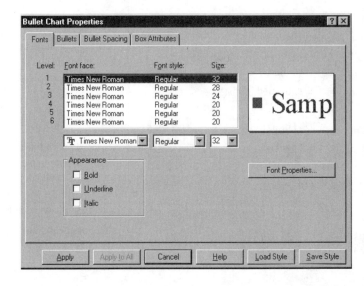

- To change the bullet style or justification, select the Bullets tab. Click the Bullet set drop-down menu to select a bullet style for *all* bullet levels. Click the Bullet button to select a bullet style for *each* bullet level.   If you select More Options from the Bullet button, you can create a bullet using the WordPerfect Characters.

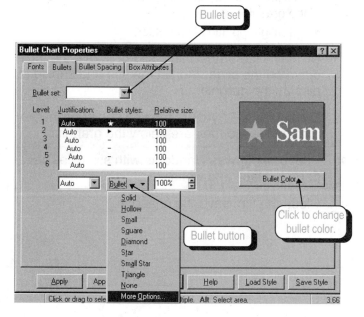

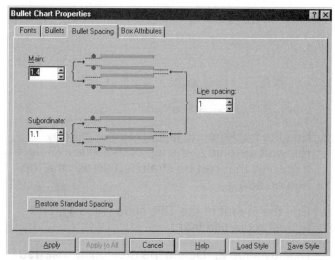

- Click the Bullet Spacing tab to adjust spacing from the bullet to the text and line spacing between bulleted text items.

- Click the Box Attributes tab to change the box shape and fill attributes of the box surrounding the bulleted text.

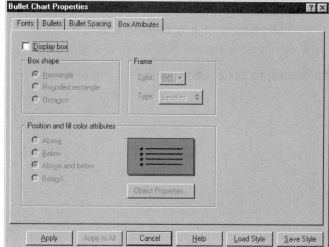

> *In this exercise, you will edit the background and layout layers by adding a graphic and changing the bullets. Note that all slides in the slide show will be affected.*

EXERCISE DIRECTIONS

1. Open ⛋**FLAGSHIP** or 🖫**10FLAGSH**.

2. Edit the background layer by inserting any relevant graphic at the top of the slide. (Select a graphic that can be stretched across the top and do so.)

3. Edit the layout of the Title slide (slide 1), and left-align the title text.

4. Display slide 2. Delete the previously inserted graphic.

5. Edit the layout of the Bullet Chart slide (slide 2):
   - Left-align the title text.
   - Move the Title and subtitle placeholder below the graphic.
   - Change the first level bullet to a red star.
   - Change the second level bullet to a blue star.

6. Switch to Slide Editor view.

7. Display slide 4 (the Data Chart slide).
   - Position and size the title placeholder to cover the top graphic.
   - Left align the title placeholder.

8. Display slide 5 (the Table slide). Move the table down on the slide. Adjust the title and subitle to display the graphic.

9. Display slide 7. Adjust the title and subtitle placeholder so they are below the graphic.

10. Print one copy as Handouts with six slides per page in black and white.

11. Close the file; save the changes.

KEYSTROKES

CUSTOMIZE SLIDE BACKGROUND

1. Click **Slide**........................... Alt + S
2. Click **Background Layer**................. B
3. Make any additions (add a graphic, if desired).
4. Click **Backgrounds** .... Alt + B
5. Click **Slide Layer**........................... S

CUSTOMIZE TEMPLATE

1. Display slide containing template you wish to customize (Title, Bullet Chart, Data Chart).
2. Click **Slide**........................... Alt + S
3. Click **Layout Layer** L

4. Make desired change.
5. Click **Layouts**......................... Alt + L
6. Click **Slide Layer**............................ S

   ✔ *To change bullet format on a Bullet Chart slide, follow steps below.*

CHANGE BULLET STYLE

1. Display slide containing Bullet Chart.
2. Double-click in bulleted text box, or select individual bulleted items.
   OR
   To change bullet style for all Bullet Chart slides, follow steps to customize template.

3. Click **Format**........................
4. Click **Bullet Chart Properties** ....
5. Click one of the following tabs and make the desired changes:
   - **Fonts** to change font attributes.
   - **Bullets** to change bullet style and/or color.
   - **Bullet Spacing** to change line spacing between bulleted items.
   - **Box Attributes** to add and/or enhance the box around bulleted text.
6. Click **Apply** ....

Exercise

11

- Draw Closed Graphic or Line Objects ■ Create Text Objects
- Group and Separate Objects ■ Combine Objects
- Order Objects ■ Contour Text

NOTES

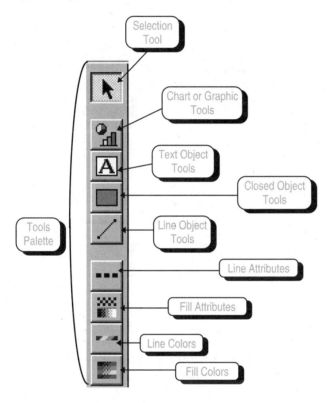

- Drawings may be added to slides only in Slide Editor or Slide Layout views. However, the drawing can be created outside the slide presentation by selecting the Create a new drawing option when starting Corel Presenations, or after selecting New from the File menu. This enables you to save your drawing using a variety of graphic formats (.PCX, GIF, JPEG). You may then insert it into another application or another Windows program.

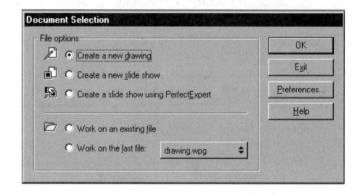

- If you select the Create a new drawing option, a blank drawing window appears for you to create your masterpiece. After the drawing is complete, save the file.

Draw Closed Graphic or Line Objects

- The Closed Object and Line Object tools located on the Tool Palette are used to create simple designs or drawings on your slides.

- Drawings created using the Tool Palette are considered graphic objects. Graphic objects include lines, shapes, and freehand designs. Closed shapes may be filled with a color or pattern.

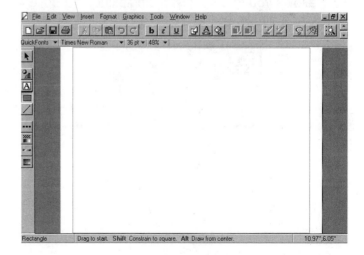

■ To draw an object (either in the blank drawing window or on a slide), first click the desired object tool you wish to use on the Tool Palette. The insertion point changes to a crosshair (+). Position the crosshair where you want to create the object; click and drag the crosshair to the point where you want to end the object. To display object handles, click the Select tool and click the object.

■ The drawing tools and their uses are described below:

- Use the Select tool to select a graphic (display its handles).

- Use Chart or Graphic tools to create bitmap images or to insert a Data Chart, Organization Chart, or QuickArt Image. (Working with Bitmap images will not be covered in this book.) Inserting a Data Chart or Organization Chart using the Chart Tools allows you to insert these items without using the Data Chart and Organization Chart templates.

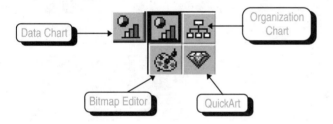

- Use Text Object tools to insert text into a drawing. The Text Area tool allows you to enter multiple lines of text; the Text Line tool allows you to enter just a single line; the Bullet Chart allows you to create a bullet list.

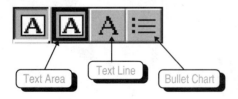

- Use Closed Object tools to create rectangles with square or round corners, circles, arrows, elipses, polygons, closed curves, arrow shapes, or polygons with equal sides.

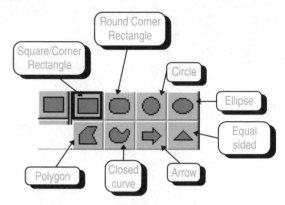

- Use Line Object tools to draw straight or curved lines, freehand lines or shapes, bezier curves, sections of ellipses or sections of circles.

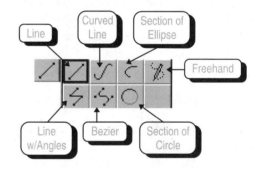

- Use the Line Attributes tool to change the width and appearance of lines. Line attributes change line appearance for lines themselves or the lines surrounding objects or text.

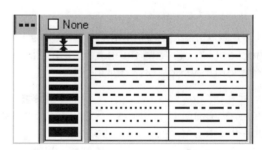

- Use the Fill Attributes tool 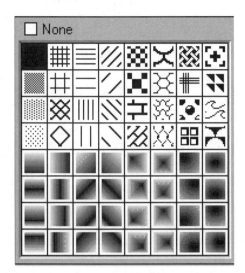 to change the fill pattern of objects and text.

- Use the Line Colors tool ⏚ to change the color of lines. Line colors change the color or lines themselves or the lines surrounding objects or text.

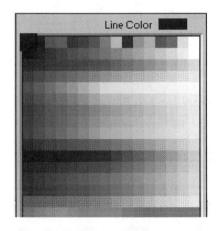

- Use the Fill Colors tool 📊 to change the fill color of objects or text.

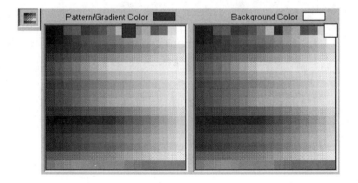

Create Text Objects

- Text entered on slides thus far has been entered into placeholders. Text added using Text Object tools creates a separate object that can be moved, sized, deleted, etc., without affecting text in placeholders.

- Use Text Object tools on the Tools Palette to add text to slides. Text Object tools include:
  - Text Area Ⓐ
  - Text Line Ⓐ
  - Bullet Chart ☰ (see explanations above).

- After selecting a Text Object tool, click once to create the object area, or click and drag to outline the area of the slide that the text should occupy using the procedures you used to draw a rectangle.

Group and Separate Objects

- When a drawing is comprised of several basic shapes, it is difficult to move, copy, or duplicate all the shapes at once. Grouping lets you select all the shapes in the group and treat them as a single object so that copying and moving the object becomes possible.

- To group an object comprised of individual shapes, select each shape (hold the Shift or Ctrl key down while you click each shape) and select Group from the Graphics menu. You can undo the grouped objects by selecting Separate from the Graphics menu.

Combine Objects

- The Combine option allows you to integrate selected objects into one drawing. For example, suppose you create a blue rectangle and place a yellow arrow within it. Select the two objects, then select Combine from the Graphics menu. The two objects will then integrate. The fill pattern or color of the two objects takes on that of the leftmost object.

Order Objects

■ Shapes may be layered or stacked on top of each other to create interesting effects. You may adjust the layers by moving them to the back or bringing them to the front. To adjust the layers of shapes or objects, click the shape or object and select <u>O</u>rder from the <u>G</u>raphics menu, then choose <u>F</u>ront, <u>B</u>ack, F<u>o</u>rward One, or Bac<u>k</u>ward One.

Contour Text

■ The **Contour Text** feature allows you to form text around a graphic object. You may choose to display both the graphic object and the text or just the contoured text. Note the samples below.

■ To contour text, select the text and the object (hold down the Shift key while you select each object), then select Contour <u>T</u>ext from the <u>G</u>raphics menu. Deselect the display text only option if you wish the graphic shape to show.

In this exercise, you will open a previously created slide show and create a logo on the background layer by using the Closed Object and Text Object tools. You will then view each slide in your presentation to see the effect. (See desired result, page 434.)

EXERCISE DIRECTIONS

1. Open ✉**FOOD** or ▭**11FOOD**.

2. Display slide 1.

3. Access the background layer.

4. Create a logo as follows:
   • Draw a circle and fill it with a contrasting shade of purple.
   • Create a text object and enter SmartFood, Inc. in 16 point. Color the text yellow.
   • Contour the text around the top center of the graphic.
   • Position the contoured graphic at the bottom left of the slide as shown in Illustration A on page 433.

5. Display slide 2.
   • Access the layout layer.
   • Right-align the text in the title placeholder.
   • Change the format of Level 1 bullets to a light pink heart.

6. Right-align the text in the title placeholder for the Data Chart, Org Chart and Combination Templates.

7. Access the slide layer.

8. Display slide 3. Insert any desired world map graphic. Adjust placeholders as necessary.

9. Display slide 6. Change the format of Level 1 bullets to a light pink heart.

10. Display slide 7. Using the tools in the Tool Palette, create a design of different shapes in different colors. Group the objects then position the graphic in the lower right corner of the slide as shown in Illustration A. Choose any desired color combination.

11. Print one copy as Handouts with eight slides per page.

12. Close the file; save the changes.

KEYSTROKES

DRAW SHAPES

1. Select desired tool from **Tools Palette**.
2. Position crosshair (+) at point where shape will start.
3. Click and drag mouse diagonally to shape ending point.
4. Release mouse button.

DRAW POLYGON OR CLOSED CURVE

1. Select **poloygon** or **closed curve** tool from **Closed Object tools** .... or
2. Position crosshair (+) at point where shape will start.
3. Move crosshair to draw shape, clicking to change direction or angle, if desired.
4. Double-click to stop drawing.

CREATE TEXT OBJECT

1. Click **Text Object tool** on the Tools Palette.. A
2. Drag to create text box.
3. Type text.

To edit text:

- Highlight text.
- Click **Fill Colors** tool .... on the Tools Palette to change text color.
- Change font and size by clicking appropriate Power Bar buttons.
4. Click outside text box.
5. Click and drag text box to desired location on slide.

LAYER OBJECTS

F6

1. Select desired object.
2. Click **Graphics** .... Alt + G
3. Click **Order**.................................... O
4. Click desired order option:

OPTION	MOVEMENT
F̲ront	Places object on top of all other objects.
Back	Places object behind all other objects.
F̲orward One	Moves object one layer up on the stack.
Bac̲kward One	Moves object one layer down on the stack.

GROUP AND SEPARATE OBJECTS

1. Select first object.
2. Shift-click remaining objects.
3. Click **Graphics**....................... Alt + G
4. Click **Group** .... G

To separate:

- Select object.
- Click **Graphics**................... Alt + G
- Click **Separate** .... E

OR

- Right-click grouped object, choose **Separate**.

CONTOUR OBJECTS

1. Draw a shape.
2. Create a text box.
3. Press the Shift key and click the shape and the text box.
4. Click **Graphics**....................... Alt + G
5. Click **Contour T̲ext** .... T

To separate:

- Click object.
- Click **Graphics**................... Alt + G
- Click **Separate** .... E

DESIRED RESULT

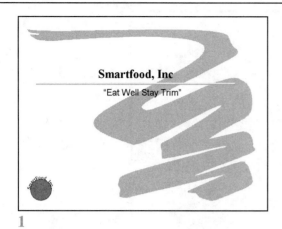

1

2

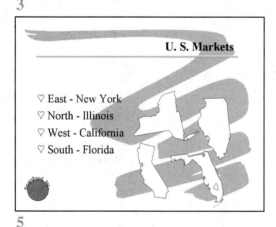

3

4

5

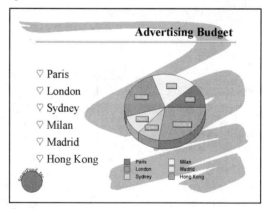

6

7

Exercise

12

- ■ **Use PerfectExpert to Create a Presentation**
- ■ **Insert Date**

NOTES

PerfectExpert

- ■ The **PerfectExpert** feature walks you through the fundamental steps for creating a presentation.

- ■ The first step in creating a presentation is to organize your thoughts. To help you plan the content of your presentation, PerfectExpert creates an outline for you and shows you what type of information you might include.

- ■ To launch PerfectExpert, select Create a slide show using PerfectExpert from the Document Selection dialog box.

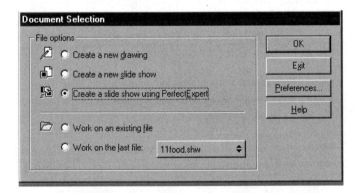

- ■ Select the template and the background as you did when you created a presentation in earlier exercises.

- ■ In the Slide Show PerfectExpert dialog box, you must indicate the type of presentation you are planning by clicking the appropriate tab.

- ■ The Content list within each tab helps PerfectExpert develop your presentation. Select an option and note the description of the presentation's objective. Then, click the Finish button.

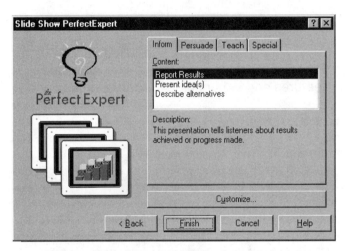

- ■ The presentation will be displayed in Outliner view. You may select the text and replace it with your own in this view, or select another view button in the Slide Show PerfectExpert dialog box. Click Close to continue.

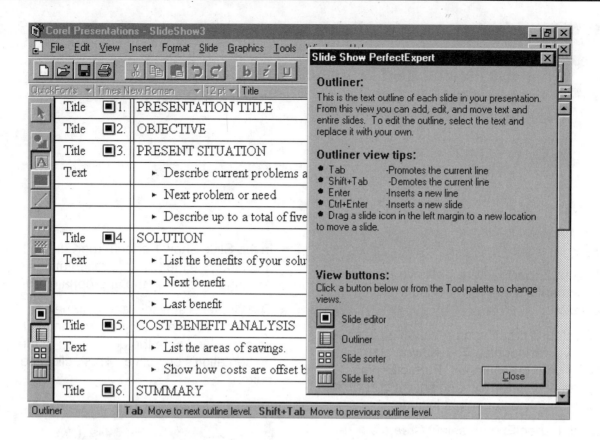

- Proceed to create your slide show using the features and enhancements learned in earlier exercises.

Insert Date

- The date may be included on individual slides or on all slides.

- To insert the date, you must first create a text box using the Text tool on the Tools Palette. Then, select Date from the Insert menu and choose either Text or Code. The Date Code option automatically updates the date whenever you retrieve or print the slide show. Remember, to include the date on all slides, you must insert it on the slide's Background Layer.

- The default date format is month, day, year. To change the format, select Date, Format from the Insert menu and select another.

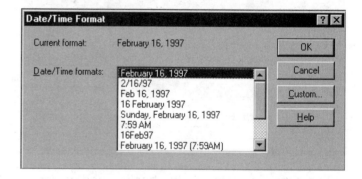

EXERCISE DIRECTIONS

1. Refer to the advertisement shown in Illustration A on page 438.

2. Use any desired light-color Background.

3. Use the PerfectExpert to create a slide presentation based on the information contained in the advertisement. Select *Persuade* as the presentation type and *Positive Audience* as the Content. (See Illustration B on page 439 for prompted topics.)

4. Edit the Layout Layer on all slide types:

   - Left-align all title placeholder text.
   - Change the first bullet level to blue stars and the second bullet level to red stars.

5. Using the design tools, create a logo and include the text, The Company of Tomorrow. Place it as desired.

6. Insert today's date (date text) on all slides in a sans serif 9 point font. Place it as desired.

7. Add relevant clip art to desired slides.

8. Spell check.

9. Print one copy as Handouts with eight slides per page in black and white.

10. Save the file; name it BUYONE.

11. Close the slide show window.

KEYSTROKES

PERFECTEXPERT

Open new document.

1. Click **File**.............................. Alt + F

2. Click **New**...................................... N

3. Click Create a slide show using **PerfectExpert**...................... Alt + E

4. Select Template and Background from Master Gallery.

5. Click **OK** .... Enter

6. Click desired tab to select a presentation type:

   - **Inform**
   - **Persuade**
   - **Teach**
   - **Special**

7. Click a desired **Content** option ... Alt + C

8. Click **Finish** .... Alt + F

9. Click **Slide Editor** view button or **Outliner View** button (depending on how you wish to compose slide text).

10. Delete PerfectExpert text and insert your own.

INSERT DATE

1. Click the **Text Object** tool on the Tools Palette.. A

2. Draw a text box.

3. Click **Insert**............................. Alt + I

4. Click **Date** .... D

5. Click an option:

   - **Text**.. T
   - **Code** C

   OR

   - **Date Format**............................... F
   - Select another format.
   - Click **OK** .... Enter

ILLUSTRATION A

PIONEER
PERSONAL COMPUTERS
For Quality Above and Beyond

The BookLife 500 Series. Notebooks perfectly designed for the mobile world. We took a close look at the way a notebook should feel, the way it travels, adapts and performs.

We saw a big need for flexibility. So, our notebooks are expandable by design—second batteries, second hard drives, available 28.8 fax/modems, CD-ROM capabilities, docking options and a full range of the latest Pentium processors.

But we also paid attention to the outside of our notebooks. A beautiful design. A smooth feel. A sophisticated color.

Now, combine these features with performance. The result is a personal computer that is above and beyond.

Introducing the BookLife 500 Series. A machine to make your daily experience with a notebook very productive. A status indicator for access to important operating information. Superb color video that's easy on the eyes. A new design because the way a notebook looks and feels is important, too. A palm rest for comfort. A newly designed keyboard for convenience. The BookLife 500 Series comes standard with CD-ROM, 16-bit sound, color video and a multi-function bay for endless expandability. And...

Multimedia equipped, powerful and expandable. So you get all the big things you need in a notebook with all the little details, too. *All for the price of **$2,500**, including a one-year warranty--for service and parts--lower than any other notebook in its class.*

Pioneer

ILLUSTRATION B

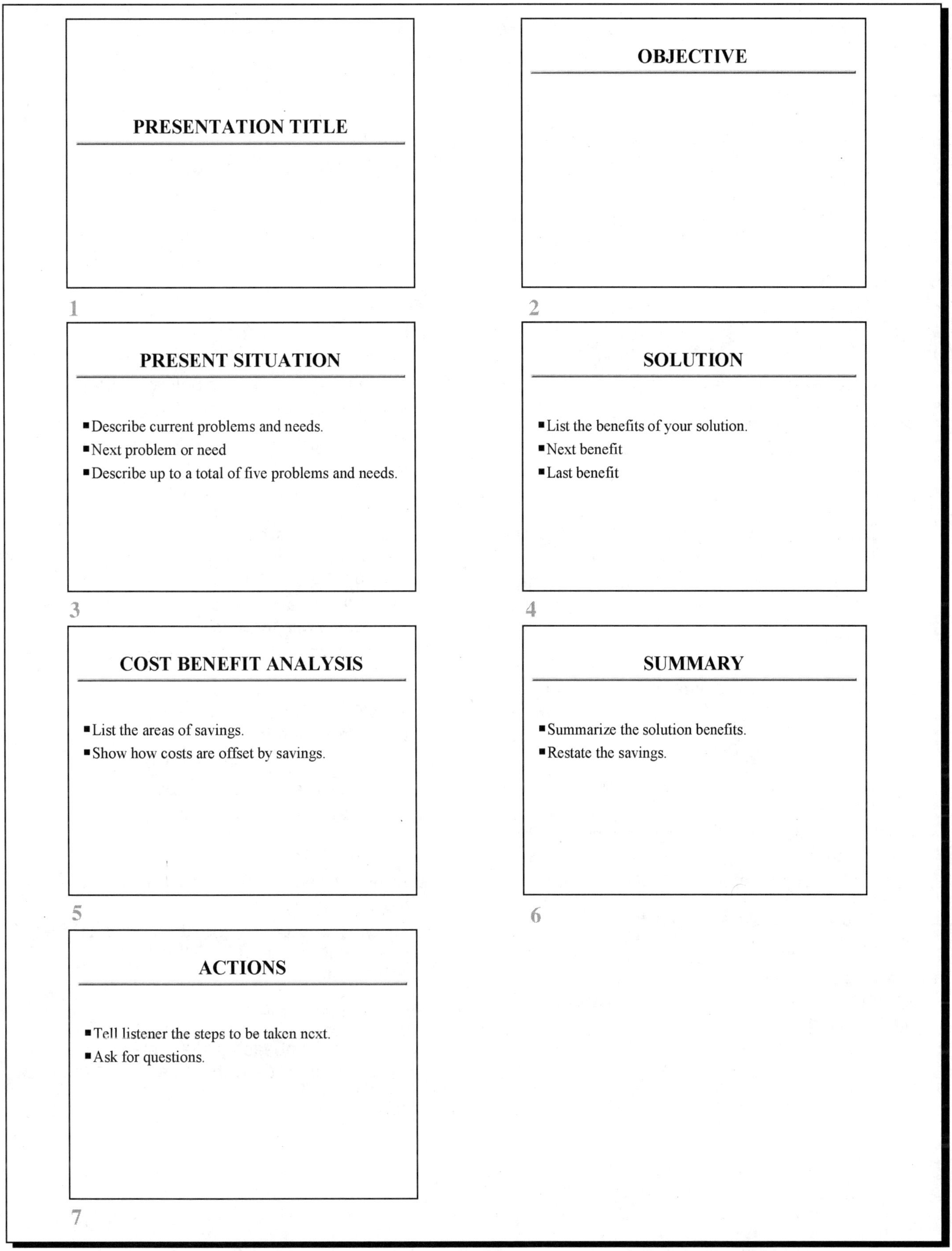
PRESENTATION TITLE
1
OBJECTIVE
2
PRESENT SITUATION
▪Describe current problems and needs.
▪Next problem or need
▪Describe up to a total of five problems and needs.
3
SOLUTION
▪List the benefits of your solution.
▪Next benefit
▪Last benefit
4
COST BENEFIT ANALYSIS
▪List the areas of savings.
▪Show how costs are offset by savings.
5
SUMMARY
▪Summarize the solution benefits.
▪Restate the savings.
6
ACTIONS
▪Tell listener the steps to be taken next.
▪Ask for questions.
7

Exercise

13

■ **Summary**

In this exercise, you will create a presentation for GreatGains Mutual Fund, a company that wants more investors to purchase their securities. This slide show will include a table, organization chart and data chart slides.

EXERCISE DIRECTIONS

1. Create a new slide show.

2. Select a Title template as the first slide.

3. Use TAUPE as the Master background.

4. Access the Background Layer.

   • Insert today's date in the top left corner of the slide in a serif 10 point italic font.
   • Create the logo on the top and bottom right corner of the slide as shown in Illustration A on page 441.

5. Create the Title Slide (1) as shown in Illustration A.

6. Select Bullet Chart template as the second slide.

7. Access the Layout Layer.

   • Change the first two bullet styles to another style and color.
   • Adjust the title placeholder so it does not interfere with the logo.

8. Access the Slide Layer.

9. Create slide 2 as shown in Illustration B on page442.

10. Create the remaining slides using the appropriate templates as shown in Illustration B, on page 442.

11. Use the names and titles below for the organization chart:

   Rachael Black: Head Fund Manager
   John Chow: Vice President
   Pamela Haupt: Vice President
   Jaime Cohen: Associate
   Harry Smith: Associate
   David Stuart: Associate
   Chandra Rao: Associate

   • Adjust the organization chart's position so it does not overlap with the logo.

12. Enter the text and data below to create the Data Chart:

   GreatGains Fund Growth Outpaces Similar Funds
   Sales (in $ millions)

	1995	1996	1997
GreatGains	200	325	420
FastMoney	156	173	165

   • Display the data labels.
   • Adjust the chart's position so it does not overlap the bottom logo.

13. Display each slide. Adjust the placeholders and/or the font size of the titles so they do not interfere with the logos.

14. Save the file; name it INVEST.

15. Print one copy of each slide in black and white. Compare each slide with those in Illustration B.

16. Close the slide show window.

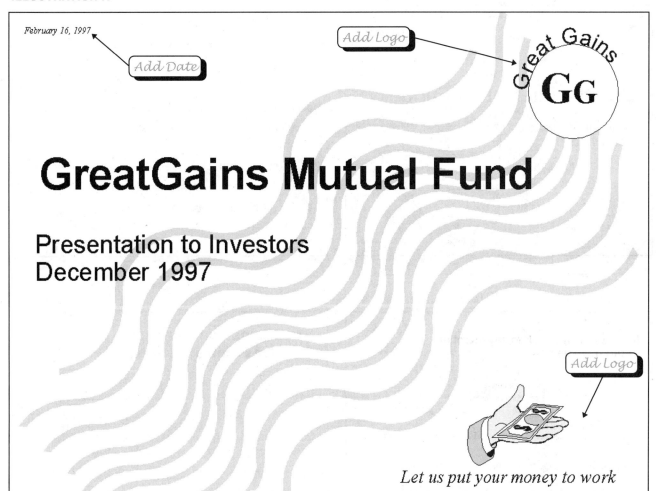

ILLUSTRATION B

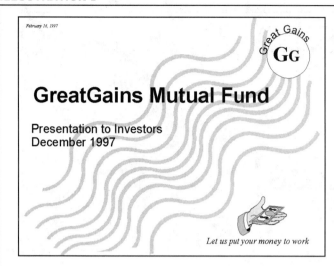

February 16, 1997

GreatGains Mutual Fund

Presentation to Investors
December 1997

Let us put your money to work

1

February 16, 1997

Why Invest in GreatGains Mutual Fund?

♦ 15% growth record for the past 3 years
♦ Most of fund invested in blue-chip stocks and bonds.
♦ Over $20 million under fund management
♦ Money managers are easily accessible
♦ Small commission fees

Let us put your money to work

2

February 16, 1997

Investors can speak to any member of our management team

Rachael Black
Head Fund Manager

John Chow
Vice President

Pamela Haupt
Vice President

Jaime Cohen
Associate

Harry Smith
Associate

David Stuart
Associate

Chandra Rao
Associate

Let us put your money to work

3

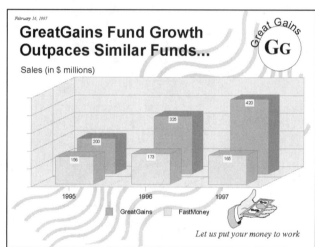

February 16, 1997

GreatGains Fund Growth Outpaces Similar Funds...

Sales (in $ millions)

	GreatGains	FastMoney
1995	156	200
1996	173	325
1997	165	420

GreatGains   FastMoney

Let us put your money to work

4

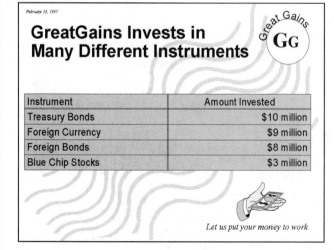

February 16, 1997

GreatGains Invests in Many Different Instruments

Instrument	Amount Invested
Treasury Bonds	$10 million
Foreign Currency	$9 million
Foreign Bonds	$8 million
Blue Chip Stocks	$3 million

Let us put your money to work

5

February 16, 1997

To invest your money with GreatGains....

♦ Call Pamela Haupt at
  ‣ 212-777-9394
♦ Write to:
  ‣ GreatGains Mutual Fund
  ‣ 686 Madison Avenue
  ‣ New York, NY 10022
♦ Inquire with your stockbroker

Let us put your money to work

6

Exercise 14

■ **Show a Presentation** ■ **Slide Transitions**
■ **Add Transitions and Animation to Bulleted Text** ■ **Animate Objects**

Slide Transition   Play Show

NOTES

Show a Presentation

■ Using a projection system or a large monitor, you can show your presentation to an audience. When a slide show is presented, each slide displays on the entire screen without showing Corel Presentations 7 screen elements.

■ Slides may be shown one at a time as an oral report is given, or they may run continuously if used at a trade show or at a demonstration counter in a store.

■ Changing slides may be activated by clicking the mouse, or pressing the Spacebar or Enter key.

■ To play a slide show, click the Play Slide Show button 🔢 on the Toolbar, or select Play Slide Show from the Slide menu. In the Play Slide Show dialog box which follows, specify the starting slide in the show and click Play. To run the show continuously. Click the Repeat slide show option. Or, select the Time delay option from the Advance tab of the Slide Transitions dialog box. (Shown in the illustration on the right.)

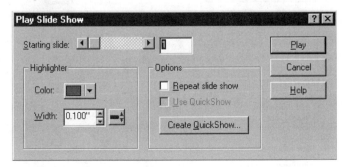

■ The **Create QuickShow** option allows you to create a QuickShow file. This separate file enables your slide show to run faster; however, this option can use a large amount of disk space.

Slide Transitions

■ **Transitions** add special effects as one slide replaces the other on the screen. Slide transitions may be added in any view.

  • To add a slide transition, click the Transition button 🔲 on the Toolbar, or select Slide Transition from the Slide menu.

■ In the Slide Transition and Sound Properties dialog box which follows, click the Transitions tab. (Check to see that the slide number and title indicated is the slide you want to receive the transition effect. If it is not, click the Next or Previous button to select the desired slide.) Then, select the Transition effect you desire. A sample of the effect will display. You may also control the speed of the transition by clicking a Speed option.

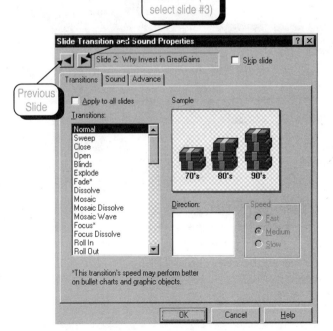

Add Transitions and Animation to Bulleted Text

- In addition to adding a transition effect to a slide, you can also create special effects to change the way bullets display on Bullet Chart slides during the show.

- You can apply two effects to bullet charts: transitions and animation. The transition options are similar to those used on slides. The animation option allows you to add movement to the bulleted items.

- To add a bullet-transitions effect, click the bulleted list to select it. Then, select Object Animation from the Slide menu. In the Bullet Chart Animation Properties dialog box which follows, deselect No effect to display the Transition options. Select a transition effect from the Effects list box and note its effect in the Sample window. If you wish to display one bulleted item at a time and/or highlight it as it displays on screen, or if you wish to display bulleted items in reverse order, click the appropriate check boxes.

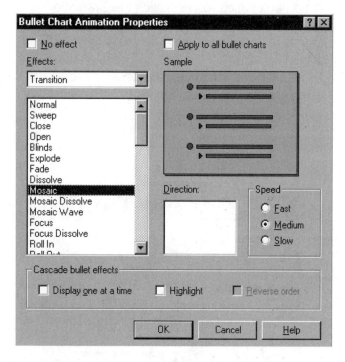

- To create animation effects, click the Effects list arrow, select Animation and new choices will appear in the list box. Select an animation effect from the list box and note its effect in the Sample window.

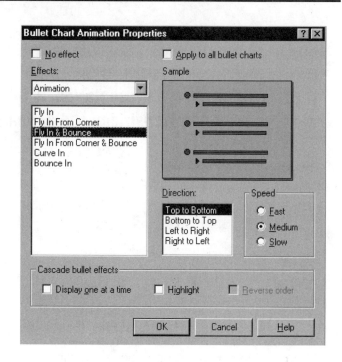

Animate Objects

- In addition to creating transitions and animations to bulleted text, Corel Presentations 7 allows you to animate a graphic object or drawing. For example, you can have a picture bounce into place or crawl into view on the slide.

- To animate a graphic object or drawing, select the object you want to animate. Then, select Object animation from the Slide menu. In the Object Animation Properties dialog box which follows, deselect the No effect check box and make the Transition and Animation choices as you did with bullets.

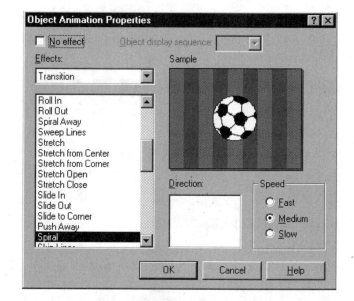

- To see a summary of the slides you created and the transition effects applied, click the Slide List View button 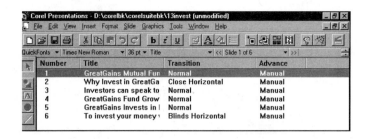.

In this exercise, you will edit a previously created slide show by adding graphics, transitions and animation to selected slides and slide objects. You will then run your slide show. Check your slide show with the desired result shown on page 446.

EXERCISE DIRECTIONS

1. Open BRAZIL or 14BRAZIL.
2. Access the Background Layer.
3. Insert the company name in the left corner of the slide in a serif 24 point yellow font as shown in Illustration A below.
   - Using WP Characters, create a star following the company name.
   - Insert December 1997 in the right corner of the slide in a serif 10 point italic font. Color the text yellow.
4. Access the Slide Layer.
5. Switch to Slide Sorter view.
   - Delete slide 8 (Stocks in Specific Industries).
6. Display the Slide Transition dialog box and select a transition type for each slide in the show.
7. Create a different animation effect for the text on each Bullet Chart slide.
8. Display slide 5 (Political Stability).

- Add a graphic and animate it using any desired effect.
9. Display slide 4 (Rising Exports).
   - Create upward pointing arrows in different colors and animate each using any desired effect.
10. Display slide 6 (Undervaluation).
    - Move the bullet placeholder to place the text in the center of the slide.
11. Save the changes to the presentation; do not close the file.
12. Switch to Slide List view.
13. Play the slide show manually.
14. Print one copy as Handouts with 5 slides per page in black and white.
15. Print one copy of the Slide List.
16. Set the slide show to run continuously and view the slide show again.
17. Close the file; save the changes.

ILLUSTRATION A

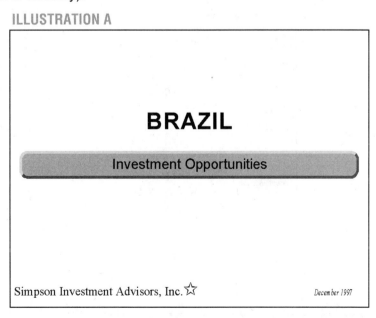

DESIRED RESULT

BRAZIL

Investment Opportunities

Simpson Investment Advisors, Inc. ☆   December 1997

1

Brief History of the Brazilian Economy

- Debt crisis in the 1980s
  - ‣ Increased foreign borrowing
  - ‣ Rising international interest rates
- Recent recovery of the economy
- Research Department's report on the history of the economy

Simpson Investment Advisors, Inc. ☆   December 1997

2

Why is the Brazilian Economy Ready for Foreign Investment?

Simpson Investment Advisors, Inc. ☆   December 1997

3

Rising Exports

- To the U.S.
- To Europe
- To Latin America

Simpson Investment Advisors, Inc. ☆   December 1997

4

Political Stability

- Current Leadership
- Free Elections

Simpson Investment Advisors, Inc. ☆   December 1997

5

Undervaluation

- Specific stocks
- Government debt

Simpson Investment Advisors, Inc. ☆   December 1997

6

Overview of Possible Investments

Simpson Investment Advisors, Inc. ☆   December 1997

7

Bonds

- Short term
- Long term

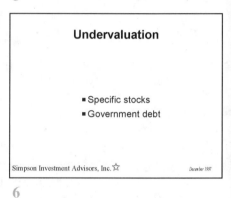

Simpson Investment Advisors, Inc. ☆   December 1997

8

Invest in Brazil

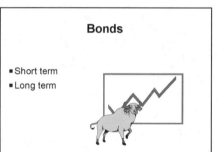

Buy Stocks in the Most Profitable Industries

Coffee   Steel   Chemical

Simpson Investment Advisors, Inc. ☆   December 1997

9

Conclusion

- Reasons to invest through Simpson Investment Advisors
  - ‣ Rate of return on investments
  - ‣ Global trading
  - ‣ Highly trained professionals
- To Summarize...

Simpson Investment Advisors, Inc. ☆   December 1997

10

KEYSTROKES

SHOW PRESENTATION

1. Open desired presentation.

2. Click **Play Show** button on

    Toolbar .... `[▣]`

    OR

    • Click **S**lide .... `Alt`+`S`

    • Click **P**lay Slide Show .... `P`

    • Change Starting Slide number, if needed.

To run show continuously:

    • Click **R**epeat slide show

        check box .... `Alt`+`R`

3. Click **P**lay .... `Alt`+`P`

4. Click left mouse button or press the Spacebar to advance from slide to slide through the presentation.

To have slides advance automatically:

1. Click **S**lide .... `Alt`+`S`

2. Click S**l**ide Transition .... `I`

3. Click **Advance Tab**.

4. Select **T**ime Delay .... `T`

    • Enter Number of seconds per build.

    • Click **A**pply to all slides .... `A`

5. Click **OK** .... `Enter`

ADD SLIDE TRANSITIONS

1. Open desired slide show.

2. Click **Slide Transition** button on

    Toolbar .... `[▣]`

    OR

    • Click **S**lide .... `Alt`+`S`

    • Click S**l**ide Transition .... `I`

3. Click **Previous** or **Next** button to go to

    desired slides .... `<<` or `>>`

4. Select desired transition type and options.

5. Click **OK** .... `Enter`

ADD TRANSITIONS AND ANIMATION TO BULLETED TEXT

1. Open a slide show.

2. Display a Bullet Chart slide.

3. Click bullet list to select it.

4. Click **S**lide .... `Alt`+`S`

5. Click **Object Animation** .... `J`

6. Deselect **N**o effect .... `Alt`+`N`

7. Click **E**ffects box .... `Alt`+`E`

8. Click **Transition** or **Animation**... `↓` `↑`

9. Click a **Transition** or

    Animation Effect .... `Tab`, `↓` `↑`

10. Choose a desired speed:

    • **F**ast .... `Alt`+`F`

    • **M**edium .... `Alt`+`M`

    • **S**low .... `Alt`+`S`

11. Choose a (cascade) bullet display effect:

    • Display **o**ne at a time ...... `Alt`+`O`

    • Hig**h**light .... `Alt`+`I`

    • **R**everse order .... `Alt`+`R`

12. Click **OK** .... `Enter`

ANIMATE OBJECTS

1. Open a slide show.

2. Display slide containing object.

3. Click object list to select it.

4. Click **S**lide .... `Alt`+`S`

5. Click **Object Animation** .... `J`

6. Deselect **N**o Effect .... `Alt`+`N`

7. Click **E**ffects box .... `Alt`+`E`

8. Click **Transition** or **Animation**... `↓` `↑`

9. Click a **Transition** or

    Animation Effect .... `Tab`, `↓` `↑`

10. Choose a **D**irection... `Alt`+`D`, `↓` `↑`

11. Choose a desired speed:

    • **F**ast .... `Alt`+`F`

    • **M**edium .... `Alt`+`M`

    • **S**low .... `Alt`+`S`

12. Click **OK** .... `Enter`

Exercise

15

- ■ **Set Slide Timings and Object Animation**
- ■ **Add Sound**

NOTES

Set Slide Timings and Object Animation

■ In the previous exercise, you learned that the slide stays on the screen until you advance it manually either by clicking the mouse or pressing the Spacebar. This is the default setting. You can, however, set a time limit for how long each slide stays on the screen. Timings are set in seconds, with .05 representing five seconds.

■ By default, object animation or transition is activated only when you click the mouse. You can have the objects appear automatically in various sequences: immediately after the slide transition; in an automated sequence after the first object is displayed; in an interrupted sequence after the first object is displayed; before or after bullet chart text displays.

■ To set slide timings and/or object animation, select Slide Transition from the Slide menu, or click the Slide Transition button 🖳 on the Toolbar. In the Slide Transition and Sound Properties dialog box which follows, click the Advance tab. (Check to see that the slide number indicated is the slide you want to add a timing.) Then, select the Time delay option and enter the number of seconds in the Number of seconds per build text box that you wish to leave the slide on screen.

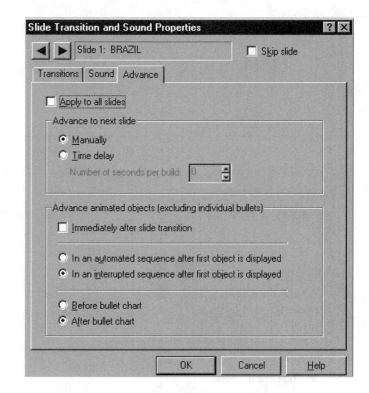

■ To advance animated objects automatically, select the object you wish to affect, then select an Advance animated objects option in the Slide Transition and Sound Properties dialog box, illustrated above.

Add Sound

■ In addition to adding visual transitions to slides, you may add a sound effect so your slide show becomes truly entertaining. You can add into a slide recorded music from a CD, a sound clip, or your own narration.

- Sounds may be added by selecting Sound from the Slide menu, or by clicking the Slide Transition button on the Toolbar and selecting the Sound tab. In the Slide Transition and Sound Properties dialog box that follows, select the slide to which you wish to add a sound. Then click the type of sound you wish to insert: Wave, Midi or CD. Corel Presentations 7 comes with numerous sound clips. Click the Browse button and choose the sound from the Open file management dialog box that appears.

- If you wish the sound to remain until the next sound effect is encountered on a slide, click the Options button, then click Loop sound in the Sound Options dialog box.

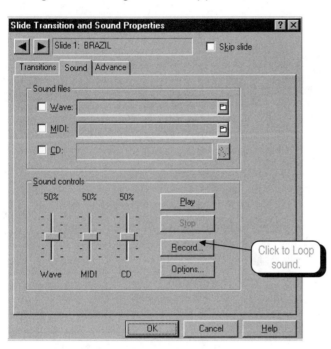

In this exercise, you will edit a previously created presentation by adding sound and timings to selected slides. You will then view your slide show.

EXERCISE DIRECTIONS

1. Open FLAGSHIP or 15FLAGSH.

2. Create a transition effect for each slide.

3. Create a different animation effect for the text on each Bullet Chart slide.

4. Display slide 3 (Our Sales Force).
   - Animate the graphic using any desired effect.
   - Set the animation to automatically appear immediately after the slide transition.

5. Add a 5-second timing for each slide.

6. Create a sound effect on slides 1 and 3.

7. Switch to Slide List view.

8. Print one copy of the Slide List.

9. Set the slide show to run continuously.

10. Play the slide show.

11. Close the file; save the changes.

KEYSTROKES

SET TIMINGS AND/OR OBJECT ANIMATION

1. Open slide presentation.
2. Display slide to receive the timing.
   OR
   Select the object to receive the animation setting.
3. Click **Slide**.............................. `Alt`+`S`
4. Click **Slide Transition** .... `I`
5. Click the **Advance** tab.
   To set slide timings:
   - Click **Time delay** option ..... `Alt`+`T`
   - Enter Number of seconds per build.
   To advance animated objects automatically, select an option:
   - **Immediately after slide transition** .... `Alt`+`I`

- **In an automated sequence after first object is displayed** ..... `Alt`+`U`
- **In an interrupted sequence after first object is displayed** ..... `Alt`+`N`
- **Before bullet chart**............ `Alt`+`B`
- **After bullet chart**............... `Alt`+`F`
6. Click **OK**................................... `Enter`

ADD SOUND

1. Open presentation.
2. Display desired slide.
3. Click **Slide** .... `Alt`+`S`
4. Click **Sound** .... `U`
   OR
   - Click **Slide Transition** button..... `⬒`
     on Toolbar.
   - Click the Sound tab.

5. Click type of sound file to insert:
   - **Wave** .... `Alt`+`W`
   - **MIDI**.............................. `Alt`+`M`
   - **CD** .... `Alt`+`C`
6. Click **Browse** button (folder icon) to find file type.
   - Choose desired sound.
   - Click **Open** .... `Alt`+`O`
7. Click **Play** to preview sound... `Alt`+`P`
   OR
   To loop sound:
   - Click **Options** .... `Alt`+`I`
   - Click **Loop Sound**........................ `L`
8. Click **OK** .... `Enter`
   to insert sound on slide.

Exercise 16

- **Audience Notes Pages and Handouts**
- **Speaker Notes**

NOTES

Audience Notes Pages and Handouts

- In the previous exercises, you have printed your presentation as handouts with five to eight slides per page. Handouts may be given to the audience so they can follow along with your presentation and/or take them home for reference. Corel Presentations 7 provides other options for printing your presentation.

- Audience notes are similar to handouts, but a series of lines are printed below each miniature slide so the audience can take notes as the presentation is given.

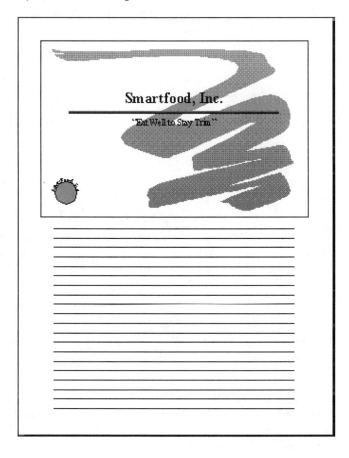

Speaker Notes

- The **Speaker Notes** option allows you to type reminders, notes and/or your script next to each slide. This will guide you through the presentation.

- You may add speaker notes in Slide Editor, Slide Sorter and Slide List views.

- To add notes to your slides, select the slide where you wish to enter such a notation. In Slide Editor view, select Speaker Notes from the Slide menu; in Slide Sorter view, right-click and select Speaker Notes from the QuickMenu; in Slide List view, highlight the slide, right-click and select Speaker Notes. In the Speaker Notes dialog box, type your note. Click the Previous and/or Next button to select another slide, and add any notations you wish in the window provided.

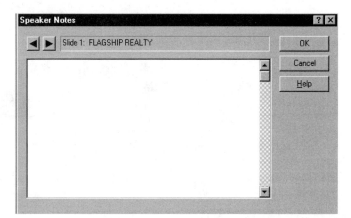

- Use the same procedures that you used to print slides and handouts to print notes pages and speaker notes.

In this exercise, you will create a table slide and add reminders on speaker note pages. See
desired result on page 454.

EXERCISE DIRECTIONS

1. Open FOOD or 16FOOD.

2. Switch to Slide Editor view.

3. Display slide 6 (Advertising Budget). Change
    the slide title to read, International Advertising
    Budget.

4. Display slide 5.

5. Add a new slide and select data chart. Use a
    Table Template. (The new slide will become
    slide 6.)

    - Enter the slide title and table data shown in
      Illustration A on page 453. Set the table data font
      size to 38 point.
    - Right-align the title placeholder.

6. Create a transition effect, transition speed and
    add a sound to each slide in the presentation.

7. Display slide 2 (SmartFood Products). Create
    an animation effect for each graphic.

8. Display slide 3 (International Expansion).
    Create an animation effect for the graphic.

9. Play the slide show. Set each slide to advance
    automatically.

10. Switch to Slide List view. Add the following
    speaker notes to the slides indicated. (See
    example shown in Illustration B on page 453.)

    Slide 1:
    - Introduce the purpose of the presentation.
    - Give a general overview of the items to be
      covered in the presentation.

    Slide 2:
    - Review the different SmartFood products
      available and identify the features of each.

    Slide 3:
    - Explain new market expansion and why
      these markets were selected.

    Slide 4:
    - Explain domestic markets and reasons for
      success in each.

11. Print one copy of the presentation as Speaker
    Notes with four slides per page.

12. Print one copy of the presentation as Audience
    Notes with four slides per page.

13. Close the file; save the changes.

KEYSTROKES

SPEAKER NOTES

1. Open desired presentation.

2. Click **Slide List View** button..........

3. Right-click slide to receive speaker
    notatation.

    OR

    - Click **Slide** ....
    - Click **Speaker Notes**.................

4. Type notes.

5. Click **Previous** or **Next** button to move
    to other slides.

6. Click **OK**.......................................

National Advertising Budget

Market	Sales	Total Ad Budget
New York	$4,666,876	$98,766
Illinois	$3,000,098	$77,888
California	$5,212,999	$100,988
Florida	$2,987,999	$65,345

ILLUSTRATION B

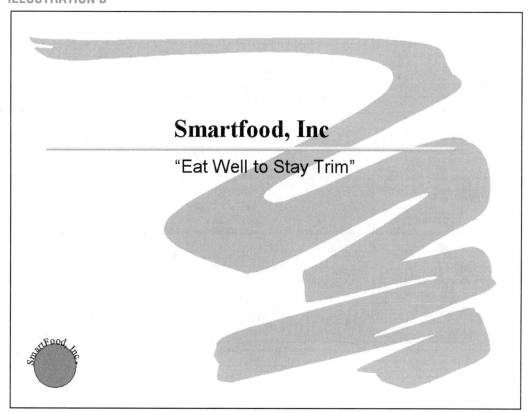

Smartfood, Inc

"Eat Well to Stay Trim"

Introduce the purpose of the presentation.
Give a general overview of the items to be covered in the presentation.

DESIRED RESULT

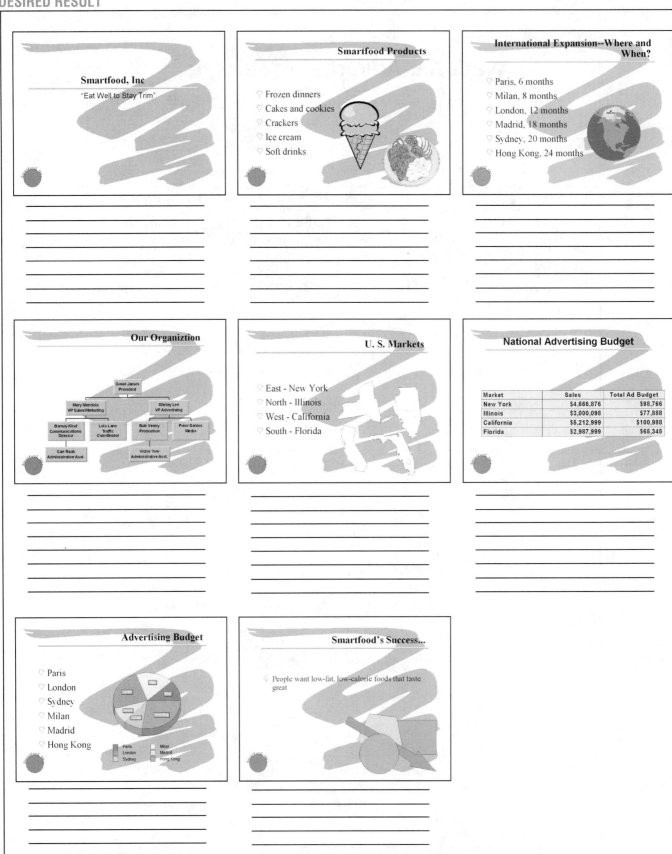

Exercise

17

■ **Summary**

In this exercise, you will get your presentation ready for a slide show. You will add transitions, builds and timings as well as prepare audience handouts and notes pages.

EXERCISE DIRECTIONS

1. Open ☐INVEST or ☐17INVEST.

2. Assign a transition effect, a transition speed, and a sound to each slide in the presentation.

3. Set a Timed Advance for each slide.

4. Create a text animation effect for the text on Bullet Chart slide 6.

5. Add the following speaker notes to the slides indicated:

   Slide 1:
   - Introduce yourself and your position in the company.
   - Explain the purpose of today's presentation.

   Slide 2:
   - Review each reason to invest in GreatGains Mutual Fund.
   - Emphasize blue-chip stocks.
   - Give three examples.

   Slide 4:
   - Explain the reasons for significant growth in 1997.

   Slide 5:
   - Review each instrument.

6. Save the changes to the presentation; do not close the file.

7. Print one copy of the slide show as speaker notes with four slides per page.

8. Print one copy of the slide show as audience notes with six slides per page.

9. Set the slide show to run continuously and view the slide show.

10. Close the file; save the changes.

Exercise

18

■ **Summary**

In this exercise, you will create a sales presentation for Maxwell Systems. This presentation will be given at the Regional Sales Meeting on October 15, 1997.

EXERCISE DIRECTIONS

1. Create a new presentation. Use any desired template.

2. Switch to Layout Layer.

3. Format the layout as follows:
   - Right-align the title.

4. Switch to Background Layer.
   - Create a company logo (company name or abbreviation and a relevant graphic) and place it where desired on the slide.
   - Include the date of the meeting in the lower right corner of the slide.

5. Switch to Slide Editor view.

6. Create the presentation as shown in Illustration A.
   - ✓   *The illustration is black and white; slide background is NOT shown.*

7. Enter the data below to create the graphic Sales by Region (in millions)

	Eastern	Central	Western
Current Year	19	17	9
Previous Year	12	9	6

8. Use the names and titles below for the organization chart:

Harry Miles	VP Sales
Tom Wiker	Eastern Region Sales Manager
Marnie Aker	Central Region Sales Manager
Joan Swanson	Western Region Sales Manager
Adrienne Hall	Eastern Region Assistant Manager

9. Spell check.

10. Save the slide show; name it MAXWELL.

11. Switch to Slide Sorter view.

12. Create a transition effect for each slide in the presentation.

13. Animate every object on each slide.

14. Create a transition effect to text on Data Chart slides.

15. Create speaker notes where necessary to help you deliver the presentation better.

16. Add a sound effect to the first and last slide.

17. Play the slide show.

18. Print one copy as Handouts with six slides per page.

19. Print one copy as Speaker Notes with four slides per page.

20. Close the file; save the changes.

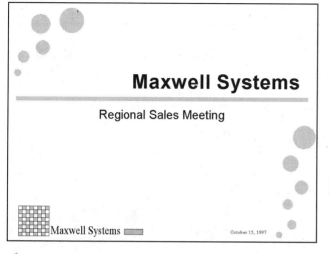

Maxwell Systems

Regional Sales Meeting

Maxwell Systems

October 15, 1997

1

BUYER INCENTIVES

- Promote bonus offers to gain new customers
- Offer discounts for
  - High volume accounts
  - Prompt payment
  - Long-term contracts

Maxwell Systems

October 15, 1997

2

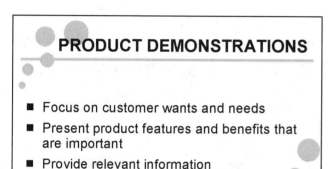

PRODUCT DEMONSTRATIONS

- Focus on customer wants and needs
- Present product features and benefits that are important
- Provide relevant information
- Close the sale

Maxwell Systems

October 15, 1997

3

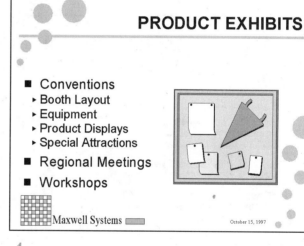

PRODUCT EXHIBITS

- Conventions
  - Booth Layout
  - Equipment
  - Product Displays
  - Special Attractions
- Regional Meetings
- Workshops

Maxwell Systems

October 15, 1997

4

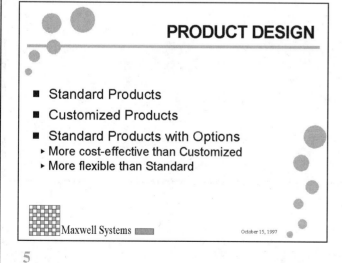

PRODUCT DESIGN

- Standard Products
- Customized Products
- Standard Products with Options
  - More cost-effective than Customized
  - More flexible than Standard

Maxwell Systems

October 15, 1997

5

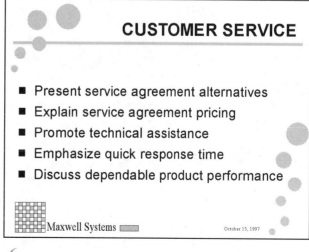

CUSTOMER SERVICE

- Present service agreement alternatives
- Explain service agreement pricing
- Promote technical assistance
- Emphasize quick response time
- Discuss dependable product performance

Maxwell Systems

October 15, 1997

6

ILLUSTRATION A *(continued)*

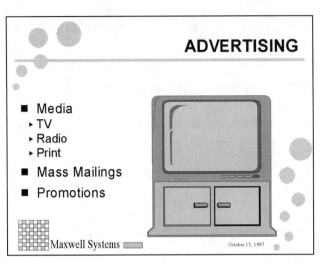

7

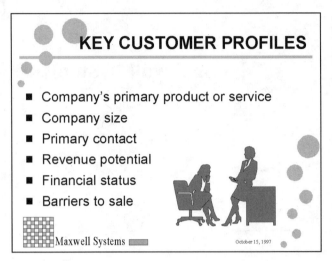

8

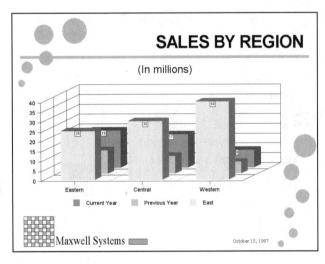

9

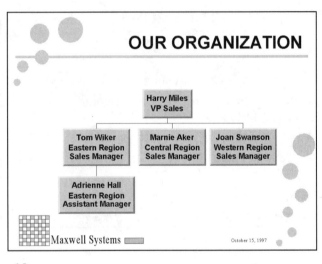

10

Corel Integration

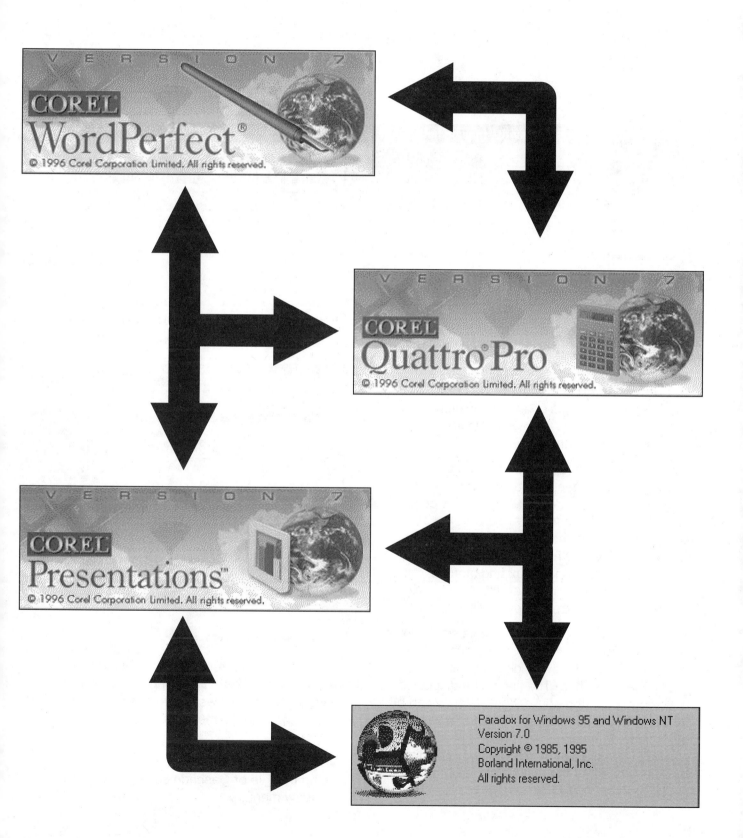

- **Window Files in One Application**
- **Window Files from Different Applications**

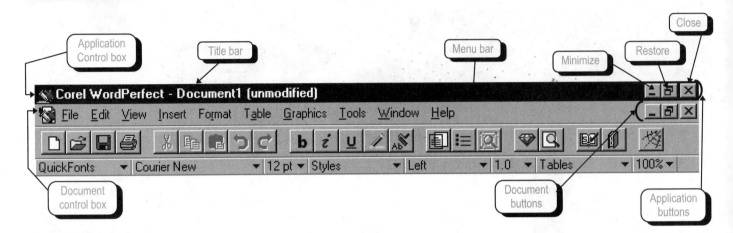

NOTES

Window Files in One Application

- Corel Office Professional 7 allows you to work with several files simultaneously in separate windows. The exact number of files that can be used at once depends on the application and available memory. (Windowing lets you view files as you work with them.)

- When you open an application, Corel Office 7 displays a full-screen, or maximized, window for your work. The control box and buttons on the title bar let you size and arrange Corel applications within the Windows screen. (See Chapter 1 - Corel Office Professional 7 Basics, Exercise 2.) The control box and buttons to the left and right of the menu bar allow you to size and arrange the current application window.

- Minimizing a window, or reducing its size, allows you to view other open files. To reduce the size of a maximized window, click the restore button 🔲 on the menu bar. The file will be displayed in a window within the application. The file can be further reduced, or minimized, to a title bar icon by clicking on the minimize button 🔲 on the file title bar. The file can be restored or maximized by selecting either the restore or maximize

button 🔲 on the title bar. Note the illustration of restored and minimized files.

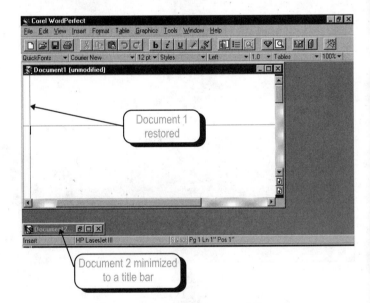

- You can resize a reduced window by dragging the window border. Dragging a corner of the window border allows you to change both the width and length simultaneously.

- If multiple files are open in the same application, you may view them all on the screen at once using the <u>T</u>ile or <u>C</u>ascade commands on the <u>W</u>indow menu.

- When files are tiled, each file is visible in a window without overlapping. The shaded title bar indicates the active window. Click any window to make it active, and click the maximize button on the title bar to maximize it.

Tiled Files

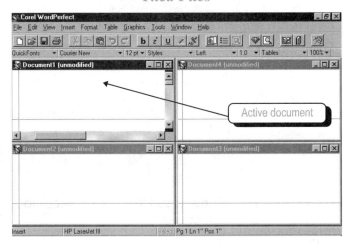

- Cascaded windows allow you to view the title bar of each open file. The windows are overlapped so that the title bar of each file is displayed. Note the illustration of four Quattro Pro files cascaded with the active notebook file on top. To make a window active, click any visible portion of the desired window.

Cascaded Windows

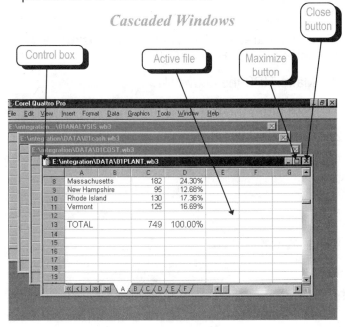

- You can also switch among file windows whether they are currently displayed or not by selecting Window from the menu and choosing the desired file from the open files listed at the bottom.

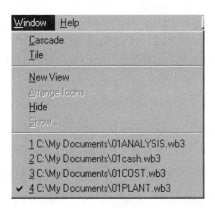

- A window can be closed by double-clicking the control box, which is at the left on the title bar or by clicking the Close button ☒.

  ✓ When you double-click, you don't get the menu.

Window Files from Different Applications

- If you wish to move between a WordPerfect document and a Quattro Pro notebook, or among files open in any Corel Office Professional 7 application, click the desired DAD icon to open the application, or click a running program icon on the Windows 95 Taskbar if the application is already open as shown in the illustration below.

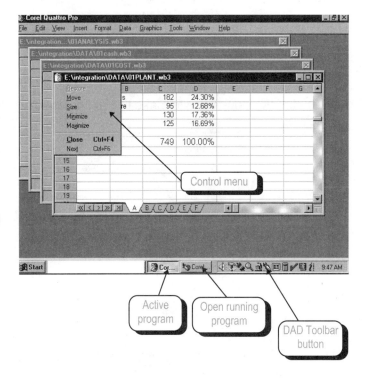

■ However, if you wish to see files from different applications on the screen at the same time, right-click the Windows 95 Taskbar and select the view option you prefer. Each application must be in a window that is not minimized in order to use these view options. Note the illustration of the menu that appears when the Taskbar is right-clicked.

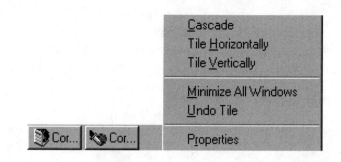

In this exercise, you will work with application and document controls, four Quattro Pro notebooks, and a WordPerfect document. You will arrange the notebooks so you can view each file, and you will use windowing to view the notebook pages and the document at the same time.

EXERCISE DIRECTIONS

1. Click the DAD Quattro Pro icon.

2. Open ✍COST.wb3 or 🖫01COST.wb3.

3. Open ✍PLANT.wb3 or 🖫01PLANT.wb3.

4. Open ✍CASH.wb3 or 🖫01CASH.wb3.

5. Open ✍ANALYSIS.wb3 or 🖫01ANALYS.wb3.

6. Use the Window menu to tile the notebooks.

7. Make COST the active notebook.

8. Minimize it.

9. Make ANALYSIS the active notebook.

10. Close the file.

11. Minimize CASH to a title bar.

12. Restore all files.

13. Use the Window menu to cascade the notebooks.

14. Use the Window menu to make the last notebook active.

15. Click the WordPerfect icon the DAD Toolbar to load WordPerfect.

16. Open ✍TIPS.wpd or 🖫01TIPS.wpd.

17. Switch back to the Quattro Pro screen by clicking the DAD icon.

   ✓ *Clicking the Taskbar is much quicker.*

18. Switch back to the WordPerfect screen by clicking the Corel WordPerfect icon on the Windows 95 Taskbar.

19. View both applications at once by right-clicking a blank area on the Windows 95 Taskbar and selecting Tile Horizontally.

20. Make TIPS the active file.

21. Size the window so that it is large.

22. Close each window and each application.

KEYSTROKES

WINDOW FILES

Positions document windows next to each other as non-overlapping tiles.

1. Click **Window** .... `Alt` + `W`
2. Click **Cascade** .... `C`

   OR

   in Quattro Pro:

   Click **Tile** .... `T`

   OR

   in WordPerfect:

   Click **Tile Top to Bottom** .... `T`

   OR

   Click **Tile Side by Side** .... `S`

CLOSE WINDOW

Ctrl + F4

Double-click Control box of active document window.

   OR

   Click **Close** button .... `X`

   OR

   a. Click Control box.

   b. Click **Close** .... `C`

MAXIMIZE WINDOW

Fills the application window with the active file.

Click **Maximize** button .... `□`
of active file (not available if window is already maximized).

   OR

   a. Click Control box.

   b. Click **Maximize** .... `X`

MINIMIZE WINDOW

Reduces active file window to a title bar icon.

Click **Minimize** button .... `▬`
of active file.

   OR

   a. Click Control box.

   b. Click **Minimize** .... `N`

SWITCH AMONG OPEN DOCUMENTS

Click any visible portion of desired document.

   OR

1. Click **Window** .... `Alt` + `W`
2. Click **name** of desired document... `↓` `↑`

   OR

   Type document number.

WINDOW FILES FROM DIFFERENT APPLICATIONS

1. Click first DAD icon.
2. Open desired file.
3. Click second DAD icon.
4. Open desired file.
5. Right-click blank area on Windows 95 Taskbar.
6. Select **Tile Horizontally** .... `H`

   OR

   Select **Tile Vertically** .... `V`

   OR

   Select **Cascade** .... `C`

<table>
<tr><td>Exercise

2</td><td>■ Copy a Notebook File into a Document File</td></tr>
</table>

NOTES

Copy a Notebook File into a Document File

■ Integration is the sharing or combining of data between Corel Office 7 tools. The source file is used to send data; the destination file is used to receive data. For example, a Quattro Pro graph or notebook page (the source file) can add supporting or visual documentation of material to a WordPerfect document (the destination file).

■ There are three methods of integrating data between Corel applications: (a.) copying and pasting, (b.) linking, and (c.) embedding. Linking and embedding will be addressed in the next exercise. The most elementary method is to copy and paste data between applications. This method is most often used when you do not expect to edit the object that is copied into the destination document.

■ You may use the DAD icons to switch or transfer information between applications, or you may display both files simultaneously as discussed in Exercise 1. To integrate a Quattro Pro table into a WordPerfect document, for example, you can copy and paste the data or use the drag and drop procedure.

• To **copy and paste** between applications: Select the data to be copied from the source file, and select Copy from the Edit menu. The copied data is temporarily placed on the system's **clipboard**. To paste the data, switch to the destination file, and select Paste from the Edit menu.

• To **drag and drop** between applications: Select the data to be copied from the source file, press Ctrl, and drag the object to the destination file on the screen or to the minimized application button on the Windows 95 Taskbar without releasing the mouse button. This will open the application and you can click or drop the object into place.

  ✓ *If you have difficulty placing the notebook data, drag it to any spot on the document, then maximize the document, and adjust the placement.*

■ If you are copying a **table**, both the copy and paste and drag and drop methods will place the table into the destination document as an object, which can then be edited as table data. However, the integrated table has no connection to the original notebook page and the formulas are not accessible. These methods should only be used when updated or linked data is not necessary and when formulas do not need editing.

In this exercise, you will copy an example of an Income Statement prepared in Quattro Pro to a WordPerfect document on small business survival. You will save the newly integrated document under a new name.

EXERCISE DIRECTIONS

1. Click the DAD Quattro Pro icon.

2. Open ANALYSIS.wb3 or 02ANALYS.wb3.

3. Click the DAD WordPerfect icon.

4. Open SURVIVAL.wpd or 02SURVIV.wpd.

5. Move to the bottom of the document.

6. Right-click on a blank area of the Windows 95 Taskbar and tile the Quattro Pro and WordPerfect applications vertically.

7. Use the Ctrl key and the drag-and-drop method to select and copy the notebook page from Quattro Pro to the bottom of the WordPerfect document.

8. Maximize the WordPerfect SURVIVAL document.

9. Select and cut the notebook table in the document.

10. Insert the additional text in the document as illustrated.

11. Switch to Quattro Pro using the program button on the Windows 95 Taskbar.
    - ✓ *If you moved the notebook instead of coping it in step 7, and it is not there, click Edit, Undo.*

12. Select and copy the notebook data.

13. Switch to the WordPerfect document.

14. Paste the notebook page after the new text in the document, as illustrated.
    - ✓ *The data will go onto a new page.*

15. Select the notebook title rows in the table and delete them.
    - ✓ *You can change data, formats, columns, etc., since this data is in table format. However, formulas cannot be changed and data is not linked to the notebook.*

16. Adjust column widths in the table, if necessary.

17. Since this is now a two-page report, create Header A with the following information:

    Small Business Survival   Page (Number)
    (Set to print on even pages.)

18. Save the file as SURVANA.

19. Print one copy.

20. Close all files.

KEYSTROKES

COPY AND PASTE DATA BETWEEN APPLICATIONS

Ctrl+X, Ctrl+V

1. Open both applications and appropriate files.

2. In the source file, highlight the data to be copied.

3. Click **Edit**............................. `Alt`+`E`

4. Click **Copy**..................................... `C`

5. Switch to the destination file.

6. Place cursor at the point of insertion.

7. Click **Edit**............................. `Alt`+`E`

8. Click **Paste**................................... `P`

COPY DATA BETWEEN APPLICATIONS WITH DRAG AND DROP

1. Open and display both applications and files.

2. In the source file, highlight the data to be copied.

3. Hold mouse button until the mouse pointer (arrow) changes to a hand.

4. Hold Ctrl while dragging the data to the desired location in the destination file.

☎☎ SMALL BUSINESS SURVIVAL TIP ☎☎

Owning a small business is an all-consuming experience. It requires the owner to constantly evaluate the company's potential and problems. All businesses experience problems. Accurate diagnosis of the severity and cause of the company problem is essential to resolving and preventing its recurrence.

How you go about diagnosing your business problems will depend on the nature of your firm and the symptoms that are being experienced.

MOST COMMON FINANCIAL DIFFICULTIES

Expenses exceed revenues.

Overly rapid growth that outpaces a business's operating systems, the skills and abilities of its personnel, etc.

Poor management skills and business know-how among business owners and key management.

Failure to maximize a business' competitive strengths and to capitalize on its competitors' weaknesses.

ACTIONS TO CONSIDER

Evaluate all expenses including business-related travel or entertainment, subscriptions, the purchase of supplies, raw materials or equipment, insurance, the use of outside professionals, phone services, etc., to determine which can be reduced, delayed or eliminated.

Eliminate or discontinue products or services that are not making money. Do a careful analysis of this during each season of the year.

Reduce staff salaries and/or benefits. Do not do both at the same time; it can be very demoralizing.

Cut prices. This action alone can sometimes provide the cash a business needs to turn itself around.

Type the text here.

SAMPLE FINANCIAL DATA

Notice the six-month analysis of Income, Expense and Net Income data below and the valuable trend analysis it provides.

Drag and drop the table.

A	A	B	C	D	E	F	G	H
1		INCOME STATEMENT ANALYSIS						
2		LOPEZ INSURANCE AGENCY						
3								
4		TOTAL	% OF	TOTAL	% OF	NET	% OF	
5	MONTH	INCOME	TOTAL	EXPENSES	TOTAL	INCOME	TOTAL	
6	JANUARY	13,457.97	14.4%	12,811.83	16.4%	646.14	4.2%	
7	FEBRUARY	14,055.45	15.0%	12,626.62	16.2%	1,428.83	9.3%	
8	MARCH	17,019.77	18.2%	13,293.92	17.0%	3,725.85	24.2%	
9	APRIL	16,414.09	17.5%	13,760.28	17.6%	2,653.81	17.3%	
10	MAY	16,109.88	17.2%	12,780.50	16.4%	3,329.38	21.7%	
11	JUNE	16,478.64	17.6%	12,894.51	16.5%	3,584.13	23.3%	
12	TOTALS	93,535.80	100.0%	78,167.66	100.0%	15,368.14	100.0%	
13								
14								

- **Integrate a Notebook File and a Document File**
- **Embed a File** ■ **Link Files** ■ **Edit a Linked File**

NOTES

Integrate a Notebook File and a Document File

■ When integrating data between Corel applications, the copy, paste method discussed in Exercise 2 does not allow the data to be connected to the source document or allow for editing of formulas. The other two methods, **linking** and **embedding**, do provide these options and are discussed in this exercise. Object Linking and Embedding, or OLE, is the system Corel Office 7 uses to link or embed objects between applications.

Embed a File

■ Embedding files enables you to edit data in the application but does not change or modify the source file. For example, double-clicking on an embedded notebook page in a WordPerfect document allows you to make edits using Quattro Pro, but will not change the source file. This is preferable if you wish to make changes within Quattro Pro that are not reflected in the source file or if the source file is not always available. Embedding creates a large destination file since it includes the embedded or integrated object. To embed a file, select Object from the Insert menu and click the Create from File option.

■ Note the illustrations of the Insert dialog box with the Create New and Create from File options selected. Use the Create New option to create a new, embedded object with tools native to the object's application while still working in the application in which the object will be inserted. In other words, if you create a new Quattro Pro notebook object from within WordPerfect, the menus and Toolbars change to Quattro Pro, and a notebook object is displayed within WordPerfect.

*Insert Object Dialog Box
with Create New options selected*

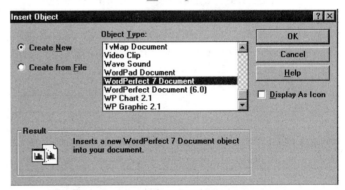

*Insert Object Dialog Box
with Create from File option selected*

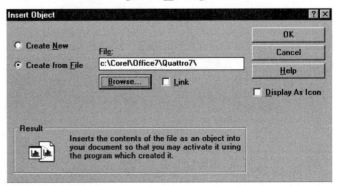

Link Files

■ Linking files allows the data in the destination file to change if the source file is updated. For example, suppose you linked a Quattro Pro notebook page (source file) into a WordPerfect document (destination file), but you need to update your notebook page data on a weekly basis. By linking the notebook page and document files, the WordPerfect document is automatically updated with the most current data. In addition, the linking procedure saves disk space since the linked file is actually stored in the source file. Linking is accomplished by selecting the source data from one application – such as Quattro Pro 7 – and pasting it into another application – such as WordPerfect 7 – using Paste Special from the Edit menu. When the Paste Special dialog box appears, click the Paste link option and identify the file type of the object as "Quattro Pro 7.0 Notebook," in the As box.

Edit a Linked File

■ As shown in the illustration below, an Edit Box button appears in the corner of a linked file when the file is linked or when the mouse is placed over the table. The **Edit Box** displays when the Edit Box button is clicked. The Edit Box can be used to modify all the properties of the object in WordPerfect.

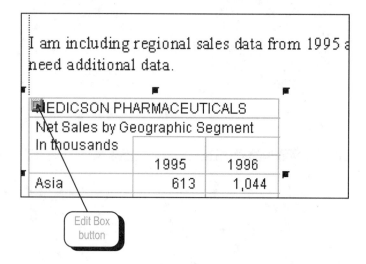

Edit Box button

■ You can also edit the linked file in the source application. When a linked file from one application is double-clicked within another application, the source application and file open for you to edit. For example, if you double-click on a linked Quattro Pro notebook page in a WordPerfect file, you are brought into the Quattro Pro application to do the edit. Therefore, if changes are made to the source file, they will automatically appear on the linked file. Conversely, if you make changes directly into the source file and then open the destination file in WordPerfect with the linked data, the updated notebook page will appear.

In this exercise, a memorandum will provide additional needed data by adding a notebook page showing financial data for the past two years. You will integrate and edit the report in linked and embedded modes.

EXERCISE DIRECTIONS

1. Click the WordPerfect icon on the DAD Toolbar.

2. Open ANNOUNCE.wpd or 03ANNOUN.wpd.

3. Make the changes indicated in the document as shown in Illustration A.

4. Click the DAD Quattro Pro icon.

5. Open PHARM.wb3 or 03PHARM.

6. Copy the notebook data as shown in Illustration B.

7. Switch to the WordPerfect document by clicking the WordPerfect button on the Windows 95 Taskbar.

8. Link the notebook page, using the Edit, Paste Special, Paste link option to link the Quattro Pro 7 notebook below the memorandum text.

   ✓ *This is a linked file that will reflect changes in the source file.*

9. Double-click on the notebook page in the WordPerfect file. (This brings you into Quattro Pro.)

10. Delete the "In thousands" text from the notebook heading.

11. Add (In thousands) to the second title line.

12. Use the Taskbar to return to the WordPerfect document and note the updated notebook page.

13. Point to the linked table and click the Edit Box button.

14. Click the Size button to set the width as close to four as possible to accommodate the new title.

15. Switch to Quattro Pro and delete the blank row under the heading.

16. Switch to WordPerfect and note the updated notebook page.

17. Select the object and move it so that it is centered horizontally on the page.

18. Save the file as ANNPHARM.

19. Print one copy of ANNPHARM.

20. Select and cut the notebook page from the document.

21. Use the Insert, Object, Create from file options to embed the notebook page into the document.

    ✓ *This is an embedded file or part of the WordPerfect file and it may be edited without changing the source file.*

22. Select the notebook page and format the numbers for the United States to bold.

23. Return to Quattro Pro and note that the notebook page did not change.

24. Close and save the Quattro Pro file, PHARM.

25. Close the WordPerfect file, ANNPHARM, without saving the changes so that the printed file is the final version.

interoffice
MEMORANDUM

To: Janice Smith

From: Your name

Subject: New Product Announcement

Date: May 12, 1997

CC: Michael Perez

As you know, we will be announcing a new product into the Canadian market in the third quarter of this year.

At our next regional sales meeting on May 26, we will discuss how this product might affect the various market segments. Since John Yule cannot attend, I would appreciate your representing him.

Call me if you need additional ~~information.~~ *data*

> *Insert*   I am including regional sales data from 1995 and 1996 below for your information.

> *Insert* ←   Quattro Pro **PHARM** data

A	A	B	C
1	MEDICSON PHARMACEUTICALS		
2	Net Sales by Geographic Segment		
3	In Thousands		
4		1995	1996
5	Asia	613	1,044
6	Canada	1,022	1,292
7	Europe	1,423	3,111
8	United States	5,906	7,929

KEYSTROKES

LINK DATA BETWEEN APPLICATIONS

1. Open both applications and the appropriate files.
2. In the source file, highlight the data to be copied.
3. Click **Edit** .... [Alt]+[E]
4. Click **Copy** .... [C]
5. Switch to the destination file.
6. Place cursor at the point of insertion.
7. Click **Edit** .... [Alt]+[E]
8. Click **Paste Special** .... [S]
9. Select **Paste link** .... [Alt]+[L]
10. Click **As** list box .... [Alt]+[A]
11. Select the Document Object linkage type .... [↓][↑]
12. Click **OK** .... [Enter]

EMBED OBJECTS

Create New:

1. Click **Insert** .... [Alt]+[I]
2. Click **Object** .... [J]

    *The **Insert Object** dialog box will appear.*

3. Click **Create new** option .... [Alt]+[N]
4. Click **Object type** list box ...... [Alt]+[T]

5. Select application from which to create object .... [↓][↑]
6. Click **OK** to create .... [Enter]

    The selected application will open.

7. Create desired information.
8. Click outside the object to return to the original application.

Create from File:

1. Click **Insert** .... [Alt]+[I]
2. Click **Object** .... [J]

    *The **Insert Object** dialog box will appear.*

3. Click **Create from file** option. [Alt]+[F]
4. Click the file folder icon.
5. Type or select drive letter or drive containing file you want to insert.
6. Double-click directory in **Directories** list box containing file you want to insert.
7. Double-click file in **File Name** list box.
8. Click **OK** .... [Enter]

EMBED DATA USING PASTE SPECIAL

1. Open both applications and the appropriate files.
2. In the source file, highlight the data to be copied.

3. Click **Edit** .... [Alt]+[E]
4. Click **Copy** .... [C]
5. Switch to the destination file.
6. Place cursor at the point of insertion.
7. Click **Edit** .... [Alt]+[E]
8. Click **Paste Special** .... [S]
9. Click **Paste** .... [Alt]+[P]
10. Click **As** .... [Alt]+[A]
11. Select Application .... [↓][↑]
12. Click **OK** .... [Enter]

EDIT OBJECT

Embedded files:

1. Double-click the object.
2. Edit the file using the source application menus. (The source file will not be changed.)
3. Switch to the destination file using the Taskbar.

Linked file:

1. Double-click the object.
2. Edit the file in the source application. (The source file will be changed.)
3. Switch to the destination file using the Taskbar.

Exercise 4

- **Integrate a Chart File and a Document File**
- **Embed a Chart** ■ **Link a Chart** ■ **Edit a Chart**

NOTES

Integrate a Chart File and a Document File

- You can insert a Quattro Pro graph into a WordPerfect document using the linking or embedding commands. The OLE system and the consequences of using linking or embedding (as described in Exercise 3) for notebook pages apply to charts as well. If the chart is part of a notebook page with data, use the Copy, Paste Special procedure since the chart can be selected and isolated. If the chart is on a separate page, the Insert, Object, Create from file procedure may be used.

Embed a Chart

- If you wish to edit a chart in WordPerfect without changing the source material, you should embed the chart. When you double-click the chart, Quattro Pro menus and Toolbars appear for editing purposes. You can return to the WordPerfect document by clicking outside the object or by clicking the WordPerfect icon on the Taskbar.

Link a Chart

- If a chart is updated periodically, or you wish to minimize the number of bytes in the WordPerfect file, you should link the chart object. Edits made on the linked chart object affect the source file; or, if the source file is changed, the object in the destination file is automatically updated.

Edit a Chart

- If you double-click on a linked or embedded chart, you will be in chart edit mode in Quattro Pro. You may make the edits and then switch back to the notebook by double-clicking the application control box or by pressing Ctrl + F4. Note the illustration of the application control button in chart edit mode.

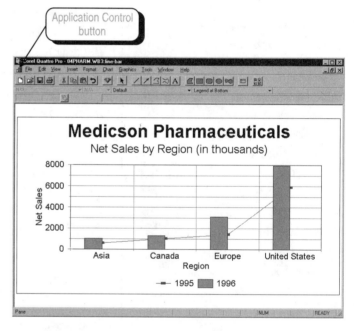

- A notebook may include multiple pages and the chart may be on a separate page. When you embed a multiple page notebook, the page that was active when the notebook was last saved will appear as the embedded object. By double-clicking on the object, you may adjust the sizing of the object, edit data, or switch to the proper page, if necessary.

In this exercise, Janice Smith of Medicson Pharmaceuticals has decided to enhance her memorandum by adding a chart comparing 1995 and 1996 data. You will integrate a chart and edit the report in linked and embedded modes.

EXERCISE DIRECTIONS

1. Click the WordPerfect icon on the DAD Toolbar.

2. Open ANNPHARM.wpd or 04ANNPHA.wpd.

3. Make the changes as illustrated on the document.

4. Click the DAD Quattro Pro icon.

5. Open PHARM.wb3 or 04PHARM.wb3.

6. Select and copy the line-column chart.

7. Switch to the WordPerfect document by clicking the WordPerfect button on the Taskbar.

8. Link the chart object, using the Paste Special, Paste link options to place the Quattro Pro 7 chart in the location shown on the document.
   ✓ *This is a linked file that will reflect changes in the source file.*

9. Double-click the chart in the WordPerfect file. (This brings you into Quattro Pro, chart edit mode.)

10. Click the Chart, Titles commands and select and delete the Main Title and Subtitle.

11. Return to the notebook view by double-clicking on the application control box in the top left corner or by pressing Ctrl + F4. (You may also click the Close button ☒.)

12. Switch to WordPerfect and note the updated chart.

13. Switch to Quattro Pro and note the level of the bar for Canada.

14. Change the Canadian sales to 5000 for 1996.

15. Note the changes on the graph.

16. Switch to the WordPerfect document and note the linked updated graph object.

17. Switch to the Quattro Pro notebook page and return Canadian sales to 1292.

18. Switch to the WordPerfect document and size the chart under the data so that it extends to the margins of the document.

19. Print one copy of ANNPHARM.

20. Close and save all files.

interoffice
M E M O R A N D U M

To: Janice Smith

From: Your name

Subject: New Product Announcement

Date: May 12, 1997

CC: Michael Perez

As you know, we will be announcing a new product into the Canadian market in the third quarter of this year.

At our next regional sales meeting on May 26, we will discuss how this product might affect the various market segments. Since John Yule cannot attend, I would appreciate your representing him.

with the related chart

I am including regional sales data from 1995 and 1996 ~~below~~ for your information. Call me if you need additional data.

Note the Canadian and European sales figures.

MEDICSON PHARMACEUTICALS		
Net Sales by Geographic Segment (In thousands)		
	1995	1996
Asia	613	1,044
Canada	1,022	1,292
Europe	1,423	3,111
United States	5,906	7,929

Insert ⟶ Quattro Pro 7 chart

Exercise 5

- Export a Paradox Database to Quattro Pro
- Insert a Paradox Database into Quattro Pro
- QuickTasks

NOTES

Export a Paradox Database to Quattro Pro

- You may wish to use a Quattro Pro notebook to summarize and analyze information saved in a Paradox database. One method of accomplishing this is to export, or send, data from Paradox to Quattro Pro. Each record will be a row in Quattro Pro, and each field will be placed in a column. Exporting is used to create a new notebook file with the database data or with part of a database table.

- To export a table from Paradox, select Export from the File menu, select the table to be exported and then select the **Export format** from the Export dialog box as illustrated below. After you select the export format, the Export Data dialog box allows you to specify the source and destination files. Click Export then switch to Quattro Pro and open the new file.

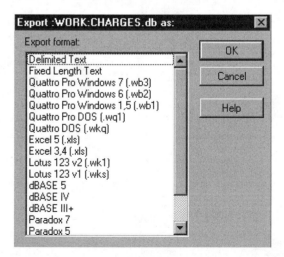

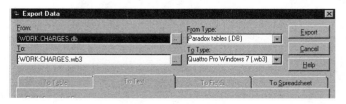

Insert Paradox Database into Quattro Pro

- You can also insert a Paradox file into a Quattro Pro file by selecting Insert from the File menu in Quattro Pro. In the Insert File dialog box, enter the file name with its extension or click the folder icon to locate the file.

- Quattro Pro translates the format of database data into spreadsheet data and vice versa. You can save a notebook as a database table using the Save As command.

QuickTasks

- The Desktop Application Director (DAD) includes a Corel QuickTasks icon for accessing frequently used automated functions, which includes several database integration tasks. The QuickTasks icon opens the screen illustrated below and offers a variety of QuickTask functions. The Share Data Between Applications option (on the Utilities tab) can be used to integrate files between all Corel Applications.

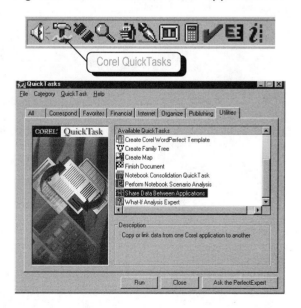

In this exercise, Kitchen Korner would like to analyze the data in the Hardware table to develop depreciation values for the year. You will use all methods (export, insert and Quick Tasks) to bring the database into Quattro Pro from Paradox. Notebook data will be formatted for presentation and analysis purposes.

EXERCISE DIRECTIONS

1. To practice sharing files with Quick Tasks:
   a. Click the DAD Quick Tasks icon.
   b. Run the Share Data Between Applications task on the Utilities tab.
      - Copy data from: Borland Paradox 7.
      - Copy data to: Corel Quattro Pro 7.
      - In Paradox 7: Open ⌨HARDWARE.DB or 🖫05HARDWA.DB.
      - Click the Edit, Select All commands.
      - Click the Continue button in the top right corner.
      - Quattro Pro will open with the cursor in A1. Click Continue.
      - ✓ *The selected table will be copied into Quattro Pro.*
   c. Close the Quattro Pro file without saving the data.

2. To practice exporting a table from Paradox to Quattro Pro:
   - Switch to Paradox 7 and use the File, Export command to export HARDWARE to a Quattro Pro Windows 7 (.wb3) file.
   - Click Export in the Export Data dialog box.
   - Switch to Quattro Pro and open the new file.
   - ✓ *The file will be in the same directory as the Paradox table.*

3. Close the file in Quattro Pro without saving the data.

4. To insert a Paradox database table into a Quattro Pro workbook:
   - In Quattro Pro, click the Insert, File commands.
   - Enter HARDWARE.db or 05HARDWARE.db and click OK.
   - ✓ *You can also click the file folder icon at the right of the file name field to locate the file.*

5. Make the following changes to the file in Quattro Pro:
   a. Insert three rows above the table to create room for a heading.
   b. Enter a two row heading that reads:
      KITCHEN KORNER
      DEPRECIATION SCHEDULE
   a. Delete the WTY and ASSIGNED TO: columns.
   b. Move the COST column to the last position.
   c. Create a new column after the COST column and enter the title: DEPRECIATION.
   d. Find the annual DEPRECIATION by dividing the COST by 5.
      - ✓ *We are depreciating the hardware over five years.*
   g. Format the DEPRECIATION figures for two place decimals.

6. Save the file as DEPHW.

7. Print one copy of the notebook page.

8. Close all files.

		KITCHEN KORNER DEPRECIATION SCHEDULE				delete columns			
BRANCH	ITEM	MFG	MODEL	COST	PURDATE	WTY	ASSIGNED TO	SERIAL #	DEPRECIATION
Big Apple	Computer	GBM	PC220	$1,348.50	06/05/96	Y	Accounting	651198	
Sunset	Computer	GBM	Notepad 500C	$2,199.00	06/10/96	Y	Accounting	AB2059	
Pacific	Computer	GBM	Notepad 600	$1,399.00	06/15/96	Y	Accounting	671150	
Pacific	Hard Drive	Barton	LPS80 220 MB	$199.00	06/20/96	N	Accounting	54219	
Sunset	Hard Drive	Wilson	CFS4 300 MB	$250.00	07/10/96	N	Purchasing	12345	
Pacific	Printer	BP	LaserJet	$1,479.00	07/15/96	N	Accounting	88842	
Bean Town	Computer	Debb	Notebook 586	$1,889.00	01/10/97	Y	Shipping	1145A	
Lakeview	Computer	Debb	P200	$2,507.52	01/12/97	Y	Accounting	765498	
Lakeview	Printer	Jokidota	BJ800	$355.00	01/12/97	Y	Accounting	43567	
Astro Center	Computer	Pancard	PE166	$2,095.54	01/25/97	Y	Purchasing	VC2342	
Astro Center	Zip Drive	Howell	Z100	$169.95	01/25/97	N	Purchasing	324222	
Twin Cities	Computer	Pancard	PE166	$2,095.54	01/29/97	Y	Accounting	BV3452	
Twin Cities	Printer	BP	LaserJet	$1,303.00	01/29/97	Y	Accounting	1213H	
Wheatland	Printer	NIC	FGE/3V	$539.00	02/03/97	N	Purchasing	87098	
Sunset	Printer	BP	Deskjet	$429.00	02/05/97	Y	Purchasing	99911	
Pacific	Printer	BP	Deskjet	$429.00	02/06/97	Y	Purchasing	22230	
Wheatland	Computer	Canton	Notebook	$2,436.00	02/10/97	Y	MIS	98793	

KEYSTROKES

EXPORT A TABLE FROM PARADOX

1. Open Paradox.
2. Click **File** .... Alt + F
3. Click **Export** .... T
4. Type the **File name** .... Alt + N

   OR

   a. Select the table directory from the **Look in** box .... Alt + I , ↓ ↑
   b. Select the desired table ... Tab , ↓ ↑
5. Click **Open** .... Enter
6. Choose the Export format .... ↓
7. Click **OK** .... Enter
8. Verify **From** and **To** destinations in the Export Data dialog box.

9. Click **Export** .... E
10. Open the destination application.
11. Open the exported file.

INSERT A PARADOX TABLE INTO QUATTRO PRO

1. Open Quattro Pro.
2. Click **Insert** .... Alt + I
3. Click **File** .... F
4. Enter file name and extension.
5. Click **OK** .... Enter

USE QUICKTASKS TO SHARE FILES BETWEEN APPLICATIONS

1. Click the DAD Quick Tasks icon .
2. Select **Utilities** tab.
3. Select **Share Data Between Applications** ..
4. Click **Run** .... Enter
5. Select application to **Copy data from**.
6. Select application to **Copy data to**.
7. Click **Next** .... Enter
8. Open file in source application.
9. Click **Continue**.
10. Place cursor at point of insertion in destination application.
11. Click **Continue**.

<table>
<tr><td>Exercise
6</td><td>■ **Merge a Paradox Table with a WordPerfect Document**</td></tr>
</table>

NOTES

Merge a Paradox Table with a WordPerfect Document

■ Table data from Paradox can be merged with a document created in WordPerfect. This process is automated with the Merge feature, as was discussed in WordPerfect, Exercise 43. Tabular data from a Quattro Pro notebook page or a WordPerfect table may also be used for a merge.

■ Merge is a WordPerfect procedure that combines a table of variable information in a data file with a form file that includes merge codes in the variable data locations. You must prepare a **data file** (which in this exercise is a Paradox table) and the **form file** for a merge. For example, a form letter may be merged with a data file of names and addresses. This will produce a file or printed output of a form letter for each person in the data file.

■ The **form file** contains the document to be merged and merge codes with the field names of the table data in the appropriate locations. For example, as shown in Illustration A, the form letter inviting the members to a meeting has the merge codes for the inside address and salutation entered in the appropriate locations. A form file must be prepared using the names of the fields in the Paradox table in preparation for the Merge procedure.

■ You have two options in creating a **data file** for a Paradox table. You can:

• Merge the data directly into WordPerfect without importing the file.

• Import or link the data into a WordPerfect table or data file and then merge the files as WordPerfect files.

■ To merge the data directly into WordPerfect without importing the file, enter the Paradox table filename in the Data Source box in the Perform Merge dialog box. The merge codes in the form letter reference the field data in the table and merge to new documents. This method ensures that the latest Paradox table information is being merged into the form letter. Note in the illustration of the Perform Merge dialog box below, you can Select Records to limit the data to be merged.

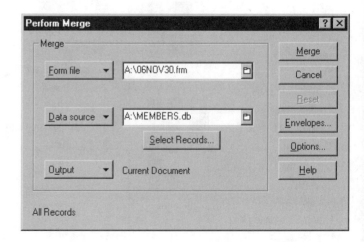

■ You can also import the data from a Paradox table by selecting Spreadsheet/Database, Import from the Insert menu or you can link the data by selecting Spreadsheet/Database, Create Link from the Insert menu. As you will note by the two illustrations on this page, both commands present similar dialog boxes. You can select the Data type and Link or Import settings from the drop-down lists. When the Filename is entered or selected, the table Fields will display. You can deselect any fields you will not need for the merge and/or you can use Query to select records that meet certain specifications. The difference between the import and link procedures is that importing the data brings in the data as it is now while linking the data will provide for update of the file data with changes in the Paradox table.

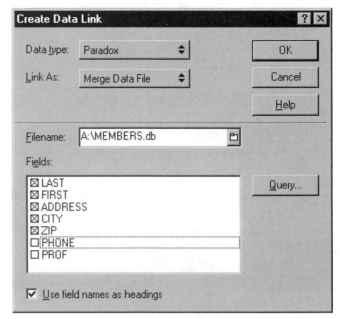

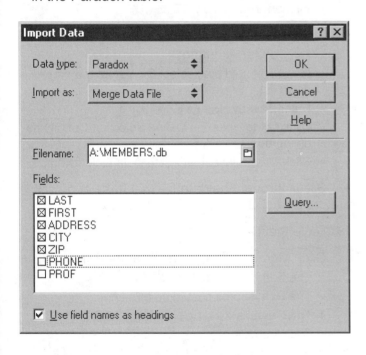

In this exercise, the CUG club would like to send a letter to its members using the information from its MEMBERS table and a letter previously created in WordPerfect. You will insert merge codes into the form letter and merge the table information to create a letter for each member.

EXERCISE DIRECTIONS

1. Click the DAD WordPerfect icon.

2. Type the letter on the following page or open 🖫06NOV30.wpd.

3. Replace the inside address and salutation information with merge codes as follow:

   a. Select Merge from the Tools menu and click Form. Select Use File in Active Window to make the current document a form file.

   b. Type MEMBERS.db as the data file.

   ✓ *Use the path or drive with the filename to locate this file that was created earlier.*

   c. Delete the three lines of the inside address.

   d. Click Insert Field on the Merge Feature Bar.

   e. Select FIRST, Click Insert, press Spacebar, Select LAST, click Insert, press Enter.

   f. Complete the remaining two inside address and salutation lines using the spacing, punctuation, and the State entry as shown in Illustration A.

   g. Close the dialog box.

   h. Save the file as NOV30.

   ✓ *The file will be saved as NOV30.frm (a form file).*

4. Click Merge on the Merge Feature Bar.

   - Current document should be set as the form file on the Perform Merge dialog box.
   - The MEMBERS.db table should be set as the Data source.
   - The Output should be set to a New Document.

5. Click Merge in the Perform Merge dialog box.

   ✓ *A new document will be created with the merged letters (22 pages), one for each member on the list. This merge method uses the Paradox table directly and provides the data in the Paradox table.*

6. Scroll down through the merged document and note the merged information and the separation of each letter by a page break.

7. Save the document as NOV30ALL.wpd. Close the file.

8. On the form letter, enter the following two-line postscript below the letter closing:

   ¶ P.S. We are asking Beverly Hills members to arrive at 5:15 p.m. and act as greeters.

9. Open a new file in WordPerfect using the New File button on the Toolbar.

10. Click Insert, Spreadsheet/Database, Create Link.

    - Data type should be set to Paradox.
    - Link As should be set to Merge Data File.
    - Filename should be MEMBERS.db.
    - Deselect the PHONE and PROF fields.

11. Click the Query button.

    - In the first field box, select CITY from the drop-down list.
    - Enter Beverly Hills as Condition 1.
    - Click OK to close the Define Selection Conditions dialog box.
    - Click OK to close the Create Data Link dialog box.

12. Scroll through the data file that has been created of Beverly Hills members.

13. Save the file as MEM.dat.

14. Click Merge on the Merge Feature Bar.

    - The Form file should be NOV30.
    - The Data source should be MEM.dat.
    - The Output should be New Document.
    - Click Merge.
    - Scroll through letters to check if they are all for Beverly Hills. Save the file as BHILLS30.frm.

    ✓ *The MEM.dat data file is linked to Paradox. If any data changes in the Paradox file, it will automatically update in this file when it is reopened. If you have time, you can make a change in Paradox to the MEMBERS table and note the change in the MEM.dat file when reopened.*

15. Print the first letter in the file.

16. Close and save all files.

California User's Group
Barry Boot, President
6 Terminal Drive
North Hollywood, CA 91615
Telephone (817)-555-1122 ■ Fax (817)-555-1020 ■ E-mail: Baroot@earth.com

November 15, 1997

FIELD(FIRST) FIELD(LAST)
FIELD(ADDRESS)
FIELD(CITY), CA FIELD(ZIP)

Dear FIELD(FIRST):

If you missed our last meeting, you may not have heard about our November dinner/seminar with the San Francisco User's Group.

We will be hosting the seminar in Beverly Hills at the Beverly Hills Hotel at 493 Sepulveda Drive on November 30, 1997, at 6:00 p.m. Our speakers will be Gary Williams of DataComm and Marge Cortez of NetLink. There will be ample time to network and meet our presenters.

The tariff for this dinner/seminar will be $40. Please e-mail your reservation and charge authorization or send a check to CUG before November 25.

See you there.

Sincerely yours,

Barry Boot
President

KEYSTROKES

USE PARADOX TABLE FIELDS TO CREATE A FORM FILE

1. Open form document.
2. Click **Tools** .... `Alt`+`T`
3. Click **Merge** .... `E`
4. Click **Form** .... `Alt`+`F`
5. Select **Use file in active window** .... `Alt`+`U`
6. Click **OK** .... `Enter`
7. Click **Associate a data file** ..... `Alt`+`A`
8. Enter a Paradox filename, or click folder to locate.
9. Click **OK** .... `Enter`
10. Place the cursor at desired location in form document.

11. Click **Insert Field** on the Merge Feature Bar.
12. Select **Field Names** .... `↓`
13. Click **Insert** .... `Alt`+`I`
14. Repeat 10-13 until all fields are entered.
15. Click **Close** .... `Alt`+`C`
16. Save the file.
    *WordPerfect will give the file a **.frm** extension.*

LINK A PARADOX TABLE TO A WORDPERFECT DATA FILE

1. Click **Insert** .... `Alt`+`I`
2. Click **Spreadsheet/Database** .... `R`
3. Click **Create Link** .... `C`

4. Select **Data type** .... `Alt`+`T`, `↓`
5. Select **Link As** Merge Data File .... `Alt`+`L`, `↓`
6. Enter **Filename**.
7. If desired, deselect unnecessary fields.

To query table:

8. Click **Query** .... `Alt`+`Q`
9. Select field for query .... `↓`
10. Enter Condition 1.
11. Repeat 9-10 as required.
12. Click **OK** to close the Define Selection Conditions dialog box.
13. Click **OK** to close the Create Data Link dialog box.

Exercise 7

- ■ **Insert a WordPerfect Outline into a Presentations Slide Show**
- ■ **Link a Quattro Pro Chart to a Presentations Slide Show**

NOTES

Insert a WordPerfect Outline into a Presentations Slide Show

■ An outline created in WordPerfect may be used as the text in a Presentations Slide Show. The outline file is inserted into Presentations in Outliner view by selecting File from the Insert menu. The WordPerfect outline must be closed before it can be inserted.

■ In a WordPerfect outline, heading levels provide the structure for the data. When the outline is inserted into Presentations, each first level paragraph number becomes the title on a separate slide. The other levels are shown as subtopics or text on the slide. The formatting or styles in the WordPerfect outline will be imported into Presentations. See the illustration below and on page 484:

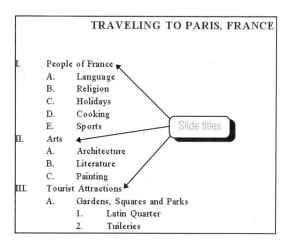

Link a Quattro Pro Chart to a Presentations Slide Show

■ Data from WordPerfect or another application can be linked to Presentations so that the Presentations slide will update if the linked file is changed. You can take Quattro Pro data, link it

to the slide show and bring it into Presentations as a chart. In preparation for this procedure, you should name the block of data to be charted. Any charts you have already created in Quattro Pro are automatically named.

■ To link Quattro charts or data to a slide, add a Data Chart slide template by selecting Add Slides from the Slide menu and clicking **Data Chart**. In Slide Editor view, double click on the slide background to add the data chart. The Data Chart Gallery dialog box will appear. Presentations will display a data chart slide with the format and layout you desire with sample data.

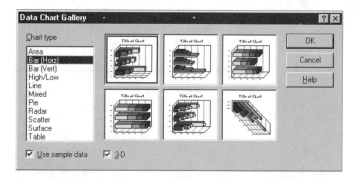

■ After selecting a chart type in Slide Editor, select Import from the Data menu. The Import Data dialog box will display, as illustrated on the next page. You can select Link to spreadsheet and Clear current data to replace the sample data and link the Quattro Pro block of data or chart to the slide. When the filename and block range is selected and entered, the Quattro Pro data and chart will replace the sample data.

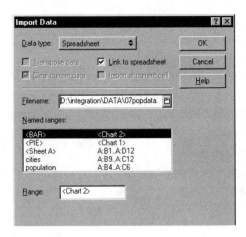

■ A Quattro Pro chart or notebook page can also be linked or embedded into a Presentations slide using Copy/Paste Link procedures. To link a chart, the chart should be selected in Quattro Pro, copied, and linked using the Paste Special, Paste Link options on a data chart slide in Presentations. The Copy/Paste Link procedure places the chart on the slide but it does not take on the slide background. The chart created using the first method has a better appearance since Presentations brings the chart into the slide layout.

In this exercise, a WordPerfect outline about traveling to France will be imported into a Presentations slide show. The slides will be edited and a Quattro Pro chart will be linked to the slide show.

EXERCISE DIRECTIONS

1. To insert a WordPerfect outline into Presentations:
   a. Click the DAD Presentations icon.
   b. Click New Slide Show.
   c. Click OK.
   d. Change to Outliner view.
   e. Click Insert, File.
   f. Choose the file 📄FRANCE.wpd or 💾07FRANCE.wpd.
      ✓ *The outline is inserted into Presentations.*
   g. Click the Slide Sorter to view the outline as slides.

2. Edit the first slide:
   a. Change the slide template to Bullet Chart.
   b. Add the following subtitle:
      Allez-Vous Travel Consultants, Inc.
   c. Add the following text:
      ★ *Panel Members:*
      – *John LeByron, President*
      – *Celeste Montrachet, Guide*
      ★ *Presenter:*
      – *Claudine Vilmay, Vice President*

3. Add a slide for chart data:
   a. Place cursor on slide 2.
   b. Click Slide, Add slides.
   c. Set the slide template to Data Chart.
   d. Switch to Slide Editor view and double-click on the data chart area.
   e. Select the pie chart and the style that includes a data table at the bottom.
      ✓ *Sample data and a pie chart will appear.*

4. View the Quattro Pro file to be linked to Presentations:
   a. Click the DAD Quattro Pro icon.

   b. Open 💾07POPDAT.wb3, or create the notebook from the illustration on the next page. Note the data and charts.
   c. Exit Quattro Pro.

5. Link Quattro Pro chart to slide show:
   a. Switch back to Presentations in Slide Editor view.
   b. Click Data, Import.
   c. Select 💾07POPDAT.wb3 as the spreadsheet data.
   d. Click Link to Spreadsheet.
   e. Select PIE named range. Data and chart will move into slide.
   f. Size chart to fit chart area.
   g. Double-click on slide title and enter: French Population.
   h. Double-click on slide subtitle and enter: Urban and Rural Populations – 1996.

6. Repeat the procedures above to add a data chart slide and import the horizontal bar chart in the BAR named range from 07POPDAT to the next slide. Add title and subtitle as follows:
   French Population
   Largest Cities-1990

7. Switch to Outliner view. Note that the Tourist Attractions segment is too long for one slide.

8. Using Shift+Tab, Tab and outlining procedures, create three slides from the Tourist Attractions section of the outline with the following headings and with the bullets as listed in the outline:

   Slide 6: Title: Tourist Attractions
             Subtitle: Gardens, Squares and Parks
   Slide 7: Title: Tourist Attractions

Subtitle: Famous Buildings and
Monuments
Slide 8:   Title: Tourist Attractions
Subtitle: Museums and Art Galleries

9. Add a Bullet Chart slide to the end of the presentation.

10. Enter the following title, subtitle and bullets:

Allez-Vous Travel Consultants, Inc.

Travel Services

- Bookings – Deluxe Level
- Restaurant Reservations
- Tours
- Guides

- Group Rates
- Historical Notes
- Demographic Notes

11. Return to the first slide and play the slide show.

12. Switch to Slide Sorter view and add a Slide Transition Property to apply to all slides.

13. In Slide Editor view set Bullet Chart Animation to apply to all slides.

14. Check the presentation by playing the slide show.

15. Save the file as FRANCE and close it.

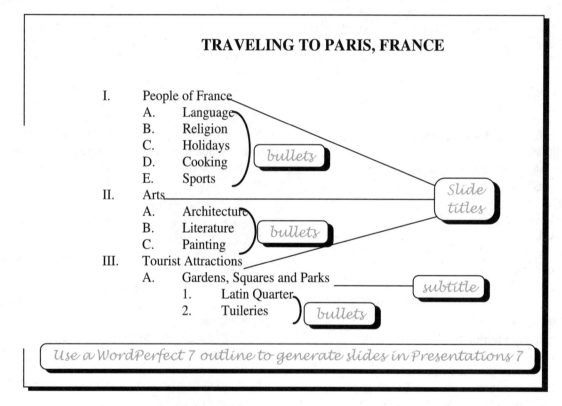

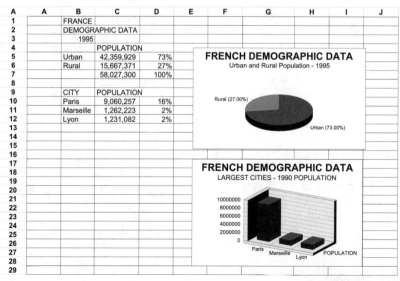

KEYSTROKES

INSERT WORDPERFECT OUTLINE INTO PRESENTATIONS

1. Click the Presentations icon on the DAD Toolbar.

2. Click **Create a new slide show** .... `Alt` + `S`

3. Click **OK** .... `Enter`

4. Select a Bullet Chart template .... `Tab` , `↓`

5. Click **OK** .... `Enter`

6. Click **View** .... `Alt` + `V`

7. Click **Outliner** .... `O`

8. Click **Insert** .... `Alt` + `I`

9. Click **File** .... `I`

10. Select the file.

11. Click **Insert** .... `Enter`

LINK QUATTRO PRO CHART TO PRESENTATIONS SLIDE

✓   *Quattro Pro data should be charted or the block of data for the chart should be named prior to performing these steps. Add a slide for chart data.*

Slide Sorter view of Presentations:

1. Click **Slide** .... `Alt` + `S`

2. Click **Add slides** .... `A`

3. Select **Template** .... `Alt` + `T`

4. Select **Data Chart** .... `↓`

5. Click **OK** .... `Enter`

6. In Slide Editor, double-click on data chart area.

7. Select **Chart type** .... `↓` `↑` , `Tab` , `↕`

8. Click **OK** .... `Enter`

9. Click **Data** .... `Alt` + `D`

10. Click **Import** .... `M`

11. Click **Data type** .... `Alt` + `D`

12. Click **Spreadsheet** .... `↓`

13. Click **Link to Spreadsheet**.

14. Select file name to import.

15. Select desired named range .... `Alt` + `N` , `↓`

16. Click **OK** .... `Enter`

Exercise 8

- Copy Presentations Text into a WordPerfect Document
- Convert Presentations Slide Shows to .wpg Format
- Insert a Presentations Slide into a WordPerfect Document

NOTES

Copy Presentations Text into a WordPerfect Document

- You can bring text developed in Presentations into a WordPerfect document. You can select the desired text in Outliner view and Copy and Paste the selection into the document. When text is brought into WordPerfect, bulleted text will be organized in outline form and subtitles will be given a level letter or number. You may have to adjust text as desired.

Convert Presentations Slide Shows to .wpg Format

- You may wish to insert a slide into a WordPerfect document. To accomplish this, however, you must first convert the Presentations slide show file to **.wpg** format. Presentations provides a macro that will automatically convert a .shw file to a .wpg file. A macro is a set of instructions that are recorded and played back to complete a task with several steps automatically. To convert a Presentations file, click Tools, Macro, Play, or simply press Alt+F10. A Play Macro dialog box will appear with a listing of pre-written macros, ready to automate various tasks. The **Shw2wpg macro**, for example, converts each slide in a slide show to separate .wpg files. Note the illustration of the Play Macro dialog box below.

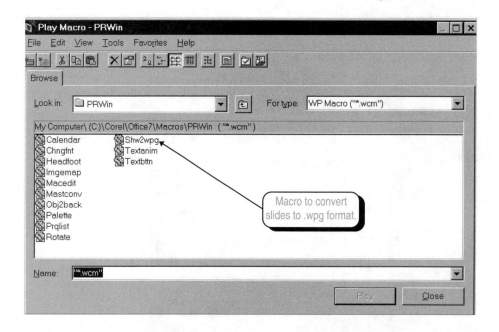

- To convert the presentation file, double-click Shw2wpg in the Play Macro dialog box. The SHW to WPG dialog box will appear. Enter the name of the slide show to convert (including the extension) and enter a directory name for saving the .wpg files. When you click Convert each slide will be converted to a separate .wpg file in the directory you specified. For example, in the illustration below, the new files will be saved to the A:\FR08 directory. The .wpg files are named using the slide titles.

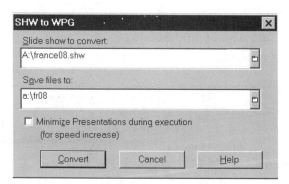

Insert a Presentations Slide into a WordPerfect Document

- Presentations slides that have been converted to .wpg format may be inserted into a WordPerfect document by selecting, File from the Insert menu. Select the file from the Insert File dialog box and click Insert. The slide will be inserted into the document as an image with an edit box. You can then size, move and enhance the image with the Edit Box features as discussed in WordPerfect, Exercise 46.

In this exercise, Claudine Vilmay of Allez-Vous Travel Consultants is continuing to prepare for her presentation on French travel. Slide text will be used to create a WordPerfect document for prospective clients. In addition, the slide show will be converted to .wpg format so that a slide can be added to a letter about the presentation.

EXERCISE DIRECTIONS

1. Open Presentations using the DAD bar.

2. Open ☞FRANCE.shw or ▢08FRANCE.shw.

3. To use slide text in a WordPerfect document:

   a. In Outliner view, move to the last slide containing the Allez-Vous Travel Consultants, Inc., Travel Services listing.
   b. Select and copy the text in the last slide.
   c. Open WordPerfect using the DAD icon.
   d. Paste the text into a new document and change font, if necessary.

4. Delete the Travel Services line.

5. Center the company name and format to 19 points.

6. Enter John LeByron, President, as a centered subtitle.

7. Insert an appropriate clipart or graphic file at the left margin, as shown in Illustration A on the following page.

8. Insert the text, as shown in Illustration A, below the slide text and graphic.

9. Save the file as FORM.wpd.

10. Print a copy of the document.

11. Switch back to Presentations.

12. Add the same graphic to the first slide, TRAVELING TO PARIS, FRANCE.

13. Save the slide show. Do not close the file.

14. Switch to WordPerfect.

15. Open ▢08GRAM.wpd, or type the letter shown in Illustration B on page 489.

16. Insert the additional text as illustrated.

17. To insert a slide into a WordPerfect document:

   a. Switch to Presentations. (The .shw file must be converted to a .wpg file.)
   b. Click Tools, Macro, Play, or press Alt+F10.
   c. Double-click the Shw2wpg macro.
   d. Enter the name of the slide show to convert, with the extension. (drive: FRANCE.shw)
   e. Enter a directory name for the .wpg files. (drive:directory name)
   f. Click Convert.
   ✓ *Each slide will be converted to a separate .wpg file in the directory you specified.*
   g. Switch to WordPerfect.
   h. Move the cursor to the insertion point for the slide.
   i. Click Insert, File on the menu.
   j. Select the directory that contains the converted slides and select the TRAVELING TO PARIS, FRANCE slide from the Insert File dialog box.
   k. Click Insert.
   ✓ *The slide will be inserted into the document as an image with an edit box.*
   i. Adjust the size and placement so that the slide is centered under the letter text.

18. Print a copy of the letter.
19. Save the file as GRAM.wpd.
20. Close all files and applications.

ILLUSTRATION A

Copy text from Presentations slide.

Allez-Vous Travel Consultants, Inc.

John LeByron, President

Insert clipart.

a. Bookings - Deluxe Level
b. Restaurant Reservations
c. Tours
d. Guides
e. Group Rates
f. Historical Notes
g. Demographic Notes

If you are interested in our services, please complete the form below.
We will send you our French information and travel packet which includes rates and tours.

NAME_____
ADDRESS_____
CITY_____STATE_____ZIP_____

TELEPHONE: DAY_____EVENING_____

Insert text.

Allez-Vous Travel Consultants, Inc.
145 Fifth Avenue
New York, NY 10016

December 1, 1997

Mr. Robert Vida
Gramercy Park Owners Association
123 Park Avenue
New York, NY 10014

Dear Mr. Vida:

Thank you for asking our group to present at your December 15 meeting on French Travel. I will present a brief slide show about France and will bring the necessary equipment. We will need a power supply and a screen.

After the presentation, our French guide and our President will be available to field questions from your group.

Insert ←

Thank you.

Sincerely yours,

I am including the first slide below so that you can prepare your agenda and include all participants.

Claudine Vilmay
Vice President

Insert

TRAVELING TO PARIS, FRANCE slide

KEYSTROKES

TO CONVERT .SHW FILES TO .WPG FORMAT

In Presentations:

Alt + F10

1. Click **Tools** .... `Alt` + `T`
2. Click **Macro** .... `M`
3. Click **Play** .... `P`
4. Click **Name** field .... `Alt` + `N`, `↓`
5. Type **Shw2wpg**.

   OR

   Click the **Shw2wpg** macro .... `↓` `↑`

6. Click **Play** .... `Enter`
7. In **Slide show to convert**, enter filename of slide show.
   Drive:*filename.shw*
8. In **Save files to**, enter a directory name for .wpg files.
   drive:directory name
9. Click **Convert** .... `Alt` + `C`

TO INSERT .WPG SLIDES INTO A DOCUMENT

In WordPerfect:

1. Move the cursor to the insertion point for the slide.

2. Click **Insert** .... `Alt` + `I`
3. Click **File** .... `I`
4. Select directory with converted slides.
5. Select **Name** .... `Alt` + `N`
   • Enter Slide Name.
   OR
   Click slide name .... `↓`
6. Click **Insert**.

Exercise 9

■ **Help Online** ■ **Use the Internet for Research**
■ **Use Internet Data**

NOTES

Help Online

■ Corel Office 7 provides online help for WordPerfect, Quattro Pro and Presentations. You must have a modem and Internet software to connect to an online information service. It may be easiest to connect to your Internet service provider prior to accessing the help feature.

■ Once you are connected to the Internet, click Help, Help Online to display the Help Online dialog box, as illustrated below. If you are connected to CompuServe, select that service to go to the User Forum, or else select Internet to use Netscape Navigator or Internet Explorer go to directly to the Corel home page on the World Wide Web. If you have installed CompuServe software and have a connection to a CompuServe account, there are user forums for Corel WordPerfect Suite and Corel Office Professional. If necessary, you can click Configure to select the application you want to use. Then click Connect.

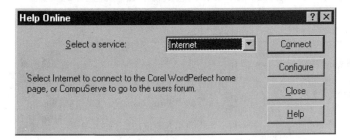

■ If you are unable to select your service or connect using this option, you can sign on to your Internet provider and use your World Wide Web browser to reach http://www:corel.com/help. You will also find application-specific Web sites, such as http://www.corel.com/products /wordperfect/cwp7/index.htm, as well as

locations for resources, new product information, and "freebies". Note the illustration of the Corel Presentations 7 home page below.

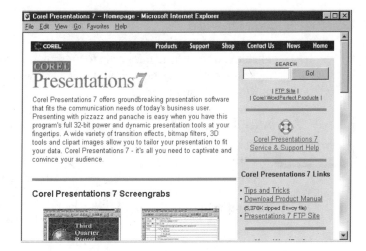

Use the Internet for Research

■ The Internet provides access to countless Web sites, many of which contain information and documentation that can be used for researching a particular subject or topic.

■ To connect to a Web site, you must use a Web browser application. A Web browser, such as Netscape Navigator or Microsoft Internet Explorer, is a graphic interface program that enables you to view the World Wide Web. Your Internet Service provider should provide you with a Web browser free of charge.

■ Each Corel Office 7 application, with the exception of Paradox7, contains a Web browser button on the Toolbar. Clicking the Web browser button should launch the browser application you currently have installed in your system.

- Once you have access to a browser, you can search the World Wide Web. You can search for specific information by going to a search site. A search site (such as Yahoo, Excite or Alta Vista) enables you to search other Web sites for information based on keywords or phrases. A search site contains a search engine, which is a database of Web site information that is continually updated. At the search site simply type the name of the item, topic, or subject about which you are seeking information, and the search engine will generate a list of results.

- When conducting a search at a Search site, you may sometimes end up with more information that you need. For example, if you entered the word *France* as the search criteria, you may get thousands of documents that include that word, many of which are unrelated to your interest. To fine-tune your query, you could use words such as AND, OR, and NOT. If you entered <u>France</u>

<u>AND restaurants</u> as the search criteria, the web sites would have to contain both references to be found. If you entered <u>France OR restaurants,</u> as the search criteria, the documents would have to contain either France or restaurants, which would return more documents since OR is less restrictive. If you entered <u>France NOT restaurants</u>, the search engine would find occurrences of France that do not include restaurants.

Use Internet Data

- When you locate information that you would like to utilize, you can print the document, or highlight to select certain information, select copy, and then paste the information into WordPerfect. You can also download the entire file, but this may be more time consuming.

Although Claudine Vilmay has a travel network, she will use the Internet to obtain a listing of three and four star hotels and interesting restaurants in Paris. This information will be added to her presentation on France and the details about the hotels and restaurants will be added to her speaker notes.

EXERCISE DIRECTIONS

✓ *Integration Exercise 9 and 10 involve live Internet research. If you do not have Internet access, Data files - containing research information obtained from the Internet - are available on DDC's separately purchased Data disks. Research information obtained from these files may be used in place of live Internet data.*

1. Click the DAD Presentations icon.
2. Open ▦FRANCE.shw or ▯09FRANCE.shw.
3. To access help online:
   ✓ *There are three sets of steps for this procedure. Use the one that fits your installation.*

I. If you have Netscape Navigator, Internet Explorer or CompuServe:

a. Click Help, Help Online to access Corel Help online.
b. Select Internet (to prompt your Web browser) or CompuServe.
c. Click Connect.
d. Look through the Corel 7 Presentations home page document.
e. Click on the Corel Presentations 7 hyperlink with the life preserver symbol on the right side of the page.

f. Click on Corel Presentations 7 FAQ's (frequently asked questions).
g. Click on any question you wish to have answered.
h. Exit from your browser and disconnect from your service provider.

OR

II. If you have a provider that is not supported through Corel Office 7:

a. Minimize the Presentations window.
b. Sign on to your Internet service provider.
c. Select your World Wide Web browser.
d. Go to http://www.corel.com/porducts/wordperfect/cwp7/indes.htm, or search for Corel Presentations 7 to reach the home page illustrated at the beginning of this exercise.
e. Complete steps d-h in the previous set of steps.

OR

III. If you do not have Internet access:

a. Use the menu steps to view the dialog box for help online.
b. Use the Help Topics menu items to view the help screens for Web browser and help online.

c. Click on the DAD WordPerfect icon.
d. Open 🖫09COREL.wpd to view the screens discussed in the procedures above.

4. Return to Presentations.

5. In Slide Sorter view, note the Restaurants and Hotels slides that need completion.

6. Edit the Restaurant slide, and change the title to Cafés.

7. Our goal is to find four Paris cafés that have good reviews. To research Paris Cafés:

   If you are connected to the Internet:

   a. Sign on to your Internet provider.
   b. Open your Web browser.
   c. Go to the Yahoo! Search site by typing http://www.yahoo.com on the location line and pressing the enter key.
   d. Search on Paris cafés or you can search for The Paris Pages.
   ✓   *You may use other search methods as well. Your provider may supply Travel pages for different countries that provide this type of information.*
   e. View the sites that might provide a list of good cafés in Paris.
   f. Select four cafés from these sites and copy or record their names or print the Web page. DO NOT DISCONNECT.

   OR

   If you do not have Internet access:

   a. Access a sample Web page document from the separately purchased data disk. Open 🖫09FRCAFE.wpd.
   b. Select four cafés and record their names or print the document.

8. Our goal is to find four hotels in Paris that have four-star rankings. To research Paris hotels:

If you are connected to the Internet:

a. Search on Paris and hotels, or France and hotels, or The Paris Pages.
✓   *You may use other search methods. Your provider may supply Travel pages for different countries that provide this type of information.*
b. View the sites that might provide a list of four star hotels in Paris.
c. Select four hotels from these sites and record or copy their names, or print the Web page.

OR

If you do not have Internet access:

a. Access a sample Web page document from the separately purchased data disk. Open 🖫09FRHOTE.wpd.
b. Select four hotels and record their names, or print the document.

9. Exit from your browser and disconnect from your service provider.

10. Maximize the Presentations icon.

11. Enter the names of the four cafés on the Cafés slide.

12. Click Slide, Speaker Notes and add any information you have found about the cafés to assist in the presentation.

13. Enter the names of the four hotels on the Hotel slide.

14. Click Slide, Speaker Notes and add any information you have found about the hotels to assist in the presentation.

15. Print copies of the Speaker Notes pages for each slide.

16. Save the presentation, name it FRANCE.

17. Close all files.

KEYSTROKES

USE ONLINE HELP

You must have a modem, Internet access (through Compuserve or another Internet Service Provider) and a Web browser (such as Netscape Navigator or Microsoft Internet Explorer).

1. Click **Help** .... `Alt`+`H`
2. Click **Help Online** .... `N`
3. Select **Internet** to launch your Internet browser.
   OR
   Select **CompuServe**.

1. Click **Configure** to select .... `Alt`+`N` application.
2. Click **Connect** .... `Alt`+`O`

Exercise 10

■ Summary

In this exercise, Martin Mackenny, of the Finance department at Boynton College, is making a presentation about investing in Brazil to his fellow college professors. He would like to obtain input from Ms. Williamson, his investment advisor affiliate, who will assist him at the meeting, as well as add further economic information on Brazil from your findings on the Internet. Once the new information is incorporated into the presentation, a memo will be sent to the college professors that will be attending the meeting using the Merge procedure with a Paradox table of staff members. A slide will be incorporated into the memorandum.

Since this is a comprehensive exercise and it may take more than one work session, we are indicating locations in the problem where you might stop and resume the scenario at a later time. The ☞ symbol before a step number indicates that this section should not be started unless you have time to complete the segment.

EXERCISE DIRECTIONS

✓ *Integration Exercise 9 and 10 involve live Internet research. If you do not have Internet access, Data files - containing research information obtained from the Internet - are available on DDC's separately purchased Data disks. Research information obtained from these files may be used in place of live Internet data.*

1. Click the DAD WordPerfect icon.
2. Open ▢10PRESENT.wpd in WordPerfect, or create the letter as shown in Illustration A.
3. Click the DAD Presentations icon.
4. Open ▢BRAZIL.shw or ▢10BRAZIL.shw in Presentations and switch to Outliner view.
5. Copy the outline from Presentations into the WordPerfect document as indicated in Illustration A on the following page.
6. Delete all the bullets under each title so that only the slide headings or main topics are included.
7. Since this is now a two-page letter, place an appropriate header on the second page of the letter.
8. Save the file as PRESENT.wpd and print one copy.
9. Close the file.
10. Open ▢10REPLY.wpd or create the response as shown in Illustration B on the following page.

11. Click the DAD Quattro Pro icon.
12. Open ▢10INFLAT.wb3 in Quattro Pro, or create the notebook and chart in Illustration C.
13. Select the chart and use the Copy, Paste Special procedure to embed the chart into the WordPerfect letter where indicated in the text.
14. Save the file as REPLY.wpd and print one copy.
15. Switch to Quattro Pro and close the file.
🖐16. Switch to Presentations and modify the slide show as follows:
    Insert a new slide as slide 7 with the heading, "Low Inflation."
17. Switch to WordPerfect and select the Quattro Pro chart object in the letter and copy it below the Low Inflation heading on slide 7 in the Presentations slide show.
18. Continue to modify the presentation as follows.
    - Edit slide 1 to read:
      Economic and Historical Prospectives on Investing in Brazil.
      Presenter: Michael Mackenny, Finance Department
      Assistant: Jennifer Williamson, Simpson Investment Advisors
    - Switch to Slide Sorter view and add a slide transition for slide 7.

19. Play the slide show.

20. To research additional information on Brazil's economy:

    If you have Internet access:

    a. Connect to your Internet provider and research Brazil and economy to develop additional data for the presentation.

    b. From the information on Brazil, add speaker notes to the second slide with additional data that can be used in the introduction.

    If you do not have Internet access:

    a. Open ⌷10BRECO.wpd, or read through the document in Illustration E and extract some pertinent information. (You will then have to type the desired text into a separate document.)

    b. From the information on Brazil, add speaker notes to the second slide with additional data that can be used in the introduction.

21. Print the Speaker Notes page.

22. Save the presentation.

23. Switch to WordPerfect and close REPLY.

24. Open ⌷10INVITE.wpd or create the memorandum shown in Illustration D.

25. Switch to Presentations and convert the .shw file for Brazil to a .wpg format by selecting Macro, Play from the Tools menu (Alt + F10) and then opening the Shw2wpg macro.

26. Switch to WordPerfect and insert the first slide from the new .wpg format slide directory into the memorandum below the text.

27. Save the file as INVITE.wpd.

28. Click Tools, Merge, Form to make the memorandum in the active window a form file.

29. Type STAFF.db or ⌷10STAFF.db as the data file.

    ✔ *Use the path or drive with the filename to locate the previously created file, or the file on disk.*

30. Insert the fields from the table necessary to create the data links for the first section of the memorandum, as indicated in Illustration D.

31. Save the form file as INVITEFF.frm.

32. Merge the files to a new document.

33. Scroll through the newly merged document to check the merge.

34. Save the file as INVITMER.wpd.

35. Print the first memorandum in the file.

36. Close and save all files.

ILLUSTRATION A

Today's date

Ms. Jennifer Williamson
Simpson Investment Advisors
255 Madison Ave
New York, NY 10016

Dear Ms. Williamson:

I am writing regarding the upcoming presentation we will be making to the staff at the college about investments in Brazil. I will be using the historical and economic background of the country to interest the group in Brazilian investment. It is my position that the Brazilian economy has substantially recovered since the Brazilian debt crisis of the 1980s and that this may be a good time to invest profitably in specific markets in Brazil.

I am including the draft outline that I expect to use for the presentation below:

If you have any suggestions or anything to add to this outline, please contact me as soon as possible. Otherwise, I will be in touch with you a week prior to the meeting to confirm hotel arrangements.

Sincerely yours,

Martin Mackenny
Finance Department

Insert Presentations outline.

ILLUSTRATION B

Today's date

Mr. Martin Mackenny
Boynton College
342 Palm Boulevard
Ocean City, VA 05555

Dear Mr. Mackenny:

Thank you for your letter regarding our presentation on Brazilian investments at the college. I trust that you will be filling in the historical and economic background from your extensive knowledge of the country. You may also be able to obtain some new statistics or other economic data from the Internet.

In addition to setting up an introductory heading in the outline, I would suggest that you include some data on the vast changes in the inflation rate. A chart showing the trend of the inflation rate over the last 15 years is included below. This is a clear indication of the changes that have taken place and it should be incorporated into the segment where you discuss the current low inflation rate.

I look forward to seeing you in two weeks and will call to confirm my arrangements for the visit. Thank you.

Sincerely yours,

Jennifer Williamson
Investment Advisor

Insert chart.

ILLUSTRATION C

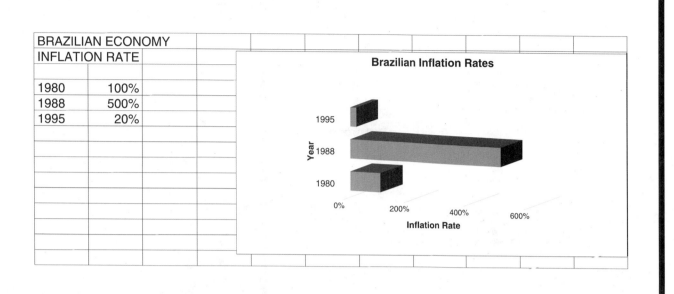

BRAZILIAN ECONOMY			
INFLATION RATE			
1980	100%		
1988	500%		
1995	20%		

Brazilian Inflation Rates

MEMORANDUM

TO: Title First Last

DEPARTMENT: Dept.

BUILDING: Bldg.

Field names for data link with Paradox table

FROM: Martin Mackenny
                               Finance Department

RE: Monthly Investment Seminar

DATE: Today's date

This month our meeting will focus on Brazil. We will be joined by Ms. Jennifer Williamson of the Simpson Investment Advisors group. The meeting will be held in the Faculty Lounge in Shepard Hall at 8:00 p.m. on the last Tuesday evening of the month.

As in the past, please note below the introductory slide of our presentation and post this notice in your department office. Thank you.

Insert slide.

ILLUSTRATION E

BRAZIL

Business and Economy Sites

DOE FOSSIL ENERGY ACTIVITIES RELATED TO BRAZIL
•Speech: "Independent Power Production and the New Model for the Electric Sector", presented by Barbara McKee at the IV International Workshop for Independent Power Production in Brazil (Sao Paolo, Brazil; June 1996)

LINKS TO BUSINESS INFORMATION SOURCES ON BRAZIL

US-DOE Energy Information Administration - Country Analysis Brief on Brazil. A description of Brazil's energy economy, including Oil, Natural Gas, and Electricity.

CIA World Factbook - Information on Brazil's geography, people, government, economy, transportation, and communications infrastructure.

U.S. Department of Commerce - 1996 Country Commercial Guide for Brazil. including economic trends, political environment, marketing information for U.S. products and services, an overview of the investment climate, leading sectors for U.S. exports and investments, Brazil's trade regulations and standards, trade and project financing, and business travel.

International Trade Adiminstration - An overview of the key economic indicators for Brazil, plus information on Brazil's big emerging sectors, market access and competition, and how the ITA can help U.S. exporters.<Picture: ita seal>

Price Waterhouse - Information Guide on Brazil, including a country profile plus information on Brazil's investment climate and incentives, business environment, banking and finance system, and taxation system.

Trade Point USA - U.S. Global Trade Outlook for Brazil, including a summary overview of the Brazilian economy with sections on trade climate & trends and export opportunities for U.S. companies. Elsewhere at this site is a 10-year summary of Brazil's National Economic Indicators and International Trade.<Picture: tpusa>

Country Commercial Guide - Brazil

Brazil: Economic Trends and Outlook

USDOC, INTERNATIONAL TRADE ADMINISTRATION

SOURCE: USDOC, INTERNATIONAL TRADE ADMINISTRATION
SOURCE KEY: IT
PROGRAM: COUNTRY COMMERCIAL GUIDES
PROGRAM KEY: IT CCG
UPDATE: Annually
ID NUMBER: IT CCG   BRAZIL02
TITLE: Brazil: Economic Trends and Outlook
DATA TYPE: TEXT
END YEAR: 1995
UPDATED: 08/23/95
COUNTRY:
| Brazil
TEXT
II. ECONOMIC TRENDS AND OUTLOOK

Major Trends and Outlook

Brazil is in the midst of a stabilization program originally developed by President Fernando Henrique Cardoso when he was Finance Minister (May 1993 - April 1994). On July 1, 1994 a new currency, the "Real", was introduced. Inflation, which had reached 50 percent/month by June 1994, has declined to monthly rates between 1 and 3 percent.

GDP growth may reach 6.4 percent in 1995, compared to 5.7 percent last year. The Real plan initially effected a 15 percent increase in income for salaried workers. Demand for goods exploded and Brazilian manufacturers have been running at full capacity to meet demand. Demand exceeding local production has been met by imports. While the administration is predicting a trade surplus of USD 3 billion by the end of the year, other sources expect Brazil to break even on its trade accounts, and some forecast a deficit. IPEA, the Institute for Applied Economic Research, has predicted a slowdown in economic growth for the latter part of 1995, as consumption levels stabilize.

In response to large monthly trade deficits in the last quarter of 1994 and the first quarter of 1995, in March 1995 the government significantly increased import tariff levels on a range of consumer goods and on shoes. The tariff increase did not affect capital goods, which constitute a significant portion of United States exports to Brazil. In June 1995, the government imposed quotas on the importation of automobiles. These measures are temporary, and the government maintains that they do not represent a reversal in Brazil's trade liberalization efforts.

The government has taken several measures to cut consumption, including a severe limitation of both consumer and business credit, but has thus far failed to introduce promised fiscal reform.

Principal Growth Sectors

The Brazilian Statistical Institute (IBGE) reported that the Brazilian economy grew 5.7 percent in 1994, an eight year high. Growth in 1994 was attributed to agricultural production (7.5 percent), industry (7.0 percent), and services (4.0 percent). Within these aggregates, crop production was up 10.4 percent and animal husbandry was up 3.6 percent. In the manufacturing area, civil construction was up 7.9 percent, other industry was up 3.2 percent and general manufacturing up 7.9 percent. The commercial sector was up 5.9 percent, transport was up 3.7 percent, and other services were up 3.4 percent.

Industrial growth in percentage terms is detailed as follows:

Category	1994	1995 (est.)
Mineral Activity	4.7	1.3
Manufacturing	7.6	4.9
Capital goods	18.6	21.9
Intermediate goods	6.5	2.3
Consumer goods	15.5	12.8
Non-durable goods	1.9	7.8

Growth in GDP in 1995 is expected to be approximately 6.4 percent.

Government Role in the Economy

Under the development policies of previous Brazilian administrations, the government established a tradition of being the dominant force in shaping economic growth by means of planning and management. Its influence was felt not only directly through the day-to-day activities of government entities, but also through governmental wage, price, and credit policies, and subsidy and fiscal incentive programs. While the central government still retains an important economic role, the policies of the current administration focus on reducing the role of the government in economic activities and concentrating government activities on more traditional roles, such as improving public health, safety, and education. As a result, the government is emphasizing creating greater economic opportunities for the private sector through privatization, deregulation, and removal of impediments to competition. Thus the engine of Brazilian economic growth is more and more the private sector.

The petroleum and telecommunications sectors are constitutionally mandated federal monopolies. A constitutional reform effort is currently underway and, if successful, will allow private sector participation in these and other sectors. Privatization, "flexibilization" of the oil and telecommunications monopolies, and the new concessions law represent recent government initiatives to create more opportunities for the private sector in areas previously reserved for the state.

Balance of Payments Situation

Brazil's trade surplus is expected to decline dramatically in 1995, due to declining export growth and rising imports. Government sources estimate the 1995 surplus will be USD$3.0 billion. Others predict a zero balance or even a deficit.

Brazil's process of trade liberalization has produced significant changes in the country's trade profile. Imports are increasing in response to lower tariffs and generally freer markets, and are now composed of a wide variety of industrial, agricultural and consumer goods. The trade deficit at the end of April, 1995, was approximately USD$2.7 billion.

In 1994 the U.S. trade deficit with Brazil was USD$590 million, USD$810 million less than in 1993. U.S. merchandise exports to Brazil were USD$8.1 billion, up USD$2.1 billion or 35 percent compared to 1993. Brazil was the United States' nineteenth largest export market in 1993. U.S. imports from Brazil totaled USD$8.7 billion in 1994 or 16 percent more than 1993.

Infrastructure Situation

Most products reach Brazil by sea and must pass through Brazil's

inefficiently run seaports. Costs are high and turn-around time
is long. Port reform legislation, enacted in 1993, has not been
effective. Esp rito Santo is the only port with privately run
berths along the southeastern coast. Costs are lower and
turnaround time shorter there.

Internal transportation is primarily by truck. Highway are
adequate, but only reach first world standards in the state of
S o Paulo and the south. Fuel costs are high, and add
significantly to the cost of transportation. Rail transportation
is limited. Geographical constraints have limited river
transport development.

Telecommunications is a government monopoly. Telephone service
is limited and of poor quality. International long distance
rates subsidize internal service. Telephone lines are costly and
waiting periods for installation are lengthy.

Electric power generation is currently adequate, but needed
investment in new capacity has been limited by the precarious
financial situation of the government.

A new law regulating concessions granted by the government is
opening up the transportation and power generation sectors to the
private sector. Legal and constitutional reforms are also
underway to allow private sector participation in coastal and
river transport, natural gas distribution, telecommunications,
and petroleum. Privatization of federally-owned railroads is
also planned.

SOURCE: National Trade Data Bank-a product of STAT-USA, U.S. Deparment of Commerce.

Index

DDC® Quick Reference Guides
find software answers faster because you read less

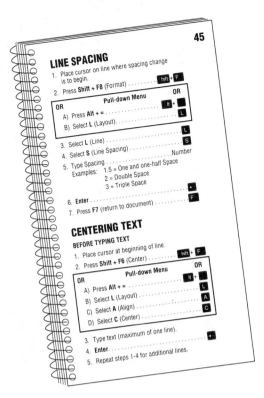

FREE TEMPLATE ON BACK COVER

What took you five minutes now takes one minute.

The illustrated instructions put your fingers on the correct keys – fast. We tell you what to do in five or six words. Sometimes only two.

No narration or exposition. Just "press this – type that" illustrated commands.

Spiral binding keeps pages flat so you can type what you read.

The time you save will pay for the book the first day. Free template on back cover.

Office Managers

Look at the production time you can gain when these quick-find, low-cost guides go to work for you. It will pay for the guides the first day you use them.

--------------------------------**ORDER FORM**--------------------------------

QTY.	GUIDE	CAT. NO.
___	Access 2 for Win	O-AX2
___	Access 7 for Win 95	AX95
___	Computer Terms	D-18
___	Corel WordPerfect Suite Win 95	G-11
___	Corel WordPerfect 7 for Win 95	G-12
___	DOS 6.0 - 6.22	O-DS62
___	Excel 5 for Win	F-18
___	Excel 7 for Win 95	XL7
___	Internet	I-17
___	Laptops & Notebooks	LM-18
___	Lotus 1-2-3 Rel. 3.1 DOS	J-18
___	Lotus 1-2-3 Rel. 3.4 DOS	L3-17
___	Lotus 1-2-3 Rel. 4.0 DOS	G-4
___	Lotus 1-2-3 Rel. 4.0 Win	O-301-3
___	Lotus 1-2-3 Rel. 5.0 Win	L-19
___	Lotus 1-2-3 Rel. 6 Win	G-13
___	Lotus Notes 3	O-LN3
___	Lotus Notes 4	G-15
___	Lotus Smartsuite	SS-17
___	Microsoft Office	MO-17
___	Microsoft Office for Win 95	MO-95
___	MS Project for Win 3.1&95	MP-17
___	Mosaic/World Wide Web	WW-17
___	MS Works 3 for Win	O-WKW3
___	PageMaker 5 Win & Mac	PM-18

QTY.	GUIDE	CAT. NO.
___	Paradox 4.5 for Win	PW-18
___	PerfectOffice	PO-17
___	PowerPoint 4.0 for Win	O-PPW4
___	PowerPoint 7 for Win 95	PPW7
___	Quattro Pro 6 for Win	QPW6
___	Quicken 8 for DOS	QKD8
___	Windows 3.1 & 3.11	N3-17
___	Windows 95	G-6
___	Word 6.0 for Win	O-WDW6
___	Word 7 for Win 95	WDW7
___	WordPerfect 5.1+ DOS	W-5.1
___	WordPerfect 5.1/5.2 Win	Z-17
___	WordPerfect 6.0 for DOS	W-18
___	WordPerfect 6.1 for DOS	G-10
___	WordPerfect 6.0 for Win	O-WPW6
___	WordPerfect 6.1 for Win	W-19
___	Works 4 for Win 95	WKW4

Desktop Publishing

QTY.	GUIDE	CAT. NO.
___	Word 6.0 for Win	G-3
___	WordPerfect 5.1 for DOS	R-5

SEE OUR COMPLETE CATALOG ON THE INTERNET
@:http://www.ddcpub.com

DDC Publishing
275 Madison Avenue,
New York, NY 10016

$12 each **$15** hardcover edition

BUY 3 GUIDES GET ONE FREE

Phone: 800-528-3897
Fax: 800-528-3862

☐ Visa   ☐ MasterCard

No._____ Exp._____

☐ Check enclosed. Add $2 for postage & handling & $1 postage for ea. add. guide. NY State res. add local sales tax.

Name _____

Firm _____

Address _____

City, State, Zip _____

Telephone No. _____

FREE CATALOG
AND
UPDATED LISTING

We don't just have books that find your
answers faster; we also have books that teach
you how to use your computer without the
fairy tales and the gobbledygook.

We also have books to improve
your typing, spelling
and punctuation.

Return this card for
a free catalog and
mailing list update.

275 Madison Avenue,
New York, NY 10016

☐ Please send me your catalog
and put me on your mailing list.

Name

Firm (if any)

Address

City, State, Zip

Phone (800) 528-3897   Fax (800) 528-3862

**SEE OUR COMPLETE CATALOG ON THE
INTERNET** @: http://www.ddcpub.com

FREE CATALOG
AND
UPDATED LISTING

We don't just have books that find your
answers faster; we also have books that teach
you how to use your computer without the
fairy tales and the gobbledygook.

We also have books to improve
your typing, spelling
and punctuation.

Return this card for
a free catalog and
mailing list update.

275 Madison Avenue,
New York, NY 10016

☐ Please send me your catalog
and put me on your mailing list.

Name

Firm (if any)

Address

City, State, Zip

Phone (800) 528-3897   Fax (800) 528-3862

**SEE OUR COMPLETE CATALOG ON THE
INTERNET** @: http://www.ddcpub.com

FREE CATALOG
AND
UPDATED LISTING

We don't just have books that find your
answers faster; we also have books that teach
you how to use your computer without the
fairy tales and the gobbledygook.

We also have books to improve
your typing, spelling
and punctuation.

Return this card for
a free catalog and
mailing list update.

DDC Publishing

275 Madison Avenue,
New York, NY 10016

☐ Please send me your catalog
and put me on your mailing list.

Name

Firm (if any)

Address

City, State, Zip

Phone (800) 528-3897   Fax (800) 528-3862

**SEE OUR COMPLETE CATALOG ON THE
INTERNET** @: http://www.ddcpub.com

BUSINESS REPLY MAIL
FIRST CLASS MAIL   PERMIT NO. 7321   NEW YORK, N.Y.

POSTAGE WILL BE PAID BY ADDRESSEE

DDC *Publishing*

275 Madison Avenue
New York, NY 10157-0410

BUSINESS REPLY MAIL
FIRST CLASS MAIL   PERMIT NO. 7321   NEW YORK, N.Y.

POSTAGE WILL BE PAID BY ADDRESSEE

DDC *Publishing*

275 Madison Avenue
New York, NY 10157-0410

BUSINESS REPLY MAIL
FIRST CLASS MAIL   PERMIT NO. 7321   NEW YORK, N.Y.

POSTAGE WILL BE PAID BY ADDRESSEE

DDC *Publishing*

275 Madison Avenue
New York, NY 10157-0410